ASHEVILLE-BUNCOMBE TECHNICAL INSTITUTE STATE DEPT.

Asheville-Buncombe Technical Institute
LIBRARY
340 Victoria Road
Asheville, North Carolina 28801

DISCARDED

JUN 2 2025

Information Sciences Series

Editors
ROBERT M. HAYES
University of California
Los Angeles, California

JOSEPH BECKER
President
Becker and Hayes, Inc.

Consultant
CHARLES P. BOURNE
University of California
Berkeley, California

Joseph Becker and Robert M. Hayes:
INFORMATION STORAGE AND RETRIEVAL

Charles P. Bourne:
METHODS OF INFORMATION HANDLING

Harold Borko:
AUTOMATED LANGUAGE PROCESSING

Russell D. Archibald and Richard L. Villoria:
NETWORK-BASED MANAGEMENT SYSTEMS (PERT/CPM)

Launor F. Carter:
NATIONAL DOCUMENT-HANDLING SYSTEMS FOR SCIENCE AND TECHNOLOGY

Perry E. Rosove:
DEVELOPING COMPUTER-BASED INFORMATION SYSTEMS

F. W. Lancaster:
INFORMATION RETRIEVAL SYSTEMS

Ralph L. Bisco:
DATA BASES, COMPUTERS, AND THE SOCIAL SCIENCES

Charles T. Meadow:
MAN-MACHINE COMMUNICATION

Gerald Jahoda:
INFORMATION STORAGE AND RETRIEVAL SYSTEMS FOR INDIVIDUAL RESEARCHERS

Robert M. Hayes and Joseph Becker:
HANDBOOK OF DATA PROCESSING FOR LIBRARIES,
Second Edition

Allen Kent:
INFORMATION ANALYSIS AND RETRIEVAL

Robert S. Taylor:
THE MAKING OF A LIBRARY

Herman M. Weisman:
INFORMATION SYSTEMS, SERVICES, AND CENTERS

Jesse H. Shera:
THE FOUNDATIONS OF EDUCATION FOR LIBRARIANSHIP

Charles T. Meadow:
THE ANALYSIS OF INFORMATION SYSTEMS, Second Edition

Stanley J. Swihart and Beryl F. Hefley:
COMPUTER SYSTEMS IN THE LIBRARY

F. W. Lancaster and E. G. Fayen:
INFORMATION RETRIEVAL ON-LINE

Richard A. Kaimann:
STRUCTURED INFORMATION FILES

Dagobert Soergel:
INDEXING LANGUAGES AND THESAURI: CONSTRUCTION AND MAINTENANCE

Thelma Freides:
LITERATURE AND BIBLIOGRAPHY OF THE SOCIAL SCIENCES

Manfred Kochen:
PRINCIPLES OF INFORMATION RETRIEVAL

Indexing Languages and Thesauri: Construction and Maintenance

DAGOBERT SOERGEL

College of Library and Information Services
University of Maryland

A WILEY-BECKER & HAYES SERIES BOOK

MELVILLE PUBLISHING COMPANY
Los Angeles, California

Copyright © 1974, by John Wiley & Sons, Inc.
Published by **Melville Publishing Company,**
a Division of John Wiley & Sons, Inc.

All rights reserved. Published simultaneously in Canada.

No part of this book may be reproduced by any means, nor transmitted, nor translated into a machine language without the written permission of the publisher.

Library of Congress Cataloging in Publication Data:

Soergel, Dagobert.
   Indexing languages and thesauri.

   (Information sciences series)
   "A Wiley-Becker & Hayes series book."
   Bibliography: p.
   1. Indexing. 2. Thesauri. I. Title.

Z695.9.S63   029.5   73–20301
ISBN 0–471–81047–9

Printed in the United States of America

10 9 8 7 6 5 4 3 2 1

Information Sciences Series

Information is the essential ingredient in decision making. The need for improved information systems in recent years has been made critical by the steady growth in size and complexity of organizations and data.

This series is designed to include books that are concerned with various aspects of communicating, utilizing, and storing digital and graphic information. It will embrace a broad spectrum of topics, such as information system theory and design, man-machine relationships, language data processing, artificial intelligence, mechanization of library processes, nonnumerical applications of digital computers, storage and retrieval, automatic publishing, command and control, information display, and so on.

Information science may someday be a profession in its own right. The aim of this series is to bring together the interdisciplinary core of knowledge that is apt to form its foundation. Through this consolidation, it is expected that the series will grow to become the focal point for professional education in this field.

Preface

This book has two objectives. First, to reassess thoroughly the functions of an indexing language or thesaurus in an information storage and retrieval system and in the light of this reassessment to analyze the structure of indexing languages and thesauri. Most importantly, this reassessment is based on a unified view of indexing languages (classification schemes) and thesauri as used in *traditional* libraries on the one hand and in *modern* (mechanized) information storage and retrieval systems on the other. It results in general principles that are applicable to a wide range of situations.

The second objective is to give a comprehensive overview of the state of the art of the display and the construction and maintenance of indexing languages and thesauri.

The first objective is a prerequisite for the second. A separate textbook on information storage and retrieval would perhaps be a more appropriate form to deal with it, and there are indeed plans for such a textbook incorporating much of the material presented in chapters B and C.

Information from many sources has been evaluated and synthesized to compile the state of the art of thesaurus construction and display as completely as possible. Some sources—for example, the rules used for the TEST thesaurus—have been referenced in detail in the footnotes. For other sources this was not possible.

I wish to give my acknowledgements for numerous examples that have been taken from Thesaurofacet, from Mandersloot et al. 1970, and from Thomas et al. 1953. In all other cases the sources of examples are given in the notes.

The table of contents has an unusual three-level format. This is to illustrate the display of a classification scheme with "summaries" or "synopses" on several levels.

I wish to thank the many people who contributed to the completion of this book. First of all, the book is based on the German "Klassifikationssysteme und Thesauri" which I wrote on behalf of the Committee for Thesaurus Research of the German Society for Documentation, using materials prepared by the committee and with the benefit of the review and comments of the committee members, especially Ingetraut Dahlberg and Alwin Diemer, Chairman (the other members of the committee were: R. Fugman, G. Heinzmann, H. Krieg, E. Lutterbeck, E. Meyer, C. v. Rothkirch-Trach, M. Scheele, H. Schneider, M. Simon, D. Soergel). The German Society for Documentation, which published the book in 1969, gave permission to use the material without restriction.

William Kurmey of the Faculty of Library Science of the University of Toronto thoroughly reviewed the whole manuscript and made many valuable suggestions to improve the content and the clarity of presentation. His contribution should enhance considerably the usefulness of the book. Katherine Packer, a member of the Faculty of Library Science of the University of Toronto and also a Ph.D. candidate at the University of Maryland, and my wife Lissa both read the whole manuscript for style and clarity and spent many hours with me discussing individual formulations.

Tom Wilson of the Graduate Library School of the University of Sheffield contributed various ideas, especially for chapter K, "Thesauri as a basis for cooperation in information services". The acronym ISAR (or, as he prefers, isar) for Information Storage And Retrieval was first used by him.

The excellent work of Faith Bange, who diligently typed and retyped the many versions and expertly interpreted my handwriting, was a great help in finishing the manuscript.

Above all, my thanks go to Calvin Mooers who, back in 1962, encouraged my interest in the field and started a process of thought without which this book would not have been possible.

College Park, Maryland   DAGOBERT SOERGEL

HOW TO READ THIS BOOK

1. This book is a handbook as well as a textbook; not every section is for every reader. Nor should every section be read in the first reading. Therefore, a number of sections have been marked as follows:

   Technical—The information contained in these sections is not important for a general understanding of the problems and the procedure or for the overall planning of a thesaurus development project. The information is needed only as one comes to the step in question. These sections can therefore be omitted in the first reading.

   Special topic—These sections deal with problems that occur only in special situations. They can therefore be omitted without any loss in understanding of other sections. An example is Section D5, "Multi-lingual thesauri".

   Advanced—These sections are meant only for the reader who is interested in depth.

   A reader with sufficient background in the structure of indexing languages and thesauri might turn immediately to chapter F, "Flow of work in the construction of indexing languages and thesauri", and return to previous sections as the need arises.

   Readers who are interested only in a general orientation and those who have the task of constructing a small indexing language/thesaurus, need only read the sections of the book given in the following guide.

   A reader interested only in a general orientation about indexing languages and thesauri and their role in an information storage and retrieval system should read the following sections:

   A1;
   B;
   C through C1.3;
   possibly C2 through C2.5 (if interested in conventional systems like subject headings and shelving classification);
   D through D1.3.2
   (omitting, of course, sections labeled "advanced", "special topic", or "technical".)

   A reader who has the task of constructing a small indexing language/thesaurus need not concern himself with the details and ramifications important for large systems. The following sections should provide sufficient information.

How to Read this Book

    A;
    B;
    C through C4, C5, possibly C5.0 (but not C5.1-C5.3), C7;
    D1-D3, D4.0, D4.1, D4.3.3, D4.4;
    E0, E1.0, E.1.1, E1.5, E1.6, E1.8;
    F;
    J;
    K0, K1 through K1.2.1, K1.2.3.

2. The problems dealt with in this book are highly interrelated. A second reading might be helpful.
3. Chapters B and C provide a limited background in classification theory, they are not intended to give a full treatment of this topic. A number of good books are available (see the first note to chapter C), and it is strongly recommended that the reader who does not have the background in information storage and retrieval and classification consult one of these books first.
4. All notes are at the end of the book. They are identified by section number and are formulated in such a way that the particular point referred to is readily clear. This procedure made it possible to omit any numbers referring to notes from the main text and thus improve readability. The reader interested in further references and other background material for a given section should simply look in the back under the section number (and possibly under a broader section number).

    The notes for each chapter or major subsection can also be considered as a bibliographical supplement that can be read separately.

5. Documents mentioned in the notes are cited by author and date of publication, e.g., Lancaster 1969.4. The bibliography is arranged by author.

Content: Overview

Introduction		**1**
A	General overview of the functions and structure of a thesaurus. Major tasks to be performed and resources and work required for the construction of a thesaurus	3
Part I	**Conceptual structure of indexing languages and thesauri**	**15**
B	Concepts and terms. Indexing language and thesaurus and their functions in an ISAR system	17
C	The structure of indexing languages and thesauri	68
Part II	**Presentation of indexing languages and thesauri**	**181**
D	Thesaurus format	183
E	Rules concerning the form of terms and related problems	298
Part III	**Procedures for the construction and maintenance of indexing languages and thesauri**	**323**
F	Flow of work in the construction of indexing languages and thesauri	325
G	Use of computers in thesaurus construction	420
H	Automatic methods in the construction of indexing languages and thesauri, starting from the texts of documents and/or search requests. Automatic classification	449
J	Updating and maintenance of indexing languages and thesauri	457
Part IV	**Thesauri as a basis for cooperation in information services**	**469**
K	Thesauri as a basis for cooperation in information services	471
Appendices		**521**
Chapter Notes		**535**
Bibliography		**559**
Index		**609**

Condensed Table of Contents

Introduction   1

  A   General overview of the functions and structure of a thesaurus. Major tasks to be performed in and resources and work required for the construction of a thesaurus   3

       A0   Introduction   3

       A1   Overview of functions and structure of a thesaurus in an Information Storage And Retrieval (ISRA) system   3

       A2   Administrative considerations. Resources and work required for the development of a thesaurus   10

Part I   Conceptual structure of indexing languages and thesauri   15

  B   Concepts and terms. Indexing language and thesaurus and their functions in an ISAR system   17

       B0   Introduction   17

       B1   Plane of concepts versus plane of terms; the synonym-homonym structure   17

       B2   Treatment of nearly related concepts: the equivalence structure   22

       B3   Indexing language   26

       B4   Thesaurus. Summary of and further remarks on the definition of preferred term, descriptor, concept, and indexing language   29

       B5   The functions of the indexing language within an ISAR system. A preliminary overview of the structure of indexing languages in relation to their functions in an ISAR system   39

       B6   The functions of the lead-in vocabulary in an ISAR system   61

       B7   "User's" or "author's" vocabulary versus logical structure and request-oriented indexing as implemented through the checklist technique   66

  C   The structure of indexing languages and thesauri   68

xiv Condensed Table of Contents

	C0	Introduction	68
	C1	Classificatory structure	69
	C2	Problems of file organization related to classification. Practical applications of semantic factoring	112
	C3	Concept formation in thesaurus building. Definition and scope notes	142
	C4	Types of concepts, descriptors, terms to be included in an indexing language or thesaurus	147
	C5	The lead-in structure. USE and SEE	155
	C6	Synonyms proper versus spelling variants	171
	C7	Summary of relationships displayed in a thesaurus	174

Part II Presentation of indexing languages and thesauri 181

    D Thesaurus format 183

D0	Introduction	183
D1	The different parts of a thesaurus	183
D2	Format of entries in the main part	228
D3	How to display descriptors and their interrelationships (methods for the design of a classified index)	235
D4	Notation	273
D5	Multilingual thesauri	293

    E Rules concerning the form of terms and related problems 298

E0	Introduction. Difference in requirements between systems using notations and systems using terms	298
E2	Spelling and transliteration	317
E3	Alphabetization	320

Part III Procedures for the construction and maintenance of indexing languages and thesauri 323

    F Flow of work in the construction of indexing languages and thesauri 325

F0	Overview and general problems	325
F1	Collect and record material (concepts, terms, relationships between and among them)	355
F2	Sort into alphabetical order and merge information on identical terms on one card	366

Condensed Table of Contents   xv

F3	Work out the preliminary structure of the thesaurus: the synonym-homonym structure, the equivalence structure, and the classificatory structure. Select preferred terms	384
F4	Work out first draft of the classified index (schedule)	392
F5	Complete first draft of the thesaurus as a whole	397
F6	Test the thesaurus by indexing and retrieval experiments	411
F7	Duplicate or print the user version of the thesaurus	412
F8	Further remarks concerning the work-flow and modifications of the standard work-flow	413
F9	Use of punched paper tape and punched cards in thesaurus construction	417

G   Use of computers in thesaurus construction   420

G0	Rationale for computer application. Overview	420
G1	Computer assistance in the collection and recording of material	428
G2	Computer assistance in sorting into alphabetical order and in merging information on identical terms into one record	429
G3	Computer assistance in working out the preliminary structure of the thesaursus	434
G4	Computer assistance in working out the classified index	441
G5	Computer assistance in completing the first draft of the thesaurus as a whole	442
G7	Printing the final thesaurus by computer	443
G8	Updating a computer-stored thesaurus	443
G9	Devices for the input (keying) of thesaurus data	447

H   Automatic methods in the construction of indexing languages and thesauri, starting from the texts of documents and/or search requests. Automatic classification   449

H0	Introduction	449
H1	Definition of units of text and counting methods	450
H2	Identification of descriptor candidates from frequency patterns	451
H3	Detection of terms or concept relationships from co-occurrence patterns	451
H4	Automatic derivation of classification schemes ("global" structures)	455

	J	Updating and maintenance of indexing languages and thesauri	457
	J0	Introduction	457
	J1	Types of changes	457
	J2	Sources for new terms, concepts and relationships to be included in the thesaurus	458
	J3	Procedures for regular updating	460
	J4	Revision of the indexing language or the thesaurus at longer intervals	463
	J5	Remarks on the flexibility of structured indexing languages (classification schemes)	464
	J6	Problems of re-indexing (re-classification)	465
	J7	Thesaurus updating and thesaurus compatibility: common problems	467

Part IV	Thesauri as a basis for cooperation in information services		469
K	Thesauri as a basis for cooperation in information services		471
	K0	Introduction	471
	K1	Cooperation in the construction of indexing languages and thesauri	472
	K2	Cooperation through sharing the results of subject indexing	493
	K3	The idea of a Universal Source Thesaurus (UST)	516

Appendices   521

Chapter Notes   535

Bibliography   559

Index   609

Contents

Preface	vii
How to Read this Book	ix
Content: Overview	xi
Condensed Table of Contents	xiii
Table of Contents	xvii
List of Figures	xli
Introduction	**1**

A General overview of the functions and structure of a thesaurus. Major tasks to be performed in and resources and work required for the construction of a thesaurus   3

   A0 Introduction   3
   A1 Overview of functions and structure of a thesaurus in an Information Storage and Retrieval (ISAR) system   3

       A1.1 Requirements for an ISAR system: conceptual structure and terminological control   3
       A1.2 Thesaurus   4
       A1.3 The thesaurus in the context of an ISAR system as a whole   5

           A1.3.1 Parameters determining thesaurus size   6
           A1.3.2 Estimating parameters; dangers of a thesaurus of inappropriate size or quality   7

       A1.4 Use of a thesaurus for improving indexes   8
       A1.5 Use of a classification scheme or a thesaurus for purposes other than ISAR   8
       A1.6 Intellectual problems in the development of a thesaurus   9
       A1.7 Criteria for the evaluation of a thesaurus   9
       A1.8 Concluding remarks   9

   A2 Administrative considerations. Resources and work required for the development of a thesaurus   10

       A2.1 Justifying the creation of a new thesaurus   10
       A2.2 Staff needed for the development of a thesaurus   10

A2.3 Time-frame for the development of a thesaurus 12
A2.4 Necessity of continuous updating 13

Part I Conceptual structure of indexing languages and thesauri 15

B Concepts and terms. Indexing language and thesaurus and their functions in an ISAR system 17

B0 Introduction 17
B1 Plane of concepts versus plane of terms: the synonym-homonym structure 17

    B1.1 Homonyms and homographs (advanced) 20

B2 Treatment of nearly related concepts: the equivalence structure 22

    B2.0 Equivalent concepts (equivalent terms) 22
    B2.1 Forming ISAR concepts and naming them. Preferred terms 23
    B2.2 Classificatory structure 23
    B2.3 Summary of B1 and B2 23
    B2.4 A more realistic but less practical model 26

B3 Indexing language 26

    B3.0 Definition of "descriptor 1 (retrieval cue)", "descriptor 2 (subject descriptor)", and "indexing language" 26
    B3.1 Remark on terminological control 29

B4 Thesaurus. Summary of and further remarks on the definition of preferred term, descriptor, concept, and indexing language 29

    B4.1 Simple definition of "thesaurus". Use of the lead-in structure in indexing 29
    B4.2 Summary of and further remarks on the definition of preferred term, descriptor, concept, indexing language, and thesaurus 30

        B4.2.0 Summary of definitions 31
        B4.2.1 Preferred term and descriptor 31
        B4.2.2 Concept, preferred term, descriptor 34
        B4.2.3 Indexing language, system vocabulary, classification scheme 34
        B4.2.4 Subject access vocabulary, thesaurus, indexing language, and classification scheme 35

    B4.3 Complex thesaurus structures. Use of the lead-in structure for terminological control in searching (advanced) 36
    B4.4 Formal definition of "thesaurus" (advanced) 38

B5 The functions of the indexing language within an ISAR system. A preliminary overview of the structure of indexing languages in relation to their functions in an ISAR system 39

    B5.0 "Indexing" versus "grouping of documents" I. Solutions to the retrieval problem 39

  B5.0.1 Elementary solution: search whole (un-indexed) collection 40
  B5.0.2 First economy measure: batch search requests 40
  B5.0.3 Second economy measure: prepare abstracts 41
  B5.0.4 Third economy measure: anticipated search requests: collect anticipated search requests and analyze documents in advance 41
  B5.0.5 Fourth economy measure: provide a retrieval mechanism 42
  B5.0.6 Concluding remarks 43
 B5.1 A preliminary view of the structure of indexing languages (classification schemes) 44
 B5.2 Request-oriented indexing and the checklist technique 45
  B5.2.0 Introduction 45
  B5.2.1 Disadvantages of the method of indexing commonly used (document-oriented indexing) 45
  B5.2.2 Implementation of request-oriented indexing; the checklist technique described 46
  B5.2.3 Summary: request-oriented indexing and the checklist technique 49
  B5.2.4 The checklist technique for search request formulation 49
  B5.2.5 Request-oriented indexing and cost-benefit considerations 50
 B5.3 Adding descriptors through supplementary document-oriented indexing 50
 B5.4 Representation versus filing of documents or catalog cards 51
  B5.4.1 Use of relatively broad descriptors in filing arrangement 51
  B5.4.2 Use of relatively broad descriptors for peek-a-boo cards or other indexes 55
  B5.4.3 Use of additional descriptors beyond those used for filing or manual indexes 56
  B5.4.4 The use of free (open-ended) terms supplementing the descriptors from the indexing language 57
  B5.4.5 Note on "descriptor" and multi-purpose systems 58
 B5.5 Summary of the functions of hierarchy and classified arrangement 59
 B5.6 Indicative versus informative representation of documents 60
 B5.7 Cost-benefit consideration for the design of an indexing language 61
B6 The functions of the lead-in vocabulary in an ISAR system 61
 B6.1 Advantages of a lead-in vocabulary for human indexing and search request formulation 62
  B6.1.1 Alphabetical index to the indexing language is more effective 62

Contents

- B6.1.2 Thesaurus as store of intellectual decisions made in day-to-day indexing and search request formulation 62
  - ,1 Gradual development of a thesaurus over time 63
- B6.2 Mechanization of indexing or search request formulation (special topic) 63
  - B6.2.1 Semi-mechanized versus fully mechanized indexing and search request formulation: description of methods 63
  - B6.2.2 Problems and implications for thesaurus building 64
  - B6.2.3 Discussion: advantages and disadvantages of mechanized indexing 65
- B6.3 Thesauri for terminological control in the searching stage 66
- B7 "User's" or "author's" vocabulary versus logical structure and request-oriented indexing as implemented through the checklist technique 66

C The structure of indexing languages and thesauri 68

- C0 Introduction 68
- C1 Classificatory structure 69
  - C1.0 Introduction: "representation" versus "grouping of documents" II (continuation of Section B5.0) 69
  - C1.1 Decomposition of concepts into semantic factors—concept combination (concept coordination) 74
    - C1.1.0 Foundations of semantic factoring and concept combination 74
    - C1.1.1 Advantages of semantic factoring 77
  - C1.2 Polyhierarchical structure. Definition of hierarchy 78
  - C1.3 Interaction of hierarchy and concept combination 83
    - C1.3.1 Limitations of the model for the generation of hierarchical structures 91
    - C1.3.2 Application of the model to hierarchy construction. Facet analysis 91
  - C1.4 Further topics in hierarchy and its use in indexing and searching 95
    - C1.4.1 Further considerations on pragmatic hierarchy building 95
      - ,1 Extending the definition of concepts or introducing new broader concepts 95
      - ,2 Introduction of additional broader concepts for searching 95
      - ,3 Introduction of a broader concept to replace a number of specific concepts 97
      - ,4 Introduction of new broader concepts to serve as headings ("organizational headings") 97
      - ,5 Antonyms 97

Contents   xxi

,6 Hierarchical relationships versus associative relationships in indexing and searching   98
,7 Introduction of new broader concepts as a creative activity   99

C1.4.2 Kinds of hierarchical relationships (advanced)   99
C1.4.3 Special cases of hierarchical structure   102

,1 Coarse hierarchy: subdivision of the preferred terms into subject fields   102
,2 Facets   103

C1.4.4 "General descriptors" and "Other descriptors" as a special type of heading applicable throughout the classification scheme   103
C1.4.5 Implementation of inclusive searching. Generic posting and the POST TO instruction   103
C1.4.6 Descriptors "..., inclusive" and "..., general references"   105

,1 Descriptor usage depends on hierarchy   106

C1.4.7 Descriptors "..., other"   106

C1.5 Associative relationships between concepts   107

C1.5.1 Concepts similar in meaning   108
C1.5.2 Concepts connected empirically ("contextual contiguity")   108

,1 Contiguity based on definition   108
,2 Contiguity based on empirical knowledge   109
,3 Contiguity and frequency of combination   109

C1.5.3 Instructional scope note   109

C1.6 Transitions between the synonym-homonym structure, the equivalence structure, and the classificatory structure   110
C1.7 Psychological dimensions of relationships   112

C2 Problems of file organization related to classification. Practical applications of semantic factoring   112

C2.0 Introduction   112
C2.1 On the relationship between conceptual structure and file organization in classification theory   113
C2.2 The problem defined   114
C2.3 Principal solutions: post-combination versus pre-combination—a quantitative view   115

C2.3.1 Post-combination and pre-combination (post-coordination and pre-coordination) defined   115
C2.3.2 Conceptual indexes (auxiliary ISAR systems) I (special topic, for systems using pre-combination only)   119

Contents

- C2.3.3 Summary 121
- C2.4 Selection and arrangement of descriptors with particular reference to ISAR systems using pre-combination (special topic) 122
- C2.5 A unified classification scheme for different kinds of file organization: core classification and extended classification (partly special topic) 126
  - C2.5.1 Special problems arising in the implementation of this proposal (technical) 128
    - ,1 Multiple entry versus entry under a precombined descriptor 128
    - ,2 Multiple entry using a faceted classification 129
- C2.6 Summary: strategies for the application of semantic factoring 129
  - C2.6.1 Considerations in the choice of a strategy 130
- C2.7 Rules for the use of precombined descriptors in an intermediary strategy not using roles and links 131
  - C2.7.1 What compound concepts should be used as precombined descriptors? 132
  - C2.7.2 What compound concepts should be represented by a combination of descriptors rather than by a precombined descriptor? 134
- C2.8 Optimization of an indexing language with a constraint as to the number of descriptors (advanced) 134
  - C2.8.1 Semantic super-imposed coding 135
  - C2.8.2 Considerations to be taken into account in reducing the number of concepts used as descriptors 137

- C3 Concept formation in thesaurus building. Definition and scope notes 142
  - C3.1 Concept formation in thesaurus building 142
  - C3.2 Definition and scope note 145
    - C3.2.0 Introduction 145
    - C3.2.1 Formal definition 145
    - C3.2.2 Scope notes for the thesaurus user 146

- C4 Types of concepts, descriptors, terms to be included in an indexing language or a thesaurus 147
  - C4.0 Typology of concepts, descriptors, terms 148
    - C4.0.1 Remarks on descriptive versus subject indexing 149
  - C4.1 The treatment of proper names used as subject descriptors 151
  - C4.2 Treatment of elements of nomenclatures 152
    - C4.2.1 Nomenclatures as adjunct thesauri 152
    - C4.2.2 Alternative possibility: inclusion of selected elements of nomenclatures into the thesaurus proper 153

Contents   xxiii

    C4.3 Concepts of general application (common attributes, common isolates)   153

  C5 The lead-in structure. USE and SEE   155

    C5.0 Introduction   156

        C5.0.1 The lead-in problem: alphabetical index method versus main part method   156
        C5.0.2 The lead-in problem: the crude form and the detailed form   158

           ,1 Further illustrative examples of the crude lead-in form   160

        C5.0.3 Use of the lead-in structure   161

    C5.1 The detailed lead-in form   162
    C5.2 Alternative lead-in forms   165

        C5.2.1 Simpler forms   165
        C5.2.2 More detailed form: expressing the equivalence structure (advanced)   166

    C5.3 OR-type USE instructions   167

        C5.3.1 Homonymous lead-in terms   168
        C5.3.2 Broad lead-in terms   168
        C5.3.3 Leads to related terms   169
        C5.3.4 OR-combination of descriptors as semantic factor   170

    C5.4 Other matters related to USE instructions   171

        C5.4.1 Qualified USE instructions (special topic)   171

  C6 Synonyms proper versus spelling variants   171

    C6.1 Synonyms proper   171
    C6.2 Spelling variants   172

        C6.2.1 Distinction between synonyms proper and spelling variants   172
        C6.2.2 Number of spelling variants to be included in the thesaurus   173
        C6.2.3 Where to store the spelling variants   174

  C7 Summary of relationships displayed in a thesaurus   174

    C7.1 Cross-references and inverse cross-references   180

Part II Presentation of indexing languages and thesauri   181

D Thesaurus format   183

  D0 Introduction   183
  D1 The different parts of a thesaurus   183

Contents

D1.0 Introduction 183
D1.1 Thesaurus format: the Roget-Soergel model 184

- D1.1.0 Rationale 184
  - ,1 Classified index required for the checklist technique of indexing and search request formulation 184
  - ,2 A descriptor should always be seen in its place in the overall structure before it is used in indexing and searching 192
  - ,3 Not too much information should be given in the alphabetical index 193
  - ,4 Roget-Soergel model appropriate for systems using notation 193
  - ,5 Parts of the thesaurus 193
- D1.1.1 Classified index (the schedule) 193
  - ,0 Summary (overview, synopsis) of the main subject fields 193
  - ,1 Display of the checklist descriptors and the important relationships among them 193
  - ,2 Classified index 194
  - ,3 Note on ,1 and ,2 194
- D1.1.2 Main part of the thesaurus 194
- D1.1.3 Alphabetical index 195

D1.2 Thesaurus format: the TEST model 196

- D1.2.0 Parts of TEST 196
- D1.2.1 Classified listings in TEST 196
  - ,1 Subject category index 196
  - ,2 Hierarchical index 196
- D1.2.2 Thesaurus of terms (main part) 197
- D1.2.3 Alphabetical index 197

D1.3 The look-up problem and how to arrange the entries in the main part 198

- D1.3.1 Where the look-up problem occurs 198
- D1.3.2 Finding the appropriate descriptor for a term that comes to mind 198
- D1.3.3 Variations of the TEST model 202
  - ,1 Inclusion of spelling variants in the main part 202
  - ,2 Always look in the alphabetical index first 202
- D1.3.4 Necessity of notation 202

D1.4 What Broader and Narrower Terms should be listed in the fields BT or NT, respectively? 202

Contents   xxv

    D1.4.1 Inverse cross-references to broad descriptors of general application (advanced)   205
    D1.4.2 Listing coordinate terms (advanced)   207

D1.5 Alphabetical index   207

    D1.5.1 General considerations   207
    D1.5.2 KWIC or KWOC format   209

D1.6 Guidance devices to facilitate look-up   209
D1.7 Description of selected thesauri   209

    D1.7.1 Thesaurus of the Vision Information Center, Harvard Medical School   211
    D1.7.2 FR Thesaurus (problems of developing countries)   211
    D1.7.3 UDC, DDC, LCC   211
    D1.7.4 Thesaurofacet   212
    D1.7.5 Medical Subject Headings (MeSH)   216
    D1.7.6 Euratom-Thesaurus   220
    D1.7.7 Thesaurus of education terms   221
    D1.7.8 American Petroleum Institute (API) Subject Authority List   221
    D1.7.9 ERIC thesaurus   223
    D1.7.10 Library of Congress Subject Headings (LCSH)   223
    D1.7.11 Other thesauri   225

D1.8 Introduction to the thesaurus   225

D2 Format of entries in the main part   228

D2.1 Information given for each term   228
D2.2 Rationale for the sequence of data fields (cross-reference types) (advanced)   228
D2.3 Arrangement of terms within one data field (technical)   232

    D2.3.0 General   232
    D2.3.1 Synonyms and equivalent terms (quasi-synonyms)   232
    D2.3.2 BT, NT, RT   233

        ,1 What Broader Terms and Narrower Terms to list   233
        ,2 Broader Terms   233

            ,2.1 Broader Terms and Semantic Factors   233
            ,2.2 USE instructions containing Broader Terms   233
            ,2.3 Upward hierarchical chains   233

        ,3 Narrower Terms   234
        ,4 Display of different kinds of hierarchical relationships   234
        ,5 Related Terms   234
        ,6 Arrangement by notation   234
        ,7 How descriptors are entered in the data fields BT, NT, RT   234

xxvi   Contents

D2.4 Typographical design of entries   235

D3 How to display descriptors and their inter-relationships (methods for the design of a classified index)   235

    D3.0 Relational displays vs. classification principles   236

        D3.0.1 Alternate classified index (advanced)   237

    D3.1 Displays for hierarchical relationships   237

        D3.1.1 Linear arrangement of descriptors (and possibly other preferred terms) in classified order with cross-references   237

            ,1 Preferred monohierarchical structure and cross-references   237

            ,2 Sequence of descriptors on the same level   239

                ,2.1 How to achieve helpful arrangement (technical)   239

            ,3 Details of presentation (technical)   241

        D3.1.2 Graphical display of hierarchical relationships   243

            ,1 Usual tree display   243

            ,2 Tree display with horizontal arrangement of hierarchical levels   246

            ,3 Circular display of hierarchical relationships   246

    D3.2 Network structures for the combined display of hierarchical and associative relationships   249

    D3.3 Comparison of different methods   255

    D3.4 Use of different type fonts (technical)   255

    D3.5 Methods for compressing the display of checklist descriptors   263

    D3.6 Auxiliary ISAR systems ("conceptual indexes") II   263

        D3.6.0 Introduction and rationale   263

        D3.6.1 Implementation of ISAR systems for descriptors (auxiliary ISAR systems)   265

            ,1 Mechanized auxiliary ISAR systems   265

            ,2 Combinatorial indexes   265

    D3.7 On-line display of thesauri (special topic)   272

D4 Notation   273

    D4.0 Definition   273

    D4.1 Purpose of notation   275

        D4.1.1 Changes in notations (advanced)   275

        D4.1.2 Notation and machine-internal code in computerized ISAR systems (special topic)   276

    D4.2 The fallacy of overstressing notation   277

D4.3 Design of a notation (technical, especially Sections D4.3.3-D4.3.6)   277

    D4.3.1 Design criteria   278
    D4.3.2 Types of notation   278

        ,1 Expressive notation   278
        ,2 Purely ordinal notation   280

            ,2.1 A special device for intercalating new serial numbers   282

        ,3 Example   282

    D4.3.3 A partly expressive, partly ordinal system of notation (mixed notation)   282

        ,1 Mixed notation 1: small indexing languages/classification schemes (less than 1,000 descriptors)   282
        ,2 Mixed notation 2: large indexing languages/classification schemes   283
        ,3 Notations for compound concepts   285

    D4.3.4 An easy-to-produce expressive notation   286
    D4.3.5 Notation for precombined descriptors   286
    D4.3.6 Notations for preferred terms that are not descriptors   288

D4.4 Specific problems in notation (technical)   289

    D4.4.1 "Incorporating" standard classification schemes   289
    D4.4.2 Descriptors with "data field"   291

        ,1 Numerical data field   291
        ,2 Data field proper name   292

    D4.4.3 The UDC method of handling time, modified   292

D5 Multilingual thesauri (special topic)   293

    D5.0 Definitions   293
    D5.1 Format of a type-1 multilingual thesaurus (lead-in only)   294
    D5.2 Format of a type-2 multilingual thesaurus (indexing language in different languages)   294

        D5.2.1 Separate editions for each language (recommended)   294
        D5.2.2 One all-language edition (not recommended)   295

    D5.3 Production of a type-2 multilingual thesaurus   295
    D5.4 Production of an English thesaurus that contains translations in other languages   296
    D5.5 Interlingual thesauri   296

E Rules concerning the form of terms and related problems   298

    E0 Introduction. Difference in requirements between systems using notations and systems using terms   298

Contents

E1 Rules for the form of terms ... 299

    E1.0 Preliminary remarks   299

        E1.0.1 Selection of rules   299
        E1.0.2 When to apply the rules for the form of terms in the process of thesaurus building   299
        E1.0.3 The application of the rules in the alphabetical index   300
        E1.0.4 Preview   300

    E1.1 Formulating terms more precisely   300

        E1.1.1 Disambiguation of homonyms through parenthetical qualifiers   301
        E1.1.2 Homonymous multiword or composite terms   301
        E1.1.3 Omission of parenthetical qualifiers in classified listings (technical)   302
        E1.1.4 Artificial homonyms   303

    E1.2 Rules on what parts of speech (nouns, adjectives, verbs) are allowed (technical)   303

        E1.2.1 Permit-all rule   303
        E1.2.2 Prefer-nouns rule   304
        E1.2.3 Grammatical form to be used for each part of speech   304

    E1.3 Designation of actions and processes, on the one hand, and of their results on the other (technical)   305

        E1.3.0 The problem   305
        E1.3.1 Rules   305

            ,1 Verb-noun rule   305
            ,2 "-ing"- "-ation" rule   305
            ,3 Explicit disambiguation   306
            ,4 Recommended rules   306

    E1.4 Singular vs. plural (technical)   306

        E1.4.0 When rules are necessary   306
        E1.4.1 Terms that are used in singular or in plural only   307

            ,1 Terms that are used in singular only   307
            ,2 Terms that are used in plural only (pluralia tantum)   307

        E1.4.2 Simple rules   308
        E1.4.3 More complicated rules: rules used in the TEST thesaurus   308

    E1.5 Sequence of words in multiword or composite terms (technical)   308

        E1.5.1 Direct entry (TEST)   309
        E1.5.2 Inverted entry   312

E1.6 Terms formed as strings of terms, interpreted as OR combination 313
E1.7 Symbols, especially numerals, as components of terms 313
E1.8 Acronyms and abbreviations 314

    E1.8.1 Commonly used acronyms 314
    E1.8.2 Use of abbreviations to save space 315
    E1.8.3 Standardized abbreviations for descriptors 315

E1.9 Term length 316
E1.10 Terms in foreign languages 316
E1.11 Proper names and trademarks 316

E2 Spelling and transliteration (technical)   317

    E2.1 Authorities 317
    E2.2 Punctuation 317
    E2.3 Capitalization 318
    E2.4 Character set available 319
    E2.5 Transliteration 319

E3 Alphabetization (technical)   320

Part III Procedures for the construction and maintenance of indexing languages and thesauri   323

F Flow of work in the construction of indexing languages and thesauri   325

    F0 Overview and general problems   325

        F0.1 The major steps 325
        F0.2 Cooperative thesaurus development 326
        F0.3 Collaboration of experts from different subject areas 326

            F0.3.0 Necessity of full-time staff and collaboration of subject experts 326
            F0.3.1 Supply of material 334
            F0.3.2 Answering questions on single problems that come up during the work on the thesaurus 334
            F0.3.3 Discussion sessions for review and/or decisions on difficult problems 335
            F0.3.4 Inter-disciplinary approach 336
            F0.3.5 Briefing of subject experts on thesaurus functions 336
            F0.3.6 Source codes for subject experts and panels 336

        F0.4 Criteria for the selection of terms and descriptors 336

            F0.4.1 Criteria for the selection of terms (whether nonpreferred lead-in terms, preferred lead-in terms, or descriptors) to be included in the thesaurus 337

Contents

        F0.4.2 Criteria for the selection of a preferred term from a class of synonyms and quasi-synonyms (arranged according to decreasing priority)   337
        F0.4.3 Criteria for the selection of descriptors   338
        F0.4.4 The use of frequency data in the selection of descriptors (technical)   340

            ,0 Introduction   340
            ,1 Gathering of frequency and co-occurrence data   341
            ,2 Use of frequency data in descriptor selection   343

        F0.4.5 Central area versus peripheral areas   345

F0.5 Use of a thesaurus form and related problems   345

        F0.5.1 Instructions on how to use the thesaurus form (technical)   345
        F0.5.2 Reasons for having an index card for each term   347
        F0.5.3 Reasons for having a form rather than blank cards   347
        F0.5.4 Size   348
        F0.5.5 Width of lines   348
        F0.5.6 Sequence of data fields   348

F0.6 Working file and user version   348
F0.7 Source indications for data elements entered in the thesaurus   349

        F0.7.1 Why source indications?   349

            ,1 Use of the source indications for the elaboration of the thesaurus   349
            ,2 Why source indications in the user version of the thesaurus?   349

        F0.7.2 Keeping track of the sources in the working file (technical)   350
        F0.7.3 Experts and lexicographers as sources (technical)   352
        F0.7.4 Keeping track of deletions (technical)   352

F0.8 Keeping track of decisions and dates   352

        F0.8.1 Keeping track of decisions and dates in working file (technical)   353

            ,1 Keeping track of decisions made   353
            ,2 Keeping track of decisions still to be made   354
            ,3 Keeping track of why decisions have been made   354

        F0.8.2 Giving dates in the user version of the thesaurus (technical)   354

F1 Collect and record material (concepts, terms, relationships between and among them)   355

        F1.1 Kinds of sources. Criteria for selection of sources   355

Contents xxxi

    F1.1.1 Sources in which terms are already arranged according to some principle (prearranged sources) 355
    F1.1.2 Sources in which terms are not ordered or from which terms must first be derived (open-ended sources) 355
    F1.1.3 Selection of the sources to be used 356
    F1.1.4 Term-association lists (special topic) 358

F1.2 Technical procedures for the recording of terms, etc. 358

    F1.2.0 Introduction 358
    F1.2.1 Preparation of sources (technical) 359

        ,0 Source identification codes 359
        ,1 Preparation of prearranged sources 359

            ,1.1 Adding an auxiliary notation 360

        ,2 Preparation of open-ended sources: mark terms to be transferred 360
        ,3 Pre-processing of open-ended sources 362

    F1.2.2 Transfer to terms to cards (thesaurus forms) (technical) 362

        ,1 Entering Synonymous, Broader, Narrower, and Related Terms 362
        ,2 Entering the source indication 365
        ,3 Transfer of terms and other information with manual procedures 365

    F1.2.3 An alternative procedure 366

F2 Sort into alphabetical order and merge information on identical terms on one card 366

    F2.1 Sort into alphabetical order. Rules for preliminary alphabetical sorting 366
    F2.2 First round of merging: merge information for identical terms 367

        F2.2.1 Procedure for merging cards and keeping track of sources (technical) 367
        F2.2.2 Steps after the first round of merging 368
        F2.2.3 "Pulling" information from additional sources (match and merge) 374

            ,1 Procedure for "pulling" (technical) 374

    F2.3 Second round of merging: merge information for terms in the same concept class (advanced and technical) 376

        F2.3.1 The procedure (algorithm) 376
        F2.3.2 Treatment of terms that consist of a string of Synonymous Terms 380
        F2.3.3 Editing during or prior to the second round of merging 380

Contents

F2.3.4 Concluding remark 381

F2.4 Remarks regarding both rounds of merging 381

    F2.4.1 Spelling and morphological variants 381
    F2.4.2 Homonyms 384

F3 Work out the preliminary structure of the thesaurus: the synonym-homonym structure, the equivalence structure, and the classificatory structure. Select preferred terms   384

    F3.1 Define broad subject fields and sort terms into these broad fields 385
    F3.2 Define subfields within each subject field and sort terms accordingly 386
    F3.3 Work out detailed thesaurus structure. Select preferred terms. Merge information for terms in the same concept class 386

        F3.3.1 Work out the synonym-homonym structure and the equivalence structure 388
        F3.3.2 Work out the classificatory structure 389
        F3.3.3 Use of judgment and creative thinking in processing the information collected from different sources 390
        F3.3.4 Introducing more specific concepts 391
        F3.3.5 Scope notes and definitions 391
        F3.3.6 Preliminary selection of descriptors from among the preferred terms 391
        F3.3.7 Some suggestions for the technique to be used (technical) 392

F4 Work out first draft of the classified index (schedule)   392

    F4.0 Classified index and cross-references in BT, NT, and RT 392
    F4.1 Type preliminary classified index. Amend working file 393
    F4.2 Improve the classificatory structure 394
    F4.3 Type improved classified index and amend working file 395
    F4.4 Discuss classified index with subject experts. Select descriptors and checklist descriptors 395
    F4.5 Assign notational symbols 397
    F4.6 Make a systematic search for additional cross-references 397

F5 Complete first draft of the thesaurus as a whole   397

    F5.0 Introduction 397

        F5.0.1 Special problems of smaller projects not using computer assistance (special topic) 398

    F5.1 Revise entries in the working file 398
    F5.2 Produce the main part of the thesaurus in list form 402
    F5.3 Check inverse cross-references and insert where necessary 402
    F5.4 Duplicate preliminary version of the thesaurus 403
    F5.5 Review the whole thesaurus. Consult with subject experts 403
    F5.6 Enter modifications in the master copy 404

F5.7 Production of the alphabetical index (technical) 404

    F5.7.1 Production of a KWIC index 404
    F5.7.2 Manual production of the alphabetical index 406
    F5.7.3 TEST model: produce alphabetical main part and alphabetical index 406
    F5.7.4 Remark 408

F5.8 Check homonyms and improve cross-reference structure using the alphabetical index 408
F5.9 Reproduce test version of the thesaurus 409
F5.10 Remarks on some technical problems arising in F5, F6, and F7 (technical) 409

    F5.10.1 Use of notations as "shorthand" for descriptors 409
    F5.10.2 Technical considerations as to the production of the main part of the thesaurus in smaller projects without computer assistance 410

F6 Test the thesaurus by indexing and retrieval experiments 411
F7 Duplicate or print the user version of the thesaurus 412

    F7.1 Duplication or printing of main part and the alphabetical index 412
    F7.2 Duplication or printing of the classified index 412
    F7.3 Proofreading 413

F8 Further remarks concerning the work-flow and modifications of the standard work-flow 413

    F8.0 Introduction 413
    F8.1 Sequence of the Steps F3, "Work out the preliminary structure of the thesaurus" and F4, "Work out the first draft of the classified index" 413
    F8.2 When should the notation be introduced? 414
    F8.3 When should the main part be typed (smaller projects without computer assistance)? 415
    F8.4 Drawing up and using a "core classification" consisting of elemental concepts early in the process 416
    F8.5 Extending the collection of conceptual relationships, especially for cooperative information services 417

F9 Use of punched paper tape and punched cards in thesaurus construction (special topic, in part technical) 417

    F9.1 Use of punched-paper-tape typewriters in thesaurus construction 417

        F9.1.1 Modifications in the flow of work 417
        F9.1.2 Conversion of punched paper tape to punched cards 418

    F9.2 Use of conventional punched card equipment 419

xxxiv   Contents

    F9.2.1 Punched-card-controlled typewriters (for example, the IBM 870 Document Writing System) 419
    F9.2.2 Keypunch and unit-record equipment 419

G Use of computers in thesaurus construction (advanced; technical with the exception of Sections G0.1 and G0.2) 420

 G0 Rationale for computer application. Overview 420
   G0.1 Rationale for computer application 420
    G0.1.1 Performing routine operations 420
    G0.1.2 Continuous modification of data base 421
   G0.2 Overview. "Entry points" for computer processing. Modifications in work flow 421
   G0.3 Record organization in the computer 424
    G0.3.1 Complete summary of the organization of cross-reference subrecords 425

 G1 Computer assistance in the collection and recording of material 428
    G1.2.2 Recording the data from the sources in machine-readable form 428

 G2 Computer assistance in sorting into alphabetical order and in merging information on identical terms into one record 429
    G2.2.3 Computer assistance in "pulling" information from big thesauri by computer 432
   G2.3 Second round of merging by computer 433
   G2.4 Standardization of spelling variants by computer 433
   G2.5 Miscellaneous problems 433
    G2.5.1 Cross-references given using notations 433
    G2.5.2 Record identification 434
    G2.5.3 Substituting numbers for terms to save storage space 434

 G3 Computer assistance in working out the preliminary structure of the thesaurus 434
   G3.3 Computer assistance in clerical tasks to be performed in F3.3, "Work out the detailed structure of the thesaurus" 435
    G3.3.1 Merging information for each class of synonyms 436
    G3.3.2 Rearranging the working file in classified order 436
   G3.4 Computer assistance for intellectual tasks in working out the detailed thesaurus structure 436
    G3.4.1 Computer assistance in hierarchy construction 436
    G3.4.2 Use of the decomposition of compound concepts into elemental concepts in working out the preliminary structure of the thesaurus 438

,1 Use of the decomposition of compound concepts in sorting terms into subject fields and subfields, and in forming groups of synonyms (Steps F3.1, F3.2, and F3.3.1)   439
,2 Use of the decomposition of compound concepts in working out the classificatory structure (Step F3.3.2)   439

    G3.4.3 Computer assistance in semantic factoring   440

G4 Computer assistance in working out the classified index   441
G5 Computer assistance in completing the first draft of the thesaurus as a whole   442

    G5.1 Computer assistance in revising entries in the working file   442
    G5.3 Check of inverse cross-references by computer   442

G7 Printing the final thesaurus by computer   443
G8 Updating a computer-stored thesaurus   443

    G8.1 Types of changes   443
    G8.2 Input of updating information   445

        G8.2.1 Line-oriented input of updating information   445
        G8.2.2 Term-oriented input of updating information   446
        G8.2.3 Comparison of the two methods   446

G9 Devices for the input (keying) of thesaurus data   447

H Automatic methods in the construction of indexing languages and thesauri, starting from the texts of documents and/or search requests. Automatic classification (advanced)   449

H0 Introduction   449
H1 Definition of units of text and counting methods   450
H2 Identification of descriptor candidates from frequency patterns   451
H3 Detection of term or concept relationships from co-occurrence patterns   451

    H3.0 Nearness measures   451
    H3.1 Interpretation of high association between two terms A and B   452
    H3.2 Second-order associations for the detection of definitional relationships   453
    H3.3 The use of inconsistent association profiles for the detection of homonyms   453
    H3.4 Detection of hierarchical relationships   454
    H3.5 Combined application of different methods   454

H4 Automatic derivation of classification schemes ("global" structures)   455

    H4.1 Automatic derivation of classification schemes by clustering methods   455

xxxvi   Contents

    H4.2 Automatic derivation of classification schemes by graph-theoretical methods   455

J Updating and maintenance of indexing languages and thesauri   457

J0 Introduction   457
J1 Types of changes   457
J2 Sources for new terms, concepts, and relationships to be included in the thesaurus   458

    J2.1 Sources within the ISAR system   458

        J2.1.1 Search request statements, search request formulations, and search performance   458
        J2.1.2 Documents and indexing of documents   459
        J2.1.3 Collection of updating information from sources within the ISAR system   459

    J2.2 Sources outside the ISAR system   460

        J2.2.1 Information on changes in user needs   460
        J2.2.2 Information on new developments in the subject fields of the ISAR system   460

J3 Procedures for regular updating   460

    J3.1 Use of thesaurus forms in updating   460
    J3.2 Processing of updating information   461
    J3.3 Issuing supplements and/or revised versions   461

        J3.3.1 Time schedule for updating   461
        J3.3.2 Physical form of supplements   462
        J3.3.3 Listing of changes made   462

    J3.4 Organization for and decision-making in thesaurus updating   462
    J3.5 "Interactive" updating of thesauri   463

J4 Revision of the indexing language or the thesaurus at longer intervals   463
J5 Remarks on the flexibility of structured indexing languages (classification schemes)   464
J6 Problems of re-indexing (re-classification)   465

    J6.1 Re-indexing problems due to introduction of new descriptors   465
    J6.2 Re-indexing problems due to changes in descriptor usage   466

J7 Thesaurus updating and thesaurus compatibility: common problems (advanced)   467

Part IV Thesauri as a basis for cooperation in information services   469

K Thesauri as a basis for cooperation in information services   471

K0 Introduction   471
K1 Cooperation in the construction of indexing languages and thesauri   472

K1.1 Cooperation in material collection and merging only 472
K1.2 Cooperation in the development of the terminological and classificatory structure 473

  K1.2.1 Cooperation between two (or a few) institutions 473
  K1.2.2 Generalized cooperation: the concept of a source thesaurus (advanced) 473

    ,1 The structure of a source thesaurus 475
    ,2 Extraction of indexing languages or thesauri for special applications from a source thesaurus 477

      ,2.1 Specific extraction of indexing languages from a source thesaurus 477

        ,2.1.1 Format for "extraction specifications" (technical) 478

      ,2.2 General extraction of indexing languages from a source thesaurus 479
      ,2.3 Use of a source thesaurus in the revision of existing indexing languages and thesauri 479

  K1.2.3 Adjunct thesauri 481

K1.3 The concept of a cumulative thesaurus (advanced) 485

  K1.3.0 Definition and use 485
  K1.3.1 Record organization for a cumulative thesaurus (technical) 486

    ,1 Treatment of the recommended structure and of source indications in a cumulative thesaurus 486

      ,1.1 Treatment of the recommended structure 486
      ,1.2 Group of data fields F-L 486
      ,1.3 Use of the data fields C1, K, and L for increasing the precision of source indications 487
      ,1.4 Further refinements 489

    ,2 Keeping track of decisions and dates in a cumulative thesaurus 489

  K1.3.2 Development of a cumulative thesaurus 489
  K1.3.3 Display of a cumulative thesaurus 490

K1.4 Incorporation of an additional thesaurus into the cumulative thesaurus and/or analysis and improvement of that thesaurus using a cumulative thesaurus (advanced and technical) 491

K2 Cooperation through sharing the results of subject indexing (special topic) 493

  K2.1 Introduction. Statement of the problem. Searching conversion versus indexing conversion 494

xxxviii   Contents

        K2.1.1 Multilateral shared subject indexing using a "switching language"   501

    K2.2 Framework for the comparison of two indexing languages or thesauri   502

        K2.2.1 Convertibility categories (advanced)   503

            ,1 Searching convertibility categories   503
            ,2 Indexing convertibility categories   504

    K2.3 Production of conversion tables   510

        K2.3.1 Ideal situation: the indexing languages of the cooperating institutions are still to be built   511

            ,1 The development of a total thesaurus through parallel development of constituent thesauri   512
            ,2 Alphabetical index for the total thesaurus   512

        K2.3.2 Usual situation: each of the cooperating institutions already has its own indexing language long in use   513

            ,1 The local approach and the global approach to the construction of conversion tables   513

        K2.3.3 Updating of the individual indexing languages or thesauri   514

    K2.4 Compatibility on a general level. The concept of an umbrella classification   514

        K2.4.1 Shared subject indexing on a general level   514
        K2.4.2 The concept of an umbrella classification   515

  K3 The idea of a Universal Source Thesaurus (UST) (special topic)   516

    K3.0 Universal Source Thesaurus versus universal classification   516
    K3.1 The structure of UST   517
    K3.2 Neutrality of UST with regard to classification principles   518
    K3.3 UST as a framework for "semi-universal" indexing languages for shared subject indexing   519
    K3.4 Implementation of a Universal Source Thesaurus   519

Appendices   **521**

Appendix 1: Thesaurus guidelines and thesaurus books   **523**

Appendix 2: Bibliographies of subject access vocabularies and dictionaries. Specific subject access vocabularies and documents on specific subject access vocabularies included in the bibliography   **529**

Contents xxxix

Chapter Notes 535

Bibliography 559

Index 609

List of Figures

Figure 1. *Examples of relationships displayed in a thesaurus* (A1.2)   5

Figure 2. *Flowchart: Considerations for the construction of a thesaurus* (A2)   11

Figure 3. *The structure of an information system* (B0)   18

Figure 4. *The structure of an ISAR (Information Storage and Retrieval) system* (B0)   19

Figure 5. *Examples of synonyms, quasi-synonyms, and homographs* (B2.3)   25

Figure 6. *Summary of definitions and further illustrations* (B4.2)   32

Figure 7. *Examples of semantic factoring* (C1.1.0)   75

Figure 8. *Some questions that might be useful for semantic factoring* (C1.1.0)   76

Figure 9a. *Example of (poly-) hierarchical relationships in tree-like representation* (C1.2)   82

Figure 9b. *Representation of the hierarchical structure of Figure 9a in linear arrangement with cross-references* (C1.2)   82

Figure 10a. *Hierarchical structure generated by two facets, no within-facet combinations, no hierarchy within facets* (C1.3)   86

Figure 10b. *Different possible linear arrangements of the concepts given in Figure 10a* (C1.3, D3.1.1)   87

Figure 10c. *Same as Figure 10a, but different semantic content* (C1.3)   88

Figure 11. *Hierarchical structure generated by two facets, no within-facet combinations, hierarchy within facets* (C1.3)   89

Figure 12. *Hierarchical structure generated by three generating concepts without hierarchical relationships among generating concepts* (C1.3)   92

Figure 13. *Hierarchical structure generated by five generating concepts with hierarchical relationship among generating concepts* (C1.3)   93

Figure 14. *Examples of different kinds of hierarchical relationships* (C1.4.2)   100

Figure 15. *Transitions between the synonym-homonym structure, the equivalence structure, and the classificatory structure* (C1.6)   111

Figure 16. *Document representations in different file systems* (C2.3.1)   117

Figure 17. *Typology of international organizations* (C3.1)   144

Figure 18. *Example illustrating the detailed lead-in form* (C5.1)   163

Figure 19. *Example illustrating the detailed lead-in form* (C5.1)   164

xlii   List of Figures

Figure 20. *Treatment of spelling variants* (C6.2)   173
Figure 21. *Types of cross-references and other data elements given in the entry for a term* (C7)   176
Figure 22. *Example worked out according to the Roget-Soergel model and the TEST model* (D0)   185
Figure 23. *Look-up in the Roget-Soergel model* (D1.3.2)   199
Figure 24. *Look-up in the TEST-model* (D1.3.2)   200
Figure 25. *Alphabetical index in KWIC and KWOC format* (D1.5.2)   210
Figure 26. *Thesaurofacet: sample page of the classified index* (D1.7.4)   214
Figure 27. *Thesaurofacet: sample page of the main part* (D1.7.4)   215
Figure 28a. *Medical Subject Headings: sample page of the classified index (subject category listing)* (D1.7.5)   216
Figure 28b. *Medical Subject Headings: sample page of the classified index (tree structures)* (D1.7.5)   217
Figure 29. *Medical Subject Headings: sample page of the main part* (D1.7.5)   219
Figure 30. *Arrangement of types of cross-references and other data elements within a record or entry in the user version of the main part of the thesaurus* (D2.1 and D2.2)   229
Figure 31. *Sample main party entry: Roget Soergel model* (D2.1 and D2.2) 229
Figure 32. *Sample main part entry: TEST* (D2.2)   231
Figure 33. *Sample main part entry: BASF* (D2.2)   232
Figure 34. *Alphabetical versus meaningful sequence of descriptors on the same level* (D3.1.1,2)   240
Figure 35. *Segment of the classified index of the FR thesaurus* (D3.1.1,3) 242
Figure 36. *Display of a large classified index with summaries* (D3.1.1,3) 244
Figure 37. *Simple tree display (following SYNTOL)* (D3.1.2,1)   246
Figure 38. *Tree display using space-saving devices. Also example of how to show a part of a big tree (following SYNTOL)* (D3.1.2,1)   247
Figure 39. *Tree display using space-saving devices* (D3.1.2,1)   248
Figure 40. *Tree display with horizontal arrangement of hierarchical levels* (D3.1.2,2)   250
Figure 41. *Circular display: hierarchical levels arranged in concentric circles (following TDCK)* (D3.1.2,3)   256
Figure 42. *Network display of conceptual relationships following EURATOM 1: Group 15 Anatomy (EURATOM 2, see Figure 46)* (D3.2) 258
Figure 43. *Network display within a coordinate grid* (D3.2)   259
Figure 44. *The descriptors and their relationships from Figure 43 displayed in a linear sequence with indention* (D3.2)   260
Figure 45. *Network display based on a sequence of processes and their results* (D3.2)   261

List of Figures   xliii

Figure 46. *Network display following EURATOM 2: Group 05 Blood system (EURATOM 1, see Figure 42)* (D3.2)   262

Figure 47. *Illustration of a combinatorial index to both LC Subject Headings and LC Classification* (D3.6.1,2)   266

Figure 48. *Example showing two types of notation* (D4.0; also used for D4.3)   274

Figure 49. *An easy-to-produce expressive notation* (D4.3.4)   286

Figure 50. *"Relative" alphabetical index to DDC* (E1.1.4)   304

Figure 51. *Guidelines to singular—plural usage* (E1.4.3)   310

Figure 52. *Flow of work in thesaurus construction: overview flowchart* (F0.1)   327

Figure 53. *Flow of work in thesaurus construction: detailed flowchart* (F0.1)   328

Figure 54. *Thesaurus form* (F0.5)   346

Figure 55. *Example of filled-in thesaurus form* (F1.2.2)   363

Figure 56. *Merging of data elements from different cards for the same term* (F2.2)   369

Figure 57. *Further examples to illustrate merging in the first round* (F2.2)   370

Figure 58. *Example of result of merging in the first round on a thesaurus form* (F2.2)   372

Figure 59. *Sample file for the second round of merging* (F2.3.1)   376

Figure 60. *Flowchart for the second round of merging (identifying classes of synonyms)* (F2.3.1)   378

Figure 61. *Examples illustrating the second round of merging* (F2.3.1)   382

Figure 62. *"Road map" for the analysis of terms* (F3.2)   387

Figure 63. *Example of revisions in the working file* (F5.1)   399

Figure 64. *Construction of a hierarchy by "chaining" hierarchical cross-references* (G3.4.1)   437

Figure 65. *Example of second-order association* (H3.2)   453

Figure 66. *Sample guidance classification scheme of a source thesaurus* (K1.2.2, 2.1.1)   480

Figure 67. *Simple extraction specification and resulting classified index* (K1.2.2, 2.1.1)   481

Figure 68. *More elaborate extraction specification and resulting classified index* (K1.2.2, 2.1.1)   482

Figure 69. *Searching conversion and indexing conversion* (K2.1)   498

Figure 70. *Two sample indexing languages for the illustration of convertibility categories* (K2.2.1)   505

Figure 71. *Searching convertibility categories (conversion from A to B)* (K2.2.1,1)   506

Figure 72. *Indexing convertibility categories (conversion from B to A)* (K2.2.1,2)   507

Introduction

Chapter A

General Overview of the Functions and Structure of a Thesaurus. Major Tasks to Be Performed in and Resources and Work Required for the Construction of a Thesaurus

A0 INTRODUCTION

This chapter should be especially helpful for the administrator planning or considering the development of a thesaurus. It begins with an overview of the functions and the structure of a thesaurus and the major tasks to be performed in its development (A1) and proceeds to a discussion of the resources required in terms of personnel, materials, and time (A2).

A1 OVERVIEW OF FUNCTIONS AND STRUCTURE OF A THESAURUS IN AN INFORMATION STORAGE AND RETRIEVAL (ISAR) SYSTEM

A1.1 Requirements for an ISAR System: Conceptual Structure and Terminological Control

An Information Storage and Retrieval (ISAR) system is a system to store and retrieve or select "retrieval objects" or their substitutes. The retrieval objects are usually documents, but they may also be research projects, institutions, experts, job offerings, job-seeking persons, data elements (such as census data), or whatever. (Throughout this book, to facilitate understanding, the term "documents" will be used instead of the more cumbersome "retrieval objects"; this in no way implies that the considerations are limited to document or reference storage and retrieval systems.) Retrieval or selection can be either for selective dissemination of information (SDI) or for retrospective searching. In either case the following requirements have to be met (or functions have to be fulfilled):

(a) *Conceptual structure.* There has to be a well-thought-through conceptual system which allows for proper organization and retrieval of material.

(a1) In indexing it should be possible to characterize (describe, mark) the documents adequately, that is, at the appropriate level of generality or specificity.

(a2) In retrieval it should be possible to search the store from a large variety of aspects or viewpoints—some of which may emerge only in the future—in such a way that the relevant material is retrieved with a reasonable degree of completeness without retrieving at the same time too much irrelevant material. Also, it should be possible to perform searches quickly and without too much effort.

(b) *Terminological control.* In cases where there are several terms designating one and the same concept, terminological control is required to ensure that an indexer or searcher is led to the appropriate concept no matter with which term he starts. In systems that use terms rather than notations, terminological control ensures, furthermore, that the same term is used in both indexing and searching for designating one and the same concept.

Any inadequacy of the conceptual system and of the terminological control leads to both under-retrieval (relevant documents are missed) and over-retrieval (non-relevant documents are retrieved). The more the size of the store and the number of searches increase, the more are felt the losses incurred by such low search performance.

A1.2 Thesaurus

Conceptual structure and terminological control are provided by a thesaurus which contains (see Figure 1):

(a) a structured system of concepts with indication of hierarchical and associative relationships between the concepts, and

(b) for each concept all terms that designate that concept. All the terms designating the same concept are called synonymous; to bring them together is terminological control.

A thesaurus contains a set of descriptors to be used in indexing and retrieving documents. This set of descriptors is called the indexing language, classification scheme, or system vocabulary.

Conceptual structure and terminological control are not dependent on the method used for indexing (indexing by humans or mechanized indexing) or on the technical devices (conventional catalogs, peek-a-boo cards, com-

(a) Conceptual structure
Electron tubes
   Vacuum tubes   *Also broader term:* Thermionic tubes
   Electron beam deflection tubes   *Related term:* Electron beam
                                                                    modulation
      Tuning indicator tubes
      Trochotrons
      Cathode ray tubes
         Image converter tubes   *Related term:* Fluorescent screens
         Image intensifiers
   . . .
   Thermionic tubes   *Also narrower term:* Vacuum tubes
                        Also broader term: Thermionic devices

(b) Synonymous term structure

Electron tubes	*Synonymous*	Electron valves
Image intensifiers	*Synonymous*	Image amplifiers
Trochotrons	*Synonymous*	Radial beam tubes
Attorney	*Synonymous*	Lawyer; Barrister; Solicitor

Figure 1. Examples of relationships displayed in a thesaurus (A1.2).

puter) that are used for storage and retrieval in a particular system. However, the higher the degree of mechanization of an ISAR system, the greater is the need for a good thesaurus that indicates conceptual relationships. "Conceptual relationships" refers to two kinds of relationships:

(a) relationships among concepts, such as hierarchical relationships;
(b) relationships among terms that result from the meanings of these terms. For example, as mentioned above, if two terms have the same meaning (designate the same concept) they are synonymous.

These relationships are stored as a network of associations in the human brain, and the human searcher makes use of them continuously, if unconsciously. In mechanized searches these relationships can be used if and only if they are included explicitly in a machine-stored thesaurus.

A1.3 The Thesaurus in the Context of an ISAR System as a Whole

It is most important to see a thesaurus and its functions in the context of the whole ISAR system in which it is to be used. Therefore, the design of the ISAR system as a whole and its role within a broader institution or within a communication network have to be clear before one can start with the development of a thesaurus. The scope and structure of the thesaurus must reflect the specific needs, viewpoints, and priorities of the users to be served by the ISAR system. Its structure and size must be adapted to the amount of use made of the ISAR system, to the collection, and to the retrieval techniques, as detailed in the next section.

A1.3.1 Parameters determining thesaurus size

The size of a thesaurus and, accordingly, the effort necessary for its development are dependent on the following parameters:

(1) scope and complexity of the subject field;
(2) kind of retrieval objects or data to be processed;
(3) intended exhaustivity and specificity of indexing.

A note of explanation is in order here. Exhaustivity of indexing is the degree to which the concepts for which the document is relevant are covered (exhausted) by the descriptors assigned to the document. Specificity of indexing is the level of specificity at which these concepts are expressed. (A document on *Image converter tubes* may be indexed by that concept, if it is available as descriptor, or else by *Cathode ray tubes* or even *Electron tubes*.) It is obvious that indexing cannot be more specific than the descriptors provided by the indexing language. It might seem that the exhaustivity of indexing, on the other hand, is not affected by the indexing language. However, this is only partly true. Certain aspects useful for the retrieval of documents (e.g., level of treatment) can be brought out in indexing only if appropriate descriptors (e.g., *Advanced, Graduate, Undergraduate, Other*) are available in the indexing language.

In determining the appropriate level of exhaustivity and specificity one should consider the following parameters:

(3a) required recall and precision of the search results;
(3b) the amount of time available to do a search;
(3c) the expected frequency of search requests;
(3d) size of the collection.
(4) retrieval techniques and technical devices used in the ISAR system.

Pre-combination versus post-combination of concepts, to be discussed in detail later, are especially important in this connection.

Occasionally quantitative formulae for the determination of thesaurus size based on these or other parameters are offered. It is our belief, however, that the assumptions from which these formulae are derived have no foundation in reality and that the formulae are therefore useless and even dangerous. It is much better to develop the thesaurus as described in this book, using the expected search requirements as decision criterion in the selection of descriptors, and then to see what size the resulting thesaurus turns out to be.

A1.3.2 Estimating parameters; dangers of a thesaurus of inappropriate size or quality

In estimating the parameters discussed in the previous section one should not be too conservative since assuming values that are too low is more damaging than assuming values that are too high. Starting from values that are too low one is inclined to be satisfied with a simple alphabetical list of descriptors, compiled with moderate effort, that does not display the conceptual structure and that does not give synonyms. If, however, the collection and the number of search requests increase faster than expected (and they do so more often than not) such a procedure results in major disadvantages. If an ISAR system is started with a thesaurus that has a conceptual and terminological structure inappropriate to handle the real growth of the collection and/or the number of incoming search requests there are only three alternative routes:

(1) Continue operation using the inappropriate thesaurus. This will give more and more inadequate retrieval results. The ISAR system will not fulfill its functions properly and it might come to the point where the users will stop asking questions and the ISAR system will break down.

(2) One can modify and complement the thesaurus by a piece-meal approach as the need for the introduction of new descriptors becomes obvious. This will lead in a short time to a confused and contradictory maze of descriptors. The results will be inadequate indexing, especially the omission of indexing terms, and inadequate search request formulation with the consequence of bad retrieval performance.

(3) The third alternative is to start anew by developing a thoroughly structured thesaurus which is appropriate for an ISAR system with the real (as distinct from the estimated) collection size and search request frequency. This means either that all the items already in the collection have to be re-indexed or that searches must be split in two parts: (a) search in the new part of the collection using the new system; (b) search in the old part of the collection using the old system. Experience has shown that the second part of the search is usually omitted after some time has passed, which means that the old part of the collection is not used anymore. (If the items in the old part of the collection become outdated anyway, this is not a disadvantage.)

Each of these alternatives obviously incurs high costs. It is apparent, therefore, that it is more economical to start with thorough thesaurus development. This may include a collection phase in which documents are indexed without using a thesaurus in order to collect terms, as described later. Of course, one should not go to the other extreme of developing a huge thesaurus for a small ISAR system. It is quite reasonable to start with a small thesaurus appropriate for the needs in the present and the near future of the system. The important point is that the basic conceptual structure of the thesaurus should be thoroughly thought through from the beginning so that one has a sound basis for future expansion. If time and resources allocated to thesaurus development are too small to permit this then the disadvantages described above cannot be avoided. Too often false economy leads to these unwanted consequences.

A1.4 Use of a Thesaurus for Improving Indexes

Indexes to abstracting/indexing services, bibliographies, or books are ISAR systems. The use of a thesaurus to improve such indexes does not, therefore, differ in principle from the use of a thesaurus in any other ISAR system.

Sometimes the same thesaurus (more precisely: the same indexing language) is used for a mechanized ISAR system as well as for a printed index to an abstracting service (API, ERIC, NLM, NASA). This practice is not without problems since the requirements for the descriptors to be used in a mechanized ISAR system on the one hand and a printed index on the other are quite different, as we shall see in Section C2. A big advantage is, of course, that documents need to be indexed only once. (Typically, 10–20 descriptors are assigned to a document for the mechanized ISAR system; the 3–5 most important ones are selected for the printed index.)

A1.5 Use of a Classification Scheme or a Thesaurus for Purposes Other than ISAR

In addition to its use within an ISAR system a thesaurus may serve the following purposes:

(1) In collecting data, be it for a management information system (MIS), for statistical purposes (like data collection by the U. S. Bureau of the Census), or for research, a classification scheme serves as guideline, and it enters into the very definition of the data collected. Of course, it serves also for later retrieval of these data.

(2) In decision-making one needs a classification of alternatives and factors affecting the choice among alternatives.

(3) A thesaurus can be used as a terminological standard in writing articles, instructions, standards, etc.

(4) A multilingual thesaurus can be used as a special multilingual dictionary in its field.

Related to thesauri are other tools used in language processing, such as

(a) monolingual, bilingual, and multilingual dictionaries;
(b) dictionaries for content analysis and similar purposes;
(c) dictionaries for machine translation.

Whereas these tools are not explicitly discussed in this book many of the considerations apply to them as well.

A1.6 Intellectual Problems in the Development of a Thesaurus

The development of a good thesaurus requires a major intellectual effort as well as clerical operations like typing and alphabetical sorting. The intellectual problems may be characterized as follows:

(1) *Concept formation*: The concepts important for retrieval have to be delineated. Starting from a raw list of terms one identifies groups of synonymous or quasi-synonymous terms, each group representing one concept to be used in ISAR. One has to decide, then, whether the meanings of two terms are sufficiently close that it is justifiable to consolidate or "lump together" the two terms in the same group, or whether two different groups, that is, two different concepts, should be established.

(2) *Definition of concepts*: The intension and extension of concept and the boundaries separating it from related concepts have to be determined. (By intension of a concept is meant its meaning, the characteristic by which we distinguish objects, e.g., redness. By extension is meant the set of all objects to which the characteristic applies, e.g., all red objects.)

(3) *Arrangement of concepts* in a structured system or network, that is, establishing for each concept its hierarchical and associative relationships.

A1.7 Criteria for the Evaluation of a Thesaurus

The following criteria are useful in the evaluation of a thesaurus:

(1) *Degree of conceptual completeness*: does the thesaurus include all concepts necessary for an adequate treatment of the subject field?

(2) *Terminological completeness*: are the synonymous terms for each concept covered? Have all the relationships of synonymity among terms been detected?

(3) *Thesaurus display*: is the display of the thesaurus clear and helpful for finding the appropriate concepts in indexing or search request information?

These factors will influence the performance of the thesaurus.

A1.8 Concluding Remarks

A sizeable body of experience and knowledge relating to thesaurus development has been accumulated, especially in the last ten or fifteen years. This book attempts to organize this knowledge into a coherent framework and to describe and evaluate the methods that have been used in thesaurus development. However, there are no easy recipes. In each project of thesaurus development a thorough evaluation has to be made to determine which methods and procedures are most appropriate for the situation, and new methods may have to be developed. Above all, the development of an appropriate conceptual structure calls for a creative and well-organized mind.

The methods suggested in this book are independent of the subject field for which the thesaurus is to be developed, the size of the thesaurus, and other factors.

A2 ADMINISTRATIVE CONSIDERATIONS. RESOURCES AND WORK REQUIRED FOR THE DEVELOPMENT OF A THESAURUS (COMPARE FIGURE 2)

A2.1 Justifying the Creation of a New Thesaurus

Obviously the development of a thesaurus is a major project. Before starting such a project, one should determine whether there is an existing thesaurus suitable to the needs of the planned ISAR system or requiring only slight modifications. While judging whether an existing thesaurus is suitable for the specific ISAR system or not it is important to keep in mind that an ISAR system is usually established in connection with specific needs. As was stressed earlier the scope and structure of the thesaurus must reflect the specific needs, viewpoints, and priorities of the users to be served by the ISAR system. On the other hand, unnecessary duplication of effort should be avoided and opportunities for cooperation should be used.

For evaluation of existing thesauri the criteria mentioned in Section A1.7 are useful. Before a thesaurus is actually accepted for an ISAR system one should try to express a number of search requests using the thesaurus. More thorough testing by indexing and retrieval experiments (as described in Section F6) is often advisable. If the results of the evaluation are negative a new thesaurus has to be developed or an existing thesaurus has to be modified. The rationale for developing a new thesaurus should be given in the introduction to the thesaurus.

The plan to develop a new thesaurus or to make major modification in an existing one should be communicated to the appropriate thesaurus collection center so that other institutions having similar plans may join the effort. Upon completion of the thesaurus, a copy or at least a notice should be sent to the appropriate center. The same is true for supplements or revised editions.

A2.2 Staff Needed for the Development of a Thesaurus

A good thesaurus does not—as is sometimes assumed—emerge out of discussions by panels of subject experts meeting now and then. The development of a good thesaurus requires the work of full-time staff in the following categories:

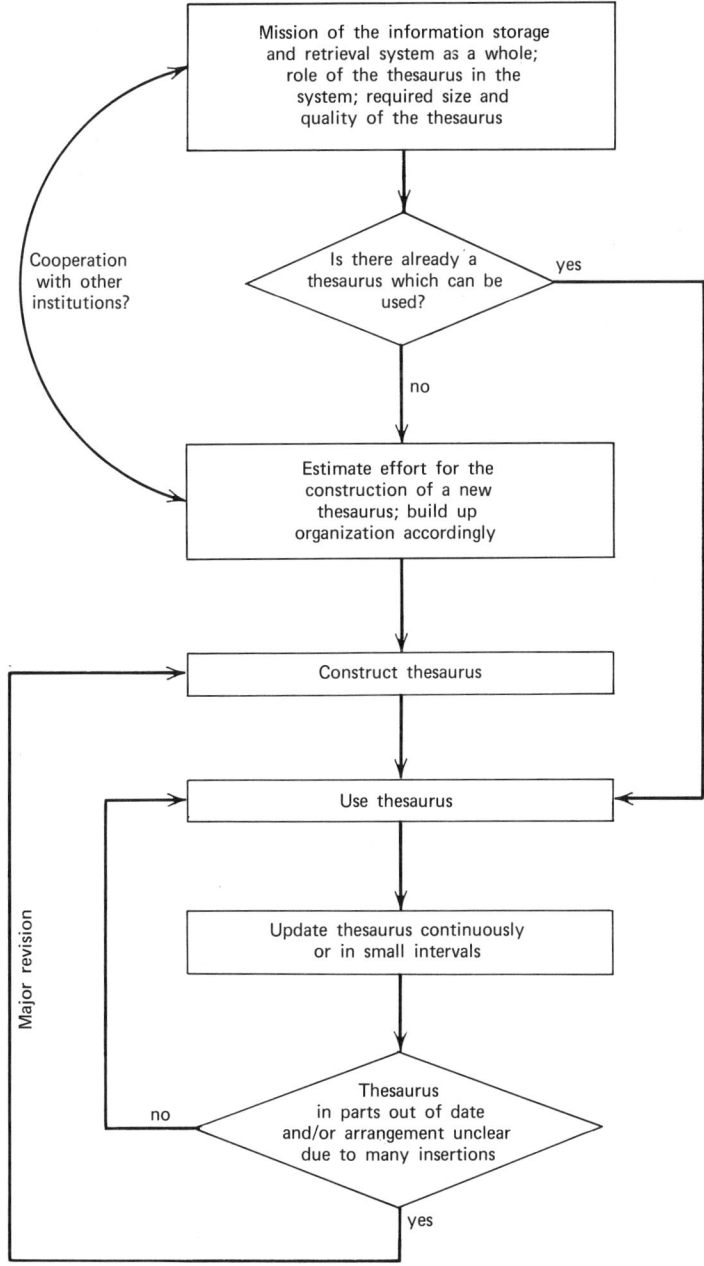

Figure 2. Flowchart: Considerations for the construction of a thesaurus (A2).

(1) information scientists or librarians with some knowledge in the subject fields covered.
(2) lower professionals or para-professionals with some knowledge of information work and of the subject fields covered;
(3) typists;
(4) clerical staff for simple clerical operations.

The number of staff members needed in each category is dependent on the size of the project. The need for staff in the different categories may vary in the different stages of the thesaurus development; large projects need detailed planning in this respect. In large projects the use of mechanical aids, such as punched paper tape typewriters, punched card equipment, or computers, is advisable. In small systems the regular staff can often do the thesaurus development; this may take up about half the time of the head of the department for a year or so. Also, typing and other clerical operations may perhaps be performed by personnel who are permanently employed in other departments of the institution. Large projects, such as the TEST thesaurus or the Dewey Decimal Classification, require their own task forces for thesaurus development and thesaurus updating.

In addition it is necessary to enlist the cooperation of experts in the subject fields covered. A note of caution must be added here, however: subject experts in the field without experience in information service tend to over-emphasize their own specialty. Furthermore they are often not aware of the practical requirements for the arrangement and retrieval of documents and of the advances in classification theory. Therefore, the development of a good thesaurus requires a cooperative effort in which the subject knowledge of the specialist in the subject field and the experience of the information scientist are combined.

A2.3 Time-Frame for the Development of a Thesaurus

In many cases one can base the development of a thesaurus on existing thesauri, classification schemes, dictionaries, and other sources that display terms and concepts in a systematic way, even if no existing thesaurus is acceptable for use in its entirety. In this case thesaurus development should be speedy in order to avoid changes in the participating staff. Working in a limited time span has the additional advantage that the staff is familiar with the whole system or large parts of it during the whole period. The requirement of speed influences, of course, the number of staff required. In addition the timing of thesaurus development must be seen in the context of the overall development of the ISAR system.

In some cases, especially in new fields, indexing languages or thesauri reflecting practical experience with respect to the actual importance of terms in formulating search requests and indexing documents in real-life systems may not yet exist. In this case scheduling a period of experimental indexing and search request formulation, using either a combination of preliminary indexing language and free-term indexing or free-term indexing alone, is recommended. In this experimental phase concepts and terms occurring in the documents and search requests processed are collected. In order to ensure a reasonable degree of completeness the experimental phase should be extended over a period of three to twelve months. Only after this period should thesaurus development proper begin, based on the concepts and terms collected. No re-indexing is necessary in ISAR systems that allow synonyms in indexing and take care of the synonym problem in searching; the thesaurus grows with the collection.

It is very difficult to give quantitative data for the time and effort needed in constructing a thesaurus. Times between 6 months and 3 years are reported. For a small-scale thesaurus (ca. 2,500 terms) the following data have been reported: 1 scientist and 1 clerical staff full-time for 6 months. (A conventional procedure using index cards was followed; a classified and an alphabetical part of the thesaurus were produced, both in form of an index file duplicated in several copies, no other publication form.)

A more typical situation for small to medium-sized ISAR systems has been alluded to above. For a period of 12–24 months, the head of the special library or information center devotes about half of his time to directing the thesaurus development. His or her secretary will be occupied about half-time with typing. Other staff members on both the para-professional and the clerical level will be involved, too, as will selected users. The actual time needed depends on the complexity of the subject field to be covered, the size of the thesaurus (about 3,000 terms is a mean figure), and other factors.

A2.4 Necessity of Continuous Updating

A thesaurus is never complete. It has to be updated continuously based on the experience gathered in its practical application so as to reflect the most recent developments in the subject field. A staff member responsible for the updating should be designated.

Part I

Conceptual Structure of Indexing Languages and Thesauri

Chapter B

Concepts and Terms. Indexing Language and Thesaurus and Their Functions in an ISAR System

B0 INTRODUCTION

In order to develop a good indexing language or a good thesaurus one needs some background knowledge of the role of terminological control in ISAR systems and of the functions and structure of indexing languages within such a system. Since this book is written for readers with widely varying backgrounds some basic viewpoints will be summarized in this chapter and in Chapter C. Figures 3 and 4 provide a summary of the structure of an information system and of an ISAR system that may serve as a framework for the considerations that follow.

Information storage and retrieval is always concerned with retrieving a document (or another retrieval object) relevant to a concept. But since concepts can be referred to only by using the appropriate terms one must be concerned with the relationships between concepts and terms (Sections B1 and B2). These considerations provide the basis for the definition of indexing language (classification scheme) and thesaurus (Sections B3 and B4). Sections B5 to B7 deal with the functions of an indexing language and of a thesaurus in an ISAR system and related problems.

B1 PLANE OF CONCEPTS VERSUS PLANE OF TERMS: THE SYNONYM-HOMONYM STRUCTURE

One has to be very careful to distinguish between the plane of concepts and the plane of designation of these concepts. Much confusion arises if one ignores this distinction.

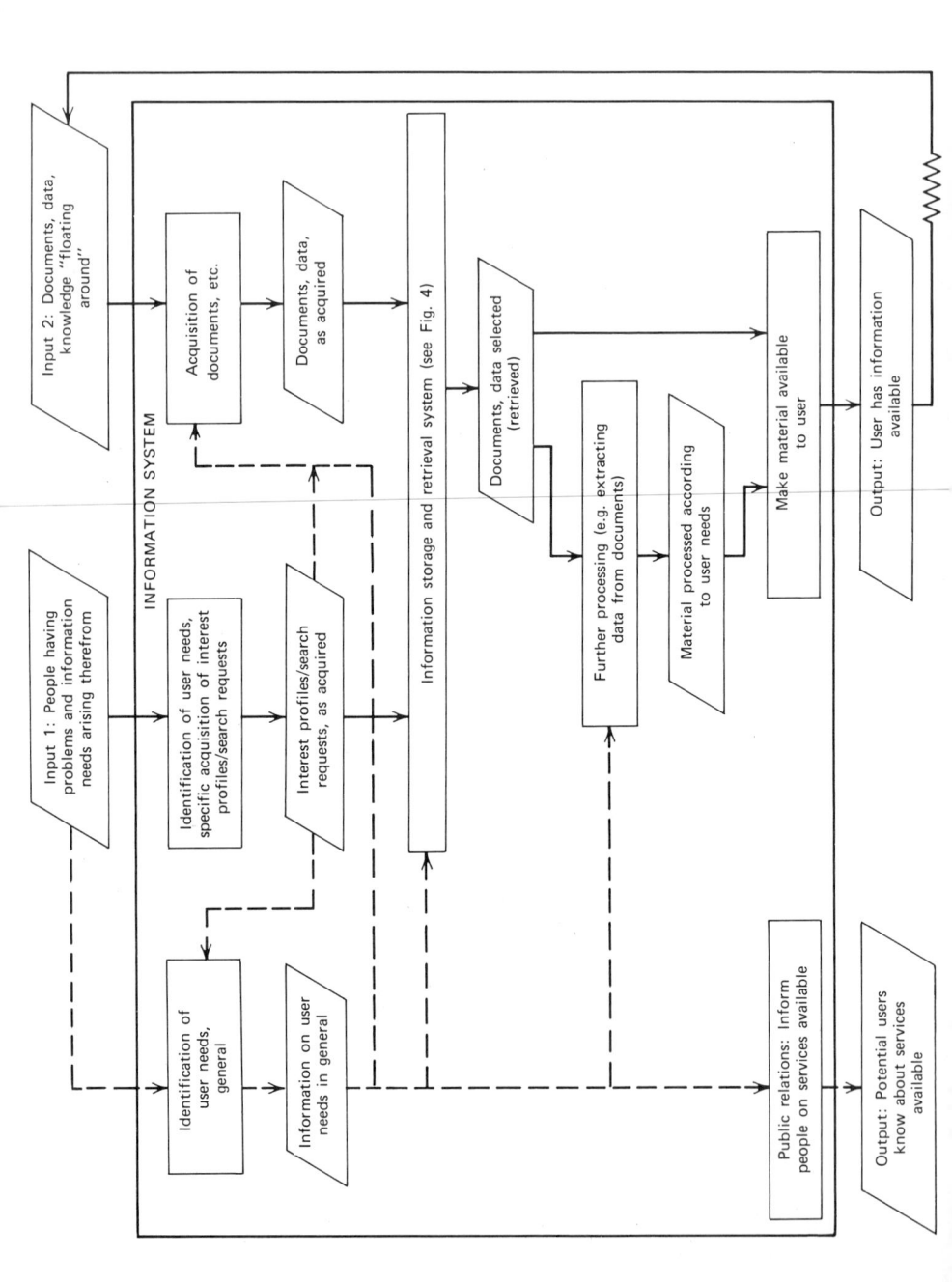

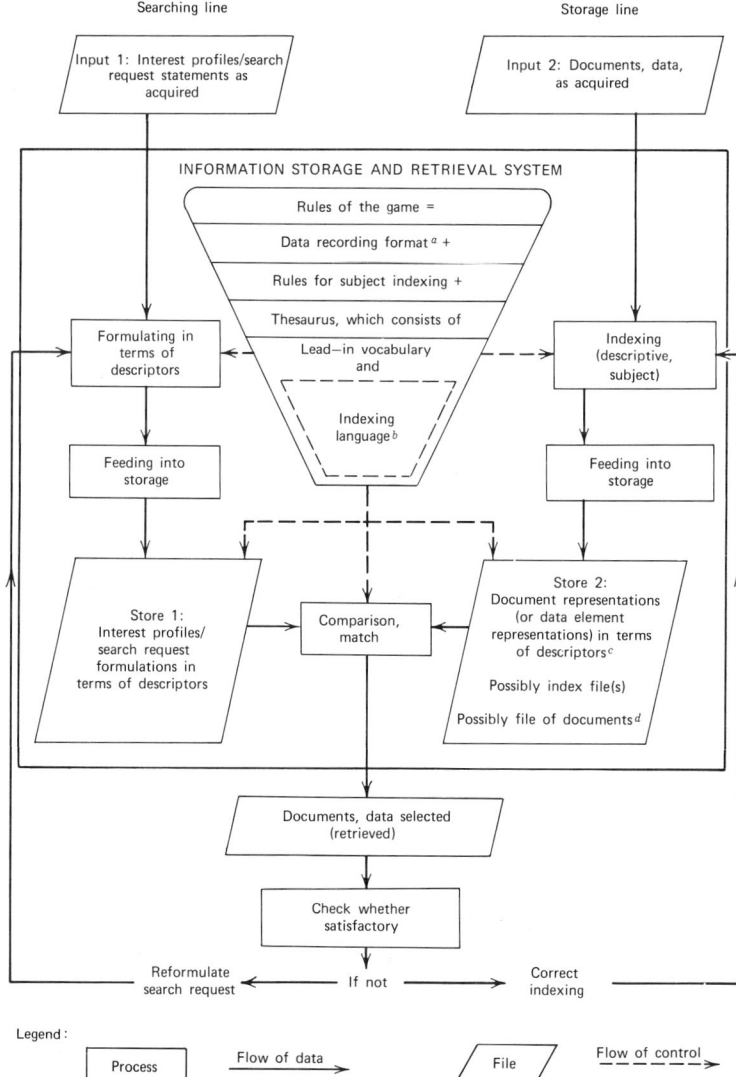

Figure 4. The structure of an ISAR (Information Storage and Retrieval) system (BC). (a) The control functions of the data recording format are not shown. (b) For many purposes, the terms indexing language, system vocabulary, and classification scheme are synonymous. (c) Document representation in this diagram is defined broadly to include both the bibliographic description of the document and the subject representation of the document. Since this book is concerned with subject retrieval, document representation will be used in the narrower sense of subject representation from this point on. (d) The organization of Store 2 is not shown in detail. The document representations in terms of descriptors are the elements entering into the comparison with the search request formulations. One or more index files can be used to implement the comparison operation, but the comparison can be performed without an index file. Physical access to the documents is often separated from the matching process; it does not concern us here.

In language, terms (single-word terms or multiword terms) are used to designate concepts. The relationships between concepts and terms are governed by the rules of terminology. However, as is well known, there is much confusion in this area. Firstly, there is no one-to-one relationship between concepts and terms. In the case of synonyms several terms designate the same concept. For example, *Lawyer* and *Attorney*, *Ethyl alcohol* and *Ethanol*, *Fixed in concentration* and *In exchange capacity* (both designating the same state of ions in chemistry), and *Place under government ownership* and *Nationalization* are synonyms. On the other hand homonyms are terms that correspond to different concepts (have different meanings): *Bank 1 (economics)* and *Bank 2 (waterways)* or *Socialization 1 (economics)* and *Socialization 2 (social psychology)* are examples. Secondly, different people use the same term with different meanings. Things are complicated even more by the well-known fact that different persons (or even the same person at different times) associate different concepts with one and the same term. It is therefore necessary to control the relationship between concepts and terms. In most fields this problem is far from solved. In developing thesauri it is necessary, therefore, to deal with terminological problems and to introduce terminological control. This is done by the synonym-homonym structure, which establishes a one-to-one correspondence between concepts and terms. As we shall see in more detail later, this is done by selecting a preferred term from a group of synonyms and by distinguishing different meanings of a homonym by a number and/or a "parenthetical qualifier" (disambiguation of homonyms).

In addition to terms there are other designations of concepts, such as mathematical symbols or pictorial symbols (iconographic designations). Again, there is no one-to-one relationship between concepts and symbols. In some fields it might be useful to include nonverbal designations in a thesaurus. Strictly speaking, the heading of this section should read "plane of concepts versus plane of designations of concepts".

A problem related to synonyms but of a more technical nature is the problem of spelling variants, which will be dealt with in Section C6.

B1.1 Homonyms and Homographs (Advanced)

The problem of homonyms is more complicated than it might seem from the previous considerations. First of all, the fact that language can be both written and spoken gives rise to the following distinction:

A homonym (broadly defined) is a term or other designation that represents several distinct concepts or, in other words, that is ambiguous. One speaks of homonyms (narrowly defined) if the sameness of a term is judged from the spoken language and of homographs if the sameness is judged from the written language.

B1   The Synonym-Homonym Structure

Examples:
> *Course* and *Coarse* or *Right, Rite, Write,* and *Wright* are homonyms, not homographs;
> *Wind 1* (air) and *Wind 2* (rotate) are homographs, not homonyms (narrowly defined).

(Different inflections of one word are considered as different terms in this context.)

ISAR, especially mechanized ISAR, is concerned almost exclusively with homographs because it deals with written, not spoken, language. The majority of authors, however, use the term "homonyms". In the following the term "homonyms" shall be used in its broader sense.

Some authors distinguish between homonymous terms and polysemous terms as follows: Homonyms designate concepts that are completely different semantically.

Examples:
> *Seal 1 (marine animal)*
> *Seal 2 (documents)*
> *Drill 1 (instruction)*
> *Drill 2 (agriculture)*
> *Drill 3 (fabric)*

Sometimes the additional criterion is added that homonyms should not have a common origin. This criterion is not very useful, however, as may be seen from the examples *Fire 1 (fire)* and *Fire 2 (dismiss)*, or *Mercury 1 (metal)* and *Mercury 2 (planet)*.

Polysemous terms, on the other hand, designate concepts that share semantic characteristics.

Examples:
> *Integration 1 (mathematics)* and *Integration 2 (economics)* (e.g., economic integration of Europe).
> *In both cases integration means putting together parts into a whole.*
> *Plasma 1 (biology)* and *Plasma 2 (physics)*.

This situation may be described as follows: There is a broader concept, e.g., *Integration*, usually a concept of general application. There are a number of narrower concepts, each used in a special field or discipline. The same term, e.g., *Integration*, is used to designate the broader concept and all the narrower concepts. In this situation it might be useful to introduce the broader concept as a separate descriptor.

The distinction between homonymous and polysemous terms is not a dichotomy but a continuum.

Examples:
Constitution 1 (character) and Constitution 2 (politics);
Field 1 (mathematics), Field 2 (sports),
Field 3 (subject field), Field 4 (data processing),
and Field 5 (agriculture);
Bridge 1 (trafficway) and Bridge 2 (dental)

(On the usefulness of concepts of general application like *Integration*, see Section C4.3.1. On the treatment of homonyms, see Sections C5.3.1 and E1.1.)

B2 TREATMENT OF NEARLY RELATED CONCEPTS: THE EQUIVALENCE STRUCTURE

B2.0 Equivalent Concepts (Equivalent Terms)

There are not too many true synonyms. True synonyms can be, for example: different terms for the same concrete object or process, a case which especially occurs in connection with new developments; common names and scientific names for chemical substances. More often than not, differences in the language indicate subtle differences in meaning or in the affectional component of a concept—for example, *Developing countries* and *Underdeveloped countries*. For purposes of ISAR, it is often useful to neglect these subtle differences and to consolidate (lump together) nearly related and/or widely overlapping concepts, resulting in a class of equivalent concepts. The terms designating the concepts in one class are called quasi-synonyms.

Examples:
Transportation and Traffic; or Form of state and Form of government; or Beer, Ale, and Malt liquor; or Socialization 1 (economics) and Nationalization, or Duration and Time, or Lightning and Illumination.

This procedure prevents the scattering of documents on the same theme or nearly related themes under a number of descriptors in the indexing stage and thus allows for searching under one descriptor instead of under a number of nearly related descriptors.

These considerations lead to the following *definition*:

> Two concepts A and B that are closely related are called *equivalent* in a given ISAR system if, within that ISAR system, no distinction is made between these concepts for indexing and retrieval purposes.

It is important to note that two concepts that are considered to be equivalent in one ISAR system may be kept distinct in another. In a special ISAR system for economic law one may, for example, wish to distinguish between *Socialization 1 (economics)* and *Nationalization*. Contrariwise, true synonyms remain true synonyms, no matter what the ISAR system is.

There is another procedure which is, in a sense, similar to yet to be distinguished from the consolidation of quasi-synonyms: one may, for purposes of indexing and searching, replace a very specific concept by the appropriate broader concept. In some cases one may even create a broader concept, replacing a number of clearly distinguishable (not widely overlapping) very specific concepts. (This procedure will be dealt with in Section C1.4.1,3; on the transitions between the different cases, see Section C1.6.)

B2.1 Forming ISAR Concepts and Naming Them. Preferred Terms

By consolidating a number of widely overlapping concepts one arrives at a new concept that contains all of the original concepts. In this book these newly formed concepts are called ISAR concepts, and the structure leading to them is called the equivalence structure. In most systems it is advisable to choose a term or form a new term that unambiguously designates the ISAR concept. These terms are called preferred terms.

To summarize: it is useful in most circumstances to group terms into classes of identical or very similar meaning and select from each class a preferred term as representative.

More precisely "preferred designation" should be used instead of "preferred term". The preferred designation may in fact be a notation, such as a class number or even a running number.

The introduction of preferred terms is one method to achieve terminological control, that is, to avoid the negative effects of terminological confusion on the performance of an ISAR system. (Other methods will be discussed later.)

B2.2 Classificatory Structure

The totality of the ISAR concepts as represented by the preferred terms together with the relationships among these ISAR concepts will be called the classificatory structure of the thesaurus. Note that it is by no means necessary or advisable to use all preferred terms in indexing (i.e., as descriptors). Many of them may be too specific for that purpose. Sections B3 and B4 will discuss this point in detail.

B2.3 Summary of B1 and B2 (See Figure 5)

The considerations in B1 and B2 may be summarized as follows: starting from a list of terms, the designer of an indexing language must develop a list

24   B   Indexing Languages and Thesauri

of concepts useful for ISAR, or ISAR concepts. A two-step reduction is useful for this purpose (leaving aside the problem of homonymy for the moment):

   Step 1: Consolidate synonymous terms
   Step 2: Consolidate nearly related concepts

Through these two steps classes of terms are formed. Each class contains synonymous and quasi-synonymous terms that correspond to the same ISAR concept. One of these terms is selected, or a new term is created, to designate the ISAR concept; this term is called the preferred term. Homonyms are disambiguated. By this procedure terminological control is introduced.

In reality there is no sharp delineation between "true" synonyms and quasi-synonyms (terms designating nearly related concepts). The following picture comes nearer to reality: a distance measure between terms is defined based upon the concepts they designate so that the distance is zero if two terms designate exactly the same concept, small if the terms designate two widely overlapping concepts, and large if the terms designate two totally different concepts. Now two terms may be called "truly" synonymous if their distance is below a very small threshold. When the distance is above that threshold but still small, the two terms may be called quasi-synonymous if this seems to be useful in the system at hand. Consider the following list of terms as a final example.

Example:
   Street, Road, Lane, Drive, Avenue, Boulevard, Route, Highway, Divided highway, Expressway, Throughway, Parkway, Turnpike, Motorway, Beltway, Ringroad.

A system that gives "distances" between terms rather than forming equivalence classes and selecting preferred terms (a process that by necessity is somewhat arbitrary) will be described in Section B4.3.

	Terms	Concepts	Preferred Terms
Homonyms Synonyms	Cu Copper		Copper
	Cable		Cable 1 (physical object) Cable 2 (telegram)
Equivalent Terms	Cable 1 Wire		Wire, cable

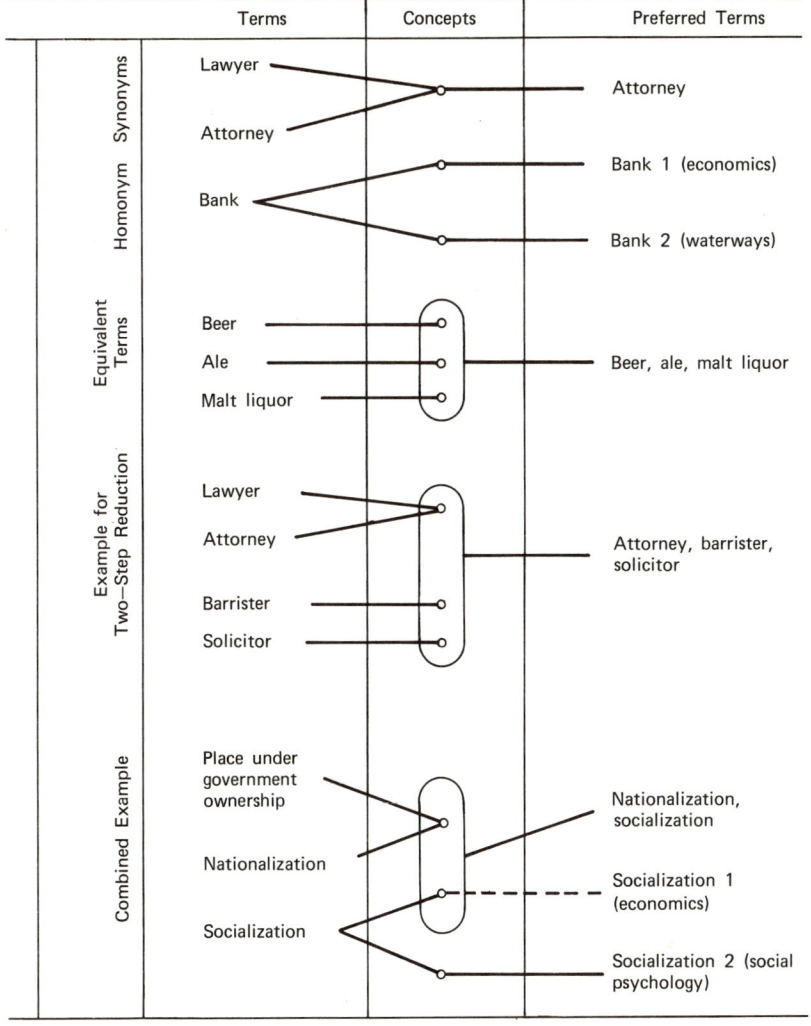

Figure 5. Examples of synonyms, quasi-synonyms, and homographs (B2.3). (left page) Wire, cable is one term that is used to designate all objects that might be called either Wire or Cable 1 or both.

B2.4 A More Realistic But Less Practical Model

The view of the relationship between concepts and terms that has been presented here is deliberately simplistic. It is assumed that concepts exist as abstract entities independently from terms or other designations and that terms can be chosen to designate uniquely these concepts. Philosophers concerned with the philosophy of language or epistemology, linguists, and psychologists concerned with concept formation will find much to quarrel with in this assumption. However, deliberate simplifications are often useful, and the simplified picture has two merits in the context of information storage and retrieval: it makes clear that one is interested in retrieving documents relevant to a certain concept and not documents indexed by or containing a certain term or other sign, and it allows for the construction of indexing languages and thesauri that take this basic fact into account. To be sure, if one wants to construct a system that uses automatic indexing or interactive searching through natural language text, one has to take a more realistic and more complicated view of the relationship between language and concepts. But for the ISAR systems operational today and for many years to come, which use human indexing and human translation of the search request into the indexing language, the simplistic view is sufficient. The reduction process described above is, by the way, not dependent on this simplistic view. One may derive some measure for the nearness of two terms without referring immediately to the meaning of those terms (for example, by psychological experiments on how people associate the terms or by observing the pattern of co-occurrence of terms in texts, see Chapter H). In this way one views a term just as a string of characters without necessarily viewing it as the designation of a concept. The plane of concepts (if it in fact exists) is, so to speak, left out of the picture.

B3 INDEXING LANGUAGE

B3.0 Definition of "Descriptor 1 (Retrieval Cue)", "Descriptor 2 (Subject Descriptor)", and "Indexing Language"

The previous two sections were concerned with the relationship between concepts and terms. This section deals with the representation or indexing of documents (or other retrieval objects). It therefore starts with a general definition not immediately related to the previous considerations:

Descriptor 1 (retrieval cue) = any string of symbols or other marks used (1) in the description and representation of documents and (2) in the selection and/or arrangement of documents (retrieval

B3 Indexing Language

objects) or their substitutes in a given system by a given mechanism.

This definition includes author and title (in an author/title catalog), date of publication (in a mechanized system or in a card catalog if sequential scanning of the card by the human eye is the "given mechanism"), subject headings (in a catalog arranged by subject headings), a term or notation causing the appropriate peek-a-boo card to be selected for searching or to be punched in file building (if the ISAR system uses peek-a-boo cards), and the words and phrases or whole sentences in an abstract (if sequential scanning by a human searcher is considered to be the "given mechanism").

This general definition is given because "descriptor" is sometimes used in this general sense, especially in mechanized systems. The following definition corresponds more nearly to the common use of the term "descriptor".

> *Descriptor 2 (subject descriptor)* = Descriptor 1 narrowed to include only strings of symbols designating ISAR concepts used in subject indexing and searching. Descriptor 2 may be a term or a notation or another string of symbols used to designate the ISAR concept. In the rest of the book the term "descriptor" will be used with the meaning of descriptor 2; whenever descriptor 1 is meant, it will be so designated.

Terminological control has not been included in the definition. This has consequences for the concept of an indexing language (to be defined shortly). However, in the remainder of the book terminological control shall be assumed unless specified otherwise. A descriptor then designates unequivocally an ISAR concept actually used (or intended to be used) for indexing and retrieval purposes. In other words every descriptor is a preferred term (but not vice-versa). Most commonly the term "descriptor" is used with these connotations. (If it is necessary to refer specifically to the string of characters that constitutes a preferred term, we shall speak of the "text of the descriptor". Notation has been mentioned in the definition because in many systems the notation is the string of symbols used in indexing and searching. Again, if it is necessary to refer specifically to the notation, we shall speak of the "notation of the descriptor".) The definition of "descriptor" provides the basis for the definition of "indexing language".

> *Indexing language (documentary language)* as used in this book = any language (broadly defined) for the representation and/or for the arrangement of retrieval objects and/or their substitutes with the objective of making the items retrievable.

An indexing language comprises:

(a) (mandatory) a *list of descriptors, the system vocabulary or lexicon*. Relationships among descriptors (such as hierarchical relationships or associative relationships) may be indicated. The system vocabulary or lexicon is often called classification scheme, especially if the descriptors are brought into some sort of classified arrangement.

Examples of descriptors are: *Hammer*; *Form of government*; *Theory*; *France*; *Graduate-level text*; *621.21* (*Water wheels*, from DDC); *SB211.P8* (*Potatoes*, LCC); *NQCL.MACH.003* (*Reactor*, Semantic Code); *Ph Rab Ssd Zb* (*Dimensional stability of plastic at high temperature*, a faceted classification).

(b) (optional) a *list of role indicators and/or relators* (relational descriptors). Hierarchical or associative relationships may be indicated among role indicators or among relators, too.

Examples *(role indicators or relators, respectively, in bold face):*
Role indicators:
(Effect : *Noise)* : **(Cause** : *Children);*
(Starting materials : *Hydrogen and Oxygen)* : **(Final product** : *Water);*

Relators:
Noise : **Caused by** : *Children;*
Hydrogen and Oxygen : **Produce** : *Water;*

One could say that the role indicators and/or the relators have a syntactical function and therefore belong to the syntax of the indexing language (as distinguished from the vocabulary given in (a)). However, there is no clear-cut frontier between descriptors and role indicators. The distinction serves more practical than theoretical purposes, and we shall not attempt to define the distinction beyond the illustration provided by the examples.

(c) *a set of formation rules* for constructing expressions in the indexing language as detailed below. In more elaborate indexing languages these rules are made explicit. More often than not, however, the rules are not spelled out explicitly but are assumed to be obvious.

(c1) (mandatory) A set of rules for the construction of more or less compound expressions, using descriptors from the lexicon and syntactical elements. These compound expressions may either be document representations or formulations of search requests.

(c2) (optional) A set of rules for the deduction of relationships between compound expressions and descriptors and between compound expressions themselves.

(c3) (optional) A set of rules for the arrangement of compound expressions in a linear sequence. These rules may be used for the filing of catalog cards or for the shelving of documents.

For further elaboration on the definitions of "descriptor" and "indexing language" and comparison with other usages see Section B4.2.

B3.1 Remark on Terminological Control

A special remark on terminological control is in order. The above considerations did not assume terminological control in the indexing language; this keeps the definition sufficiently general to include operational systems that have no terminological control at all. There are also well-known systems that have terminological control but exert it not in the indexing stage but in the searching stage (synonyms are allowed in indexing and all documents indexed by any one of a number of synonyms are retrieved) to be discussed in Section B4.3 (if there is no terminological control in indexing, one speaks of free-term indexing). The generality of the definition covers the use of the natural language as indexing language.

On the other hand it is now widely recognized that indexing languages using terminological control give better results, and most indexing languages do use terminological control in indexing. Therefore, the terms "indexing language", "system vocabulary", or "classification" are most commonly used with the understanding that terminological control is applied in the indexing stage. We shall follow that usage unless specified otherwise.

B4 THESAURUS. SUMMARY OF AND FURTHER REMARKS ON THE DEFINITION OF PREFERRED TERM, DESCRIPTOR, CONCEPT, AND INDEXING LANGUAGE

B4.1 Simple Definition of "Thesaurus". Use of the Lead-In Structure in Indexing

In the previous section it was strongly recommended that the indexing language contain preferred terms only. But the exclusive use of preferred terms has the following disadvantage. Often a thesaurus user, whether an indexer or a searcher, is looking for a certain concept and has in mind a particular term designating that concept, as suggested by a document, his own language usage, or whatever. He looks up this term in the alphabetical index. If he is lucky his term happens to be the preferred term used to designate the concept; but often this will not be the case, and then the user has to think up some other term for the concept and look up that term, and so on, until he has found the preferred term. It would be much easier for the user if he could find a reference in the alphabetical index whether he looks under the preferred term itself or under any of the synonymous and quasi-synonymous terms designating the same concept. Such terms had been eliminated when selecting a preferred term from a class of synonymous and quasi-synonymous terms, but they should be included in the alphabetical index, thereby expanding again the total vocabulary. These reintroduced synonymous and quasi-synonymous terms serve the purpose of leading to the appropriate descriptor; they are part of the lead-in vocabulary.

There is a second problem that has to be dealt with in this connection: In systems of combination indexing (frequently termed coordinate indexing), compound concepts are often eliminated and a combination of descriptors is used instead for indexing and searching purposes. In this case it is useful to tell the user which combination of descriptors to use. We thus have the following situation: the lead-in vocabulary gives the preferred term for the compound concept and refers to the combination of descriptors to be used. In addition the lead-in vocabulary may include synonymous terms designating the same compound concept with a reference to the preferred term and possibly the combination of descriptors to be used. These relationships are displayed in Figure 6a. The whole system is called "thesaurus" in this book. A thesaurus thus consists of an indexing language or a system vocabulary, including all the relationships among descriptors, and a lead-in vocabulary that includes all the relationships among the lead-in terms and that leads from the terms not used as descriptors to the appropriate descriptors in the indexing language, possibly specifying the nature of the relationship between lead-in term and descriptor.

These considerations apply also to the case where the look-up of the appropriate descriptors in indexing and/or formulating of search requests is performed by a computer program instead of by the indexer or searcher. The thesaurus has to be much larger in size in this case because the computer program cannot deal with minor variations in spelling as easily as people can or find as easily another term if the term looked for is not there.

One would like to collect in a thesaurus all the terms of a given subject field and to detect the relationships among them as completely as possible. In all practical situations there is, however, the problem of costs and of competence, and the thesauri available are more or less complete. It is therefore not useful to include completeness as a criterion in the definition of "thesaurus".

B4.2 Summary of and Further Remarks on the Definition of Preferred Term, Descriptor, Concept, Indexing Language, and Thesaurus

In an area that abounds with conceptual and terminological confusion the preceding sections lay out a system of definitions that is useful and logically consistent and at the same time reflects whatever consensus on the usage of terms can be found in the field. These definitions form the basis of all that follows. It is therefore appropriate to summarize these definitions, elaborate them further, and contrast them with other usages.

B4.2.0 Summary of definitions

Figure 6 gives a summary of definitions and further illustrations.

B4.2.1 Preferred term and descriptor

Preferred term was defined as the term that is selected from a class of synonymous and quasi-synonymous terms to designate unequivocally the concept underlying the class.

Descriptor (descriptor 2, subject descriptor) was defined as any string of symbols designating a subject and used (1) in the representation of documents (in indexing) and (2) in the selection and/or arrangement of documents or their substitutes in a given system by a given mechanism. As they stand, these two definitions are independent. A preferred term need not be a descriptor, that is, there are preferred terms that are not admissible in document representations and search request formulations. A descriptor need not be a preferred term (there are ISAR systems that do not use terminological control in indexing). However, a closer relationship between "preferred term" and "descriptor" is established if one requires, as indeed in most of this book we do, that only preferred terms be used as descriptors. This stipulation leads to Figure 6b. Common usage goes further: it does not allow for preferred terms that are not descriptors. "Preferred term" and "descriptor" are considered to be synonymous. As shall be discussed in more detail in Section C5, it is important to maintain the distinction between "preferred term" and "descriptor", and a deviation from common usage in this point can therefore not be avoided.

(Sometimes *descriptor* is even used synonymous to *terms in the thesaurus*. The reader who wants to see for himself how confused things can get may look at the following quotation from the explanation of the KWOC-index of TEST:

"Index words (words preceding a group of terms in a KWOC-type index, D.S.) that are themselves descriptors appear in boldface italics, otherwise in boldface. Terms that are USE references rather than descriptors are preceded by a centered dot (·)" In the first sentence, *descriptor* means *term in the thesaurus* (there are plenty of index words in boldface italics preceded by a dot (·)!). In the second sentence, *descriptor* clearly means *descriptor 2* as defined above. In reading the literature, one has to be exceedingly careful to determine what is really meant.)

Synonymous with "descriptor" are the terms "keyword", "clueword", "cueword", "index term", and others. A "subject heading" is a specific type of descriptor, namely, a descriptor used in an alphabetical subject catalog or printed index. Some people use "descriptor" only in connection with

1. *Synonym-homonym structure* — Relates terms to concepts

2. *Equivalence structure* (quasi-synonyms or equivalent terms) — Groups together widely overlapping concepts resulting in "ISAR-concepts" expressed by preferred terms (1-1 correspondence)

3. *Classificatory structure* — Made up of ISAR-concepts, as expressed by preferred terms, and their interrelationships. May refer from an ISAR-concept not used for indexing and searching to the appropriate descriptor(s).

4. *Indexing language* (system vocabulary, classification scheme) — Made up of descriptors, i.e. preferred terms designating ISAR-concepts that are actually used in document representations and search request formulations.

5.

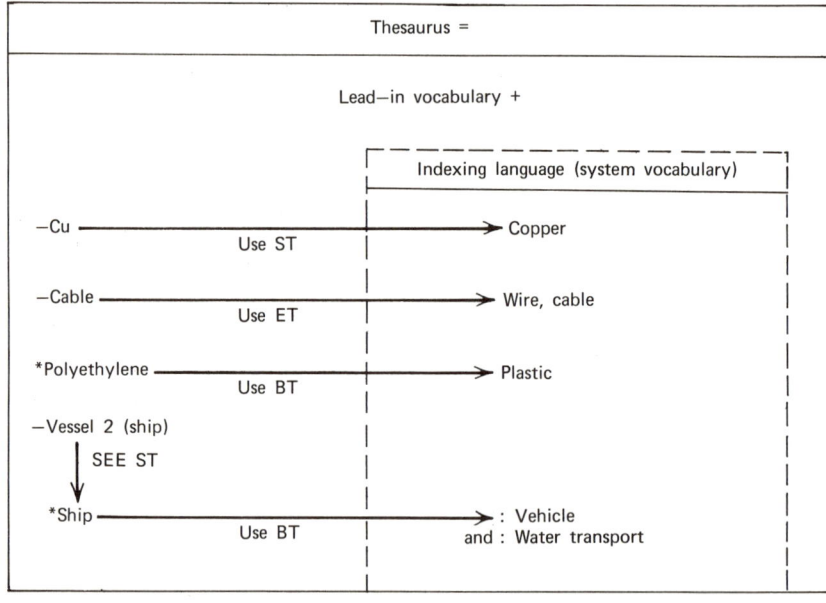

Legend: ST Synonymous term — Not a preferred term
         ET Equivalent term   * Preferred term but not a descriptor
         BT Broader term

Figure 6a. (left) Summary of definitions.
Figure 6b. (right) Further illustrations (B4.2).

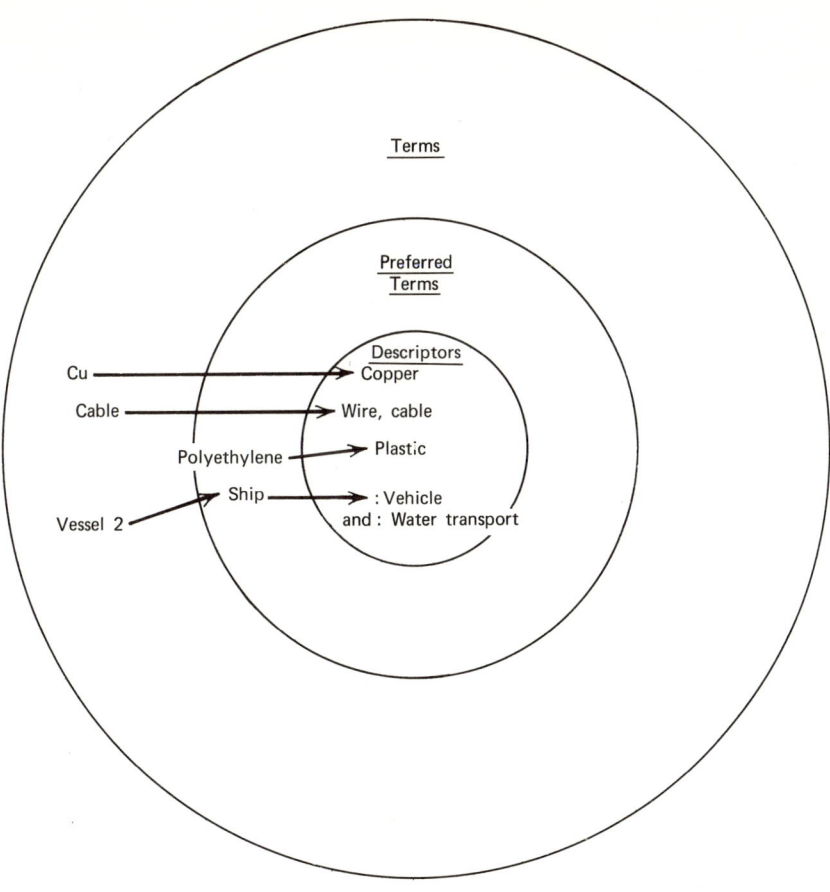

Type of term	Part of thesaurus		Relationship belongs to
P D	I	Copper	
N	L	Cu USE ST Copper	Syn-Hom Structure
P D	I	Wire, Cable	
N	L	Cable USE ET Wire, Cable	Equivalence Structure
P D	I	Plastic	
P	L	Polyethylene USE BT Plastic	Classificatory Structure
P D	I	Vehicle	
P D	I	Water transport	
P	L	Ship USE BT :Vehicle and :Water transport	Classificatory Structure
N	L	Vessel 2 (ship) SEE ST Ship	Syn-Hom Structure

Type of term:
N = Non-preferred term
P = Preferred term
D = Descriptor

Part of thesaurus:
L = Lead-in vocabulary
I = Indexing language, system vocabulary

34   B   Indexing Languages and Thesauri

ISAR systems using combination indexing (usually implemented through edge-notched cards, peek-a-boo cards, or computerized methods). Descriptors in this usage represent predominantly elemental concepts, whereas subject headings represent predominantly compound concepts. While this usage corresponds to the original definition of "descriptor" it has not gained currency in the profession. A "class number" is another specific type of descriptor, namely the notation from a classification scheme such as the Dewey Decimal Classification or the Library of Congress Classification.

B4.2.2 Concept, preferred term, descriptor

In Section B1 and elsewhere it was stressed how important it is to distinguish between the "plane of concepts" and the "plane of terms" (more general, the "plane of concept designations"). However, since there is a one-to-one relationship between concepts and preferred terms, the terminology can be relaxed a little: in order to avoid the rather awkward phrases "the concept designated by the preferred term X" or "the preferred term designating concept X", "concept" and "preferred term" shall often be used interchangeably. The same remark applies to "concept represented in the indexing language" and "descriptor".

B4.2.3 Indexing language, system vocabulary, classification scheme

The definition of indexing language given in Section B3.0 is deliberately very general. In fact it includes any language used for indexing and retrieval purposes, and it does not rule out any language because of any properties which that language may or may not have. Even natural language can be used as an indexing language as defined above. The definition does not assume that there is any terminological control (there may be different descriptors contained in the indexing language, designating the same concept without indication of appropriate relationships between these descriptors). Nor does the definition assume that any relationships between descriptors are indicated; specifically, it does not assume that there is any degree of hierarchy. The definition is valid for traditional as well as for modern mechanized methods of information storage and retrieval, and it is valid for document or reference storage and retrieval as well as for data storage and retrieval or storage and retrieval of other objects, and it is valid for retrospective searching as well as for selective dissemination of information.

A term often used in connection with indexing language is "classification" or, more precisely, "classification scheme". There are about as many definitions of "classification" as there are writers on the subject, and we shall not try to give a new one. But it might be useful to point out the range of meanings associated with the term "classification". Of particular interest is the definition contained in the conclusions of the Elsinore Conference

(1964): "By classification is meant any method creating relations, generic or other, between individual semantic units, regardless of the degree of hierarchy contained in the systems and of whether those systems would be applied in connection with traditional or more or less mechanized methods of document searching." This definition, which formed the starting point for the definition of indexing language used in this book, has not become popular in the field. In general usage the term "classification" is used to designate the list of descriptors, the system vocabulary or lexicon. Many authors use the term "classification" only if there is terminological control in indexing (if the descriptors correspond unequivocally to concepts), if hierarchical relationships are indicated between the descriptors, and if the descriptors are arranged in a classified order. If these conditions do not hold, these authors would use the term "descriptor list" or "subject heading list" or a similar term. In this book the terms "classification" and "system vocabulary" will be considered synonymous.

In most indexing languages used in operating ISAR systems only the system vocabulary is given explicitly, and the designers of these indexing languages in effect refer to the system vocabulary if they use the term "indexing language". In this book "system vocabulary", "classification" (or "classification scheme"), and "indexing language" are therefore used interchangeably for most purposes. Sometimes a distinction is made between indexing language as the set of descriptors that *could* be used in indexing and the systems vocabulary as the set of descriptors that actually *have been* used in indexing. However, this distinction is useful only for ISAR systems that use free-term indexing (so that the number of potential descriptors is very much larger than the number of descriptors actually used).

B4.2.4 Subject access vocabulary, thesaurus, indexing language, and classification scheme

The terms "thesaurus" and "indexing language" or "thesaurus" and "classification scheme" are often used synonymously. Some authors associate with the term "classification" traditional schemes like Library of Congress Classification or DDC and with the term "thesaurus" the method of combination indexing or a particular kind of representation of relationships between concepts. Some authors also associate with "thesaurus" a list arranged alphabetically (not in classified order). None of these criteria is valid as characteristic for a definition, and we therefore have tried to clarify in our definitions the following issues:

(1) By "indexing language" should be designated the language to be used in document representations and search request formulations. This does not include the lead-in vocabulary because the elements of the lead-in vocabulary, by definition, are not used in document representations or search request formulations.

36 B Indexing Languages and Thesauri

Often "indexing language" is defined as it is here, but later on it is understood to include lead-in terms. In our view a lead-in entry tells how to use the indexing language, and including lead-in terms in the indexing language is about as sensible as including German terms in the English language because they are lead-in terms in a German-English dictionary.

(2) There should be a clear distinction between systems that provide an indexing language (system vocabulary) only and systems that in addition provide a lead-in vocabulary. These latter systems have been given the name "thesaurus" by those writers who gave some thought to the concept. In Sections B4.3 and B4.4 we shall extend the definition of "thesaurus" to more general structures.

(3) The issue of the structure of an indexing language (conventional classification versus concept combination) should be kept separate from the issue of whether or not a lead-in vocabulary is given. It is therefore not useful to understand by "thesaurus" a system that gives a lead-in vocabulary *and* which is made for combination indexing.

(4) The arrangement in which descriptors are presented (alphabetically versus classified) is still another issue.

A good general term to cover "classification scheme", "system vocabulary", "descriptor list", etc., and "thesaurus" might be "subject access vocabulary".

In systems using terminological control in indexing the term "authority list" is used both in the sense of "indexing language" ("system vocabulary") and of "thesaurus". The emphasis is on the fact that the authority list specifies those terms that are allowed as descriptors (authorized terms). The term "controlled vocabulary" is also used for the indexing language of such systems. Correspondingly, "vocabulary control" is often used for "terminological control".

The remainder of Section B4 deals with complex thesaurus structures that may be used in advanced ISAR systems (Section B4.3) and goes into the problem of a formal definition of the concept "thesaurus" connected therewith (Section B4.4). The reader who is not interested in these specialized topics may turn immediately to Section B5.

B4.3 Complex Thesaurus Structures. Use of the Lead-In Structure for Terminological Control in Searching (advanced)

There are ISAR systems that do not use preferred terms at all in document representations and search request formulations. The title and/or an abstract and/or the full text of the document might serve as document representation in such a system. In this case the indexing language consists of all terms of the natural language (common words, such as articles and pronouns, are often explicitly excluded from the indexing language). However, terminological control is a necessity in these systems, too. It can be achieved as follows: Terms are grouped into classes of synonymous and equivalent terms as above. A group might be, for example, *Attorney; Barrister; Lawyer; Solicitor*. Whenever *Lawyer* occurs in a search request, it is expanded to *Attorney OR Barrister OR Lawyer OR Solicitor*. So far, we have the same information in the thesaurus as discussed in Section B4.1 except that the user need not select a preferred term. We call such a thesaurus a "simple" thesaurus. (It is fairly obvious that for purposes of *storing* such a thesaurus we would select a preferred designation (term or number) for each class. All terms of the class would be listed under that preferred designation, and a reference to it would be made from each term in the class.) However, putting together synonyms and quasi-synonyms in a class and thereby treating them as equal is a rather crude procedure (see Section B2.4). A more complex thesaurus structure can reflect more of the complexities of language. An example may illustrate such a structure by contrasting it with the "simple" thesaurus structure described in Section B4.1.

Assume the search request statement as turned in by the user consists of one term only, namely, *Lawyer*. By expanding the search request formulation as described above, documents which contain in their text *Attorney* or *Barrister* or *Solicitor* are judged by the system as being of equal relevance as documents which contain in their text the term *Lawyer*. However, documents containing *Lawyer* or *Attorney* are probably more relevant than documents containing *Barrister* or *Solicitor*. We could quantify this judgment by assigning the relevance coefficient 1.0 to documents containing *Lawyer* or *Solicitor*. Furthermore, we might assign the relevance coefficient .5 to documents containing *Judge*. In the "simple" thesaurus we might have the cross-reference *Attorney* Related Term *Judge*, which could be used to expand the search request formulation to *Lawyer OR Attorney OR Barrister OR Solicitor OR Judge*. Again, in the simple system a document containing *Judge* is not distinguished in its relevance from a document containing *Lawyer* or *Attorney* in this simple system. The information contained in a complex thesaurus structure can be represented in table form (see following page).

If the search request combines two terms, e.g., *Lawyer* AND *International politics*, the coefficients for both have to be considered to determine the degree of relevance of a document containing, say, *Barrister* and *Foreign policy*. The figure .8 in column 3 thus indicates the strength of a relationship between the terms *Lawyer* and *Barrister*. We call this relationship a "relevance relationship" because it is used in determining the coefficient of relevance of a document containing the term *Barrister* to a search request containing the term *Lawyer*. These relevance relationships are often not symmetric. The problem of how these relevance relationships can be determined cannot be dealt with here.

Term in search request	Term in document	Relevance coefficient
1st example:		
Lawyer	*Lawyer*	1.0
	Attorney	1.0
	Barrister	.8
	Solicitor	.8
	Judge	.5
2nd example:		
International	*International politics*	1.0
politics	*World politics*	1.0
	Global politics	1.0
	International relations	.7
	Foreign policy	.6
	Foreign relations	.5

A large number of terms is necessary for this procedure, and "relevance relationships" of the form shown in the example have to be indicated. Note that with this kind of thesaurus we may stay in the plane of terms without referring in any way to the plane of concepts. Therefore, the indexing language remains on the plane of terms without explicit reference to concepts, whereas in the simple thesaurus structure the elements of the indexing language are in a one-to-one relationship to concepts. As a consequence, there is no such thing as a lead-in vocabulary in the complex thesaurus system described here. (All terms may be used in document representations and search request formulations, so there is no problem of leading from forbidden terms to allowed terms.) But it is useful to define "thesaurus" broadly to include such a structure of terms and their interrelationships. In ISAR systems using free terms, the searcher is free to use or not to use the thesaurus. He could include all the terms needed in the search request himself and weight them as he wishes (he may want to assign 60% to *Judge* instead of 50%).

The considerations of Sections B4.1 and B4.3 will be taken up again in Section B6.

B4.4 Formal Definition of "Thesaurus" (advanced)

The following definition includes both the simple case described in Section B4.1 and the complex case described in Section B4.3.

A thesaurus in the field of information storage and retrieval is a list of terms and/or of other signs (or symbols) indicating relationships among these elements, provided that the following criteria hold:

(a) the list contains a significant proportion of non-preferred terms and/or of preferred terms not used as descriptors;
(b) terminological control is intended.

Some amplification of this definition is in order: in the case B4.1 criterion (a) serves to distinguish between systems that contain an indexing language only and systems that provide in addition a lead-in vocabulary. Only the latter are called "thesaurus". The requirement of a "significant proportion" (which somewhat arbitrarily may be set to be 10% or more, to give an order of magnitude) excludes those systems from among the thesauri that list in a random manner a few synonyms with cross-references in addition to the descriptors in the indexing language. While it would be logical to include such systems among the thesauri, it is more useful to speak of a thesaurus only in those cases where there is a serious intent of including such additional terms systematically. If such an intent is implemented to any reasonable degree, it results in all practical cases in a proportion of non-preferred terms and/or preferred terms not used as descriptors of the order of magnitude given. One could, of course, conceive of a field in which a one-to-one correspondence between concepts and terms exists. However, this is not realistic.

The structures discussed in Section B4.3 are included in the definition because there are no preferred terms at all; therefore, 100% of the terms are non-preferred terms, and terminological control is intended.

B5 THE FUNCTIONS OF THE INDEXING LANGUAGE WITHIN AN ISAR SYSTEM. A PRELIMINARY OVERVIEW OF THE STRUCTURE OF INDEXING LANGUAGES IN RELATION TO THEIR FUNCTIONS IN AN ISAR SYSTEM

In developing an indexing language or thesaurus one has to have in mind the application of these tools in the ISAR system as a whole. Sections B5 to B7 summarize the functions of an indexing language and the additional functions of a thesaurus within an ISAR system as a whole and indicate implications for the design of an indexing language.

B5.0 "Indexing" versus "Grouping of Documents" I. Solutions to the Retrieval Problem

It is logical to start with a reassessment of the retrieval problem. The following considerations may seem very obvious; however, it is often the obvious which is forgotten, and we shall see that these obvious considerations lead to important consequences that are not at all so obvious.

The purpose of an ISAR system is to select documents relevant to a given search request, be it (a) for selective dissemination of information

40   B   Indexing Languages and Thesauri

(SDI) (identifying all documents acquired in, say, the last month and relevant to a "standing" search request or interest profile, and sending appropriate notices to the user), or (b) for retrospective searching (identifying all documents in the collection relevant to a search request to be answered once for the whole collection, not at regular intervals for recent accessions).

B5.0.1 Elementary solution: search whole (un-indexed) collection

The most elementary method for selecting documents relevant to a given search request is the following: Look at every document in the collection, having in mind the search request, and decide whether this document is or is not relevant to the search request. If the collection consists of 100 documents, the following "unit operations" are necessary for one search request:

—1 unit operation to read and understand the search request;
—100 unit operations to read and understand the documents;
—100 unit operations to compare the documents with the search request and decide for each whether or not it is relevant.

Reading and understanding the documents is the most time-consuming of these operations. The following discussion assumes that several requests can be kept in memory at the same time and that each unit operation comparing a document with a search request takes the same time whether there is only one search request or several search requests in parallel.

As is well known, this elementary method is not efficient if the system receives numerous search requests. Look at a situation where we have, say, 50 search requests per week. Processing these search requests according to the elementary method described above would require the following unit operations:

—50 unit operations to read and understand the search requests;
—5,000 unit operations to read and understand the documents;
—5,000 unit operations to compare with search requests.

It is the purpose of ISAR systems to organize this basic process in a more efficient way.

B5.0.2 First economy measure: batch search requests

A first improvement can be achieved as follows: Wait until all 50 search questions have come in. Then proceed as follows: Read and understand all 50 search requests and store them in memory. Thereupon read and understand each of the 100 documents, comparing it with each of the search requests in memory in order to decide whether it is relevant to that search request or not. Using this procedure, the following unit operations are necessary.

B5 Functions of the Indexing Language 41

—50 unit operations to read and understand the search requests;
—100 unit operations to read and understand the documents;
—5,000 unit operations to compare the documents with the search requests.

By this procedure the number of the time-consuming unit operations for reading and understanding of documents has been drastically reduced. This increase in efficiency is due to the fact that one does not process each incoming search request individually; instead, one batches together a number of search requests and processes them in parallel.

This method is often used by scientists writing major studies. For example, consider a Ph.D. student writing his dissertation: He divides the theme of the study into a number of subtopics and, in reading documents, he indicates for which of the subtopics the document is relevant.

B5.0.3 Second economy measure: prepare abstracts

There is another possibility for increasing efficiency. We could shorten the time necessary for reading and understanding documents by summarizing the essential aspects of a document in an abstract so that, in processing a search request, only the abstract has to be perused. However, there is one major drawback in this approach: The abstract has to contain all aspects of the document that may be important for the decision on whether or not the document is relevant to a certain search request. These aspects are often not known beforehand.

B5.0.4 Third economy measure: anticipated search requests: collect anticipated search requests and analyze documents in advance

Neither batching of search requests nor preparing abstracts is efficient enough for large ISAR systems. Greater efficiency is achieved through combining and carrying further the methods of batching search requests and of preparing abstracts. In batching search requests even more effort could be saved by processing more than 50 search requests in parallel. Why not collect all search requests that are to be served on a regular basis in a system for SDI (e.g., in a company, all search requests that are pertinent to the program of research and development)? Why not, in addition, think about what search requests are to be expected and list those search requests, too? If we do this we obtain a list of search requests to which we may assign numbers. Each incoming document is now processed by assessing its relevance for each of these search requests and the numbers of those search requests for which the document is relevant are noted. By this process of indexing we arrive at a representation of the document similar to abstracts. If a user now comes with a search request, all we have to do is to look up the number of the search request and then look through all the document representations to see whether this number is recorded or not. This is a purely mechanical process.

This method is a logical development of batching search requests: all possible search requests are listed so that the contents of each document has to be read and understood only once. The method is also a logical development of preparing abstracts: the aspects to be considered in writing the document representations are rendered explicit by the list of anticipated search requests; therefore, the effort needed later to read and understand the document representation in processing a search request approaches zero. Of course this method fails if a search request comes in that has not been anticipated and therefore has not been considered in indexing the documents. In this case one has to go back, at least in principle, to the elementary method of reading all documents in the store.

The search requests or their numbers are descriptors, and the list of search requests is an indexing language as defined earlier. In a real system the whole process is more complicated, as we shall briefly outline in Section B5.1 and describe in detail in Section C1.

B5.0.5 Fourth economy measure: provide a retrieval mechanism

Using the method of anticipated search requests we still have to look through all the document representations as a search request comes in. This procedure is called sequential scanning. Manual sequential scanning is feasible only in very small collections. In medium-sized collections it is possible to perform sequential scanning using suitable devices (punched card equipment, computers). In a very large collection even these mechanical devices are not sufficient. We therefore have to look for ways to improve our retrieval method further. Numerous mechanisms are available for this purpose. A simple mechanism is grouping documents by subject. Since this mechanism has had considerable impact on the development of classifications, it will be discussed in some detail. This simple mechanism works as follows: Groups of documents (or of substitutes for documents, such as catalog cards) relevant to the same search request are formed. If a search request comes in all one has to do is to pull the appropriate group. Originally (especially before the card catalog came into use) people thought it would be possible to arrange the documents (books) themselves in such groups on the shelves. However the arrangement on shelves imposes two technical constraints:

(1) as a rule, every document can be shelved in one and only one location;
(2) the documents have to be arranged in a linear sequence.

These constraints force the designer of a system to assume that every document is relevant to one and only one search request. This assumption is far from correct.

From this approach a classification scheme is viewed as a list of headings or labels for groups of documents (or pigeonholes). Classifying of a document means, then, to assign the document to one of these groups. Obviously the assignment of a document to a group says something about the content of the document and is thus a representation of the document. Very often this representation is very incomplete. (Sometimes "classifying" is still used in a narrow sense to mean only "grouping of documents". Other authors use it almost synonymously with indexing, implying a classified indexing language.)

Another aspect has to be considered in connection with "shelving classifications". In arranging documents or their substitutes for the purpose of retrieval, an additional requirement has to be met, as illustrated in the following example:

Example:
Search request no. 35   *Elementary education in Peru,*
Search request no. 47   *Elementary education in Chile, and*
Search request no. 123   *Elementary education in Brazil*
are related to each other.

The corresponding groups of documents should therefore appear in the same neighborhood on the shelves, so that in a search for a broader request one can look at all these groups at once. This means a hierarchical arrangement of the groups. The technical constraints mentioned above require that a specific group belong to one and only one broader group; a specific concept must not have more than one broader concept (we may view the group headings as concepts). A system that imposes this constraint is called a mono-hierarchical system. Whereas such a system might have seemed reasonable in 1850, it certainly cannot represent the complexity of today's world and today's knowledge.

We shall come back to the problems of shelving classification in general and of mono-hierarchy in particular in Sections B5.2 and C1.

B5.0.6 Concluding remarks

It is most important to note that all these methods have the purpose of organizing more efficiently the basic retrieval process: look at a document and decide whether or not it is relevant for a given search request. The search request (the problem of the user) is the primary concern, and the documents have to be looked at in the light of the search request. This is perfectly clear in the elementary method, where we have one search request and look in turn at each document in the collection. The basic problem might be obscured, however, in the method of anticipated search requests, where for every incoming document we look at a list of search requests. One has to be very careful to retain the basic purpose of the process in this case, too. The indexer has to read and understand the document, look at the document from the point of view of each of the search requests listed, and for each of these search requests make a decision as to whether or not the document is relevant. We shall come back to this problem in Section B5.2.

B5.1 A Preliminary View of the Structure of Indexing Languages (Classification Schemes)

Using the method of anticipated search requests one may have to compare a document with 100 or 1,000 or more search requests. This task is obviously not manageable unless the search requests are brought into a meaningful order so that whole groups can be eliminated at once. In any real situation we have so many search requests—either listed as interest profiles or anticipated—that it may not be possible to arrange them in a meaningful order or that even a meaningful order would not allow for an easy overview. To solve this problem, search requests are split into components, as illustrated by the following example:

Example:
Search request:
  I need material on the corrosion of steel pipes
Components:
  Corrosion AND Steel AND Pipes
Search request:
  German technical schools in India
Components:
  Technical schools AND Germany AND India AND Activity taking place in developing country AND Activity sponsored by industrial country.

The system of these components will be much simpler than the system of all search requests. Only these components are then used in the representation of documents. In other words they are used as descriptors. Instead of looking for the number of a search request in the document representation, one looks for the appropriate combination of descriptors which expresses the search request. It is obvious that this procedure is much more flexible because it allows the expression of search requests that have not been anticipated, as long as the appropriate components are available in the system.

B5.2 Request-Oriented Indexing and the Checklist Technique

B5.2.0 Introduction

Request-oriented indexing is a logical development of the method of anticipated search requests. It is of utmost importance for the performance of an ISAR system and it has a decisive influence on the design of an indexing language. In spite of the importance of the orientation towards search requests, indexing is very often done in a document-oriented mode. We therefore consider request-oriented indexing in detail, carrying further the deliberations of Section B5.0.

We start our considerations by describing two disadvantages of "shelving classification schemes" so that we may then contrast the advantages of request-oriented indexing with the traditional approach.

B5.2.1 Disadvantages of the method of indexing commonly used (document-oriented indexing)

Section B5.0.5 dealt with the approach that reduces the classification scheme to the function of arranging documents on shelves. This approach has two negative consequences:

(a) *In the design of the indexing language* or classification scheme: the selection of the descriptors to be included in the classification scheme, their arrangement, and the indication of relationships between them is done in such a way as to create suitable headings for groups of documents in the collection to be organized. Descriptors denoting form characteristics of the documents or descriptors like *Graduate level text* are considered only insofar as they are useful as headings for groups of documents, otherwise they are omitted. The same is true for descriptors that represent general aspects, e.g., *Threshold, Effects*, and for very specific descriptors. All of these elements would be very useful for the formulation of search requests. In addition only those hierarchical relationships needed for the shelving arrangement are considered; this leads to an artificial mono-hierarchical structure.

(b) *In indexing*: one looks for a "pigeonhole" where the document fits in. If the cataloger has found such a pigeonhole, he is satisfied, regardless of whether or not the document is relevant for other search requests. The indexing is document-oriented rather than, as it should be, request-oriented.

In shelving and to a lesser degree in conventional card catalogs there are technical constraints leading to this procedure, as we have seen earlier. The basic attitude has been transferred, however, to systems of combination indexing in which the technical constraints no longer exist. This attitude may be briefly summarized as follows: The document is primary, and we have to find a class number for the document in the classification scheme or express the content of the document by an appropriate combination of descriptors.

The usual procedure for indexing arising from this attitude is the following. The indexer reads the document or an abstract of the document, notes the subjects dealt with in the document or, even worse, just underlines important terms in the abstract. Thereupon he "translates" his own terms or the terms underlined in the abstract into the indexing language, often using an alphabetical index. As soon as the indexer has found descriptors for every subject he has identified, he is satisfied; the indexing is finished. This is obviously a complete reversal of the basic retrieval operation, where the search requests are primary and the documents are looked at in light of the search requests. This reversed approach has a very unfortunate consequence: the fact that the document is possibly of interest for other problems and that additional aspects should be considered in indexing is not taken into account.

Consider the following examples:

(1) In July, 1967, shortly before an important session of the Romanian National Assembly, the official Soviet newspaper *Pravda* published an article issuing a warning to nationalist movements in countries of the Communist bloc without naming any specific country. It is immediately clear to the knowledgeable indexer that Romania is addressed and that, therefore, "bilateral relationships USSR-Romania" is an important descriptor in indexing the article so that the article may be retrieved in a search for that subject. Note that the term *Romania* appears nowhere in the article.

(2) Documents with the following titles should be retrieved in a search for, and therefore indexed by, *Seismonastic movements of plants*:

Mechanics of the movement of the leaf of Dionaea
Sensitivity of the flowers of Catasetida
The stimulative substance of Mimosa

B5.2.2 Implementation of request-oriented indexing; the checklist technique described

These examples again illustrate the point made amply clear earlier—that indexing should be request-oriented, not document-oriented. The search requests are primary and the documents are analyzed with a view to the search requests. The indexer has to think of all the possible search requests (or aspects occurring in search requests) and decide for which search requests the document at hand is relevant. To say it another way: The list of search requests serves as a checklist which is to be compared with the document so that all aspects for which the document is relevant are elicited. Those search requests to which the document is relevant are checked. This statement applies also to the case where the original search requests are broken up into components; these components, too, are questions or aspects to be considered in the analysis of documents.

This point is so important that it is useful to illustrate it further with additional examples. In the reference storage and retrieval system of a company it is very useful to have the following descriptors:

B5 Functions of the Indexing Language 47

Technological developments that might put us out of business;
Technological developments that might be used to improve our products;
Market gaps for our products.

These might well prove to be the most important descriptors in the system.

The second example is an ISAR system for curriculum development. The purpose of such a system is to retrieve topics that contribute to specified educational objectives. The retrieval objects are therefore topics, and each topic has to be indexed by the educational objectives it serves. But how could this be done without drawing up a list of all educational objectives in the first place? As it happens this list will be hierarchically structured because there are objectives, sub-objectives, sub-sub-objectives, and so on.

This all boils down to a procedure for indexing that is quite different from the procedure usually applied: having read and understood the document (or at least what the document is about) the indexer looks at each descriptor (each request) in turn and decides whether the document is relevant to that descriptor (that request) or not (the list of descriptors serves as a checklist to be compared with the document). This is how indexing really should be done. An objection comes immediately to one's mind, however: it is not possible in any practical situation to look at a thousand or five thousand or even more descriptors for every document to be indexed. We therefore have to look for realistic means of implementing this indexing procedure or, in other words, of implementing the principle that the search requests are primary. This can be done as follows:

(1) *Checklist descriptors.* There are a limited number of descriptors that are particularly important to the organization setting up the ISAR system in terms of their expected occurrence in search requests. These descriptors should be considered especially in indexing; they will therefore be called "checklist descriptors". In order to ensure that the checklist descriptors receive the required considerations the following policies should be followed:

(1.1) The indexer has to learn the checklist descriptors and have them in his mind so that he goes through them more or less unconsciously while indexing documents.

(1.2) The descriptors, especially the checklist descriptors, should be displayed on a few pages in such a way that the overall structure of the indexing language and the different relationships between the descriptors become clear. Various typographical and graphical means that can be used for that purpose will be discussed in Chapter D, especially Section D3. Such a display is particularly useful for leading the indexer or searcher almost automatically to the appropriate descriptors and for making sure that no important aspects are overlooked. This will enhance inter-indexer consistency as well as intra-indexer consistency, (that is, it will make sure that different indexers, as well as the same indexer at different times, will use the same descriptors in indexing a document).

(2) *Subdivision into subject fields.* The set of descriptors (search requests) is

subdivided into subject fields (usually overlapping) in such a way that the indexer looking at the heading of a subject field can already decide whether or not there is an expectation that the document is relevant to any of the descriptors contained in the subject field.

Example:
Education
Communication and language
Society
Politics
International politics
Law
Economics
Technology
Problems of developing nations
Socio-cultural change

In that way the indexer discards many of the subject fields, thus narrowing down considerably the number of descriptors to be looked at. Within a field the same procedure is applied: The field is subdivided into subfields (usually overlapping), and the indexer again starts by looking at the headings of the subfields.

Example:
Politics
    System of government
    State and organs of the State
        ...
        Constitution
        ...
    Political process
    Internal politics
    Public administration

This leads to a polyhierarchical structure. *Constitution*, for example, is also narrower than *Public law*, a subdivision of *Law*. In this way, the indexer is led to consider *Constitution* whether he approaches that subject from the viewpoint of *Politics* or from the viewpoint of *Law*. This structure is complemented by the introduction of numerous Related Term cross-references, so that the indexer is led almost automatically to the descriptors for which the document is relevant.

The selection of checklist descriptors is obviously specific for a specific institution. The division of descriptors into fields and subfields should reflect the interests of the specific institution, too. (Note the field *Socio-cultural change* in the example above.) As a consequence, the adaptation of an indexing language to the specific needs of the institution at hand is a prerequisite for request-oriented indexing. However, the display of the checklist descriptors alone doesn't do the job. It only reminds the indexers what to look for. The indexer has to have the expertise to judge for each descriptor whether or not the document is relevant for that descriptor.

In a very crude form, request-oriented indexing can be reduced to a few indexing instructions such as:

> Index each chemical compound, its effects described, and possible applications
> OR
> Index each topic by the educational objectives to which it might contribute.

This is better than nothing, but hardly sufficient.

B5.2.3 Summary: request-oriented indexing and the checklist technique

The representation of documents serves two purposes

(a) to select documents (or their substitutes) for the notification of users in a system of SDI;
(b) to select documents in retrospective searches.

What is at stake in both cases is a decision whether or not the document is of interest for a given search request. Request-oriented indexing means to make these decisions when a document enters the ISAR system so that their results may then be used in later searches. An indexing language is consequently viewed as a checklist of anticipated search requests or of components of search requests. In indexing, each document has to be analysed against this checklist. Knowing the document, the indexer decides for each of the search requests in the checklist whether or not the document should be retrieved by that search request.

B5.2.4 The checklist technique for search request formulation

Since descriptors are, in practice, not search requests but components of search requests, a checklist technique should also be used in formulating search requests. Going down the list of descriptors one asks oneself: "Are documents indexed by that descriptor likely to be relevant to my (or the client's) problem?" and "Could this descriptor be used to narrow down the search request formulation?" In medicine, for example, one should always consider the possibility of narrowing down the search request formulation by adding *Male* or *Female* or *Human* (as opposed to material on animals). In general a user can clarify and make more precise his own image or concept of what it is he needs by browsing through an indexing language or classification scheme that is displayed properly. This will result in a better search request formulation and better retrieval results.

B5.2.5 Request-oriented indexing and cost-benefit considerations

We have argued the case that better performance of an ISAR system can be achieved by request-oriented indexing. However, a price has to be paid for this better performance: The indexers have to be subject experts capable of judging the relevance of a document for a given question. The indexing has to be done thoroughly. Request-oriented indexing is hardly amenable to mechanization. For each individual ISAR system viewed in its function within a larger system a decision has to be made whether the benefits to be derived from better performance are worth the price.

B5.3 Adding Descriptors Through Supplementary Document-Oriented Indexing

On the other hand, it might be dangerous to index documents only by comparison with a preconceived set of search requests or components thereof, as it is done in pure request-oriented indexing using the checklist technique: The representation of documents may become too much biased by the anticipated search requests, especially with respect to the degree of specificity of descriptors used. This bias may result in the loss of parts of the information which might be important for unexpected search requests coming up in the future.

For example, in an ISAR system on transportation technology only the technical aspects of transportation systems may be of interest in search requests, and the place where these transportation systems operate is therefore not indexed. If a search request involving place comes up unexpectedly, it cannot be answered. Or in an ISAR system on research projects and experiments performed in foreign countries one might index by country and broad subject field. If a search request involving a specific topic comes up unexpectedly, it can be answered only with very low precision.

It is therefore recommended that, in addition to request-oriented indexing, the contents of the documents be represented as closely as possible. In looking for descriptors expressing the content of a document, the indexer will often use the alphabetical index (which is barely used in the checklist technique of indexing). However, the indexer should not rely on the alphabetical index in this case either; he should look up the appropriate descriptor in a classified listing, as we shall explain further below. The alphabetical index should be used only as an entry to a classified listing.

We have stressed above that the set of descriptors assigned to a document through request-oriented indexing using an appropriately structured indexing language is biased by the anticipated search requests represented in the indexing language. Therefore, many authorities conclude that hierarchically structured indexing languages and request-oriented indexing using the checklist technique should not be applied at all and that one should rely solely on a faithful description of the contents of the document, preferably in the terminology of the document itself. However, this conclusion is not warranted at all: through request-oriented indexing important retrieval clues are derived above and beyond the descriptors assigned in the usual document-oriented approach to indexing. As we have seen in this section it is not necessary to choose between request-oriented indexing and faithfully describing the contents of a document; both can and should be used together.

A closely related point is this: It is claimed that the author's vocabulary should be used in indexing because terminological control as such would introduce bias. This claim is debatable, as we shall see in Section B7. But again, it is quite possible to give the author's terminology in addition to the standardized descriptor.

B5.4 Representation Versus Filing of Documents or Catalog Cards

B5.4.1 Use of relatively broad descriptors in filing arrangement

In many cases the filing arrangement of documents or catalog cards is still an important problem. Examples are all libraries with open stacks (in particular smaller libraries intended for browsing); subject catalogs for manual use; and archives of newspaper clippings, where the arrangement of the clippings presents a serious problem. The purpose of filing arrangement is to group documents or catalog cards according to subjects and thus maintain an overview of a vast collection and make it possible to perform searches. The descriptors used for filing must be neither too specific nor too numerous because otherwise the very purpose of filing arrangement would be defeated. In addition one has to consider a situation illustrated by the following example:

Example:
U. S. Senate, U. S. House of Representatives, and U. S. President are specific descriptors that are all narrower than U.S. Government. It is likely that they co-occur in documents; therefore, the group of documents indexed by U. S. Senate widely overlaps the group of documents indexed by U. S. House of Representatives.

In shelf arrangement of documents, this situation conflicts with the principle of a single storage location. In a card catalog, filing a card (making an entry) under both *U.S. Senate* and *U.S. House of Representatives* conflicts with the principle of keeping the number of cards per document down. Also in an inclusive search for *U.S. Government* many cards have to be looked at twice. If for documents relevant to the specific concepts *U.S. Senate* and/or *U.S. House of Representatives* only one card is filed under *U.S. Government*, all these problems disappear. There is still another consideration favoring broader descriptors for arrangement: it is useful in many cases to arrange books, newspaper clippings, or catalog cards chronologically within a broader subject group.

In most ISAR systems it is recognized that relatively broad descriptors should be used for filing. The usual practice is to consider indexing only as a preliminary step for filing. Only those descriptors are used in indexing that later on will be used in filing. However, this is a short-sighted procedure; it neglects the ultimate purpose of the ISAR system. For example, it does not take into account that the references found under a given descriptor (heading) in a card catalog are screened for relevance and that more specific indexing is extremely valuable in screening. In general the optimal specificity of the document representations should be determined independently of the specificity necessary for filing, considering all the uses made of the document representations. In many systems it will prove useful to make the representation of the documents as specific as possible so as to retain as much information as possible. Ergo, the following principle evolves:

Use specific concepts in document representations (in indexing)—use more general concepts for filing arrangement.

Example 1:

C688 *Airplanes*	*Used in indexing and filing*
...	
— *C688.5 Airbus*	
— *C688.6 Variable geometry airplanes*	*Used in indexing only*
— *C688.7 V/STOL airplanes*	

Example 2:

U.S. Government
— *U.S. Senate*
— *U.S. House of Representatives*
— *U.S. President*

Example 3:

For airport locations, use individual cities in indexing, but states for filing.

Example 4:

The British National Bibliography provides specific document representations, e.g., Bureaucratic organization. Personnel. Job mobility. Mathe-

B5 Functions of the Indexing Language

matical models. The documents are arranged by broader DDC classes, in the example
   331.127 Labor force. Mobility.
In this case the specific representation serves two purposes, namely (1) to give more information for screening and (2) to produce an index that provides specific subject access to documents beyond the arrangement by DDC classes.

Example 5:
   If a library determines that
      331.127 Labor force. Mobility.
   is too specific for shelving its books it might shelve under
      331.1 Industrial relations (Labor-management relations)
   or   331 Labor economics
   instead. Still the specific class number is useful for screening.

The principle 'specific descriptors in indexing—more general descriptors for filing' has the following *advantages*:

(1) *Document representations more informative.* The document representations give more information, and this allows for better decisions in "screening" the references retrieved by the system, for example, in looking through all the cards filed under a given subject heading in a card catalog. If abstracts are given this point holds only insofar as one can make many decisions using the descriptors alone, thereby saving the work needed for reading the abstracts.

Example:
   In a search for V/STOL airplanes *one has to look through all the cards under the nearest "filing descriptor" (heading), namely* Airplanes. *If* V/STOL airplanes *appears on the cards for the relevant documents, the search is much faster and will not miss relevant documents.*

(2) *Connection from specific to broad descriptors.* If only broad descriptors are used in indexing, there is always a chance that the indexer cannot make the connection from the specific concept dealt with in the document to the appropriate broad descriptor to be used in indexing. This type of error can be avoided by using the specific concepts in indexing (see (6) for an example).

(3) *Rearrangement possible.* If experience with the system shows that the arrangement should be reorganized and that, for example, separate headings should be established for each type of airplane, this rearrangement is possible without re-indexing each of the documents concerned.

(4) *Change to mechanized system.* In mechanized ISAR systems the specific descriptors, e.g., *V/STOL airplanes*, may be used immediately in the search by the system, thus giving better search results. The above principle offers two advantages in this connection:

(4a) it is possible to use the same indexing for mechanized ISAR as well as for the production of manual ISAR tools;

(4b) one can easily change from a manual system to a mechanized system. If the indexing in the manual system has been specific, it is not necessary to index the documents anew in order to fully exploit the advantages of the mechanized system for the old part of the collection.

(5) *Shared subject indexing.* In sharing the results of subject indexing, some of the participating institutions can use the specific indexing for a more detailed arrangement meeting their purposes and/or for their mechanized ISAR system (compare example 5, British National Bibliography).

On the other hand, the following *arguments* are introduced *against* specific indexing:

(6) *Indexing more difficult?* It is asserted that the use of specific descriptors increases the effort necessary for indexing.

Comment: It is true that in some cases more effort is needed to choose the appropriate specific descriptor.

Example:
Radio wave propagation
   Atmospheric propagation
   Scatter propagation
     Ionospheric propagation
     Tropospheric propagation
   ...
Strategies
   Flexible response
   Massive retaliation
   Direct stategy
   Indirect strategy
   ...

But in other cases it is easier to index by a specific descriptor that might be more familiar to the indexer than the appropriate broader descriptor. For example, it is easier to index nuclear reactors by giving the specific name or type than by giving their general characteristics, as may be seen from the following.

Example:
Reactor Beta = Graphite moderated reactors: Carbon dioxide cooled reactors
Reactor Karlsruhe = Zirconium hydride moderated reactors: sodium cooled reactors

If the specific name is used in indexing one can be sure that the appropriate broad descriptor will be used in filing.

B5 Functions of the Indexing Language 55

(7) *Filing more difficult?* It is asserted that the mechanical process of filing catalog cards is made more difficult if the descriptor given on the card is not always the same as the descriptor under which to file.

Comment: this is simply a question of suitable procedures:

(7a) in a classified catalog a guidecard is made up for each descriptor used for arrangement, and the range of notations to be filed under that guide card is shown, e.g.,

C688 - C688.7 or *A35 - A39*

(7b) in an alphabetical catalog the term to be used for arrangement must be written down on the card, followed by the specific term. A possible format is

*Vegetables*Beans*

(In a system where the index entries or catalog entries are prepared by computer, the sequence may also be reversed if this is judged to be more legible and easier to understand.) This procedure is similar to alphabetico-classified arrangement, where we would write

Vegetables–Beans
Vegetables–Carrots

so as to achieve collocation of *Beans* and *Carrots*.

In summary the following possibilities are open in an alphabetical subject catalog:

(0) Write only *Vegetables* on the catalog cards even if the document is on *Beans*.

(1) Write **Vegetables*Beans* on the catalog cards, but disregard *Beans* in filing.

(2) Write *Vegetables–Beans* on the catalog card and consider *Beans* in filing.

(3) Write *Beans* on the catalog card and file under *Beans*.

If *Vegetables* is used as the catalog entry but **Vegetables*Beans*, **Vegetables*Carrots* and so on are written on the cards, it is easy to subdivide and establish the new catalog entries *Vegetables–Beans, Vegetables–Carrots*, etc. (conversion from (1) to (2)). If only *Vegetables* were written on the cards re-indexing would be needed. Conversion from (1) or (2) to (3) or from (2) to (1) are simple, too. If we want to convert from (3) to (2) or (1) we have to find all vegetables in the catalog.

B5.4.2 Use of relatively broad descriptors for peek-a-boo cards or other indexes

The above principle can be applied to other cases than arrangement or filing *stricto sensu*. One can, for example, establish a peek-a-boo file with peek-a-boo cards for broader descriptors only, so that the number of peek-a-boo cards is kept small and a sufficient percentage of document numbers is punched in each card. Again, the indexing may be more specific so that the screening of the documents retrieved by the peek-a-boo cards is easier. Examples 1-3 from the previous section apply here, too.

56 B Indexing Languages and Thesauri

Another form of the same principle is to use, for example, *Agrarian reform* in indexing and punch the peek-a-boo cards for the semantic factors *Agriculture* and *Reform*. Still another form of the principle is to use roles and links in indexing for a peek-a-boo file. While the roles and links cannot be used in searching with the peek-a-boo cards, they are useful in scanning the representations of the documents retrieved in the first stage.

The procedure described might also be useful within mechanized ISAR systems that use an inverted file but want to keep the number of descriptors in the inverted file small. The system search can proceed in two steps:

Step 1—Search the inverted file.

Due to the broad descriptors used in the inverted file, this step may result in low precision.

Step 2—Scan the representations of the documents retrieved in Step 1 and check whether or not the specific descriptor(s) asked for are present.

In the second step precision is increased.

B5.4.3 Use of additional descriptors beyond those used for filing or manual indexes

The principle of specific representation can be viewed from another aspect: It is possible to use more descriptors in the document representations than are used as entries for that document in a subject catalog. There are two situations which give rise to such a procedure:

(a) The document deals with several specific concepts that are all narrower than the broader concept to be used for arrangement. For example, a document may be indexed by *C688.5 Airbus* and *C688.7 V/STOL airplanes* but filed only with *C688 Airplanes*. However, in a card catalog produced by manual means the document would be filed twice under *C688 Airplanes* unless special measures are taken.

A modification of this principle can be used if the specific descriptors are used for filing, too: If there is only one of the specific descriptors an entry is made for it. If there are two or more specific descriptors (or to give another possible rule, if there are more than 50% of the specific descriptors) a filing entry is made for the broader descriptor only. In searching one always has to look under the specific descriptor itself and under the appropriate broader descriptor. A corresponding procedure is possible in peek-a-boo systems.

(b) Only a few descriptors representing the main subject (or theme) of the document are used as entries in a card catalog or printed index. For a more precise representation of the document it is useful to add further descriptors representing minor subjects or aspects under which the main subject is treated (for example, a statistical method used). In effect this is a form of weighting the descriptors. The descriptors used as index entries are marked accordingly. All descriptors assigned to a document can be used in mechanized ISAR since size is not nearly as critical as in printed indexes. Many systems that produce printed indexes and maintain a machine-searchable file use this procedure.

(c) A combination of (a) and (b) is possible: In indexing specific descriptors are used, and those that are most important to represent the document for retrieval are marked, e.g., by a star (*). Each starred descriptor gives rise to an entry in an index for manual use. However, this entry will often be under a descriptor that is broader than the specific descriptor used in indexing.

Example:
Descriptors used in indexing (document representation):
  *Aquadrones; *V/STOL airplanes; *New York City; *Intercity traffic; Concrete; Models; Helicopters; Local rail transit; New Jersey; Traffic planning
Entries will be made under the following filing descriptors:
  Small airports   (broader than Aquadromes)
  Airplanes   (broader than V/STOL airplanes)
  New York City   (itself a filing descriptor)
  Intercity traffic (itself a filing descriptor)
No entries are made for the non-starred descriptors.

B5.4.4 The use of free (open-ended) terms supplementing the descriptors from the indexing language

In some ISAR systems the indexer may use, in addition to the descriptors found in the indexing language and assigned to a document, other terms that are not contained in the indexing language (the system vocabulary). It does not matter whether or not they are contained in the lead-in vocabulary. These terms are then called "free terms" or "open-ended terms". These might be, for example, terms designating very specific concepts (of course, the appropriate descriptor from the indexing language designating the broader concept must also be assigned). This procedure serves the purpose of giving more information about a document, thus facilitating final screening. In a sense the additional free terms substitute for an abstract. As long as only this purpose is to be served, additional free terms are fine. As soon as one wants to use these free terms in retrieval by a formalized retrieval procedure, e.g., in a mechanized ISAR system, one encounters a problem: There is no terminological control for the free terms, and so all the problems dealt with in B1 and B2 arise. If it is beneficial to use very specific concepts in retrieval, these concepts should be represented in the indexing language. We have shown above that this does *not* imply the use of these very specific concepts in shelves arranged by subject, in card catalogs, peek-a-boo files, or other inverted files. The importance of request-oriented indexing is another point militating against the use of free terms. (Compare the discussion of semi-mechanized indexing in B6.2.)

If the main purpose of free terms is to express concepts to be used in indexing on a level more specific than the indexing language, the following form is useful: Write down the notation or text of the appropriate descriptor, and then add the text of the free term (possibly omitting the text of the descriptor). The concept for which the document is relevant is thus registered in two ways: In a more general but standardized way and in a more specific but not standardized way.

B5.4.5 Note on "descriptor" and multi-purpose systems

If free terms are used in a mechanized search procedure, they are descriptors for that procedure. If specific preferred terms are used in indexing but only more general preferred terms are available for mechanized searching, the specific preferred terms are *not* descriptors for mechanized searching. Recall the definition of descriptor (subject descriptor) as a "string of symbols designating a concept and used for selection and/or for sorting/arranging documents or their substitutes in a given system by a given mechanism". The present context shows the importance of the clause "by a given mechanism". Whereas in principle scanning by a knowledgeable searcher is included in the possible mechanisms, this discussion is restricted to retrieval mechanisms that rely solely on strictly mechanical/clerical operations. Under this restriction only preferred terms should be used as descriptors except in rather sophisticated systems. The use of free terms as descriptors runs counter to that recommendation. On the other hand, the use of specific preferred terms merely to increase the amount of information on a document to be used in scanning the results of a system search might be wasteful, unless there is a chance that these preferred terms might be used as descriptors later and/or in another version of the ISAR system as described above.

Section B5.4.3 mentioned multi-purpose ISAR systems that provide more than one retrieval tool, more than one retrieval mechanism, e.g., a printed index and computer retrieval or two search steps within a computerized search procedure. Indexing is done simultaneously for both subsystems. Two parameters of indexing may vary from subsystem to subsystem:

(1) Exhaustivity of indexing—for example, more descriptors per document are used for the mechanized ISAR system than for the printed retrieval tool. The indexer has to mark the descriptors accordingly.

(2) Specificity of indexing—more specific descriptors are used for one subsystem than for the other. This may mean that specific preferred terms as assigned by the indexer can be used as descriptors in mechanized searches, whereas they are converted to broader terms for the printed index. Or a system may allow free terms as descriptors for machine searches but not for the printed index.

B5   Functions of the Indexing Language   59

These considerations have enormous implications for thesaurus building. Assume a thesaurus for a new abstracting/indexing service has to be built. One has to determine first whether one wants to be able later on to do retrospective searches in the data base. If the answer is yes an elaborate thesaurus including specific descriptors is needed. If the answer is no a much smaller thesaurus containing only broader descriptors will be sufficient for, say, yearly indexes. Also it has to be clear whether retrospective searching will be in a printed index or by computer because the requirements for the indexing language will be different in each case, as we shall see in Section C2.

B5.5 Summary of the Functions of Hierarchy and Classified Arrangement

In different contexts hierarchy and classified arrangement of descriptors emerged as important features of an indexing language. It is convenient to list all the reasons for the introduction of hierarchy and classified arrangement at one place in this section.

(a) *Facilitate the use of the checklist technique for indexing and search request formulation* (especially browsing through the descriptors available).

(b) *Assist the indexer in the choice of the appropriate level of generality.* Two useful rules in this connection are the following: If a broader descriptor, say *Aircraft,* is dealt with as a whole or if more than 50% of the narrower descriptors of *Aircraft* are dealt with, *Aircraft* should be used in indexing. *Aircraft* should also be used if the indexer cannot determine which specific narrower descriptor should be used—in other words, what specific type of aircraft the document is about. The document will then be retrieved in a search for *Aircraft, general references* (as opposed to *Aircraft, inclusive;* see Section C1.4.6).

Note that the "more than 50%" rule involves a loss of information because the document representation does not tell exactly which narrower descriptors are dealt with and which are not. If one is willing to pay for the additional effort, one may stipulate that all descriptors dealt with should be used in indexing but only the broader descriptor should be used in filing, as described in Section B5.4.3.

(c) *Facilitate implementation of the principle: specific indexing—more general filing.*

(d) *Facilitate inclusive searches:* (if one searches for a broader descriptor A, documents on the narrower descriptors B, C, or D are retrieved as well). This point holds for manual systems (including systems based on shelving) and in mechanized systems. It is especially important for SDI, where broad search requests are common.

(e) *Facilitate the collocation of related items in files.* Collocation in turn facilitates inclusive searching and browsing and often allows faster look-up of a number of related items.

(f) The hierarchy is important for *shared subject indexing,* as we shall discuss at length in Chapter K.

Aside from these functions in the application of the thesaurus as a finished product, hierarchy plays an important role in thesaurus-building (see Sections F3 and F4).

B5.6 Indicative Versus Informative Representation of Documents

An abstract or another representation of a document may be

(a) indicative—indicating the topic dealt with in the document; or
(b) informative—summarizing or extracting actual information given in the document.

Examples:

(1a) *The economic situation in the United States in March, 1971.*

(1b) *In March, 1971, the jobless rate was 6%; the investment rate was low; and the prices were still rising.*

(2a) *Negotiations US–USSR on the limitation of strategic arms.*

(2b1) *In 1970 the US and the USSR were involved in negotiations on the limitation of strategic arms. The positions taken by each side were . . .; the negotiations had the following results. . . .*

(2b2) *The planned negotiations between the US and the USSR concerning the limitation of strategic arms could not take place because. . . .*

(3a) *Problems caused by root-knot nematodes in growing sweet potatoes in Mississippi are discussed. Experiments with commercial and experimental nematocides are described.*

(3b) *The yield and quality of sweet potatoes can be increased by soil fumigation or the addition of solid nematocides in some areas of Mississippi. The commercial fumigants Vorlex, Dow W-85, and DD significantly increased yields and quality in the treatment rows.*

An indicative abstract cannot replace the document itself because it does not transmit actual information. An informative abstract, however, gives at least some of the information contained in the document and can therefore replace the document itself if the information given is sufficient for the purpose at hand.

A set of descriptors assigned in indexing is an indicative representation of a document. Since in this book we are concerned mainly with indexing and not with abstracting, one might ask why we deal with indicative and informative abstracts. The reason is that it is quite possible and often useful to use a controlled vocabulary in writing abstracts. The descriptors selected from this vocabulary can be strung together either by natural language or by an elaborate artificial syntax suitable for machine processing. If such a procedure is to be used for informative abstracts, the indexing language must contain very specific descriptors (compare example (3a) with (3b)). The same is true of an indexing language to be used in data storage and retrieval systems.

B5.7 Cost-Benefit Considerations for the Design of Indexing Languages

The degree of detail involved in the representation of documents is a major factor for the costs, as well as for the benefits, of an ISAR system. In many cases more detailed representation involves higher costs. This high cost is not in all cases warranted by corresponding benefits in searching. One may, for example, have only a few searches to be performed, or it may be completely sufficient to retrieve a few relevant documents in the average search. On the other end of the scale special requirements arise in data storage and retrieval systems. From such considerations one can determine the necessary degree of detail of the document representations and can in turn draw conclusions concerning the design of the indexing language. Two aspects have to be considered:

(a) *Specificity of the descriptors* to be included in the indexing language. Specific descriptors allow for a precise representation of the documents and therefore for high precision in searching (if the emphasis in searching is on recall, one may always use broader descriptors for inclusive searches). Since the number of descriptors increases very fast with increasing levels of specificity, it is particularly important to display the structure of the indexing language or classification scheme in the best possible way so that indexers and searchers may find their way through the scheme.

(b) *Syntactical devices,* such as roles and links or relators, complicate indexing and searching and should be used only if a high precision is required and cannot be achieved otherwise. Syntactical devices are essential in data storage and retrieval systems that are not confined just to numerical data such as physical constants or statistical data.

B6 THE FUNCTIONS OF THE LEAD-IN VOCABULARY IN AN ISAR SYSTEM

Section B5 dealt with the functions of the indexing language (classification scheme, system vocabulary). A thesaurus also contains a set of terms not used as descriptors, called lead-in terms (or non-descriptors) (see the definition in Sections B4.1 and B4.3). It is to the functions of this lead-in vocabulary that we now turn.

A lead-in vocabulary that makes the thesaurus an as-complete-as-possible collection of the terms of the subject field is essential for mechanized indexing and search request formulation (B6.2). But a lead-in vocabulary is also very useful for human indexing and search request formulation, especially for the complementary indexing starting from the document and not from the checklist descriptors (B6.1). Finally, Section B6.3 discusses systems that do not exert terminological control in indexing.

B6.1 Advantages of a Lead-In Vocabulary for Human Indexing and Search Request Formulation

B6.1.1 Alphabetical index to the indexing language is more effective

The addition of the lead-in vocabulary, that is, of synonyms and quasi-synonyms of the descriptors as well as of specific preferred terms and their synonyms, makes the alphabetical index a much better tool. An indexer or a searcher who has found a term in the document or the search request he is working on or a term designating a pertinent concept that came to his mind otherwise then looks up that term in the alphabetical index. If the alphabetical index is more complete by virtue of the addition of the lead-in vocabulary, the probability of finding the term is much higher. Only seldom will it be necessary to think of another term for the same concept, look up this term, and so on. The look-up in the more complete alphabetical index is much speedier.

B6.1.2 Thesaurus as store of intellectual decisions made in day-to-day indexing and search request formulation

In indexing it often happens that a concept needed in the representation of a document is not available as a descriptor. The same is true for search request formulation. In this case an appropriate descriptor or an appropriate combination of descriptors has to be found. Without a lead-in vocabulary the indexer or searcher has to decide by himself which descriptor or which combination of descriptors to use. Nowhere in the system is this intellectual decision recorded explicitly. Another indexer (or the same indexer after some time has elapsed) coming to the same concept in indexing another document has to go through the same intellectual effort, and there is no assurance that the outcome will be the same. This problem is even more serious in search request formulation where the searcher has to outguess the indexer. Given a lead-in vocabulary the situation is quite different: either the concept is already represented in the lead-in vocabulary with a reference to the appropriate descriptor or combination of descriptors or it is included in the lead-in vocabulary at its first occurrence. Thus the intellectual effort need not be repeated when the concept occurs for the second time and indexer-indexer as well as indexer-searcher consistency is increased. In addition scope notes are added as the meanings of descriptors are clarified in day-to-day use in indexing and search request formulation. In sum the results of any intellectual effort spent once are stored in the thesaurus so that they can be used again at later occasions.

,1 **Gradual development of a thesaurus over time.** Some institutions (including some institutions using established classification schemes, such as UDC or DDC) build a thesaurus over time by including in the lead-in vocabulary synonymous and quasi-synonymous terms as well as new concepts as they occur in the documents and/or search requests. In this case it is of advantage to maintain the lead-in vocabulary in the form of a card file.

B6.2 Mechanization of Indexing or Search Request Formulation (Special Topic)

B6.2.1 Semi-mechanized versus fully mechanized indexing and search request formulation: description of methods

In mechanized indexing a list of free terms and/or the title and/or an abstract and/or the full text of a document are processed by a computer program, which derives descriptors for the document. There are different degrees of automation involved. At the one end of the scale a human indexer prepares a list of terms representing the document, using any terms that occur to him. He may underline terms in the document and/or add his own terms. Correspondingly the user uses any terms that come to his mind in formulating his search request (this is particularly relevant in the context of interactive ISAR systems). These terms are then fed into the computer, and the program looks up the appropriate descriptor(s) (text and/or notation) in a thesaurus. Section B2.2 mentioned the possibility of using notations or numbers as the preferred designations of ISAR concepts. It is mainly in systems using semi-mechanized indexing and search request formulation that this possibility is used (e.g., BASF). Note, however, that this translation process is only a crude approximation of the more intelligent procedure an indexer should use, namely, the checklist technique of indexing. Things get a little bit more involved if the descriptors are to be derived from the terms in the title and/or the abstract, using the rule that every significant term is to be translated into a descriptor. For search requests the equivalent would be to process a paragraph-long request statement as submitted by the user (note that generation of the proper *AND* and *OR* parentheses would be exceedingly difficult and is excluded from our considerations). Since this is still basically a translation process using the lead-in vocabulary, the methods described so far are called *semi-mechanized indexing*.

At the other end of the scale are procedures where the full text of a document is processed. This presents the problem of *selecting* terms that are to be used as descriptors as they stand (in a system using free-term indexing) or that are to be translated into descriptors (as in semi-mechanized indexing), or of inferring from whole passages of text what descriptors to use. This is called *fully mechanized indexing*.

64 B Indexing Languages and Thesauri

The problem of retrieving documents based on abstracts in natural language text, to be dealt with below, is very similar but not identical to the problem of fully mechanized indexing. Another closely related problem is computer assistance in translation from one language to another. Terms are isolated in the source-language text, and the target language equivalent is looked up in a computer-stored dictionary. Still another related problem is automatic abstracting, which usually is done by extracting whole phrases or sentences from full-text documents. Fairly sophisticated procedures have been developed for this purpose, and some of these use a thesaurus of "cue words" that assist in the process of selecting appropriate sentences from the document. An abstract prepared by any of these procedures may in turn be used for semi-mechanized indexing.

B6.2.2 Problems and implications for thesaurus building

The following problems exist for both semi-mechanized and fully mechanized indexing:

(1) *Morphological variants of terms.* The terms used in preliminary document representations, titles, abstracts, or the documents themselves may appear in a variety of different forms. The same is true for the terms in search request statements. As long as the equivalence between two forms can be established by fairly simple rules that can be incorporated in a computer program (e.g., nouns without -*s* = singular, nouns with -*s* = plural), only one form needs to be entered into the thesaurus. As soon as more is involved, the different forms have to be entered into the thesaurus even if they would not be needed in a thesaurus for manual use.

Examples:
>   Tumor and Tumour or
>   Thesaurus and thesauri or
>   Catalyst, catalyzer, catalyze.

As a result the size of the thesaurus increases considerably. This problem can be avoided by the use of word stems. Only stems are included in the thesaurus. Input terms are reduced to the stem before they are looked up. In some cases, it is not desirable to lump together all words with the same stem. The procedure can be modified so that full words can be included in the thesaurus where necessary.

(2) *The proper identification of multi-word terms.* In semi-mechanized indexing, where a set of terms for each document or search request is prepared by an indexer or searcher, this identification is not a problem. But in fully mechanized indexing, where the multi-word terms have to be identified from titles, abstracts, full text, or a natural language statement of the search request, it is sometimes difficult to identify multi-word terms, especially if other words intervene. In this case the thesaurus may be used for the isolation of multi-word terms within the

text (not only for the translation of these terms into the indexing language). In any case the thesaurus should contain those multi-word terms that designate concepts important in the ISAR system at hand. One problem is whether to store multi-word terms with or without prepositions or other connectives.

(3) *Homonyms*. If the terms occurring in a document or the terms used by the user on a console are homonymous it is often difficult to assess the appropriate meaning by the computer program. One solution might have the computer report back the homonymous term, giving all the meanings available in the thesaurus, so that a human editor can determine the appropriate meaning to be used. Of course homonyms have to be tagged in the thesaurus no matter whether the homonym in question occurs in different meanings or in one meaning only within the thesaurus (if a homonym occurs with one meaning only in the thesaurus the possibility that the same term is used in another meaning in a document or in a search request statement is not excluded). Syntactic and semantic information needed for the "disambiguation" of a homonym should be given in the thesaurus.

(4) *Different ways to express a subject*. In fully mechanized indexing much more so than in semi-mechanized indexing we are confronted with the fact that the same subject can be expressed in many different ways in language. It might be necessary for the program to "understand" whole passages of text in order to derive the appropriate descriptor. The problems involved are similar to those encountered in mechanical translation, and they require linguistic programs. A thesaurus for this task must contain syntactical information for each term.

(5) *Cue-words*. A thesaurus for fully mechanized indexing may contain "cue-words" that assist in the process of selecting the appropriate terms to be used as the basis for indexing.

(6) *Common words*. A thesaurus for fully mechanized indexing must contain "common words," like *and, or, it, the, which* in addition to the *"content words"* for two reasons: (a) if common words are left out, the computer program could not decide whether a word missing from the thesaurus is a common word or a term designating a concept that has not yet been included in the thesaurus; (b) common words are important for syntactical analysis. If titles and abstracts or free terms containing common words are to be processed, common words may be needed for semi-mechanized indexing, too. These common words are often stored in a separate list of "stop-words".

B6.2.3 Discussion: advantages and disadvantages of mechanized indexing

Semi-mechanized indexing or search request formulation has the advantage that it saves the time of the indexer or searcher. The indexer or searcher (a) need not look up the appropriate descriptor in the thesaurus and (b) need not write down a term contained in the text or in the abstract of the document or in the search request statement whether or not this term is a descriptor. On the other hand, this method has major drawbacks, as may be seen from the considerations on the checklist technique of indexing and search request formulation. Looking at a sensibly organized classification scheme the indexer can much better determine the descriptors for which the document being indexed is relevant, and the searcher is much better able to conceptualize his problem by browsing through the scheme. This disadvantage of semi-mechanized indexing could in part be avoided while still keeping some of the advantages by the following procedure: The indexer assigns the appropriate descriptors using the checklist technique. He then adds free terms to include aspects and/or details not covered by the checklist. These free terms are then translated into descriptors as described. The problems inherent to the translation process persist, of course.

These advantages and disadvantages identified for semi-mechanized indexing are even more marked in fully automatic indexing. An especially thorny problem is represented by concepts dealt with in a document without a corresponding term appearing in the document. Compare the Section B5.2.1 example of the *Pravda* article addressed to *Romania* without mentioning *Romania*. It is unlikely that these problems will be solved by computer programs for a long time to come. This is not to say that fully mechanized indexing should not be applied in fields where situations like this are unlikely or if a cost-benefit analysis shows that higher costs for manual indexing are not warranted in terms of the benefits gained. These few remarks must suffice here.

A less conspicuous advantage of both semi-mechanized and fully mechanized indexing is that new terms to be included in the thesaurus, whether originating from documents or from search request statements, are detected automatically. They may then be included in the thesaurus while updating according to the procedures to be described in Chapter J.

B6.3 Thesauri for Terminological Control in the Searching Stage

Some ISAR systems use free-term indexing and exert terminological control in searching (see Section B4.3 on complex thesaurus structures). The role of the thesaurus in such systems is to expand the search request formulations properly. It is obvious that request-oriented indexing can be applied only in a very limited way in this type of system and that the problem of homonyms is just as difficult as in mechanized indexing.

B7 "USER'S" OR "AUTHOR'S" VOCABULARY VERSUS LOGICAL STRUCTURE AND REQUEST-ORIENTED INDEXING AS IMPLEMENTED THROUGH THE CHECKLIST TECHNIQUE

A remark concluding Chapter B is in order. It has been stated that "in building a thesaurus the user's vocabulary should be followed up as nearly as possible and that every term that is not contained explicitly in the user's vocabulary should be omitted even if it is necessary for logical coherence". Conversely, it has also been stated that indexing of documents should use, insofar as possible or even exclusively, the vocabulary of the author, and that only terms appearing in the literature should be included in the thesaurus. These positions reflect a failure to perceive the necessity of a tool to solve the problems of communication that have been outlined in the previous sections and that are amply covered in the literature on classification. It is the task of a thesaurus to provide optimal service in indexing and retrieving documents. This task can hardly be achieved by following up the user's or the author's vocabulary as nearly as possible. There is no such thing as *the* user, and users' viewpoints often contradict each other. There is no such thing as *the* author either, and different authors use different terminology, and users again use different terminology. The use that a user makes of a document is often quite different from what the author thought the document would be useful for. The indexer has to serve as the user's agent by indicating possible uses of each incoming document. In order that the indexer can fulfill this role he has to have a clear picture of what uses his clients are interested in. Were it not for these reasons, a thesaurus would not be needed at all in reference storage and retrieval. In ISAR systems for retrieval objects other than documents or other textual units, the controversy is pointless. As it is, the thesaurus-maker is confronted with the challenge to clarify the muddled terminological and conceptual systems as far as possible, thus laying a foundation for successful communication.

Chapter C

The Structure of Indexing Languages and Thesauri

C0 INTRODUCTION

The previous chapter was concerned with the definitions of "indexing language" (or "classification scheme" or "system vocabulary") and "thesaurus", which are basic to this book. It then discussed the functions of these tools in an ISAR system. This provides the basis for a detailed analysis of the structure that should be imbedded in indexing languages and thesauri in order to achieve these functions. This analysis will be undertaken in this chapter. The first four sections are devoted mainly to conceptual problems. Section C1 deals with concept combination and hierarchy, the two structural principles on which the classificatory structure should be built. Intertwined with these purely conceptual considerations is the actual implementation of these principles, especially of concept combination in ISAR systems; this problem is examined in Section C2. Sections C3 and C4 contain additional related material: Section C3 deals with concept formation in thesaurus building, the sharpening of definitions, and ways in which these definitions can be recorded in scope notes for the thesaurus user. Section C4 deals with different types of concepts and their treatment in a thesaurus. The next two sections deal with problems related to the lead-in structure and to terminology. Section C5 discusses in detail the lead-in problem and alternative ways to solve it. Section C6 deals with the similarities and differences of synonyms and spelling variants. In view of these considerations it follows that a considerable number of cross-references and much other information has to be given for each term in the thesaurus in order to convey the complex network of relationships. For purposes of display of the thesaurus, to be dealt with in Chapter D, it is necessary to organize the various types of relationships into an orderly list. This is done in Section C7. The considerations in this chapter are illustrated by many examples. More examples can be found in Figure 22 (Section D0), the figures in Section D1.7, "Description of Selected Thesauri", and especially in Figure 35 (Section D3.1.1,3); it might be useful to look at Figure 35 before proceeding further.

C1 CLASSIFICATORY STRUCTURE

As has been shown in Sections B1 and B2, it is useful in most circumstances to form classes of terms having identical or very similar meanings and to select from each class a preferred term as a representative. Each preferred term corresponds unequivocally to an ISAR concept. The ISAR concepts, as represented by the preferred terms, and the relationships between them form the classificatory structure of the thesaurus. Section C1 is devoted to a detailed discussion of the classificatory structure.

The main types of relationships between ISAR concepts are "is semantic factor of", hierarchical relationships, and associative relationships. Since these are relationships between concepts, the appropriate cross-references are entered for preferred terms only.

The structure expounded in the following is inherent in any conceptual system, even though it is often not made explicit. Also, this structure is independent of the particular mechanical devices used in a specific ISAR system. The mechanical devices determine only how easy it is to exploit the structure of the conceptual scheme for conducting successful searches. The following exposition summarizes some principles dealt with in more detail at other places so that convenient reference to these principles can be made in other sections.

C1.0 Introduction: "Representation" Versus "Grouping of Documents" II (Continuation of Section B5.0)

Modern methods of information storage and retrieval are based on the decomposition of compound concepts into their components. Taking an analogy from chemistry, we may say that molecules are decomposed into fragments and finally into atoms.

Example:
   (a) *Vehicles for local rail transit in New York City.*
Decomposition into fragments:
   (b) *Vehicles: Local rail transit: New York City.*
Further decomposition into atoms:
   (c) *(Means: Transportation): (Rail transport: Local transit): New York City.*
(The colon stands for concept combination.)

Another example serves to illustrate the problems of traditional classifications like DDC, to be dealt with in detail below; DDC-numbers are given preceding each term.

Example:
   (a) *372.181 Attitudes of elementary school students*
   (b) *372.18 Elementary school students: 152.452 Attitudes*
   (c) *(372.1 Elementary schools: 372.8 Students): 152.452 Attitudes*

With these methods one does not make the attempt, futile from the beginning, to bring together a complete collection of all molecules. It is sufficient to have a collection of atoms from which every molecule can be generated by combination as needed. In indexing and searching, the atoms or elemental concepts are combined to yield the compound concept in question. In order to enhance the advantages of this method, it is useful to contrast it with conventional systems designed for arranging documents on shelves. These classifications are built on the following principles:

   (i) Descriptors must be mutually exclusive.
   (ii) Monohierarchy: a descriptor must not have more than one broader descriptor.

From (i) it follows that the concepts used as descriptors in conventional classification schemes are highly compound (large molecules). Many documents would have to be assigned more than one of the "fragments" shown in the examples under (b) so that these fragments would not be mutually exclusive. Whereas the compound concept given in (a) would be a good entry for arranging documents on shelves the fragments given in (b) would not be useful for that purpose because many documents would have to be assigned to two or more descriptors (classes). (There is a quite different reason why a document might have to be assigned to two descriptors (two classes): the document may deal with two or more specific concepts that are all narrower than the same broader concept. This problem is solved by shelving or filing under the broader concept, as has been explained in Section B5.4.1.)

To summarize: Traditional library classifications were intended for the retrieval of books based on shelving arrangement, since no other mechanical aids were available or thought of. This system led to a classification scheme in which compound concepts are arranged in a monohierarchy.

Such a system has the following *disadvantages*:

   (1) *In reality, any compound concept has not only one but several broader concepts.*

Examples:
Rolling stock (vehicles for railroads) has the broader concepts: *Vehicles* and *Railroads*
Reactors for power plants—broader concepts: *Reactors* and *Power plants*
Trade negotiations—broader concepts: *International negotiations* and *Foreign trade.*

The compound concepts in the previous examples have even more broader concepts.

In a monohierarchical system (such as LCC, DDC, or UDC) these concepts must appear under one broader concept only. *Trade negotiations,* for example, may appear either under *International negotiations* (field: *International politics*) or under *Foreign trade* (field: *Economics*), but not under both. If one is looking for a compound concept, one has to know, therefore, under which of several possible broader concepts it appears. If the concepts get more compound the problem gets increasingly more difficult. The example from DDC given above illustrates this. Another example is *Legal problems of the status of Berlin in the trade negotiations between the Federal Republic and the Soviet Union.*

In alphabetical schemes such as subject headings or KWIC indexes the problems of finding the descriptors appropriate for indexing or searching are even more severe.

(2) As a result, it is almost *impossible to search for concepts or aspects of general application*, e.g., for a method that may be used in different contexts or for a concept like *Structure*. Compound concepts containing *Structure* as a semantic factor are scattered all over the scheme under a wide variety of broader concepts, and it is necessary to retrieve them from among the huge number of compound concepts listed in the scheme. Lacking other means for the retrieval of relevant compound concepts, one would have to look through the whole scheme; this is obviously not a feasible solution in most situations. Instead we should have a "conceptual index" as discussed later.

These considerations tacitly assumed that the concept of general application has been taken into account somehow in the scheme. However, the introduction to request-oriented indexing made it clear that many such concepts are simply disregarded in conventional schemes, in which case they cannot be used in retrieval at all.

(3) It is *not possible to combine concepts freely*, especially concepts or aspects of general application. Therefore, only those combinations contained explicitly in the classification scheme can be used in searching. This feature creates a lack of flexibility.

(4) Finally, *a document can be indexed by one and only one descriptor* (usually representing a compound concept). Therefore, exhaustive indexing is not possible, and many aspects for which the document would be relevant cannot be taken into account. In theory there is the following possibility: Draw up a

scheme that contains very specific descriptors in such a way that for every document a descriptor containing all aspects for which the document is relevant can be found. But this approach would result in almost as many descriptors as documents, which obviously is not feasible.

As a result of these factors many search requests cannot be answered at all by an ISAR system based on shelving arrangement, and for other search requests many relevant documents are missed. By using a card catalog (either classified or subject headings), one can improve significantly upon this situation: a document may now be indexed by more than one descriptor, but still only a few. This allows for the decomposition of the large molecules into fragments so that some flexibility is gained. But still one tries to keep the number of descriptors per document small so that the card catalog does not grow to an unmanageable size. This requires that the descriptors be mutually exclusive, at least to a certain degree. It follows that the descriptors still represent compound concepts, but not as compound as needed for shelving arrangement. In other words, one is working with fragments that are combined to give larger molecules. The monohierarchical structure is retained both as a matter of habit and because in a card catalog each heading should appear in one place only (cross-references to this place are possible, of course). It follows that the disadvantages (1) through (3) and to a lesser degree (4) apply to the card catalog, too.

The transition from subject-oriented shelving arrangement to the conventional subject catalog may be viewed as a first step from the exclusive use of a classification scheme for the arrangement of documents on shelves to the representation of documents by free combination of descriptors, from "grouping" to representation. It is the step from the larger molecules to fragments. A second and perhaps more important step is the step from the fragments to the atoms. Modern technical devices like edge-notched cards, peek-a-boo cards, and computers have made this step possible. Whereas the former technical means required at least a certain degree of mutual exclusivity of the descriptors, this requirement has lost any meaning in connection with modern techniques. On the contrary, these modern technical tools are intended for searches for combinations of descriptors, and descriptors can therefore be freely combined in search request formulation. The ISAR technique thus concurs with the requirements arising from the conceptual nature of the retrieval problem. By the same token the artificial principle of monohierarchy may be dispensed with in modern systems because the technical constraints leading to that principle are no longer in force in such systems.

Using these modern methods, a document may be represented by as many descriptors as necessary so that the fragments may be decomposed to atoms. The atoms may, in turn, be put together in any way, thus allowing for a maximum of flexibility and precision in the representation of documents and the formulation of search requests. The problem has shifted from assigning (in many cases forcibly) a document into a class corresponding to a compound concept ("grouping" or "pigeonholing") to building a "tailor-made" representation for each document by a combination of elemental concepts. In this book, this method is called "combination indexing", a term that more aptly describes the method than the commonly used "coordinate indexing". The methods discussed are on a continuous scale that starts with the use of very compound concepts (large molecules) as descriptors and that ends with the use of elemental concepts (atoms) as descriptors. Section C2.3.1 will elaborate on this idea.

Conventional classification schemes, such as DDC or LCC, have been developed basically for arranging documents on shelves. Further developments meant for the adaptation to subject catalogs or even machine methods have not changed this basis and often lead to contradictions within the system itself. One may have serious doubts, therefore, whether these classification schemes, the basic structure of which is determined by the shortcomings of the technical aids of the previous century or the conventional card catalog, should be used in modern ISAR systems. However, in the construction of modern indexing languages and thesauri use should be made of the enormous intellectual effort that has been invested in these schemes.

A further remark is in order. It is possible to avoid the disadvantages of monohierarchy even in a scheme developed for shelving arrangement or filing. It is true that one is forced, for technical reasons, to start with a monohierarchical system. The group of documents on *Trade negotiations* can be shelved only within one broader group, say *International negotiations*. However, there is no reason why one should not make a note with *Trade negotiations* that *Foreign trade* is an additional broader concept and, vice versa, make a note with *Foreign trade* that *Trade negotiations* is an additional narrower concept. Using such a cross-reference structure, one can then find all descriptors narrower than *Foreign trade* and thus avoid the disadvantages mentioned above. This idea is of particular importance for concepts of general application, e.g., *Structure*. Most subject catalogs give cross-references of this type, but in a more-or-less haphazard manner. In the course of our discussion, we shall describe how such a cross-reference structure can be constructed systematically by taking into account the structure of molecules in terms of the atoms they are built from ("concept combination and hierarchy"). It will be shown that it is also possible to use compound concepts in indexing and still use free combinations of elemental concepts in searching. To summarize: classification schemes which are built according to modern principles may also be used for an improved solution of the "classical" problems. In Section C2 on file organization for information retrieval these ideas will be explored further.

C1.1 Decomposition of Concepts Into Semantic Factors—Concept Combination (Concept Coordination)

C1.1.0 Foundations of semantic factoring and concept combination

Compound concepts—for example, *Trade negotiations*—may be split or factored or decomposed into less compound concepts according to their meaning. *Trade negotiations* has the semantic factors *International negotiations* and *Foreign trade*—not just *Negotiations* and *Trade*, which would be the linguistic components of the two-word term *Trade negotiations*. This decomposition makes clear that the compound concept *Trade negotiations* should be accessible from both conceptual components (or semantic factors). In some cases the components can be decomposed in turn. Finally one arrives at concepts that cannot be decomposed further in the given system. Such concepts are called "elemental concepts" relative to that system. A concept can be decomposed into semantic factors and still be used as descriptor. The decomposition is a purely conceptual act; how its result is used in the actual implementation of an ISAR system is a technical question of file organization to be discussed later, in Section C2.

A descriptor designating an element concept shall be called "elemental descriptor". A descriptor designating a compound concept shall be called "precombined descriptor". If a compound concept has to be expressed in search request formulation or indexing, there are two possibilities: either the indexing language already contains a ready-made precombined descriptor or several descriptors have to be combined to express the compound concept.

It should be stressed again that we are not concerned with the linguistic decomposition of multi-word or composite terms but with semantic factoring of compound concepts according to their meaning. For example, *Rare earth metals* is a multi-word term designating an elemental concept. Semantic factoring is not useful in this case. On the other hand, the term *Ship*, elemental from the linguistic point of view, designates a compound concept which may be factored as shown in Figure 7a. Sometimes we have a multi-word term designating a compound concept in which the single words are not the appropriate terms for the semantic factors. A striking example is *White House* (in the sense "The White House announces" or "A White House aide"):

Example:
> *White House* = *Administrative agency: Chief executive officer: United States*

While decomposition into semantic factors is useful, the meaning of *White House* has nothing to do with *White* and *House* (for further examples see Figure 7).

C1   Classificatory Structure   75

a. Miscellaneous examples

Car	= Vehicles	: Road transport	
Ship	= Vehicles	: Water transport	
	= (Means, instruments	: Transport)	: Water transport
Aircraft	= Vehicles	: Air transport	
Highway	= Traffic ways	: Road transport	
Waterway	= Traffic ways	: Water transport	
Airway	= Traffic ways	: Air tranpsort	
Railway	= Traffic ways	: Rail transport	
Birth statistics	= Statistics	: Birth : Demography	
Socialistic society	= System of society	: Marxism, Communism[a]	

	produced by	acting upon
Atomic bound = Bound	: Electrons	: Atoms

b. Use of a series of semantic factors as a common subdivision of other concepts

Steel pipes	= Steel	: Pipes	
Steel rods	= Steel	: Rods	In these examples, the conceptual decomposition happens to be the same as the linguistic decomposition
Steel wire	= Steel	: Wire	
Copper pipes	= Copper	: Pipes	
Copper rods	= Copper	: Rods	
Copper wire	= Copper	: Wire	

Monetary theory	= Money and banking	: Economic theory
Monetary policy	= Money and banking	: Economic policy
Monetary situation	= Money and banking	: Economic situation
Theory of economic growth	= Economic growth	: Economic theory
Growth policy	= Economic growth	: Economic policy
Economic growth, measured in a real situation	= Economic growth	: Economic situation

Figure 7. Examples of semantic factoring (C1.1.0). (*a*) Socialism would not be appropriate because it usually means socialism in a democratic system, like Great Britain or Germany.

Of course, having made clear the principle, we may note that often conceptual structure *is* reflected in linguistic structure; often multi-word terms do designate a compound concept, and the single terms designate or very nearly designate the semantic factors.

Example:

   Steel pipes = Steel: Pipes

This fact can be used in thesaurus building. (See Section F5.8, "Check homonyms and cross-references using the alphabetical index" and G3.4.3, "Computer assistance in semantic factoring".)

C Structure of Indexing Languages, Thesauri

In the early fifties a number of systems were established using so-called "uniterms". In these systems compound *terms* were split into their *linguistic* components and the list of components so derived was used as indexing language without terminological control. As one may easily understand, this method is no longer applied. It is a common mistake, however, to use the term "uniterms" in connection with combination indexing (coordinate indexing). Also, this is at the root of the widespread confusion of semantic factoring with linguistic decomposition.

Determining the semantic factors of a compound concept has to be done in a pragmatic way by applying common sense. Theories of semantic factoring are difficult; they would be connected to theories of definition and theories of concept formation, especially of the formation of concepts in science. The list of questions given in Figure 8 and the considerations in Section C1.3.2 on facet analysis should be helpful in semantic factoring. Of course, not every question applies in every case. The problem whether a concept is "ultimately" elemental (cannot be decomposed further) is difficult in theory but easily settled in most practical cases by common sense.

A special aspect of semantic factoring is shown in Figure 7b. A series of semantic factors is used as a common subdivision for a number of other

Of which class is it (the concept) a member or a subclass? (distinguishing features may then be elicited by use of the other questions)
From what is it a part?
What is it made from?
What are its distinctive properties?
What is it capable of?
Is it or is it not accompanied by something else or accompanying something else?
Is it in a specific state, condition, or circumstance?
Is it in a specific environment?
Does it determine, cause, influence, produce, act upon something else? Is it determined, caused, influenced, produced by something else?
Has it a specific purpose, is it a means or instrument to achieve something else? Is it a goal or end achieved or to be achieved by something else?
Is it a theory of something or an aspect of looking at something? Is it looked at under a specific aspect or viewpoint?

These are general questions that can be asked of a concept to elicit semantic factors. In a specific subject field one may add more specific questions, e.g. in *Medicine* "What is the organ involved?". Often the semantic factors are obvious without applying any such questions.

Figure 8. Some questions that might be useful for semantic factoring (C1.1.0).

concepts. This device greatly facilitates the construction of consistent classification schemes of the conventional type.

The reverse process of semantic factoring is concept combination to yield compound concepts. Note that not all specific concepts can be expressed precisely by a combination of elemental concepts.

Example:
Helicopter *cannot be expressed precisely by semantic factors, but the broader concept* Aircraft *can be expressed by the combination* Vehicles: Air transport.

The simple combination of elemental concepts is a comparatively crude method and may lead to errors.

Example:
School libraries (libraries serving schools) *and*
Library schools (schools teaching about libraries) *would both be expressed as*
Schools: Libraries

A refinement is achieved through the use of links and roles. The introduction of these syntactical elements must always be seen in the framework of cost-benefit analysis for the whole ISAR system. Faceted classification is a system which introduces syntactical elements in a rather restricted, and therefore manageable, manner. But faceted classification is not as flexible as other more complicated systems. The reader is referred to the literature for details.

C1.1.1 Advantages of semantic factoring

(1) *All essential aspects of a concept are rendered explicit.* This explicitness allows for a thorough analysis of the relationships between concepts in a classification scheme or a thesaurus, as will be discussed in detail below. This is of special importance for establishing links between disciplines. If conventional systems, which contain a large number of compound concepts arranged in a monohierarchical structure (for example, UDC), are subjected to such an analysis, it may be seen that they display only a fraction of the relationships existing between the compound concepts and that they are therefore deficient.

Related to this is another point. Semantic factoring may lead to the detection of general concepts which later on might be useful for retrieval. For example, *Railroad stations, Harbors,* and *Airports* all contain the semantic factor *Traffic stations*, but this concept as such will certainly not be included in a classification scheme unless it is detected in the procedure of semantic factoring. In a search on how to handle passengers in a traffic station this concept is very useful, however.

An important practical suggestion evolves from these considerations: the suggestion of preparing a conceptual index or auxiliary ISAR system to such schemes as Library of Congress Classification or Library of Congress Subject Headings. In such an index precombined descriptors contained in these schemes could be found under each of their semantic factors, as described later in Sections C2.3.2 and D3.6.

(2) *One arrives at a (comparatively) small set of elemental concepts* by means of which by various combinations all compound concepts can be expressed (especially if a syntax is used). As has been shown earlier, free combination allows for the precise representation of compound subjects as dealt with in documents, whereas in traditional systems one can only select, among the available precombined descriptors, the one that comes nearest to the subject dealt with in the document, even though this descriptor is not exactly what is wanted. Another aspect of this point is related to updating. Provided that the list of elemental concepts has been carefully drawn up, the majority of new concepts coming up in search requests or documents can be expressed by combination of the elemental concepts available as descriptors. Only in a minority of cases will it be necessary to make changes in the structure of elemental concepts.

(3) *It is possible to search for any combination of elemental concepts* and thus to search for combinations which the indexers did not think of at all. As mentioned above, this possibility is due to modern technical devices. For example, even if a document is indexed by *Ships* and *Engines*, it is retrieved in a search for the combination *Vehicles* and *Engines* because *Vehicles* is a semantic factor of *Ships*.

To a certain extent, therefore, it is possible to bring new viewpoints to the material already indexed. This makes for flexibility and adaptation to new developments.

The practical applications of semantic factoring will be dealt with in Section C2, "Problems of file organization related to classification".

C1.2 Polyhierarchical Structure. Definition of Hierarchy

Due to schemes like DDC and LCC misconceptions of hierarchy are widespread. The following exposition is intended to correct these misconceptions.

Hierarchy is *not* a straitjacket in which the universe of knowledge has to fit somehow or other. On the contrary, a properly designed hierarchy is a device to assist in indexing documents and in performing searches. Whenever a hierarchy sets constraints, it is faulty; whenever it helps the indexer or searcher, it serves its purpose. Accordingly, the following definition of hierarchical relationships is pragmatic and oriented towards searching.

> Concept A is broader than concept B whenever the following holds: in any inclusive search for A all items dealing with B should be found. Conversely B is narrower than A.

Examples:
Ground transport is broader than Rail transport (in an inclusive search

for Ground transport all documents dealing with Rail transport should be found);
Electron tubes is broader than Cathode ray tubes.

A number of remarks are appropriate in order to elaborate this definition.

(1) The definition applies to all concepts, and thus it applies to descriptors. The usual expressions are "Broader Term" and "Narrower Term". These expressions represent a loose use of language (see Sections B1 and B2). Their usage is so widespread, however, that we adhere to it in spite of its looseness.

(2) In most practical situations it is sufficient to use the following less stringent formulation of the condition given above: in many (instead of any) inclusive searches for A most (instead of all) items dealing with B should be found.

(3) The condition given may be interpreted in two ways:

(3a) Ask one subject expert whether he wants to retrieve in any inclusive search for A all items dealing with B. Introduce hierarchical relationships accordingly. This procedure yields an indexing language that corresponds to the viewpoint of the particular subject expert consulted. By consulting a number of subject experts different sets of hierarchical relationships are obtained. One may integrate all these hierarchical relationships into one scheme, indicating in each case the names of the subject experts that felt that this hierarchical relationship should be introduced. The resulting structure is rather complicated.

(3b). A simpler alternative is as follows: introduce only those hierarchical relationships that are agreed upon by a sizeable majority of subject experts. One may also do a majority count based on the search requests submitted: if the search request formulation as submitted by the user contains descriptor A, the user is asked whether he wants to retrieve documents on descriptor B, too. If the answer is yes for the majority of search requests containing descriptor A, then the hierarchical relationship "A broader than B" is introduced.

(4) The function of hierarchical relationships in indexing and search request formulation using the checklist technique, as well as the further functions of hierarchy listed in Section B5.5, offer additional criteria for the introduction of hierarchical relationships. Most hierarchical relationships will serve several or all of these functions simultaneously.

(5) It is in order to emphasize the purely pragmatic nature of the definition. It is oriented toward the function of hierarchical relationships in the search process. This is not to deny that logical or philosophical considerations might be helpful in suggesting hierarchical relationships. But it is to say that the ultimate decision should be based on the pragmatic criterion, not on strict rules based on logical considerations (such as the rule: whole-part relationships should not be considered as hierarchical relationships). (The introduction of two different kinds of Related Term (RT) cross-references in the API-Thesaurus, one for what in fact amounts to hierarchical relationships that do not fit into a faceted scheme and one for truly associative relationships, shows how confusing things can get once one leaves the safe ground of pragmatics.)

Obviously, this conception of hierarchy has major implications for hierarchy building. Usually, a hierarchy is built starting from a given set of concepts. The traditional approach to hierarchy building is as follows: The given set of concepts is subdivided into mutually exclusive groups; each of these groups is in turn subdivided into mutually exclusive subgroups, and so on. The emphasis is on putting the concepts into some kind of orderly arrangement. If a concept does not fit "naturally" anywhere into that arrangement, it is arbitrarily put somewhere. If a concept would fit into different places, it is more or less arbitrarily assigned to one of them; no concept is allowed to have more than one broader concept. This principle we call monohierarchy. It is quite obvious, especially in the light of our above definition, that this approach is artificial and imposes many constraints.

The modern approach to hierarchy-building is quite different. Pairs of concepts drawn from the given set are considered. Each pair of concepts A, B is analyzed as to whether or not the condition in the above definition holds for the concepts A and B in the pair. If the answer is yes a hierarchical relationship is established between A and B. If not, no such relationship is established.

Examples:

Rail transport	*broader concept*	*Ground transport*
Traffic stations	*broader concept*	*Traffic facilities*
Constitution	*broader concepts*	*Politics*
		Public law
Social psychology	*broader concepts*	*Sociology*
		Psychology
Railroad stations	*broader concepts*	*Railroads*
		Traffic stations
Trade negotiations	*broader concepts*	*International negotiations*
		Foreign trade

In the last two examples the broader concepts are the semantic factors: *Trade negotiations* $=$ *International negotiations*: *Foreign trade*. Vice versa, if a concept has two broader concepts, this is often a hint that the concept can be decomposed into semantic factors. This interaction between semantic factoring and hierarchy is very important and will be discussed in detail later.

As may be seen from these examples some concepts may end up having only one broader concept, but by no means is this true for all concepts. It is entirely possible and, in fact, occurs fairly often that a concept has two or more broader concepts. If a scheme allows a concept to have more than one broader concept we call that scheme *polyhierarchical*.

While some concepts may have two or more broader concepts, it may turn out for other concepts that they are left without any broader concepts at all after the procedure is finished. These concepts on top of the hierarchy may be broad subject fields such as *Economics*. But they may also be specific concepts that happen to have no broader concepts such as *Packaging* (in DDC there is no class number for this concept as a whole) or *Weights and measures* (wrongly placed under *380 Commerce* in DDC). Concepts of general application are more likely to be left without a broader concept than other types of concepts.

The importance of polyhierarchy cannot be overemphasized. As was shown earlier, most existing classification schemes do not use the flexibility of polyhierarchy, but are based on the rigid principle of monohierarchy: a descriptor must not have more than one broader descriptor. If this rigid principle is used many arguments result from the question which of several possible characteristics for the subdivision of a field is the "true" or more important characteristic. If as in the above examples a concept may be placed under several broader concepts, an argument arises as to which is the "true" broader concept and which is the "true" place in the hierarchy for the concept in question. But there is no point in arguing whether *Social psychology* should be placed under *Sociology* or under *Psychology*. Either solution would be inadequate. In a polyhierarchical scheme no such futile argument arises. One simply notes both broader concepts for *Social psychology*. This example illustrates one of the most important results of modern classification research. Polyhierarchical schemes allow for a better representation of the conceptual structure of any field. Many problems encountered in the construction of rigid monohierarchical schemes are revealed as fictitious by the idea of polyhierarchy. In the following the terms "hierarchy" and "hierarchical" will be used in the sense of "polyhierarchy" and "polyhierarchical" throughout. (The terms "strong hierarchy" for monohierarchy and "weak hierarchy" for "polyhierarchy" are also used. "Polyhierarchy" is sometimes used for systems that divide the same universe according to different viewpoints, resulting in different facets. However, the schedules given in such systems may still be (and often are) monohierarchical in the sense used here (every descriptor given in the facets has one and only one broader descriptor). The compound concepts created by combination of descriptors from different facets form, of course, a polyhierarchical structure.)

A more elaborate example of hierarchical relationships is given in Figure 9a and, in different form, in Figure 9b.

The discussion up to now has dealt with hierarchy mainly from the point of view of searching—specifically, conducting inclusive searches. Another important function of hierarchy is to facilitate the checklist technique of indexing and search request formulation. For this purpose it is necessary

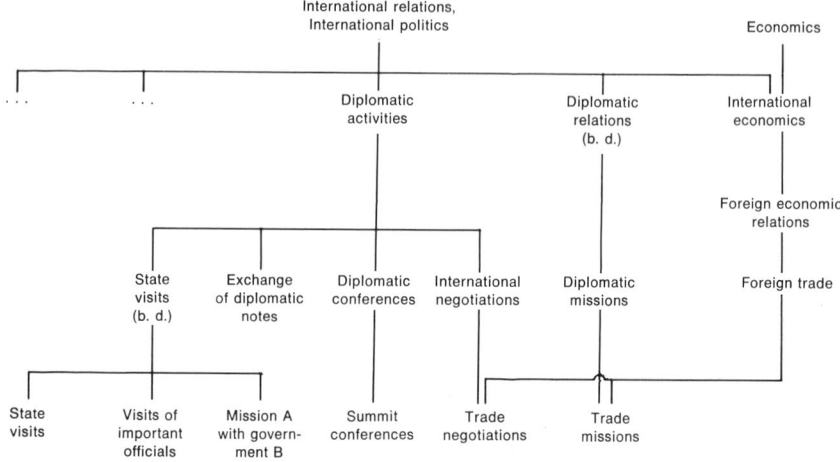

Figure 9a. Example of (poly-)hierarchical relationships in tree-like representation (Section C1.2). (Legend: b. d. = broadly defined.)

1 *International relations, international politics* NT 15
  2 Diplomatic activities
    3 State visits (broadly defined)
      4 State visits
      5 Visits of important officials
      6 Contact of mission A with government B
    7 Diplomatic conferences
      8 Summit conferences
    9 International negotiations
      10 Trade negotiations BT 17
  11 Diplomatic relations
    12 Diplomatic missions
      13 Trade missions BT 17
14 *Economics*
  15 International economics BT 1
    16 Foreign economics relations
      17 Foreign trade NT 10, 13

Figure 9b. Representation of the hierarchical structure of Figure 9a in linear arrangement with cross-references (C1.2).

to bring the concepts into an orderly arrangement with headings and subheadings for easy scanning. It is plausible that the arrangement of concepts should express as many of the hierarchical relationships as possible and that related concepts should be shown near to each other. This presents the problem of where to put a concept that has more than two broader concepts. The problem of listing at a sensible place those concepts that do not have broader concepts also arises. It may even be necessary to introduce additional hierarchical relationships geared specifically toward the checklist technique. Not all hierarchical and associative relationships can be expressed by the linear arrangement; those that are left over have to be expressed by cross-references as shown in Figure 9b. These problems of display will be discussed in Section D3.

It was the purpose of this section to give the general idea of hierarchy. More detailed considerations are deferred until Section C1.4.

Complementing the hierarchical relationships are *associative relationships,* usually called *Related Term* (RT) relationships. Concept *A* is related to concept *B* if the following holds: an indexer or searcher weighing the use of *A* should be reminded of the existence of *B*. A detailed discussion will be given in Section C1.5.

C1.3 Interaction of Hierarchy and Concept Combination

In the early days of combination indexing (coordinate indexing), it was suggested (and this is still a widespread opinion) that semantic factoring or concept combination on the one hand and hierarchy on the other are opposite principles and that systems must be based either on combination indexing or on hierarchical classification schemes, but not on both. Neither the definition of "broader than" nor the description of the functions of hierarchy given earlier contain anything to support this conception. A simple example may suffice to reveal its superficiality: *Railroad stations* may be decomposed into *Railroads: Traffic stations.* However, at the same time, the concepts *Railroads* and *Traffic stations* are both broader than *Railroad stations.* This is a simple example showing the interaction of concept combination and hierarchy to be discussed in detail below.

The development of the misconception that one can only have either concept combination or hierarchy may be explained as follows: It will become clear presently that a system of compound concepts shows a polyhierarchical structure enormously more complex than the hierarchical structure of a scheme of elemental concepts. Traditional systems, such as DDC or UDC, which try to arrange this enormously complex structure in a monohierarchy, are bound to reveal the total inadequacy of such an undertaking. On the other hand, systems using elemental concepts and free concept combination are able to cope with the complexity. Therefore, hierarchy has been

84   C   Structure of Indexing Languages, Thesauri

discredited and concept combination has been considered to be the solution. However, there may be hierarchical relationships between elemental concepts, and there are cases where it is useful to represent the complex polyhierarchical structure formed by compound concepts. It follows that semantic factoring or concept combination on the one hand and hierarchy on the other are not opposite and mutually exclusive principles. On the contrary, they interact with each other.

The *Railroad stations* example illustrates a very simple rule for the derivation of hierarchical relationships from concept combination: a compound concept is narrower than each of its components. A thorough understanding of the "derivation rules" discussed in the following is very important.

Refer to Figures 10a–c and 11, which give examples of hierarchical structures generated by two "facets". In this context, facet is understood in a specific and restricted sense: a facet is a set of concepts that are not to be combined with each other, that is, there are no within-facet combinations. In Figure 10a all possible combinations of concepts from the left-hand facet with concepts of the right-hand facet have been formed. This gives six compound concepts, so that altogether there are eleven concepts. All the hierarchical relationships resulting from the simple rule given above are represented in the picture (As the reader may verify there are no other hierarchical relationships possible). The example given in Figure 11 is more complicated in that we now have hierarchical relationships among concepts *within* one facet. The reader may easily see that the resulting hierarchical structure is meaningful. The following rules for inferring relationships between concepts, familiar from the rules for broadening (or narrowing down) search requests, have been used in its construction.

(a) Starting from a compound concept, one may get broader concepts by
(a1) dropping one of the components (dropping a restriction).

Example:

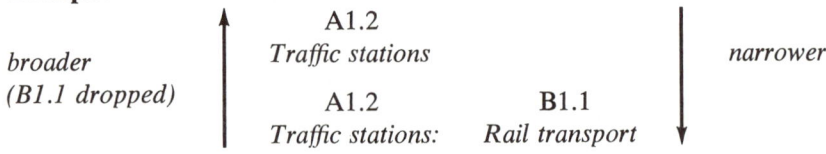

(a2) broadening one of the components (weakening a restriction)

Example 1:

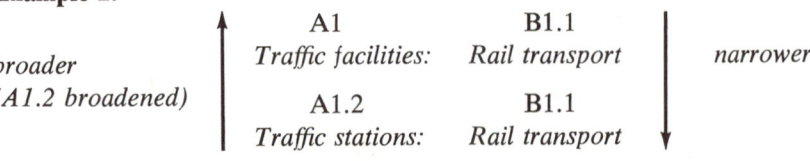

C1 Classificatory Structure   85

Example 2:

	A1.2	B1	
broader	*Traffic stations:*	*Ground transport*	*narrower*
(B1.1 broadened)	A1.2	B1.1	
	Traffic stations:	*Rail transport*	

If a restriction is weakened more and more it finally fades away. For example, *A Division by installation versus vehicles* covers the whole universe considered and therefore does not restrict anything; *A:B1.1* is nothing else than *B1.1*. Dropping a component is a special case of broadening that component.

Example 1:

	A	B1.1	
	(Universal concept):	*Rail transport*	
Broader	A1	B1.1	*narrower*
(A1.2 broadened)	*Traffic facilities:*	*Rail transport*	
	A1.2	B1.1	
	Traffic stations:	*Rail transport*	

Example 2:

	A1.2	B	
	Traffic stations:	*(Universal concept)*	
	A1.2	B1	
Broader	*Traffic stations:*	*Ground transport*	*narrower*
(B1.1.2 broadened)	A1.2	B1.1	
	Traffic stations:	*Rail transport*	
	A1.2	B1.1.2	
	Traffic stations:	*Local rail transit*	

Venn diagrams may be useful to clarify these rules, for example:

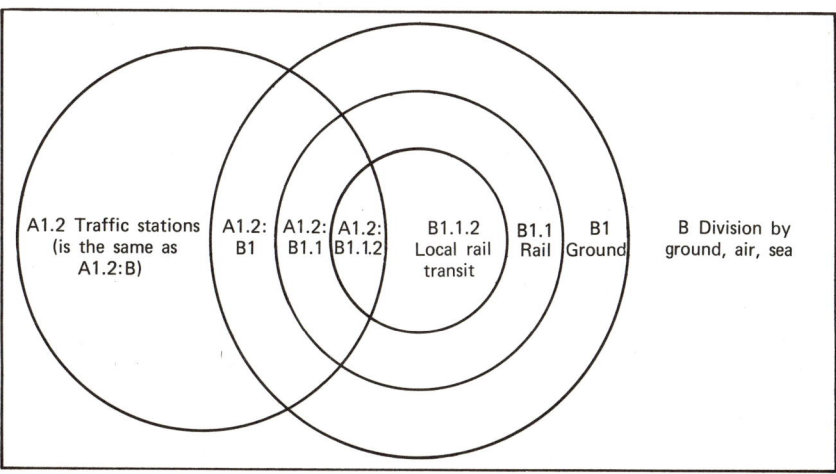

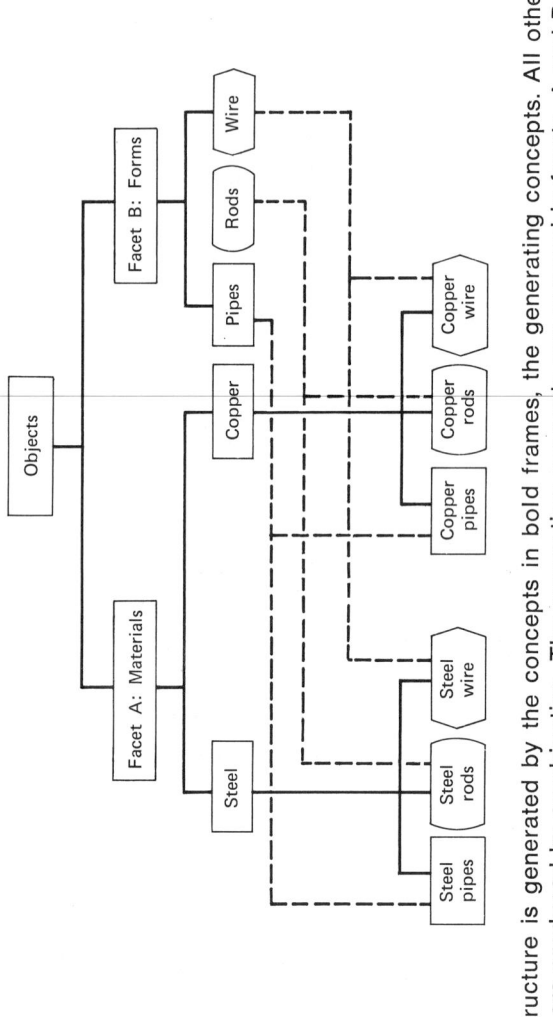

The whole structure is generated by the concepts in bold frames, the generating concepts. All other concepts (in light frames) are produced by combination. The generating concepts are grouped in facets, A and B. Each element of facet A is combined with each element of facet B. This gives 2 × 3 = 6 combination. Each combination, e.g., *Steel pipes*, is narrower than both of its components, in the example *Steel* and *Pipes*, as indicated by the solid and the broken line, respectively. The broken lines are in no way less important than the solid lines. They only serve to express the two-facet structure. Note how the pattern of facet B appears under both elements of facet A, and vice versa.

Figure 10a. Hierarchical structure generated by two facets, no within-facet combinations, no hierarchy within facets (C1.3). (Courtesy the University of Maryland.)

"Ruly" arrangement 1	"Ruly" arrangement 2	Arbitrary arrangement 1	Arbitrary arrangement 2
1 Steel	1 Steel NT 4, 7, 10	1 Steel NT 11	1 Steel
2 Steel pipes BT 9	2 Copper NT 5, 8, 11	2 Steel pipes BT 6	2 Steel pipes BT 6
3 Steel rods BT 10	3 Pipes	3 Steel rods BT 8	3 Steel rods BT 8
4 Steel wire BT 11	4 Steel pipes BT 1	4 Copper NT 7,9	4 Steel wire BT 10
5 Copper	5 Copper pipes BT 2	5 Copper wire BT 10	5 Copper NT 7, 9,11
6 Copper pipes BT 9	6 Rods	6 Pipes 2	6 Pipes NT 2
7 Copper rods BT 10	7 Steel rods BT 1	7 Copper pipes BT 4	7 Copper pipes BT 5
8 Copper wire BT 11	8 Copper rods BT 2	8 Rods NT 3	8 Rods NT 3
9 Pipes NT 2, 6	9 Wire	9 Copper rods BT 4	9 Copper rods BT 5
10 Rods NT 3, 7	10 Steel wire BT 1	10 Wire NT 5	10 Wire NT 4
11 Wire NT 4, 8	11 Copper wire BT 2	11 Steel wire BT 1	11 Copper wire BT 5

Figure 10b. Different possible linear arrangements of the concepts given in Figure 10a (C1.3, D3.1.1). (Courtesy the University of Maryland.)

This figure shows how the polyhierarchical structure displayed in Figure 10a can be expressed through a linear sequence with cross-references. In the "ruly" arrangement 1 *Steel* and *Copper* are subdivided by form. The hierarchical relationships shown by solid lines are expressed by the linear arrangement and indentation. The hierarchical relationships shown by broken lines are expressed by cross-references. In the "ruly" arrangement 2 it is just the other way around: each form is subdivided by materials, broken lines expressed by linear arrangement, solid lines by cross-references. In the arbitrary arrangement the decisions on which hierarchical relationships to express in the arrangement and which by cross-references are completely arbitrary. At this point it is important to understand that a polyhierarchical structure can be expressed by a linear arrangement with cross-references. We defer details until Section D3.1.1.

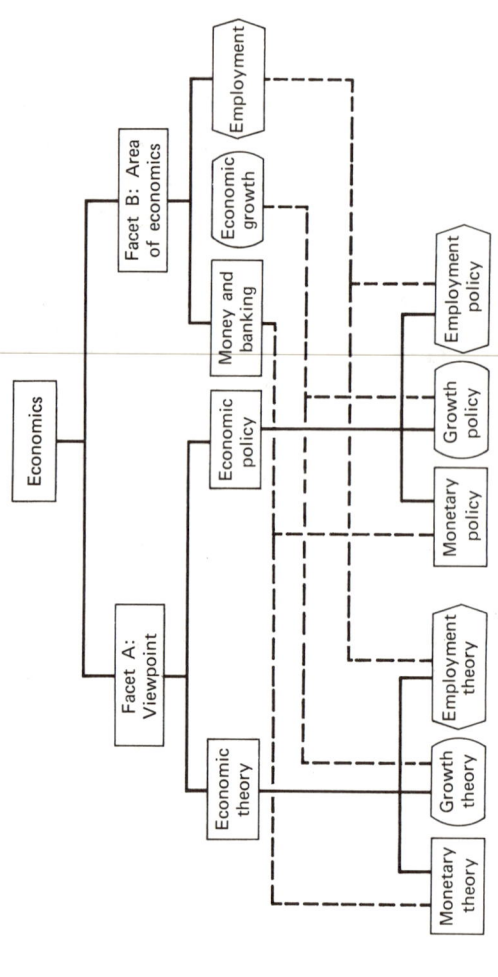

This figure shows how the same abstract structure is applicable to a different subject. It also shows that the generating concepts are not always elemental; *Economic theory* can be decomposed into *Economics* and *Theory*.

Figure 10c. Same as Figure 10a, but different semantic content (C1.3).

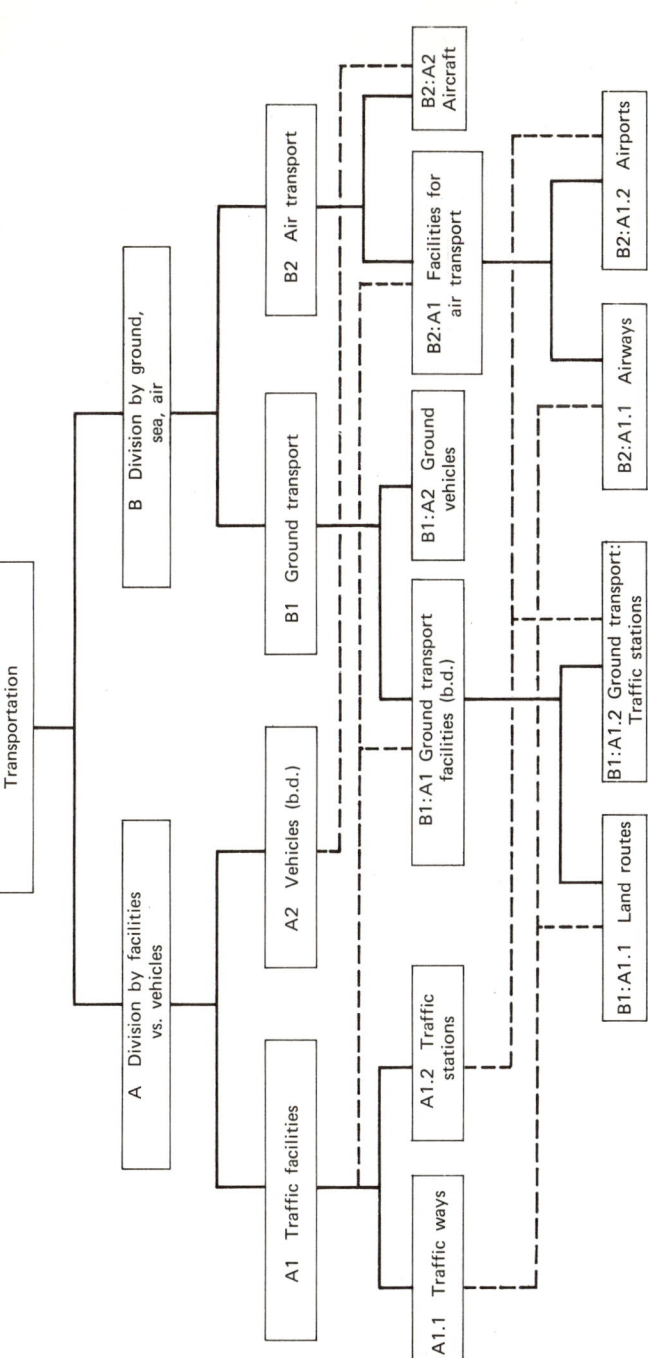

Figure 11. Hierarchical structure generated by two facets, no within-facet combinations, hierarchy within facets (C1.3). (Courtesy the University of Maryland.)

Now we have hierarchical relationships within facet A; *A1.2 Traffic stations* is narrower than *A1 Traffic facilities*. This leads to a more complicated structure. For example, *B2:A1.2 Airports* is narrower than *B2:A1 Installations for air transport*. Note how the pattern of facet A appears under both *B1 Ground transport* and *B2 Air transport*, the elements of facet B, and vice versa. This example also illustrates the fact that it is often useful to subdivide a concept, in this case *transportation*, by several characteristics of subdivision, in this case A and B. This idea will be discussed in more detail in Section D1.3.2.

90   C   Structure of Indexing Languages, Thesauri

To keep matters simple, the examples were restricted to compound concepts made up of two components. The rules hold as well if three or more concepts are present.

Example:

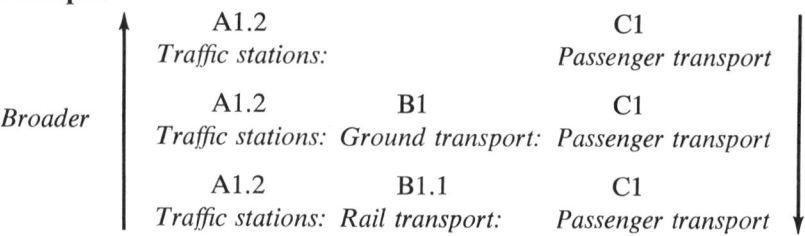

	A1.2		C1
	Traffic stations:		*Passenger transport*
Broader	A1.2	B1	C1
	Traffic stations:	*Ground transport:*	*Passenger transport*
	A1.2	B1.1	C1
	Traffic stations:	*Rail transport:*	*Passenger transport*

The rules for forming narrower concepts are just the other way around. There is, however, a third possibility not represented in the examples:

(a3) A compound concept may have a narrower concept that cannot be derived by any of these methods.

Example:

Helicopter is narrower than the compound concept *Aircraft* (which can be expressed by the combination *Vehicles: Air transport*), but *Helicopter* cannot be derived from *Vehicles: Air transport* by adding a component or narrowing down a component. Another example is *Flute* and *Music: Instruments*.

This case is important in systems that use mainly elemental concepts. If, in such a system, *Helicopter* is important for retrieval one should introduce the precombined descriptor *Aircraft* and the descriptor *Helicopter*. Otherwise, *Helicopter* can only be searched by the combination *Vehicle: Air transport*, and in every search for *Helicopter* one has to eliminate manually all the documents on other types of aircraft.

(b) Starting from a compound concept, one may get related concepts by replacing one or more components. In the example, the degree of association is higher between the 1st and 2nd line, since *B1.1.2* is related to *B1.1.1* while *B2* is not (or at least much less so).

Example:

C1	A2	B1.1.1	
Passenger transport	*Vehicles:*	*Railroad*	is strongly related to
C1	A2	B1.1.2	
Passenger transport	*Vehicles:*	*Local rail transit*	is less related to
C1	A2	B2	
Passenger transport	*Vehicles:*	*Air transport*	

C1 Classificatory Structure   91

If we remove the restriction that no within-facet combinations should be formed, we get more compound concepts (for example, ten instead of six in the case of Figure 10) and more complicated structures. The reader can follow for himself the hierarchical relationships depicted in Figures 12 and 13.

The discussion has shown how, starting from a set of elemental concepts and the hierarchical and associative relationships between them, it is possible to derive numerous hierarchical and associative relationships between compound concepts and between compound concepts and elemental concepts. However, not all relationships can be so derived. This is especially true for associative relationships of the type "connected empirically", for example, *Parochial schools* is related to *Relationships between church and state* or *State-controlled planned economy* is related to *Economy of Eastern European countries after World War II*.

C1.3.1 Limitations of the model for the generation of hierarchical structures

Consider an example: *Desert animals* can be expressed as the combination *Animals: Desert*. According to the model *Desert animals* is narrower than *Desert*. However, it is questionable whether this hierarchical relationship is useful (see the discussion of types of hierarchical relationships in Section C1.4.2). This problem can be solved only by using role indicators in forming compound concepts. The type of relationship between *Desert* and *Desert animals* could then be determined from the role indicator associated with *Desert* in the combination *Animals: Desert* (this role indicator might be *Environment*). This line of thinking leads to a rather complicated model. For the rest of this book we shall disregard these complications and assume that semantic factors are always broader concepts.

C1.3.2 Application of the model to hierarchy construction. Facet analysis

The thesaurus builder usually is confronted with a large set of compound concepts among which numerous hierarchical relationships exist, resulting in a complex and rather unwieldy structure. The model discussed in this section suggests the following approach to manage the problem:

Step 1: Decompose the compound concepts into elemental or quasi-elemental concepts.

Step 2: Arrange the elemental concepts that result from Step 1 in a hierarchy. Usually, the set of elemental concepts can be partitioned into *facets* or *characteristics of subdivision*. For example, two facets in the field of *Transportation* are *Facilities vs. vehicles* and *Ground, sea, air* (there are, of course, more). Within each facet, hierarchical relationships are established as necessary. Now we have

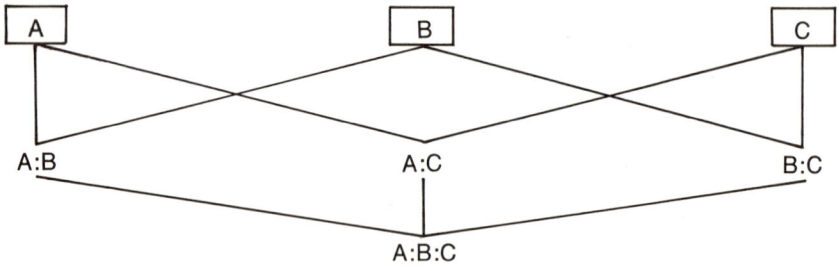

Generating concepts (in boxes):
A   Vehicles
B   Ground transport
    B1   Rail transport ⎫
    B2   Road transport ⎬ For Figure 13
C   United States

In Figure 12 each generating concept has been combined with each other generating concept. The hierarchical relationships that result are obvious.

The structure in Figure 13 derives from the structure in Figure 12. Two new generating concepts, B1 and B2, have been added; they are both narrower than B. Thus we have hierarchical relationships *within* the generating concepts as in Figure 11. Accordingly, the structure gets more complicated. The combinations B:B1 and B:B2 and their derivatives have been omitted because this would be obviously the same as B1 or B2 itself. The combination B1:B2 and its derivatives have also been omitted in order not to complicate the structure too much. Hierarchical relationships resulting from rule (a1) are depicted by oblique lines (e.g. A:B:C narrower than A:B) and hierarchical relationships resulting from (a2) by rectangular lines (e.g. A:B1 narrower than A:B because B1 narrower than B). A:B:C is narrower than A:B *due to combination,* whereas A:B1 is narrower *due to substitution* of the narrower descriptor for the broader descriptor B.

The underlined elements of Figure 13 form the structure shown in Figure 12. This simpler structure is embedded in the more complicated structure shown in Figure 13.

Figure 12.   Hierarchical structure generated by three generating concepts without hierarchical relationships among generating concepts (C1.3). (Courtesy the University of Maryland.)

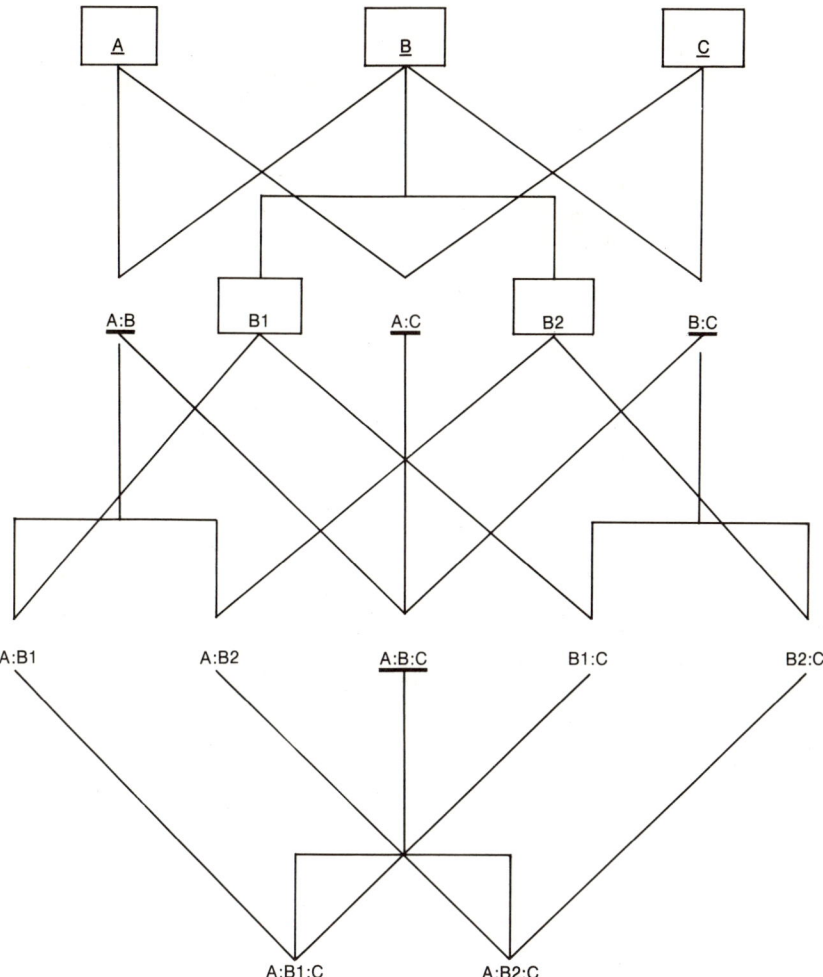

Figure 13. Hierarchical structure generated by five generating concepts with hierarchical relationship among generating concepts (C1.3). (Courtesy the University of Maryland.)

a relatively simple structure that gives a conceptual grasp of the field under investigation.

Step 3: Most of the hierarchical relationships between compound concepts can now be derived in a purely mechanical way. The resulting structure is a highly complex polyhierarchical one. The problem of representing such a structure in a linear sequence is a problem in file organization, to be dealt with in Sections C2 and D3.

The facets (characteristics of subdivision, also called "categories" or "types of terms") are specific to each field. They should emerge while working out the classificatory structure, especially from semantic factoring of compound concepts. The following facets are encountered often:

Things, object, entities (concrete or abstract), equipment
Materials
Properties, states, conditions, characteristics
Processes
Goals, objectives, purposes

(See Figure 51, Section E1.5.3, for a similar set of facets with examples.)

If the facets of a field are known beforehand they are of great assistance in semantic factoring. Most compound concepts are between-facet combinations; so for each compound concept the questions may be asked: What is the facet 1 (e.g., *Things*) component involved? What is the facet 2 (e.g., *Materials*) component involved? and so on. This leads to a list of questions like the one given in Figure 8, Section C1.1.0.

Facet analysis can be applied on different levels. First, some facets may contain concepts of general application. Second, some facets, like *Processes,* occur in different fields, and the question arises whether to arrange all processes at one place or whether to have a process facet in each field. This problem is discussed briefly in Section D3.0. Other facets are specific to a field; for example, in the field of *Transportation* we have the facet *Division by facilities versus vehicles* (see Figure 11). Third, a facet may have subfacets. For example, in the field of education the facet *Things, objects, entities* would have the subfacets *Equipment and instructional material* and *Persons.* Fourth, a concept further down in the hierarchy may be subdivided by facets. For example, *International relations* includes the narrower descriptors *Diplomatic activities* and *International organizations. Diplomatic activities* has, among others, the characteristics of subdivision *By mode of communication* and *By level.* The characteristics of subdivision for *International organizations* are shown in Figure 17, Section C3.1.

An elemental concept may belong to several facets. Other concepts may not fit in any facet.

C1 Classificatory Structure

All this shows that facet analysis should never be applied rigidly. It should help to grasp the conceptual structure of a field. Never should it be understood as a straitjacket into which the structure of a field has to be forced. Nor does the use of facet analysis mean that one is bound to make up a faceted classification with all the elaborate rules for file organization connected therewith. Whereas problems of file organization have prompted the idea of facet analysis, the major importance of this idea today is on the conceptual level.

C1.4 Further Topics in Hierarchy and its Use in Indexing and Searching

C1.4.1 Further considerations on pragmatic hierarchy building

,1 Extending the definition of concepts or introducing new broader concepts. There are cases in which a concept A, e.g., *Rail transport*, is "almost broader" than B, e.g., *Subways*—that is, most but not all documents indexed by *B Subways* should be retrieved while searching for *A Rail transport* (there are subways, at least in the design stage, that use the pneumatic tube principle instead of rails). In this case the definition of *A Rail transport* may be extended to say, A' *Track transport* (for lack of a better term), and then we will have a true hierarchical relationship between A' *Track Transport* and *B Subways*. It may even turn out that the original narrowly defined concept A is not useful for searching; in this case concept A is omitted and we have merely extended the definition of the original concept. On the other hand it might be that both A and A' are useful for searching. In this case *A Rail transport* should be retained and we have introduced a new broader concept—A' *Track transport*. (It might also be that the original concepts A and B can be expressed by combination of A' with appropriate semantic factors; see Section C2.8 for a more detailed discussion.)

Note that the introduction of A' as a new concept (rather than as a concept replacing A) gives more flexibility to the searcher, who may choose to search for the narrower concept *A Rail transport* or to search for the broader *A' Track transport* and then retrieve also the documents indexed by B. This is paid for by an increase in the number of descriptors contained in the indexing language. If it is anticipated that A' would actually be seldom used in searching, it should not be introduced, and a Related Term cross-reference *A Rail transport* RT *B Subways* should be used instead so that the person searching for A is reminded of the existence of B and can modify his search request to give A OR B. Conversely, B RT A should be introduced so that the indexer in indexing a document on *B Subways* does not overlook *A Rail transport* if the document deals with a subway using rails. This problem is further discussed in ,6 below.

,2 Introduction of additional broader concepts for searching. Broader concepts introduced by extending a definition are sometimes more useful for searching than for indexing purposes. Often there is no term for such a concept in the discipline in question.

Examples:
Broader concept to include all the following:
State
Constitution
Parliament
Administration, executive branch
or
Broader concept to include all the following:
Relation to own culture (Culture)
Relation to other culture (Culture)
Informal education (Education)
Socialization of the individual (Sociology)
Adaptation—re-adaptation (Sociology)
Culture and personality (Social psychology)
Attitudes, opinions (Social psychology)

In the second example the concepts to be included are taken from the different fields indicated in "( )". This example illustrates a number of related points. Usually, hierarchy is conceived of as an arrangement in which one intends to find a place for every concept. If this goal is achieved, then the hierarchy building is considered to be finished. We have seen that this is a misconception. The main problem is not to arrange concepts in a meaningful order, but to introduce hierarchical relationships and, if necessary, new broader concepts useful in searching. One might, of course, use in searching the OR-combination of the seven concepts, *Relation to own culture, . . ., Attitudes, opinions.* However, this procedure is cumbersome. In a computerized ISAR system seven terms have to be keyed. In a peek-a-boo system seven cards have to be pulled, and even then OR is not easily implemented. Furthermore, the procedure is not very reliable. One may easily forget one or more of the descriptors that should be included in the OR-combination. Both problems are solved by the introduction of the new broader concept. Only one term has to be keyed, only one peek-a-boo card (produced by generic posting) has to be pulled; this card immediately gives the OR-combination looked for, which can now easily be ANDed with other concepts. The new broader concept pulls together related concepts from different fields and shows them in one place, making it easier for the searcher to find a complete list of the concepts to be included. The broader concept might also be useful in indexing. One problem in the art of hierarchy building is, then, to anticipate those OR-combinations that are going to be used frequently.

,3 **Introduction of a broader concept to replace a number of specific concepts.** Another situation giving rise to the introduction of a new broader concept is the following: one has three concepts, B, C, and D, which are too specific to be used as descriptors in the given system. One solves the problem by introducing the new broader concept, A, which is used as a descriptor (or B, C, and D are used in the representation of documents, whereas A is used in the filing arrangement of documents, as discussed in B5.4.1).

Example:
    A *Stonework, glass, ceramics*
    B *Stonework*
    C *Glass*
    D *Ceramics*

(This is one subproblem of the general problem of how to design an optimal indexing language, to be discussed in Section C2.8.)

,4 **Introduction of new broader concepts to serve as headings ("organizational headings").** Broader concepts may also be introduced to serve as headings to clarify the arrangement (or organization) of the descriptors in the display of the indexing language. These "organizational headings" are very useful for the checklist technique of indexing and search request formulation. This is especially true for a broader concept designating a characteristic of subdivision.

Example:
Diplomatic activities by level;
or
Employment of specific groups
    Employment of children
    Employment of women
    Employment of handicapped persons
    Employment of jail inmates

Some systems insert such headings but do not assign notational symbols to them; examples are LCC and Thesaurofacet. This approach is not recommended because it necessitates an additional rule and is thereby confusing, and it is not possible to refer to these headings by way of notation. Also, these headings are often useful as descriptors.

,5 **Antonyms.** A special case to which all the considerations in the previous sections ,2–,4 apply is the introduction of a broader concept to cover two antonyms or two concepts representing two extreme points of a continuum.

Example:
> *Roughness versus Smoothness*
> *Roughness*
> *Smoothness*

In some cases one might wish to use only the broader concept for indexing and searching. (Often one of the antonyms is used to designate this broader concept; for example, *Roughness* might be used to designate the whole scale. However, this is a confusing practice.) In other cases one might wish to use a refined scale for the subdivision of the continuum.

,6 Hierarchical relationships versus associative relationships in indexing and searching. In some ISAR systems hierarchical relationships are used automatically in searching, either by generic posting or by other means. In such systems the searcher searching for, say, *B1 Ground transport* is compelled to retrieve documents indexed by the narrower concept *B1.1 Rail transport*, too. In a more flexible system he may have a choice between searching for *Ground transport, general references*, which would not include documents indexed by narrower terms, and *Ground transport, inclusive*, which would include such documents. But even in this flexible system we may have the following situation: *A Language processing* has two clearly narrower concepts *B Automatic translation* and *C Automatic indexing*. We are in a quandary whether also to define a hierarchical relationship between *A Language processing* and *D Manual indexing*. If we do so the searcher finds himself in the following situation: if he wants to retrieve documents on *Automatic translation* and *Automatic indexing* while searching for *Language processing* he wants to use *Language processing, inclusive*, and he is compelled to retrieve documents on *Manual indexing* as well, even if he doesn't want to. So we have exactly the same situation as described in ,1,—that is, *Language processing*, as understood by the searcher, has been broadened to include *Manual indexing*. If there are in fact many searches for *Language processing* in which a document should not be retrieved just because it is indexed by *Manual indexing* and if the introduction of a broadened concept *A' Language processing* (broadly defined) is not warranted then one should introduce an associative relationship *A Language processing* RT *D Manual indexing* (and the inverse *D* RT *A*). In this case the searcher looking for *A Language processing* is reminded of the existence of *D Manual indexing* and he can search for *A* OR *B*, if he so wishes. The searcher thus has greater flexibility paid for by more effort. The indexer, too, has to be more careful in this situation: If *Manual indexing* is narrower than *Language processing*, then the indexer having indexed a document by *Manual indexing* does not need to think at all whether he should use *Language processing* as a descriptor in indexing (except if the document is also on *Language processing* in general); the document will be retrieved in searching for *Language processing, inclusive* anyway. On the other hand, if *Manual indexing* is not hierarchically related to *Language processing*, then the indexer has to make a judgment whether or not the document should be retrieved in a search for *Language processing* proper and index accordingly (such would be the case if a document deals explicitly with manual indexing as a language-processing activity): In exercising his judgment, the indexer may start from the assumption that a searcher making a very broad search for *Language processing* will use the search request formulation *A Language processing* OR *D Manual indexing*, so that a document that is only obliquely relevant for *A* and that is indexed by *D* need not be indexed in addition by *A*.

It should be clear from these considerations that the usage of a descriptor in indexing is heavily dependent on its position in the hierarchy. This fact is very important in shared subject indexing, as we shall see later.

,7 **Introduction of new broader concepts as a creative activity.** In all these cases the introduction of new broader concepts is a most important creative activity, and the new concepts are developed by the application of the principles and methods of concept formation, as expounded in classification theory, to the analysis of the subject field in question.

C1.4.2 Kinds of hierarchical relationships (advanced)

The pragmatic definition of hierarchical relationships given in Section C1.2 was not concerned about the details of the "meaning" of a relationship. For a better understanding of the nature of hierarchical relationships, which in turn is useful for the development of the hierarchical structure, it is useful to consider the meaning of a relationship in more detail. Of special interest in connection with hierarchy are the following kinds of relationships between concepts (for examples, see Figure 14):

(1) *Class inclusion*. These are relationships of the form class/member of a class or class/subclass (hierarchy in the logical sense). In this case the narrower concepts have all the characteristics of the broader concept and, in addition, at least one further characteristic. One can always say in this case "*B* (the narrower concept) is an *A* (the broader concept) that has the characteristic *C*". For example: *B Radial beam tube* is an *A Electron tube* that has *C Several anodes arranged in a circle*.

(2) "*Topic inclusion*", which is "the relation between two areas of knowledge, one inclusive of the other (e.g., *Psychology* and *Personality*)". Another example is *Physics* and *Thermodynamics*.

(3) *Relationships of the type whole-part*.

(4) *Other types of connection, e.g.,*
    Electron tubes
        Characteristic curve of electron tubes

Electrolysis
    NT — Class inclusion
        Alternating current electrolysis
        Glow lamp electrolysis
        Fusion electrolysis
        Internal electrolysis
        External electrolysis
    NT — Connected
        Decomposition potential
        Current-potential diagram
        Residual current
        Limiting current
        Current density—potential diagram
Television camera tube
    BT — Class inclusion
        Cathode ray tubes
    BT — Whole
        Television camera
    BT — Connected
        Image transmission technology
    NT — Class inclusion
        Television color camera tube
    NT — Part
        Electrodes
    NT — Connected
        Transfer characteristics
Nuclear physics
    BT — Topic inclusion
        Physics
    NT — Topic inclusion
        High energy physics
        Elementary particles

Figure 14. Examples for different kinds of hierarchical relationships (C1.4.2).

In this case we have clearly a hierarchical relationship as defined above (that is, a document indexed by *Characteristic curve of electron tubes* should be retrieved in a search for *Electron tubes*), but we have neither class inclusion nor topic inclusion nor a relationship of the type whole-part.

Further kinds of relationships may be derived using the questions given in Figure 8, Section C1.1.0, to aid semantic factoring. An example of one such relationship is *Desert animals–Desert*.

These distinctions are different from the distinction hierarchical rela-

C1 Classificatory Structure   101

tionships—associative relationships. There are different ways to handle this two-fold set of distinctions:

(a) *Use a more refined set of relationships.* Instead of using Broader Term/Narrower Term (BT/NT) and Related Term (RT) to indicate relationships, use a more refined set, including the relationship-types (1)–(4) mentioned above, possibly other types of relationships and the residual types "hierarchical relationship, unspecified" and "associative relationship, unspecified". The searcher can then specify what relationship-types he wants the system to use as hierarchical relationships. (E.g., in searching for *Desert* he may want to retrieve documents indexed by *Sand desert, Stone desert,* etc., (narrower by class inclusion), but he may not want to retrieve documents indexed by *Desert animals* (*Desert* being the environment of the *Desert animals*). But another searcher *may* want to retrieve documents on *Desert animals*.

(b) *Use BT/NT and RT only.* Then the problem arises of how each of the other types of relationships should be treated. For each type there are three possible solutions, illustrated by using the example of the whole-part relationships:

(b1) Use all whole-part relationships as hierarchical relationships.

(b2) Use whole-part relationships as hierarchical relationships if they are to be used in inclusive searching; otherwise use Related Term relationships. For example, one might stipulate that whole-part relationships be treated as hierarchical relationships in anatomy and geography, but not otherwise.

(b3) Use no whole-part relationship as hierarchical relationship; use all whole-part relationships as Related Term relationships.

The decisions as to which possibility to choose for each type of relationship have to be made in each individual ISAR system considering the effects of a hierarchical relationship on retrieval. In this way, the structure of the indexing language can be adapted to specific user requirements.

TEST uses the following rules: "The broader term reference (BT) is employed to refer from a term representing a member of a class (or classes) of concepts to any term(s) in the thesaurus representing that class or classes: for example, *Steels* BT *Iron alloys*. . . The part-whole relationship is usually not a broader-narrower relationship; for example, *Gear teeth* BT *Gears* is incorrect. However, in certain specific areas part-whole generics can be usefully employed. These areas are anatomy and geographic locations. Also specifically excluded from the broader-narrower category are relationships based on the possible applications or uses of an entity; for example, *Platinum* is not considered to be a member of the generic family *Catalysts* because, although it is sometimes used as a catalyst, it has too many other applications to list all as broader terms. *Platinum* is, however, always a member of the class metals, so that the reference *Platinum* BT *Metals* should be entered."

With other classification schemes or thesauri, one has to check the rules and/or concrete examples in order to find out what types of relationships are used as hierarchical relationships.

(c) *Combine both solutions.* Give both the detailed type of the relationship and the BT/NT relationship. The searcher would then have a choice: he may specify the types of relationships he wants to be used as hierarchical relationships in the search. Or he may say that this is too complicated for him and that he simply wants to use the BT/NT relationships established in the system.

C1.4.3 Special cases of hierarchical structure

,1 Coarse hierarchy: subdivision of the preferred terms into subject fields. By this is meant the subdivision of the preferred terms into broad subject fields and possibly subfields and sub-subfields such as:

> *Agriculture*
> ....
> *Biological and medical sciences*
> ....
> *Chemistry*
> > *Chemical engineering*
> > *Inorganic chemistry*
> > *Physical and general chemistry*
> > *Radio and radiation chemistry*
>
> *Electronics and electrical engineering*
> > ....
>
> ....

In effect a hierarchy is thereby established. There are only a few hierarchical levels: the broad fields, possibly subdivisions, and the preferred terms assigned to them as narrower terms. Such a coarse hierarchy is useful as a tool in thesaurus construction, including the construction of conversion tables from one thesaurus to another. Sorting terms into broad subject fields is the first step in developing the classificatory structure of the thesaurus. Often a term belongs to more than one field. In this case a primary field should be indicated. (This is the field where the term should be sorted initially). The indication of a primary field also paves the way for the selection of a monohierarchical structure, which is needed in order to display a polyhierarchical structure as a linear sequence with cross-references.

In addition to these uses in thesaurus construction, a coarse hierarchy may serve for announcement purposes, be it in abstracting services or in individualized selective dissemination.

If the coarse classification of subject fields and subfields is used by several institutions, possibly in connection with shared subject indexing, it is called an "umbrella classification". This concept will be discussed in more detail in Section K2.4.2.

In some systems (for example, DGD/ET) a middle way between the coarse subdivision into subject fields and the introduction of a complete hierarchical structure is chosen. The subject fields are further subdivided, going two, three, or four levels down (a notation may be assigned to the concepts so defined). More specific concepts are simply placed under the appropriate concepts of this framework, but no further hierarchical relationships between these more specific concepts are indicated.

,2 **Facets.** Another possibility for the introduction of a hierarchical structure is the grouping of descriptors into facets, as discussed in Section C1.3.2. The facets may be viewed as broad concepts in the same way as subject fields (for example, economics) may be viewed as broad concepts. In a polyhierarchical system it is, of course, possible to represent both kinds of subdivision.

C1.4.4 "General descriptors" and "Other descriptors" as a special type of heading applicable throughout the classification scheme

These two headings might be useful for the subdivision of broad subject fields. Under the heading *General descriptors* are placed those descriptors that are of general application in the subject field in question. The heading *Other descriptors* lumps together those descriptors for which no appropriate subdivision of the subject field can be found. As descriptors are collected under this heading, additional subdivisions of the field will emerge, and the descriptors will be moved to an appropriate new subdivision when the thesaurus is updated.

The introduction of these headings should be clearly distinguished from the use of descriptors such as *Economics, general references* and *Economics, other*, to be dealt with in the Section C1.4.6.

C1.4.5 Implementation of inclusive searching. Generic posting and the POST TO instruction

An inclusive search for, say, *Rail transport* is a search in which documents indexed by the narrower descriptors *Railroads* and *Local rail transit* are retrieved as well. There are two basic methods to implement inclusive searches, and these methods will be discussed with reference to the ISAR system model given in Figure 4, Section B0.

(1) *Implementation of inclusive searching in the searching line.*
This is done simply by appropriate formulation of the search request. In the example the search request formulation would be *Rail transport* OR *Railroads* OR *Local rail transit*. This "expanding" or "exploding" of the descriptor *Rail transport* can be done by the searcher or by the system. In either case the method gets cumbersome if many narrower descriptors are involved. That is why implementation of inclusive searching in the storage line should be considered This is not the place to enter into a cost-benefit discussion comparing the two methods. (Compare Section D4.1.2 on the use of expressive codes for implementing inclusive searches in sequential scanning.)

(2) *Implementation of inclusive searching in the storage line.*

(2.1) In indexing. If a descriptor, e.g., *Local rail transit* is used in indexing a document, all its broader descriptors, e.g., *Rail transport* and *Ground transport*, are also used in indexing the document. This method may be called generic posting in indexing. It is both wasteful and harmful and therefore not recommended.

(2.2) In building the index file. Document numbers posted to, for example, *Local rail transit* are also posted to *Rail transport, inclusive* (but *not* to *Rail transport, general references*) and furthermore to *Ground transport, inclusive*. This is called *generic posting*.

If inclusive searching is implemented only through expanding the search request formulation, no Broader Term cross-reference implies generic posting. If inclusive searching is implemented only through generic posting, all Broader Term cross-references imply generic posting. In neither case is it necessary to introduce a special POST TO-instruction. However, it is sometimes useful to combine both methods. For example, one might use generic posting from *Railroads* and from *Local rail transit* to *Rail transport, inclusive* but not higher up to *Ground transport*. This makes it possible to do an inclusive search for *Rail transport* with one descriptor. In an inclusive search for *Ground transport* it is necessary to expand the search request formulation to *Ground transport* OR *Rail transport, inclusive* OR *Road transport*. (Note that it is not necessary to include *Railroads* or *Local rail transit* in the expanded search request formulation.) If both methods of implementing inclusive searching are used in combination, it is necessary to introduce special POST-TO-instructions and the inverse POSTED FROM-statements. The POST TO-instructions should be executed in building (or updating) the index file rather than in indexing. If this procedure is followed, the POST TO-instructions need not be given in the user version of the thesaurus. The POSTED FROM-statements tell the searcher what descriptors can be safely omitted from the expanded search request formulation because they are included implicitly by generic posting. If the expansion of search request formulations is done by a computer program, the POSTED FROM-statements can also be omitted from the user version of the thesaurus.

If (against our recommendation) the POST TO-instruction is to be executed by the indexer the following points should be noted. In the case of generic posting over several hierarchical levels the POST TO-instruction should contain *all* terms to which postings have to be made. The existence of POST TO-instructions forces the indexers to look up every descriptor contained in a USE-instruction unless every USE-instruction is extended to contain also the descriptors to which to post. This is particularly important in systems that use a combination of descriptors for most compound concepts.

C1.4.6 Descriptors ". . ., inclusive" and ". . ., general references"

Assume we have a system using generic posting (e.g., a peek-a-boo file). Using, for example, *Economics* in a search request, we would retrieve in this system all documents indexed either by *Economics* itself or by any narrower descriptor, e.g., *Money and banking*. For some searches, especially if we use *Economics* with other descriptors, this is extremely useful. For others, say if we want textbooks and other documents on economics in general, it would be equally harmful. The obvious way out is to introduce, at least for searching, two descriptors (two peek-a-boo cards):

(1) *Economics, inclusive* receives postings from narrower descriptors.

(2) *Economics, general references* (or *Economics, exclusive*) does not receive such postings, but just shows those documents that are indexed by *Economics* itself.

Economics, general references is used in indexing in the following cases:

(a) If the document deals with general principles that pervade the whole field of economics and cannot be expressed by one of the narrower descriptors.

(b) If the document deals with 50% or more of the descriptors narrower than *Economics*.

(c) If the document deals with another subject (e.g., education) but from an economic point of view or in relationship to economics.

In a system implementing inclusive searches through expansion of the search request formulation, no explicit distinction between the two descriptors is needed. Take a card catalog: in searching for *Economics, general references*, one looks through the cards filed under *Economics* itself. In searching for *Economics, inclusive*, one has to look through all the cards filed under any narrower descriptor, too. In some computerized systems it is possible to make the distinction by indicating *general references* or *inclusive* by a special symbol attached to the appropriate descriptor in the search request formulation. (In MEDLARS, for example, the descriptor by itself means *general references*; to obtain *inclusive* one can "explode" the descriptor.) Otherwise, it is necessary to key in all the narrower descriptors in an OR-combination.

(Special topic:) In a more refined analysis, one may choose the following somewhat modified procedure: For very broad concepts, such as economics, one would introduce *Economics, inclusive* and *Economics, general references* in the schedules and in the indexing stage (*Economics, general references* being a term narrower than *Economics, inclusive*). *Economics, inclusive* would be used for indexing documents for which case (c) holds, thus reserving *Economics, general references* to the cases (a) and (b) (one might even use separate descriptors for (a) and (b)). For broader concepts of the next lower level, for example, *Economic policy*, one would have only one descriptor, corresponding to . . ., *general references* in the schedule, but two peek-a-boo cards. The peek-a-boo card for . . ., *general references* would in this case include case (c). For still narrower descriptors like *Wage and price policy*, no distinction would be made either in the schedule or in the peek-a-boo file, in spite of the fact that these descriptors, in turn, may have narrower descriptors. In systems using links one might also introduce a separate descriptor *General references*. It would then be possible to produce *Economics, general references* by combination, and this combination would contain uses (a) and (b) only.

,1 **Descriptor usage depends on hierarchy.** From these considerations it follows that the usage of a descriptor in indexing depends on whether or not this descriptor has narrower descriptors.

Example:

indexing language A	indexing language B
A4 Aircraft	B4 Aircraft
	B4.2 Airplanes
	B4.4 Subsonic airplanes
	B4.6 Supersonic airplanes
	B4.8 Helicopters

In A, any document on any type of aircraft is indexed by *A4 Aircraft*. In B, only documents on aircraft in general are indexed by *B4 Aircraft* (unless generic posting in indexing is used, which is not recommended anyway). In other words, *B4* is the descriptor *Aircraft, general references* (not available in indexing language A), and *A4* is the descriptor *Aircraft, inclusive* (formed by *B4* OR *B4.2* OR *B4.4* OR *B4.6* OR *B4.8* in indexing language B). Furthermore, the usage of a broader descriptor in the sense . . ., *general references* depends on the narrower descriptors. This is another instance of the influence of hierarchy on descriptor usage, and it is an important consideration in updating as well as in shared subject indexing.

C1.4.7 Descriptors ". . ., other"

The descriptor *Economics, other* should be introduced for documents that deal with a specific concept from the field of economics that is neither contained as a descriptor in the indexing language nor expressible as a combination of concepts nor narrower to a descriptor listed under *Economics*. The indexer should include in the document representation as a free term the specific concept giving rise to the use of the descriptor *Economics, other* so that this specific concept can be included in the thesaurus. The documents indexed by *Economics, other* and the free terms used in their representations should be examined periodically so that descriptor candidates are detected. An example is provided by the procedures used in the U. S. Bureau of the Census. In the collection of data on occupations, subjects use a free term to describe their occupation. These free terms are then translated (coded), by man or by machine, into the appropriate descriptor of the occupation classification. Those terms translated into e.g., *Metal workers, other* are examined periodically to see whether new specific descriptors should be introduced. However, one might choose deliberately not to introduce specific concepts as descriptors and use *Economics, other* instead in order to keep the number of descriptors down. In case the descriptor *Economics, other* is not introduced *Economics, general references* has to be used instead. In systems using links, one might introduce *Other* as a descriptor in its own right and produce *Economics: Other* by combination.

C1.5 Associative Relationships Between Concepts

Definition: Concept A is related to concept B (has an associative relationship to concept B) if the following holds: an indexer or searcher weighing the use of A should be reminded of the existence of B (and there is no hierarchical relationship between A and B).

The associative relationships complement the system of hierarchical relationships. Associative relationships exist between all concepts that are sons of the same father in the hierarchy. One may extend this principle to include grandsons of the same grandfather, and so on; the degree of association becomes lower as the number of intervening levels increases. This principle may be restated with a somewhat different emphasis by saying that concepts in the same neighborhood in the classified arrangement tend to be associated (or, the other way around, the classified arrangement should take into account the associative relationships between concepts). If two concepts are in the same neighborhood in the classified arrangement, or if they are sons of the same father (so that a relationship is established at least by a hierarchical cross-reference), the associative relationship need not be indicated explicitly. In all other cases explicit cross-references are introduced. This procedure ties the introduction of explicit cross-references to the classified arrangement. While it cuts down enormously on the number of cross-references, the procedure has the following disadvantage: whenever the classified arrangement is changed, one has to check whether new RT cross-references are necessary and existing ones can be deleted (for a more detailed discussion of this problem see Section F4.0).

(Furthermore, explicit Related Term cross-references may be omitted (and the number of such cross-references kept down) due to the following consideration: If A is related to both B and C and if B and C are very near in

C Structure of Indexing Languages, Thesauri

the classified arrangement (say not more than 5 lines apart) then it is sufficient to establish one associative relationship from A to B or to C, whichever is the more important one. Following the cross-reference to B one will see C and vice versa. By the same token if D and E are very close neighbors and both related to F it might suffice (at least in the classified index) to give the relationship from D to F because, whenever one looks at E, one will also see D and the relationship indicated there.)

An associative relationship can be one-directional: one may have A related to B but not B to A. As a rule, however, associative relationships are bi-directional. One can distinguish between two kinds of associative relationships:

C1.5.1 Concepts similar in meaning

These are concepts that have common elements in their definitions.

Example:
> *Race problems (sociology) related to Race (physical anthropology)*
> or
> *Political ideas related to Social philosophy.*

In these cases one should consider the following two possibilities which are alternatives to the introduction of an associative relationship:

(1) *Consolidate the two concepts in an equivalence class* ("competition" of similar-in-meaning and quasi-synonymous).

Example:
> *Vertical take-off and landing airplanes (VTOL) and Short take-off and landing airplanes (STOL) consolidated in V/STOL.*
> *Wire and Cable consolidated in Wire, cable*

(2) *Form a new broader concept* covering the related concepts, leaving the related concepts separate.

Example:
> *Automatic indexing, Automatic abstracting*
>   *Automatic indexing*
>   *Automatic abstracting*

Some cases are on the borderline between associative and hierarchical relationships.

C1.5.2 Concepts connected empirically ("contextual contiguity")

,1 **Contiguity based on definition.** Concepts that, due to their definition, co-occur frequently in reality.

Example:
(1) Measuring instrument; Calibrating; Error
(2) Copyright; Duplication

,2 Contiguity based on empirical knowledge. An associative relationship may result from knowledge gained by empirical study.

Example:
Alcohol related to Solvents
Alcohol related to Antifreezes
Planned economy related to Eastern Europe economies after World War II

,3 Contiguity and frequency of combination. A special case of ,1 or ,2 is the following cross-reference in systems based on concept combination:

If two descriptors, say *Taxes* and *Public law*, are often used in combination, an appropriate cross-references is made from *Taxes* to *Public law*, and vice versa.

Example:

P83 Taxes	Compound concept:
	Tax law
RT *N74 Public law*	
I64 Birth	Compound concept:
	Birth customs
RT *I74 Customs*	

NKP Color Television interference
   RT *MXS Interference suppression*

This cross-reference has the following advantages:

(a) With a document on *Tax law*, the indexer using P83 *Taxes* is less likely to overlook the descriptor N74 *Public law*, and the searcher is less likely to omit N74 *Public law* as an additional specification in his search request formulation.

(b) The indexer or searcher using *P83 Taxes* has the notation or the correct spelling of *N74 Public law* immediately available, so that look-up in the alphabetical index or classified index is not necessary.

Whereas the compound concept *Tax law* is not used as descriptor, it is recognized in the system and it is made easier for the indexer or searcher to find the appropriate combination of descriptors.

C1.5.3 Instructional scope note

A generalized cross-reference to descriptors likely to be used in combination is the "instructional scope note": a cross-reference is made, not to a specific descriptor, but to one or more general classes or facets of descriptors in order to indicate that one descriptor of each facet should be used for further specification.

Example:
> *Diseases*
>> Check also RT *Part of body and Causes of disease*

That means, for instance, if a document deals with the disease *Cancer*, the indexer should check whether it deals with cancer of a specific part of the body, e.g., the lung, and if so, use *Lung* in indexing; the same holds for the cause of cancer.

Example:
> *Semiconductor modulator*
>> Combine with specific *Semiconductor device* used to achieve modulation

This can be expressed more concisely by
> LV/MH *Semiconductor modulators*
> RT MH *Semiconductor devices*

Such an instructional scope note may also be expressed by a suitable arrangement of the descriptors on the document analysis sheet or question analysis sheet.

A rudimentary form of an instructional scope note is the general instruction "Specify context in which the descriptor is used", which may be expressed, for example, by the symbol ***. The indexer or searcher is then required to find the appropriate specifications for himself (if he is using the descriptor *Administration*, for example, he should also specify the object of administration, such as school, personnel, etc.).

C1.6 Transitions Between the Synonym-Homonym Structure, the Equivalence Structure, and the Classificatory Structure

Section B1 and B2 emphasized the distinction between these three structural levels. But it was also mentioned that due to the complexity of language the boundaries are blurred. This phenomenon will be discussed with reference to the examples given in Figure 15. Let A be a descriptor and B a term in the lead-in vocabulary with a USE instruction to A. There may be different reasons behind this USE instruction:

(1) The terms A and B are synonymous, they have the same meaning, or they refer to the same "conceptual content".

(2) The terms A and B are quasi-synonymous (equivalent), that is, their meanings overlap widely. A may fully cover B, B being only slightly narrower; in

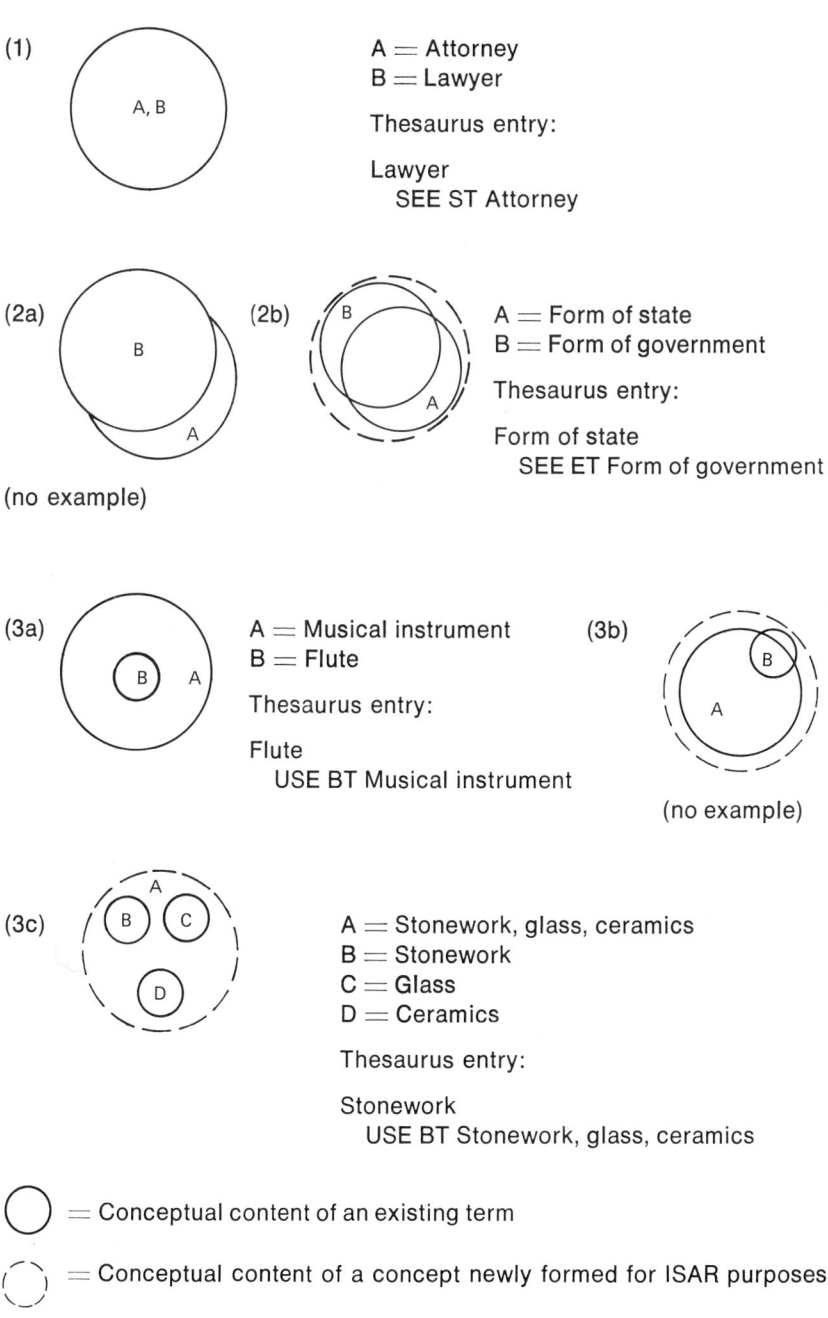

Figure 15. Transitions between the synonym-homonym structure, the equivalent structure, and the classificatory structure (C1.6).

this case *A* will be used as the preferred term (case (2a)). Otherwise, a new ISAR concept covering the meaning of *A* as well as that of *B* is formed in establishing the equivalence structure. The preferred term *A* is assigned to this newly formed ISAR concept (case (2b)).

(3) *B* designates a concept that is too specific to be used as a descriptor. The broader concept designated by *A* is used instead. The different cases shown in (3) differ gradually from the cases shown in (2): in (2a), *B* is only slightly narrower than *A*, in (3a), *B* and *A* are clearly distinct concepts. In (3b), as opposed to (2b), we also have two clearly distinct concepts. (3c) differs from (2b) in that several clearly distinguishable specific concepts are brought together under one newly formed broader concept. The transitions between these cases are fluid. In most practical cases decisions should not be difficult, however. As we shall see in Section C5 it is recommended anyway that cases (1) and (2) be treated alike and that only (3) be treated differently.

C1.7 Psychological Dimensions of Relationships

Psychologists study term-term associations that people form in their minds. From this point of view, two main types of relationships can be distinguished:

(1) *Definitional relationships.* These are: synonymity, quasi-synonymity, similarity in meaning, class inclusion, and topic inclusion.

(2) *Relationships of "contextual contiguity".* These are: part-whole, connections like *Electron tubes—Characteristic curve of electron tubes*, and empirical connectedness.

The types of relationships used in a thesaurus, namely synonymity and quasi-synonymity, hierarchical relationships, and associative relationships, have been developed based on the function of these relationships in an ISAR system. The two dimensions used by psychologists cut across this typology. They are important for the interpretation of data from word association studies and of word co-occurrence statistics, as discussed in Chapter H.

C2 PROBLEMS OF FILE ORGANIZATION RELATED TO CLASSIFICATION. PRACTICAL APPLICATIONS OF SEMANTIC FACTORING

C2.0 Introduction

A number of issues in classification theory that are important for thesaurus building are, in fact, problems of file organization. Failure to distinguish properly between conceptual structure on the one hand and file organization on the other may lead to erroneous assumptions and less-than-optimal procedures in thesaurus building. For example, it is very often assumed that semantic factoring is invariably tied to the use of post-combination (post-coordinate) indexing systems. Section C1.1 has made clear already that this is by no means true. There are several ways in which semantic factoring can be applied; they will be explored in detail in this Section. Sections C2.1–C2.5 provide a background discussion of the problems involved. This discussion is closely related to the section on semantic factoring (C1.1) and the discussion of "conceptual indexes" in Section D3.6. Section C2.6 gives a summary of the strategies for the application of semantic factoring and Section C2.7 deals with rules for the use of precombined descriptors in systems based mainly on post-combination indexing. The chapter is concluded by a discussion on how to optimize an indexing language when the ISAR techniques used impose a limit on the number of descriptors (Section C2.8).

C2.1 On the Relationship Between Conceptual Structure and File Organization in Classification Theory

Classification theory can be divided into two major areas: conceptual structure and problems in file organization. The principles of hierarchy and of concept combination which were discussed in Section C1 are problems of conceptual structure. Problems like pre-combination versus post-combination (pre-coordination versus post-coordination), synthetic versus enumerative classification schemes, or alphabetical versus classified order, to be discussed below, are problems of file organization. More precisely, we are concerned with files that serve the purpose of retrieving documents relevant to a given search request. The following considerations will concentrate on inverted files, in which retrieval is done by look-up, but some of the problems are relevant for sequential scanning, too. The file organization part of classification theory is concerned with the question: how can a file be organized in such a way that the conceptual structure developed previously can be put to maximum use in searching, given the constraints of the equipment available in a given system? In the area of file organization the problems related to classification might be considered as part of the logical organization of files. However, to some extent we shall also deal with the physical organization of files for two reasons. Firstly, the logical organization of a file determines, more or less, its physical organization (how much it does so depends on the medium used), and the boundaries between logical and physical organization are not well defined. Secondly, there is a dependence in the other direction: some storage media are so inflexible with respect to physical handling that only very few types of logical organization of the file can be implemented efficiently.

In the past many classificationists have concentrated too exclusively on the file organization aspects of classification, and they have looked on the problems of conceptual structure from the point of view of file organization. The conceptual structure has been developed for a given type of file organization, which in turn was dictated by the limitations of the medium used (such as shelving of books or card catalog). This imposed many restrictions on the consideration of conceptual structure, and many aspects important for information storage and retrieval have not been brought out. Faceted classification *stricto sensu*, with its emphasis on the linear arrangement of highly compound concepts, and the Library of Congress Classification are classic examples of this fallacy. This over-emphasis on file organization within the constraints of conventional media led to the fact that the many results of classification theory that pertain to conceptual structure are presented in a file organization framework. This might be one of the reasons why the results of classification theory have been neglected or sometimes reinvented in a rather amateurish manner in mechanized ISAR systems where the restrictions imposed by file organization are far less severe than in manual systems.

In view of the fallacious attitude just described, we restate our position as follows: The primary and basic task is to understand conceptual structure and its functions in the retrieval process. Sections B5 and C1 undertook this task without any reference to the limitations imposed by any particular kind of file organization. File organization is the secondary, technical, almost ancillary task. File organization has to serve the purpose of allowing maximum use of the conceptual structure in searching. Moreover, if different types of file organization have to be used in different systems (or within one system), they should still be based on the same conceptual structure. As we shall see later this procedure will increase considerably the effectiveness of ISAR systems. Furthermore, this principle would serve to maintain compatibility between ISAR systems with different kinds of file organization, e.g., a peek-a-boo file and a conventional card catalog, or a computerized ISAR system and a printed index.

Obviously conceptual structure and file organization are closely intertwined, and one cannot be treated without reference to the other. This will become very clear from the following discussion. Also, the presentation of an indexing language (a classification scheme) or a thesaurus is basically a matter of file organization; therefore, some duplication with Chapter D on presentation cannot be avoided.

C2.2 The Problem Defined

The problem to be solved by file organization may simply be stated as follows: Each document deals with a very compound concept, made up of many components and called *document representation*.

Example:
The Glideway system, a high speed ground transportation system in the Northeastern United States.
Components of compound concept (document representation):

Traffic networks; Traffic modelling and simulation; Traffic ways; Traffic stations; Vehicles; Propulsion of vehicles; Rail transport; High-speed transport; Schedules; Passenger traffic; United States.

Searches are also made for compound concepts, called search request formulations; but these search concepts are usually made up of fewer components.

Examples:
(1) Stations for rail transport.
Components of compound concept (search request formulation):
Traffic stations: Rail transport
(2) A regional network for passenger transport in the Northeastern United States.
Components of compound concept (search request formulation):
Transportation network: Passenger transport: United States

The problem is, then, to retrieve those documents that have a representation equal to or narrower than the search request formulation. (In the case of non-inclusive searches one wishes to retrieve only those documents with a document representation equal to the search request formulation.) We shall discuss several alternative methods to solve this problem and the influence of each alternative on file organization. As mentioned earlier we shall deal mostly with inverted (term-entry) files. It is easy to see how the discussion applies to direct (item-entry) files, too. For the following discussion we shall restrict the meaning of "descriptor" a bit: Descriptors are those concepts under which entries are made in the inverted file. An entry is defined here in a more general way; it may be a document number or call number or a condensed document description such as on a catalog card, or the full text of a document, stored on shelves or in a computer, etc. A record in an inverted file shall be defined as a descriptor, together with all the entries associated with it.

C2.3 Principal Solutions: Post-Combination Versus Pre-Combination— A Quantitative View

C2.3.1 Post-combination and pre-combination (post-coordination and pre-coordination) defined

(Remark on terminology: Post-combination and pre-combination are so much better terms than post-coordination and pre-coordination that we suggest these new terms replace the old ones. Accordingly, we suggest post-combination indexing and pre-combination indexing instead of post-coordinate indexing and pre-coordinate indexing.)

116   C   Structure of Indexing Languages, Thesauri

The most important parameter in characterizing the organization of a file in our context is the degree of compoundness of the descriptors. This is a "quantitative" version of the dichotomy post-combination versus pre-combination. The designer of a file has three strategies available:

(1) *Strategy 1: Use elemental descriptors.* At the one end of the scale are files where the descriptors are elemental or nearly elemental. The usual application of peek-a-boo cards would be a concrete example. The number of descriptors in these files is comparatively small. A document representation (the compound concept assigned to a document) is made up by listing many of the elemental or nearly elemental descriptors (see Figure 16(1)); an entry is made under each of these elemental concepts (multiple entry with numerous entries). In the same way a search request formulation is made up as a combination of elemental or nearly elemental descriptors, each of which may easily be found in the comparatively small list of descriptors. A search for this combination is then made. This type of file is useful only in the case where it is feasible, from a mechanical point of view, to search for combinations of descriptors, such as in the case of combination indexing systems (e.g., peek-a-boo cards or computerized files). All documents are retrieved that have a representation equal to or narrower than the search request formulation. More precisely, documents that have a representation that is narrower due to combination are retrieved. If documents that have a representation narrower due to substitution have to be retrieved, too, a properly expanded search request formulation or generic posting have to be used. As explained in C1.3, Figure 13, "Narrower due to combination" means $A:B:C$ being narrower than $A:B$. As we have seen, this is to be distinguished from $A:B1$ being narrower than $A:B$ due to the fact that B1 is narrower than B. The situation can be depicted as follows:

Example:

	A	B		
search request formulation	Vehicles:	Ground transport		

	A	B1	A	B	C
document representation	Vehicles:	Rail transport	Vehicles:	Ground transport:	US
	Narrower due to substitution		Narrower due to combination		
	Retrieved only if suitable measures are introduced (either search for A: (B OR B1) or use generic posting from B1 to B).		Retrieved by searching in any combination indexing system.		

(2) *Strategy 2: Use highly precombined descriptors.* On the other end of the scale are files that use highly precombined descriptors, such as files where documents are arranged on shelves by subject. In this case we have a huge number of

descriptors in the indexing language (the class numbers are the descriptors). A document representation is made up of one highly precombined descriptor (see Figure 16(2)); only one entry is made (single entry). In preparing a search the first step is to find among the huge number of highly precombined descriptors the one that is equal to the search request formulation. For an inclusive search one has to find, in addition, all descriptors narrower than the search request formulation. In a second step one can then retrieve the documents entered under these descriptors. The important problem of how to find the appropriate precombined descriptors is dealt with in Sections C2.3.2 and D3, especially D3.6.

Title:
  The Glideway system, a high-speed ground transportation system in the northeastern United States.
(1) *Document representation in a peek-a-boo system* (many elemental descriptors):
  Transportation networks; Traffic modelling and simulation; Traffic ways; Traffic stations; Vehicles; Propulsion of vehicles; Rail transport; High-speed transport; Schedules; Passenger transport; United States.
(3) *Document representation in a card catalog* (few precombined descriptors):
  Passenger transportation networks;
  Rail transport stations;
  Rail transport vehicles—high speed.
(2) *Document representation in a shelving system* (highly precombined descriptors):
  High-speed rail transportation networks for passenger transport.

Figure 16. Document representations in different file systems (C2.3.1). (Courtesy the University of Maryland.)

(3) *Strategy 3: intermediate solution: use moderately precombined descriptors.* In the middle of the scale are files using moderately precombined descriptors, such as in subject heading catalogues. The number of descriptors in the indexing language is large, but not as large as in (2). A document representation is made up of a few precombined descriptors (see Figure 16(3)); an entry is made for each of these (multiple entry with a few entries). In preparing a search one must first find the appropriate precombined descriptors from among the large number of descriptors; this poses problems similar to, but less severe than, finding the highly precombined descriptors in Strategy 2. In a second step one can then scan the entries under one of those precombined descriptors to retrieve the pertinent documents. If it is mechanically feasible one might also search immediately for a combination of precombined descriptors. In Strategy 3 precombined descriptors may be combined to form still more compound concepts. However, it is not allowed to use a combination of descriptors instead of a precombined descriptor available in the indexing language. This faulty procedure is sometimes used in card catalogs using UDC; one speaks of a "competition" between "colon-combination" and further "direct" hierarchical subdivision.

Example:
Pre-combined descriptor:
368.44 Unemployment insurance versus
Combination of two descriptors:
368.4 Workmen's insurance: 331.6 Unemployment

Using the combination of two descriptors when a precombined descriptor is available can only lead to confusion. The precombined descriptor has been included in the indexing language in order that it be used in indexing so that it can be used in searching. The searcher must be sure that the precombined descriptor has been used consistently in indexing.

On the other hand, searches for *Unemployment* now present a problem. If documents relevant for *Unemployment insurance* are indexed by *368.44*, the searcher looking for documents relevant for all aspects of *Unemployment* and looking under *331.6* should find a cross-reference there that tells him that *368.44 Unemployment insurance* is a narrower term and that he should look there, too. If many of these cross-references are missing, as in the case with UDC, it is better to exclude from the indexing language compound concepts that are not often used; that is, only a subset of UDC is used as the indexing language. If *368.44 Unemployment insurance* is excluded from the indexing language then it is correct to index a document relevant for *Unemployment insurance* by

Example:
368.4 Workmen's insurance: 331.6 Unemployment.

We shall take up the whole problem in more detail later.

The use of precombined descriptors in indexing does not preclude the possibility of searching for any combination of elemental concepts, i.e., use of post-combination in searching, if the ISAR system is designed properly. For example: A document indexed by *Ships* and *Engines* is retrieved in a search for *Vehicles* AND *Engines* because *Ships* is decomposed into *Vehicles: Water transport*.

The use of elemental descriptors may lead to so-called false combination or "false drops" and is therefore seldom applied in its pure form, as we shall see later. False drops can be prevented by the use of syntactical elements, i.e., roles and links or relators. The document representations formulated by elemental descriptors, roles, and links are completely equivalent to the document representations formulated by precombined descriptors. Using an indexing language containing a small number of elemental descriptors and syntactical elements one may achieve the same results as when using an indexing language containing a large number of precombined descriptors and at the same time gain considerably in flexibility.

(Special topic:) It is interesting to look at the relationship between the number of descriptors contained in the indexing language and the number of descriptors needed to index a document. If one assumes that the exhaustivity of indexing is held constant, as we did in the above discussion, then, as we have seen, the following holds: As the compoundness of the descriptors increases the number of descriptors contained in the indexing language increases and the number of descriptors needed to index a document decreases. In ISAR systems based on shelving or a card catalog the decrease in the number of descriptors per document is usually not matched by a corresponding increase in the compoundness of descriptors. Therefore, these systems tend to have lower exhaustivity than, say, a computerized ISAR system using elemental or quasi-elemental descriptors. Up to now, we have considered an increase in the number of descriptors due to the addition of pre-combined descriptors which do not introduce new aspects. If the new descriptors represent additional aspects which are useful to formulate anticipated search requests and which, therefore, should be considered in indexing the picture is totally different. Form descriptors such as *Level of treatment* are a good example. Such an extension of the indexing language increases, of course, the number of descriptors per document, since more aspects have to be considered in indexing. In the example a *Level of treatment* descriptor would have to be added to the representation of each document.

C2.3.2 Conceptual indexes (auxiliary ISAR systems) I (special topic, for systems using pre-combination only)

We have seen that in systems using precombined descriptors the problem arises of finding the appropriate descriptors for indexing or searching among the large number of descriptors. A further example is in order (cf. Figure 16, Section C2.3.1; arbitrary notation added):

Example:
Search request:
  Transportation networks using rail
  Descriptors that should be used (among others) for retrieving relevant documents:
  HA358.8 San Francisco. Subway system
  TM743.6 High-speed rail transportation networks for passenger transport.

Another example is: Find all class numbers in UDC (or in LC) that deal with a general aspect like *Structure*. In order to solve these problems a mechanism for the retrieval of the appropriate precombined descriptors has to be provided. We could call this mechanism a secondary or auxiliary ISAR system. In a broader sense this includes the use of cross-references as in the *Unemployment insurance* example given in Section C2.3.1(3). In a narrower sense an auxiliary ISAR system is a genuine ISAR system that accepts search requests formulated in terms of elemental concepts and that retrieves the appropriate precombined descriptors. In fact, such an auxiliary ISAR system functions in just the same way as a primary ISAR system retrieving documents: The precombined descriptors are "indexed" using elemental concepts (anticipating Section C2.5, we could call these elemental concepts "core descriptors").

Example:
HA 358.8 San Francisco. Subway system
  indexed by
    San Francisco; Local transport; Passenger transport; Rail transport; Underground transport; Transportation networks.
TM 743.6 High-speed rail transportation networks for passenger transport
  indexed by
    High-speed transport; Passenger transport; Rail transport; Transportation networks.
The search request:
  Transportation network using rails
    is also formulated in terms of elemental concepts, namely
  Rail transport AND Transportation networks.

Obviously both precombined descriptors are retrieved using this search request formulation. How the auxiliary ISAR system is actually implemented is a technical problem. It could take the form of a card catalog: For a precombined descriptor an entry is made (a card is filed) under each of the elemental concepts by which it is indexed. It could also take the form of a printed index or the form of a mechanized ISAR system. (See Section D3.6 for details.) In a broader sense the implementation of an auxiliary ISAR system is a problem of the presentation of indexing languages and thesauri to be dealt with in Section D3.

In such auxiliary ISAR systems the decomposition of compound concepts into semantic factors is used to gain a deeper insight into the structure of the indexing language which, in turn, allows the setting up of an appropriate auxiliary ISAR system.

In the majority of systems using precombined descriptors (with the notable exception of faceted classification), the auxiliary ISAR system is rather weak.

(Further explanation:) It should be clear from this discussion that there is no structural difference between auxiliary ISAR systems that retrieve precombined descriptors and primary ISAR systems that retrieve documents. If any further clarification is needed it should be provided by the following example, where one and the same ISAR system can be viewed as an auxiliary or as a primary ISAR system.

Example:

In a file of newspaper clippings the clippings are the documents; they are arranged in folders according to themes which are very compound concepts like French reactions to the development of relations between U.S. and U.S.S.R.; that means we have a shelving classification, the themes being the descriptors. Let us assume that an auxiliary ISAR system in form of a card catalog has been set up to retrieve these themes. The above theme is indexed by:

Reactions to international developments: France; Bilateral relations: U.S.: U.S.S.R.,

and an entry is made under each of these elemental concepts.

But we could also look at this catalog in another way: We could look at each *folder* as being a document; the theme of the folder would then be the title of the document and the set of elemental concepts assigned would be the document representation. In this view our catalog cards would stand for documents, the elemental concepts serving as descriptors; the ISAR system can thus be viewed as a primary ISAR system, retrieving documents (namely the folders), not an auxiliary ISAR system retrieving descriptors.

C2.3.3 Summary

Searching consists of two steps:

Step 1: Find the appropriate descriptors to be used in the formulation of the search request.

Step 2: Retrieve documents by combination of the descriptors found in Step 1.

(This two-step searching is particularly explicit in a procedure used in an ISAR system for biology; each term found in the title of any publication is used as a descriptor under which the publication may be retrieved. Then there is a core classification scheme and an index for the retrieval of these descriptors in terms of core descriptors. In this system descriptors need not be preferred terms.)

The "work load" of searching for the appropriate compound concepts may be distributed between the two steps.

In systems on one end of the scale, for example, peek-a-boo systems, the descriptors are elemental; therefore, no combination searching is necessary in Step 1, and combination of many descriptors takes place in Step 2. In systems on the other end of the scale, for example, in shelving classifications, the descriptors are highly precombined (ideally as compound as the document representations); therefore, there is combination searching involving many components in Step 1, retrieving the appropriate descriptor (or descriptors, in the case of inclusive searches), but there is no combination searching in Step 2. In intermediate systems the descriptors are moderately precombined so that both steps involve combination searching with fewer components in each step.

(Special topic:) In intermediate systems and in practice in shelving classifications one often does not find a precombined descriptor corresponding to the search request formulation. In such a case one must not conclude that there are no documents corresponding to this search request formulation. It only means that a descriptor of the specificity required is not in the indexing language so that the documents that are relevant have been indexed by one or more broader descriptors only. (In shelving classification the documents have been shelved under one broader descriptor only.) To find all descriptors under which a document relevant to the search request must have been indexed or, in shelving classification, the possible places where the document might have been shelved, one can proceed as follows: Try all possible combinations of n-1 elemental concepts. If a precombined descriptor is found, note it down and drop the combination; if not, retain the combination. For each of the retained combinations of n-1 elemental concepts try all possible combinations of n-2 elemental concepts and so on until no combinations are left. The descriptors retrieved can now be used to retrieve the relevant documents.

C2.4 Selection and Arrangement of Descriptors with Particular Reference to ISAR Systems Using Pre-Combination (Special Topic)

Two main problems in the organization of inverted files are the selection of descriptors for which records are to be included in the file and the arrangement of the records for these descriptors in the file. In manual ISAR systems like ISAR systems based on shelving by subject, card catalogs, and printed indexes these problems are especially severe. These systems have to use many precombined descriptors in order to serve their purpose properly, and so the problem arises of selecting the precombined descriptors to be included. Since the number of descriptors is much larger than in systems using elemental descriptors, the problem of arranging the records in the file is much more difficult. (A record in an inverted file has been defined above as a descriptor, together with all entries under that descriptor.) It is sensible to arrange the records in the file in the same sequence in which the descriptors are arranged in the display of the indexing language. Almost the whole burden of organizing the file is thus placed on the indexing language or classification scheme. The problems are compounded by the constraints inherent in the physical medium used in manual ISAR systems.

The problems of selection and arrangement of descriptors are usually discussed under the heading "enumerative versus synthetic classification schemes". The following more refined analysis introduces three aspects that should be used in analyzing indexing languages/classification schemes:

(1) Selection of descriptors, especially how easy or how difficult it is to introduce new precombined descriptors.
(2) Arrangement of descriptors.
(3) Designation of descriptors, especially of precombined descriptors.

Whereas these aspects are important mainly for indexing languages/classification schemes for manual ISAR systems, they apply also to indexing languages/classification schemes for mechanized ISAR systems.

(1) *Selection of descriptors.* How easy or how difficult is it to introduce a new precombined descriptor? Can the indexer introduce new precombined descriptors at his discretion or are there set procedures by which new precombined descriptors have to be approved? (Or is the introduction of new precombined descriptors forbidden at all?) What is the time needed to introduce a new descriptor? What are the criteria for approval for a new descriptor? A criterion might be, for example, literary warrant, i.e., one might require that the number of entries made under the new descriptor is expected to exceed a certain number. This problem is related to the problem of multiple entry. If multiple entry is allowed in the ISAR system in question, then one may always use several less compound descriptors to make up the representation of the document being indexed instead of introducing a new precombined descriptor. (However, a precombined descriptor available in the indexing language should always take precedence over a combination of less compound descriptors, as discussed in C2.3.1(3)). In this case one should use literary warrant and/or "search warrant" as a criterion. If multiple entry is not allowed, such as in the LCC and in those applications of faceted classification where a policy decision for single entry has been made, the situation is more difficult. In the case of LCC one must either reconcile oneself to class documents by the nearest, but still inappropriate, class number or one has to update the classification in very short intervals. Faceted classification takes a quite different approach: Only elemental concepts ("core descriptors", called "foci" in faceted classification) are listed explicitly. The indexer is free to combine elemental concepts, thus forming precombined descriptors, as he deems necessary to represent the document at hand. It is consistent to call the combination created by the indexer a precombined descriptor because it is under the combination that the document is entered in the catalog. (Note that there may be, and often are, several documents entered under the same combination.) Since the list of precombined descriptors is continually growing without any control over the introduction of new precombined descriptors, an auxiliary ISAR system is particularly important in this case. It is provided if the rules of faceted classification are followed properly. In many catalogs using subject headings new precombined descriptors, consisting of a main heading and a standardized subheading, can be freely introduced. This is essentially the same procedure as used in faceted classification, but applied only on a very limited scale.

124   C   Structure of Indexing Languages, Thesauri

The following observation should serve to further clarify the issues: A scheme of the LCC type that allows for the inclusion of very specific precombined descriptors and for "immediate updating" and that provides an auxiliary ISAR system for the retrieval of descriptors as described above is operationally equivalent to a faceted classification scheme.

(2) *Arrangement of descriptors.* Note first that once an auxiliary ISAR system for the retrieval of precombined descriptors as described above has been established, the sequence of the descriptors is less significant. They could even be numbered serially as they arise. This would then be a system in the category (3a1) below (independent symbols for precombined descriptors). Usually, however, the descriptors are arranged in a sequence that is more or less transparent for the user of the ISAR system. There are two aspects to be considered in this connection:

(a) To what extent is the place of a precombined descriptor based on its components?

(b) Is the sequence of independent elements alphabetical or classified?

(2a) *To what extent is the place of a precombined descriptor based on its components?* There are three possibilities:

(2a1) Each descriptor is considered an independent element. The place of a precombined descriptor in the arrangement is not dependent on its components. The designer of the indexing language is completely free in his decision where the descriptor should be placed. For example, if a subdivision by country is used in different places, a different sequence of countries can be chosen in each instance. (Since the designer is completely free he may choose to consider the components of a precombined descriptor in his decision; the important point is that he does not have to.)

(2a2) A precombined descriptor is placed in the classified sequence according to its components, but the order of components within the combination is free.

Example:
```
    A1
    A1:   B1
    A1:   B2:   C2
    A1:   C1:   B1
    A2
    A3:   B1
    B1:   A2
    B1:   C1
```

This procedure ensures, for example, that at every place where a subdivision by countries is used the countries appear in the same sequence. This makes it much easier for the user to comprehend the scheme. On the other hand, sometimes different subdivisions are more appropriate at different places, e.g., time periods for the history of different countries. With this method the designer still has considerable discretion with respect to the place of a precombined descriptor in the linear sequence by choosing the appropriate sequence of components in the combination (the appropriate "citation order").

(2a3) A precombined descriptor is placed in the classified sequence according to its components, *and* the order of components within the combination is prescribed in every instance (fixed citation order).

Example:
A1
A1: B1
A1: B1: C1
A1: B2: C1
A2
A2: B1
A3: B1
B1: C1

This procedure is mandatory in systems that allow the indexer to freely introduce new precombined descriptors because otherwise the same descriptor might end up at two or even more places. (Further examples for (2b2) and (2b3) are provided in Figure 10b, Section C1.3; (2b3) corresponds to "ruly arrangement" and (2b2) corresponds to "arbitrary arrangement".)

(2b) *How are the independent elements arranged?* The independent elements can be arranged either in alphabetical order (2b1) or in classified order (2b2). We do not go into the merits of each here (see Section D1.1.0).

(3) *Designation of descriptors.* The designation of descriptors should reflect their arrangement. The alternative methods of designation are therefore closely connected to the methods of arrangement, and the subdivision of Section (3) will follow the subdivision of Section (2).

(3a) *Designation of precombined descriptors.* There are three possibilities:

(3a1) Precombined descriptors are designated by their own independent symbols. Examples are LCC (the independent symbols being class numbers) and, with some exceptions, subject headings, the independent symbols being natural language terms. This method of designation is mandatory if the place of a precombined descriptor in the arrangement is not dependent on its components. It is compatible with the two other methods of placing precombined descriptors.

(3a2) Precombined descriptors are designated by a string of constituent symbols, each constituent symbol representing one of the conceptual components. The order of constituent symbols within a string (the citation order) is free. This is the most appropriate method of designation if (2a2) is the method for arrangement. It is incompatible with (2a1) as well as with (2a3).

(3a3) As (3a2), but now the citation order is fixed. Faceted classification is an example. This is the most appropriate method of designation if (2a3) is the method of arrangement.

(3b) *Choice of independent symbols.* The independent symbols used for designating precombined descriptors in (3a1) and the constituent symbols in (3a2) and (3a3) can be either terms (in case of alphabetical arrangement) or notational symbols (in case of classified arrangement).

Let us illustrate these notions using the example of subject headings. The main headings and the subheadings are independent elements designated by terms and arranged alphabetically (with minor deviations in some catalogs). Many subject headings are created by combining a main heading with a subheading, and for those headings the place in the arrangement is determined by the components. The citation order is fixed: Main heading–subheading. A closer look reveals a more complex situation. Often the linguistic structure of a main heading reflects the conceptual structure as in *Radio engineering* or *Aircraft;* in this case it is debatable whether the symbol is independent or made up of a string of constituent symbols. (In other cases, like *Ship,* the natural language text does not reflect the conceptual structure; compare Section C1.1.0 on the basis of semantic factoring.) If we consider *Radio engineering* as a string of the constituent symbols *Radio* and *Engineering* then the problem arises of what the citation order should be; should it be *Radio engineering* or *Engineering, radio.* This problem is no different from the problem of citation order in faceted classification.

C2.5 A Unified Classification Scheme for Different Kinds of File Organization: Core Classification and Extended Classification (Partly Special Topic)

The perspectives developed in this book lead to a practical proposal for the design of an indexing language (a classification scheme) to be used in connection with different kinds of file organization. One starts from a *core classification* consisting of elemental or only moderately compound concepts. These concepts are called *core descriptors,* and they are represented by an independent symbol, such as a notation or a term. The core classification is presented as a linear arrangement with cross references. In a faceted classification, the schedules would be the core classification. Starting from the core classification, descriptors are formed. In a peek-a-boo or other post-combination system only core descriptors are used as descriptors. In a card catalog or similar system the core descriptors themselves may be used as descriptors, too. But further precombined descriptors are formed by combination of core descriptors, as it becomes necessary during the development of the catalog, as described in the following. (The rest of this section is special topic—for systems using precombination only.) The following discussion on the procedure and the problems associated with it refers to Figure 13 (Section C1.3). In the beginning documents dealing with *A Vehicles: B Ground transport* are entered under both *A* and *B*. If it turns out that there are a lot of search requests for *A:B* or a lot of documents dealing with *A:B*, then *A Vehicles: B Ground transport* is introduced as a precombined descriptor and documents dealing with *A:B* are entered only there. This reduces both the number of entries and the effort necessary for searching (in searching for *A:B* it is no longer necessary to scan *all* the cards entered under *A Vehicles* or all the cards entered under *B Ground transport*). A document dealing with *Ground transport vehicles in the U.S.* is entered under *A Vehicles: B Ground transport* and under *C U.S.* (or *B Ground transport: C U.S.*, if this is a precombined descriptor). Again, if there are many search requests or many documents on the subject, *A Vehicles: B Ground transport: C U.S.* could be introduced as a more compound descriptor. Specific precombined descriptors are thus introduced as the need arises. The core classification together with the additional precombined descriptors may be called an "extended classification".

Once a fairly large number of precombined descriptors has been introduced, thorough indexing gets a bit tricky. Assume we have the precombined descriptors

A Vehicles: B1 Rail transport and
A Vehicles: B Ground transport: C U.S.

A document dealing with *Vehicles for rail transport in the U.S. (A: B1: C)* has to be entered under both *A: B1* and *A: B: C*. A general rule can be stated as follows (compound concepts denoted by lower case letters): Let *d* be the representation of a document. An entry for the document is made under every descriptor *x* with *d* narrower than *x* unless an entry is made already under descriptor *y*, *y* being narrower than *x*.

Example:

The document representation is again A: B1: C. The descriptors are A, B, B1, B2, C, A: B. Entries are made under A: B, B1, and C (not under A because A: B is narrower than A, and not under B because A: B is narrower than B). If B: C were a descriptor, an entry would have to be made there rather than under C. If A: C were a descriptor, an additional entry would be required.

Note that this rule merely makes explicit what should be done in any subject heading catalog. If this rule is not followed, retrieval failures result.

Obviously an auxiliary ISAR system or index to find the appropriate precombined descriptor while indexing documents as well as while formulating search requests is mandatory in such a system (in particular, a searcher looking for *B Ground transport* should be led to *A Vehicles: B Ground transport*).

If the extended classification is to be used for arrangement of documents on shelves or for other single-entry systems, highly precombined descriptors are necessary. (This is the way faceted classification is usually applied). If appropriate precombined descriptors are not available, the document representations formulated in terms of precombined descriptors will be less precise.

The important point in this proposal is that different institutions using the same core classification could extend it in different ways, adapted to their specific needs, but still maintain compatibility between their systems. Even nonessential features of the core classification (for example, the sequence of main classes or facets) could be changed without destroying compatibility on a conceptual level. (There may be some practical difficulties arising from the use of different notations in both systems. But these can easily be resolved if computers are used.) Existing schemes, such as LCC, could be made compatible by expressing their descriptors in terms of the core classification as shown in the examples given in Section D3.6. A properly designed core classification could thus take the role of this old dream, a universal classification. This is made possible by concentrating on the basic notions of conceptual structure and leaving aside details of arrangement and file organization on which agreement cannot be achieved and is not even always desirable.

C2.5.1 Special problems arising in the implementation of this proposal (technical)

,1 Multiple entry versus entry under a precombined descriptor. Take the above example of documents on *A:B*. In one case they are entered under both *A* and *B*. Searcher 1, looking for *A*, is lucky because he has all entries together at one place in the catalog. The same is true for searcher 2, looking for *B*. Searcher 3, looking for *A:B,* however, is disadvantaged because he has to scan all entries under *A* (or all entries under *B*) to find those on *A:B*. If the precombined descriptor *A:B* is created and arranged after *A* searcher 1, looking for *A,* is still lucky. Searcher 3, looking for *A:B*, is lucky, too. Searcher 2, looking for *B,* however, is now disadvantaged because he has to follow up a cross-reference to another place of the catalog. Giving up the advantage of having fewer entries, the designer could help searcher 2 by arranging the new precombined descriptor at a second place as *B:A* and making entries for this second place, too. For searcher 3, looking for *A:B,* this would also be convenient because he could now enter the file at either *A* or *B*. Speaking in terms of the model sketched in section C1.3 this means: the compound concept *A:B* is arranged under each of its broader concepts.

Note that such a system provides an auxiliary ISAR-system for precombined descriptors, as described above, right in the file itself. As the degree of precombination is increased and the descriptors have more components, the size of the file increases very rapidly if one uses this procedure. One must then select some particularly useful places from among all the possible ones in which to put a given precombined descriptor. This is, in essence, the purpose of the PRECIS system. For each document a representation is prepared as a combination of core descriptors, structured according to special rules. The document representation is included in the system as a precombined descriptor (if it was not already included before). This descriptor appears at different places in the arrangement, and an entry for the document is made under each of them, preferably giving the document number.

(The application of the PRECIS system in the British National Bibliography (BNB) has a little peculiarity which might be confusing: the index to BNB is an index to documents. However, the full document representations are listed in BNB by DDC class numbers, and the class number is the only means to look up a document representation. Therefore, in the BNB index class numbers are given instead of document numbers. This should not distract from the fact that the index is an index to precombined descriptors formed in PRECIS, not an index to DDC class numbers.)

,2 **Multiple entry using a faceted classification.** The descriptors for a classified catalog using multiple entry can, of course, be formed using a faceted classification. Each descriptor is then designated by a string of constituent notations. A document is indexed by as many descriptors as necessary to represent the subject, the appropriate notational strings are put on the catalog card, and the card is filed at the appropriate places.

C2.6 Summary: Strategies for the Application of Semantic Factoring

(1) *Do not include compound concepts in the indexing language.* Use only elemental concepts as descriptors. Retain compound concepts in the lead-in vocabulary and show the combination of elemental descriptors to be used.

(2) *Retain compound concepts as precombined descriptors* and use them in indexing and searching (it is possible to use these precombined descriptors to form even more compound combinations). Use the decomposition into semantic factors only for the analysis of relationships among precombined descriptors and for searching, where, through the use of semantic factoring, every combination of elemental or compound descriptors is allowed in the formulation of search requests. The indexing language contains, in this case, elemental descriptors as well as the precombined descriptors. All elemental concepts should be represented in the indexing language so that compound concepts not represented by a precombined descriptor may be formed in indexing or searching. In addition these elemental descriptors are useful in searches for general aspects.

(3) *Intermediate strategies* are possible.

C2.6.1 Considerations in the choice of a strategy

The following points should be considered in choosing a strategy or, more precisely, determining the level of precombination to be used.

(1) *Mechanical devices available in the ISAR system.* If the mechanical devices available in the ISAR system do not allow for searches using a combination of descriptors, precombined descriptors should be used; an example is the conventional card catalog. On the other hand, if combination searching is possible, such as in computerized systems or peek-a-boo card systems, elemental descriptors can be used. However, one might want to retain a certain level of precombination to avoid too many "false drops". (Another method for the elimination of false drops is the use of roles and links.)

(2) *Number of descriptors included in the indexing language.* If the descriptors are precombined, their number is much larger, and it is more difficult to find the appropriate descriptors for indexing and search request formulation. This is especially important if it is not possible to train the indexers thoroughly in the use of a complex indexing language or classification scheme, as when scientists do part-time indexing.

(3) *Number of descriptors to be used for indexing a document.* If the descriptors are elemental many have to be used in indexing a document. This requires much effort unless the descriptors (or at least the frequently used descriptors) are printed on the document analysis sheet so that they may just be checked. If the descriptors are precombined, a few are sufficient to index a document. The same considerations hold for search requests.

(4) *Difficulty of indexing and search request formulation.* In an indexing language containing many precombined descriptors it is difficult to find the appropriate descriptors for document representation or search request formulation (cf. Section C2.3.2). It is easier to combine elemental or quasi-elemental descriptors to formulate a document representation or a search request. Indexing or search request formulation using concept combination with roles and links is more difficult than either of the former. Faceted classification occupies a middle ground: The indexer combines elemental concepts according to a facet formula to obtain a document representation. This is somewhat more difficult then merely listing elemental descriptors but probably easier than finding a highly precombined descriptor. The concept combinations created by the indexer are used as descriptors, and the searcher is therefore confronted with a large set of precombined descriptors. On the other hand, a system using precombined descriptors in indexing in order to facilitate manual searching can be complemented by a mechanized searching facility that allows the searcher to formulate his search in terms of elemental descriptors (cf. Section C2.3.1).

(5) *Matching descriptor combinations used by searchers with those used by indexers.* A strategy relying heavily on elemental descriptors presents the problem of matching the combination of descriptors used by the searcher to express a given compound concept with the combination used by the indexer. This has to be achieved by an appropriate lead-in structure. A specific problem is pre-

sented by concepts of general application like *Reform.* In a system using precombined descriptors, e.g., *Agrarian reform,* we are assured that the aspect *Reform* is being considered—it is done automatically by the system. In a system where the indexer is to use the combination *Agriculture:Reform* an element of unreliability is introduced.

The rules when and when not to use a compound concept as descriptor, which follow in C2.7, are to be viewed in the light of points (1) through (5). Vice versa, the considerations set forth in Section C2.7 should be taken into account in choosing a strategy.

C2.7 Rules for the Use of Precombined Descriptors in an Intermediary Strategy Not Using Roles and Links

In the practical construction of thesauri the question arises which compound concepts to include in the indexing language as precombined descriptors and which to include in the lead-in vocabulary only. The reasons why one might want to use at least some precombined descriptors can be summarized as follows:

(1) *To prevent "false drops"*: In searching, pure combination of elemental descriptors may lead to situations of the following type: a document on "Cars for the rapid-transit link between airport and city" will be indexed by the following elemental descriptors, among others: *Vehicles*; *Subways*; *Air traffic*; *Traffic stations*. A search for *Aircraft*, expressed by *Vehicles:Air traffic* would retrieve the document. As a consequence, precision in retrieval is lowered. To say it in another way: "Specific multiword (better: precombined, D.S.) descriptors often facilitate retrieval of specific information."

(2) *To serve for the arrangement of documents or catalog cards.*

(3) *To decrease the number of descriptors needed to index a document.*

In each individual case the benefits derived from the use of a precombined descriptor have to be weighed against the costs, especially the increase of the indexing language and possibly the complication of indexing, as discussed above. The usefulness of the decisions made should be checked in practical indexing and retrieval experiments to be described in Section F6.

It is very important to understand that the rules to be applied in these decisions must refer to the conceptual plane. Semantic factoring deals with the decomposition of concepts into semantic factors according to their meaning, not with the splitting of terms according to their linguistic structure. Rules referring to the linguistic structure of terms (especially of multi-word terms) miss this point. An example is the following rule: "Do not decompose the multi-word term if the component words, taken by themselves, have a meaning different from their meaning in the combination." In this case the multi-word term designates a compound concept, but this compound concept is not a combination of the concepts designated by the single words. However, this fact is not a basis for deciding whether or not it is meaningful to decompose the concept into semantic factors. It means only that the meaning of the single words has nothing to do with the semantic factors to be used (See the example *White House* given in C1.1.0, the meaning of *White House* has nothing to do with *White* and *House*, but still it is useful to decompose it in semantic factors as indicated.) The following rules refer to the conceptual plane.

C2.7.1 What compound concepts should be used as precombined descriptors?

This section gives a list of criteria that should be used in deciding whether to use a compound concept as precombined descriptor.

(a) *Frequency in indexing and/or searching.* Use a compound concept as precombined descriptor if it is used frequently in indexing and/or searching. This rule reduces the number of descriptors needed per document representation or per search request formulation and thus reduces effort.

(b) *Frequency of components.* Use a compound concept as precombined descriptor if its components are used heavily in indexing, so that the probability of false drops is higher. However, establishing a precombined descriptor is only justified if the compound concept is expected to be used with some frequency in searching, so that the effect of false drops would be serious. This rule is of special importance if a combination of elemental descriptors would not express the compound concept exactly or if many documents are to be expected which will be indexed by both elemental descriptors but which do not deal with the compound concept.

Example:
Philosophy of culture should be retained as a precombined descriptor because there may be many documents indexed by Philosophy as well as by Culture but not relevant to Philosophy of culture. Another example is Student teacher.

(c) *Syntactical relationship of components.* A special case of (b) is illustrated by the example *Library schools* (Schools teaching about Libraries) versus *School libraries* (Libraries serving schools). Here we have two compound concepts which are made up of the same elemental concepts but in which the syntactical relationship of the two components is different.

Example:
Administrative personnel–Personnel administration

In such cases the compound concept should be used as a descriptor if it occurs frequently in indexing or searching.

C2   File Organization and Classification   133

The above example may be contrasted to the following examples, where the lack of indication of syntactic relationships does not result in ambiguity.

Example:
Transistor: Characteristic
Household: Tools

(d) *Logical completeness of hierarchy.* Use a compound concept as precombined descriptor if it is necessary to achieve logical completeness at a location in the hierarchy or if it is to be used in the checklist technique of indexing.

Example:
Agrarian reform may be an important concept in an ISAR system. It may be expressed as a combination of Agriculture and Reform. Now if a document is relevant to Agrarian reform, an indexer using the checklist technique is most likely to scan the descriptors listed under Agriculture to determine whether the document is relevant to them or not. If he finds Agrarian reform there, the use of this descriptor for indexing is made sure. If he doesn't find Agrarian reform there, he might well overlook the descriptor Reform. The document would then be missed by searches for Agrarian reform as well as by searches for Reform.

This leads to another related rule: If a concept of general application is important for searching, the most important combinations should be included as precombined descriptors if otherwise the concept of general application is likely to be overlooked in indexing.

(e) *Hierarchical relationships.* Use a compound concept as precombined descriptor if it has broader, narrower or related concepts that cannot be seen from the "derivation rules" given in Section C1.3 (see especially the *Helicopter* example in C1.3(a3)).

(f) *Doubtful cases.* If in doubt use a precombined descriptor for a compound concept. If later experience shows that it would be sufficient to use a combination of elemental descriptors instead of the precombined descriptor, the precombined descriptor can easily be eliminated from the indexing language and be replaced by the combination of elemental descriptors in the document representations. Contrariwise, if the compound concept has not been used as precombined descriptor from the beginning and if it turns out later that it should have been used, a number of documents will have to be reindexed if the compound concept is introduced as descriptor. On the other hand, in the absence of information about the expected use of compound concepts, this reindexing cannot always be avoided.

(g) *Indexing language not increased.* Finally a compound concept should be used as precombined descriptor if such use does not lead to an increase in the indexing language. For example, *Helicopter* should be used rather than *Aircraft: Rotary wing*, since the elemental concept *Rotary wing* is not useful in any other context. The introduction of *Rotary wing* rather than *Helicopter* would therefore not reduce the overall number of descriptors in the indexing language.

C2.7.2 What compound concepts should be represented by a combination of descriptors rather than by a precombined descriptor?

A combination of descriptors should be used instead of a precombined descriptor if none of the rules listed above apply. In addition, the following rules can be used:

(a) *Object–material.* Compound concepts designating an object made of a certain material can be expressed by a combination of two descriptors, one for the object and one for the material. For example: *Metal:Tubes.*

(b) Many chemical compounds can be expressed by a combination of descriptors, each standing for a specific group of atoms.

(Remark on C2.7.1 and C2.7.2: The following additional rules have been established, but they are not very sensible; they are listed only to give a complete account of the rules used in TEST.

"a. A specific multiword descriptor should be established when suitable more general descriptors are not available in the vocabulary. To provide adequate representation of the specific concept, a combination of general descriptors must include at least one descriptor that is a member of the same hierarchical class as the specific concept. Observation of this principle will promote more consistent and complete retrieval, whereas the use of a combination in which neither descriptor bears a generic relationship to the specific concept may lessen retrieval efficiency."

"c. Two or more individual descriptors should be used instead of establishing a specific multiword descriptor when the specific concept is a member of the same generic class (See Rule C-4) as each of the more general descriptors; for example, arc oxygen cutting is a member of the classes arc cutting and oxygen cutting, so may be represented by those descriptors. When individual descriptors are employed in preference to a specific descriptor, the appropriate cross reference should be added to the Thesaurus. (See Rules C-2 and C-3.)")

The rules within Sections C2.7.1 and C2.7.2 apply to individual "local" situations. A more sophisticated procedure that takes into account the overall structure of the indexing language is described in the following section.

C2.8 Optimization of an Indexing Language with a Constraint as to the Number of Descriptors (Advanced)

One of the advantages of semantic factoring is the possibility of reducing the size of the indexing language by eliminating compound concepts. There are several reasons why one might wish to have a small indexing language. In

C2 File Organization and Classification 135

ISAR systems using edge-notched cards or machine-punched cards (one card per document), one has a limited number of coding positions per document. In a peek-a-boo system it is not efficient to have too many peek-a-boo cards. To a certain extent it is also easier for an indexer or searcher to find his way through a smaller indexing language.

In a very limited subject field the number of concepts one is dealing with may be small to begin with and no special measures are necessary. This is not true for a larger subject area and one has to think how to reduce the number of concepts to be used as descriptors. The following situation is likely to occur: after every concept is decomposed into semantic factors as seems sensible, the number of elemental concepts to be used as descriptors is still too large. In this case one may have to go to "forced" decompositions. The generalization inherent in semantic factoring must be carried beyond what seems natural at the first look in order to meet the constraint regarding the number of descriptors. For a better understanding of the procedures to be applied it is necessary to understand the idea of "semantic super-imposed coding". Therefore, this idea will be expounded in the next section.

C2.8.1 Semantic super-imposed coding

In super-imposed coding as applied, for example, to edge-notched cards, a concept is coded by a combination of holes. (Each hole of course will occur in several other combinations.) In a search for a certain concept, all cards are retrieved for which the holes of the combination representing this concept have been punched. In this way it is possible to accommodate, say, a thousand concepts by, say, a hundred holes. The same principle can, of course, be applied to peek-a-boo cards; each concept is represented by a combination of several peek-a-boo cards.

Now this is exactly what happens in semantic factoring. Assume an indexing language containing, say, one hundred elemental descriptors. One hole is assigned to each of them. Each of perhaps a thousand concepts can be expressed by the appropriate combination of elemental descriptors, and if a document deals with a compound concept the holes of the appropriate elemental descriptors are punched. In searching for that concept one looks again for all cards in which the appropriate combination of holes is punched.

In super-imposed coding as usually understood, the hole-combination to be punched for a given concept is selected on a merely random basis, usually with the objective of minimizing false drops. It is therefore called random super-imposed coding. In the application of semantic factoring, on the other hand, the combination of holes is selected on a semantic basis according to the decomposition of the concepts in semantic factors. We therefore speak of semantic super-imposed coding. In this case each hole and each hole combination has a meaning in itself, and it is possible to search for all documents on one elemental descriptor; this search will retrieve all documents that deal with any compound concept containing the elemental descriptor as a semantic factor. In random super-imposed coding, on the other hand, individual holes have no meaning and only those hole combinations explicitly assigned to a concept have meaning. It is much more difficult to perform inclusive searches. (Compare to this point the following quotation ". . . the Luhn (super-imposed, D.S.) pattern code may seem to have a major disadvantage. Since none of the individual patterns which make up a pattern are in themselves significant, one cannot use pieces of different patterns in searching on a categorical basis." It is proposed to solve the problem by encoding the broader concepts separately so that the "categorical code" is independent of the "specific code" which is said to be more flexible. However, this procedure would need more coding positions, and the whole point of super-imposed coding is to save coding positions.)

In random super-imposed coding one tries to minimize the number of false drops to be expected by using appropriate statistical techniques in assigning hole combinations to concepts (a false drop occurs in the following way: By punching the holes for the concepts A, B, and C the hole combination for concept D is also produced). In semantic super-imposed coding, minimizing false drops is more involved and may not be as successful. However, this is not as serious a disadvantage as it may seem for the following reasons. The false drops appearing in random super-imposed coding are usually wholly meaningless to the theme of a search. In semantic super-imposed coding, the documents turning up as false drops often are at least obliquely relevant. The original concept and their semantic factors are:

Example:
Welfare reform = *Welfare : Reform*
Agrarian reform = *Agriculture : Reform*
A document on *Welfare reform* and *Agriculture* is indexed by *Welfare, Reform and Agriculture. In searching for Agrarian reform this document will turn up as a false drop; but indeed this document is nearly related to the search request.*

Now it might occur that the number of holes is so small that they are not sufficient if we define the elemental descriptors in a natural way. This might force us to introduce a certain amount of arbitrariness in our system, which thus may become a hybrid between random and semantic super-imposed coding.

After this introduction the problem addressed in the next section can be defined as follows: Given is a list of concepts that are of interest in our ISAR system (the original list of concepts). The number of positions available to encode these concepts is limited. The problem is to design a super-imposed

C2 File Organization and Classification 137

coding to accommodate all the concepts. The super-imposed coding shall be as semantic as possible.

A number of remarks may be added to elaborate on this exposition. The super-imposed coding may be in two stages, the first stage being a semantic factoring of concepts, the second stage being a random super-imposed coding of the elemental descriptors arrived at in the first stage. Both methods of super-imposed coding may be used simultaneously, that is, some of the coding positions may have meaning whereas others have no meaning.

In random super-imposed coding the indexer should use the mostly compound concepts from the original list, which later on are encoded by a clerk who looks them up in a code list. In this case the indexer considers the original list of concepts as the indexing language. Of course the indexer could look up the terms and record only the holes to be punched. However, this procedure would waste the time of the indexer for clerical tasks and also make the document representations totally unintelligible.

In semantic super-imposed coding the indexer may use the compound concepts from the original list, and the appropriate coding positions may be looked up by a clerk using a coding list which, in this case, is at the same time a thesaurus. However, in semantic super-imposed coding the indexer may also use the elemental concepts themselves as descriptors. In most cases the indexer will be able to determine the appropriate elemental concepts without looking into the thesaurus. The document representations would be intelligible, though less precise. In this case the indexing language consists of the elemental concepts only.

C2.8.2 Considerations to be taken into account in reducing the number of concepts used as descriptors

In the following discussion it is assumed that the "synonym-homonym structure" and the "equivalence structure" have been determined already so that there is a list of ISAR concepts. However, most of the considerations apply also if one starts with an unprocessed list of terms. Furthermore, assume that a sample collection of documents has been indexed using the complete list of original ISAR concepts so that some statistical information is available.

There are two principal methods of reducing the number of concepts represented in the indexing language:

(a) consolidate several concepts into one broader concept;
(b) decompose a compound concept into semantic factors so that it can be eliminated. Note, however, that in some cases it is better to retain a compound concept as descriptor, as discussed in Section C2.7.

Several concepts may be consolidated into a broader concept in two cases:

(a1) Specific concepts may be consolidated into one broader concept (or the specific concepts may be simply omitted if the broader concept is available already) if the benefits in searching derived from their distinction do not justify the increase in the number of descriptors. For example, a distinction between individual metals may not be needed in a particular ISAR system, so that all metals can be consolidated in the one descriptor *Metals*. Another example is *Stonework, glass, ceramics* (We discussed this already in Section C1.4.1,3).

(a2) If two concepts show a high statistical association in the sample collection, i.e., if the majority of documents that deal with concept *A* also deal with concept *B*, then a distinction between these concepts in searching is not possible (even if it should be wanted), and the two concepts may be consolidated.

Example:

Status and Role in Sociology are clearly distinct conceptually but have a strong tendency to co-occur in documents (cf. C1.5.2 "Concepts connected empirically").

In all cases where one considers consolidating several concepts, one should look at their frequency in the sample collection. In case (a1), for example, we may have three concepts *A*, *B*, and *C*, the distinctions among which are of some importance in searching. If they are all of equally low frequency, the effect of their consolidation on search results would not be too detrimental. However, if *C* is frequent and *A* and *B* infrequent, then in searching for *A* one will obtain very low precision. In case (a2) if two highly associated concepts *A* and *B* are very frequent, then the consolidation will have the effect that in a search for *A* the absolute number of irrelevant documents will be high, even though the precision may be high also (if the absolute number of documents retrieved is high it is much more important to have very good precision than if the absolute number of documents retrieved is low).

In some cases the constraint set for the number of descriptors may make it necessary to consolidate concepts one would like to keep distinct. This case will be discussed shortly.

As long as the number of descriptors is not limited, consolidation of concepts and semantic factoring are carried only as far as seems sensible in the subject field in question. As soon as it is necessary to set a limit for the number of descriptors, one may have to resort to rather "forced" semantic factoring.

Example:

Borrowed words = Syncretism: Vocabulary, grammar
Personal names = Symbols: Individual
Vehicles = Means and instruments: Transportation
(*Means and instruments is used as a semantic factor for a variety of concepts, such as Musical instruments, Weapons, or Tools*).

C2 File Organization and Classification 139

In the process of reducing the size of the indexing language by "forced" semantic factoring, functional considerations in the framework of the whole ISAR system come into play. The following discussion deals with some of these considerations.

If a first set of descriptors keeping within the limit given has been designed, one frequently encounters the difficulty that several of the concepts on the original list are expressed by the same combination of descriptors; consequently, these descriptors cannot be distinguished in searching. (The case where several concepts have been consolidated under one broader concept is a special case: the descriptor combination for all the narrower concepts consists of only one descriptor: namely, the broader concept.)

If the distinction of these original concepts is important, one must find further semantic factors that can be added to the descriptor combinations, thus serving to differentiate between concepts. First one should try to extend the definition of available descriptors so that they may serve as the additional semantic factors one was looking for. Only if no available descriptor can be found should the introduction of a new descriptor be considered.

Example:
We have the following original concepts with their descriptor combination:
Antisemitism   = Ethnic relations: Social discrimination
Anti-Chinese feelings = Ethnic relations: Social discrimination

We want to distinguish between these two concepts. Therefore, we are looking for an additional semantic factor for each of them. Among the descriptors already available we have *Israel* and *China* (concepts standing for nations/geographical subdivisions). We extend the definition of these descriptors so that they also designate ethnic origin (the descriptors are, of course, removed from their former place in the hierarchy by this extension; they are no longer part of the schedule of nations/geographical subdivisions). This results in the following combinations.

Example:
Antisemitism   = Ethnic relations: Social discrimination: Israel
Anti-Chinese feelings = Ethnic relations: Social discrimination: China

Thus, we have achieved the distinction wanted. However, this procedure has a disadvantage: now someone searching for *Israel as a nation* must use the newly defined broad descriptor and cannot avoid retrieving all documents on *Antisemitism*. A gain in distinction at the one place is paid for by a loss in distinction at the other place. In each such case a decision must be made where the distinction is more important, taking into account the needs of the users of the ISAR system.

One could think that in the example above it would be easy to search for *Israel as a nation*, rejecting all documents on *Antisemitism* by using the search request "wanted all documents dealing with *Israel*, BUT NOT with *Ethnic relations*". While it is possible to implement negation in many ISAR systems, including peek-a-boo systems, the usefulness of negation as a retrieval operation is questionable. A document dealing with *Ethnic relations between Arabs and Jews in Israel* would be rejected in spite of its relevance. These considerations lead to an important rule for semantic factoring: A descriptor D shall appear in the descriptor-combination for a concept A if and only if, in each search for the descriptor D, all documents dealing with concept A must be found. In other words the descriptor D should be used in the descriptor-combination for concept A if and only if it is broader than A. If one does not adhere to this rule then a search for D will retrieve irrelevant documents. This rule is closely related to Section C1.3.1. There we used the example *Desert animals*. If it is true that in most searches on *Desert*, all documents on *Desert animals* should be found, then *Desert animals* = *Animals: Desert* is correct. Otherwise, one should introduce a new descriptor *Environment is desert*, which would result in *Desert animals* = *Animals: Environment is desert*. Introduction of this new descriptor is subject to the optimization procedure to be described. The new descriptor could be arranged in the hierarchy as follows:

Desert (broad)
 Desert per se
 Environment is desert

In the example given above the broadening of *Israel (as a nation)* to *Israel (including ethnic origin Jewish)* is not necessarily bad. It may be a useful generalization for many searches. For example, in a search for *U.S.-Israel-relations* a document on *The situation of the Jews in U.S.* would not be completely irrelevant. In other words, the need for the expression of ISAR concepts on the original list through a limited number of descriptors may prove to be a useful source for the rethinking of the definitions of the descriptors and the introduction of useful generalizations. As new ISAR concepts turn up in updating, this process continues and leads to revisions in the system. In some cases the descriptor in the broader definition may be more useful than the descriptor as it was defined first. This is not so in our example, however. We would still like to be able to search for *Israel (as a nation)*. It should be clear by now what we should do in this case: We have to look for an additional descriptor which could be combined with *Israel (broad)* to express the concept *Israel (as a nation)*. In this case we would have to introduce a pair of descriptors A = *Used for designating a nation/geographical subdivision* and B = *Used for designating ethnic origin*. Then *Israel (as a nation)* = *Israel (broad): Used for designating a nation/geographical subdivision*. *Israel (broad)* and all other descriptors designating both a nation and ethnic origin could be dealt with the same way. Thus we would only need one basic schedule of descriptors designating both nations/geographical subdivisions and ethnic origin instead of two separate schedules, one for nations and one for ethnic origin. However, a problem would arise since there is no exact correspondence between nations and ethnic origin. Furthermore, the descriptors *A* and *B* are so broad as to be almost worthless unless links are used. Both problems are encountered often when this approach is applied, but in most cases they are much less serious than in our example.

In extending the definition of a descriptor to include another of the ISAR concepts from the original list one should make use of the frequency data in a similar way as described above for the consolidation of concepts. It would not be wise to choose a descriptor that occurs infrequently as a component for a concept that occurs frequently if the descriptor is important in searching and if it is not possible to restore its original sense by combination with another descriptor as it was in our example of *Israel (as a nation)*. On the other hand, no serious difficulties will arise if one chooses a descriptor that occurs frequently as a semantic factor of a concept that occurs infrequently even if this does not seem favorable from a semantic point of view.

If, based on these considerations, it does not seem advisable to use a descriptor *A* in order to achieve a necessary distinction it might still be possible to choose a broader descriptor *A'*. The distinction achieved will not be as fine as the distinction that would have been achieved by using *A*. On the other hand, the broadening of the descriptor *A'*, which is broad already, is not as bad as the broadening of the more specific descriptor *A*.

As a last resort one may introduce one or more new descriptors. This is paid for by the necessity of omitting other descriptors at other places in order to keep the number of descriptors within the limit. Again we have a tradeoff. Sometimes, the introduction of a pair (or a triplet,. . .) of new descriptors makes it possible to solve many "parallel" problems.

Example:
We may have the same descriptor combination for Foreign trade and Domestic trade, for Foreign traffic and Domestic traffic, for Foreign market and Domestic market, etc. By introducing the two descriptors Foreign economic relations and Domestic economic relations all these problems can be solved at once. A series of "parallel" problems where necessary distinctions cannot be made thus gives a warning that an important aspect has not been considered in the indexing language (put another way, that an important facet is missing).

This example illustrates another interesting point. It is likely that the system in its first version contains *Foreign economic relations* but not *Domestic economic relations*. In this case it would be possible to search for *Foreign trade* without retrieving documents that deal only with *Domestic trade* by combin-

142 C Structure of Indexing Languages, Thesauri

ing *Trade* with *Foreign economic relations*, but it would not be possible to search specifically for *Domestic trade*. *Domestic economic relations* is likely to be missing from the first version of the indexing language because it is less conspicuous than *Foreign economic relations*. If this omission goes unnoticed a searcher wanting to retrieve documents on *Domestic trade* has to use *Trade* without qualification as the search descriptor, and he retrieves many irrelevant documents dealing with *Foreign trade* only. This type of situation can be found very often, and the thesaurus builder should watch out for it and correct it.

If the procedure described leads to descriptors that are more suitable for encoding of the ISAR concepts on the original list than self-consistent general concepts, some features of random super-imposed coding are introduced. It is, of course, possible to go one step further and to introduce additional "descriptors" that have no semantic content and are used for encoding purposes only. This procedure could be called "mixed super-imposed coding." It is used in the ISAR system of *Inter Nationes*, where the numbers 1–99 (so called "Zusatzzahlen") are introduced as additional descriptors.

Example:
European Atomic Energy Community =
    Research   :   *Nuclear physics*   :   25
European Organization for Nuclear research =
    Research   :   *Nuclear physics*   :   37

Whenever this device is used the advantages of semantic super-imposed coding, especially the possibility of inclusive searching, is lost. In addition, one is not forced any more to rethink one's system and introduce new generalization as one is if the super-imposed coding is to be completely semantic. These are the reasons for the principle that the super-imposed coding should be as semantic as possible.

(The *Inter Nationes* system has the additional disadvantage that the encoding is done in indexing, so that the numbers 1–99 actually appear in the document representations which therefore are no longer fully intelligible.)

C3 CONCEPT FORMATION IN THESAURUS BUILDING. DEFINITION AND SCOPE NOTES

C3.1 Concept Formation in Thesaurus Building

As we have seen, one of the major concerns in thesaurus building is to develop a conceptual framework that mediates between the interest of the searcher and how he expresses his interest on the one hand and the information provided by an author and how he expresses his findings on the other.

C3 Concept Formation, Scope Notes 143

This task has to be fulfilled within the limitations of the ISAR system at hand, especially the limitations in the size of the indexing language. Special requirements for concept formation arise from this task.

Concept formation occurs if we consolidate equivalent concepts like *Beer, Ale,* and *Malt liquor,* as discussed in Section B2. The newly formed broader concept is useful even if we retain *Beer, Ale,* and *Malt liquor* individually as specific descriptors. A subtle case of consolidating equivalent concepts occurs when all concepts are named by the same term.

Example:
The term Intelligence (in Psychology) means slightly different things to different people. In our indexing language we should have a concept Intelligence (broadly defined) that includes all these meanings. (Again, this does not preclude the retaining of Intelligence 1, Intelligence 2, Intelligence 3, each carefully defined).

In semantic factoring new concepts are often formed, as discussed in Section C1.1 and especially in Section C2.8.2.

Example:
Traffic stations (extracted as a semantic factor from Railroad stations, Bus stations, Harbors, Airports, and then also found applicable to Parking garage);

Another Example:
Domestic economic relations.

New concepts are also formed in hierarchy-building, as discussed in Section C1.4.1.

Both methods are of special importance in developing concepts that are useful in several disciplines. Such concepts "should be pitched at the level of abstraction permitting them to embrace concepts that are substantially identical and whose differences are largely a consequence of the idiosyncrasies of the field in which they have been used". Such concepts would contribute both to efficiency in ISAR systems and to the "transferability of knowledge across disciplines".

Other problems of concept formation occur if the ISAR system deals with socio-economic information from different countries. Say the ISAR system deals with information on education in the *United States, France,* and *Germany.* For each country we have a list of types of educational institutions. We want to derive one list that is applicable to all countries. This would allow us to reduce the number of descriptors. But even if we retain the original lists in the indexing language, the newly developed common list allows a searcher to search easily for, say, *Elementary schools* in all countries. Such a common list is also essential for the gathering of comparative educational statistics. A lot of careful work on definitions has to be done in establishing the entries in the common list, as anybody having worked in or with comparative statistics can testify. The thesaurus builder should rely on work done by experts in comparative education in this instance.

A last example of concept formation in thesaurus building is the typology of international organizations given in Figure 17. This typology was the result of the joint efforts of a classificationist (who contributed the approach of facet analysis) and a subject expert. As is clear from this example, the necessity for clear definitions and scope notes, to be discussed in the next section, is particularly obvious for concepts newly formed in the process of thesaurus construction.

A further aspect of concept formation in thesaurus building and particularly in thesaurus updating is the broadening of the meaning of descriptors that occurs as they are used.

Facet 1: *International organizations by level*
    Private international organizations
    Quasi-governmental international organizations
    Governmental international organizations
Facet 2: *International organizations by membership*
    Universal membership
        SN (Scope Note)
            No restrictions as to geographical location, political system, main religion or other characteristics of member countries
    Limited membership
        SN Members only from one region or from, say, Islamic countries, or industrial countries
Facet 3: *International organizations by scope and orientation*
    Covers entire range of politics
        SN E.g., United Nations; International Federation of Christian Democratic Parties
    Covers only specific function
        SN E.g., World Health Organization; International Federation for Documentation
Facet 4: *International organizations by internal cohesion*
        SN Basic tendency, not momentary developments
    Loose groupings
    Cohesive organizations
Facet 5: *International organizations by organizational structure*
    Centralized structure
    Decentralized structure

Figure 17. Typology of international organizations (C3.1).

C3.2 Definition and Scope Note

C3.2.0 Introduction

A clear understanding of the meaning of a term is necessary:

(1) in thesaurus building in order to place the term properly in the thesaurus structure and
(2) in thesaurus usage for indexing and searching.

For thesaurus building it may be necessary to have a full, formal definition. In thesaurus usage the meaning of a term is often made clear through the context of thesaurus structure. But often context is not sufficient to convey the intended usage of a term, and a supplemental scope note has to be added.

C3.2.1 Formal definition

Definition has two aspects:

(1) Delineation of a concept in the plane of concepts;
(2) Assignment of a term to that concept. (Actually one often starts from a term and then delineates a concept to which this term can be assigned.)

In the following considerations aspect (1) will be emphasized. However, in decisions on synonyms and quasi-synonyms aspect (2) is the important aspect.

A definition should give the following information:

(a) Is there a broader concept from which the concept to be defined may be derived by specialization? Is there a whole of which the concept to be defined forms a part? In which context does the concept to be defined play a particular role?
(b) What concepts narrower by class inclusion are comprised in the concept to be defined? What are parts of the concept to be defined?
(c) Are there concepts that sometimes are understood as being narrower than the concept to be defined but that are to be excluded explicitly in the thesaurus at hand?
(d) What concepts are related to the concept to be defined? What is it that distinguishes the concept to be defined from these related concepts? What does it have in common with the related concept?
(e) Examples for the usage of a concept.

Sources for this information are:

—universal and specialized encyclopedias;
—dictionaries;
—treatises on the terminology of a field;
—basic textbooks of the subject field;

—search request statements for which a term has been used in the formulation of the search request;
—documents for which a term has been used in indexing;
—other terms in which the term to be defined occurs as a semantic factor.

C3.2.2 Scope notes for the thesaurus user

Every term in the thesaurus should be formulated in such a way that it conveys the intended meaning to any user of the thesaurus in an optimal way. Terms that have a commonly accepted definition should therefore be used whenever possible. Often the meaning of a preferred term is already clear from the synonymous and quasi-synonymous terms, so that a definition is unnecessary. Also, the indication of Broader and Narrower Terms (either in the thesaurus entry or in the schedule), as well as of Related Terms, serves the same purpose.

In these cases the information given in the formal definition is reflected in the structure of the thesaurus and need not be recorded explicitly in a scope note. (A parenthetical qualifier to disambiguate a homonym is still in order, even if the particular meaning of the homonym can be inferred from the context within the thesaurus structure, see Sections E1.1.3 and E1.1.4.) In other cases the meaning of a term may still not be readily apparent, especially if its connotations have changed over time or if it is used with a different meaning from country to country, e.g., *Billion,* or if it designates a concept that has been newly formed in thesaurus construction. Proper names that are not commonly known are another case in point. In other cases there remains considerable latitude as to the usage of a term. In all these cases further clarification is necessary. This point is well summarized in the following quotation:

> In a retrieval system in which the recording and communication of usage decisions has been hit and miss, the usage based on such decisions may still be consistent, passed from indexer to indexer by word of mouth or written memoranda. But more probably term usage will vary within such a system from indexer to indexer. And seldom will information on usage be passed on to the searchers in the system. If term usage is reasonably derived from thesaural relationships, the unaided indexer or searcher may arrive at it through logical processes, but there is the chance that similar logic may lead him to another, erroneous conclusion. His interpretation of the thesaurus may be reasonable but nonetheless wrong in the sense that it is different from the accepted usage decision on that term. Often thesaurus relationships permit several valid interpretations of the scope of a term, each different.

In all these cases a scope note explaining how the term is to be used in indexing and searching should be given. This is especially important for thesauri to be used in cooperative information services (shared cataloging) and for multilingual thesauri. The explanation may, in particular, point out any meanings that are excluded from the descriptor at hand. (In some thesauri there is a special field, "Excludes", where those concepts are entered. It seems to us, however, that this is not necessary and that the scope note is the appropriate place for this information.) Mathematical or chemical formulae are allowed in scope notes and may allow for a much shorter expression. Often a picture is more useful than verbal explanation. This is especially true in technical fields. If it is feasible with the printing method to be used, pictures should therefore be included.

With respect to the mutual delineation of several concepts it is sometimes useful to explain several concepts in one unified text. This unified text is then entered in the entry of one of these concepts in field SN. In the entries for the other preferred terms an appropriate reference is made in field SN. (A similar procedure has been used in this book in the terminological remark on preferred term, descriptor, concept, indexing language, and thesaurus in Section B4.2.)

Often it is useful to lead a thesaurus user who is looking for a formal definition to an appropriate source. This is much more sensible than to repeat in the thesaurus lengthy definitions that can be found in readily accessible encyclopedias. It is important to give an exact source indication including page number. In some cases it might even be possible to develop the thesaurus into a common classified index to a number of encyclopedias or lexica by thoroughly following up these source indications.

In the field SN one might indicate, then, three kinds of sources:

(i) sources that have been used in formulating the scope note given;
(ii) sources that contain a definition or further explanations that are accepted for the thesaurus;
(iii) sources that contain variant definitions or explanations.

The scope note is also the appropriate place to indicate the date when a term became or ceased to be a descriptor or when other important changes concerning the term have been made. (See Section F0.8.2 for details).

C4 TYPES OF CONCEPTS, DESCRIPTORS, TERMS TO BE INCLUDED IN AN INDEXING LANGUAGE OR A THESAURUS

In developing an indexing language or a thesaurus the designer must recognize that there are different types of concepts to be included. This is important for two reasons:

(1) One might overlook a particular class of concepts.
(2) Different types of concepts may require different treatment.

Section C4.0 gives a typology of concepts and Sections C4.1–C4.3 add specific considerations pertaining to specific types of concepts.

C4.0 Typology of Concepts, Descriptors, Terms

For the representation of documents (or other retrieval objects), the following types of concepts (or of terms designating these concepts) should be available:

(a) *Form descriptors.* Descriptors or terms denoting formal characteristics of the documents such as *Bibliographical form, Language of document, Level of treatment,* and descriptors or terms that express the assessment of the indexer as to how the document can be used most effectively, such as *Read immediately, For reference only,* or (in a system where the retrieval objects are persons or institutions) *Get in contact with.* These descriptors are often called "form descriptors" or "bibliographic descriptors". These descriptors are on the borderline between descriptive indexing and subject indexing (see Section C4.0.1).

(b) *Content descriptors.* Descriptors or terms characterizing the subject matter of documents or used in an analogous way for the representation of other retrieval objects.

(b1) *proper names,* especially the following (special topic):

(b1.1) Names of persons. In a biography of Churchill, for example, "Churchill" characterizes the subject matter of the document:

(b1.2) Names of institutions, organizations, conferences, projects.

(b1.3) Names of other human groups (such as tribes, nationalities).

(b1.4) Geographical names.

(b1.5) Names of historical events.

(b1.6) Names of treaties, doctrines, etc.

(b1.7) Names of specific legislation and assistance programs.

(b1.8) Names of books (including textbooks) and other material.

(b1.9) Names of works of art (may overlap with (b1.8)).

(b1.10) Other proper names.

(b2) *Elements of nomenclatures,* e.g.:

(b2.1) Designations of species or other groupings in biological taxonomy.

(b2.2) Designation of chemical substances.

(b2.3) Designations of different types of technical parts, e.g., electron tubes.

(b2.4) Trade names, names of specific products, designations of types (e.g., of aircraft, Boeing 747); military nomenclature.

(b3) *All other concepts or terms.*

Obviously, most of the terms contained in a thesaurus belong to type (b3) (unless it is a specific thesaurus of chemical substances or of biological species, etc.).

C4 Types of Concepts, Descriptors 149

The distinction between (b2) "elements of nomenclatures" and (b3) "all other concepts" is of practical significance (see Section C4.2), but hardly of any theoretical value. It would be difficult to formulate an abstract criterion to distinguish between the two.

According to TEST, one may subdivide (b3) into "terms of an analytical nature, such as anemometers, boundary layer, cardiovascular system, density energy conversion, heat resistant alloys, spectroscopy"; and (b3.2) "terms of an abstract nature, such as tests, measurement, and calibration".

Sections C4.1 through C4.3 discuss specific problems connected with some of these types of concepts.

C4.0.1 Remarks on descriptive versus subject indexing

In Section B3.0 *descriptor 1* is defined as "any string of symbols . . . used (1) in the description and representation of documents and (2) in the selection and/or arrangement of documents or their substitutes. . . ." In descriptive indexing (descriptive cataloging) names of authors, title of journal where published, other documents cited, etc., are used as descriptors 1. In subject indexing terms or other symbols designating ISAR concepts and proper names (terms or other symbols designating individual entities dealt with in the document) are used as descriptors.

A first remark relates to descriptive indexing itself. The set of descriptors 1 used there presents exactly the same problems of control that have been described in Section B1: There are several names for the same author: real name and pseudonym, maiden name and married name, different forms of names for corporate bodies—the synonym problem. Sometimes the same name actually refers to different people, the same title to different books—the homonym problem. A thesaurus (or authority list) approach to these problems could do much to simplify the complicated rules for the formation of entries in descriptive cataloging and/or to remove application of these rules from the day-to-day cataloger and especially from the much-plagued user to the maker of the thesaurus (or authority list). At the same time such a thesaurus would serve the purpose outlined below.

A second and perhaps more fundamental remark relates to the relationship of descriptive indexing and subject indexing. Currently these two are considered as two separate areas. In advanced ISAR systems it would make sense, however, to integrate descriptive indexing and subject indexing into one comprehensive system with one comprehensive thesaurus relating, for example, author names to concepts. One could then search for questions like "publications on politics by physicists". This example shows that for the purposes of retrieval the distinction between descriptive and subject indexing is by no means as useful or as clear-cut as is usually assumed. Another case in point is that publication date and place are very useful for narrowing down a search request.

This leads to a third remark that relates to form descriptors. Form descriptors occupy a shadow area between descriptive indexing and subject indexing. The following list moves gradually from bibliographic description to the representation of content:

Example:
Bibliographical form
Date of publication (time spans)
Place of publication (countries)
Language of document
Document contains (pictures, maps, ...)
Type of work (bibliography, textbook, ...)
Level of treatment
Quality
Use to be made of document
Ideological vantage point of author
Document contains statistical data.

Technically, form descriptors are often dealt with the same way as subject descriptors. This is especially useful if this is the only way to enable the searcher to formulate a search request combining subject aspects with bibliographic aspects. For example, in a peek-a-boo system, it is very useful to have peek-a-boo cards for publication dates:

Example:
Publication date before 1950
Publication date 1950–1959
Publication date 1960–1964
...

Or peek-a-boo cards may be used for the country of publication as well. (In a computerized ISAR system, the publication date in the bibliographic document description could be used for this purpose.)

This discussion leads to a fourth point:

The reasons for treating descriptive and subject indexing differently are mainly practical: there are many more authors and titles of documents than subject descriptors needed to represent documents. New authors turn up at an increasing rate whereas new subject descriptors are the exception. It would be impractical to publish in book form a list of all the authors of books in the Library of Congress. Conversely, it is practical to publish Library of Congress Subject Headings. Different sets of rules apply in forming the descriptors. It is often a technical necessity to use different files and

C4 Types of Concepts, Descriptors 151

different types of files for bibliographic searches on the one hand and subject searches on the other. Now from a technical point of view form descriptors behave like subject descriptors. It is therefore possible to treat them technically like subject descriptors, and we have shown that it is useful to do so. On the other hand, proper names that are used as subject descriptors behave like authors (except proper names that are used very often, like *U.S., UN, NATO*). Also the rules for forming descriptors are the same as in descriptive indexing in this case. Therefore, it might be quite appropriate to enter documents *about* persons and institutions in the author-title catalog.

C4.1 The Treatment of Proper Names Used as Subject Descriptors

The use of proper names often allows for specific and quick selection of documents. Proper names should therefore be allowed in document representations and search request formulations. However, this is not as simple as it may seem at the first look: In many cases a document indexed by a proper name, for example, *Nixon* (in 1971), should also be retrieved in searches for broader descriptors, for example, *United States* and *Chief executive*. In other words, we have a hierarchical relationship between the proper name as the Narrower Term and one or more concepts as the Broader Terms. One has to make sure that these relationships between proper names and concepts are taken into account appropriately.

One may achieve this purpose in two ways:

(a) Proper names are dealt with exactly as all other descriptors, that is, they are included in the indexing language, and the appropriate hierarchical relationships are introduced and are used in searching and possibly in filing.

(b) Proper names may be used in indexing without being listed explicitly in the indexing language. The indexer, while using such a proper name, adds the appropriate broader descriptor.

In manual systems it is recommended for practical reasons that only the most important proper names be listed in the indexing language explicitly. All other proper names are used in indexing but supplemented by the appropriate broader descriptors (alternative (b)). Proper names that are not listed in the indexing language but that are allowed to be used in indexing are sometimes called "identifiers" and distinguished from descriptors, which have to be listed explicitly in the indexing language. In computerized systems one may maintain a large proper-name dictionary and thereby save the additional effort of adding the appropriate broader descriptors whenever a proper name is used in indexing.

The explicit inclusion of proper names in the indexing language poses enormous updating problems. On the other hand, if proper names are used freely by the indexers it is possible that the same proper name will be entered in different forms or that different proper names for the same individual object or person will be used without the appropriate control. As an intermediate solution it is recommended that an authority file be maintained at a central location. Also strict rules on the form of proper names should be set up. As far as applicable the same authority file and the same rules that are used for descriptive cataloging should be used.

Proper names can be included in a classified arrangement of descriptors in two ways. One may list them all together in a proper-name dictionary, or one may include smaller lists at appropriate places in the classified arrangement.

Compare Section B5.4 "Representation versus filing of documents or catalog cards", where similar problems are discussed in a more general framework.

Further remarks:

One system divides proper names into the following sections: Company names, chemical names, geographical (including geological) names. ERIC includes as identifiers "acronyms and coined terminology" in addition to proper names. No control whatsoever is exercised on identifiers. The dangers of such a procedure have been outlined above. (In the ERIC index, documents on ERIC appear in four places: *ERIC* (5 times); *Educational Resources Information Center* (25 times); *Educational Resources Information Center (ERIC)* (2 times); *Educational Resources Information Centers* (1 time). Compare Section B5.4.4 to the whole problem. In Section D4.4.2,2 we describe a notation that ties proper names to the appropriate broader descriptor in the classified arrangement.

In an ideal ISAR system the proper-name dictionary would also contain the authors of documents so that it would be possible to search for "Publications on politics by physicists", as discussed in Section C4.0.1. However, this is usually not feasible since the number of persons who authored documents is so much bigger than the number of persons dealt with in documents.

C4.2 Treatment of Elements of Nomenclatures

C4.2.1 Nomenclatures as adjunct thesauri

One may treat nomenclatures (especially internationally accepted nomenclatures) as "adjunct" thesauri and either use an available publication containing the nomenclature in addition to the thesaurus proper or incorporate the nomenclature into the thesaurus. (For a definition of "adjunct thesaurus" see Section K1.2.3.)

C4.2.2 Alternative possibility: inclusion of selected elements of nomenclatures into the thesaurus proper

An alternative procedure is used by TEST. TEST treats elements of nomenclatures as all other terms, subject to the following rules:

(1) *For biological nomenclatures:* "Where possible, consistent use should be made of established nomenclature systems for describing plants and animals. Where departures are necessary, cross-references should be provided to maintain continuity."

(2) *For names of chemical substances* and other organic or inorganic materials, the following rules are given. These rules are intended to keep the number of such names in reasonable limits:

(2.1) chemistry

"To avoid proliferation of terms in the field of chemistry, the names of specific chemical compounds as descriptors should be restricted. Instead, a vocabulary of descriptors representing generic compound classes, functional groups, and structural features should be devised. This will permit indexing and searching by coordinating appropriate descriptors to denote specific compounds, as well as classes of compounds.

Names of specific compounds that occur frequently in the literature may be entered as descriptors; for example *sulfuric acid, carbon tetrachloride, morphine, progesterone.*"

(2.2) alloys:

"Descriptors should be established for certain generic alloy families: for example, *aluminum copper alloys, molybdenum steels, zinc alloys.* This will permit indexing and retrieval on a somewhat general level, but will prevent proliferation of descriptors to represent specific alloy systems."

These rules are not useful in ISAR systems dealing with special fields in chemistry or specifically with alloys.

C4.3 Concepts of General Application (Common Attributes, Common Isolates)

There are concepts of very general application, such as *Capability, Planning, Theory, Function, Structure,* and *Means and instruments.* Further examples are *Modern* vs. *Traditional; Domestic affairs* vs. *Foreign relations* (applied to politics, economics, etc.); *Education in home country* vs. *Education in foreign country; Reforms; Governmental; Vulnerability.*

As single descriptors these concepts of general application convey little information. Some authors recommend, therefore, not using them at all. As a reason corroborating this recommendation they mention the fact that these concepts are often overlooked in indexing and therefore cannot be used in searching with a reasonable degree of reliability.

However, there are important reasons for the use of concepts of general application:

(1) *Use in combinations.* Often these concepts are needed in order to express a specific concept by a combination of descriptors. They are especially useful for the modification of less general concepts.

Examples:
Theory; Testing; Measuring; Application; Trend; Threshold

The advantages gained from the possibility of combining descriptors freely are especially important in connection with these concepts; search requests can be formulated more precisely.

Example:
Blood pressure AND Measuring
Blood pressure AND Threshold
X-rays   AND Measuring
X-rays   AND Threshold

A general concept may appear as component in a precombined descriptor. Or it may be indicated as part of a descriptor combination to be used to express a compound concept. In both cases the concept of general application is taken into account in indexing. The consistent use of these concepts in other cases should be achieved by a consequent application of the checklist technique of indexing, by the introduction of *see also* cross-references, and by appropriate training of the indexers.

(2) *Standard subheadings.* A special case of (1) is the use of standard subheadings for the subdivision of less general descriptors in a conventional subject catalog.

Examples (from the Library of Congress Subject Headings):
Libraries   —Centralization
Schools   —Centralization
Agriculture   —Accidents
Agriculture   —Costs
Agriculture   —Mathematical models
Agriculture   —Research
Transportation—Accidents
Transportation—Costs
Transportation—Mathematical models
Transportation—Research

(3) *Points to enter hierarchy.* Some concepts of general application, espe-

cially those designating general categories or facets, may serve as entry points that lead to more specific terms to be used in indexing.

Example:
Losses 1407
Scope note: Use of a more specific term is recommended; consult the terms listed as narrower terms:
NT *Core loss*
      Damage
      Eddy currents
      Fire losses
      Head losses
      Insertion losses
      Lost circulation
      Power loss
      Rejects
      Scattering loss
      Seepage
      Transmission loss
      Wastes
      Water loss
      Yield

Often concepts of general application are located near the borderline between subject descriptors on the one hand and role indicators or relators (that is, elements of the syntax) on the other.

C5 THE LEAD-IN STRUCTURE. USE AND SEE

Section B6 expounded on the functions of the lead-in vocabulary in an ISAR system. The present section describes in detail the lead-in structure that is to serve these functions. In a small thesaurus with a limited lead-in vocabulary a very simple rule suffices: with each lead-in term (each term not used as descriptor) give a USE instruction that directs the indexer or searcher to the descriptor(s) to be used. However, the lead-in problem is really more complex, and in larger thesauri one has to take this complexity into account. This is true especially for the thesaurus construction phase. It is also very important if a thesaurus system for shared subject indexing is being built. If none of these situations applies we suggest that the reader read only Section C5.0, not Sections C5.1–C5.3; even Section C5.0 is not a must, but it will enhance understanding.

156   C   Structure of Indexing Languages, Thesauri

C5.0 Introduction

C5.0.1 The lead-in problem: alphabetical index method versus main part method

Sections C1–C4 have dealt with conceptual structure, mainly the structure of the indexing language. However, this is only part of the structure of the thesaurus as a whole. As has been shown earlier, one important function of a thesaurus is to lead from a term in the lead-in vocabulary to the appropriate descriptor or descriptors to be used. This problem will be addressed now.

The whole problem is closely related to the format of the thesaurus. It is therefore necessary to make a few remarks on thesaurus format here; this topic is treated fully in Section D1. The two parts of the thesaurus important in the present context are the *main part* and the *alphabetical index*. The main part must contain an entry for every descriptor, giving additional information such as Synonymous, Broader, Narrower, and Related Terms and possibly a scope note. Depending on the design of the thesaurus the main part may contain, in addition, all preferred terms that are not descriptors or even an entry for every term contained in the thesaurus (the reader not familiar with the distinction between *preferred term* and *descriptor* is advised to take a look at Figure 6, Section B4.2). The arrangement of the main part may be either classified or alphabetic. In either case an alphabetical index is necessary if only because a multi-word term such as *Low altitude nuclear explosion* appears at only one place in the alphabetical sequence in the main part (in the example, under L).

The lead from a lead-in term to a descriptor may be achieved in two ways, called the *alphabetical index method* and the *main part method.*

The two methods may be illustrated using the example *Air explosions* (descriptor) and *Air blasts* (synonymous lead-in term).

Example:

(1) Alph. index method

Main part	T23 *Aerial explosions* UF *Air blasts*
Alph. index	*Aerial explosions* T23 *Air blasts* T23 *Air transport* M76 *Air blasts* T23 *Aerial explosions* T23

C5 The Lead-In Structure. USE and SEE

(2) Main part method

Main Part	Aerial explosions 　UF Air blasts Air blasts 　USE Aerial explosions
Alph. index	Aerial explosions Air blasts Air transport Air blasts Aerial explosions

The rules to be seen from this example are as follows:

(1) In the *alphabetical index method* no entry is made for the lead-in term in the main part. In the alphabetical index one or more entries, as necessary, are made for the descriptor, as well as for the lead-in term. In each entry the descriptor to be used is given either in the form of a notation or in the form of full text. The use of notation is more appropriate for this method, however.

(2) In the *main part method* the main part contains an entry for the lead-in term at one place in the alphabetical sequence (this method is useful only if the main part is arranged in alphabetical sequence). The entry for the lead-in term will give a USE-instruction to the descriptor to be used. In the alphabetical index one or more entries, as necessary, are made for the descriptor as well as for the lead-in term; no further information is given in the entries. The user wanting, for example, *Blasts* and looking in the alphabetical index under B will find *Air blasts* there. He will then go to the main part and find *Air blasts* under A, where he will find the USE instruction USE *Air explosions*.

It is preferable to use the alphabetical index method only for those cases where just one descriptor (not a combination of descriptors) is to be used, depending on how much space is allowed for the notation, and to resort to the main part method if a combination of descriptors is to be used.

For reasons to be discussed later we suggest the alphabetical index method for the leads from non-preferred terms to preferred terms, whether these preferred terms are descriptors or not, and the main part method for the leads from preferred terms that are not used as descriptors to the appropriate descriptor(s). However, most existing thesauri use the main part method for all the leads. The following discussion is therefore in terms of the main part method. However, all main part entries that would be superfluous in the alphabetical index method are marked by an asterisk (*).

158   C   Structure of Indexing Languages, Thesauri

C5.0.2 The lead-in problem: the crude form and the detailed form

The form commonly used for providing the leads is the *crude form* (our term). However, in the working file used for the construction of the thesaurus and often in the user version, the *detailed form* (our term) is more appropriate, as will be shown by way of examples taken from TEST. TEST uses the crude form. USE is introduced as a cross-reference of the same type as Broader Term, Narrower Term, and Related Term. If a term is not used as descriptor it can have a USE cross-reference only. This USE cross-reference refers to the descriptor(s) to be used, no matter whether these descriptors are Synonymous or Equivalent Terms, Broader Terms, or semantic factors. With the descriptor an appropriate inverted cross-reference USED FOR (UF) is entered. Again, no distinction is made whether the descriptor is synonymous to or broader than the term entered in the inverse cross-reference. The term in the inverse cross-reference is marked by a dagger (†), however, if the descriptor is a semantic factor.

Examples:
    1. *Aerial explosions*
        UF *Air blasts*   *Synonym/Equivalent*
        †*Low-altitude nuclear explosions*   *Narrower Term,*
                                                    compound

        Inverse cross-references:
        Air blasts
            USE *Aerial explosions*   *Synonym to be used*
        Low altitude nuclear explosions
            USE *Aerial explosions*   *two semantic factors*
            and *Nuclear explosions*   *to be used*

    2. *Logic circuits*
        UF *AND circuits*   *Narrower Term, not compound*
        Inverse cross-reference
        AND circuits:
            USE *Logic circuits*   *Broader Term to be used*

The crude form does not distinguish between the display of the synonym/homonym structure, the equivalence structure, and the classificatory structure on the one hand and the instructions indicating the term to be used as descriptor on the other. This point is further illustrated by the following example (slightly modified from TEST).

Example:

Data processing	is in fact
UF Automatic data processing	ST
Data analysis	NT
Data handling	NT ⎫ Synonymous
Data management	NT ⎬ to each other
Electronic data processing	ST

The entries for the inverse cross-reference are as follows (all of them would be superfluous with the alphabetical index method):

*Automatic data processing
  USE Data processing
*Data analysis
  USE Data processing
*Data handling
  USE Data processing
*Data management
  USE Data processing
*Electronic data processing
  USE Data processing

Now *Automatic data processing* and *Electronic data processing* are synonymous to *Data processing; Data handling* and *Data management* are synonymous to each other and narrower than *Data processing; Data analysis* is narrower than *Data processing.* Furthermore we might wish to give a definition for the concept expressed by *Data handling* or *Data management* in spite of the fact that it is not used as a descriptor. This definition would have to be given both in the entry for *Data handling* and in the entry for *Data management,* which is a waste of space. Why not, then, choose *Data management* as the preferred term, give the definition there, and refer from *Data handling* to *Data management,* at the same time showing that the two terms are synonymous? And why not distinguish in USE instructions between the case where the descriptor to be used is a synonym and where the descriptor(s) to be used is (are) Broader Term(s)? This is exactly what we shall describe as the *detailed form* in Section C5.1. As we shall see in detail there, the purpose is achieved by detaching the USE *instructions* from the ST, BT, NT and RT *cross-references.*

Example:
  Air blasts
    USE ST *Aerial explosions*

Low-altitude nuclear explosions
USE BT :Aerial explosions
and :Nuclear explosions

However, one should keep in mind that we thereby provide more information than in the crude form. The additional information may mean higher costs for the preparation of the user version of the thesaurus. The user may not need this information, and it might even confuse him. So the point is not that the detailed form is unconditionally superior but that it offers an alternative which should be considered and which often, in fact, is better than the crude form. In the construction phase the detailed form is definitely superior. First, the mass of all terms is reduced to the preferred terms. Then the descriptors are selected from the preferred terms. The fact that in the crude form the underlying conceptual relationships are not specified in the USE instructions is especially awkward in the case where the thesaurus is to be used by some other ISAR System. In this other system the decisions on which specific concepts and which compound concepts to use as descriptors might well be different, whereas synonyms remain synonyms no matter in what system we are. Also the comparison of thesauri is much more difficult if the crude lead-in form is used. (We come back to these problems when we talk about thesauri and cooperation in Chapter K.) To avoid these problems it is recommended that at least the working file of the thesaurus be kept in the detailed form, even if, for the user version, the crude form is better in the specific application.

There is another way to solve the problem discussed here. We could simply stipulate that all preferred terms should be descriptors, thereby eliminating instructions like USE BT. We could then use the crude lead-in form without any disadvantage. However, the indexing language would grow too large for most ISAR systems.

,1 **Further illustrative examples of the crude lead-in form.**

Example 1:
Manufacturing
  UF Fabrication   *Synonym*

  Manufacturing methods   *Synonym among*
  Manufacturing techniques *themselves, designating narrower concept*

Example 2:
School integration
  UF School desegregation
  Desegregated schools
  Integrated schools

Example 3:
  Automatic Language Translation
     Note   Whenever possible, specify NATURAL LANGUAGES or ARTIFICIAL LANGUAGES.
     Use   APPLICATIONS; ELECTRONIC DIGITAL COMPUTERS; LANGUAGE TRANSLATION

  Automatic Translation
     Note   If automatic translation of languages is meant, use LANGUAGE TRANSLATION; APPLICATION; and ELECTRONIC DIGITAL COMPUTERS. Whenever possible, specify ARTIFICIAL LANGUAGES or NATURAL LANGUAGES.
     Use   APPLICATIONS; ELECTRONIC DIGITAL COMPUTERS; TRANSLATION

  Language Translation, Automatic
     Note   If natural language translation is meant, add NATURAL LANGUAGES. If translation of a particular natural language is meant, name them.
     Use   ELECTRONIC DIGITAL COMPUTERS; LANGUAGE TRANSLATION

  Machine Translation
     Note   If machine refers to ELECTRONIC DIGITAL COMPUTERS, use that term as well, and also APPLICATIONS. If translation refers to LANGUAGE TRANSLATION, use that term in preference to TRANSLATION.
     Use   TRANSLATION

  Mechanical Translation
     Use   APPLICATIONS; ELECTRONIC DIGITAL COMPUTERS; LANGUAGE TRANSLATION

C5.0.3 Use of the lead-in structure

The instruction USE in, say,
  Kinescopes
     USE ST -*Television picture tubes*
seems to imply that the indexer or searcher, thinking of the term *Kinescopes,* should indiscriminately use *Television picture tubes* instead. However, such is not the case. *Television picture tubes* is merely the proper entry point in the indexing language. It might have narrower descriptors, e.g., *Black and white television picture tubes* and *Color television picture tubes,* and the indexer or searcher has to decide whether one of these would be appropriate.

Further examples:
> *Helicopter*
> *USE BT -Aircraft*
> where the entry for *Aircraft* is
> *Aircraft*
> *NT Civilian aircraft*
> *Military aircraft.*

Depending on whether the document is on civilian or military helicopters, the indexer should choose *Civilian aircraft* or *Military aircraft*. This situation is particularly important when a concept is expressed by a combination of descriptors.

Example:
> *Passenger aircraft*
> *USE BT :-Aircraft*
> *and : Passenger transport*

where again we might have *Civilian aircraft* or *Military aircraft*.

Descriptors that have narrower descriptors are marked by '-' so that the indexer or searcher is alerted to the fact that he should look up the descriptor and consider the narrower descriptors, too.

C5.1 The Detailed Lead-In Form

In the detailed lead-in form the SEE and USE *instructions* are expressed independently from the ST, (ET), BT, NT, and RT *cross-references*. Consequently, the cross-reference structure can be worked out first without paying any attention to the question which of the preferred terms are to be used as descriptors and which are not. The cross-references present in the example of *Data processing* used above are displayed (with some added information) in the left column in Figure 18. The thesaurus builder now decides which preferred terms should be used as descriptors and which ones are so specific that a Broader Term should be used as descriptor, and adds the appropriate SEE and USE instructions; the result is shown in the right column in Figure 18. A second example is given in Figure 19. As may be seen from the examples the following rules apply:

(1) SEE instructions usually lead from non-preferred terms to preferred terms that are not descriptors. They may also lead from a preferred term to a broader preferred term that is not descriptor.

(2) USE instructions lead from lead-in terms (be they preferred terms or not) to descriptors.

(3) A SEE instruction may be followed by the appropriate USE instruction for the convenience of the user (see examples *Data handling* and *Vessels 2*).

Conceptual relationships	SEE and USE instructions and SF (seen from) and UF (used for) statements added

Data processing
  ST Automatic data processing
       Electronic data processing
  NT Data analysis
       Data management
       Data recording
       Data transmission
	Data processing
	  UF ST Automatic data proc.
	            Electronic data proc.
	  UF NT Data analysis
	            Data management
	      NT Data recording
	            Data transmission

Entries for the inverse cross-references

Automatic data processing
  ST Data processing
	*Automatic data procesing
	  USE ST Data processing

Data analysis
  BT Data processing
	Data analysis
	  USE BT Data processing

Data handling
  ST Data management
	*Data handling
	  SEE ST Data management
	  USE BT Data processing[a]

Data management
  ST Data handling
  BT Data processing
	Data management
	  SF ST Data handling
	  USE BT Data processing
	  SN Storage and retrieval of data, updating data files. Excludes *Data acquisition*, *Data recording* and *Data analysis*[b]

Data recording
  BT Data processing
	Data recording
	  BT Data processing

Data transmission
  BT Data processing
	Data transmission
	  BT Data processing

Electronic data processing
  ST Data processing
	*Electronic data processing
	  USE ST Data processing

Figure 18. Example illustrating the detailed lead-in form (C5.1). (*) Designates entries not needed if the alphabetical index method is used for lead-in. (*a*) This line is optional. It saves the reader the two-step procedure of going from *Data handling* to *Data management* in order to see there that he should use the descriptor *Data processing*. In many cases it might be advisable to the user, however, to do exactly this in order to look at a scope note and other information given with the preferred term, and the usefulness of the optional line is therefore questionable. (*b*) Note that this scope note appears only with the preferred term *Data management*, not with the synonymous term *Data handling*. Having the preferred term is therefore useful, even though it is not a descriptor. The scope note is important because *Data acquisition* and *Data recording* are descriptors in their own right.

164 C Structure of Indexing Languages, Thesauri

Conceptual relationships   SEE and USE instructions and SF and UF statements added; more information on preferred terms included

Attorney
  ST Lawyer

Attorney
  UF ST Lawyer
  UF ET Barrister
              Solicitor
  UF NT Tax attorney
  NT   Patent attorney
  BT   Law personnel

Flute
  BT Musical instruments

Flute
  SF NT Recorder
  USE BT Musical instruments

Lawyer
  ST Attorney

*Lawyer
  USE ST Attorney

Musical instruments
  NT Flute

Musical instruments
  UF NT Flute

Recorder
  BT Flute

Recorder
  SEE BT Flute
  USE BT Musical instruments

Ships
  ST Vessels 2 (ships)
  BT :Vehicles
  and :Water transport

Ships[a]
  SF ST Vessels 2 (ships)
  SF NT Aircraft carriers
              Cargo ships
              Passenger ships
  USE BT :Vehicles
    and   :Water transport
  RT   Boats
           Barges
  SN   Used for deep-water transport

Vessels 2 (ships)
  ST Ships

*Vessels 2 (ships)[a]
  SEE ST Ships
  USE BT :Vehicles
    and   :Water transport

Figure 19. Example illustrating the detailed lead-in form (C5.1). (*) Designates entries not needed if the alphabetical index method is used. (*a*) Note again the economy of having the preferred term Ships and recording NT and RT only there.

(4) From every lead-in term there must be either a SEE instruction or a USE instruction or both.

(5) For every USE instruction there must be an appropriate inverse UF (USED FOR) statement. For every SEE instruction there must be an appropriate SF (SEEN FROM) statement. (See Section D2.4 for the use of typography in achieving optimal intelligibility when using the detailed lead-in form.)

The following example illustrates a special case of the *Recorder–Flute–Musical instrument* situation.

Example:
>   Helicopter
>   SEE BT   Aircraft
>   Aircraft
>   SF   NT   Helicopter
>   USE BT   :Vehicles
>   and   :Air transport

Note that simply writing
>   Helicopter
>   USE BT   :Vehicles
>   and   :Air transport

would not bring out the fact that Helicopter is actually narrower than the combination Vehicles: Air transport. However, as in the case of Recorder, we could write
>   Helicopter
>   SEE BT   Aircraft
>   USE BT   :Vehicles
>   and   :Air transport

Remark: The following combinations of SEE and USE with relationships are possible:

(1) SEE ST, SEE ET, USE ST, USE ET
(2) SEE BT, USE BT (and possibly USE NT, but compare C5.3)
(3) SEE RT, USE RT
(1′) SF ST, SF ET, UF ST, UF ET
(2′) SF NT, UF NT
(3′) SF RT, UF RT

In the Roget-Soergel thesaurus format recommended in D1 none of the combinations in (1) appears explicitly because the alphabetical index method for lead-in is used. In the field ST/ET, SF and UF can then be omitted; this might be done even in other formats because in the field ST/ET SF and UF can always be inferred.

C5.2 Alternative Lead-In Forms

C5.2.1 Simpler forms

If the detailed lead-in form is used together with the alphabetical index method of lead-in, separate entries are needed in the main part for preferred terms that are not used as descriptors; this results in an increase in the size of the main part. A simpler alternative is as follows.

Example:
>Data processing
>>UF ST Electronic data processing
>>UF NT Data management
>>   Data handling
>>NT   . . .

The fact that *Data management* and *Data handling* are synonymous would not be brought out by this procedure. Also, if the lead-in is to a combination of descriptors rather than to a single descriptor the alphabetical index entries must provide enough space to list several notations.

A further simplification, namely merging the UF NT field with the UF ST field leads to the crude form described in Section C5.0.2. (Refer to that section for a discussion of the relative merits of the crude and detailed form.)

C5.2.2 More detailed form: expressing the equivalence structure (advanced)

On the other hand a more detailed form is possible. One may emphasize the equivalence structure by treating it in the same way as the classificatory structure and not like the synonym-homonym structure (as has been suggested in C5.1).

Example:
>Academic achievement
>>UF ST Scholastic achievement
>>UF ET Educational achievement
>>   Educational attainment

The corresponding inverse entries are:
>*Scholastic achievement
>>USE ST Academic achievement
>
>*Educational achievement
>>USE ET Academic achievement
>
>*Educational attainment
>>USE ET Academic achievement

Clearly the first two terms are synonymous. The last two terms are equivalent to the Main Term, and that is shown by the prefix ET. But still we have not expressed the fact that *Educational achievement* and *Educational attainment* are true synonyms. This could be accomplished as follows.

C5 The Lead-In Structure. USE and SEE

Example:
   Academic achievement
      UF   ST   Scholastic achievement
      UF   ET   Educational achievement
   Educational achievement
      SF   ST   Educational attainment
      USE ET   Academic achievement

The inverse entries would be as follows:
   *Scholastic achievement
      USE ST   Academic achievement
   *Educational attainment
      SEE ST   Educational achievement
      USE ET   Scholastic achievement *(optional line)*

Further Examples:
   Acoustic insulation
      UF   ST   Sound insulation
      UF   ET   Acoustic insulators
                 Sound insulators
      UF   NT   Sound absorbing materials
                 Sound reflecting materials

In this example the last two terms designate concepts narrower than *Acoustic insulators*.

   Administrative personnel
      UF   ST   Administrative staff
                 Management personnel
      UF   ET   Business managers
                 Business officials

In an even more detailed method, one would distinguish:
—plane of spelling;
—plane of synonym-homonym structure;
—plane of equivalence structure;
—plane of classificatory structure.

C5.3 OR-Type USE Instructions

Some thesauri contain USE instructions that specify several descriptors, one of which is to be used in indexing. (This is not to be confused with a USE instruction that specifies a combination of descriptors to be used in indexing.) The following discussion analyzes the situations where this can occur and shows how the OR-type USE instruction can be avoided in each case.

C5.3.1 Homonymous lead-in terms

The lead-in term from which the USE instruction is made is homonymous, and each of the descriptors given corresponds to one of the meanings of the lead-in term.

Example:
>   Charges
>   USE   Charges (Law)
>   OR   Electric charges
>   OR   Expenses
>   OR   Explosives
>   OR   Payload

A different procedure is recommended: the homonym should be disambiguated so that one entry is made for each of its meanings. Each of these entries would contain a USE instruction specifying uniquely the descriptor to be used. The above example would then look as follows.

Example:
>   Charges (Electricity)
>   USE   Electric charges
>   Charges (Explosives)
>   USE   Explosives
>   Charges (Finance)
>   USE   Expenses
>   Charges (Law)
>   Charges (Missile technology)
>   USE   Payload

C5.3.2 Broad lead-in terms

The lead-in term may designate a broader concept that is not used in itself as a descriptor. The USE instruction specifies narrower descriptors from which to choose in indexing ("downward" USE instruction).

Example:
>   Amide
>   USE NT   C-Amide
>   OR NT   Aryl-C-Amide
>   OR NT   P-Amide

(In most existing thesauri it would be simply USE, without NT). A different procedure is recommended for this situation, too. The broader concept should be allowed as a descriptor and the Narrower Terms should be listed in field NT. In general, rules for indexing should specify that the most specific descriptor that covers the subject in question should be used in indexing. If it seems necessary in connection with a particular broader concept to remind the indexer of this rule it should be done in a scope note, such as "consider a narrower descriptor for indexing".

Together these two regulations eliminate the need for the OR-type USE instructions. The structure of the thesaurus is thereby clarified. The following example from the Thesaurus of ASTIA descriptors is slightly more complicated:

Example:
1st ed.:
   Actuators
      USE   *Explosive actuators*
      OR   *Hydraulic actuators*
      OR   *Magnetic actuators*
      OR   *Servo mechanisms*
      OR   *Synchros*

2nd ed.:
   Actuators
      NT   *Explosive actuators*
              Hydraulic actuators
              Magnetic actuators
      RT   *Servo mechanisms*
              Synchros

The following complication can arise: In systems where the number of descriptors that can be used in indexing is limited it might be necessary to exclude a broader concept from the indexing descriptors (the broader concept should always be available as a searching descriptor!). In this case the scope note should read "Use a narrower term in indexing. Term allowed in searching". The narrower terms are then listed in the appropriate field without USE.

C5.3.3 Leads to related terms

An apparently similar but conceptually different situation occurs.

Example:
   Dementia
      USE RT *Psychiatry*
      OR   RT *Encephelopathy*
      OR   RT *Geriatrics*

170 C Structure of Indexing Languages, Thesauri

Dementia is connected empirically to the three concepts offered in the USE instruction. Again, *Dementia* should be kept as a descriptor to be used in addition to one or more of the descriptors listed as RT.

If the number of descriptors to be used within a system is very limited, it might be more efficient to omit the broader concept or additional aspects, such as *Dementia*, from the descriptors if these concepts are not expected to be important for searching. In this case a scope note "Use the appropriate term(s) listed in RT" should be made.

C5.3.4 OR-combination of descriptors as semantic factor

There is a fourth situation, especially in thesauri that refer often to descriptor combinations. Consider the following example.

Example:
> *Meat as food*
>   NT   *Food from hunting*
>   *Food from animal husbandry*

Meat is not a descriptor in the particular system. Both Narrower Terms are expressed by a combination of descriptors. In such cases it would be awkward to create two entries for the lead-in term or to use leads to narrower terms.

Instead one writes as follows:

Example:
> *Meat as food*
>   USE BT   :*Q92 Food, beverages*
>   and :   *P31 Hunting*
>   or *P42 Animal husbandry*

Instead of using the OR-combination of descriptors one might also use a broader concept covering both components in the OR-combination of descriptors. It would then be the responsibility of the indexer to substitute a more specific descriptor if the subject dealt with in the document can be better expressed this way, as discussed in Section C5.0.3, "Use of the lead-in structure". In some cases it is useful to suggest to the indexer a narrower descriptor that is particularly relevant.

Example:
> *Political statements by a church*
>   USE BT :*Politics*
>   or *Internal politics*
>   or *Political interest groups*
>   and :*Church*
>   and :*Commentary*

Agricultural technology
   USE BT :*Agriculture*
       and : *Technology*
           or Tools

C5.4 Other Matters Related to USE Instructions

C5.4.1 Qualified USE instructions (special topic)

If a thesaurus is established for simultaneous use by two or more institutions, the decisions on which term is to be used may differ from institution to institution. In this case different USE instructions may have to be entered:

(1) An unqualified USE instruction to be applied by indexers of institutions for which no qualified USE instruction is provided;
(2) Qualified USE instructions to be followed by the indexers of an institution that does not agree to this unqualified USE instruction.

The qualification consists of a code for the institution, preceding, following, or replacing, *USE*.

Example:
               Claw
           USE   *Nail*
   VETDOC USE   *Hoof*
               Bloat
   RINGDOC USE   *Gastroenteropathy*

In the latter example the absence of an unqualified USE instruction means that *Bloat* is to be used except for the ISAR system of RINGDOC.

C6 SYNONYMS PROPER VERSUS SPELLING VARIANTS

As we have seen in Section C5, synonyms are needed in the lead-in structure to lead to the appropriate preferred term and ultimately to the appropriate descriptor. The same is true for spelling variants, including morphological variants. However, there is a difference between synonyms and spelling variants: Whereas synonyms should appear in the main part entry for the preferred term, spelling variants should not. Furthermore, not all spelling variants are needed in the lead-in structure. The present section addresses these problems.

C6.1 Synonyms Proper

Synonyms convey additional information as to the scope and usage of the preferred term, and they should therefore appear in the main part entry for the preferred term. We might also formulate this as follows: The indexer or searcher looking at a main part entry can see that there is no need to look elsewhere in the thesaurus for the terms listed as synonymous or quasi-synonymous.

In the working file used for the elaboration and the updating of the thesaurus it might be useful to make the distinction between Synonymous Terms (ST) and quasi-synonymous or Equivalent Terms (ET). This distinction is especially useful in thesauri that are likely to be used for the construction of other indexing languages or thesauri, since the decisions about term equivalence are dependent upon the purpose of the thesaurus. In the user version of the thesaurus—the edition actually used for indexing and searching—the distinction between ST and ET can usually be neglected.

C6.2 Spelling Variants

Spelling variants (including morphological variants and possibly inverted forms) do not convey additional information on the usage of the preferred term and should therefore not appear in the main party entry. Some spelling variants are considerably apart from the preferred spelling in the alphabetical sequence, and they should therefore appear in the alphabetical index. They are called external spelling variants (SP-EX). Other spelling variants are so near to the preferred spelling in the alphabet that they should not even be included in the alphabetical index. They might be needed for mechanized ISAR systems, however; in this case they should be included as spelling variants internal to the system (SP-IN).

The examples in Figure 20 may serve to illustrate these considerations.

This procedure could be rephrased as follows: Within the plane of the synonym-homonym structure we distinguish in the working file a "plane of spelling variants". A preferred spelling is selected for each term and applied everywhere in the thesaurus. In the working file the spelling variants of the preferred term, as well as those of its synonyms, are stored together unless the more detailed procedure to be described in Section C6.2.3 is chosen. In the user version of the thesaurus the (external) spelling variants appear in the alphabetical index only.

C6.2.1 Distinction between synonyms proper and spelling variants

The basic criterion for the distinction between synonyms and spelling variants is, to repeat, whether or not the term in question contributes to an explanation of the meaning and the usage of the preferred term. Consider the descriptor *Automation* and the term *Automated*. *Automated* may be used as an Equivalent Term, but some systems might use it as a separate descriptor, and users might look for it as a separate descriptor. Therefore, *Automated* should

C6 Synonyms Versus Spelling Variants

Working file		Main part	
M27	Esthetics	M27	Esthetics
SP-EX	Aesthetics		
U63	Molding sands	U63	Molding sands
SP-EX	Moulding sands	ST	Baked sands
ST	Baked sands		
S34	Melanosaroma	S34	Melanosaroma
SP-IN	Tumour	ST	Tumor
ST	Tumor		
T45	Monotony	T45	Monotony
SP-IN	Monotone		
N36	Morality	N36	Morality
SP-IN	Morals		

Alphabetical index

Aesthetics	M27
Baked sands	U63
Esthetics	M27
Melanosaroma	S34
Molding sands	U63
Monotony	T45
Morality	N36
Moulding sands	U63
Tumor	S34

Figure 20. Treatment of spelling variants (C6.2).

be listed in the main part entry for *Automation*; it should *not* be treated as a spelling variant. *Morality* and *Morals* is a borderline case.

C6.2.2 Number of spelling variants to be included in the thesaurus

The number of spelling variants to be included in the thesaurus is determined by the following considerations:

(1) For look-up of terms by human indexers and searchers only external spelling variants are needed.

(2) In some systems the descriptor texts are used in indexing and searching. They are compared to the appropriate form of the descriptor as stored in the machine. In this case it is useful to include frequently occurring erroneous forms of the descriptors (caused, for example, by typing errors) as internal spelling variants (for singular/plural see (3)).

(3) If the thesaurus is to be used for mechanized indexing or for searching based on free indexing, more spelling variants have to be included, as has been explained in Section B6.2.2(1). In this case frequent erroneous forms of non-descriptors and of spelling variants should be included as well (again, these can be left out of the alphabetical index for manual use). Erroneous forms of terms

174   C Structure of Indexing Languages, Thesauri

used in indexing are one of the major sources of recall failure in mechanized systems using no terminological control at all or terminological control in searching only. However, spelling variants that can easily be transformed to the main form (e.g., obtaining the plural by appending -s) need not be included in the thesaurus.

C6.2.3 Where to store the spelling variants

A further problem is where to store the spelling variants internally. In the Roget-Soergel thesaurus format recommended in Chapter D, main part entries will be made for preferred terms only. This does not present a problem for spelling variants of the preferred term; they are simply stored in field SP-EX or field SP-IN, as the case may be. It does present a problem, however, for spelling variants of Synonymous or Equivalent Terms. It would be easiest to store these spelling variants in field SP-EX or SP-IN too.

Example:
> *Melanosaroma*
> *SP- IN   Tumour*
> *ST   Tumor*

This procedure would be sufficient for purposes of producing the alphabetical index and for mechanized indexing. However, the information on what spelling variant belongs to what term would be lost. Two possibilities exist to prevent this. One could number the terms in field ST; the preferred term would get the number 0. With each spelling variant the number of the term would be given. The other possibility is to allow for a "secondary" field for spelling variants after each term in field ST. (Details of file organization in a computer-stored thesaurus are dealt with in Section K1.3.1,1.3.) If a main part entry is made for every term and not only for preferred terms, the problem does not exist. Spelling variants appear in field SP-EX or SP-IN in the entry for the appropriate terms. However, we do not recommend this procedure.

C7 SUMMARY OF RELATIONSHIPS DISPLAYED IN A THESAURUS

The previous sections made clear that a series of cross-references and other data elements has to be given for each term in the thesaurus. It must be possible to identify uniquely the type of each cross-reference or other data element. For this purpose it is necessary to have a unique label for each type of data element. This is true for manual as well as for computerized procedures. A complete listing of the types of data elements, together with the labels we suggest, is given in Figure 21. This list is both a summary of the relationships to be displayed in a thesaurus, as discussed in Chapters B and C, and a list of data element types to be used in the recording, manipulation, and display of these relationships, to be discussed in Chapters D, F, and G.

C7 Summary of Relationships 175

The division into types of data elements given in Figure 21 is very fine and detailed. With most thesauri it would not be advisable to make such fine distinctions in the edition actually to be used by indexers and searchers. Even so, it might be advantageous in many cases to make the fine distinctions in the working file used for thesaurus construction and maintenance.

Figure 21 gives data element labels in the form of letter codes for both the detailed subdivision (Column 3) and the less detailed subdivision (Column 4). These labels are constructed in such a way that the part preceding the hyphen in the detailed label is, at the same time, the less detailed label. The less detailed labels are the same as the ones used in the TEST thesaurus as far as applicable. These labels are now commonly agreed upon. The labels for the detailed subdivision are suggested in this book.

It is appropriate to sketch briefly the use of these labels in record organization, to be discussed in more detail later. There are two ways to organize the entry or record for a term. One way is to subdivide the record into data fields, where each data field contains one or more data elements of the same type. The whole field is identified by the appropriate label. The second way is to identify each individual data element by the appropriate label. (We shall call such a labeled data element a subrecord; see Section G0.3 "Record organization in the computer".) A mixed procedure is also possible: Define fields for the general data element types and label the data elements in each field according to its specific type. For example, have a data field for ST/ET, and label true synonyms ST, Equivalent Terms ET (the part of the label appearing after the hyphen is sufficient for labeling a data element within a data field.). For manual processing it is best to subdivide the record for a term into data fields according to general data element types. If it is necessary to distinguish specific data element types the mixed procedure should be used.

Some examples of thesaurus entries are shown in Figure 22 (Section D0) and in Sections D1.7 and D2.2.

In developing a thesaurus, it is recommended that a thesaurus form be designed to reflect the structure of the entries to be used so that the data elements may be entered in an orderly fashion as they are encountered in the work. Such a thesaurus form is depicted in Figure 54, Section F0.5.

The meanings of the columns in Figure 21 are as follows:

(1) A number label for data fields, using the less detailed subdivision and reflecting the position of this data field within the entry in a practical arrangement. These number codes appear on the thesaurus form (Figure 54, Section F0.5).

(2) Data element type.

(3) Detailed letter label for the data element type, to be used for internal storage as well as for printouts of the thesaurus.

(4) Same as (3), but for the less detailed subdivision. This less detailed divi-

The meaning of the different columns and further explanation of the table are given in the text.

1	2	3	4	5	6 Main section	7 Additional sections
01	Hierarchical level	HL	—	—	F0.5.1	
02	Type of term or record[a]	TY	—	—	F0.5.1	
03	Subject field Subject category[b]	FD	—	—	C1.4.3,1	
05	*Notation*	NO	—	—	D4	D1.3.4
07	Internal code	CD	—	—	D4.1.2	
10	Main Term	MT	—	—		
12	Standardized abbreviation	AB	AB	—	E1.8.3	
17	Syntactical information	SY	—	—		B6.2.2(7); F5.1(b)
20	Spelling variants for the alphabetical index	SP-EX	—	(SP-EX)	C6.2	
23	Spelling variants for internal purposes only	SP-IN	—	(SP-IN)	C6.2	B6.2.2(1)
30	*Synonyms*[c]	ST-ST ST	ST ST	ST-ST* ST	B1, C6.1	C6.2.1
30	*Equivalent Terms, quasi-synonyms*[c]	ST-ET ET	ST ET	ST-ET* ET*	B2, C6.1	C6.2.1
35	*Translations*[d]	TR	TR	TR	D5	
40	Definition, scope note[e]	SN	SN	—	C3.2.2	
41	Subject field, subject category[b]	FD	FD	—	C1.4.3,1	D3.0
42	Facet	FA	FA	—	C1.4.3,2	C1.3.2, D3.0

44	Is combination of[f]	BT-CM	BT	NT-IS*	C1.1	C2, D2.3,2,2.1
44	Broader Terms—other[f]	BT-OT	BT	NT-OT*	C1.2, C1.4	B5.5; D1.4; D2.3,2,2; F4.0
45	Is semantic factor of[f]	NT-IS	NT	BT-CM*	C1.1	C2, D2.3,2,3
45	Narrower Terms—other[f]	NT-OT	NT	BT-OT*	C1.2, C1.4	B5.5; D1.4; D2.3,2,3; F4.0
44	Broader Terms—class inclusion[g]	BT-CL	BT	NT-CL*	C1.4.2(1)	
45	Narrower Terms—class inclusion[g]	NT-CL	NT	BT-CL*	C1.4.2(1)	
44	Broader Terms—topic inclusion	BT-TO	BT	NT-TO*	C1.4.2(2)	
45	Narrower Terms—topic inclusion	NT-TO	NT	BT-TO*	C1.4.2(2)	D2.3,2,4
44	Broader Terms—whole[h]	BT-WH	BT	NT-PT*	C1.4.2(3)	
45	Narrower Terms—part[h]	NT-PT	NT	BT-WH*	C1.4.2(3)	
44	Broader Terms—connected	BT-CN	BT	NT-CN*	C1.4.2(4)	
45	Narrower Terms—connected	NT-CN	NT	BT-CN*	C1.4.2(4)	
46	Coordinate Terms	RT-CR	RT	RT-CR*		
46	Coordinate—class inclusion	RT-CL	RT	RT-CL*		
46	Coordinate—topic inclusion	RT-TO	RT	RT-TO*		D2.3,2,5
46	Coordinate—parts	RT-PT	RT	RT-PT*		
46	Coordinate—connected	RT-CN	RT	RT-CN*		

Figure 21. Types of cross-references and other data elements given in the entry for a term (C7).

Figure 21 (continued).

1	2	3	4	5	6 Main section	7 Additional sections
46	*Related Terms, associated terms*	RT	RT	RT(*)	C1.5	F4.0, D2.3
46	Related reflexive	RT-RF	RT	RT-RF*	C1.5	
46	Related to	RT-TO	RT	RT-FR	C1.5	
46	Related from	RT-FR	—	RT-TO*	C1.5	
46	Similar in meaning	RT-SI	RT	RT-SI(*)	C1.5.1	
46	Empirically connected	RT-EC	RT	RT-EC(*)	C1.5.2	
46	Check also to	RT-CT	RT	RT-CF	C1.5.3	
46	Check also from	RT-CF	—	RT-CT*	C1.5.3	
50	Translations[d]	TR	TR	TR	D5	
60	Definition, scope note[e]	SN	SN	—	C3.2.2	F0.8.1,3
61	Internal scope note	SN-IN	—	—	F0.8.1,3	
70	Terms in unspecified relationship to the Main Term in data field 10	UN	—	UN		F1.2.2,1; F3.3.3; F5.1(d)
81	Editor (lexicographer) and date when entered[i]	ED	—	—	F0.8.1,1	
82	Provisional; look again[i]	PR	—	—	F0.8.1,2	
85	Expert to whom questions should be directed[i]	EX	as many pairs as needed		F0.8.1,2	
86	Question(s) to be asked from that person[i]	QU			F0.8.1,2	

	Indications to be used in any field				
89	Source$_i$	SR	SR	—	F0.7
	Relative frequency	FQ	%	—	
	Instructions for the user to be used in any field:				
—	See	SEE	SEE	SF*	C5
—	See from	SF	SF	SEE*	C5
—	Use	USE	USE	UF*	C5
—	Used for	UF	UF	USE*	C5
—	Post to	PT	PT	PF*	C1.4.5
—	Posted from	PF	PF	PT*	C1.4.5

In the graphical displays described in D3 letter symbols may be replaced by graphical symbols as follows:

BT—CM: =
BT: → or -≥ (for: go up to)
NT: ← or ≤- (for: come from below)
RT: ↗ or /

(a) The following codes can be used in the data field 02 Type of Term or record: Descriptor, DS; Other preferred term, OP; Non-preferred term, NP; Eliminate term (whole record), EL; Change in existing term, CH. *(b)* One of two locations can be chosen for the data field Subject field: either 03 or 41. Once a choice is made it should always be adhered to. *(c)* If no distinction between ST and ET is to be made in the user version of thesaurus, then ST-ST and ST-ET should be used. If a distinction is to be made, then ST and ET should be used. Inverse cross-references can be implemented through the alphabetical index. *(d)* One of two locations can be chosen for the data field Translations: either 35 or 50. Once a choice is made it should always be adhered to. *(e)* One of two locations can be chosen for the data field Scope note: either 40 or 60. The location may vary from entry to entry: short scope notes in 40, long scope notes in 60. *(f)* Here we assume that all semantic factors are broader terms and that the part-whole relationship, for example, is considered a hierarchical relationship. In other words, we disregard the complications mentioned in Section C1.3.1 (example: Desert animal). BT-OT is meant to contain all Broader Terms that are not labeled specifically; this may include BT-CM. See Section D2.3.2.1 for details. Also, sections given for BT-OT hold for all BT; same for NT *(g)* *UNESCO 71.12 suggests BTG (Broader Term Generic) and NTG (Narrow Term Generic) (3.4.3, p. 16). *(h)**UNESCO 71.12 suggests BTP (Broader Term Partitive) and NTP (Narrow Term Partitive) (3.4.3, p. 16). *(i)* The labels 81, 82, 85, and 86 can be used to append this editorial information to individual data elements or to data fields as well as to label a separate data field that contains editorial information for the record as a whole. *(j)* In the working file the label 89 is used to append a source indication to individual data elements. A separate data field is used only in the user version of the thesaurus, see F0.7.1.2.

sion is suggeted for the user version of the thesaurus. If no code is given in Column 4 it is suggested that the data elements of this type be omitted entirely in the user version.

(5) This column gives the appropriate inverse cross-references (see Section C7.1). The inverse cross-reference should in each case be entered in the working file. The * indicates that the inverse cross-reference must also be entered in the user version of the thesaurus. (Non-starred inverse cross-references may or may not be entered in the user version.)

(6) Main section in the book where the data element type is dealt with.

(7) Other sections in the book particularly relevant to that data element type.

C7.1 Cross-References and Inverse Cross-References

For each cross-reference from A to B an appropriate inverse cross-reference (also called reciprocal cross-reference or tracing) from B to A is necessary, in all cases in the working file and in most cases in the user version of the thesaurus. The appropriate inverse cross-reference is indicated in Figure 21, Column 5. The purpose of the inverse cross-references in the user version has already been discussed in connection with the particular relationships involved:

— With Synonymous and Equivalent Terms the inverse cross-references have the effect that all synonymous and equivalent terms are listed in the entry for the preferred term, thus contributing to an explanation of the meaning of that term.

— With hierarchical relationships the introduction of inverse cross-references leads to a complete representation of the hierarchical structure. If from A a cross-reference to the additional narrower term B is made then the inverse cross-reference with B to the additional Broader Term A makes sure that this additional Broader Term is not overlooked.

— The usefulness of inverse cross-references in connection with the Related Term cross-reference has been discussed in Section C1.5. It was also mentioned there that the inverse cross reference need not always be introduced in the user version of the thesaurus.

In the working file the inverse cross-references are extremely valuable in the updating of the thesaurus. If any changes are made for a term (for example, a term is deleted or its use as a preferred term is discontinued), all cross-references to that term have to be changed. Through the inverse cross-references to Term A the entry for term A shows all the places where a cross-reference to term A has been made and where changes have to be made accordingly.

Part II

Presentation of Indexing Languages and Thesauri

Chapter D

Thesaurus Format

D0 INTRODUCTION

This chapter deals mainly with the user version of the thesaurus. The user version is used by indexers and searchers (as opposed to the working file used for thesaurus construction and updating). It is geared toward thesauri that are presented in hard-copy form, be it printed, mimeographed, or whatever. However, many of the considerations are also applicable to thesauri that are stored in computer memory and consulted via computer terminal.

It seems useful to provide a concrete example in which the reader can follow the methods and alternatives discussed in this chapter. Such an example is given in Figure 22. It illustrates two basic alternatives in thesaurus format, the Roget-Soergel model and the TEST model, using the same set of terms and relationships in each case.

D1 THE DIFFERENT PARTS OF A THESAURUS

D1.0 Introduction

Roget's thesaurus consists of the following parts in the order listed:

(0) Introduction to the thesaurus.
(1) Classified index (schedule).
(2) Main part in classified arrangement.
(3) Alphabetical index.

Notwithstanding the deviation in the arrangement of most other thesauri, notably TEST, Roget has found the most meaningful form, the one most appropriate to the intended use of a thesaurus.

The classified index (schedule) fulfills the function of providing an overview of the classificatory structure, thus giving an opportunity to browse through in order to find the appropriate descriptor.

184 D Thesaurus Format

The function of the main part is to provide detailed information on every term (more precisely, on every preferred term). The function of the alphabetical index is to provide quick access via a term that comes to mind.

However, not everybody agrees with this format, and other possibilities have to be discussed. A number of points have to be considered that are rather intricately related to one another. Furthermore, the problem of thesaurus format is closely intertwined with the lead-in problem discussed in Section C5. A linear presentation of the points is therefore difficult. We shall proceed as follows: First of all, two problems can be isolated and deferred until later sections: Section D2 deals with the problem of how to arrange the items in the entries in the main part, and Section D3 deals with methods of displaying the classificatory structure. The problem of what should go into the introduction of the thesaurus can also be isolated and is dealt with in Section D1.8, enabling us to concentrate on the more complicated and controversial issues in Sections D1.1 to D1.7. We shall first discuss the two models illustrated in Figure 22, namely, the Roget-Soergel model (D1.1) and the TEST model (D1.2). Partly based on these two models the discussion proceeds to a number of specific points, elucidating further advantages and disadvantages of the two models. (D1.3-D1.6). Finally, descriptions of selected thesauri are presented to illustrate further the points made and to introduce further possibilities for the formatting of a thesaurus (D1.7).

The description of a thesaurus should give for each part:

(a) the entries made and how they are arranged;
(b) what information is given in each entry.

This is the scheme that will be followed. At the end of this introduction a remark of caution is in order: the considerations in Chapter D are based on plausible assumptions as to how indexers and searchers should work for optimal performance of the ISAR system and how they are assisted by the thesaurus display. The validity of the conclusions reached would have to be checked in actual performance studies.

D1.1 Thesaurus Format: The Roget-Soergel Model

D1.1.0 Rationale

,1 Classified index required for the checklist technique of indexing and search request formulation. First of all we recall that the indexing language (classification scheme, system vocabulary) contained in the thesaurus has to be viewed as a checklist of topics and aspects against which the documents have to be analyzed. Whenever the question "Should this document be retrieved in searching for this descriptor?" is answered with *yes*, the document is indexed by the descriptor. This is the essence of the checklist tech-

a. Roget-Soergel model

a1: Roget-Soergel model: classified index (displayed with
    level indicator lines on the top and bottom)
1 2 3 4 5 6 7

M20 Electron tubes
   M25   Vacuum tubes ← M73; → PVN Vacuum devices
      M27   X-ray tubes → M60, M90, YDY X-ray apparatus
      M30   Electron beam deflection tubes → M60
         M33   Tuning indicator tubes → M90
         M37   Trochotrons → M93
         M40   Cathode ray tubes /M97
            M42   Image converter tubes → M90, NJ3 TV cameras
               M43   Image intensifiers
            M45   Storage tubes → M90; /M72
            M47   Television camera tubes → M90, NJ3 TV cameras
               M47.5   Black and white TV camera tubes
               M47.7   Color TV camera tubes → NLC Color TV cameras
            M48   Television picture tubes → M97, NVU TV receivers
               M48.5   Black and white TV picture tubes
               M48.7   Color TV picture tubes → NVW Color TV receivers
   M50   Gaseous tubes ← M74, M77
   M60   Thermionic tubes ← M27, M30
   M70   Cold cathode tubes
      M72   Phototubes → KVW Photoelectric devices; /M42, M49
         M73   Vacuum phototubes → M25
         M74   Gaseous phototubes → M50
         M75   Photomultiplier tubes → M85
      M77   Cold cathode glow discharge tubes → M50
      M78   Numerical indicator tubes → M93
   M85   Electron multiplier tubes ← M75
   M90   Electron tubes by application ← M27, M33, M42, M45, M47
      M93   Counting tubes ← M37, M78
      M97   Display tubes ← M48; /M40
1 2 3 4 5 6 7

Figure 22. Example worked out according to the Roget-Soergel model and the TEST model (DO).

```
a2: Roget-Soergel model: main part in classified sequence
1+   M20   Electron tubes                                    5+   M47   Television camera tubes
     UF  ST   Electron valves                                     UF  ST   Pick-up tubes
         RT  —EJ2      Electrons                                          BT  —M90       Electron tubes by application
             —JPL      Electron tube rectifiers                               —NJ3       Television cameras
             —LL/MA    Electron tube oscillators                 UF  NT   *See the following nondescriptor entries
             —LV/MA    Electron tube modulators                      RT  —M72       Phototubes
              LW/MA    Electron tube demodulators
              LX/MA    Electron tube mixers               6     M47.3$   Television camera tubes by construction
              XRM      Electron tube voltmeters                USE BT  —M47       Television camera tubes

2+   M25   Vacuum tubes                                     7    M47.3.23$   Iconoscopes
         BT  —PVN      Vacuum devices                            SF  ST   Storage type camera tubes
         RT   JPX      Thermionic rectifiers                     USE BT  —M47       Television camera tubes
              JPY      Voltage multiplier rectifiers
             —MF       Electron tube components             7—  M47.3.25$   Emitrons
              PVB      Outgassing                               USE BT  —M47       Television camera tubes
             —PVD      Degassing
              QNS      Glass metal seals                   7—  M47.3.27$   Image iconoscopes
                                                               SF  ST   Superemitrons
3+   M27   X-ray tubes                                         USE BT  —M47       Television camera tubes
         BT  —M60      Thermionic tubes
             —M90      Electron tubes by application       7—  M47.3.40$   Orthicons
              YDY      X-ray apparatus                         USE BT  —M47       Television camera tubes
         RT   DT4      X-rays
              NJR      Low light level television          8—  M47.3.45$   Image orthicons
              YDE      X-ray radiography                       SEE BT  :M47.3.40$   Orthicons
             —YDX      X-ray analysis                              and  :M43        Image intensifiers
                                                               USE BT  :—M47       Television camera tubes
3+   M30   Electron beam deflection tubes                        and  :M43        Image intensifiers
     UF  ST   Beam tubes
         BT  —M60      Thermionic tubes                    7—  M47.3.60$   Vidicons
         RT  —EHD      Electron beams                          USE BT  —M47       Television camera tubes
              EHH      Electron beam modulation                RT   DNT        Photoconductivity
              K4K      Beam switches
                                                           8—  M47.3.63$   Infrared vidicons
4+   M33   Tuning indicator tubes                              SEE BT  :M47.3.60$   Vidicons
     UF  ST   Magic eye tubes                                      and  :—DWX      Infrared devices
         BT  —M90      Electron tubes by application           USE BT  :M47        Television camera tubes
         RT   WC8      Tuning                                      and  :—DWX      Infrared devices

4+   M37   Trochotrons                                     9—  M47.3.67$   Thermicons
     UF  ST   Radial beam tubes                                SEE BT  :M47.3.63$   Infrared vidicons
              Additrons                                            and  :M42.5$     Infrared image tubes
              Cyclophones                                      USE BT  :—M47       Television camera tubes
         BT  —M93      Counting tubes                              and  :—DWX      Infrared devices
                                                                   and  :—M42      Image converter tubes
4+   M40   Cathode ray tubes
     UF  ST   CRT                                          7—  M47.3.85$   Dissector tubes
         RT   DUB      Cathodoluminescence                     USE BT  —M47       Television camera tubes
              EHF      Cathode rays
              ENR      Raster                              6+   M47.5    Black and white television camera tubes
              ENW      Scanning circuits
             —M97      Display tubes                       6+   M47.7    Color television camera tubes
              WON      Character generators                    UF  ST   Color television pick-up tubes
             —WOQ      Cathode ray tube displays                   BT  —NLC       Color television cameras
              ...                                              UF  NT   M47.7.5$   Plumbicons

                                                           7—  M47.7.5$   Plumbicons
                                                               USE BT  Color TV camera tubes
```

Figure 22. (continued)

a3: Roget-Soergel model: alphabetical index in KWOC format and giving notations

Additrons	M37		**Radial**	
Beam			Radial beam tubes	M37
Beam tubes	M30		**Ray**	
Electron beam deflection tubes	M30		Cathode ray tubes	M40
Radial beam tubes	M37		X-ray tubes	M27
Black			**Storage**	
Black and white television camera tubes	M47.5		Storage type camera tubes	M47.3.23$
Camera			**Superemitrons**	M47.3.27$
Black and white television camera tubes	M47.		**Television**	
Color television camera tubes	M47.7		Black and white television camera tubes	M47.5
Storage type camera tubes	M47.3.23$		Color television camera tubes	M47.7
Television camera tubes	M47		Color television pick-up tubes	M47.7
Television camera tubes by construction	M47.3$		Television camera tubes	M47
Cathode			Television camera tubes by construction	M47.3$
Cathode ray tubes	M40		**Thermicons**	M47.3.67$
Color			**Trochotrons**	M37
Color television camera tubes	M47.7		**Tubes**	
Color television pick-up tubes	M47.7		Beam tubes	M30
Construction			Black and white television camera tubes	M47.5
Television camera tubes by construction	M47.3$		Cathode ray tubes	M40
CRT	M40		Color television camera tubes	M47.7
Cyclophones	M37		Color television pick-up tubes	M47.7
Deflection			Dissector tubes	M47.3.85$
Electron beam deflection tubes	M30		Electron beam deflection tubes	M30
Dissector			Electron tubes	M20
Dissector tubes	M47.3.85$		Magic eye tubes	M33
Electron			Pick-up tubes	M47
Electron beam deflection tubes	M30		Radial beam tubes	M37
Electron tubes	M20		Storage type camera tubes	M47.3.23$
Electron valves	M20		Television camera tubes	M47
Emitrons	M47.3.25$		Television camera tubes by construction	M47.3$
Eye			Tuning indicator tubes	M33
Magic eye tubes	M33		Vacuum tubes	M25
Iconoscopes	M47.3.23$		X-ray tubes	M27
Image iconoscopes	M47.3.27$		**Tuning**	
Image			Tuning indicator tubes	M33
Image iconoscopes	M47.3.27$		**Type**	
Image orthicons	M47.3.45$		Storage type camera tubes	M47.3.23$
Indicator			**Vacuum**	
Tuning indicator tubes	M33		Vacuum tubes	M25
Infrared			**Valves**	
Infrared vidicons	M47.3.63$		Electron valves	M20
Magic			**Vidicons**	M47.3.60$
Magic eye tubes	M33		Infrared vidicons	M47.3.63$
Orthicons	M47.3.40$		**White**	
Image orthicons	M47.3.45$		Black and white television camera tubes	M47.5
Pick-up			**X-ray**	
Color television pick-up tubes	M47.7		X-ray tubes	M27
Pick-up tubes	M47			
Plumbicons	M47.7.5$			

Figure 22. (continued)

b: TEST model
b1: TEST model: thesaurus of terms (main part)

Additrons
  USE   Trochotrons

Beam tubes
  USE   Electron beam deflection tubes

Black and white television camera tubes
  BT   Cathode ray tubes
          Communication systems
          Electron beam deflection tubes
          Electron tubes
          Electron tubes by application
          Television
          Television apparatus
          Television camera tubes
          Television cameras
          Thermionic tubes
          Vacuum devices
          Vacuum engineering
          Vacuum tubes

Cathode ray tubes
  UF   CRT
  BT   Electron beam deflection tubes
          Electron tubes
          Thermionic tubes
          Vacuum devices
          Vacuum engineering
          Vacuum tubes
  NT   —Image converter tubes
          Storage tubes
          —Television camera tubes
          —Television picture tubes
  RT   —Cathode ray tube displays
          Cathode rays
          Cathodoluminescence
          Character generators
          Display tubes
          Rasters
          Scanning circuits

Color television camera tubes
  UF   Color television pick-up tubes
          Plumbicons
  BT   Cathode ray tubes
          Color television
          Color television apparatus
          Color television cameras
          Communication systems
          Electron beam deflection tubes
          Electron tubes
          Electron tubes by application
          Television
          Television apparatus
          Television camera tubes
          Television cameras
          Thermionic tubes
          Vacuum devices
          Vacuum engineering
          Vacuum tubes

Color television pick-up tubes
  USE   Color television camera tubes

CRT
  USE   Cathode ray tubes

Cyclophones
  USE   Trochotrons

Dissector tubes
  USE   Television camera tubes

Electron beam deflection tubes
  UF   Beam tubes
  BT   Electron tubes
          Thermionic tubes
          Vacuum devices
          Vacuum engineering
          Vacuum tubes
  NT   —Cathode ray tubes
          Trochotrons
          Tuning indicator tubes
  RT   Beam switches
          Electron beam modulation
          Electron beams

Electron tubes
  UF   Electron valves
  NT   —Cold cathode tubes
          —Electron multiplier tubes
          —Electron tubes by application
          —Gaseous tubes
          —Thermionic tubes
          —Vacuum tubes
  RT   Electrons
          Electron tube demodulators
          Electron tube mixers
          Electron tube modulators
          Electron tube oscillators
          Electron tube rectifiers
          Electron tube voltmeters

Electron valves
  USE   Electron tubes

Emitrons
  USE   Television camera tubes

Iconoscopes
  USE   Television camera tubes

Image iconoscopes
  USE   Television camera tubes

Image orthicons
  USE   Television camera tubes
  and   Image intensifiers

Infrared vidicons
  USE   Television camera tubes
  and   Infrared devices

Magic eye tubes
  USE   Tuning indicator tubes

Orthicons
  USE   Television camera tubes

Pick-up tubes
  USE   Television camera tubes

Plumbicons
  USE   Color television camera tubes

Radial beam tubes
  USE   Trochotrons

Storage type camera tubes
  USE   Television camera tubes

Superemitrons
  USE   Television camera tubes

Television camera tubes
  UF   Camera tubes
          Dissector tubes
          Emitrons
          Iconoscopes
          Image iconoscopes
          †Image orthicons
          †Infrared vidicons
          Orthicons
          Storage type camera tubes
          Superemitrons
          Television camera tubes by construction
          Television pictures tubes
          †Thermicons
          Vidicons
  BT   Cathode ray tubes
          Communication systems
          Electron beam deflection
          Electron tubes
          Electron tubes by applica
          Television
          Television apparatus
          Television cameras
          Thermionic tubes
          Vacuum devices
          Vacuum engineering
          Vacuum tubes
  NT   Black and white television
          Color television camera t
  RT   —Phototubes

Television camera tubes by construc
  USE   Television camera tubes

Thermicons
  USE   Television camera tubes
  and   Infrared devices
  and   Image converter tubes

Trochotrons
  UF   Additrons
          Cyclophones
          Radial beam tubes
  BT   Counting tubes
          Electron beam deflection
          Electron tubes
          Electron tubes by applica
          Thermionic tubes
          Vacuum devices
          Vacuum engineering
          Vacuum tubes

Tuning indicator tubes
  UF   Magic eye tubes
  BT   Electron beam deflection
          Electron tubes
          Electron tubes by applicat
          Thermionic tubes
          Vacuum devices
          Vacuum engineering
          Vacuum tubes
  RT   Tuning

Vacuum tubes
  BT   Electron tubes
          Vacuum devices
          Vacuum engineering
  NT   —Electron beam deflection t
          Vacuum phototubes
          X-ray tubes
  RT   Degassing
          Electron tube components
          Glass metal seals
          Outgassing
          Thermionic rectifiers
          Voltage multiplier rectifiers

Vidicons
  USE   Television camera tubes
  RT   Photoconductivity

X-ray tubes
  BT   Electron tubes
          Electron tubes by applicat
          Thermionic tubes
          X-ray analysis
          X-ray apparatus
  RT   Low light level television
          X-ray radiography
          X-rays

Figure 22. (continued)

b2: TEST model: alphabetical index in KWOC format

- *Additrons*

Beam
- Beam tubes
- Electron beam deflection tubes
- Radial beam tubes

Black
- Black and white television camera tubes

Camera
- Black and white television camera tubes
- Color television camera tubes
- Storage type camera tubes
- Television camera tubes
- Television camera tubes by construction

Cathode
- Cathode ray tubes

Color
- Color television camera tubes
- Color television pick-up tubes

Construction
- Television camera tubes by construction

- *CRT*
- *Cyclophones*

Deflection
- Electron beam deflection tubes

Dissector
- Dissector tubes

Electron
- Electron beam deflection tubes
- Electron tubes
- Electron valves

- *Emitrons*

Eye
- Magic eye tubes

- *Iconoscopes*
- Image iconoscopes

Image
- Image iconoscopes
- Image orthicons

Indicator
- Tuning indicator tubes

Infrared
- Infrared vidicons

Magic
- Magic eye tubes

- *Orthicons*
- Image orthicons

Pick-up
- Color television pick-up tubes
- Pick-up tubes

- *Plumbicons*

Radial
- Radial beam tubes

Ray
- Cathode ray tubes
- X-ray tubes

Storage
- Storage type camera tubes

- *Superemitrons*

Television
- Black and white television camera tubes
- Color television camera tubes
- Color television pick-up tubes
- Television camera tubes
- Television camera tubes by construction

- *Thermicons*
- *Trochotrons*

Tubes
- Beam tubes
- Black and white television camera tubes
- Cathode ray tubes
- Color television camera tubes
- Color television pick-up tubes
- Dissector tubes
- Electron beam deflection tubes
- Electron tubes
- Magic eye tubes
- Pick-up tubes
- Radial beam tubes
- Storage type camera tubes
- Televsion camera tubes
- Television camera tubes by construction
- Tuning indicator tubes
- Vacuum tubes
- X-ray tubes

Tuning
- Tuning indicator tubes

Type
- Storage type camera tubes

Vacuum
- Vacuum tubes

Valves
- Electron valves

- *Vidicons*
- Infrared vidicons

White
- Black and white television camera tubes

X-ray
- X-ray tubes

Figure 22. (continued)

b3: TEST model: subject category index (coarse hierarchy)

0900
Electronics and Electrical Engineering

0901
Components
Adding circuits
Air blast circuit breakers
Air circuit breakers
Air gaps
Anodes
Antitransmit receive tubes
Armatures
Armored cables
Astable multivibrators
Audiofrequency oscillators
Automatic frequency control
Automatic gain control
Avalanche diodes
Backward wave oscillators
Backward wave tubes
Ballasts (electric)
Bandpass filters
Bandstop filters
Beam power tubes
Blocking oscillators
Bundled conductors
Bus conductors
Cable insulation
Camera tubes
Capacitors
Carbon brushes
Carbon electrodes
Carbon fuel cell electrodes
Carbon resistors
Carcinotrons
Cathode followers
Cathode ray tubes
Cathodes
Cavity resonators
Ceramic capacitors
Ceramic vacuum tubes
Cesium electron tubes
Channel selectors
Circuit breakers
Circuit interconnections
Circuit protection
Circuits
Clamping circuits
Clipper circuits
Coated electrodes
Coaxial cables
Coaxial filters
Coincidence circuits
Cold cathode tubes
Communication cables
Commutators
Comparator circuits
Condenser tubes
Control circuits
Correlators
Counting circuits
Coupling circuits
Crossbar switches
Crossed field devices

Cryotrons
Crystal detectors
Crystal filters
Crystal holders
Crystal mixers
Crystal oscillators
Crystal ovens
Crystal rectifiers
Dark trace tubes
Deflection coils
Delay circuits
Differentiating circuits
Differentiators
Digital filters
Diodes
Directional couplers
Discriminators
Dispenser cathodes
Drift transistors
Dynatrons
Dynodes
Electrical insulating papers
Electrical insulation
Electrical insulators
Electrical tapes
Electric coils
Electric conductors
Electric connectors
Electric contacts
Electric cutouts
Electric filters
Electric fittings
Electric fuses
Electric outlets
Electric raceways
Electric relays
Electric switches
Electric terminals
Electric wire
Electroacoustic transducers
Electrodes
Electrolytic capacitors
Electromagnetic wave filters
Electron emitters
Electron guns
Electronic commutators
Electronic packaging
Electron tube heaters
Electron tubes
Equivalent circuits
Feedback circuits
Field effect transistors
Film resistors
Fire control circuits
Fixed capacitors
Fixed resistors
Flip flops
Frequency discriminators
Gas discharge tubes
Gates (circuits)
Germanium diodes
Getters
Glass capacitors
Glass resistors
Gunn diodes
Gyrators
Harmonic generators
High pass filters
Hydrogen electrodes
Iconoscopes
Ignitrons
Image converters

Image orthicons
Image tubes
Inert anodes
Infrared image tubes
Infrared thermistors
Infrared vidicons
Insulated conductors
Insulated wire
Integrated circuits
Interrupters
Inverter circuits
Ion guns
Junction boxes
Junction diodes
Junction transistors
Klystrons
Ladder networks
Limiter circuits
Limit switches
Logic circuits
Low pass filters
Magnetic amplifiers
Magnetic circuits
Magnetrons
Matched filters
Matrices (circuits)
Mechanical filters
Mesa devices
Metal oxide transistors
Mica capacitors

0902
Computers
Accumulators (computers)
Airborne computers
ALGOL
Analog computers
Analog to digital converters
Aperture cards
Arithmetic and logic units
Assembler routines
Assembly languages
Associative storage
Asynchronous computers
Autocoders
Auxiliary equipment (computers)
BASIC (programming language)
Binary processors
Bombing computers
Buffer storage
Calculators
Card punches (data processing)
Card readers (data processing)
Card reproducers
Card sorters
Card to tape converters
Central processing units
Character generators
Character processors
Character recognition devices
COBOL
COGO
Collators
Compilers
Computer components
Computer driven punches
Computerized simulation
Computer logic
Computer programming
Computer programs
Computers
Computer storage devices

(Figure 22b3 Courtesy Engineers Joint Council, New York, N.Y.)

```
b4: TEST model: hierarchical index
Electron tubes
  · Cold cathode tubes                         ·  · Electron beam deflection tubes
  ·  · Cold cathode glow discharge tubes       ·  ·  · Cathode ray tubes
  ·  ·  · Numerical indicator tubes            ·  ·  ·  · Image converter tubes
  ·  · Phototubes                              ·  ·  ·  ·  · Image intensifiers
  ·  ·  · Gaseous phototubes                   ·  ·  ·  · Storage tubes
  ·  ·  · Photomultiplier tubes                ·  ·  ·  · Television camera tubes
  ·  ·  · Vacuum phototubes                    ·  ·  ·  ·  · Black and white television camera tubes
  · Electron multiplier tubes                  ·  ·  ·  ·  · Color television camera tubes
  ·  · Photomultiplier tubes                   ·  ·  ·  · Television picture tubes
  · Electron tubes by application              ·  ·  ·  ·  · Black and white television picture tubes
  ·  · Counting tubes                          ·  ·  ·  ·  · Color television picture tubes
  ·  ·  · Numerical indicator tubes            ·  ·  · Trochotrons
  ·  ·  · Trochotrons                          ·  ·  · Tuning indicator tubes
  ·  · Display tubes                           ·  ·  · X-ray tubes
  ·  ·  · Television picture tubes             · Vacuum tubes
  ·  ·  ·  · Black and white television picture tubes   ·  · Electron beam deflection tubes
  ·  ·  ·  · Color television picture tubes    ·  ·  · Cathode ray tubes
  ·  · Image converter tubes                   ·  ·  ·  · Image converter tubes
  ·  ·  · Image intensifiers                   ·  ·  ·  ·  · Image intensifiers
  ·  · Storage tubes                           ·  ·  !  · Storage tubes
  ·  · Television camera tubes                 ·  ·  ·  · Television camera tubes
  ·  ·  · Black and white television camera tubes   ·  ·  ·  ·  · Black and white television camera tubes
  ·  ·  · Color television camera tubes        ·  ·  ·  ·  · Color television camera tubes
  ·  · Tuning indicator tubes                  ·  ·  ·  · Television picture tubes
  ·  · X-ray tubes                             ·  ·  ·  ·  · Black and white television picture tubes
  · Gaseous tubes                              ·  ·  ·  ·  · Color television picture tubes
  ·  · Cold cathode glow discharge tubes       ·  ·  · Trochotrons
  ·  ·  · Numerical indicator tubes            ·  ·  · Tuning indicator tubes
  ·  · Gaseous phototubes                      ·  · X-ray tubes
  · Thermionic tubes
```

Figure 22. (continued)

Remarks on the example

The main consideration in the design of the example was to illustrate the two lead-in methods (alphabetical index versus main part) and the two lead-in forms (detailed versus crude). This leads to a high percentage of lead-in terms (preferred terms not used as descriptors, as well as synonyms), and the difference in size of the main part in the Roget-Soergel model and in th TEST model is thereby exaggerated.

If in the TEST model narrower terms are listed all the way down in the main part, 39 more lines would be needed. In a real situation the effect would be much worse because one would have a higher percentage of descriptors that are further down in the hierarchy.

nique of indexing. The same use of the thesaurus is made in search request formulation, where the user can clarify in his own mind what it is he needs by browsing through the indexing language. As Section B5.2 has shown earlier, a classified arrangement of the descriptors is mandatory for the practical implementation of the checklist technique. Moreover, those descriptors that are particularly important in the checklist technique or, for short, the *checklist descriptors* should be displayed in such a way that they can be surveyed in a glance, their relationships becoming clear immediately. This will ensure that the indexer will consider the important descriptors while indexing a document.

,2 A descriptor should always be seen in its place in the overall structure before it is used in indexing and searching. In selecting a descriptor for indexing a document or in formulating a search request, the indexer or searcher must be aware of the broader, narrower, and related descriptors (or, in other words, of the place of the descriptor in the structure of the indexing language). This is true for descriptors assigned through the checklist technique of indexing as well as for additional descriptors suggested by the document. Descriptors used in indexing and search request formulation should, therefore, never be selected using an alphabetical index alone. In many cases one should consult the definitions of several descriptors in one section of the hierarchy in order to decide which descriptor to use. These purposes are best achieved through a classified arrangement.

Further elaboration: Librarians and other information workers often have the preconception that a classified arrangement is too complicated for the users. This conception sometimes persists even in the face of practical experience to the contrary. For example, one author argues against structuring on the grounds that "Simplicity is (necessary, D.S.) for certain classes of users (e.g., non-librarians)", therefore: "For retrieval, a relatively unstructured IRL (information retrieval language) is given to the users who are doctors, engineers, etc., quite unused to the indexing subtleties which are the stuff of life to librarians and information officers. The main terms, about three hundred, are simply listed in alphabetical order. The trigraph terms, with their three letter codes, are in a separate section, in facet clumps. Users have to scan the entire list until they locate descriptors which might express the concepts they wish to search for." The user reaction to this concept is reported as follows: ". . ., but users have complained about having to scan the entire list of main headings for the terms they want. They have also shown dislike of having to look in two different places (main terms and trigraph terms) for their descriptors. This has given rise to our most recent development of combining the two sections, and putting them all into facet groups."

But even though the users did not like the alleged simplicity because it was not functional, the same author goes on to say: "This has had to be balanced by the need to keep our published IRL, and the guide to its use, as simple as possible for our 'lay' users."

,3 **Not too much information should be given in the alphabetical index.** We have seen that the indexer or searcher weighing the use of a descriptor should always look in a classified listing to get the structural context of that descriptor. It follows that an alphabetical listing should not contain information about the terms listed but should refer to a classified listing. Otherwise the indexer or searcher is tempted to rely solely on the alphabetic listing. This practice leads to poor results in indexing and search request formulation (A classic example is the following: A document on "speedy decision-making in the battlefield" was indexed by the UDC number for (mathematical) decision theory, a branch of format logic!). Additional considerations have to be weighed in deciding whether to arrange a subject catalog in alphabetical or in classified sequence. A short note must suffice here: many reasons speak for classified sequence and many of the advantages mentioned for alphabetical sequence are fallacious.

,4 **Roget-Soergel model appropriate for systems using notation.** The Roget-Soergel model is designed mainly for a system where the indexer records notations that later on may be supplemented by the descriptor text, either through a typist or through a machine (type 1 system of Section E0). However, it might also be used in systems where the indexer records the actual text of descriptors in the proper form, as described in Section D1.3.2.

,5 **Parts of the thesaurus.** The parts of the thesaurus in the Roget-Soergel model have been listed above:

(0) Introduction.
(1) Classified index.
(2) Main part in classified arrangement.
(3) Alphabetical index.

For leads from synonyms to preferred terms the alphabetical index method is used. For leads from preferred terms that are not used as descriptors to the appropriate descriptor the main part method, detailed form, is used. It is possible to modify the model by using the simplified lead-in form discussed in Section C5.2.1 or even the crude lead-in form.

D1.1.1 Classified index (the schedule)

,0 **Summary (overview, synopsis) of the main subject fields.** This summary should include the first and second levels of the hierarchy. Corresponding page numbers to the main part can be indicated.

The summary may be omitted if the main subject fields can be easily recognized in the display of the checklist descriptors to be discussed next.

,1 **Display of the checklist descriptors and the important relationships** among them. (This part is an extract from the classified index to be discussed next.) Since the checklist descriptors are usually the more heavily used descriptors it might be useful to print them on the document analysis sheet. The indexer then just encircles the relevant descriptors or their notation. This procedure enhances both speed and consistency of indexing. Often only the most frequently used descriptors are printed on the sheet, and other descriptors have to be written in as needed. A similar technique is very useful for search request forms.

,2 **Classified index.** This is a display of all descriptors and possibly some or all other preferred terms in classified order. It is a classified index to the main part of the thesaurus. A monohierarchy is shown by classified order with indention, and the most important additional relationships between the concepts are shown in abbreviated form. If preferred terms that are not descriptors are included they must be clearly marked as such, e.g., by the typefont used or by their notation. If the number of descriptors contained in the indexing language is restricted, the display of checklist descriptors and the display of all descriptors may be the same.

,3 **Note on ,1 and ,2.** Both parts should be arranged in such a way that they provide for easy overview; it should be possible to survey the display of checklist descriptors in one glance (double letter-size format or European format DIN A3). Therefore, only the most important cross-references can be indicated. Graphical symbols should be used to indicate the kind of relationship (symbols suggested for this purpose are given in Figure 21, Section C7). Only the notational symbols for the descriptors or preferred terms referred to need be given. (In both displays, look-up of descriptors and other preferred terms by notation is fast, so that this is not a serious disadvantage).

Other signs that should be used are:

* Especially important aspect to be considered in indexing.
! Used with a specific meaning; look up scope note.

Section D3 contains detailed considerations on the format in which such displays can be set up. In some cases it might be useful to prepare both a printed display (linear arrangement with indentions) and a graphical display because different users may have different preferences.

D1.1.2 Main part of the thesaurus

(a) *Entries and arrangement of entries*
(a1) An entry is made for every preferred term, whether it is a descriptor or not.
(a2) Entries are arranged in classified sequence.

The arrangement of the main part in classified sequence follows the rationale given above (Section D1.1.0). A specific point may be added: It is often ad-

D1 The Different Parts of a Thesaurus   195

vantageous to compare the scope notes for several related descriptors (e.g., descriptors that are included in a common broader descriptor). In this case it is convenient to have all these scope notes at one place. In delineating related descriptors it is often useful to write *one* scope note for several descriptors, list it with one of them, and refer from the others. Again, all these descriptors ought to be together in the main part.

(a3) Indentions are not used. (This saves space.) If the Main Term is a descriptor it is printed in boldface. The entry for a descriptor is often followed by entries for lead-in terms that are narrower; these lead-in terms are printed in italics; they are preferred terms designating a more specific concept. In field UF NT of the descriptor the following note should be made: "See the following non-descriptor entries". Through this procedure one can avoid listing in field UF NT many terms that can be seen easily because they follow in the classified arrangement.

(a4) The hierarchical level is shown by a number on the left margin for both descriptors and lead-in terms. The number is followed by '+' for descriptors and by '—' for lead-in terms.

(b) *Information given for each entry*. All the data elements listed in Figure 21, Section C7, should be given unless they are of interest for the working file only. For details see Section D2. Only those Broader and Narrower Terms are given that cannot be seen from the classified arrangement, and only one level up or down.

D1.1.3 Alphabetical index

In the discussion of the rationale for the Roget-Soergel model a major argument was that the indexer or searcher should use mainly the classified index (schedule) for identifying all relevant descriptors and get supplementary information from the main part as necessary. Even so, the necessity for an alphabetical index to the classified arrangement is obvious.

(a) *Entries*. One or more entries are made for every term, whether it is a preferred term or not, and for every spelling variant (except spelling variants that are internal to the system only, as discussed in Section C6.2). In the case of multiword terms an entry is made under every significant word. The KWIC or KWOC format is used (for details see Section D1.5).

(b) *Information given in each entry*. Only the notation is given. The notation will lead the user to the appropriate location in the main part, where he will then find out whether the term is a descriptor, a synonym to a descriptor, or a preferred term but not a descriptor—and, in the latter case, which descriptor(s) to use. In addition he will find further information he should consider before using the descriptor for indexing. The notation will also lead the user into the classified index, where he can get a good view of the place of the term in the overall structure. Since the alphabetical index gives the notation only, it serves only as a lead to the main part or to the schedules, and the indexer has to look up the term there. This fact is by no means a disadvantage; on the contrary, it is desirable.

As has been explained earlier an indexer or searcher who intends to use a term should consult the main part or at least the classified index (schedule); he should not rely solely on the little amount of information that could be given in the alphabetical index.

D1.2 Thesaurus Format: The TEST Model

D1.2.0 Parts of TEST

TEST consists of the following parts in the order listed (the numbers refer to our recommended order given in Section D1.0):

- (0) Introduction.
- (2) Thesaurus of Terms (main part).
- (3) Permuted index (alphabetical index).
- (1) Classified indexes.
- (1.1) Subject category index.
- (1.2) Hierarchical index.

This model may be summarized as follows: the main part is arranged alphabetically; the main part method for lead-in is used in the crude form. Therefore, there are no preferred terms that are not descriptors. (The detailed form could be used within the basic setup of TEST.) The classified listings are, in a way, added afterwards; they are not essential to the model.

D1.2.1 Classified indexes in TEST

,1 Subject category index. Presents a 3-level coarse hierarchy: 22 subject fields (subject categories), subdivided into an average of 8 subject groups each. The subject fields, the groups within a subject field, and the descriptors within a group are arranged in alphabetical order. Groups have a four-digit notation, and in the main part the notation(s) of the appropriate group(s) are given for each descriptor.

Since each group still contains a large number of descriptors, this list is not of much use in day-to-day indexing and search request formulation. It is useful as a source for the construction of specialized thesauri where the whole vocabulary presented in TEST would be too big.

,2 Hierarchical index. This is a classified index with some peculiarities: It contains 700 "descriptor families", each headed by a main entry (the "head" of the family) and consisting of all descriptors narrower than the main entry term. Only descriptors that, in the *Thesaurus of Terms,* have no Broader Terms and two or more levels of Narrower Terms were selected as main entries. All descriptors that do not have Broader Terms and that have only one level of Narrower Terms are omitted. (The reason is that the display of the corresponding "descriptor family" in the hierarchical index would merely repeat the list given under NT for the term in the *Thesaurus of*

D1 The Different Parts of a Thesaurus 197

Terms.) All descriptors that have none of the main entry terms as Broader Term are excluded. The main entries are arranged alphabetically. Within a descriptor family descriptors are arranged according to the hierarchical structure, but on each level they are arranged alphabetically. No notation is given.

It is not difficult to see that this hierarchical index is not at all suitable for the checklist technique. Its only use, therefore, is to locate a given descriptor in its hierarchical context. However, due to the fact that there is no notation it is rather cumbersome to look up a known descriptor in the hierarchical index.

D1.2.2 Thesaurus of terms (main part)

(a) *Entries and arrangement of entries.* An entry is made for every term, including spelling variants (as far as they are considered at all) but excluding inverted forms. The entries are arranged in alphabetical order.

(b) *Information given for each entry.*

(b1) *For lead-in terms:* A USE instruction giving the descriptor to be used.

(b2) *For descriptors:* UF, BT, NT, RT; in some cases a scope note is given. In giving Broader and Narrower Terms, all hierarchical chains are considered, all the way up and one level down. For details see D2.

D1.2.3 Alphabetical index

One might think that an alphabetical index is unnecessary in the TEST model since the main part is arranged in alphabetical order. However, an alphabetical index is needed in spite of this for two reasons:

(1) Multi-word terms appear in the main part only once, namely under the first word.

(2) The main part contains only a limited number of entries per page; looking for a certain term in the main part requires, therefore, a lot of page turning.

The alphabetical index is organized as follows: An entry is made for every term under every significant word. The KWOC format is used. The proper form of the term can be seen from its listing in the KWOC index. The only other information given is whether the term is a descriptor or not; this is shown by a centered dot before lead-in terms (i.e., nondescriptors). Once a term has been found in the alphabetical index the established form has to be looked up at its place in the alphabet in the main part. This is mandatory for lead-in terms since the reference to the appropriate descriptor is to be found only in the main part. It is recommended for descriptors, too, in order to interpret the descriptor in the context of the additional information given in the main part. In this model spelling variants have to appear in the main part so that the appropriate USE instruction can be given. The inverse UF statement could be omitted for spelling variants, but this is not done in TEST.

D1.3 The Look-up Problem and How to Arrange the Entries in the Main Part

D1.3.1 Where the look-up problem occurs

First, with proper procedures for indexing and search request formulation (namely, the checklist technique) the indexer or searcher looks most often through the classified index (the schedule) first. If he needs more information on a certain descriptor in order to decide whether it should be used for indexing or searching, he then turns to the main part. In this case he has the notation already available; consequently, his look-up is much faster if the main part is arranged in classified order.

Second, the indexer or searcher should look up Broader, Narrower, and Related Terms given for a descriptor. (In the Roget-Soergel model BT's and NT's exclude those that can be seen from the classified arrangement, thereby drastically reducing the number of terms to be looked up separately). Again, if a notation is given this look-up will be much faster in a classified arrangement than look-up using the actual text in an alphabetical arrangement. Often it will not be necessary to go beyond the classified index.

The third look-up problem occurs when an indexer or searcher has a certain term in mind and wants to find the appropriate descriptors. In indexing techniques actually used, as distinct from the method that we recommend, this is the most common problem. It will be dealt with in the next section.

D1.3.2 Finding the appropriate descriptor for a term that comes to mind

In the following discussion it is assumed that a conscientious indexer or searcher will always look up a descriptor in the main part or at least in the classified index before using it. It is easy to see the modification to be made in the flowcharts (Figure 23 and Figure 24) for the case in which the indexing is not done in such a conscientious manner.

The discussion analyzes the four cases illustrated by the following example; the descriptor is in each case *Tuning indicator tubes,* which has the synonym *Magic eye tubes* serving as lead-in term.

Example:

Case	Indexer or searcher has in mind	Proper form of term is
Case 1:	Tuning indicator tubes	same
Case 2:	Magic eye tubes	same
Case 3:	Indicator tubes	Tuning indicator tubes
Case 4:	Eye tubes	Magic eye tubes

The procedure can be followed in the worked-out example given in Figure 22 (Section D0).

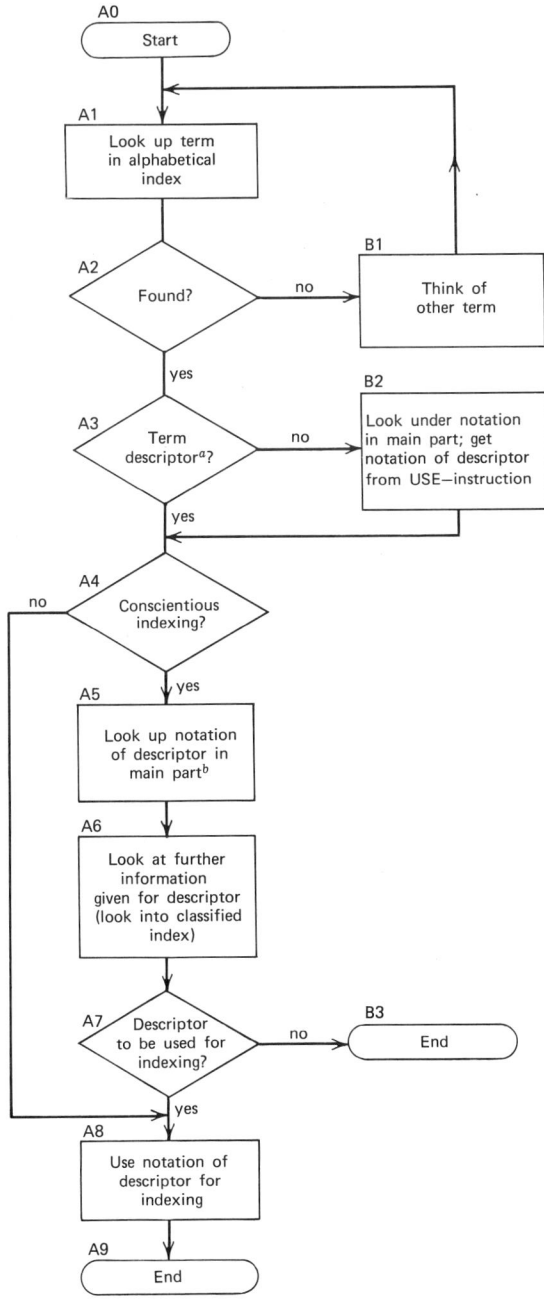

Figure 23. Look-up in the Roget-Soergel model (D1.3.2). (*a*) More precisely: is the notation given the notation of a descriptor? If conscientious indexing is used this decision box can be omitted since one looks into the main part anyway. (*b*) Note that in the main part the descriptor is usually within the range of a page or so from the lead-in term. Therefore, very little effort is needed for this look-up when coming from B2.

200 D Thesaurus Format

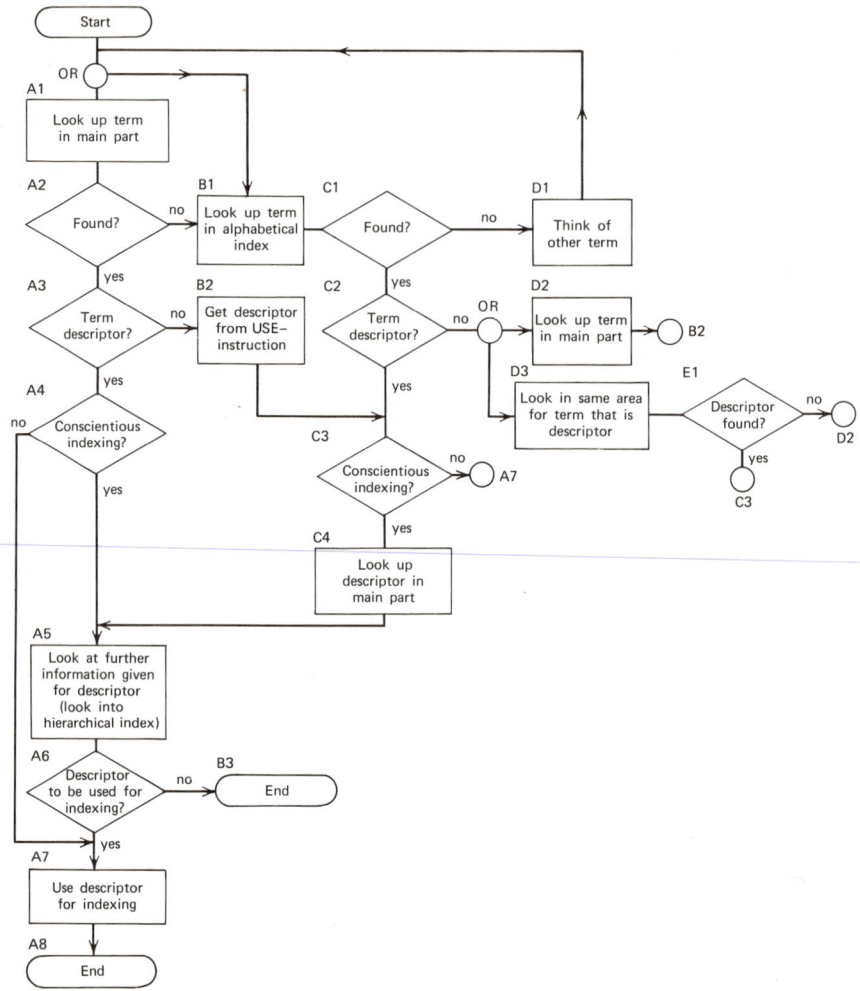

Figure 24. Look-up in the TEST Model (D1.3.2).

(1) *Look up in the Roget-Soergel model* (Figure 23).

All cases: look up term in the alphabetical index. Find the notation M33. Go to the main part and find the descriptor M33 *Tuning indicator tubes* with all the information on that descriptor. Go to the classified index and find the hierarchical environment. Note that a sloppy indexer could make do with one step in this case—simply using M33 (the notation of a descriptor) in indexing without bothering to examine the descriptor first.

(2) *Look up in the TEST model* (Figure 24)

In the Roget-Soergel model one always needs two steps, alphabetical index and

D1 The Different Parts of a Thesaurus 201

main part (unless sloppy procedures are used). The proponents of the TEST model argue that the alphabetical arrangement in the main part provides "direct" access without the detour through an alphabetical index. Let us examine this argument, considering the different cases:

Case 1: Look up *Tuning indicator tubes* in the main part; find all information. One step needed; the argument is valid.

Case 2: Look up *Magic eye tubes* in the main part; find USE instruction to *Tuning indicator tubes;* look this up. Two steps needed.

Case 3: Look up *Indicator tubes* in the main part; make sure it is not there (this takes longer than to find a term that is there!). Look up *Indicator tubes* in the alphabetical (KWOC) index; find the proper form *Tuning indicator tubes.* Look that up in the main part; and there find out that it is a descriptor. Three steps needed.

Case 4: Same as Case 3 starting with *Eye tubes* except that having found *Magic eye tubes* in the main part, one has to follow the USE instruction from there. Four steps needed. Often, however, Case 4 can be reduced to Case 3 by intelligent searching.

Example:
Starting term Cleaning by electrolytic means. Look into alphabetical index, find Electrolytic cleaning, but it is not descriptor. Look around a little bit and find Electrochemical cleaning, which is a descriptor (Non-descriptors are marked in the alphabetical index!)

In addition in many Case-4 instances the descriptor will not be far away from the lead-in term in the alphabetical sequence in the main part, e.g., *Numerical methods* USE *Numerical analysis.*

If the detailed lead-in form is used in the Roget-Soergel model (as in the example in Figure 22, Section D0) things get slightly more complicated.

Example:
Look in the alphabetical index under Mask tubes. Find the term Shadow mask tubes with the notation M48.7.2$. Go to the main part. There find
    M48.7.2$ Shadow mask tubes
        USE BT M48.7 Color TV picture tubes.
Look up this descriptor. Since the descriptor to be used will be very near, this is actually not a third look-up.

In comparing the two models, one should have in mind two points:

(a) Look-up in the alphabetical index is faster than in the alphabetical main part because the alphabetical index has a much higher "term density" per page.

(b) Look-up by notation is much faster than look-up by term in an alphabetical sequence provided the notation is constructed properly.

This analysis shows that the one-step argument is valid for Case 1 only, and even there weakened by point (a), longer look-up time in the main part. In Cases 2–4, look-up in the TEST model takes longer than in the Roget-Soergel model. An evaluation to determine which of the two models is better for the third look-up problem has to be based, therefore, on an estimate of the relative frequency of the different cases. An overall evaluation will have to take into account all three look-up problems discussed in D1.3.1. Finally, one has to take into account the habits of the people who use the thesaurus and whether it would be worthwhile or possible to educate the thesaurus users to use the method that has been proved to be better if that method is different from the one they are accustomed to.

D1.3.3 Variations of the TEST model

,1 Inclusion of spelling variants in the main part. One could include in the main part *all* forms of each term (bringing components to the front by inversion), thus doing away with the alphabetical index and simplifying the flowchart given in Figure 24. However, this would make the main part rather unwieldly and distract from its main function of providing detailed information on preferred terms.

,2 Always look in the alphabetical index first. One could *always* start by looking into the alphabetical index, thus skipping step 1. But why, then, arrange the main part alphabetically? It would only avoid the use of a notation, which is not a useful purpose, as will be shown below. Incidentally, if one uses this procedure one could eliminate all nonpreferred terms from the main part and indicate in each entry in the alphabetical index the appropriate preferred term. This would then approach the Roget-Soergel model except that the text of the preferred terms would be used instead of notation and the main part would be arranged alphabetically. However, this would not be a very sensible procedure.

D1.3.4 Necessity of notation

The elegance of the Roget-Soergel model rests on the use of notation. For those who are afraid of the introduction of a notation it may be added that a notation is needed anyway if one accepts our earlier reasoning demonstrating the importance of a classified schedule in indexing. The problem of how to construct a flexible notation that can be expanded to accommodate new descriptors is dealt with in Section D4.

D1.4 What Broader and Narrower Terms Should Be Listed in the Fields BT or NT, Respectively?

This is an important point in thesaurus display. It properly belongs to D2, where the information to be given in the entries in the main part is discussed.

D1 The Different Parts of a Thesaurus

But it is so closely intertwined with thesaurus format as a whole that it is dealt with here, recognizing that some repetition will inevitably result. Refer to Figure 22 (Section D0) for an illustration of some of the alternatives discussed. The following discussion applies to Related Terms, too.

The question is how to express the hierarchical structure within the set of descriptors and preferred terms. There are three main possibilities, namely,

(a) provide a classified index (schedule) with a notation and give additional BT-NT cross-references only (Roget-Soergel model);

(b) express the complete hierarchical structure by BT-NT cross-references, regardless of whether or not there is a classified index (TEST model);

(c) provide a "conceptual index" or auxiliary ISAR system that lists each descriptor under each of its semantic factors, as described in Section D3.6. If it is properly constructed such an index can show more hierarchical relationships than a classified index (schedule).

For the construction of (a) or (b) it is not necessary in principle that the compound concepts be expressed by semantic factors, as long as all hierarchical relationships are known. However, the task becomes much easier if one expresses the compound concepts by semantic factors, since the derivation of hierarchical relationships, the determination of the arrangement, and the introduction of cross-references can then be done much more systematically and can even be automated, as discussed in Sections C1.3 and G3.4.2. A conceptual index, on the other hand, by its very nature requires that compound concepts be decomposed into semantic factors.

From each possibility different requirements for the main part arise, as shown below.

The question of what Broader and Narrower Terms to list has two aspects:

(1) What hierarchical chains should be considered?
(2) How far up or down should one go in each chain?

We shall take up these aspects in sequence.

(1) *What hierarchical chains should be considered?*

(1a) If a classified index (schedule) with a notation is provided, one may disregard those hierarchical chains that can be seen from the linear classified arrangement. Only the "additional" hierarchical chains going up or down need be considered. This rule cuts the size of the main part of the thesaurus considerably. Furthermore, if a good classified index is provided, the number of RT cross-references can be cut substantially; this also reduces the size of the main part, as has been shown in Section C1.5.

The following exception to the above-mentioned rule is recommended: if a broader descriptor forms part of a USE instruction, it should be listed in the field BT, whether or not it can be seen from the linear classified arrangement.

(1b) The other possibility is to express the complete hierarchical structure by BT-NT cross-reference. This possibility must be used if there is no classified schedule at all (as in the first edition of the EJC-Thesaurus) or if the classified schedule is not complete and/or not amenable by a notation (as in TEST). All hierarchical chains going up or down from the term in question must be considered in this case. This course may be followed even if there is an appropriate classified schedule.

(1c) If there are many highly precombined descriptors, the hierarchical structure is so complex that both methods fail. One should provide a classified index of the core descriptors (which are mostly elemental) and a conceptual index (auxiliary ISAR system).

(2) *How many levels should one go up or down?*

In either case (1a) or (1b) one must decide how many levels one should go up for BT and how many levels one should go down for NT in each chain. The following possibilities exist; (2a) is recommended, (2c) seems not useful.

(2a BT) List only the Broader Term immediately above the concept in question (one level up in the chain).

(2a NT) List only the Narrower Term immediately below the concept in question (one level down in the chain).

(2b BT) List all Broader Terms in the chain (all the way up in the chain).

(2b NT) List all Narrower Terms in the chain (all the way down in the chain).

(2c BT) List Broader Terms n levels up (e.g., $n = 3$).

(2c NT) List Narrower Terms m levels down (e.g., $m = 3$).

When going all the way up or all the way down it might be useful to indicate with each BT or NT the number of levels above or below, respectively. Hierarchical chains should be given in correct order upward or downward, respectively, and different hierarchical chains resulting from polyhierarchy should be kept separate. An alternative is to list all BT in alphabetical sequence.

Example:
The hierarchical chain is
Transmission
   Wave propagation
      Electromagnetic wave transmission
         Radio transmission
            Ionospheric propagation
The entry in TEST is
Ionospheric propagation
   BT *Electromagnetic wave transmission*
      Radio transmission
      Transmission
      Wave propagation

This arrangement makes it difficult to enter the classified index at the right place, which would be the broadest term listed. Therefore, this arrangement is not recommended.

Any of the nine BT-NT combinations may be used in a thesaurus. The best solution is to omit hierarchical chains that can be seen from the classified arrangement and to go one level up and one level down. This method saves room, and it has almost no disadvantages as long as the user of the thesaurus has a classified schedule available and is referred to the appropriate place in that schedule by notation, as is the case in the Roget-Soergel model. In the TEST model the user has to do a considerable amount of path-tracing upward or downward if hierarchical chains are given one up or down only (unless he is willing to go to the bother of consulting the hierarchical index). There is a trade-off between user effort and amount of storage space (printed pages, magnetic disk, or other computer storage) needed. This problem is even more serious with Related Term cross-references.

Remark: The first edition of the EJC thesaurus, forerunner of TEST, considers all hierarchical chains and goes all the way up and all the way down. Since this thesaurus does not have a classified index at all this procedure is the only way to assist the indexer in the selection of the proper level of generality, which is a function of the hierarchy. TEST proceeds as EJC except that it goes only one level down. It thereby enables the user to see the place of the term in question in the hierarchy from above; this view is somewhat obscured, however, by the alphabetical arrangement of the terms in the field BT (see the example given above). It is difficult in TEST to find all Narrower Terms since the classified index given in TEST cannot be entered by notation. The easiest way is probably to identify the broadest BT, look it up in the hierarchical index, and search from there for the descriptor in question.

D1.4.1 Inverse cross-references to broad descriptors of general application (advanced)

Concepts of general application, like *Materials,* often have a large number of Narrower Terms, the hierarchical relationships being obvious without using a thesaurus in most cases. (Many of the Narrower Terms are likely to be narrower due to the fact that the concept of general application appears as a semantic factor within them, e.g., *Social stability = Social structure: Stability.*)

There is general agreement that it is useful in these cases to list all the narrower concepts with the very broad concept because this assists the indexers and searchers in finding the appropriate more specific concept, starting from the concept of general application.

There is disagreement with respect to the inverse cross-references from the specific concepts to the concept of general application. TEST argues that these inverse cross-references inflate the thesaurus unnecessarily and prescribes that they be omitted:

"In a few instances, terms will be so broad in meaning that their utility as indexing terms will be doubtful, yet they must be retained for use in disciplines of peripheral interest or merely as a guide to more specific terminology. Under these circumstances, list under the very broad descriptor the terms to which it is desirable to refer the thesaurus user omitting cross-reference designators. Append to the broad descriptor the scope note 'Use of a more specific term is recommended—consult the terms listed below.' For example, the term *Materials* is of little use in indexing documents that deal with materials in any but the most general way, but in a vocabulary in which many specific materials types are represented by indexing terms, the term is a useful point at which to display certain more specific terms or related terms for further study without carrying a useless BROADER TERM reference to materials on each of many specific terms. No reciprocal cross-references should be made from listed specific descriptors to the broad descriptor, although such records should be maintained (in the working file, D.S.) for housekeeping purposes (see Rule C-9)."

However, this rule should not be used for the following reasons. If a classified arrangement is used the concept of general application can often be seen from the arrangement, and in the Roget-Soergel model it would not be listed as BT with the specific concept.

Example:
T20 Materials
. . .
T27 Ceramics
. . .

It is not necessary to say
T27 Ceramics
BT T20 Materials

If no classified arrangement is given, or if the Broader Term cannot be seen from that arrangement, the inverse cross-references should be retained for the following reasons: (1) Often the concept of general application is a semantic factor of the specific concept and should be listed as such (the concept of general application may, in fact, be part of a USE instruction). (2) The alleged savings do not warrant the introduction of a new rule. (3) It might sometimes be useful for the indexer or searcher to go from a specific concept to the concept of general application and look through the list of the specific concepts listed there.

Example:
> The indexer considers the descriptor H85 Social stability, listed under H Society. He finds BT A23 Stability; following this cross-reference he comes to the entry
> A23 Stability
> > NT E17 Stability of the educational system
> > > H85 Social stability
> > > P74 Economic stability
> > > Y27 Religious stability
> > . . .

The document in question is possibly relevant for one of these other descriptors.

If the classified arrangement is subject-oriented (as opposed to facet-oriented), the inverse cross-reference to the concept of general application will often be accomplished by listing it under 41 'Facet'. As discussed in D3.0.1 one might provide an alternate classified index based on the facet principle. The inverse cross-reference would then be accomplished by giving the alternate notation, leading to the appropriate place in the alternate classified index.

D1.4.2 Listing coordinate terms (advanced)

Related to the problem of listing Broader and Narrower Terms is the problem of listing coordinate (collateral) terms. "Coordinate terms" means here (following British terminology) sons of the same father (not to be confused with coordination in the sense of combination). In a thesaurus following the Roget-Soergel model, coordinate terms should not be listed at all. If there is no classified index that can be entered by a notation, it would certainly be useful to list coordinate terms in the field RT, but the resulting size of the thesaurus would be prohibitive. Only the most important coordinate terms should be listed.

D1.5 Alphabetical Index

D1.5.1 General considerations

(Compare Sections D1.1.3 and D1.2.3.)

(a) *Entries.* One or more entries should be made for every term, including spelling variants. For multi-word terms an entry should be made for every significant word. For composite terms significant components should be considered.

Example:
> *Gold-fish*
> *Pre-test*
> *Over-compensation*

If the index is in the KWIC or KWOC format, multi-word terms do not present problems. If it is not KWIC format, suitable forms of the terms have to be created by inversion.

Example:
> *Flexible couplings*
> > *Couplings, flexible*
>
> *Television camera tube*
> > *Camera tube, television*
> > *Tube, television, camera*
>
> *Overcompensation*
> > *Compensation, over-*

In the first example the inverted form is less important if *Couplings* is a descriptor and *Flexible couplings* is a narrower descriptor. (Compare Sections E1.1.3 and E1.1.4 for the treatment of homonyms and artificial homonyms in the alphabetical index.)

(b) *Information given for each entry.* In the TEST model one can see the proper form of the term under which to look in the main part. In the Roget-Soergel model the notation is given. It might also be useful to indicate whether or not the term is:
—a descriptor;
—synonymous to a descriptor;
—a preferred term not used as a descriptor;
—a synonym of such a term.

(According to D4.3.6 preferred terms that are not descriptors have a notation that contains either : or $ and can be recognized thereby. Moreover, one might arrange that, whenever a term is a nonpreferred synonym, a spelling variant, or a translation, the notation given in the alphabetical index will be followed by $ST or $RT, respectively.) No additional information should be given. Otherwise, the indexer or searcher may be tempted not to look into the main part or into the classified index; this procedure may result in ill-considered and wrong use of descriptors in indexing or searching (see Section D1.1.0,2).

If one does not agree with this philosophy, one may introduce additional information in the alphabetical index, namely USE instructions giving the appropriate descriptor(s) to be used and SEE instructions giving the text of the appropriate preferred term if that preferred term is not a descriptor. In addition to the dangers just mentioned look-up will be slower due to the increase in size of the alphabetical index. (It is not useful to give page numbers referring to the main part of the thesaurus. The notation is sufficient for locating a term in the main part; if the main part is properly ar-

D1 The Different Parts of a Thesaurus 209

ranged, look-up by notation is as fast as look-up by page number. The page numbers are more likely to change than the notations, and they have to be done all over again if the thesaurus is revised.)

D1.5.2 KWIC or KWOC format (see Figure 25)

The most convenient format for an alphabetical index as described above is a KWIC format. A KWOC format that lists the look-up terms only once, such as in Figure 25c, may be better. (There are KWOC displays that are worse than KWIC.) The preparation of some sample pages in order to determine user preference is recommended.

D1.6 Guidance Devices to Facilitate Look-up

In all parts of the thesaurus it is important to have running titles and similar guidance devices that help the user to quickly locate the entry he is looking for. In all classified parts the notation of the first term on the page should appear in the upper left-hand corner, the notation of the last term in the upper right-hand corner. In alphabetical parts the same holds for the actual terms. Page numbers should appear at the bottom.

In addition it is very useful to use differently colored paper for the different parts of the thesaurus.

D1.7 Description of Selected Thesauri

This section describes briefly a few selected thesauri for the purpose of further illustrating the considerations dealt with in the preceding sections and providing introductory illustration for the considerations to follow in Sections D2–D4. The sequence of thesauri is chosen according to increasing difference from the Roget-Soergel model. The numbers used to identify the parts are those given in Section D1.0, namely,

(0) Introduction,
(1) Classified index,
(2) Main part,
(3) Alphabetical index.

If the sequence of the parts of a thesaurus differs from this pattern, this will be indicated at the beginning of the description. The existence of an introduction is assumed. In all thesauri the crude form for lead-in is used unless mentioned otherwise. Note that this section is only concerned with the format of presentation and *not* with the content. So the statement that LCC is relatively near to the Roget-Soergel model does in no way imply a judgment on LCC as a classification; it only refers to the presentation. Also it makes no difference from this point of view whether the classified arrange-

a: Actual KWIC: ERIC Thesaurus	b: Constructed KWIC: Same terms as shown in Column c[a]		c: Actual KWOC: TEST[a]
Ratios (mathematics)			
Rats			***Inflow***
Parent reaction		influence fuses	**Influence**
Student reaction		influence mines	•Influence fuses
Reactive behavior	•Operating	influence (instruments)	•Influence mines
Readability		influenza	•Operating influence (instruments)
Retarded readers		influenza virus	***Influenza***
Readiness	Swine	influenza virus	Influenza virus
Readiness (mental)	Haemophilus	influenzae	Swine influenza virus
Handwriting readiness	Water	influx	***Influenzae***
Integration readiness		informal organization	Haemophilus influenzae
Learning readiness		information	***Influx***
Reading readiness	Combat	information centers	Water influx
Reading readiness tests		•information analysis centers	***Informal***
Reading		information capacity	Informal organization
Reading ability		•information engineers	***Information***
Reading achievement		•information processing language	Combat information centers
Directed reading activity		information retrieval	•Information analysis centers
Applied reading		information retrieval effectivenes	Information capacity
Reading assignments		•information retrieval precision	Information centers
Basic reading		information sciences	•Information engineers
Beginning reading		information scientists	•Information processing language
Reading centers		information systems	Information retrieval
Reading clinics		information theory	•Information retrieval effectiveness
Remedial reading clinics	•Recorded	information	•Information retrieval precision
	•Science	information specialists	Information sciences
	•Technical	information centers	Information scientists
			Information systems
			Information theory
			•Recorded information
			•Science information specialists
			•Technical information centers

Figure 25. Alphabetical index in KWIC and KWOC format (D1.5.2).

(a) Single word terms that appear in the Thesaurus of Terms section are in bold italics. • Indicates USE reference. (Figure 25a from USERIC 1972, 1969 version; Figure 25c courtesy Engineers Joint Council, New York, N.Y.)

D1 The Different Parts of a Thesaurus 211

ment is based on faceted classification or on more traditional principles or whether the scheme uses monohierarchy or polyhierarchy.

The interested reader is strongly urged to look at the thesauri described. Sample pages cannot transmit the "flavor" of a thesaurus; therefore, sample pages are included only for two of the thesauri described.

D1.7.1 Thesaurus of the Vision Information Center, Harvard Medical School

This thesaurus very nearly approaches the Roget-Soergel model. The main part is arranged in classified order. Since only a list of synonyms and no other information is given for a descriptor, the main part can at the same time be used as classified index, so no separate classified index is provided. The alphabetical index is KWIC. The notation is given for each term, and nondescriptors are enclosed in parentheses. (The notations used are rather lengthy.)

D1.7.2 FR thesaurus (problems of developing countries)

The alphabetical index method for lead-in is used.

(1) *The classified index* contains descriptors only (there are no other preferred terms) and is printed on the document analysis sheet, so that the indexer can just encircle them (a segment of the classified index is displayed in Figure 35, Section D3.1.1,3). All NT and BT and the most important RT cross-references are given for each descriptor. (In the cross-references descriptors are cited by their notation.) The partly expressive, partly ordinal notation for small schemes to be described in Section D4.3.3,1 is used.

(2) *Main part.* The main part contains entries for all terms and many inverted forms. The entries are arranged alphabetically. Semantic factors to be used, NT, BT, RT, and sources are given in that order. BT and NT are given only if they cannot be seen from the linear arrangement in the classified index and only one level up or one level down, respectively. Descriptors are cited by notation and standardized abbreviations. Some very short scope notes are given as well.

(2.1) Some descriptors in this thesaurus needed rather lengthy scope notes which would not easily fit into the main part. A separate listing of these scope notes in classified order is therefore given. Many of these scope notes deal with a whole group of descriptors and their mutual delineations.

(3) There is no alphabetical index, the main part is to be used instead.

D1.7.3 UDC, DDC, LCC

The reader might wonder why these "traditional" schemes appear here. The reason is that they are, in fact, thesauri as defined in this book. In addition to the indexing language they contain a lead-in vocabulary. This is especially true for UDC and DDC. UDC, for example, gives in its alphabetical index synonyms for its descriptors, terms too specific to be descriptors, and terms designating compound concepts that are to be expressed by a combination of descriptors. The alphabetical index method for lead-in is used in each scheme.

(1) All schemes have a *classified index,* preceded by "summaries", i.e., outlines showing the major subdivisions or main classes (first subdivision) and then successively adding further levels of the hierarchy (second and third subdivision). The classified index also gives some cross-references and some scope notes. The notation of both UDC and DDC uses digits and some special characters only; in both cases the notation is expressive down to the lowest level of specificity (DDC notation is not consistently expressive, however). LCC uses the partly expressive, partly ordinal notation for large schemes to be described in Section D4.3.3,2.

(2) None of the schemes has a *main part* as defined in this book.

(3) All schemes have an *alphabetical index* (however, LCC has a separate alphabetical index for each class). In the case of both UDC and DDC the alphabetical index contains the descriptors, spelling variants (especially inverted forms), and synonyms for the descriptors, and terms designating concepts that are not used as descriptors. The notation of the descriptor or the descriptor combination to be used is given in each entry (in UDC this might be a single main number, a main number with auxiliary, or a combination of two main numbers). The index to LCC has entries for descriptors, giving their notation; inverted forms of descriptors; and a few other lead-in terms. For lead-in terms only the text of the descriptor to be used is given, so that the user has to look a second time to find the notation.

Example
Building design see Architecture, rather than
Building design: NA
or *Engraving, copper see Copper engraving, rather than*
Engraving, copper: NE 1750-1775

The index to LCC also contains some see-also cross-references.

In the case of LCC, there is an additional consideration: In a somewhat oblique way, the list of LC Subject Headings can be considered to be the main part of LCC. Since LCSH is arranged alphabetically, it is often used as a substitute for the still-missing comprehensive alphabetical index to LCC.

D1.7.4 Thesaurofacet
(See Figures 26 and 27.)

The main-part method for lead-in is used. For preferred terms that are to be expressed by a combination of descriptors (rather than by one broader descriptor), the detailed lead-in form is used.

D1 The Different Parts of a Thesaurus

(1) *Schedules (classified index)*
An overview of the main fields of the thesaurus is given in the table of contents. In the schedules all descriptors and a number of preferred terms that are expressed by a combination of descriptors are displayed. For some descriptors narrower or related descriptors not to be seen from the linear arrangement are given in the schedules (as a rule such cross-references are given only in the part labeled "thesaurus"—see below); these cross-references are all designated by '*', and no distinction between Narrower Term and Related Term is made. A few scope notes are also given in the schedules. The notation is ordinal, using both numeric and alphabetic characters as the base.

(2) *"Thesaurus" (main part)*
The part labeled "thesaurus" is the main part and is organized as follows:
(a) An entry is made for every term, including some spelling variants and, in some cases, inverted forms. The entries are arranged in alphabetical order.
(b) The following information is given in each entry:
—For most lead-in terms: The text of the appropriate descriptor (not the notation).
—For descriptors and for other preferred terms that are expressed by a combination of descriptors: UF, NT(A), BT(A), RT, S BT, S BT(A), S RT. S indicates a descriptor to be used in a combination. The symbol BT(A) is used for those Broader Terms that cannot be seen from the linear arrangement in the schedules. Broader Terms to be seen from the schedules are designated by BT; they are given only in the case they are used as a semantic factor (the distinction between BT and BT(A) seems rather unnecessary). NT(A) includes preferred terms that contain the main term as a semantic factor. Broader and Narrower Terms are given one level up or down, respectively. In the cross-references to other descriptors, only the text of these descriptors is given, while the notation is omitted. If one wants to enter the schedules at the descriptor given in a USE instruction or at an additional broader descriptor given as a cross-reference, a second look-up to obtain the notation of that descriptor is necessary.

(3) There is *no alphabetical index*; the main part is to be used instead.

Thesaurofacet comes close to the recommended format, but the differences should be noted:
—Only a very few cross-references are given the schedules. There is no differentiation in the schedules between BT, NT, and RT cross-references.
—The main part is arranged alphabetically, and notations are omitted in the cross-references in the main part.
—There is no alphabetical index. Therefore, spelling variants, especially inverted forms, have to be included in the main part, loading the main part with information that does not properly belong there. Also, look-up by alphabet is slower since the main part is considerably larger than an alphabetical index would be (by an estimated factor of 4). It should be noted, on the other hand, that the recommended format, consisting of a main part

MA	**ELECTRON TUBES**		MBE	Electron wave tubes
	*Electron tube theory EKA		MBF	Travelling wave tubes
			MBH	Backward wave tubes
	By frequency:		MBJ	Carcinotrons
			MBM	Magnetrons
	Combine with notation for frequency,		MBP	Velocity modulated tubes
	for example:—		MBQ	Klystrons
MA/DYD	Very high frequency tubes		MBT	**Electron beam deflection tubes**
	*Resnatrons MDC		MBV	Indicator tubes (tuning)
MA/DYF	Microwave tubes		MBW	Trochotrons
	*Backward wave tubes MBH		MC	Cathode ray tubes
	*Carcinotrons MJB		MC2	Image converter tubes
	*Electron wave tubes MBE		MC4	Image intensifiers
	*Klystrons MBQ		MC6	Storage tubes
	*Magnetrons MBM		MCE	Television camera tubes
	*Resnatrons MDC		MCI	Television colour camera
	*Travelling wave tubes MBF			tubes
	*Velocity modulated tubes MBP		MCL	Television picture tubes
			MCO	Television colour picture
	By construction:			tubes
			MCQ	**X ray tubes**
MA2	**Vacuum tubes**		MCS	**Phototubes**
	*Cathode ray tubes MC		MCT	Photomultipliers
	*Electron beam deflection tubes		MCW	**Electron multipliers**
	MBT			*Photomultipliers MCT
	*Electron multipliers MCW			
	*Phasitrons MD6			**By number of electrodes:**
	*Resnatrons MDC			
	*X ray tubes MCQ		MD	Diodes (tubes)
MA4	**Thermionic tubes**			*Plasma diodes (tubes) MAR
	*Cathode ray tubes MC		MD3	Triodes (tubes)
	*Dynatrons MDB			*Thyratrons MAI
	*Electron beam deflection tubes		MD5	Multielectrode tubes
	MBT			*Trochotrons MBW
	*Electron wave tubes MBE		MD6	Phasitrons
	*Hot cathode arc discharge tubes		MD7	Reactance tubes
	MAG		MDA	Tetrodes
	*Resnatrons MDC		MDB	Dynatrons
MAC	**Gas discharge tubes**		MDC	Resnatrons
	*Cold cathode glow discharge		MDG	Pentodes
	tubes MB2		MDH	Pentagrid converters
	*Counting tubes MER		MDL	Multiple unit tubes
	*Phototubes MCS			
MAE	Ionisation tubes			**By application:**
MAG	Hot cathode arc discharge tubes			
MAI	Thyratrons			*Storage tubes MC6
MAJ	Hydrogen thyratrons			*Television camera tubes MCE
MAL	Pool tubes		MER	*Television picture tubes MCL
MAM	Excitrons			Counting tubes
MAO	Ignitrons			*Indicator tubes (numerical)
MAP	Plasma tubes			MB7
MAR	Plasma diodes (tubes)			*Trochotrons MBW
MAT	Flash tubes		MET	Dekatrons
MAW	Transmit receive tubes			*For other applications combine*
	(duplexers)			*notation for Electron tubes with*
MB	**Cold cathode tubes**			*application. For manual systems*
	*Counting tubes MER			*the preferred order is application*
	*Photomultipliers MCT			*followed by tube, but permuted*
	*Phototubes MCS			*entries may be made, for example:—*
MB2	Cold cathode glow discharge			*Electron tube amplifiers LE/MA
	tubes			*Electron tube demodulators
MB4	Neon tubes			LW/MA
MB5	Controlled cold cathode glow			*Electron tube mixers LX/MA
	discharge tubes			*Electron tube modulators LV/MA
	*Dekatrons MET			*Electron tube oscillators LL/MA
MB7	Indicator tubes (numerical)			*Electron tube rectifiers JPL
MB8	Trigatrons			

Figure 26. Thesaurofacet: sample page of the classified index (D1.7.4). (Courtesy English Electric Co. Ltd., Whetstone, Leicester LE8 3LH, England.)

Gas Discharge Tubes   **MAC**
UF   Discharge tubes
       Gas tubes (electronic)
RT   Discharge lamps
       Gas discharge
       Gas filled radiation detection
       Photo tubes
NT(A)   Cold cathode glow discharge tubes
       Counting tubes
BT(A)   Thermionic tubes

Television Cameras   **NJ3**
RT   Television camera tubes
       Television transmitters
NT(A)   Colour television cameras
       Television recording cameras
BT(A)   Television studio apparatus

Television Camera Tubes   **MCE**
UF   Camera tubes (television)
       Emitrons
       Iconoscopes
       Image iconoscopes
       Image orthicons
       Orthicons
       Pick up tubes (television)
       Vidicons
RT   Phototubes
       Photomultipliers
       Television cameras
BT(A)   Television apparatus

Television Centres *use*
Television Studios

Television Channels   **NHC**
UF   Channels (television)
RT   Television links

Television Circuits   **NJA**
RT   Clamping circuits
       Television interference
       Television receivers
       Television scanning
       Television synchronisation
       Television transmitters
       Video circuits
NT(A)   Colour television circuits
       Combining amplifiers
       Equalising pulses
       Horizontal deflection oscillators
       Limiters
       Phase detectors
       Scanning circuits
       Synchronising pulse generators
       Synchronising separators
       Television time bases
       Vertical deflection oscillators
       Videofrequency amplifiers
       Vision mixers

Television Colour Camera Tubes   **MCI**
UF   Colour camera tubes (television)

       Colour cell
       Pick up tubes (colour television)
       Plumbicons
RT   Colour television cameras
BT(A)   Colour television apparatus

Television Colour Picture Tubes   **MCO**
UF   Apple tubes
       Banana tubes
       Colour picture tubes (television)
       Chromatrons
       Display tubes (television colour)
       Flat picture tubes
       Gabar tubes
       Kaiser Aiten thin tubes
       Kinescope (colour)
       Reflected beam kinescope
       Shadowmask tubes
       Television display tubes (colour)
RT   Colour television receivers

Television Communication Systems *use*
Television Transmission Systems

Television Display Tubes (colour) *use*
Television Colour Picture Tubes

Thermionic Tubes   **MA4**
UF   Hot cathode tubes
       Thermionic valves
RT   Filaments (tube)
       Heaters (tube)
       Metal vapour rectifiers
       Thermionic cathodes
       Thermionic emission
       Thermionic power generation
       Thermionic rectifiers
NT(A)   Cathode ray tubes
       Dynatrons
       Electron beam deflection tubes
       Electron wave tubes
       Hot cathode arc discharge tubes
       Resnatrons
BT(A)   Thermionic devices

Triodes (semiconductor) *use*
Transistors

Triodes (tubes)   **MD3**
RT   Grids (tube components)
NT(A)   Thyratrons

Trioxides   **HNH**

Trip Coils *use*
Tripping Mechanisms (circuit breakers)

Trochotrons   **MBW**
UF   Radial beam tubes
BT(A)   Counting tubes
       Multielectrode tubes

Trolley Buses   **R7L**

Figure 27. Thesaurofacet: sample page of the main part (D1.7.4). (This page has been composed from various entries to show the relationship to Figure 26.) (Courtesy English Electric Co. Ltd., Whetstone, Leicester LE8 3LH, England.)

216   D   Thesaurus Format

A - ANATOMICAL TERMS

A9 - Sense Organs

SENSE ORGANS
EAR (A1)
EYE (A1)
OLFACTORY MUCOSA (A4, A10)
TASTE BUDS (A3)

ANTERIOR CHAMBER	EYE (A1) (Continued)	ORGAN OF CORTI (A8)
Aqueous Humor (A12)	Conjunctiva	PUPIL
AQUEOUS HUMOR (A12)	Cornea	RETINA
CHOROID	Lacrimal Apparatus	Fundus Oculi
CILIARY BODY	Lens, Crystalline	Macula Lutea
COCHLEA	Retina	Rods and Cones (A8)
Organ of Corti (A8)	Sclera	RODS AND CONES (A8)
CONJUNCTIVA	Uvea	SCLERA
CORNEA	Vitreous Body	SEMICIRCULAR CANALS
EAR (A1)	EYEBROWS (A1)	SENSE ORGANS
Ear, External	EYELASHES (A1)	Ear
Ear, Middle	EYELIDS (A1)	Eye
Labyrinth	FUNDUS OCULI	Olfactory Mucosa (A4, A10)
EAR CANAL	IRIS	Taste Buds (A3)
EAR, EXTERNAL	Pupil	TASTE BUDS (A3)
Ear Canal	LABYRINTH	TYMPANIC MEMBRANE
EAR, MIDDLE	Cochlea	UVEA
Ear Ossicles	Semicircular Canals	Choroid
Eustachian Tube	Vestibular Apparatus	Ciliary Body
Tympanic Membrane	LACRIMAL APPARATUS	Iris
EAR OSSICLES	LENS, CRYSTALLINE	
EUSTACHIAN TUBE	MACULA LUTEA	VESTIBULAR APPARATUS
EYE (A1)	OLFACTORY MUCOSA (A4, A10)	VITREOUS BODY
Anterior Chamber		

Figure 28a. Medical Subject Headings: sample page of the classified index (subject category listing) (D1.7.5). (Source: MeSH 1972, published by the National Library of Medicine.)

arranged in classified order, giving entries for preferred terms, only, and including an alphabetical index, would need a little more space (a factor of about 1.1 to 1.2) than the part labeled "thesaurus" of Thesaurofacet.

Note that the authors of Thesaurofacet use the term "thesaurus" where we would use the term "main part of the thesaurus". In our usage the schedules are included in the thesaurus; in Thesaurofacet usage they are not.

D1.7.5 Medical Subject Headings (MeSH)

This thesaurus is between the Roget-Soergel model and the TEST model. The main part method for lead-in is used. The intermediate form of lead-in (described in Section C5.2.1) is used as detailed below. MeSH consists of the following parts in the sequence given:

    Introduction (0)
    Updating information (*)

D1 The Different Parts of a Thesaurus 217

A9 - SENSE ORGANS

SENSE ORGANS	A9.		
EAR	A9.22.	A1.72.26.	
EAR, EXTERNAL	A9.22.16.		
EAR CANAL	A9.22.16.1		
EAR, MIDDLE	A9.22.32.		
EAR OSSICLES	A9.22.32.1		
EUSTACHIAN TUBE	A9.22.32.1		
·TENSOR TYMPANI	A9.22.32.1	A2.72.62.	
TYMPANIC MEMBRANE	A9.22.32.1		
LABYRINTH	A9.22.48.		
COCHLEA	A9.22.48.1		
ORGAN OF CORTI	A9.22.48.1	A8.75.32.1	
SEMICIRCULAR CANALS	A9.22.48.1		
VESTIBULAR APPARATUS	A9.22.48.1		
EYE	A9.44.	A1.72.52.1	
ANTERIOR CHAMBER	A9.44.4.		
AQUEOUS HUMOR	A9.44.4.1	A12.13.12.	
CONJUNCTIVA	A9.44.9.		
CORNEA	A9.44.14.		
·DESCEMET'S MEMBRANE	A9.44.14.1		
EYEBROWS	A9.44.19.	A1.72.52.1	A1.90.5.1
EYELASHES	A9.44.24.	A1.72.52.1	A1.90.5.1
EYELIDS	A9.44.29.	A1.72.52.1	
LACRIMAL APPARATUS	A9.44.34.		
LENS, CRYSTALLINE	A9.44.39.		
RETINA	A9.44.44.		
FUNDUS OCULI	A9.44.44.1		
MACULA LUTEA	A9.44.44.1		
RODS AND CONES	A9.44.44.1	A8.75.32.1	
SCLERA	A9.44.49.		
UVEA	A9.44.54.		
CHOROID	A9.44.54.1		
CILIARY BODY	A9.44.54.1		
IRIS	A9.44.54.1		
PUPIL	A9.44.54.1		
VITREOUS BODY	A9.44.59.		
OLFACTORY MUCOSA	A9.70.	A4.60.13.1	A10.88.48.1
TASTE BUDS	A9.88.	A3.54.42.1	

* INDICATES PROVISIONAL HEADING

Figure 28b. Medical Subject Headings: sample page of the classified index (tree structures) (D1.7.5). (Source: MeSH 1972, Tree structures, published by the National Library of Medicine.)

Main part (2)
Provisional headings (2.1)
Subject category listing (1.1)
Tree structures (1.2)
Permuted medical subject headings (3)
These parts will be discussed in the sequence of the numbers indicated in parentheses.

(0) *Introduction.* In addition to the usual material the introduction contains a list of subheadings that do not appear anywhere else in the thesaurus. These subheadings are very important in indexing and search request formulation.

(1) *Classified index*

D Thesaurus Format

(1.1) In the published version there is the *"Subject Category Listing,"* which consists of an overview of the categories and sub-categories—the outline of the scheme, and a rather peculiar classified index (see Figure 28a). In each subcategory all descriptors are listed in alphabetical sequence. Indented under each descriptor are his "sons" (narrower descriptors one level down). Thus, many descriptors appear twice, and still the hierarchy is not expressed well at all. For descriptors that belong to other subcategories, the other subcategories are also given. If a descriptor appears under two broader descriptors within one sub-category it is simply listed twice without indication.

(1.2) In addition there is a less widely distributed separate document, called *"Tree Structures"* (see Figure 28b). This is a classified index in the normal form, with a more detailed expressive notation that continues the subject category code in the way described in Section D4.3.4. (There are still sets of descriptors that all have the same notation, so there is no 1–1 correspondence between notation and descriptors.) Since these detailed notations are not given in the main part, linkage between main part and tree structures is on a general level only. The "Tree Structures" are much more useful than the "Subject Category Listing."

(2) *Main part* (see Figure 29).

(a) An entry is made for every term, including spelling variants, especially selected inverted forms. The entries are arranged alphabetically.

(b) For each term the subcategory number(s) leading to the general area in the classified index are given; the detailed notation is not included. (Within the National Library of Medicine there seems to exist a version, called "Searcher's MeSH, where the detailed notation is written in. This version also gives the date when a descriptor has been introduced.)

Furthermore, the cross-references are given for lead-in terms or descriptors, as appropriate.

Cross-reference		Inverse cross-reference	
MeSH designation	Our designation	MeSH designation	Our designation
See	USE ST	X	UF ST
See under	USE BT	XU	UF NT
See also related	RT-TO (related to)	XR	RT-RF (related from)
See also specific	NT	XS	BT

The intermediate form for lead-in, described in Section C5.2.1, is used: from both *Insurance, surgical* and *Surgical insurance* there is a cross-reference *see under* (USE BT) *Insurance, health*. Both terms appear in the entry for *Insurance, health* in the field XU (UF NT). Only NT's or BT's not to be seen from the classified index are given, one level up or down. RT's are given mainly to descriptors that are in a different subcategory of the classified index. (Other related terms can be seen by looking into the classified index). For the layout and further details see Figure 29.

E39 see BAYER E39 (D4)

EAR (A1, A9)

EAR CANAL (A9)
see also related
CERUMEN (A12)

EAR DEFORMITIES, ACQUIRED (C11)

EAR DISEASES (C11)
see also related
OTORHINOLARYNGOLOGIC DISEASES
(C5, C11)

EAR, EXTERNAL (A9)

EAR, INTERNAL see under LABYRINTH (A9)

EAR, MIDDLE (A9)
XU TYMPANIC CAVITY (A9)
XU TYMPANUM (A9)

EAR NEOPLASMS (C2)

EAR OSSICLES (A9)
see also related
STAPES SURGERY (E4)

XU INCUS (A9)
XU MALLEUS (A9)
XU STAPES (A9)

EARTHWORMS (B1)

EAST COAST FEVER see under THEILERIASIS
(C1, C15)

EATING BEHAVIOR see FEEDING BEHAVIOR (F1)

EATON AGENT see MYCOPLASMA (B3)

INOSITOL (D11)
XU PHYTIC ACID (D11)
XU PHYTIN (D11)

INOSITOL, PHOSPHATIDYL see under
PHOSPHOINOSITIDES (D11)

INOSITOLHEXAPHOSPHATE
PHOSPHOHYDROLASE see PHYTASE (D9)

INSANITY see MENTAL DISORDERS (F2)

INSECT BITES AND STINGS (C14)

INSECT CONTROL (G3)
see also related
CHEMOSTERILANTS (D3)
INSECTICIDE RESISTANCE (G1)
JUVENILE HORMONES (D8)

INSECT HORMONES see under INVERTEBRATE
HORMONES (D8)

INSECT REPELLENTS (D3)

INSECT VECTORS (B1)

INSECT VIRUSES (B4)

INSECTICIDE RESISTANCE (G1)
XR INSECT CONTROL (G3)

INSECTICIDES (D3)
see also related
CHOLINESTERASE INHIBITORS (D5, D9)

see also specific
DDD (D2)
ISOFLUROPHATE (D5)

XR ANTI-INFECTIVE AGENTS (D3)
XR CHOLINESTERASE INHIBITORS (D5, D9)

INSTINCT (F1)
see also related
LIBIDO (F2)

XU ENERGY ACCUMULATION ACTIVITY (F1)
XU INNATE BEHAVIOR (F1)

INSTITUTES see under ACADEMIES AND
INSTITUTES (N3)

INSTITUTIONAL PRACTICE (N4)

INSTITUTIONALIZED CHILD see CHILD,
INSTITUTIONALIZED (I, M)

INSTRUMENTAL LEARNING see under
CONDITIONING, OPERANT (F1)

INSULA OF REIL see under CEREBRAL CORTEX
(A8)

INSULIN (D8)
see also related
HYPERINSULINISM (C7)
SHOCK THERAPY, INSULIN (E2, F3)

INSULIN ANTIBODIES (D12)

INSULIN RESISTANCE (G1)

INSULINASE see under PEPTIDE
PEPTIDOHYDROLASES (D9)

INSURANCE (N3)

INSURANCE, ACCIDENT (N3)
X ACCIDENT INSURANCE (N3)

INSURANCE, DENTAL (N3)
XU DENTAL CARE PLANS (N3)
XU PREPAID DENTAL CARE (N3)

INSURANCE, HEALTH (N3)
X HEALTH INSURANCE (N3)
XU HEALTH BENEFIT PLANS, EMPLOYEE (N3)
XU INSURANCE, SURGICAL (N3)
XU MEDICAL CARE PLANS (N3)
XU PREPAID MEDICAL CARE (N3)
XU SICKNESS INSURANCE (N3)
XU SURGICAL INSURANCE (N3)

INSURANCE, HEALTH, FOR AGED see HEALTH
INSURANCE FOR AGED, TITLE 18 (N3)

Figure 29. Medical Subject Headings: sample page of the main part (D1.7.5). (This page has been composed from segments from two pages to show the relationship to Figures 28a and b.) (Source: MeSH 1972, published by the National Library of Medicine.)

(3) *Alphabetical index.* This is a most peculiar KWOC index issued as a separate publication. The main part can also serve as an alphabetical index.

D1.7.6 Euratom-Thesaurus

The main-part lead-in method is used. The thesaurus consists of the following parts in the order listed:

Dictionary of index terms (main part) (2).
Alphabetical index to the terminology charts (3.1).
Terminology charts (classified index) (1).

Some background knowledge about the structure of the vocabulary in this thesaurus is necessary in order to understand the descriptions of the parts. The thesaurus contains the following types of terms:

All terms	*19,183*
Descriptors	*15,695*
Core descriptors ("keywords")	*4,665*
"General purpose descriptors"	*1,199*
Inorganic compounds, nuclides & alloys	*3,466*
Other descriptors ("accepted terms")	*11,030*
Non-descriptors ("forbidden terms")	*3,488*

(1) *Terminology charts (classified index).*
(1.1) Overview of the 57 charts.
(1.2) The charts display core descriptors, selected noncore descriptors, and a few lead-in terms in a graphical method (see Section D3.2, Figure 46). A core descriptor may appear in only one chart, a noncore descriptor may appear in more than one chart according to its semantic factors. Each chart has a number which serves as notation for each of the terms displayed in the chart. For each keyword the number of occurrences within the first 545,000 documents is given.

(2) *Dictionary of index terms (main part)*
(a) Entries are made for all terms (including lead-in terms). The arrangement is alphabetical.
(b) Information given in each entry:
—For lead-in terms: simple USE instructions, expressed by USE, or OR-type USE instructions expressed by SEE . . . OR . . . OR. Lead-in terms are preceded by '-'.
—For descriptors: For all descriptors the frequency of occurrence (presumably after generic posting) within the first 360,000 documents in the EURATOM collection is given.

For the majority of descriptors that are not core descriptors, a POST TO instruction, (expressed by USE), is given but only one level up. Since generic posting is done by computer, the indexer need not care. The USE (POST TO) instructions contain a Broader Term or more often, two or more semantic factors. Ultimately, the indexing of a document by a non-core descriptor will, in the majority of cases, cause the posting of that document to one or more core descriptors. For a minority of non-core descriptors Related Terms are given, preceded by SEE. By policy, no descriptor has both USE and SEE.

No inverse cross-references are given at all. That means, for example, that it is not possible to see from what other terms a term is being posted.

No notations are given in the main part.

Note: Since the main part gives so little information, the term density is almost as high as in an alphabetical index (200 terms per page). However, multi-word terms appear under the first term only.

(3) The main part serves as *alphabetical index*.

(3.1) There is an alphabetical index of the general purpose core descriptors (excluding descriptors for chemical substances), giving the notation (the number of the chart where the descriptor appears). Actually, this index precedes the charts. The index does *not* include noncore descriptors or lead-in terms. (The index is necessary because in the main part no reference to the chart number is made.)

D1.7.7 Thesaurus of education terms

The main-part method for lead-in is used. The thesaurus consists of the following parts in the order listed:

Alphabetical array (main part) (2).
Faceted array (classified index) (1).
Alphabetical index (3).

(1) *Part 2: Faceted array (classified index)*. Three-level monohierarchy: facets, subfacets, descriptors. Descriptors grouped within subfacets. All descriptors within one subfacet have the same notation, the subfacet number. The BT-NT relationships given in the main part are *not* displayed here, even though they seem to follow a monohierarchical pattern. An overview of the facets and subfacets is given in the introduction.

(2) *Part 1: Alphabetical array (main part)*
  (a) One entry is made for each term.
  (b) Information given for each entry.
—For lead-in terms, a USE instruction is given.
—For descriptors, SN, UF, BT, NT, RT are given in that order. BT's and NT's are given one level up or down, respectively. The data field RT always contains the notation of the subfacet to enter into the faceted array and often other descriptors. Descriptors given in USE, BT, NT, RT are not accompanied by their notation.

(3) *Alphabetical index*. KWIC-type, no information except the proper form of the term.

D1.7.8 American Petroleum Institute (API) Subject Authority List

This is a most idiosyncratic thesaurus, and its description will therefore be lengthy. The reader is advised that the discussion is difficult to follow without a copy of the API thesaurus at hand.

D   Thesaurus Format

The main part lead-in method is used. The thesaurus consists of the following parts in the order given.

Alphabetical thesaurus (main part) (2).
Chemical aspects (1.1).
Bibliographical descriptors (1.2).
Hierarchy of descriptors (1.3).
Hierarchy index (3.1).

In the following, the parts are described in detail.

(1) *Classified index*
This consists of three parts:
(1.1) Chemical aspects;
(1.2) Bibliographical descriptors;
(1.3) Hierarchy of descriptors.

The hierarchy (1.3) is a meaningful arrangement of descriptors based on a faceted classification. Columns are numbered, and the column number is used as notation for each descriptor in the column.

In addition the lists of section headings for each of the four abstract bulletins issued by API are given, preceding (1.3). They are arranged in classified order. A statement of scope is included for each heading. The section headings also appear in the main part (preceded by an unexplained number and with a scope note referring to this part). The same term may occur as a section heading and as a normal descriptor.

(2) *Alphabetical thesaurus (main part)*
(a) One entry is made for each term.
(b) Information given in each entry.
—For lead-in terms USE instructions and sometimes OR-type USE instructions expressed by *See* are given. Inverse for USE is USED FOR. There is no inverse for *See*. A USE instruction sometimes refers to a combination of descriptors.

Example:
Paint dryer
  USE Drying agent
    PLUS Paint
The inverse looks as follows:
Drying agent
  USED FOR Paint dryer
    PLUS Paint

—For descriptors SN, BT, NT, RT, and UF are given. However, the matter is not as easy as that: BT is actually split into three cross-reference types. The cross-reference type *Broader Terms (autoposted)* contains the Broader Terms to be seen from the classified index, going all the way up (inverse: *Narrower Terms*). The cross-reference type *Related Terms (auto-*

posted) contains what in our definition are additional Broader Terms. They seem to go all the way up (inverse: *See also* with term followed by an *). The cross-reference type *Chemical aspects (autoposted)* contains those Broader Terms that are chemical aspects (no inverse given). The cross-reference type *Narrower Terms* contains the Narrower Terms to be seen from the hierarchy going all the way down. The other Narrower Terms, which are inverse to entries in *Related Terms (autoposted)* appear under *See also* and are followed by an *. Unstarred terms in *See also* are genuine Related Terms as defined by us (there is not always an inverse cross-reference in this case). Thus, the hierarchy displayed in the classified index is expressed completely by the terms listed under *Broader Terms* and *Narrower Terms* with one exception. Some descriptors, like *Direction*, do not receive postings from their narrower descriptors as shown in the classified index, e.g., *Upward*. Therefore *Upward* appears in the field *See also* in the main part. If there are too many Narrower Terms like this, as with *Material*, a scope note referring to the classified index replaces the list of terms in *See also*. The notation leading to the classified index is not given.

Remark: Of interest are chains with two types of hierarchical relationships (in API notation):

Example:
  A Related terms (autoposted) B
  B Broader terms (autoposted) C.
In this case we have B See also A*, but not C See also A*. Whether A is posted on C is unclear.

  (3) The main part is to serve as *alphabetical index*.
  (3.1) *Hierarchy index*
  This is an alphabetical index containing only descriptors appearing in (1.3) (and some Broader Terms that are not descriptors but have been added to the hierarchy for logical coherence and structure). Multi-word descriptors are entered under the first word only. The notation is given for each descriptor.
  The introduction to this thesaurus is issued as a separate publication.

D1.7.9 ERIC thesaurus

This thesaurus follows very nearly the TEST model with the following major exceptions: In the main part Broader Terms are listed only one level up; Narrower and Related Terms that have in turn Narrower Terms are not indicated as such. There is no hierarchical index, only a subject category index. The alphabetical index is KWIC.

D1.7.10 Library of Congress Subject Headings (LCSH)

This thesaurus consists of a main part only. The main part method for lead-in must therefore be used.

(a) *Entries.* Since the main part must also serve the function of an alphabetical index, spelling variants, inverted entries (in case the descriptor is in direct entry form), and direct entries (in case the descriptor is in inverted entry form) are included in a consistent manner. As a result, the list of terms included is rather complete, but at the same time the main part gets rather unwieldy.

(b) Information given for each entry:
—for lead-in terms: a USE instruction, expressed by *See*
—for descriptors:
—Library of Congress Classification class number (if there is one corresponding to the descriptor).
—Scope note (if necessary).
—NT and RT-TO (related to) in one data field, labeled sa (See also)
—UF-statements in a data field labeled x (*B x A* is the inverse of *A* see *B*)
—BT and RT-FR (related from) in one data field, labeled xx (*B* xx *A* is the inverse of *A* sa *B*)

The last two fields are not meant to appear on the subject card in the catalog. They are important, however, for the maker of the catalog: A synonym with a see-reference is not entered in the card catalog until the corresponding descriptor is entered. Likewise, a see also cross-reference is not introduced until the target-descriptor is introduced.

Example:
If Architectural models is not a heading in the card catalog at hand, then the cross-reference
    Miniature objects
        See also Architectural models
does not make sense in that catalog. As soon as Architectural models is introduced the cross-reference has to be added to the subject card for Miniature objects. The xx-statement in the entry for Architectural models reminds the maker of the catalog to do this.

Example:
A complete LCSH entry looks as follows:

    Architectural models (NA2790)
        sa *Architectural casts*   *RT*
            Structural frames—Models   *NT*
       x *Models, Architectural*   *SP*
      xx *Architectural casts*   *RT*
            Miniature objects   *BT*
            Models and modelmaking   *BT*

As can be seen from this description, hierarchical and RT relationships

D1   The Different Parts of a Thesaurus   225

are confounded in the sa—xx structure. As a matter of policy there are no upward see-also references, no BT in sa (there are still some cases from earlier times where this policy has not been followed). In the example *Architectural casts* appears twice, under sa and xx. On the subject card for *Architectural models* in the catalog, it will appear only once since the xx-field does not appear there. The example leads us to surmise that terms appearing under both sa and xx are in fact RT, whereas terms appearing under sa only are NT and terms appearing under xx only are BT.

An LCC class number is given only if the heading corresponds closely to a class in LCC. Nevertheless, the Subject Heading List may serve as a limited substitute for the still-missing comprehensive alphabetical index to LCC.

Another feature of LCSH (and some other subject heading lists) is the space-saving device used in listing terms consisting of a main heading and a subheading.

Examples:
  Aeroplanes
      . . .
    —Escape devices
        See *Pilot ejection seats*
      . . .
  Architecture
      . . .
    —Modular design
        See *Modular coordination (Architecture)*
      . . .
    —Orders
        x *Architectural orders*
        Orders, architectural

D1.7.11   Other thesauri

There are many more thesauri exhibiting interesting features than could be discussed in this section. Appendix 2 gives a list of all thesauri mentioned anywhere in this book, other important thesauri, and in addition, bibliographies of thesauri.

D1.8   Introduction to the Thesaurus

The thesaurus should have an introduction that gives the following information:

  (1) *Information of interest to all users.*

(1.1) Range of the thesaurus. This includes:

—subject coverage. (In delineating the subject covered one might state whether the thesaurus is discipline-oriented or mission-oriented. A discipline-oriented thesaurus contains the vocabulary of a scientific discipline, e.g., *Biology, Chemistry, Physics;* of an area created by grouping together several disciplines, e.g., *Technology, Science, Social sciences, Humanities;* or of a subfield of a discipline for example, *Chemistry of ferroorganic compounds.* A mission-oriented thesaurus, on the other hand, contains the vocabulary necessary for the representation and retrieval of documents needed for a certain mission, such as *Pest control, Pollution control, Space research.*)

—language(s) of the thesaurus: Is the thesaurus monolingual (but possibly giving translations into other languages) or multilingual (to be used for indexing in several languages);

—degree of specificity of the concepts included (the number of descriptors and of preferred terms that are not used as descriptors included in the thesaurus may be indicative);

—type of the thesaurus with respect to its relationship to other thesauri. The following types can be distinguished:

—independent thesaurus (none of the below);
—source thesaurus (definition see Section K1.2.2);
—adjunct thesaurus (definition see Section K1.2.3);
—cumulative thesaurus (definition see Section K1.3);
—total thesaurus (definition see Section K2.3.1);
—constituent thesaurus (definition see Section K2.3.1);
—umbrella thesaurus (umbrella classification) (definition see Section K2.4).

(1.2) Description of the conceptual structure of the thesaurus and of the thesaurus format (parts of the thesaurus, what information is given in each part). Explanation of signs used. The discussion of the conceptual structure of thesauri in Chapter C, especially the summary table of relationships given in Figure 21, Section C7, and the discussion of thesaurus format in Chapters D and E suggest the points to be covered. As to thesaurus format the descriptions of various thesauri in Section D1.7 may serve as illustration.

(1.3) Instructions how the thesaurus is to be used in indexing and searching. (For this purpose it might be useful to reprint or to refer to parts of this book, see the guide given in "How to read this book".

This section may well entail a brief description of the ISAR system for which the thesaurus is to be used: Is indexing manual, semi-mechanized, or fully mechanized? Is it based on post-combination (post-coordination: only elemental or quasi-elemental concepts are used as descriptors), or is it based on precombination (precoordination: many compound concepts are used as descriptors as well)? How much precombination? Is terminological control applied in indexing or in searching, or are both approaches possible (as in the case where both free terms, either taken from the abstract or freely assigned by the indexer, and the corresponding descriptors are stored). Is the retrieval tool a subject catalog or an index, produced by conventional means or by computer, arranged in alphabetical or in classified order? Or is it a simple mechanized tool, such as peek-a-boo

D1 The Different Parts of a Thesaurus

cards, edge-notched cards, machine punched cards, or coded microfilm? Or is computerized retrieval used, batch or interactive? Is generic posting used? How else can inclusive searches be implemented? Are descriptors cited in the document representations by their notation only or by text only or by notation and text?

(1.4) Information on the procedures for updating the thesaurus:

(1.4.1) The users should be encouraged to give comments and suggest new terms or relationships between terms. The procedure for submitting these comments and suggestions should be explained.

(1.4.2) Plans for publishing supplements and revised editions should be outlined (with time-frame). It should be explained how the materials can be obtained, and the user should be made aware of the importance of having an updated version.

(2) *Information of interest for a limited number of users and information specialists only.* This is partly the same information as in (1) but in more depth. In addition sources and procedures used in thesaurus construction are of interest here. (The paragraphs 2.1, 2.2, etc., are analogous to the paragraphs 1.1, 1.2, etc.)

(2.1) The relationship of this thesaurus to other thesauri in the same area should be explained. If a similar thesaurus already exists, the reasons for developing a new thesaurus and the characteristics distinguishing it from the existing one should be stated explicitly.

(2.2) The conceptual structure and the format of the thesaurus should be explained in depth, with reasons for the alternatives chosen. This implies that the rules, conventions, and principles used in building (and updating) the thesaurus be given, including the rules for the form of entries.

(2.3) No additional information on thesaurus use is needed.

(2.4) Updating procedures should be explained in more detail in the context of procedures used in thesaurus construction in general (2.6).

(2.5) A list of the sources used in constructing the thesaurus should be given. Indicate for each source whether all or only part of the terms contained in it have been included in the final thesaurus.

(2.6) The procedures used in thesaurus construction should be described briefly. In particular, it should be clear whether intellectual effort was used to select concepts and terms and to establish terminological and classificatory relationships or whether these tasks were performed by deriving concepts, terms, and relationships on a statistical basis, starting from texts and/or from results of indexing using free terms. Whereas the second approach presupposes computer use, in the first approach it is of interest to know whether or not a computer has been used for clerical tasks. Furthermore, the criteria used to select terms to be included in the thesaurus, the criteria used to select a preferred term from a class of synonyms and quasi-synonyms, and the criteria used to select descriptors from the preferred terms should be given. Finally the procedures used for processing updating information and producing updated versions should be described.

(2.7) It should be indicated whether the working file for the thesaurus is available for other thesaurus projects, what information beyond the user version it contains, and whether it is available in machine-readable form.

D Thesaurus Format

D2 FORMAT OF ENTRIES IN THE MAIN PART

It seemed useful to isolate this problem from the discussion of the thesaurus format as a whole in order not to overload that discussion. The following considerations are independent of the model used. Only the entries for preferred terms need to be considered, since entries for non-preferred terms do not exist in the Roget-Soergel model and are trivial in the TEST model.

The following discussion will focus on the entries in the user version of the main part and also deal briefly with the problems arising with the working file that is used in constructing and updating the thesaurus. (The working file may be either a card file or a computer-stored file). The reader is advised to look at the thesaurus form displayed in Figure 54, Section F0.5, and then reread Section C7, "Summary of relationships displayed in a thesaurus", before reading further.

D2.1 Information Given for Each Term

A complete list of the types of cross-references and other data elements is given in Figure 21, Section C7. Figure 30 gives an excerpt of this list, showing the types of cross-references (gross subdivision) important for the user version. For each individual thesaurus the designer must decide what information in what detail should be given (1) in the working file and (2) in the user version. Figure 30 may serve as a guideline on what to include in the user version. The problem of gross versus detailed subdivision will be discussed in Section D2.3.

Data elements of the same type are best grouped into data fields. The letter codes given in Figure 21 and in part repeated in Figure 30 are suggested for labeling the data fields.

If the main part is arranged in classified order, the hierarchical level, together with a "+" for descriptors and a "−" for other preferred terms, should be shown on the left margin outside the entry proper.

Figure 31 shows a sample main part entry following these considerations. Figure 32 and 33 show examples of other arrangements.

D2.2 Rationale for the Sequence of Data Fields (Cross-Reference Types) (Advanced)

The notation (if any) and the preferred term itself form the heading of the entry (in contrast to the other data fields no label is necessary in the user version). The standardized abbreviation (if any) may almost be considered to be part of the heading. Synonyms and quasi-synonyms follow immediately because they contribute to the explanation of the meaning of the preferred term (Main Term) as discussed in Section C6.1. Except for special cases to

05	+10	Heading: Notation (if any) and preferred term (Main Term)	
12	AB	Standardized abbreviation (if any)	
30	ST	Synonyms and quasi-synonyms	
40	SN	Scope note (alternative place, especially if very short)	
41	FD	(Subject field, subject area)	
42	FA	(Category, facet)	
44	BT	Broader Terms and semantic factors	possibly in reverse order
45	NT	Narrower Terms and "is semantic factor of"	
46	RT	Related Terms	
50	TR	Translations	
60	SN	Definition or scope note (preferred place, especially for long scope notes)	
89	SR	Source indications	possibly after TR

Figure 30. Arrangement of types of cross-references and other data elements within a record or entry in the user version of the main part of the thesaurus (D2.1 and D2.2).

6+	M48.7	**Color TV picture tubes**	
		AB	Col TV pic tu
	UF	ST	Color kinescopes
			Color TV display tubes
		BT	-F75 Color TV receivers
		NT	P23.7 Color TV Screens
		RT	M48.2 Flat picture tubes
			-U83 Radiation hazards
		SN	Descriptor introduced Jan. 1, 1960. In searching for documents indexed before that date, USE BT M48 TV picture tubes.
		SR	AR;KL:TC904;SK;TM:659.5

Note that neither the Broader Term *M48 TV Picture tubes* nor the Narrower Terms *M48.7.2 Shadow mask tubes* and *M48.7.3 Chromatrons* are given because they can be seen from the classified index. The line SR (Sources) is given only if deemed useful in the particular thesaurus. This main part entry is produced from the working file card displayed in Figure 63 (Section F5.1).

Figure 31. Sample main part entry: Roget-Soergel model (D2.1 and D2.2).

be discussed below, the information on the position of the term (or better: concept) in the classificatory structure comes next. It contributes to the clarification of the concept, and it suggests further concepts that the indexer or searcher should consider. Broader Terms and Narrower Terms are both more closely related to the Main Term and should therefore precede the Related Terms.

The question whether to choose the sequence BT - NT or NT - BT is not easy to decide. The contribution of both to the definition of the Main Term is about the same. BT - NT has the following advantage: if there is a USE BT instruction it is early in the entry. NT - BT has the following advantage: a UF NT statement, if one exists, appears after UF ST or immediately after the Main Term. In addition to grouping the UF statements together this is useful because the indexer knows that he need not consider these specific concepts, and the searcher knows that he will retrieve material on them, too, and that he cannot get more specific in his search request by using the more specific concepts in the search request formulation.

Translations are, in effect, synonyms or quasi-synonyms, and it would therefore make sense to put them after data field ST. However, further clarification of the meaning of the Main Term by reading translations would be open only to readers knowing the appropriate language(s) well enough, usually a minority. Furthermore, the translations would usually not add much beyond the synonyms and quasi-synonyms in explaining the Main Term. Therefore, it makes more sense to put translations toward the end of the entry, thereby providing space for Broader Terms, etc., at the beginning. In a type 1 (lead-in only) multilingual thesaurus, however, translations should be entered after the synonyms.

Longer scope notes should also be placed toward the end of the entry. Many users of the thesaurus will know the definition or scope note after some time anyway so that they need not look at it anymore, whereas other information like BT and NT is more important for day-to-day memory assistance. However, if the scope note is very short, such as "Consider narrower descriptors in indexing", it might be more useful to give it at the alternate place at the beginning.

The sequence of scope note and translations is not a critical issue. Placing the scope note at the end offers some advantages in the technical preparation of the thesaurus. For the same reason it might even be useful to have the source indications precede the scope note.

We have purposely omitted from this discussion types of cross-references and other data elements that do not appear in the user version or that play only a minor role there. Their sequence is determined by the requirements of processing, as reflected in the thesaurus form depicted in Figure 54, Section F0.5.

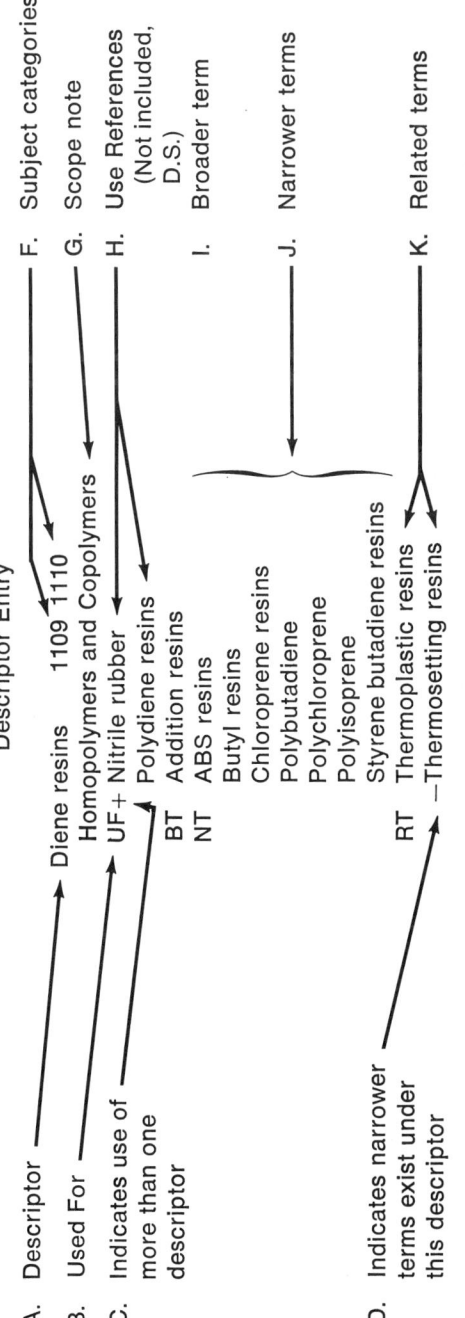

Figure 32. Sample main part entry: TEST (D2.2). (Courtesy Engineers Joint Council, New York, N.Y.)

D Thesaurus Format

Field designators

Standard	BASF		
MT	b	Zone melting	Terms designating the concept (no preferred term is selected)
	b	Zone separation	
	b	Zone purification	
SP	c	Zone melting processes	
TR-G	g	Zonenschmelzen	
	g	Zonentrennen	
	d	Zonenreinigen	
SN	g	Separation of certain constituents (impurities) from a solid by zone heating to the melting point; the dissolved impurities move with the melted zone which is then separated after cooling	
FD	k	V0	Code for subject field
NO	n	2337	Notation (unique expression of concept)
SR	q	ABC 1574;G0 1119;R0 5810; TA 6.3, UL 2/1-VF 6	Source codes
BT-CL	o	Purification	
	o	Thermal processes	
NT-CL	u	Horizontal zone melting	
	u	Zone melting without crucible	
	u	Microzone melting	
RT	v	Crystallizing	

Figure 33. Sample main part entry: BASF (D2.2). (Source: BASF, p. 16, translated and adapted.)

D2.3 Arrangement of Terms Within One Data Field (Technical)

D2.3.0 General

The number of data fields in the user version should be kept small in order not to confuse the user. The same is true for worksheets used in thesaurus construction. The definition of data fields should therefore be based on the gross subdivision in Figure 21, Section C7, also shown in Figure 30, Section D2.1. Within the data fields so defined, one may keep distinctions by labeling the individual terms listed. This is especially important for a working file kept on thesaurus forms or in the computer.

D2.3.1 Synonyms and equivalent terms (quasi-synonyms)

Synonyms and Equivalent Terms should be lumped together in the user version. The distinction is difficult and of limited operational significance. Only

D2 Format of Entries in the Main Part   233

for purposes of cooperation and cumulative thesauri is the distinction important, and it is therefore recommended that it be kept in the working file if that is possible without too much effort.

Within this data field one might give the Synonymous Terms first and then the Equivalent Terms. Other criteria for arrangements to be used instead or as a secondary criterion are:

—importance (frequency of use being an indicator);
—alphabetical sequence.

D2.3.2. BT, NT, RT

These types of cross-references have some problems in common, whereas other problems are specific to one type of cross-references. The sequence in which these problems are taken up is somewhat arbitrary.

,1 **What Broader Terms and Narrower Terms to list.** On the question of what Broader and Narrower Terms should be listed in the data fields BT and NT respectively, see Section D1.4.

,2 **Broader Terms.**

,2.1 **Broader Terms and Semantic Factors.** According to Section C1.3 every Semantic Factor of a concept is also a Broader Term for that concept. Therefore, it is useful in most situations to lump them together in one data field. One might distinguish Semantic Factors from other Broader Terms by a ":" (colon) in front, as in the examples given in Figure 22a2 (Section D0). In this case, all Semantic Factors should be put at the beginning of data field BT.

,2.2 **USE instructions containing Broader Terms.** In case there is a USE instruction containing Broader Terms two data fields should be established: The first data field is designated by SEE BT and contains the Broader Terms not in the USE instruction; the second data field is designated by USE BT and contains the Broader Terms to be used.

Example:
Recorder
   SEE BT   Flute
   USE BT   Musical instrument
(*Compare Section C5.1 "The detailed lead-in form" and the examples given there; further examples are found in Figure 22a2, Section D0).*

,2.3 **Upward hierarchical chains.** If Broader Terms are given more than one level up, they should be arranged from specific to general. If there are several hierarchical chains they should be listed separately. However, the separate listing of USE instructions takes precedence over these rules. (In the Roget-Soergel model hierarchical chains are not given except in cases illustrated by the example in ,2.2.)

,3 Narrower Terms. The considerations on Broader Terms apply here too. The distinction between Is Semantic Factor Of and Narrower Term can again be expressed by a special sign, e.g., "†" (dagger). "NT†" is thus the inverse of "BT:". If necessary, two data fields, UF NT and NT, should be established in that sequence. Downward hierarchical chains should be arranged from general to specific. One might even use an arrangement with indention, but considerably more space is needed. (about 1.3 times as much). If there are several hierarchical chains they should be listed separately. (In the Roget-Soergel model only one level down is given.).

,4 Display of different kinds of hierarchical relationships. If a differentiation between the different kinds of Broader or Narrower Terms is necessary, a tabular arrangement is probably more useful for the user version than labeling the individual terms listed.

Example:
Television camera tube

	Class inclusion	Whole-part	Other connected
BT	Cathode ray tubes	Television camera	Image transmission
NT	Television color camera tube	Electrodes	Transfer characteristics

,5 Related Terms. Again, it is not recommended to use the detailed subdivision. USE RT or UF RT should precede RT, as in BT and NT.

Remark: If the detailed subdivision is used, terms appearing in RT-RF (Related Term - Reflexive) belong by definition to RT-TO (Related Term —To) and RT-FR (Related Term—From) and therefore need not be repeated there. It is also possible to omit the data field RT-RF. Then the terms from this data field have to be listed twice, in RT-FR and RT-TO. RT-FR need not be listed in the user version. (Compare, however, the description of LCSH in Section D1.7.10.)

,6 Arrangement by notation. Within BT, NT, RT, if several terms go into the same place according to the rules discussed, they should be arranged by notation, following the rules of the particular system used. If no notation is used, alphabetical arrangement or arrangement by importance can be used instead.

,7 How descriptors are entered in the data fields BT, NT, RT. Descriptors and other preferred terms are entered in these data fields by giving their notation (if any) and the text or an abbreviation of the text that can be understood immediately (compare E1.8.2 and E1.8.3).

If a descriptor has narrower descriptors, its notation (or text if there is no notation) is preceded by "-" (or some other sign). This shows the indexer or searcher that he should look up this descriptor to find out about narrower descriptors he should consider. The usefulness of this procedure is obvious for Narrower Terms and Related Terms. That it is also useful for Broader Terms and Semantic Factors follows from Section C5.0.3, "Use of the lead-in structure" (see the examples there). If a descriptor or other preferred term has Narrower Terms that are not descriptors, it is *not* preceded by a "-". From the examples in Figure 22a2 and b2 (Section D0) it can be seen that the hyphen should not disturb the alignment of the descriptors by first character of notation or text.

In thesauri following the TEST model it is useful to mark the broadest term in a hierarchical chain (e.g., by "#"), so that the user can see immediately where to enter the hierarchical index. In TEST the user has to do some guesswork since all Broader Terms are arranged alphabetically, and the broadest term is not marked. A more elaborate system of signs can be devised, e.g.,

> Head of hierarchy without scope note
+ Head of hierarchy, with scope note.
. Both Broader and Narrower Terms, with scope note
/ No Narrower Terms, with scope note

D2.4 Typographical Design of Entries

See Figure 32 (Section D2.2) for an example of overall arrangement.

A maximum of four typefonts (or types of underlining) should be used to distinguish between the following:

(1) Main Term, if Main Term descriptor (e.g., 8 point, bold face)
(2) Main Term, if Main Term is not descriptor (e.g., 8 point, italics)
(3) Within entry: descriptors forming part of a USE instruction (e.g., 6 or 8 point, bold-face)
(4) Within entry: All other information (e.g., 6 or 8 point, normal)

See Section D3.4 for various typefonts available on typewriters and types of underlining or capitalizing that may also be used.

D3 HOW TO DISPLAY DESCRIPTORS AND THEIR INTER-RELATIONSHIPS (METHODS FOR THE DESIGN OF A CLASSIFIED INDEX)

This section deals with displays that by the very arrangement of descriptors and possibly the use of graphical means like lines and arrows express relationships between descriptors (and possibly other preferred terms).

It should be clear from the outset that such a display can show only the most important relationships between descriptors. Otherwise it would become so crowded as to be unintelligible. However, it is possible to indicate additional important relationships with each descriptor given in the display in an abbreviated form; for an example see Figure 35, Section D3.1.1,3. A complete listing of all relationships for each term is possible only in the main part of the thesaurus.

Section D3.1–D3.3 will deal with various possibilities for the design of such displays, most of them illustrated by a sample page. In some cases it might be useful to give the same information (for example, the listing of checklist descriptors) in two different forms so that each thesaurus user can pick the form that is most useful to him.

It is useful to clarify some underlying issues in Section D3.0 before discussing the details of how to present a relational display.

D3.0 Relational Displays vs. Classification Principles

It is one problem to detect and record the hierarchical and associative relationships between descriptors and other preferred terms. It is another problem to display as many of these relationships as possible in, say, a linear sequence with indentions. Very often these two issues are confused. Part of the confusion stems from the fact that people think only the hierarchical relationships that can be displayed can be in the system, thus falling into the error of monohierarchy. An ideological debate then ensues over what hierarchical relationships should be defined and displayed in the system. The most basic decision is between a subject-oriented arrangement and an arrangement based on facets. A subject-oriented arrangement would put *Teachers* under *Education*, *Diplomats* under *Foreign relations*. A faceted arrangement would put both under *Persons*. A subject-oriented arrangement ("Fachsystematik") is easier to grasp for the user. This is true at least for ISAR systems within one traditional area. In interdisciplinary areas or ISAR systems spanning several areas the situation might be different. It is important to recognize that both approaches do not exclude each other. As soon as it is clear that both the hierarchical relationships detected in a subject-oriented approach *and* the hierarchical relationships detected in a faceted approach should be included in the system and that it is only a question of relative importance which ones should be shown by the arrangement of descriptors, the whole question can be tackled in a much more pragmatic way.

The problem of designing a relational display is an optimization problem under constraint. The utility of the display has to be maximized. The constraint is that the designer have only one or two dimensions so that he cannot, for example, collocate every two terms that are related to each other. *Utility* can be operationalized as follows: A benefit arises if two terms that

D3 Descriptor Displays 237

are often looked for together or that *should* be seen together are neighbors in the display. (This statement applies also, and especially so, if the classified sequence is to be used for the arrangement of documents or catalog cards). In a more precise formulation: the benefit of a term-pair is the product: strength of the relationship between the terms multiplied by their nearness in the display, where nearness is the inverse of the number of lines intervening between the two terms increased by 1. The sum of these products over all pairs of terms has to be maximized. Of course this optimization cannot be done literally by actual computation, but it suggests a way of thinking. Furthermore, utility depends on the clarity of the arrangement; this should be maximized so that the user can easily grasp the underlying structure. It is reasonable to assume that, in order to maximize utility, as many hierarchical relationships as possible have to be expressed by the arrangement. But this still leaves considerable latitude: the designer has to decide what hierarchical relationships should be displayed; then he has to decide on the sequence of the broadest terms and the sequence of the sons of the same father. There exists a number of formal principles that can assist in attaining a sensible arrangement; they will be dealt with in Section D3.1.1,2. It should be emphasized, however, that these principles should assist, not govern. If in a given instance the formal principle does not lead to the optimization described above, it should not be used for that instance. This point is often missed in the literature.

D3.0.1 Alternate classified index (advanced)

In most areas there is a choice between a subject-oriented arrangement and a faceted arrangement as a basis for the classified index. In making this choice the designer should have in mind the pragmatic optimization discussed above. But one arrangement does not exclude the other. One may, for example, choose a subject-oriented arrangement for the principal classified index and the main part; this arrangement determines the notation. In addition one might have an alternate classified index based on the facet principle. An alternate notation would be used in that index. According to Section C4.3 general terms to head the facets are included in the indexing language anyway. The NT listings for these in the main part can be reduced drastically if an alternate classified index is provided.

D3.1 Displays for Hierarchical Relationships

D3.1.1 Linear arrangement of descriptors (and possibly other preferred terms) in classified order with cross-references

,1 **Preferred monohierarchical structure and cross-references.** The best way to display a polyhierarchical structure is as follows: Select a preferred monohierarchical structure and display it in a linear arrangement with indentions. That means: if a descriptor has two or more broader descriptors, decide under which of these broader descriptors it should appear (decide on its place in the linear sequence). This place in turn determines the notation of the descriptor. A cross-reference is made for each hierarchical relationship not expressed by the linear sequence. Figure 10b (Section C1.3) and the classified index in the Roget-Soergel model in Figure 22a1 (Section D0) provide examples of how this can be done. As may be seen from there, there are three forms to give a cross-reference from A to B:

(1) Put a symbol ($\rightarrow$ or BT, $\leftarrow$ or NT, / or RT) after descriptor A, followed by the notation of descriptor B. This is appropriate if descriptor B is not too far away in the linear sequence, so that it can be looked up easily.

(2) As (1), but add the text of descriptor B (or its standard abbreviation) to the notation. This is appropriate if much page-turning would be necessary to look up B and if space is not a problem.

(3) For NT cross-references there is a third possibility (not shown in Figure 22a1): put the descriptor B (notation and text) indented after descriptor A at the logical place among the other sons of A, but enclose it in parentheses.

Example:
M25 Vacuum tubes
M27 X-ray tubes
M30 Electron beam deflection tubes
(M73 Vacuum phototubes)

This is appropriate if B should appear at a particular place among the sons of A to make a logical pattern.

It is useful to put a "-" in front of B if B has narrower descriptors (see Section D2.3.2,7). This is particularly important in forms (2) and (3). If one lists B a second time in the linear sequence (form (3)), one might give all the narrower descriptors of B with proper indentions at the second place also. However, this requires a great deal of space.

This leads to the rationale for selecting a monohierarchical structure. It is best explained by reference to the classified index of the TEST model in Figure 22b (Section D0). TEST simply lists a descriptor B (say, *Electron beam deflection tubes*) under each of its broader descriptors. If B has narrower descriptors they are listed at all these places, too. In the example of Figure 22b this doubles the size of the classified index. Also, at none of the two (or more) places is the user told that *Electron beam deflection tubes* has a second Broader Term. If notations are used (as is to be recommended in connection with a classified index) many descriptors would have two or more notations, which would only lead to confusion. If the main part is to be arranged in classified order and/or if a catalog and/or books on shelves are to be arranged in classified order, selection of a monohierarchical structure is even more important.

In selecting a monohierarchical structure the information in the data fields FD (Subject field) and/or FA (Facet) might be useful, especially if the selection is to be computer assisted (compare Section G3.4.1). One should be careful to keep in mind that the hierarchical relationships selected for presentation in the linear arrangement are in no way distinguished from, or more important than, the hierarchical relationships that are shown through cross-references.

If there are many precombined descriptors with three or more conceptual components, the hierarchical structure gets so complex that a linear arrangement with cross-references is not adequate anymore. An auxiliary ISAR system, possibly in form of a combinatorial index (to be discussed in Section D3.6), should be considered in this case.

If preferred terms other than descriptors are to be included in the classified arrangement, "descriptor" in this section should be read to mean "descriptor or other preferred term".

,2 **Sequence of descriptors on the same level.** The sequence of the descriptors on the highest level, as well as the sequence of coordinate descriptors (sons of the same father), is not determined by the hierarchy. In many classification schemes or thesauri, alphabetical sequence is chosen for coordinate descriptors; this decision is based on the argument that a classified sequence would be arbitrary and that a descriptor looked for could be found more easily in an alphabetical sequence. However, this argument is fallacious and alphabetical sequence does not lead to the optimal arrangement discussed above, as is illustrated by the example given in Figure 34.

Furthermore, the purpose of the classified display is not easy look-up of a term that is known—that can be done using the alphabetical index—but to show the relationships among the descriptors. If anything more is needed the following reasoning may serve as an additional demonstration of the fallacy of arranging coordinate terms in alphabetical sequence. Assume a multilingual thesaurus. The notations for the descriptors are determined by the sequence of the descriptors in, say, the English edition. The notations in turn determine the sequence of descriptors in the editions in other languages, say, in the French edition. If the English arrangement on which the notation was based were alphabetical, the sequence of descriptors in the French edition would be completely devoid of any meaning or principle whatsoever.

,2.1 **How to achieve helpful arrangement (technical).** Developing a helpful arrangement often leads to improvements of the hierarchy: In looking for a useful arrangement, one often detects additional hierarchical levels so that collocation is achieved by the improved hierarchy. In the example of

Figure 34 one sees several clearly discernible blocks corresponding to different facets of *Organization of development aid*. One should look out for such blocks, whether the criterion for subdivision is facet-oriented or subject-oriented. Then one should try to find or coin a heading for each block ("organizational headings"). If no heading can be found or coined, then the block should be displayed as a distinguishable entity without heading, as will be discussed in Section ,3.

Organization of development aid
    Bilateral aid
    Development aid by churches
    Documentation on development aid
    Evaluation of development aid projects
    Financing of development aid
    Government aid
    Institutions giving development aid
    Multilateral aid
    Private aid
    Procedures for the approval of aid projects

The following arrangement would make much more sense:
Organization of development aid
    Bilateral aid
    Multilateral aid

    Institutions giving development aid
    Government aid
    Development aid by churches
    Private aid

    Financing of development aid
    Procedures for the approval of aid projects
    Evaluation of development aid projects

    Documentation on development aid

Figure 34. Alphabetical versus meaningful sequence of descriptors on the same level (D3.1.1,2).

After the hierarchy has been carried as far as seems sensible, the following principles can assist in arranging terms on the same level in a sequence that is helpful (useful, meaningful) according to the criteria discussed in Section D3.0.

(1) Increasing complexity (this is the essence of the theory of integrative levels).

(2) Evolutionary—arrange entities in the order they evolved, e.g., biological species, ideas.

(3) Sequence of steps—e.g., production processes, research methods, sequence of logical steps.

(4) Chronological—e.g., historical events.

(5) Geographical—spatial proximity.

(6) Canonical—arrange in an order given by an authority, e.g., books of the Bible.

(7) Consistency—if comparable subdivisions appear in two or more different places, the sequence should be the same at all these places unless there are good reasons to do otherwise. In most of these cases the elements of the comparable subdivisions can, in fact, be decomposed into semantic factors and the sequence can be based on the combination of concepts as discussed in Section C2.4(2).

(8) Importance—put those descriptors first that are most important for indexing and search request formulation, especially indexing and search request formulation using the checklist technique.

Sometimes two of these principles lead to the same sequence, for example, increasing complexity and evolutionary in the case of biology. One can apply, for example, the sequence of steps principle on one level and then arrange the narrower descriptors within each step by increasing complexity.

,3 **Details of presentation (technical).** There are different possibilities for indicating the hierarchical level of a descriptor or other preferred term in the linear arrangement:

(a) *One can indent narrower terms under the broader term.* This is the most usual form, and we have encountered several examples already. Difficulties arise if one turns from one page to the next because then the reference line is lost. Possibilities for resolving this difficulty are:

(a1) One can use a level indicator line at the top and at the bottom of the page, as shown in Figure 22a1 (Section D0) and in Figure 36. A level indicator line shows the position of each hierarchical level.

(a2) One can indicate each level by a dot (see classified index of the TEST model in Figure 22b (Section D0)) or by a vertical stroke (no example).

(a3) One can use vertically lined paper, each line corresponding to a hierarchical level (no example).

(b) *One can use different typefonts* and/or different kinds of underlining to indicate the hierarchical level (see Section D3.4 for details).

(c) *One can indicate the hierarchical level by a number on the left margin.* This method is recommended for the main part, as shown in Figure 22a2 (Section D0).

Figure 35 shows how a sizeable indexing language (660 descriptors and 590 cross-references among them) can be displayed in a linear sequence with indentions in an intelligible way. At the same time this figure shows how

J00 **Politics** (↗ *J92ff)
  J01 Politics, general references
  J02 Political ideas (ideologies) (↗Z20)
  J05 Political awareness (↗F87)
  J20 Systems of government → SC32
    J22 Democracy
    J23 Dictatorship, authoritarian government
    J25 Totalitarian government
    J26 Charismatic government
    J27 Kingship
    J28 Chieftainship
    J29 Feudalism (↗ J20)
  J32 Autonomy, self government (↗ J87, L06)
  J33 Independence, sovereignty
    (↗ D89, K00, L00, Z25) → SC49
  |J34 **The state** (↗*J92ff, N74)
    J35 State territory (K38)
    J36 Nationality, citizenship
    J38 Constitution (↗ N77) → N74
    J39 Council system
    J42 Legislative body, parliament → SC39
    J45 Executive branch (↗ *J90ff)
    J48 Federalism, decentralization
    J49 Centralization, centralized structure
  |J52! **Formation of political opinion** (↗ F82)
  |J53! Elections and votes
  |J55! Pressure politics, lobbyism
  |J57! Subversion
  J60 Internal politics (↗J80)
      ← J86, J87
    |J62 Political interest groups (↗D89, *J92ff)
    |J63 Political elites (↗ *J92ff) H80!
    |J65 Political parties (↗Z20, *J92ff)
    |J67 Opposition (↗ *J92ff)
    J69 Political conflicts → SC37
    J70 Political planning → SC41
    J73 Educational and cultural policy (↗E23)
    J75 Social policy → SC43
    J76 Social reform → D82
  J80 Administration (↗ J00, J60, *J92ff)
    J81 Administrative structure (↗J32, J48, J49)
    J82 Bureaucracy, agencies
    J83 Public utilities
    J84 Financial planning and control, accounting
    J86 Law and order, internal security → J60
    J87 Regional administration (↗J32, J48) → J60
    J89 Standardization (↗Q43) → SC62
  J90! Institutions, organizations in general
    (↗H62, H65, 5080)
  *J92! **Sponsor in/from developing country**
  *J93! — industrial country ← M30
  *J94! **Activity/process takes place in developing country**
  *J95! — in industrial country
  *J97! **Public**
  *J98! **Private**
  K00 Int. and foreign relations
      ← M30, fr. p. 4; → SC46
    K01 Int. and for. rel., gen. ref.
    K05 —, planning, goals → SC41
    K06 —, bilateral
    K07 —, multilateral
    K10 Global internal, org.
      (↗ *J92ff, M20) ← fr. p. 4;
      → K07, SC47
    K20 Regional internat. org. (↗ *J92ff, K36, M20) ← fr. p. 4; → K07, SC47
    K27! National org. for internat. problems
      (↗ *J92ff, M20) → SC47
  |K32 **Diplomacy, internat. conf.** ← 5305
    K35 Treaties, agreements (↗ N86)
    K36 Alliances, pacts, treaties (↗ *J92ff, K20, K70, Q84) ← fr. p. 4; → SC47
    K37 Non-alignment, neutrality → SC48
    K38 Borders, border conflicts (↗ J35)
    K39 Conquest, subjugation (↗ K70)

  K43 Immigration, emigration → SC29
  K44 Refugees, displaced persons → SC29
  K50 Internat. cultural exchange
    (↗ B30, X80) ← E77
  |K62 **Peace**
  |K63 Coexistence
  |K65 International conflicts (↗ K77)
  |K70 Military affairs
  |K72 Armament, disarmament
  |K74 Armed forces (↗ H57) → SC45
  |K77 Combat actions, wars (↗ K39, K65)
  L00 Problems of colonies
      ← M03; → SC46
    L05 Colonial policy → SC41
    L06 Status of colony (↗ J32)
    L07 Use of colony
    L09 Position and treatment of native people

  Descriptors from other areas to which cross-references are made:

  B00 Culture
    B30 Cultural relations, culture contact
    D82 Reforms
    D89 Movements

  E00 Education
    E77 Education and training in foreign
        countries
  F50 Communication
    F82 Public relations, propaganda

  H00 Society
    H57 Military, warriors (as a profession)
    H62 Social institutions
    H65 Groups
    H80 Non-resident groups

  L00 Problems of colonies
    L06 Status of the colony

  M00 Problems of developing countries
    M03 After-effects of colonial rule
    M20 Development institutions
    M30 Development aid

  N00 Law
    N74 Public law
    N77 Civil rights

  P00 Economy
    Q43 Streamlining of operations
    Q84 Foreign economic relations

  X50 Recreation
    X80 Travel, tourism

  Z20 Ideologies
    Z25 Nationalism

  Example of a sum card:

    SC41 *Political planning etc.* → SC40
    E23 Educational planning, curricula (↗ J73, P15)
    J70 Political planning
    K05 Int. and foreign relations, plans, goals
    L05 Colonial policy
    SCM10 Development policy etc. (↗ J90ff)
    P10 Economic policy
    P15 Economic planning (↗ E23)
    U25 Regional and urban planning → SC60

  Signs:
    *   Do not overlook in indexing and search request formulation
    !   Note scopenote in main part
    (↗) See also; consider descriptor after ↗ also
    →   Additional broader descriptor (BT)
    ←   Additional narrower descriptor (NT)
    J34   example: for searching, the broader descriptor *SCJ34*
    :   *The state, etc.*, is available; it will retrieve everything indexed
    J45   by *J34*, or *J35* or *J36* or *J38* or *J39* or *J42* or *J45*.

Figure 35. Segment of the classified index of the FR thesaurus (D3.1.1,3). (The figure shows a segment of a two-page display of the indexing language, consisting of about 660 descriptors, with 590 cross-references among them, which is printed on pages 2 and 3 of a four-page document analysis sheet.) (Courtesy Forschungsstelle fuer Weltzivilisation, Freiburg, Germany.)

D3 Descriptor Displays 243

descriptors can be emphasized through the use of different typefonts and special signs. A method combining (a1) and (b) is recommended for the display of larger classified indexes; it is illustrated in Figure 36. Note the use of summaries at different levels; these summaries are very important to facilitate easy overview of the indexing language. (Another example of summaries is provided by the tables of contents of this book.) The following rules have been followed in Figure 36:

—A level indicator line is given at the top and at the bottom of the page.

—Major fields have been assigned level 0; areas, level -1. In the general summary all hierarchical relationships are shown by indention. The left margin corresponds to level -1. In the summary of one area the left margin corresponds to level 0 and the area is underlined using "=" (boldface type would do as well) because its level cannot be shown by indention. In the detailed classified index the left margin corresponds to level 1, and the subject field has to be underlined using "=" as well. This procedure saves a lot of space (two indentions are omitted in the classified index), and the hierarchical relationships not shown by indention can always be seen from a summary page.

—Underlines other than "=" have no meaning for the hierarchy. They merely serve to facilitate the perusal of the scheme. For another example see Figure 48, Section D4.0.

As discussed in Section ,2.1 a block of related descriptors for which no heading can be found or coined should be displayed as a separate block. This can be achieved by a space or another typographical symbol, e.g., a short line, preceding and following the block.

Remark: One may add a level -2 with such headings as
Bibliographic descriptors
Content descriptors: Subjects
Content descriptors: Geographical subdivisions
and a general summary displaying these and the areas within each, with the level indicator line
-2 -1 0 1

D3.1.2 Graphical display of hierarchical relationships

,1 **Usual tree display.** A simple example is given in Figure 37. In Figure 39 oblique lines are used instead of rectangular ones. If the pure tree method is used down to the lowest level, it involves a great deal of space. Therefore, various space-saving devices have been introduced, as can be seen from Figure 38 and Figure 39. In Figure 39 some of the hierarchical levels have been brought into a horizontal sequence instead of the usual vertical one.

The tree method is suitable for giving an overview of the interrelationships between a small number of terms. For the actual display of a whole classification scheme it has serious disadvantages: If one wants to display

a: We start from the following hierarchy:

   A/B General descriptors
   . . . .
   G/K Culture and society, politics, administration, and law
   . . . .
       H00 Education and research
          H10 Education
             H12 Pedagogics
                H14 Teaching methods
                    H14.3 Programmed instruction
             . . .
          H30 Schools for general education
          . . . .
       H200 Certificates, examinations
       H300 Scientific disciplines
       . . . .
       I00 Society
       . . .
   N/P Economics and related areas

This information is presented as follows:

b1: <u>General summary</u>
   -1 0 1   (level indicator line)
   A/B <u>General descriptors</u>
   . . . .
   G/K <u>Culture and society, politics, administration, and law</u>
   . . . .
       H00 Education and research
       H300 Scientific disciplines
       . . .
       I00 Society
   N/P <u>Economics and related areas</u>
       . . .

Figure 36. Display of a large classified index with summaries (D3.1.1,3). (*a*) Only important descriptors of that level, having a larger number of narrower descriptors, are included in the overview. (Source: extracted and translated from Soergel, et al., 1970.8, issued by DATUM, Bonn, Germany.)

b2: Summary of one area

0 1 2

G/K Culture and society, politics, administration, and law
===============================
...

H00 Education and research

   H10 Education

      H30 Schools for general education[a]

      ...

   ....

   H200 Certificates and examinations

H300 Scientific disciplines

...

I00 Society

...

b3: Detailed classified index

1 2 3 4 5

G/K Culture and society, politics, administration, and law
===============================
...

H00 Education and research

H10 Education

   H12 Pedagogics

      H14 Teaching methods

         H14.3 Programmed instruction

         ...

   ...

   H30 Schools for general education

      H32 Elementary school

      ...

1 2 3 4 5

Figure 36. (Continued)

246 D Thesaurus Format

the whole scheme in a one-piece tree, one may well need a wall over thirty feet long. At least for printing the whole tree has to be divided into a large number of small trees. This gives rise to the problem of showing the connection between the various small trees. For a good solution of this problem see Figures 37 and 38.

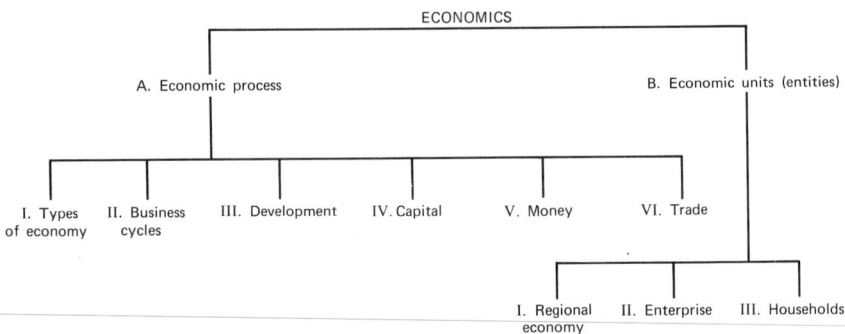

Figure 37. Simple tree display (following SYNTOL) (D3.1.2,1). (Source: SYNTOL 1964.)

The tree format can be expanded to express a limited number of polyhierarchical relationships, as may be seen from Figures 9–11, Sections C1.2 and C1.3; rectangular lines are to be preferred in this case. A limited number of associative relationships (in addition to those shown by collocation) might also be displayed using a different kind of line (e.g., dotted line).

,2 Tree display with horizontal arrangement of hierarchical levels (see Figure 40). Implementation of this method in printing is easier, but it does not allow for the expression of polyhierarchical and associative relationships.

,3 Circular display of hierarchical relationships (Figure 41). The different hierarchical levels are arranged in concentric circles in this method. This has the following advantage: The lower hierarchical levels, which often contain more terms, correspond to the outer circles which provide more space. On the other hand, the method has the following disadvantages:

—It is difficult to divide one big circular scheme into several small circular schemes. Therefore, the method is suited only for subject fields that can easily be subdivided into relatively small, relatively closed subfields.

—The number of hierarchical levels allowed for on a letter-size sheet is limited.

—Polyhierarchical relationships may be displayed within one circular scheme only and are limited even there.

—The same is true for associative relationships.

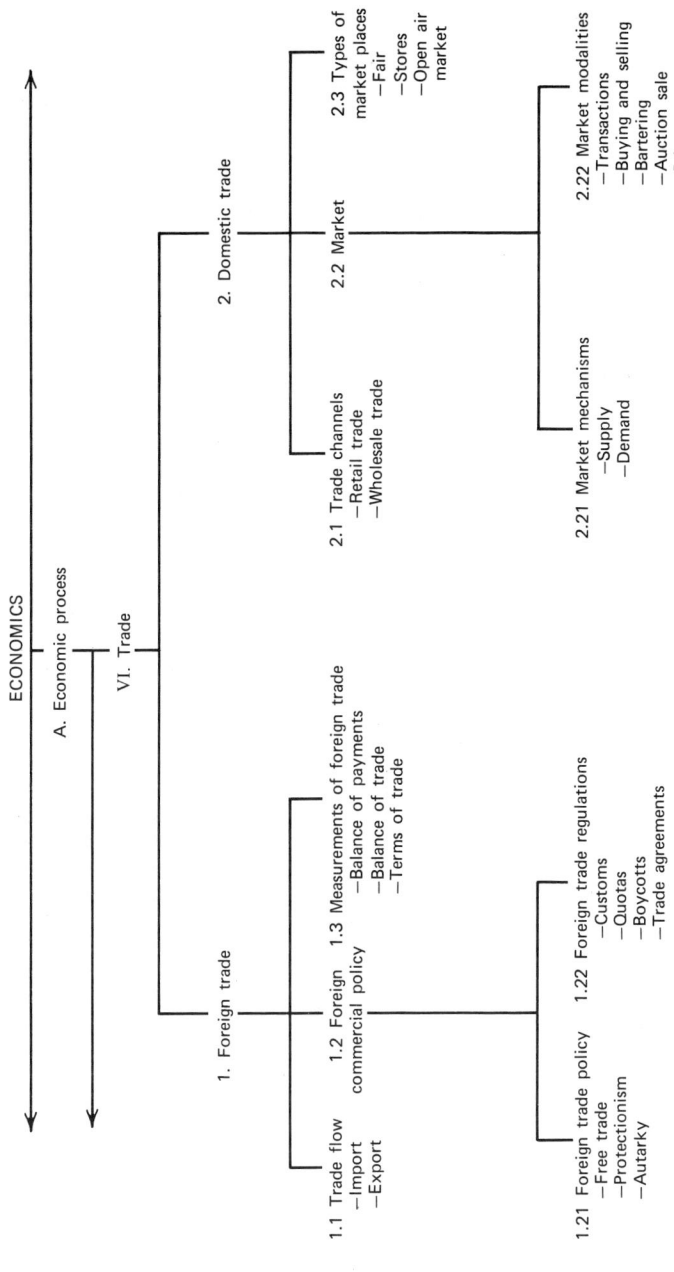

Figure 38. Tree display using space-saving devices. Also example of how to show a part of a big tree (following SYNTOL) (D3.1.2.1). (Source: SYNTOL 1964.)

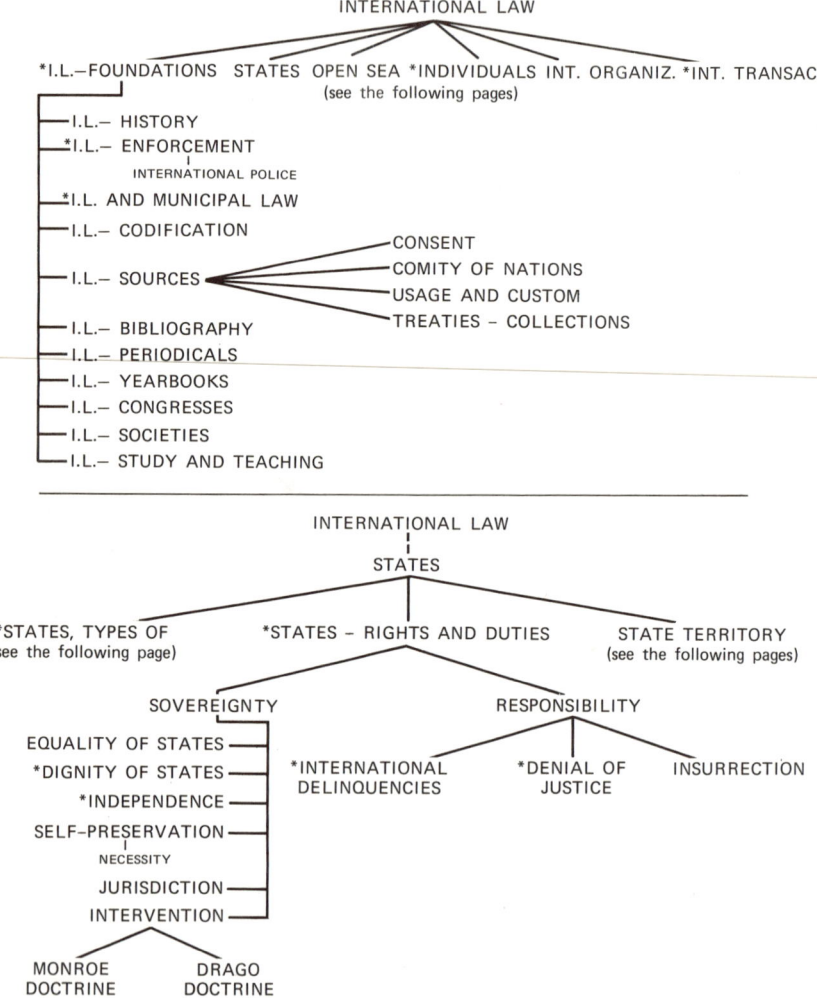

Figure 39. Tree display using space-saving devices (D3.1.2,1). (Courtesy John Wiley & Sons, New York, N.Y.)

D3.2 Network Structures for the Combined Display of Hierarchical and Associative Relationships (See Figures 42–46)

The network method illustrated by Figure 42 is similar to the circular scheme. Again, the terms have to be divided into groups that can be displayed on one sheet each. A term that may serve as heading for the group is placed in the center of the sheet. The terms in the next lower level of the hierarchy as well as possibly related terms appear in a first round (which now need not be of circular shape). As distinct from the circular scheme there is no line connecting the terms on the first round. There are arrows from a Broader Term to its Narrower Terms, and there are two-way arrows between Related Terms. From the terms in the first round one proceeds in the same way. (The rounds of the second level are not closed, however.) There are numerous relationships between terms belonging to different rounds, resulting in a network of interrelationships. Relationships to descriptors belonging to other groups are indicated. These descriptors are placed outside a rectangular frame, and their group number is given.

Each group has a number which is given on the sheet for that group.

It is, of course, possible to display the relationships between groups as a whole in a graph containing the group headings, corresponding to the summary recommended for a linear arrangement in Section D3.1.1,3.

There are variants of this method:

—Place the graph in a coordinate grid and identify each descriptor by the two coordinates (these identifications form a notation as defined in Section D4) (Figure 43).

—The example given in Figure 45, where relationships based on a sequence of processes and their results are shown by downward arrows and hierarchical relationships are shown by horizontal arrows.

—EURATOM 2 (see Figure 46). This method gives much more detail and takes more space accordingly. (The group *Anatomy* shown in Figure 42 has been split into two groups in the second edition of the EURATOM thesaurus, and the area used to display a group has been doubled in the second edition).

Network structures allow for the display of more complex interrelationships among descriptors than the methods described in the previous section. Often this is done at the cost of clarity and intelligibility, but that is a matter of individual preference. It is especially important in this method that a careful selection be made of those relationships most useful for indexing and searching and that the network be designed in such a way as to display these relationships as adequately as possible.

Figure 40. Tree display with horizontal arrangement of hierarchical levels (D3.1.2,2). (All the hierarchical reationships displayed in Figures 38 and 39 are shown; the hierarchical relationships from Figure 38 are shown down to level 5. The subdivisions for descriptors marked "*" are not shown.)

Level 0	1	2	3	4	5
		History Enforcement	International police		
		And municipal law			
		Codification			
	Foundations		Consent		
			Comity of nations		
		Sources	Usage and custom		
			Treaties— collections		

INTERNATIONAL LAW		Bibliography		
		Periodicals		
		Yearbooks		
		Congresses		
		Societies		
		Study and teaching		
	States	States, types of*		
		States—rights and duties	Sovereignty	Equality of states
				Dignity of states
				Independence
				Self-preservation	Necessity
				Jurisdiction
				Intervention	Monroe Doctrine
					Drago Doctrine

(Continued)

Figure 40. (Continued)

Level 0	1	2	3	4	5
INTERNATIONAL LAW			Responsibility	International delinquencies	
		State territory*		Denial of justice	
				Insurrection	
	Open sea*				
	Individuals*				
	International organization*				
	International transactions*				
		I. Types of economy*			
		II. Business cycles*			

ECONOMICS

A. Economic process

III. Development*			
IV. Capital*			
V. Money*			
VI. Trade	1. Foreign trade	1.1 Trade flow	Import
			Export
		1.2 Foreign commercial policy	1.21 Foreign trade policy
			1.22 Foreign trade regulations
		1.3 Measurements of foreign trade	Balance of payments
			Balance of trade
			Terms of trade
	2.1 Trade channels		Retail trade
			Wholesale trade

(Continued)

Figure 40. (Continued)

Level 0	1	2	3	4	5
ECONOMICS			2. Domestic trade	2.2 Market	2.21 Market mechanisms
					2.22 Market modalities
				2.3 Types of marketplaces	Fairs
					Stores
					Open air markets
	B. Economic entities	I. Regional economy*			
		II. Enterprise*			
		III. Household*			

D3 Descriptor Displays 255

D3.3 Comparison of Different Methods

This section is not intended to give a thorough analysis of the comparative advantages and disadvantages of each method. It merely discusses some examples from which the reader may form his own judgment. In order to get a first impression of the advantages and disadvantages of the graphical methods described, as compared to a listing with indentions, one may look at Figures 43 and 44; these figures display the same descriptors and the same relationships as a network and a linear arrangement, respectively. In this particular case the display in Figure 43 gives almost exclusively hierarchical relationships (it could, therefore, be represented just as well by a circular scheme according to D3.1.2,3). In the linear arrangement of Figure 44, the sequence of descriptors on the same hierarchical level has been copied exactly from Figure 43 (counterclockwise). Without this restriction one could have chosen another, more meaningful sequence. Note that this comparison is based on an example in which the relationships to be displayed are mostly hierarchical. If this condition did not hold the situation would be different. See, for example, Figure 42. It would not be possible to express the relationships displayed there by a linear arrangement with indentions; cross-references would have to be added.

D3.4 Use of Different Type Fonts (Technical)

In all the methods described above it is, of course, possible to enhance the intelligibiity by using different typefonts and different kinds of underlining. It is advisable, for example, to emphasize descriptors that are heavily used as well as descriptors that otherwise might easily be missed, regardless of their hierarchical level. One has to be careful, however, to avoid confusion in the case where certain type fonts or kinds of underlining are used to indicate hierarchical level. By using various typewriters, one may have different-size typefonts if the original is to be typed. Some typefonts available on typewriters are:

Very large type: Olivetti primary typewriter (used in libraries for typing call numbers) and IBM 72, type element ORATOR (upper case only)
Slightly above normal size: IBM Executive
Normal size: 10 characters per inch (pica)
Slightly below normal size: 12 characters per inch (elite)
Very small type: Mikron type
Types of underlining available are as follows:
Underline using = = = = = =
Solid underline ─────────
Broken underline ── ── ── ──

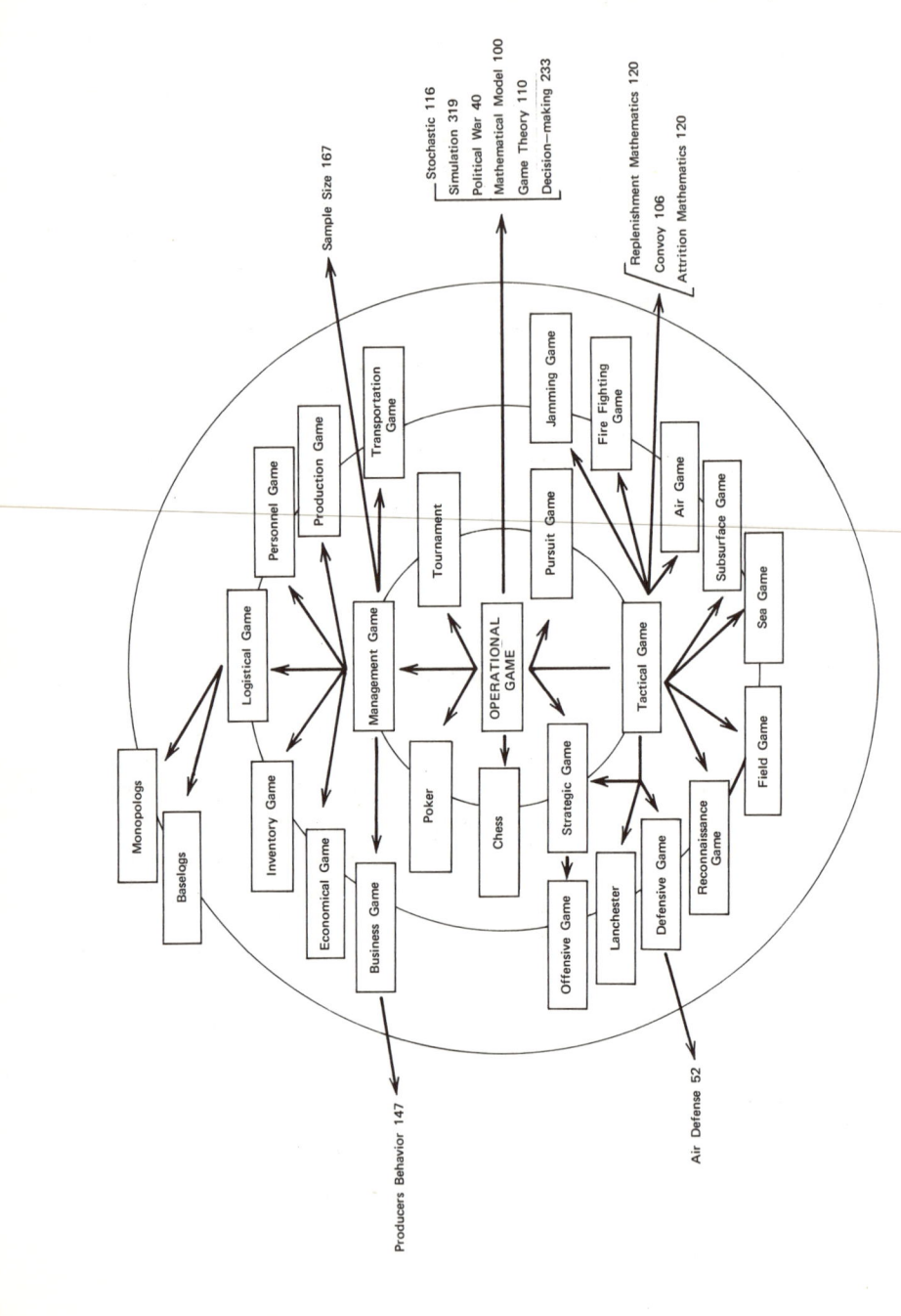

E 13 Q	Air Game	
O 6 D	Baselogs	
E 14 Q	Business Game	
E 15 Q	Chess	
E 16 Q	Defensive Game	
E 17 Q	Economical Game	
E 18 Q	Field Game	
X 7 W	Fire Fighting Game	
E 4 R	Game, Operational	
E 19 Q	Inventory Game	
E 20 Q	Jamming Game	
O 4 D	Lanchester	
E 1 R	Logistical Game	
E 2 R	Management Game	
O 5 D	Monopologs	
E 3 R	Offensive Game	
E 4 R	Operational Game	
E 5 R	Personnel Game	
E 6 R	Poker	
E 7 R	Production Game	
E 8 R	Pursuit Game	
E 9 R	Reconnaissance Game	
E 10 R	Sea Game	
E 11 R	Strategic Game	
E 12 R	Subsurface Game	
E 14 R	Tactical Game	
E 13 R	Tournament	
E 15 R	Transportation Game	

Figure 41. Circular display: hierarchical levels arranged in concentric circles (following TDCK) (D3.1.2,3). (Source: TDCK 1966.5.)

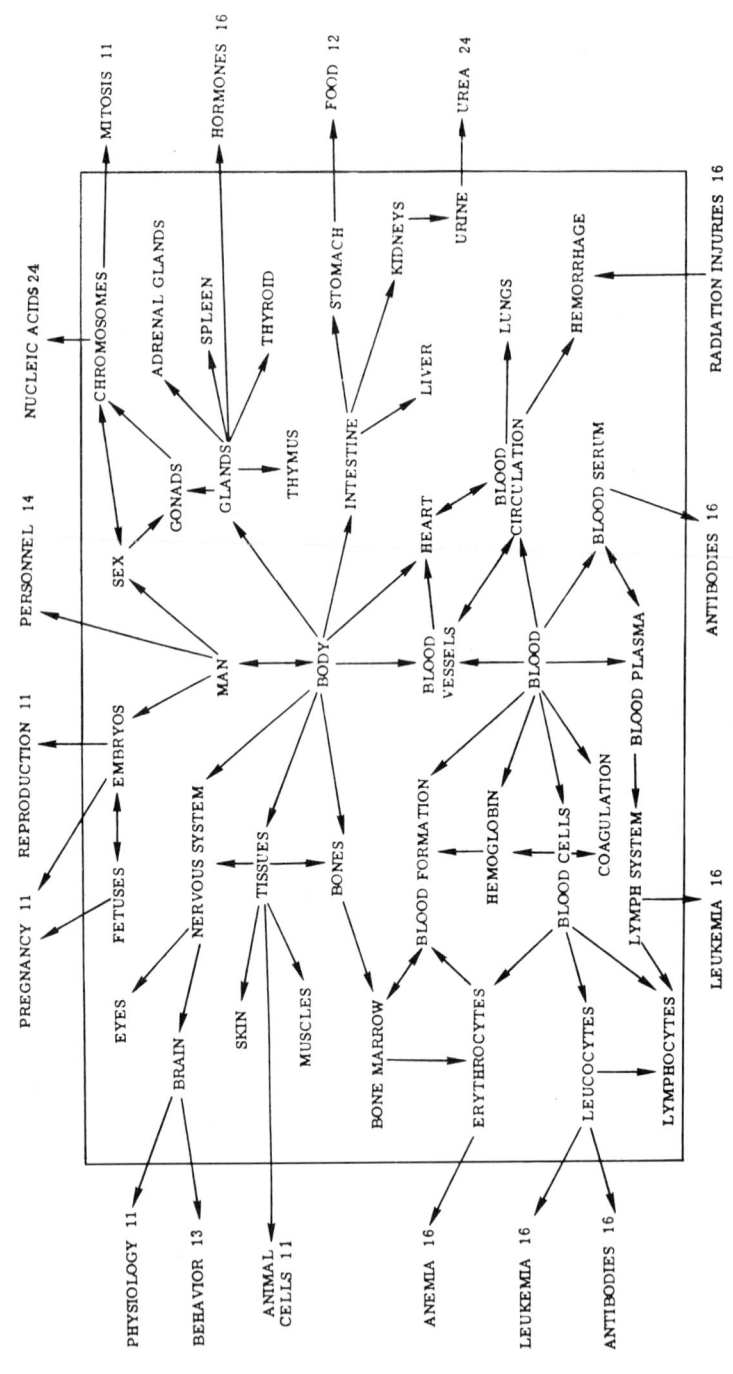

Figure 42. Network display of conceptual relationships following EURATOM 1: Group 15 Anatomy (EURATOM 2, see Figure 46) (D3.2). (Source: EURATOM 1967, 1964 ed., issued by EURATOM, Brussels, Belgium.)

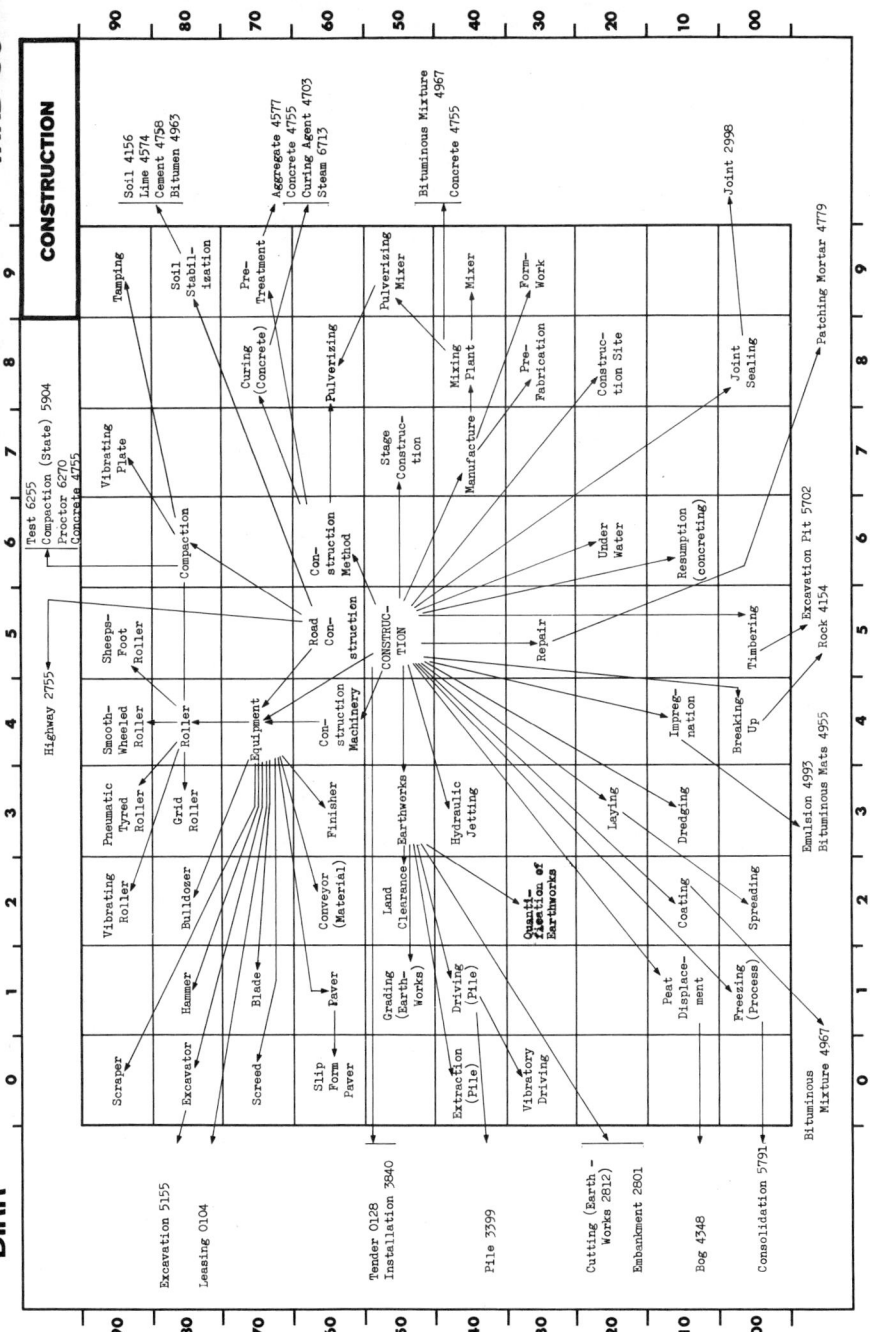

Figure 43. Network display within a coordinate grid (D3.2). (Source: IRRD thesaurus 1972, issued by OECD, Paris.)

Construction

0	Construction method		0	Earthworks
1	Pulverizing		1	Land clearance
1	Pre-treatment		1	Grading (earthworks)
1	Curing (concrete)		1	Extraction (pile)
0	Road construction		1	Driving (pile)
1	Soil stabilization		2	Vibratory driving
1	Compaction		1	Quantification of earthworks
2	Tamping		0	Hydraulic setting
2	Vibrating plate		0	Peat displacement
0	Equipment		0	Freezing (process)
1	Roller		0	Coating
2	Sheeps-foot roller		0	Laying
2	Smooth-wheeled roller		1	Spreading
2	Pneumatic roller		0	Dredging
2	Vibrating roller		0	Impregnation
2	Grid roller		0	Breaking up
1	Bulldozer		0	Repair
1	Scraper		0	Timbering
1	Hammer		0	Resumption (correcting)
1	Excavator		0	Under water
1	Blade		0	Joint scaling
1	Screed		0	Construction site
1	Paver		0	Manufacture
2	Slip form paver		1	Prefabrication
1	Conveyer (material)		1	Form work
1	Finisher		1	Mixing plant
			2	Mixer
			2	Pulverizing mixer

Figure 44. The descriptors and their relationships from Figure 43 displayed in a linear sequence with indention (D3.2). The numbers at the left designate the hierarchical level.

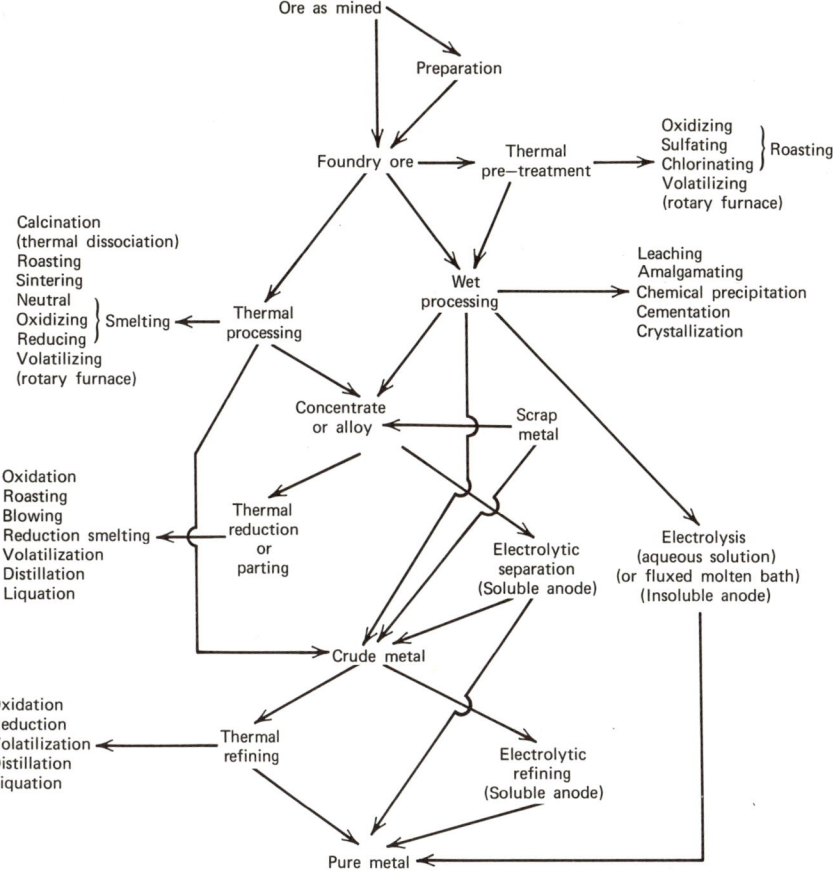

Figure 45. Network display based on a sequence of processes and their results (D3.2). (Courtesy Verlag Chemie, Weinheim, Germany.)

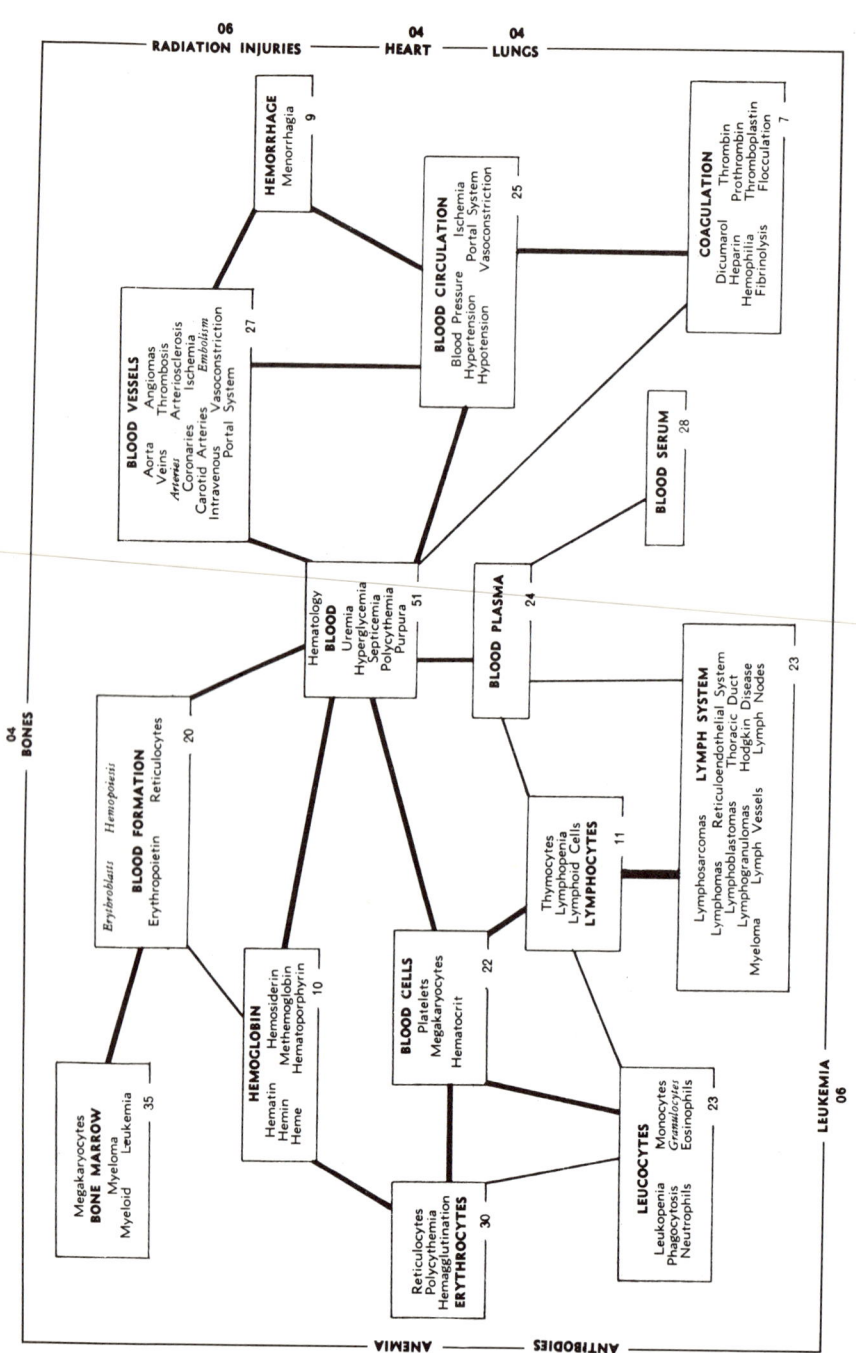

Figure 46. Network display following EURATOM 2: Group 05 Blood system (D3.2). (In the original, the print is black and the boxes and the lines between them are green. A variant of this form, considered first for the EURATOM thesaurus, is shown in EURATOM 1967, pt I, back.) (Source: EURATOM 1967, issued by EURATOM, Brussels, Belgium.) (EURATOM 1, see Figure 42)

D3.5 Methods for Compressing the Display of Checklist Descriptors

It should be possible to grasp the display of the checklist descriptors and their interrelationships in one glance (see Section D1.1.1). This display should therefore fit on a double letter-size sheet (Europ. size DIN A3). A printed display is best because one may use various typefonts, including very small ones (which are still legible in quality printing). Also a great number of special characters are available in printing. However, the cost of typesetting will usually be prohibitive unless the checklist descriptors are printed on the document analysis sheet, as suggested in D1.1.1,1.

The use of a typewriter in producing this display presents difficulties. It has been suggested that the descriptors be abbreviated to six letters, which would allow for a thousand descriptors on a double letter-size format, if indention is not used. However, this procedure not only neglects indention but also the notation preceding a descriptor. The six-letter abbreviations are very often too short to be intelligible. A better procedure is to prepare an original of two times the linear size (four times area size) and to reduce it 2:1.

D3.6 Auxiliary ISAR Systems ("Conceptual Indexes") II

D3.6.0 Introduction and rationale

Basically the displays discussed so far in Section D3 are mechanisms to retrieve concepts based on their relationships to other concepts. (Section D3 is not at all concerned with the retrieval of concepts based on the terms used to designate those concepts; that problem is solved by an alphabetical index.) There are two modes of retrieval of concepts:

(1) The retrieval mode might be browsing as when applying the checklist technique of indexing. For this purpose it is essential that for any concept all narrower concepts be easily retrieved so that they can be scanned to see whether or not they are relevant.

(2) The search might be for a certain concept someone has in mind for indexing or for searching. If he is using a classified arrangement, he will enter at a broader concept which he knows. He will then go downward into the classified arrangement as well as follow Narrower Term cross-references until he finds the appropriate descriptor.

The process is best illustrated in a system where precombined descriptors are expressed by semantic factors. Someone has expressed his search concept by $A:B:C:E$. He enters the list at any of the components, say A. There he looks through the narrower descriptors, either listed at the same place or indicated through cross-references. Either he finds the descriptor he is looking for or he finds a descriptor broader than his search concept, say

A:B:E. In the latter case he looks through the narrower descriptors given for *A:B:E*, and there he finds *A:B:E:C* (which, of course, is the same as *A:B:C:E*, the system using a different order of the components from that of the searcher). Starting from *A:B:E:C* he also finds all narrower descriptors, either listed immediately or indicated by cross-references. The process is not dependent on semantic factoring (but it is more easily understood in these terms). It is dependent only on the inclusion of all hierarchical relationships. If there are many descriptors that are, in effect, precombined (no matter whether this is shown through semantic factoring or not), than we have a very intricate polyhierarchical structure. The number of cross-references grows to the point where the above process is too cumbersome and inefficient to be practical. In other words, if the number of descriptors is large and many of the descriptors are precombined, cross-references do not provide a convenient means for retrieving descriptors, as anybody following the cross-reference in LC Subject Headings can confirm. This may be reformulated by saying that in this case cross-references do not provide a convenient means for displaying the hierarchical structure.

What, then, can the designer of the indexing language do? The answer is very simple. He can set up an *ISAR system for descriptors,* called an auxiliary ISAR system.

(The following quote elaborates on this idea: "It seems to the program team that the problem of indexing is, in fact, an information retrieval problem in and of itself. The indexer is attempting to retrieve relevant information, i.e., appropriate descriptor terms, from the universe of terms available to him. The data base consists of all appropriate or valid descriptors which can or should be used, and his criteria of selection are based upon the requirements of the article or book he is indexing, the system, and the user. An indexing aid, then, is that device or technique which enables him to rapidly select or retrieve from the data base those descriptors which are most accurate and/or appropriate.")

Such a system makes it possible for the thesaurus user to express the concept looked for by a combination of "core descriptors" contained in a "core classification" consisting of elemental or nearly elemental concepts and then retrieve all descriptors (subject headings, LC class number, etc.) that are equal to or narrower than the concept looked for. Or he may find that there is no such descriptor. Note that it is easier to retrieve, say, three core descriptors which by combination form the concept looked for among a thousand core descriptors than to retrieve the compound concept looked for among, say, 30,000 precombined descriptors.

In the following section we shall discuss possible implementations of such an auxiliary ISAR system.

D3.6.1 Implementation of ISAR systems for descriptors (auxiliary ISAR systems)

,1 Mechanized auxiliary ISAR systems. One could use any mechanical system used for combination indexing, for example, peek-a-boo cards or edge-notched cards or an on-line computerized ISAR system (an off-line computerized system would not be very useful since the retrieval tasks in indexing or formulating search requests cannot wait). Note that the possibility for inclusive searching must be built into the system; with peek-a-boo cards or edge-notched cards this means generic posting. In such a system one could see at once whether a compound concept containing the core descriptor combination being searched for is represented in the system or not.

,2 Combinatorial indexes. By combinatorial index we mean a printed index that makes it possible to retrieve combinations in terms of their components, in our case to retrieve precombined descriptors in terms of their semantic factors.

The simplest example is a KWIC index as shown in Figures 47c and 47d, using strings of terms or strings of notational symbols, respectively. The use of notations makes more sense because related compound concepts are collocated. Take the example *N2800* (which stands for *Architectural Acoustics*) and *Buildings-Soundproofing*. In the KWIC index based on terms (Figure 47c) the entries based on the second component (*Acoustics* or *Soundproofing* respectively) are far apart. In the KWIC index based on notations (Figure 47d) the second component is expressed by *T30* or *T37*, respectively, and as a result the entries are in the same area.

The KWIC index allows for look-up of "combinations" consisting of one component only; it is based on one-component entry. If one is searching for a combination of two components, any one of these components may be selected, and all entries containing this component have to be scanned. More convenient but also of much larger size would be an index showing each descriptor under each combination of components (for example, a SLIC index). As an intermediate solution, it has been suggested that entries be made only for "useful combinations". The chain-indexing method presents another possibility for reducing the number of combinations.

(However, the chain indexing method rather confuses the matter by being two things at once: an index to descriptors in terms of their constituents and broader concepts as well as an alphabetical index. To some degree the "relative" alphabetical index to DDC and even, if to a still lesser degree, the alphabetical indexes for the LCC schedules serve at the same time as combinatorial indexes based on conceptual components. It would be much clearer and probably much more useful to separate these two func-

266   D   Thesaurus Format

tions and to provide a chain index in which the constituents are expressed by their notation and an alphabetical index to the schedules. This is not to say that the chain index is the best form of a combinatorial index.)

As may be seen from Figure 47 an index constructed according to one of these methods would facilitate considerably the use of indexing languages containing many precombined descriptors, such as the LC Subject Headings or the LC Classification, both in indexing and in searching.

A remark of caution is in order with respect to combinatorial indexes: Combinatorial indexes usually are designed in such a way that it is easy to retrieve those descriptors that are equal to the search request formulation or narrower than the search request formulation due to combination—that is, for the search request formulation $A:B$ the narrower descriptor $A:B:C$ is found easily. Retrieving also the narrower concept $A:B1$, where $B1$ is narrower than B, or $A1.1:B1.1$ is much more difficult. Whereas in mechanized systems this problem can be solved easily by generic posting from $A1.1$ to $A1$ to A and $B1.1$ to $B1$ to B, in a combinatorial index we would need 9 entries, namely $A1.1:B1.1$, $A1.1:B1$, $A1.1:B$; $A1:B1.1$, ... $A:B$. For reasons of space these entries are usually omitted. An exception to this is the chain index, where some of these entries are made.

Figure 47. Illustration of a combinatorial index to both LC Subject Headings and LC Classification (Section D3.6.1,2).

a: Core classification

          A70   Military vs. civilian
                 A73   Military
                 A77   Civilian
          N00   Transportation and traffic
                 N10   Vehicles
                 N20   Traffic installations
                        N25   Traffic stations
                 N33   Air transport
                 N37   Water transport
          R00   . . .
                 R23   Buildings
                 R27   Architecture
                 R43   Construction
          S00   Engineering
                 T30   Acoustics
                        T37   Soundproofing
          U00   America
                 U15   US

Figure 47. (Continued)

b: LC Subject Headings and LC Class Numbers with decomposition into semantic factors

LC subject headings

Aeroplanes—Soundproofing = N10 Vehicles: N33 Air transport: T37 Soundproofing

Airports—Buildings = R23 Buildings: N25 Traffic stations: N33 Air transport

Buildings—Soundproofing = R23 Buildings: R43 Construction: T37 Soundproofing

Ships—Soundproofing = N10 Vehicles: N37 Water transport: T37 Soundproofing

LC class numbers

H550-560 Ports, harbors, docks, wharves, etc.
  = N25 Traffic stations: N37 Water transport: A77 Civilian

NA2800 Architectural acoustics
  = R27 Architecture: T30 Acoustics

NA6300-6307 Airport buildings
  = R23 Buildings: N25 Traffic stations: N33 Air transport: A77 Civilian'

NA6330 Dock buildings, ferry houses, etc.
  = R23 Buildings: N25 Traffic stations: N37 Water transport: A77 Civilian

TC350-374 Harbor works
  = N25 Traffic stations: N37 Water transport: S00 Engineering

TM1725 Soundproof construction
  = R23 Buildings: R43 Construction: T37 Soundproofing

TL725-726 Airways (routes), airports, and landing aerodromes
  = N20 Traffic installations: N33 Air transport

VA67-79 Naval ports, bases, reservation, docks, etc.
  = N25 Traffic stations: N37 Water transport: A73 Military: U15 US

Figure 47. (Continued)

c: Index (KWIC—format, using terms)

	→ Architecture: Acoustics.	NA 2800 Architectural acoustics
Buildings: Traffic Stations:	Air transport.	Airports—Buildings
Traffic installations:	Air transport.	TL 725–726 Airways, airports
Buildings: Traffic Stations:	Air transport: Civilian.	NA 6300–6307 Airport buildings
Vehicles:	Air transport: Soundproofing.	Aeroplanes—Soundproofing
:	Architecture: Acoustics.	NA 2800 Architectural acoustics
:	Buildings: Construction: Soundproofing.	TM 1725 Soundproofing construction; Buildings—Soundproofing
		Airports—Buildings
:	Buildings: Traffic Stations: Air transport.	NA 6300–6307 Airport buildings
:	Buildings: Traffic Stations: Air transport:	NA 6300 Dock buildings, ferry houses, etc.
:	Buildings: Traffic Stations: Water transport:	
Civilian.		
Civilian.		
Traffic Stations: Air transport:	Civilian.	NA 6300–6307 Airport buildings
Traffic Stations: Water transport:	Civilian.	NA 6330 Dock buildings, ferry houses, etc.
Traffic Stations: Water transport:	Civilian.	HE 550–560 Ports, harbors, docks, etc.
Buildings:	Construction: Soundproofing.	TM 1725 Soundproofing construction; Buildings—Soundproofing
Traffic Stations: Water transport:	Engineering.	TC 350–374 Harbor works
Traffic Stations: Water transport:	Military: US.	VA 67–79 Naval ports, bases, etc.
→ Buildings: Construction:	Soundproofing.	TM 1725 Soundproofing construction; Buildings—Soundproofing

Vehicles: Air transport:	Soundproofing.
Vehicles: Water transport:	Soundproofing.
: Traffic installations: Air transport.	
Buildings: Traffic Stations: Air transport.	
Civilian. Buildings: Traffic Stations: Air transport:	
Civilian. : Traffic Stations: Water transport:	
Civilian. Buildings: Traffic Stations: Water transport:	
Engineering. : Traffic Stations: Water transport:	
Military: US. : Traffic Stations: Water transport:	
Water transport: Military: US. Traffic Stations:	Soundproofing.
Vehicles: Air transport:	Soundproofing.
Vehicles: Water transport:	Soundproofing.
Buildings: Traffic Stations: Water transport: Civilian.	
Traffic Stations: Water transport: Civilian.	
Traffic Stations: Water transport: Engineering.	
Traffic Stations: Water transport: Military: US.	
Vehicles: Water transport:	Soundproofing.

Aeroplanes—Soundproofing.	
Ships—Soundproofing.	
TL 725–726	Naval ports, bases, etc.
Airports—Buildings	
NA 6300–6307	Airport buildings
HE 550–560	Ports, harbors, docks, etc.
NA 6330	Dock buildings, ferry houses, etc.
TC 350–374	Harbor works
VA 67–79	Naval ports, bases, etc.
VA 67–79	Naval ports, bases, etc.
Aeroplanes—Soundproofing.	
Ships—Soundproofing.	
NA 6330	Dock buildings, ferry houses, etc.
HE 550–560	Ports, harbors, docks, etc.
TC 350–374	Harbor works
VA 67–79	Naval ports, bases, etc.
Ships—Soundproofing.	

A sample search request might be: *Soundproofing of Vehicles*. This is expressed by the combination *Soundproofing: Vehicles*. One may enter the index under either term and scan the entries there for the other term. In this example one will find the two subject headings *Aeroplanes—Soundproofing* and *Ships—Soundproofing*.

Figure 47. (Continued)

d: Index (KWIC—format, using notations)

```
N25: N37: A73: U15              VA 67–79 Naval ports, bases, etc.
N25: N37: A77                    HE 550–560 Ports, harbors, docks, etc.
R23: N25: N33: A77               NA 6300–6307
R23: N25: N37: A77               NA 6330 Dock buildings, ferry houses, etc.
             N10: N33: T37       Aeroplanes—Soundproofing
             N10: N37: T37       Ships—Soundproofing
             N20: N33            TL 725–726 Airways, airports, etc.
        R23: N25: N33            Airports—Buildings
        R23: N25: N33: A77       NA 6300–6307 Airport buildings
             N25: N37: A73: U15  VA 67–79 Naval ports, bases, etc.
             N25: N37: A77       HE 550–560 Ports, harbors, docks, etc.
        R23: N25: N37: A77       NA 6330 Dock buildings, ferry houses, etc.
             N25: N37: S00       TC 350–374 Harbor works
             N20: N33            TL 725–726 Airways, airports, etc.
        R23  N25: N33            Airports—Buildings
        R23  N25: N33: A77       NA 6300–6307 Airport buildings
             N10: N33: T37       Aeroplanes—Soundproofing
```

N25:	N37:	A73:	U15	VA 67–79 Naval ports, bases, etc.
N25:	N37:	A77		HE 550–560 Ports, harbors, docks, etc.
R23:	N25:	N37:	A77	NA 6330 Dock buildings, ferry houses, etc.
	N25:	N37:	S00	TC 350–374 Harbor works
	N10:	N37:	T37	Ships—Soundproofing
	R23:	N25:	N33	Airports—Buildings
	R23:	N25:	N33: A77	NA 6300–6307 Airport buildings
	R23:	N25:	N37: A77	NA 6330 Dock buildings, ferry houses, etc.
	R23:	R43:	T37	TM 1725 Soundproof construction; Buildings—Soundproofing
	R27:	T30		NA 2800 Architectural acoustics
	R43:	T37		TM 1725 Soundproof construction; Buildings—Soundproofing
R23:				TC 350–374 Harbor works
N25:	N37:	S00		NA 2800 Architectural acoustics
→	R27:	T30		Aeroplanes—Soundproofing
N10:	N33:	T37		Ships—Soundproofing
N10:	N37:	T37		TM 1725 Soundproof construction; Buildings—Soundproofing
→ R23:	R43:	T37		VA 67–79 Naval ports, bases, etc.
N25:	N37:	A73:	U15	

D3.7 On-Line Display of Thesauri (Special Topic)

For most purposes hard-copy display of a thesaurus is most efficient, and the previous considerations were intended mainly for hard-copy display. In some situations, however, on-line display may be preferable, and it will become more important as terminal technology improves and the costs for visual display terminals decrease. A few remarks are, therefore, in order.

The main advantages of on-line display are:

(a) *Availability of the thesaurus:* The user of an on-line ISAR system does not need a copy of the thesaurus while searching. This is especially important in networks where a user sitting at one terminal may use a number of ISAR systems that employ different thesauri.

(b) *Flexibility of display and use:* First of all, automated auxiliary ISAR systems to retrieve descriptors, as described in Section D3.6, can be implemented. Second, in a hard-copy display, space is limited if one wants to stay within reasonable costs. Therefore, the information that can be given in each entry is limited. For example, in the classified index cross-references are indicated by notation only—the descriptor text is omitted to save space. On-line presentations do not have these restrictions because only a segment of the whole structure is displayed at any one time.

It is plausible to assume that a computer file organization along the lines of the Roget-Soergel model is best. For the user only three "parts" of the thesaurus are needed:

(0) Introduction
(1) Classified index
(2) Main part.

The introduction should be available on-line to instruct the user in the on-line use of the thesaurus at hand. The classified index is displayed in segments according to user request. The user should have a choice of the form used in the display (linear sequence with indention, tree method, network arrangement, etc.). Also he should be able to call for summaries on different levels of specificity, as discussed in Section D3.1.1,3 and exemplified in Figure 36. Looking at the general summary, the user decides on an area that he wants to have "expanded", that is, displayed in more detail (narrower descriptors 1 or 2 levels down). This process can then be repeated until the proper descriptor is found. It is especially convenient if the instruction to "expand" a particular descriptor can be given by pointing to the descriptor with a light pen. It can be seen from this discussion that the considerations on the display of the classified index apply in the main to on-line display as well. The same is true for the considerations on main part entries in section D2. It might be useful to let the user specify, if he so chooses, what information he wants from the main part and in what detail he wants that information. If the user does not give these specifications, a standard default option would apply. If the screen is big enough, one may use about two-thirds of the screen to display a segment of the classified index and the other third to display the main part entry for the descriptor being examined.

The main difference between hard-copy display and on-line display occurs in the look-up problem. The discussion in Section D1.3 applies to hard-copy display only. In on-line display all look-ups can be done by computer. Specifically the user does not need an alphabetical index. An exception to this occurs if a term is not found by the program; then it is useful to display an appropriate section of the alphabetical index (KWIC format).

D4 NOTATION

D4.0 Definition

A notational symbol or, for short, a notation is a string of characters used to identify each descriptor and possibly some or all preferred terms. The most important function of notation is to facilitate the look-up of a given descriptor in a classified arrangement. The set of all notational symbols and/or the system of forming notational symbols is also called a notation. The necessity for notation arises from the use of descriptor displays arranged in classified order as pointed out in Section D1.3.4. We have shown that the use of such displays is essential in achieving good results in indexing and search request formulation.

There should be a one-to-one correspondence between descriptors and other preferred terms on the one hand and notational symbols on the other. That is, to each preferred term there is assigned one and only one notational symbol, and each notational symbol belongs to one and only one preferred term. Notation and preferred term are thus only different expressions for the same concept.

Examples:
H14.3 Programmed instruction
NA2800 Architectural acoustics

A more elaborate example is given in Figure 48.

It is also possible to proceed as follows: One forms classes of synonymous and quasi-synonymous terms, but instead of selecting a term as the preferred designation of the ISAR concept one assigns to each class a notational symbol which serves as the preferred designation. (One might also say "the same notational symbol is assigned to each term in the class", which amounts to the same thing.) In this case there is no one-to-one correspondence between ISAR concepts and terms (since there are no preferred

D Thesaurus Format

	1	2	3	4	5	6	7

Expressive notation	Partly expressive partly ordinal notation
1	**A00 General categories of a more general nature** (for combinations)
1.1	A05 General, others
1.2	A09'3 All subject fields
...	...
1.5	A09'9 *Data versus analysis*
1.5.1	A10 *Data, description, experimental*
1.5.1.1	A13 Process-produced data
1.5.1.2	A15 News
	...
1.5.1.5	A20 Quantitative data, figures, statistics
1.5.1.5.1	A22 Figures given in text
1.5.1.5.2	A24 1-3 statistical tables
	...
1.5.1.6	A30 *N.N. (document, table contains; figure is)*
1.5.1.6.1	A32 Base figure
1.5.1.6.2	A33 Sum
1.5.1.6.2.1	A33.2 Figures given are sums
1.5.1.6.2.2	A33.4 Summation in a table
	...
1.5.1.6.6	A38 Parameters of the distribution of a variable
1.5.1.6.6.1	A38.2 Position parameters
1.5.1.6.6.1.1	A38.3 Average, arithmetic mean
1.5.1.6.6.1.2	A38.4 Median, percentile
1.5.1.6.6.1.2.1	A38.5 Median
1.5.1.6.6.1.2.2	A38.5'5 Percentile (with data field)
1.5.1.6.6.1.3	A38.6 Mode, most frequent value
1.5.1.6.6.2	A38.7 Parameters of scatter
1.5.1.6.7	A39 Descriptive measures for the connection between several variables
1.5.2	A50 *Analysis, results of theoretical work*

	1	2	3	4	5	6	7

Figure 48. Example showing two types of notation (D4.0; also used for D4.3). (The arrangement follows the method recommended in D3.1.1,2.) (Source: Soergel et al. 1970.8, issued by DATUM, Bonn, Germany.)

terms), but there is a one-to-one correspondence between ISAR concepts and notational symbols.

D4.1 Purpose of Notation

In order to avoid any misunderstandings it should be stressed from the outset that the primary purpose of notation is *not* to facilitate computer processing. On the contrary, its primary purpose is to facilitate external operations of indexing and search request formulation, of the input of data, and of filing in conventional ISAR systems. In more detail the purposes of notation can be stated as follows:

(a) *Fast look-up in descriptor lists arranged in classified order.* Linkage from alphabetical index to classified index and main part.

(b) *Short denotation of descriptors.* This serves the convenience of the indexer or searcher or anybody who has to write down descriptors. It is also useful for making cross-references within the classified index. One *caveat* should be added, however: in all material to be read by users of the ISAR system (catalog cards, print-out of search results) the abbreviated text of the descriptor should be added to the notational symbol whenever the effort in terms of time and space needed seems justified. This is necessary because the notational symbols alone are not intelligible to the user.

(c) *Speeding up clerical processes,* such as writing, punching, filing. Sorting and filing using a properly designed notation are much faster than the same operations working on natural language terms.

(d) *Facilitate the detection of errors* by mechanical checks.

We shall discuss in Section D4.3 how a notation serving these purposes can be designed.

D4.1.1 Changes in notations (advanced)

None of these purposes requires that the notational symbol for each descriptor remain unchanged over a long period of time provided that in document representations (and in stored interest profiles) the notational symbols are always accompanied by an abbreviated form of the text of the descriptor. Therefore, some notational symbols can be changed if the necessity arises. There are, of course, difficulties connected with such changes similar to the difficulties connected with a change in phone numbers. But these difficulties can be coped with. Severe inconveniences arise from changes in notational symbols if, for economic reasons, it is not possible to give an abbreviated text with every notational symbol. In mechanized systems the problems arising therefrom can be solved in two ways. A brute-force approach would be to replace the old notation for descriptor A by the new notation in all the records where it appears. A more elegant solution is as follows: One uses a code designed specifically for machine internal operations, which is different from the notation. If descriptor A occurs in a document representation, it is always represented by this internal code. The internal code never changes. There is a conversion table, leading from the notational symbol to the appropriate internal code, and vice versa. If a notational symbol has to be changed, the only thing one has to do is to change the conversion table accordingly.

In non-mechanized systems the problems are more difficult. Take, as an example, a collection of newspaper clippings which increases by 500 clippings a day. On each clipping the appropriate notational symbols have to be written in order to ensure correct filing. The effort to add to each notational symbol an abbreviated text would be prohibitive; it could not be justified in terms of a cost/benefit analysis. The user can get the text of the descriptor from the label on the folder and so this text need not be repeated on every single clipping. The only thing that can be done in this situation is to keep an exact record of changes in notation so that the meaning of a certain notational symbol can be inferred from the time at which the clipping has been indexed. One may also replace the old notational symbol by the new one as the folders concerned are actually used, but even this possibility is precluded as soon as one puts the clipping collection on microfilm. It should not be surprising that changes in notation are most inconvenient in those cases where one relies most heavily on notation. It is advisable in such a case to change notations only if absolutely necessary and to weigh the disadvantages of a change in notation against the disadvantages of the alternatives, namely, using longer notations or inserting a new descriptor in a place where there is a gap in the notational symbols, even if this is not the best place in terms of logical sequence.

D4.1.2 Notation and machine-internal code in computerized ISAR systems (special topic)

We have already alluded to the fact that it is by no means necessary to use the notation for machine internal operations. There are several possible ways of representing a descriptor in the computer:

(a) Descriptor text,
(b) Notation,
(c) A machine-internal code independent from both text and notation.

The use of a machine-internal code requires translation from the descriptor text or the notation into the code, and vice versa. Even so, overall efficiency is often higher because brief internal codes mean storage savings and higher processing speed. The internal code for a descriptor remains the same, whereas text or notation may change, as discussed above.

Another aspect is the possibility of performing inclusive searches as easily and cheaply as possible. In a system based on sequential scanning this would be facilitated by a code with a structure similar to an expressive notation (see Figure 48, Section D4.0); however, such codes tend to be rather lengthy. Another possibility is the use of level-indicators.

Example:
A10/2 Data, description, experimental
A13/3 Process-produced data

However, these are problems to be solved by computer programmers, and they must not be a main concern in thesaurus development.

D4.2 The Fallacy of Overstressing Notation

The reader should be aware of a serious fallacy which is to be encountered especially in the Universal Decimal Classification, namely, the fallacy of basing an indexing language/classification scheme on notation. The notation is neither an indexing language/classification scheme nor an essential part of such a scheme. It would be completely wrong first to devise a notation and then adapt the hierarchical structure of the indexing language to that notation. The logical order of steps is exactly the opposite. First the hierarchical structure of the indexing language has to be developed without paying any attention to any notation whatsoever. Only then is it possible to devise a notation for that particular indexing language which serves best the above-mentioned purposes. Depending on the type of notation used it may then be necessary to make small changes in the hierarchical structure in order to avoid inconvenient notational symbols. This is especially true for systems in which the mechanical devices used set some constraints for the notation. An example may illustrate this point. Assume a system using the MIRACODE microfilm retrieval device. In this device, three-digit codes are used to represent descriptors. In order to facilitate input to the MIRACODE device, notation and machine code should be identical. This limits the notation to three-digit numbers. If one wants to use expressive notation for doing inclusive searches, the hierarchy to be designed for that purpose is limited to three levels. Such an artificial limitation may work better in that particular system than an ideal hierarchy. One has to keep in mind that the ultimate purpose is not to have an ideal indexing language/classification scheme but to have an optimal overall ISAR system.

D4.3 Design of a Notation (Technical, Especially Sections D4.3.3-D4.3.6)

This section is not intended to deal with the design problems in detail. The interested reader is referred to the literature cited in D4.1. We give only a brief summary, which is followed by some suggestions of our own. In our discussion we shall refer repeatedly to the example given in Figure 48 (Section D4.0).

D4.3.1 Design criteria

In order to serve the purposes discussed in Section D4.1 a notation should meet the following criteria:

(a) *Simplicity*. The notation should be simple:
(a1) to look up and to sort (it should convey order clearly);
(a2) to remember;
(a3) to write or type (this is partly a function of (a2)—if a notation is easy to remember it is also easier to type or transcribe, and the probability of errors in these operations is reduced). The characters used in notational symbols should be available on the keyboards of the machines used;
(a4) to pronounce (easy pronunciation may contribute to memorability). (Some authors have even devised notations consisting of pronounceable syllables. To us this seems rather fanciful, basing the design mainly on a criterion of minor importance. If, however, one wants to use this type of notation one might use existing tables of 3- and 4-character pronounceable syllables.)

(b) *Brevity*. The more frequently a descriptor is used, the shorter its notation should be.

(c) *Hospitality*. One should be able to insert new descriptors at any place without having to reorganize the notation.

(d) *Redundancy* for purposes of error detection, mainly in computerized systems. A check digit, added to the notation proper, is useful for that purpose. The check digit may be derived from the notation by a special formula, or one may use the first two letters of the descriptor text. This latter method is particularly useful if, along with the notation, the descriptor text is entered anyway. Or one may append to the notation proper a digit indicating the hierarchical level. A fixed structure of the notational symbols can also be used (e.g., only capitals in the first position, only digits thereafter). If many gaps are left in the notation a typing error will often result in an invalid notation, which will thus be detected.

(e) *Ease of designing* the notation (especially if the notation is to be used in the process of thesaurus construction only).

D4.3.2 Types of notation

,1 **Expressive notation.** An expressive notation is defined by the following characteristic: If B is narrower than A then the notation for B is derived by adding characters to the notation of A.

Example:
hierarchical chain from UDC:
5   Science
52   Astronomy
523   Descriptive astronomy
523.8   Stars
523.85   Star clusters
523.854   Milky Way

D4 Notation 279

Another example is given in Figure 48 (Section D4.0).

(a) *Advantages.*

(a1) An expressive notation reflects a monohierarchical structure; given the notation, the place of the descriptor in a monohierarchical structure can be inferred at least to some extent. This may also add to the memorability of the notation to a certain extent but the length of expressive notations for specific concepts tends to decrease memorability.

(a2) If one wishes to subdivide a term that does not already have Narrower Terms the additional notations can be inserted without any difficulty (hospitality in chain).

Remarks on the advantages of expressiveness:

(1) It is claimed that, with an expressive notation, one may infer from the notation for a concept the whole hierarchical chain leading upwards from that concept. If we have *523.854 Milky Way,* we may conclude from this that *523.85* is the notation of a broader concept. This helps us little, however, unless we know what *523.85* stands for, which is unlikely. We therefore have to look into the schedules in order to see that *523.85* stands for *Star clusters.* The alleged advantage of expressiveness is lost because we have to look into the schedule anyway. However, it is easy to memorize the notations for the top elements of the hierarchy, for example, *5 Science* and *52 Astronomy.* Here expressiveness is of advantage. However, it is sufficient in this case to carry the expressiveness to the second level of the hierarchy and then use more or less ordinal notations, as, for example, in the notation for LCC or in the notation suggested in Section D4.3.3.

(2) If the notation is used for machine internal purposes, too, then the expressiveness may be used to facilitate inclusive searching. Expressive notations may also be used to facilitate inclusive searches in classified catalogs; there are, however, other means to achieve the same purpose.

(b) *Disadvantages.*

(b1) The number of main classes (highest terms), as well as the number of narrower terms each term may have, are limited by the notational base (that is, the number of characters to be used in the notational symbols at the position in question, for example, digits *0* to *9* = 10 characters, upper case letters *A* to *Z* = 26 characters, digits *0* to *9* and upper-case letters *A* to *Z* = 36 characters). This disadvantage can be overcome by introducing a separator, e.g., the period, for separating hierarchical levels in the notation (see the example in Figure 48, Section D4.0). However, the length of the notations is almost doubled by this procedure. Another procedure is the *octavizing device*: symbols on the same level run as follows: *0 ... 8, 90 ... 98, 990 ... 998,* etc. This leads to longer notations for the last descriptors in any array, and it also tends to obscure expressiveness.

(b2) The length of a notation is determined by the hierarchical level of the descriptor so that one has long notations for specific descriptors. In some systems this disadvantage is avoided by arbitrarily limiting the number of hierarchical levels. This is, however, an example of the fallacy of adapting the hierarchical structure to the notation instead of the reverse, discussed in Section D4.2.

(b3) Any change in hierarchical structure leads to a change in notation.

,2 Purely ordinal notation. The descriptors are numbered serially (but leaving gaps, see below), where *number* is understood in a more general sense to mean any string of characters (usually alphabetical characters and/or digits and a few special characters) provided there is a rule which determines how these character strings are to be arranged in a linear sequence.

The advantages and disadvantages are the reverse of those of an expressive notation:

(a) *Advantages.*

(a1) Every term can have any number of Narrower Terms on the level immediately below. The number of main classes is not limited.

(a2) The length of the notational symbols is not determined by the number of hierarchical levels but only by the total number of descriptors (and possibly other preferred terms). (This number may have to be increased if one wants to leave gaps.) Ordinal notations are therefore shorter than expressive ones.

(a3) A change in the hierarchy does not necessarily lead to a change in notation as long as the sequence of descriptors is not changed.

Example 1:
Introduction of new Broader Terms (notation after "." is ordinal)

Before		After	
I12 Age		I12 Age	
I12.23	Age 0- 5	I12.22	Age 0-20
I12.27	Age 5-10	I12.23	Age 0- 5
I12.33	Age 10-15	I12.27	Age 5-10
I12.37	Age 15-20	I12.33	Age 10-15
I12.43	Age 20-25	I12.37	Age 15-20
....		I12.42	Age 20-40
		I12.43	Age 20-25
		....	

Example 2:
Elimination of a hierarchical relationship

Before		After	
N36	Economic growth	N36	Economic growth
N37	Cycles of the economy	N37	Cycles of the economy

(b) *Disadvantages.*

(b1) The hierarchical structure is not reflected in the notation. From the notation one cannot draw any inference about the place of a descriptor in the hierarchy; one has to look into the classified index in order to get that information (compare, however, the remark in Section D4.3.2,1).

This disadvantage can be alleviated by appending a symbol indicating the hierarchical level to each notation.

Example:
A10/2 Data, description, experimental
A13/3 Process-produced data.

Instead of *A10/2* one might also write *A10b* or whatever seems meaningful.

(b2) It is not possible to subdivide a term unless there happens to be a sufficiently large gap in the number following that term (no hospitality in chain).

It is advisable to leave gaps in the sequence of numbers so that descriptors can be inserted later on. If one is lucky, these gaps allow for the insertion of a new descriptor without any changes in existing notations. If one is not lucky and the new descriptor logically belongs between two descriptors where there is no gap in the sequence of notations, one has to shift the notation either backward or forward until one comes to the next gap. Changes in notation are thus limited to the range between the new descriptor and the next gap. Alternatives are to insert the descriptor where there is a gap at the cost of having a not-so-logical sequence, or one might use the special device for intercalating new numbers described below. (The criteria to be considered in choosing the best alternative are discussed in Section D4.1.1). The distribution of gaps may be based on substantive considerations. (In which parts of the scheme are additions highly unlikely? In which parts are they to be expected?) If such criteria are lacking, one should proceed in a purely formal way and distribute the gaps equally within an array. The following table may be used in calculating gaps.

1	2	3	4	5	6	7	8
							2
						2	3
					2	3	4
			2	2	3	4	5
	3	3	4	4	4		
5		5	4	5	6	6	6
	7	7	6	7	7	7	7
			8	8	8	8	8
						9	9

number of descriptors (top row)

digits assigned (body)

For example, if $A50$ has five narrower descriptors, they will be given notations ending with the digits in column 5, namely, $A52, A54, A55, A57, A58$. (The digits 0 and 1 have special meanings in the system for which this table has been devised; compare Section D4.3.3.)

In some cases it might be advisable to leave gaps of 10 or 100 by appending 0 or 00 to every notation initially. This makes for ample flexibility, paid for by longer notational symbols.

,2.1 A special device for intercalating new serial numbers. It is useful to introduce the following convention: Between two adjacent numbers, for example, $A54$ and $A55$, new numbers $A54'0$ . . . $A54'9$ can be inserted. (Originally the comma was suggested instead of the apostrophe because the apostrophe is reserved for other purposes in UCD (and DDC). However, the comma is not easily distinguished from the period, which is very often used in notational symbols.)

One should be careful to understand that, for example, $A54'3$ need not be narrower than $A54$. It is simply a serial number after $A54$, just as $A55$ is. The principle may be applied several times: Between $A54'6$ and $A54'7$, the serial numbers $A54'6'0$ . . . $A54'6'9$ may be intercalated. Of course, the policy of leaving gaps is followed after the apostrophe: If there is only one number to be intercalated between $A54$ and $A55$ this number will be $A54'5$. In case more than ten numbers have to be inserted one may also create numbers as $A54'00$ . . . $A54'99$ or even $A54'a1$ . . . $A54'z9$. This principle of intercalation of serial numbers enables one to insert new descriptors at any place without any changes in existing notations. This is paid for by lengthier notations for the new descriptors and by having an additional rule to be learned by the user.

The principles of leaving gaps and of intercalating serial numbers may also be applied with expressive notations for the determination of the numbers within an array.

,3. Example. For an example comparing an expressive notation with a modified ordinal notation see Figure 48 (Section D4.0). In UDC-type notation (omitting the "." used as a separator) the expressive notations would be shorter but still lengthy.

D4.3.3 A partly expressive, partly ordinal system of notation (mixed notation)

Neither a completely expressive nor a purely ordinal notation is completely satisfactory. One might therefore try to derive a system of notation that combines characteristics of both. Such a system is described in the following, first for small indexing languages/classification schemes and then in the extended version for larger schemes.

,1 Mixed notation 1: small indexing languages/classification schemes (less than 1,000 descriptors). Assign capitals to the major subject areas (main classes). To conserve letters it will sometimes be useful to lump together under one capital several main classes that contain few descriptors each; on the other hand two or three capitals may have to be assigned to main classes containing many descriptors. One can extend the base for the main classes by assigning a digit instead of a capital to the main classes of form descriptors and/or by assigning a 2-digit number instead of a capital to major geographic areas (for example, *51* for *Europe*, *52* for *Asia*, etc.). All capitals may then be used for subject field descriptors. Within one capital descriptors are simply numbered serially, using 2-digit numbers starting with *00* and leaving gaps as described above.

The use of capitals in the way described makes this notation partly expressive. The expressiveness can be enhanced if one follows some principles in serial numbering in those places where it is possible without difficulties:

—Use of the digit *0*: the combination *00* is used for main classes only; *0* as a last digit is used only for more important Broader Terms which have a number of Narrower Terms. The notational symbols for a main class always end with *0*.

—Use of the digit *1*: *1* as last digit is used only for descriptors of the form *Economics, general references*.

—It is possible to "simulate" to a certain extent expressive notation in the serial numbering. (Compare, for example, in Figure 48, Section D4.0, *A20* or *A30*). This principle is not applied, however, if it would lead to difficulties (see, for example, *A10*). For an example of this notation, see Figure 35, Section D3.1.1,3.

Such a notation is easy to sort, brief, and easy to remember. According to psychological experiments it is easier for most people to remember character strings consisting of alphabetical characters and digits than to remember character strings consisting of digits only or alphabetic characters only.

,2 Mixed notation 2: large indexing languages/classification schemes (see Figure 48, Section D4.0, for an example).

(a) The basic notations are formed as before, possibly using the following extension: After, for example, *D99*, one may continue with *D100 . . . D999*. In this case one would assign the notations *D100, D200*, etc., to major Broader Terms or possibly even to main classes, thus extending the base available for notations for main classes. Another possibility, used in LCC, is to start with two capitals.

(b) The notation for a narrower descriptor can be formed by "fractional subdivision", but it need not be formed in that way.

Example:
    U17   Catastrophes
        U17.3   Earthquakes
        U17.7   Tornados

(Note the use of the period as a separator.)
It would also be possible to write the notations for the Narrower Terms as follows:

Example:
> U17 Catastrophes
>   U18 Earthquakes
>   U19 Tornados

It is even possible to use both methods at the same time.

Example:
> U17 Catastrophes
>   U17.3 Landslides
>   U18 Earthquakes
>   U19 Tornados

This last possibility should be used seldom, however. If a Narrower Term also has Narrower Terms the notation for these can again be formed using fractional subdivision or by continuing in an ordinal sequence.

Example:
> C79 Gross national product: production, distribution, utilization
>   C79.3 Distribution and redistribution of the GNP
>   C79.3.2 Distribution of the GNP, income distribution

But again, we could also write:
> C79 Gross national product: production, distribution, utilization
>   C79.3 Distribution and redistribution of the GNP
>   C79.4 Distribution of the GNP, income distribution

Fractional subdivision should be used only in those cases where the Broader Term—Narrower Term relationship is certain beyond doubt. If one were to detect later on that descriptor *B* was not in fact narrower than descriptor *A*, then the notation of descriptor *B*, formed by fractional subdivision, would have to be changed.

Two-digit numbers or even character-digit combinations may also be used after the period. It is recommended in this case that simulation of expressive notation be applied.

Example:
> N68 Income
>   N68.20 Income scale
>   N68.40 Types of receivers of income
>   N68.50 Sources of income
>   N68.52 Wages, salaries
>   N68.54 Business income
>   N68.56 Transfer incomes
>   N68.56.20 Pensions
>   N68.56.30 Welfare
>   . . . .

Often there is the alternative of using either further fractional subdivision or two-digit numbers after the period.

Example:
    N68.5   *Sources of income*
        N68.5.2   *Wages, salaries*
        N68.5.4   *Business income*
        N68.5.6   *Transfer incomes*
                N68.5.6.2   *Pensions*
       . . . .

Usually two-digit numbers are to be preferred because the notations for the numerous specific descriptors are then shorter by one character. Only if these specific descriptors are expected to be used very seldom as compared with the descriptors of the next higher level should further fractional subdivision be used, thereby keeping the notations of the broader descriptor shorter by one character.

(c) Arrangement of these notations in linear sequence. In simple cases the sequence is intuitively clear. For more complicated cases and for computer processing, one has to have formal rules:

—Each notation is subdivided into groups as follows:

- - Each non-digit character forms a group in itself.

- - A group of digits included between two non-digit characters (or being at the beginning or the end) forms a group which is to be sorted according to its numerical value.

—The collating sequence is as follows: :) . ' , all numbers A . . . Z
Disregard "(" in collating; see the example (H84:P33).3 below. This collating sequence takes into account the rules to be discussed in Sections D4.3.5 and D4.3.6.

,3 Notations for compound concepts. In Sections D4.3.5 and D4.3.6 we shall discuss the possibility of forming the notation of a compound concept by a *colon chain* containing the notations of its constituents.

Example:
    H84:P33:D50   *Cooperatives: Agriculture: History*

In this example the components are arranged in increasing order. This is not necessary, however. If the designer wants the compound concept listed under *D50 History*, he would write:

Example:
    D50:H84:P33   *History: Cooperatives: Agriculture*

In other words, the sequence of the components determines the place of the compound.

Fractional subdivision may be applied to these compound notations, too.

286 D Thesaurus Format

Example:

H84:P33 stands for *Cooperatives in Agriculture*. Kolchoses are a specific type of such cooperatives, and the notation for this term could therefore be *(H84:P33).3*.

However, it might be preferable to add a further component, if possible.

The sorting rules and the collating sequence given in Section ,2 lead to the following sequence.

Example:

H84	*Cooperatives*
H84:P33	*Cooperatives: Agriculture*
H84:P33:D50	*Cooperatives: Agriculture: History*
H84:P33:J84	*Cooperatives: Agriculture: Accounting*
(H84:P33).3	*Kolchoses*
H84:P33.7	*Cooperatives: Animal husbandry*
H84:P72	*Cooperatives: Buying*
H87	*Unions*

D4.3.4 An easy-to-produce expressive notation

The following notation is easy to produce and therefore recommended as auxiliary notation for schemes to be used as sources in thesaurus construction. It is best explained by Figure 49.

Notation	Terms
1	A
1.1	. B
1.2	. C
1.2.1	. . D
1.2.2	. . E
1.3	. F
2	G

Figure 49. An easy-to-produce expressive notation (D4.3.4).

The notation is completely expressive. By using the period as a separator of the different hierarchical levels we may have, for example, *2.13.2*, thus avoiding the limitations of the number of narrower descriptors a descriptor can have which is inherent in the usual decimal notation. (See Figure 48, Section D4.0, for a worked-out example.)

D4.3.5 Notation for precombined descriptors

(To understand this section the reader should be familiar with the notions discussed in Sections C2.4, "Selection and arrangement of descriptors with particular reference to manual ISAR systems", and C2.5, "Core classification and extended classification".)

In the discussion so far it has been tacitly assumed that all descriptors would have their own independent notation. However, there are situations where it is preferable to form the notation for a precombined descriptor by combining the notations of its constituents. Faceted classification is a case in point.

Example:
The notation for the precombined descriptor Dimensional stability of plastic at higher temperature is formed by combining the components
   Ph   *Plastics*
   Rab   *Dimensions*
   Ssd   *High temperature*
   Zb   *Stability (general)*
to result in PhRabSsdZb.

More generally, this principle is often useful if a core classification and extended classification are used. The core descriptors are assigned their own independent notation (even if they are moderately precombined), all other descriptors are assigned notations formed by combination. For example:

H84:P33:D50 Cooperatives: Agriculture: History

Note, however, that the notations formed by combination tend to be lengthy; this disadvantage is particularly serious if the indexing language/classification scheme is to be used for arranging books on shelves.

In systems where the notion of a core classification is not applied, descriptors should always be assigned their own independent notation. We shall illustrate the reasoning behind this rule using the example *Philosophy of culture*. If *Philosophy of culture* is a preferred term in the lead-in vocabulary, it might be assigned the notation *B00:Z50* (*B00 Culture, Z50 Philosophy*), as we shall see in the next section. If *Philosophy of culture* is a descriptor it has to be assigned a notation like *B02*. Thus the thesaurus user can tell from the notation whether he has a preferred term or a descriptor. Second, in some systems the indexer is allowed to form compound concepts like *B00:Z50* to be included in the document representation; this is more precise than just using the isolated descriptor *B00 Culture* and *Z50 Philosophy*. (In effect this is a form of linking descriptors.) Again, it is possible to distinguish between precombined descriptors having their own independent notation and compound concepts formed by the indexer. If the notion of a core classification is applied, other measures have to be taken if it is necessary to distinguish between precombined noncore descriptors and preferred terms in the lead-in vocabulary. This matter will not be discussed here, however.

D4.3.6 Notations for preferred terms that are not descriptors

In thesauri following the Roget-Soergel model it is necessary to assign a notation to *all* preferred terms, even to those that are not used as descriptors, in order to have the proper lead from the alphabetical index to the main part. In small systems one might simply use the same type of notations for both descriptors and other preferred terms. However, in larger systems this might become inconvenient, especially if descriptors are in general elemental concepts and if many other preferred terms are expressed as descriptor combinations. Also it is sometimes useful to design the notation in such a way that one can tell descriptors from lead-in terms simply by looking at the notation. The following example and the accompanying explanation show how this can be achieved.

Example:
    C642   **Traffic installations**
         . . .
         Water transport installations
         Air transport installations
         . . .
         Traffic stations
    C670   **Water transport**
    C680   **Air transport**

Descriptors are in boldface, the rest are other preferred terms. Notations could be assigned according to one of the alternatives.

Example:
    (a) C642:C670   *Water transport installations*
         C642:C680   *Air transport installations*
         . . .
         C642.3$ *Traffic stations*
    (b1) C642.4$ *Water transport installations*
         C642.6$ *Air transport installations*
         . . .
         C642.8$ *Traffic stations*
    (b2) C644$ *Water transport installations*
         C646$ *Air traffic installations*
         . . .
         C648$ *Stations, terminals*

In the example *C642 Traffic installations* has two kinds of Narrower Terms that are not used as descriptors: those generated by adding additional semantic factors and those generated by direct subdivision. They should always be listed in that order. This is achieved if one stipulates that ":" sorts before ".".

The rules used in this example are as follows:

(a) If the preferred term is a compound, its notation is formed as a "colon chain" of the notations of the constituents, or simply as a chain if the individual elements of the combination can be identified without a separator (e.g., by a capital at the beginning). The sequence of the constituents determines the place of the compound in the linear arrangement, or vice versa. Note that this method is not a must for compound terms; method (b) can be used as well. (Compare C1.1.0, especially the end of that section. Note that the colon does not specify the *kind* of relationships between the components. One can do so by introducing more differentiated relational indicators).

(b) The preferred term is assigned its own, independent notation followed by "$" to show that the notation does not stand for a descriptor. This notation can be formed by fractional subdivision.

These two methods can be used together in the same thesaurus, and it depends on the specific situation what method should be used for the preferred term in question. Advantages and disadvantages of the two methods can be shortly described as follows: Notations using alternative (a) are easy to produce and highly hospitable; the sequence of the preferred terms usually makes sense; furthermore, the structure of the notation reflects the conceptual structure of the term. But the notations are lengthy. Notations using alternative (b) are more difficult to produce, especially if hospitality has to be ensured. The main advantage is that one needs only to take off the $-sign if the term becomes a descriptor. The notations of descriptors should never contain "$", thus preserving the possibility, given in many systems, to tell descriptors from preferred lead-in terms by the notation.

Remarks:
(1) Of course, another suitable special character may be used instead of $.
(2) One might also think of the following possibility: Use, for example, *C642*, *C642$*, or *C642$NT* as the notation for all nondescriptor preferred terms listed after *C642 Traffic installations*, and list these terms in alphabetical order. However, this would lead to complications, as one can easily see from this example: The entry *Sea transport installations* in the alphabetical index would give *C642$* as notation, but the user would have to look under *C642$ Water transport installations*.

D4.4 Specific Problems in Notation (Technical)

D4.4.1 "Incorporating" standard classification schemes

The considerations on "adjunct" thesauri in Section K1.2.3 will show that it is often useful to consider standard classification schemes as part of an indexing language. Often it is useful to reflect this in the notation and to have a notation for every element of the standard classification scheme incorporated. This is most easily done by an "incorporation rule".

Example:
> A standard geographical subdivision of the US runs as follows:
> 1 Northeastern States
>   11 New England
>   111 Maine
>
>   . . . .
>
>   12 Middle Atlantic
>
>   . . . .
>
> In our scheme we have Y25 United States
> By an "incorporation rule" we get
>   Y25.111 Maine
>   or
>   Y25.123.B5 Philadelphia

The standard scheme uses an expressive notation assuming that each additional digit belongs to a lower level (as in UDC). If one wants to be consistent with the mixed notation for large schemes described above, one might prescribe that the notation for *Maine* be written as follows:
   Y25.1.1.1 Maine.

The whole geographic subdivision of the US is now incorporated in the indexing language by just including one line—*Y25 US*—and providing the user with the book containing the geographic subdivision for the US.

A second example to illustrate this method is in order.

Example:
> The United Nations Statistical Office has an "International Standard Industrial Classification of all Economic Activities (ISIC)". In this scheme 5 is Construction.

In our scheme, we include:
>   N89 Classification of economic activities
>   N89A Classification of economic activities used by the US Bureau of the Census
>
>   . . . .
>
>   N89G ISIC

Then we have:
>   N89G.5 Construction

This allows for the use of the scheme most appropriate for the specific application (for example: ISIC scheme for international statistical data, Bureau of Census scheme for US statistical data).

However, this example demonstrates a problem: since there are several classifications of economic activities, we might have several different notations for *Construction*. For example, if in the US Bureau of the Census scheme *Construction* has the notation 7, then we would also have *N89A.7 Construction*.

In the case of indexing statistical data this situation cannot be avoided since the data should always be indexed using the same scheme that has been used in collecting as well as in sorting, and/or aggregating these data. It is well known that this problem has to be faced using statistical data. However, it is possible to work out a conversion table between different classifications that would then show that *N89A.7* and *N89G.5* are actually the same (for details see Section K2). An incorporation rule is mandatory if one does not list the elements of, say, the ISIC scheme explicitly and refers to the ISIC book instead (implicit inclusion of an adjunct thesaurus), but it is also useful if the elements of the adjunct thesaurus are listed explicitly in the thesaurus to be constructed (explicit inclusion).

D4.4.2 Descriptors with "data field"

,1 Numerical data field in the notation. Many descriptors denote variables that have numerical values. It would enhance the possible specificity of indexing if the indexer could give the actual value or value range dealt with in the document or data element indexed.

Example:
```
I12         Age
I12=18      Age 18 years
I12=20-25   Age 20 until below 25
```

In a sophisticated ISAR system it is then possible to specify a value or value range in searching. In a less sophisticated system one could search only for age, or for value ranges included explicitly in the indexing language with an appropriate notation.

Example:
```
I12    Age
       I12.0   Age  0-10
       I12.1   Age 10-20
       I12.1   Age 20-30
       I12.3   Age 30-40
       . . . .
```

One might also assign the following notation to the fixed age ranges.

Example:
> *E12 Age*
> *E12=0-10   Age 0-10*
> *E12=10-20   Age 10-20*
> *E12=20-30   Age 20-30*
> *E12=30-40   Age 30-40*
> . . . .

Note that this is just a specific way to formulate the fixed notations for fixed ranges and that the indexer is not allowed to use ranges of his own.

It is also possible to index by a descriptor with data field and by the appropriate descriptor(s) giving a fixed range.

Example:
> *Index by*
> > *I12=20-25 and by I12.2*
>
> *or index by*
> > *I12=18-28 and by I12.1 and I12.2*

This is only a special case of the principle: use specific descriptor for representation—use more general descriptors for filing. The fixed-range descriptors would be used in a less sophisticated ISAR system (e.g., in a card catalog); the descriptors with the indication of a variable data field would be used in scanning the document representations for final selection or in a more sophisticated ISAR system (for example, a computerized ISAR system to be developed or used in parallel with the card catalog).

,2 Data field proper name.

Example:
> *4315   Programming languages*
> *4315=FORTRAN IV*

In many systems proper names are allowed as descriptors (often called identifiers, see Section C4.1). By the procedure described here proper names are bound to the appropriate descriptor contained in the indexing language.

D4.4.3 The UDC method of handling time (modified)

The idea of descriptors with data field is especially appropriate for indicating the time period dealt with in the document. If time is used very often in indexing, a simplified procedure should be used: T (or other letter) stands for time. The "=" sign is omitted for convenience.

Example:
> *T69.5*   *1969 May*
> *T69.5.13*   *1969 May 13*

T69.5.13-7.19	*1969 May 13–July 19*
T69.5-7	*1969 May–July*
T65-70	*1965–1970*
T1700-1800	*1700–1800*

Note that, in the mixed notation for large schemes, *T69.5.13* is narrower than *T69.5* so that in a search for events in May, 1969, a document describing an event on the 13th of May, 1969, will be retrieved.

Again, fixed time spans can be introduced. They should be expressed by the same kind of notation.

Example:
T60–64
T65–69
   T65
   T66
   ...

In a sense this notation "speaks for itself". For purposes of clarity and sorting sequence it is even better to write *T1969.5*. However, this is paid for by longer notations. Other time concepts may be given a notation starting with *TT*.

D5 MULTILINGUAL THESAURI (SPECIAL TOPIC)

(The main problems to be dealt with here are problems of thesaurus format. For this reason this section is contained in Chapter D in spite of the fact that we also discuss problems of the flow of work which properly would belong in Chapter F.)

D5.0 Definitions

A multilingual thesaurus is a thesaurus to be used for indexing and searching in several languages, for example, English, French, and German. The fact that a thesaurus gives translations in other languages for every term does not by itself make this thesaurus a multilingual thesaurus.

There are two types of multilingual thesauri. In type 1, the descriptors and other preferred terms are all in one language, say English. In order to facilitate the use of the thesaurus for, say, French users, the appropriate French terms are added to the lead-in vocabulary. Type 2 goes one step further: There are two versions of the indexing language, one English and one French. English-speaking indexers and searchers use English descriptors in indexing documents and formulating search requests; French-speaking indexers and searchers use the equivalent French descriptors. Furthermore, in the French edition, French preferred terms appear in the heading of an entry and in the data fields BT, NT, RT.

In the following we assume that a thesaurus has to be developed for use in the languages English, French, and German. The generalization for more than three languages is obvious. We deal first with thesaurus format (D5.1 and D5.2), then with production of a type-2 multilingual thesaurus, starting from an English thesaurus giving French and German translations (D5.3), and then with problems of producing a thesaurus giving translations (D5.4).

D5.1 Format of a Type-1 Multilingual Thesaurus (Lead-In Only)

In a thesaurus designed according to the Roget-Soergel model one simply adds a French alphabetical index and a German alphabetical index, or one prepares an alphabetical index containing terms from all three languages.

In a thesaurus following the TEST model the situation is more complicated. The French and German lead-in terms have to be entered in the main part. The main part may have either a separate alphabetical sequence for each language or one alphabetical sequence containing all languages. Accordingly, one will have three alphabetical indexes, one for each language, or one alphabetical index covering all languages.

D5.2 Format of a Type-2 Multilingual Thesaurus (Indexing Language in Different Languages)

There are two possibilities: (1) separate editions for each language (recommended) and (2) one all-language edition (not recommended).

D5.2.1 Separate editions for each language (recommended)

Three editions of the thesaurus are established, one for each language. These editions could be completely separate. However, one might give French and German translations in the English main part, English and German translations in the French main part, etc.

The connection between the three editions is furthermore established by the notation, which would be, of course, the same in all editions. This format is recommended because the separate editions for each language are much easier to use than one all-language edition.

One could extend the alphabetical index to the English edition to give a rather superficial fast look-up multilingual dictionary by arranging it in four columns as follows:

Column 1:   English term
Column 2:   Notation and possibly English preferred term
Column 3:   French preferred term
Column 4:   German preferred term

D5 Multilingual Thesauri

The English edition can be used as a multilingual dictionary even without this addition to the alphabetical index in the following way: Look up a term in the English alphabetical index, find the notation, look under the notation in the French or German edition of the main part, find there *all* French or all German terms designating the same concept.

D5.2.2 One all-language edition (not recommended)

In this case the classified index as well as the main part of the thesaurus gives all terms and other information in each of the three languages. It would also be possible to use three parallel columns, one for each language. However, each part of the thesaurus would be three times as big as a monolingual thesaurus on the same subject. This format would therefore be rather difficult to use. A consequent application of this idea to the alphabetical index would mean that English, French, and German terms are all given in one alphabetical sequence, also inconvenient.

D5.3 Production of a Type-2 Multilingual Thesaurus

Assume that there is an English thesaurus that gives one or usually several French and German translations for each preferred term and that a multilingual thesaurus is to be produced therefrom. First, some additional intellectual work has to be done:

—Often there are several French and several German terms for an English preferred term. From among these a French preferred term and a German preferred term have to be selected.

—The definitions or scope notes have to be translated unless one stipulates that the definitions or scope notes be given in one language, the *language of definition*, only. Separate French and German editions in the format recommended in Section D5.2.1 can now be produced in a merely clerical procedure

At least in larger projects a computer should be used.

The flow of work is as follows. For each concept a notation is given as well as a preferred term in each language: English, French, and German. From these data the French edition is produced in these steps:

Step 1: In the classified index replace the English preferred terms given after each notation by the appropriate French preferred term.
Step 2: In the main part proceed as follows:
Step 2.1: In the heading of every entry replace the English preferred term by the French preferred term. Place the other French terms in the data field ST.
Step 2.2: (If English translations are to be included) In the data field TRanslations, delete the subfield *French* and add the subfield *English*. Place the English preferred term and the English synonyms and quasi-synonyms in that subfield.
Step 2.3: In all other data fields replace after each notation the English pre-

ferred term by the appropriate French preferred term. (In all these data fields only preferred terms, preceded by a notation, are given.)

Step 3: The production of the alphabetical index for the French edition is trivial.

Actually the operation becomes a little bit more complicated if one considers, in addition, the data fields Syntactical Information and Spelling Variants. Obviously the data elements in these fields would have to be developed separately for the French edition.

D5.4 Production of an English Thesaurus That Contains Translations in Other Languages

A simple, but not very good method is simply to translate the English terms using a big English-French (English-German, etc.) dictionary. French translations of an English preferred term are data elements just as are English synonyms and translation can be interpreted as pulling information from a big thesaurus (the dictionary) by the matching and merging process, to be described in Section F2.2.1. Missing translations must be supplied by subject specialists fluent in both languages. All translations should be checked by a subject specialist who has the target language as his mother tongue and who is fluent in the starting language. The best check is independent retranslation into the starting language.

A better procedure, ensuring fuller coverage of French terminology, is as follows: include in the sources from which the thesaurus is to be built sources in French (French thesauri, French abstracts, etc.) as well as specialized bilingual or multilingual dictionaries. In the process of forming groups of synonymous and quasi-synonymous terms, to be described in Sections F2.3 and F3, it is then advisable to treat translations in the same way as synonyms (the preferred term being English in each case). Multilingual lexicographers are needed, especially for the sorting of terms into subject fields and subfields in steps F3.1 and F3.2 and in the subsequent working-out of the preliminary detailed structure of the thesaurus in step F3.3. This is of particular importance for type-2 (indexing language in different languages) multilingual thesauri.

In either case for each language an alphabetical index of all the terms in that language should be prepared to detect homonyms and other problems, as dealt with in Section F5.8.

D5.5 Interlingual Thesauri

The above discussion of multilingual thesauri is over-simplified in one respect: terms in different languages very often do not designate the same concept but differ slightly in meaning. This simplification is justified, however, because for the preferred terms sameness in meaning has to be established (if necessary by suitable definitions and scope notes). Difficulties arise if one wants to maintain the distinction between synonyms and quasi-synonyms. Furthermore, one will be made more aware of the fact that concepts for which there is an English preferred term may not have an appropriate term in French, and vice versa. In such cases it is recommended that the concept be included with the English term in the French thesaurus, or vice versa, so that the classificatory structure is identical in both editions.

A more refined solution of these problems would require an interlingual thesaurus. Terms of all languages at hand would be collected into one big vocabulary. Starting from this vocabulary one would then develop a thesaurus according to the method to be described in Chapter F without paying attention to the language to which each term belongs. In particular, one would form groups of synonymous and quasi-synonymous terms—English, French, German, etc., all mixed—and one would then select a preferred term which might belong to any of the languages.

Chapter E

Rules Concerning the Form of Terms and Related Problems

E0 INTRODUCTION. DIFFERENCE IN REQUIREMENTS BETWEEN SYSTEMS USING NOTATIONS AND SYSTEMS USING TERMS

Every term in the thesaurus should be formulated in such a way that it conveys the intended meaning in an optimal way. "Optimal" refers both to the proportion of prospective users who understand the term and to the speed and completeness of their understanding. Furthermore, terms often have to be looked up in an alphabetical arrangement, and this process should be as speedy as possible, avoiding look-up at different places. These two requirements are valid for a thesaurus used in any ISAR system, and appropriate rules for the form and alphabetical arrangement of terms must be set up in order to meet these requirements.

However, there is a difference between two types of ISAR systems as to the importance of these rules. This difference is based on the method used for recording the descriptors in the document representations and the arrangement of descriptors in retrieval tools (catalogs, indexes). Type-1 systems use notational symbols for both purposes. The notational symbols may be accompanied by the term itself for the convenience of the user, but all functions of arrangement and retrieval are performed on the notational symbols alone. In type-1 systems the exact form of terms does not matter as long as the proper meaning is conveyed.

Type-2 systems use terms in the document representations and for the arrangement in retrieval tools. In these systems it is important that exactly the same form of the descriptor be used consistently. Otherwise all sorts of errors arise (cards are misfiled, computer will reject improper form). (In mechanized systems one could, of course, reduce non-standard forms to a

E1 Rules for the Form of Terms

standard form, for example, a wrongly used plural form to the singular form. However, this would require a considerable increase in the vocabulary to be used by the program and/or a special program to standardize nonstandard forms. Both mean more storage space and/or more processing time.) The alphabetical arrangement is more important also because the user should be able to go directly to the location where the entries are actually filed in as many cases as possible. Type-2 systems require, therefore, a more stringent set of rules for the form of entries and a more consistent application of these rules than type-1 systems.

E1 RULES FOR THE FORM OF TERMS

E1.0 Preliminary Remarks

E1.0.1 Selection of rules

This chapter deals with a number of problems such as singular vs. plural form and noun vs. adjective form. Alternative rules are discussed for each problem. One of the alternatives should be selected for the thesaurus to be constructed and then be applied consistently to all terms, including synonymous lead-in terms. Only spelling variants are exempt from the rules as discussed below.

E1.0.2 When to apply the rules for the form of terms in the process of thesaurus building

The rules should be applied when the main part of the thesaurus is formed into shape in Step F5.1. Some of the rules given in the following have a major impact on the place of a term in the alphabetical sequence (for example, direct vs. inverted entry). These rules should be applied earlier, namely, while transferring terms from sources on thesaurus forms in Step F1, if the following conditions hold:

(a) The terms taken from the different sources are *typed* on the thesaurus forms (not cut and pasted).

(b) One does not wish to keep track of the specific form in which a term occurs in a particular source.

The early application of the rules influencing the place in the alphabetical sequence offers a distinct advantage: if the same term occurs in different sources but in different forms, the introduction of uniformity makes sure that all thesaurus forms (index cards) on that term are brought together and all information can be cumulated on one card in Step F2. This is of particular importance if the elimination of duplicates and the cumulation of the information on a term from different sources is done by computer.

E1.0.3 The application of the rules in the alphabetical index

There are two problems:

(1) *Spelling variants*. Application of the rules selected may result in the elimination of spelling variants, especially internal spelling variants (for example, the singular of a term may be eliminated if the rules prescribe the use of plural). As discussed, external spelling variants (SP-EX) should be included in the alphabetical index for manual use, and additional internal spelling variants (SP-IN) may be needed in mechanized indexing or searching of natural language text. To the extent necessary, spelling variants that do not conform to the rules for the form of terms selected should therefore be included in the thesaurus.

(2) *Composite words in a KWIC index*. As discussed in Section D1.5, "Alphabetical index", it is useful to split composite words or to split a prefix from the word stem in punching the entries for the alphabetical index in order that the term appear at the appropriate places in a KWIC or KWOC index. As a result, a term might appear in hyphenated form in the alphabetical index, whereas its standard form appearing in the main part is one unhyphenated word. It is not possible, then, to find the standard form of a term from the alphabetical index alone. (Note that there are terms where the hyphenated form *is* standard!) However, in ISAR systems that use terms in document representations and search request formulations an indexer will often look up in the alphabetical index a descriptor he knows just to verify the standard form. The use of a nonprinting separator instead of the hyphen is an elegant solution to this problem.

E1.0.4 Preview

The problems discussed in the following may be grouped roughly as follows: Disambiguation of homonyms (E1.1); grammatical form of terms (E1.2–E1.4); multiword terms of different kinds (E1.5–E-1.7); abbreviations and term length (E1.8–E-1.9); miscellaneous (E1.10–E1.11).

E1.1 Formulating Terms More Precisely

As has been stated above every term in the thesaurus should be formulated in such a way that it conveys the intended meaning to any user of the thesaurus. In the following cases special measures are necessary to meet this requirement:

(a) for terms that are homonyms;
(b) for terms the meanings of which widely overlap in general usage but that have been more clearly delineated in a thesaurus;
(c) for terms that are used in the thesaurus in a meaning other than that generally accepted (e.g., broadening or narrowing the definition);
(d) for terms that have been coined in building the thesaurus.

E1 Rules for the Form of Terms

In all these cases the term has to be made more precise by a parenthetical qualifier as described in the following. If this is not possible, a scope note must be given for the term. The scope note (as distinct from a parenthetical qualifier) is not part of the term.

According to the criteria for the selection of preferred terms given in Section F0.4.2 terms that are homonymous or otherwise unclear should be avoided as preferred terms if an unambiguous synonymous term exists, unless there are overriding criteria. In each case the homonym has to be entered in the lead-in vocabulary. The following rules apply then, too.

E1.1.1 Disambiguation of homonyms through parenthetical qualifiers

The clarification of the meaning of a homonym is achieved by a parenthetical qualifier; the parenthetical qualifier (as distinct from a scope note) is part of the term. Parenthetical qualifiers should not be used for any other purpose. (Parenthetical qualifiers should never be used for compound concepts, e.g., *Tubing (metal)*; if one wants use the inverted form, one should write *Tubing, metal.*)

For further clarification the terms that correspond to the different meanings of a homonym might be distinguished by numbers.

Examples:
Mercury 1 (metal)
Mercury 2 (planet)
Resistance 1 (electrical part)
Resistance 2 (characteristic of an electrical part)
(ZIID puts a hyphen between term and number, such as Mercury-1.)

A parenthetical qualifier is needed for every homonymous term, even if the term is used in only one of its meanings within the thesaurus ("lonely homonym"). If numbers are used, it might seem that the number 1 could be omitted for a lonely homonym; however, this is not recommended because it might prove necessary in future revisions to use the term in other meanings, too. This is of particular importance in connection with mechanized indexing, where the number following a term might be used as an indicator of homonymy (compare Section B6.2.2(3)).

E1.1.2 Homonymous multiword or composite terms

Multiword or composite terms are sometimes homonymous.

Examples:
Water cooling may mean both Cooling of water and Cooling by water.
Computer models may mean both Models of computers or Models to be used for the treatment of a problem by computer. These terms have to be dealt with in the same way as all other homonyms. Often a phrase like Cool-

ing by water is preferable and is found as easily in an alphabetical index in the KWIC format as *Water cooling*.

The conceptual background for this type of homonym is as follows: the multiword term stands for two compound concepts that are made up of the same components, the relationships between these components being different. The problem arises only if it is really necessary to include the compound concept in the thesaurus, either as a precombined descriptor or as a lead-in term. (Compare the rule C2.7.1(c) on the use of compound concepts as precombined descriptors.)

E1.1.3 Omission of parenthetical qualifiers in classified listings (technical)

If the Broader Term is known, the meaning of a homonym can usually be inferred.

Example:
Economics
Banks
Calculus
Integration.

Clearly we are not dealing here with *Banks (waterways)* or *Integration (politics)*. One might conclude, therefore, that parenthetical qualifiers can be omitted in classified listings. However, this omission would have two disadvantages:

(1) In the construction of the thesaurus one would have to keep two forms of homonyms: one with parenthetical qualifier for the alphabetical index, one without parenthetical qualifier for the classified listing(s). Otherwise it would be necessary to add the parenthetical qualifiers while constructing the alphabetical index. In the above example one could not just enter *Integration* in the alphabetical index but *Integration (mathematics)*.

(2) In the use of the thesaurus: the indexer should be able to take a descriptor from the classified index and use it in a document representation as it is. The document representation does not always provide the context to imply the proper meaning of a homonym.

It might be better, then, to use the parenthetical qualifier even if it is somewhat more cumbersome:

Example:
Economics
Banks (economics)
Calculus
Integration (mathematics).

E1.1.4 Artificial homonyms

Especially in classification schemes of the UDC or LCC types we often encounter the following situation.

Example:
  Religious behavior
    Tolerance
  Solvents
    Alcohol.

Tolerance here stands, in fact, for the compound concept *Religious tolerance*; and *Alcohol* stands for the compound concept *Alcohol as solvent*. This situation can be characterized as follows: A compound concept, like *Alcohol as solvent*, is listed under one of its semantic factors, in this case *Solvents*. The term chosen for the compound concept actually designates only the second semantic factor, *Alcohol*. *Alcohol* thereby becomes an artificial homonym; in some other place in the hierarchy it might be used in the sense *Alcohol as antifreeze*. The reasoning behind this procedure is similar to that for the omission of parenthetical qualifiers discussed in the previous section. With artificial homonyms there are even more disadvantages. The users of the thesaurus might think of the term in question in its broad meaning and then question whether it has been properly placed in the hierarchy. Or an indexer dealing with a document on *Political tolerance* might turn to the index, find *Tolerance*, and use that term in spite of the fact that it really means *Religious tolerance*. This is especially likely if *Tolerance* appears nowhere else in the scheme. Correspondingly, a searcher might be misled into believing that *Tolerance* stands for the broad concept, whereas it really stands only for *Religious tolerance*. Therefore, it is better to use the full term *Religious tolerance*.

The "relative" index to DDC solves most of the problems arising from artificial, as well as from natural, homonyms, as shown in Figure 50. Note, however, that the production of this type of alphabetical index is not just a mechanical procedure; it requires intellectual effort.

The remainder of Chapter E is technical. For a small thesaurus, only the rules discussed in Sections E1.5, E1.6, and E1.8 are important. The other sections may be consulted if the need is felt.

E1.2 Rules on What Parts of Speech (Nouns, Adjectives, Verbs) Are Allowed (Technical)

E1.2.1 Permit-all rule

Follow the general rule and use the term which expresses the concept most appropriately, be that term a noun, an adjective, or a verb. In the case of many properties the adjective is more appropriate than the noun.

304 E Rules Concerning the Form of Terms

Entries from the DDC schedule (slightly modified):
523.4 Planets
    523.41 **Mercury** ←
546 Inorganic chemistry   Homonyms
    546.663 **Mercury** ←
623 Military and naval engineering
    623.741–.746 **Aircraft** ←
629 Other branches of engineering   Artificial
    629.1 Flight vehicles and engineering   homonyms
        629.133 **Aircraft** ←
672–673 Specific metals manufactures
    673.71 **Mercury** ←   Artificial homonym
                                         to 546.663

Entries from the "relative index":
Aircraft
    engineering   629.133
    military
        engineering   623.741–.746
Mercury
    Descriptive astronomy   523.41
    Inorganic chemistry   546.663
    Manufacture   673.71

Figure 50. "Relative" alphabetical index to DDC (E1.1.4).

E1.2.2 Prefer-nouns rule

Avoid terms that consist only of an adjective (or several adjectives); wherever possible use noun form instead.

Example:
    not Rough—but Roughness
    not Hot—but High temperature
(Note that Heat would not be the appropriate noun to express the property Hot.)

"In a limited number of instances, needed retrieval concepts can be represented only by adjectives or equivalent expressions. These usually take the form of words or phrases that describe in some manner the operation of equipment or systems; for example: *airborne, mobile, portable.*"

On the use of verbs, see Section E1.3.

E1.2.3 Grammatical form to be used for each part of speech

Once we have decided what parts of speech to allow we have to decide in which form each should be used. In the case of nouns the question is when to use singular and when to use plural. Section E1.4 has been set aside to deal with this problem. No problems arise with adjectives. (In German the adverbial form should be used.) With verbs one has to decide between the infinitive form and the gerund. (One might argue that the gerund is a noun. Compare Section E1.3.)

E1.3 Designation of Actions and Processes, on the One Hand, and of Their Results on the Other (Technical)

E1.3.0 The problem

(a) In many cases an action or a process may be expressed either by a verb or by a noun (which usually is a derivative of the verb).

Examples:
Flee—Flight
Emigrate—Emigration
Catalyze—Catalysis
Concentrate—Concentrating and Concentration
Build—Building

(b) Often the noun derived from a verb designates both the process and the result of that process. For example, *Concentration*, meaning both a process and a state; the same is true for *Building*. These nouns represent, therefore, a special class of homonyms (more precisely, polysemous terms). Whenever it is necessary to distinguish clearly between a process and its result, the corresponding term(s) has (have) to be disambiguated using one of the following rules. (There are cases where it is *not* necessary to bother about the distinction!)

E1.3.1 Rules

One may disregard the use of natural language and stipulate the following rules, thereby eliminating a part of the homonymy of these nouns in the particular thesaurus. It is possible to use these rules in parallel—that is, to decide in each single case which rule to apply (compare Section ,4).

,1 Verb-noun rule.

(a) Designate processes by a verb in the infinitive form.
(b) Designate the result of a process by a noun derived from the corresponding verb.

,2 "-ing"-"-ation" rule.

(a) Designate a process by the gerund, e.g., *Concentrating, Precipitating*.
(b) Designate the result of a process by a noun derived by using the suffix "-ation" or "-ion" or another appropriate suffix, e.g., *Concentration, Precipitation*.
(c) If only one of these nouns exists, use explicit disambiguation as in the next rule. In many cases this rule approximates normal usage in the English language.

,3 Explicit disambiguation. The rules set forth in the foregoing paragraphs eliminate homonymy only in the particular thesaurus and only for those users familiar with the rules. There is another possibility that does not suffer from these limitations: Simply treat these homonyms as all other homonyms and add a parenthetical qualifier.

Example:
Concentration 1 (process)
Concentration 2 (result)
Building 1 (process)
Building 2 (result)

One may wish to replace the general qualifying expression (result) by a more specific qualifying expression which makes clear the kind of the result.

Example:
Concentration 2 (state)
Building 2 (structure)

,4 Recommended rules. Our recommendation on the rules to be applied is as follows: In any case enter all possible forms as terms: the verb in the infinitive form; the process noun, disambiguated through a parenthetical qualifier; and the result noun, disambiguated. For the process use the verb as the preferred term and the process noun as spelling variant (or, less desirable, use the process noun as the preferred term and the verb as spelling variant). For the result use the result noun as preferred term.

E1.4 Singular vs. Plural (Technical)

E1.4.0 When rules are necessary

In ISAR systems that use notations (possibly amended by the term) in document representations and search request formulations (type-1 systems) the choice between singular and plural is determined solely by the general consideration that the term should be formulated in such a way as to best convey the intended meaning. The designer may therefore use his own sense of language in order to determine whether a term should be entered in singular or plural form. In many cases both will be suitable; for the sake of simplicity one may decide to use the singular form in these cases. But consistency does not matter; nor does it matter whether both singular and plural are used in indexing (that means the indexer need not consult the thesaurus just to make sure that he has the right form). Some people may prefer to assist their sense of language by establishing some rules selected from the alternatives given in the following.

E1 Rules for the Form of Terms 307

In ISAR systems that use terms in document representations and search request formulations (type-2 systems) strict rules are advantageous. The rules should be as simple as possible so that an indexer who knows a descriptor does not need to look into the thesaurus just to make sure whether singular or plural form should be used. It should be emphasized that the main purpose of rules is to save the indexer's and searcher's time. If they are going to have to look up every descriptor in the thesaurus they might as well take the form prescribed there whether this form follows a rule or not. Unfortunately, rules reflecting a sense of language are not simple. The requirement of simplicity therefore conflicts to some extent with the requirement of best conveying the meaning. The requirement of simplicity takes precedence, however.

E1.4.1 Terms that are used in singular or in plural only

There are a number of terms that are used in singular only or in plural only; the rules given later do not apply to them.

,1 Terms that are used in singular only.

Examples:
Radiation
Pollution
Biology

,2 Terms that are used in plural only (pluralia tantum).

Examples:
Scissors
Pants

In a broader sense this category also comprises terms that, when used in the plural form, designate a collectivity.

Example:
X-rays

In some cases there exists a singular form of a term that is used in plural only, but the singular form has a different meaning.

Example:
Woods—singular form Wood
Supplies—singular form Supply
Glasses—singular form Glass

The latter example shows how complicated things can get: there is *Glass 1 (material)*, no plural; *Glass 2 (drinking glass)*, singular and plural; and *Glasses 3 (spectacles)*, plural only. From these cases there is a gradual transition to terms like *Light*. *Light* is a homonym: *Light 1 (phenomenon)* and *Light 2 (light source)*. Only *Light 2 (light source)* has a plural.

E1.4.2 Simple rules

Enter nouns in the singular form (more precisely, nominative singular).

The following exception is optional: Use plural if the term designates a generic concept, e.g., *Measuring instruments, Characteristic values*. This rule is in accordance with a natural sense of language.

Example:
> *Characteristic value*
> *Pressure*
> *Volume*
> *Temperature.*

The normal user would expect the entry *Characteristic values* as a heading for the characteristic values then listed. On the other hand, this rule leads to complications, especially if one uses "generic concepts" in a broad sense. One might then well conceive of a good many concepts as generic concepts which have more specific concepts as narrower concepts. The "exception" would then lead to the result that a sizeable proportion of all terms is entered in plural, thus undercutting the general rule. Therefore, it might be advisable not to use the exception.

The use of the singular is in accord with standard lexicographic procedure.

E1.4.3 More complicated rules: rules used in the TEST thesaurus

"In choosing between singular and plural noun forms, a useful rule of thumb may be applied as follows: Use the plural form when the proposed term is a count noun, that is, a noun which may be used to answer the question 'how many?' (for example, devices such as *gauges, nozzles, fuses*); use the singular form for mass nouns, those that express 'how much?' (for example, *iron, wood, charcoal*); use the singular for specific processes, properties, or conditions. Table 1 [reproduced as Figure 51, D.S.] provides a summary of the recommended procedure. Common usage should be followed for term types not covered in the above general rule or in the table."

E1.5 Sequence of Words in Multiword or Composite Terms (Technical)

In the case of multiword terms, like *Radar antenna*, there is a choice between natural word order (direct entry) and the form *Antenna, radar* (inverted entry). With three or more words there are even more possibilities. Similar problems arise with composite terms, such as *Electrooptics* which might be entered as *Optics, electro*. The problem of composite terms, while not very conspicuous in English, is of paramount importance in other languages, e.g., German.

The whole problem is irrelevant for ISAR systems using notations in document representations and search request formulations (type-1 systems) and having a KWIC- or KWOC-type alphabetical index for their thesaurus. A multiword or composite term can be found in the alphabetical index under each of its components. The most natural form of a term should be used in such systems.

The problem is important in other systems for two reasons:

(a) The rule used determines the *form of terms*. This is important for ISAR systems that use terms in document representations and search request formulations (type-2 systems).

(b) The rule used determines *where to look for term in an alphabetical sequence*. This is important for an alphabetical index that is not KWIC- or KWOC-type. In this case both the direct and the inverted form should be entered in the alphabetical index, no matter which one is the preferred form (or whether notations are used). We mentioned this already in Section D1.5.1(a). The question of where to look is more important if the main part is arranged in alphabetical order. It is advantageous if in most cases the user can find the looked-for term in the main part without consulting the alphabetical index (compare the discussion of look-up in Section D1.3.2, especially (2)). This is even more important for alphabetically arranged subject catalogs. Especially there one might also wish to group together in one neighborhood all kinds of *Antennas*, for example, be they *Radar antennas, Television antennas,* or whatever.

Several kinds of terms are distinguished in the rules given below:

(1) *Multiword terms*
(1.1) Noun-noun, e.g., *Television antennas.* In many languages, e.g., German, this type seldom occurs and composite words are used instead.
(1.1.1) Special case: abbreviation-noun, e.g., *PNP transistors.*
(1.2) Adjective-noun, e.g., *Refractory materials.*
(2) *Composite one-word terms.* The problem here is that we have a whole spectrum from *Railroads*, which is not perceived as a composite term and to which, therefore, the considerations here do not apply; to *Metalworking*, which more often would be written *Metal working* and to which the rules *do* apply.

The designer of the thesaurus may choose among the following alternative rules.

E1.5.1 Direct entry (TEST)

"Descriptors consisting of two or more words should be listed in their natural word order, that is, the order normally used in English sentences.

Figure 51. Guidelines to singular–plural usage (E1.4.3). (Courtesy Engineers Joint Council, New York, N.Y.)

Type of Term	Use Singular Form	Use Plural Form
Material terms, such as: chemical compounds, mixtures, materials	When term is specific, as: urea, cellophane, beeswax	When term is generic, as: amines, solvents, plastics
Terms representing properties, conditions, characteristics	When term is specific, as: viscosity, temperature, purity, opacity	When term is generic, as: physical properties, process conditions
Terms representing equipment, devices, physical objects, and elementary particles	Do not use singular	Use plural, as: pulverizers, regulators, mesons, teeth, stars

Class of use terms	Do not use singular	Use plural, as: adhesives catalysts
Process terms	Use singular, as: constructing installing modulating	Do not use plural
Proper names (A proper name is defined as the name for a *single unique* item)	Use singular, as: Hooke's Law Pluto	Do not use plural
Disciplines, fields, subject areas	Use singular according to common usage, as: chemistry hydraulics engineering	Do not use plural (Words such as "hydraulics" are actually singular)
Events or occurrences	Do not use singular	Use plural, as: ambushes explosions discharges

Example:
> *Radar antennas*
> *not: Antennas, radar*
> *Refractory materials*
> *not: Materials, refractory"*

E1.5.2 Inverted entry

Strictly speaking, the inverted entry rule applies only to terms consisting of two words. With terms consisting of three or more words one has to select that sequence of words which best corresponds to the gist of the following considerations. In many two-word terms one word designates the "focus of definition" whereas the other designates a specific characteristic or "difference", narrowing the meaning of the term. In *Radar antennas*, *Antenna* is the focus and *Radar* the difference. The rationale for the inverted entry is to have the focus in the first position and then give the difference.

Example:
> *Antennas, radar*
> *not: Radar antennas*
> *Materials, refractory*
> *not: Refractory materials*

There are some multiword terms to which this line of thinking does not apply and for which an exception from the inversion rule should be made.

Examples:
> *Gross national product*
> *not: Product, gross national*
> *First aid*
> *not: Aid, first*
> *Rare earths*
> *not: Earths, rare*
> *pH value*
> *not: Value, pH*

The problems discussed in this section arise from the attempt to introduce features of helpful arrangement or collocation in systems based on the alphabetical sequence of terms. This attempt is severely hindered, to say the least, by the fact that there is no one-to-one correspondence between the linguistic structure of terms and the structure of the concepts they express. To the extent that the linguistic structure of a multiword or composite term does reflect the conceptual structure of the concept designated by the term, the problem of direct versus inverted entry is a problem of citation order, as we have remarked at the end of Section C2.4.

E1.6 Terms Formed as Strings of Terms, Interpreted as OR Combination

Section B2 dealt with the formation of concepts by consolidating several widely overlapping concepts. Very often a single word or term designating the newly formed concept is missing. The best thing to do in order to convey the intended meaning is to form a string of terms designating each one of the original concepts.

Example:
Nationalization, socialization
    or
Beer, ale, malt liquor.

This means that the ISAR concept is formed by the union (logical *OR*) of the original concepts. The same principle can be applied for naming broader concepts for which no appropriate term exists. This is often the case with broader concepts representing a whole scale.

Example:
Roughness, smoothness

(compare Sections C1.4.1,2–5). In some cases it might also be useful to string together true synonyms. The constituents of a string need not be repeated in the field ST if a KWIC-type alphabetical index is used. Instead of ",", one might also use "/", e.g., *Beer/ale/malt liquor* or one might write *Beer and ale and malt liquor.*

E1.7 Symbols, Especially Numerals, as Components of Terms

Instead of words as linguistic components of terms we may also have symbols.

Examples:
Asymmetrical C-atom
H-bond
n-body problem
PNP-transistors
γ-rays

Numerals are a special type of symbol often used in terms. They occur in chemical names. In simple cases the numerals can be put at the end. All other cases are too complex to be treated here.

Numerals also appear in other contexts, e.g., *Fourth grade*. A sensible rule is to display numeric elements as arabic numerals following the word to which they belong, e.g., *Grade 4*. Confusion with numbers used to distinguish homonyms should not occur because there is no parenthetical qualifying expression. If one wants to distinguish more clearly, one might write *Grade-4* and *Field 4 (data processing)* or vice versa.

E1.8 Acronyms and Abbreviations

Abbreviations may be used for different purposes, as explained in the following paragraphs.

E-1.8.1 Commonly used acronyms

In the specialized language of the different disciplines numerous abbreviations for the designations of concepts, for substances, for trade names, and for proper names are in general use. Some of these acronyms, like *Radar* and *Laser*, are actually regarded as full words and do not concern us here. For the others one of the following procedures should be used, as appropriate:

(a) If the meaning of an acronym is well established and known among the vast majority of the prospective users of the thesaurus and the products of the ISAR system, and "when significant gain in convenience can be demonstrated", then the acronym may be used as descriptor (or other preferred term). The unabbreviated form should then be treated as a synonym.

Examples:
ACTH for Adrenocorticotropic hormone;
PETN for Pentaerythritol tetranitrate;
VTOL aircraft for Vertical takeoff and landing aircraft.

(b) If the acronym is in general use but a sizeable minority of prospective users may not be familiar with it, one may use the abbreviation and add the unabbreviated form as a parenthetical expression; for example, *CPM (critical path method).*

(c) If an acronym is well-known only to some of the users, the full text should be used and the abbreviation should be added as a parenthetical expression—for example, *Crisis management (CM).*

Rationale for these rules. Rule (a) is a device for saving space and reading time; since most people know the acronym, nothing is lost by omitting the unabbreviated form. Those who do not know the acronym can look in the main part of the thesaurus and find the full form listed as a synonym. In case (b) many people need to read only the acronym, but a full explanation has to be given immediately (rather than only in the main part of the thesaurus) for the sizeable minority who don't know the acronym. In case (c) nothing is lost by adding the acronym because it doesn't require much space and one does not need to enter the acronym as a synonym, as would be otherwise necessary. In all cases acronym and full form appear in the alphabetical index (if this index is designed as a KWIC index, as suggested in D1.5.2),

E1 Rules for the Form of Terms 315

and in the cases (b) and (c) acronym and full form will appear together at all places. (One might argue that the advantages of the procedures in cases (b) and (c) do not warrant the use of parentheses, otherwise reserved for parenthetical qualifiers of homonyms. An alternative in dealing with cases (b) and (c) would be always to choose the full form as the preferred term and to give the acronym as a synonym.)

E1.8.2 Use of abbreviations to save space

Abbreviations may be used in the same way as in other natural language texts (for example, in the articles of some encyclopedias) in order to save space in printing and/or in order to keep the number of characters of a term within a given limit (according to rule E1.9). It should be possible to infer the unabbreviated form of the term from the abbreviation given. One might, for example, chop off "-ation" in *Compens.* or even "-eviation" (or similar endings), as in *Abbr.*, or "-ary", as in *Libr.*, or one might omit letters within a word, as in *Childhd* or *Gvt*. There is a standard that gives abbreviations for often-used words. (A rule for German is: If an adjective precedes a noun, omit the letters "-ich" or "-isch" and replace them by a period.)

E1.8.3 Standardized abbreviations for descriptors

For many purposes it is useful to establish a list of short standardized abbreviations for the descriptors. These standardized abbreviations may be used, for example, in document representations or in the thesaurus itself in the cross-references in the fields BT, NT, RT. In all these cases space and work is saved by using standardized abbreviations. The standardized abbreviations should be very short (not exceeding fifteen characters).

Examples
(notation and full form from Thesaurofacet):

MBT	*El beam defl tu*	Electron beam deflection tubes
MBW	*Trochotrons*	Trochotrons
MC	*Cath ray tubes*	Cathode ray tubes
MCL	*TV col pict tu*	Television color picture tubes
TLF	*Hor bor mach tls*	Horizontal boring machine tools

As may be seen from these examples (which are selected with a bias toward lengthy descriptors), the meaning of the descriptor is perfectly clear in most cases from the standardized abbreviation. In a few cases the abbreviation can serve only as a kind of mnemonic device for those who know the descriptor. In systems using notation the notation is considered part of the standardized abbreviation. The use of standardized abbreviations is a viable compromise between giving the notation or class number only (as is usual in the application of UDC or DDC) and giving the full text of the descriptors.

E1.9 Term Length

"It is usually desirable to establish a maximum term length for the purpose of maintaining succinctness of terms or for other special purposes, such as maintaining the capability for a particular page format in a printed thesaurus" or meeting specific data processing requirements. Succinctness of terms is less important if one uses notational symbols and/or standardized abbreviations according to E1.8.3. Constraints in printing can be overcome by allowing several lines for one descriptor. TEST recommends a maximum of 36 characters per term. Often it is not possible to convey the intended meaning within this constraint. If the constraint must be kept, a scope note may be used.

E1.10 Terms in Foreign Languages

Sometimes there is no English term which adequately expresses a concept. The preferred term selected according to the criteria given in Section F0.4.2 is then a foreign-language term. It might be useful in this case to give the language after the term, using the official language symbol, e.g., *Bremsstrahlung /G/*. In other cases there might be terms in foreign languages that are used often enough in the English-speaking scientific community, especially in the literature, to warrant inclusion as synonyms in field ST (*not* only in the field TRanslations).

Example:
 Eigenvalue
  ST Eigenwert /G/.

This is not to be confused with establishing a multilingual thesaurus.

E1.11 Proper Names and Trademarks

Proper names should be identified by a qualifying expression, at least in the working file used in thesaurus construction; it may even be useful to distinguish the different kinds of proper names listed in Section C4.0. Product names and registered trademarks should in each case be identified in the user version of the thesaurus by the qualifying expression *(product name)* or *(trademark)* or *(R)* or ® (if available in typefont) or *(Warenzeichen)* or *(Wz)* (in German). With trademarks this is important because they are recognized by law as being proprietary.

E2 SPELLING AND TRANSLITERATION (TECHNICAL)

E2.1 Authorities

In case of doubt the following sources should be consulted:

Webster's;
Oxford English Dictionary (OED).
for French: *Petit Larousse*;
for German: *Duden* ("fachsprachliche Schreibweise" to be preferred, if given).

If the term is not contained in any of these sources, other appropriate sources such as the ones listed below should be consulted.

McGraw-Hill Encyclopedia of Science and Technology;
Chamber's Technical Dictionary;
International Encyclopedia of the Social Sciences;
Other accepted special dictionaries;
National and International Standards;
Newest edition of *UDC*.

E2.2 Punctuation

In the case where a term consists of a string of terms, the constituent terms should be separated by "," or by "/" (not by ".").

Example:
Nationalization, socialization
Intelligence satellites/early warning satellites/military communication satellites.

If inverted entries are used they will also contain ",", e.g., *Material, refractory*. In certain types of computer processing this double use of "," may cause trouble. In a string of terms "/" is to be preferred in this situation.

In order to avoid the repetition of the same word or stem within one term one may follow the common dictionary practice and use a hyphen.

Example:
Division of labor, organization of -

The use of parentheses for enclosing qualifiers or abbreviations has been dealt with in Sections E1.1.1 and E1.8.1, respectively.

In general, punctuation should follow general usage and enhance comprehensibility of the terms. Deviations from this principle can be justified only by constraints imposed by filing rules and/or machine processing. In an ISAR system where notations are used in document representations and search request formulations (type-1 systems) filing rules are of importance only for the alphabetical index (even there their importance is decreased by using the KWIC format). It might be worth the effort to transform the form that is most comprehensible to the form that files correctly, either while punching the KWIC lines for the alphabetical index (compare Section F5.7) or by a computer routine written for that purpose.

TEST imposes the following restrictions: "Punctuation marks in descriptors should be restricted. . . . Commas, periods, apostrophes, and most hyphens should be excluded, since they are difficult to handle consistently, complicate machine-processing of the thesaurus, and are not necessary to convey the meaning of the terms. Hyphens should be used only in terms whose intended meaning would be altered by omission of the hyphen. When omitting a normally occurring hyphen the space occupied by the hyphen should be handled according to these criteria:

(1) Retain the space for compound adjectives, combinations, and letter-word combinations.

Examples:
High temperature testing
Man machine systems
n body problem

(2) Drop the space in attaching prefixes to the base words.

Examples:
Countermeasures
Microanalysis
Ultrahigh frequency."

Rule (2) has the consequence that *Microanalysis* does not appear under *Analysis* nor *Ultrahigh* under *High* in the KWIC index unless a nonprinting separator is used.

E2.3 Capitalization

In English one may choose between the following possibilities:

(a) Capitalize each word in a term except words such as *in*, *of*, etc. (to be included in a stop-word list).
(b) Start all terms with a capital, but do not capitalize words within a multi-word term (this rule is followed in this book).
(c) Start the Main Term (the heading of an entry) with a capital, terms in all other data fields with a lower-case letter.
(d) Start all terms with a lower-case letter.

If one chooses alternative (b) or (c), one would still retain the rule that proper names start with a capital. On the other hand, if one chooses alternative (a) one might make an exception for terms starting with a symbol that is customarily written in lower case.

Examples:
n-body problem
pH value
gamma-rays.

Other languages may require different rules. Even if the main language of the thesaurus is English, this may be important for entries in the field TRanslations.

For German one of the following rules can be selected:

(bG) Start all terms with a capital.

(cG) Start the Main Term (the heading of an entry) with a capital, all other terms as they would start within a sentence.

(dG1) Start all terms as they would start within a sentence, e.g., *optisch*; *Aktivität*; *optische Aktivität*.

(dG2) Start all terms with a capital except terms that are not nouns and not attached to a noun,
e.g., *optisch; optisch aktiv*
but *Optische Aktivität*.

Some thesauri, especially those that are reproduced from computer print-outs, use all capitals. However, this does not make for easy reading.

E2.4 Character Set Available

The character set available is dependent upon the equipment used (typewriter keyboard, punching equipment keyboards, data processing equipment, programming language used). The character set available should be clearly identified from the beginning.

E2.5 Transliteration

The appropriate standards should be used for transliteration. If other rules are applied, a reference should be made in the introduction to the thesaurus. In case there are several alternatives for the transliteration of a word, the one not using diacritical marks should be chosen.

Greek letters, be they single or elements of a compound term, are usually written out phonetically.

Examples:
alpha
gamma-rays.

320   E   **Rules Concerning the Form of Terms**

A list of Greek characters with phonetic transliterations may be found in every good lexicon.

The use of Greek letters in chemical names is too complicated to be dealt with here. See E1.7, references.

E3 ALPHABETIZATION (TECHNICAL)

In most cases common-sense alphabetization will do. The precise rules of alphabetization really matter only in very large alphabetical arrangements. Furthermore, in most cases a program to do the alphabetization by computer is available, and one is then bound to use the rules implemented in this program unless one writes his own program.

There are two problems in alphabetization:

(a) *Word-by-word versus letter-by-letter.* Word-by-word really means that the string of characters forming a term is sorted without any modifications, counting blank and hyphen, as well as other special characters, as normal characters. Letter-by-letter means to ignore blank and possibly other special characters, especially hyphen, in sorting. In other words, from the original term a new string of characters is formed by leaving out these characters. These modified strings are then sorted. (Somebody working on the USCOSATI guidelines was so mystified by computers as to create a third type, "Computer sort". From the USCOSATI guidelines this type derived a permanent existence in many other guidelines.)

(b) *Filing sequence (or sorting or collating sequence) of the characters.* It is possible to consider two characters to be alike for sorting purposes, for example, to sort blank and hyphen the same way. Through suitable programming it is possible to use any filing sequence on any computer.

TEST uses these rules:

"Alphabetize descriptors letter-by-letter, according to the following rules:
(1) Ignore all spaces between words.
(2) Ignore all characters other than left parenthesis, numerals, and letters.
(3) File according to the sequence:
   (a) left parenthesis
   (b) numerals in usual order
   (c) letters in usual order

A representative sequence of terms filed according to the above rules is:

Example:
Mercury (metal)
Mercury (planet)
Mercury amalgams
Mercury arc retifiers

Mercury lamps
Metal finishing
Metallurgy
Metals
Metal working

Note: *Metal working* is sometimes spelled as one word, *Metalworking*. In letter-by-letter alphabetization, the sequential position of *Metalworking* is unaffected by the spelling selected for the authorized descriptor. Similarly, the sequential position of *Metal-working* is unaffected by the use of a hyphen."

For alternative rules and/or a more detailed treatment of the subject we may refer to the ALA filing rules, to national or international standards on alphabetization, and to other literature.

Part III

Procedures for the Construction and Maintenance of Indexing Languages and Thesauri

Chapter F

Flow of Work in the Construction of Indexing Languages and Thesauri

F0 OVERVIEW AND GENERAL PROBLEMS

F0.1 The Major Steps (See Overview Flowchart, Figure 52)

The logical sequence of major steps is as follows: The flow of work naturally starts with the collection of material (F1). (Many ISAR systems start without a thesaurus, and terms chosen freely by the indexer are used in indexing. This may be considered the collection phase. Unless the ISAR system is very small, one will soon detect that this approach is insufficient and then proceed with the construction of a thesaurus based on the terms collected in indexing using free terms.) Thereupon follow the steps F2 to F5. Step F2, "Sort into alphabetical order and merge information on identical terms", consists of a series of purely clerical procedures which are geared to reduce the redundancy found in the material as originally collected. This frees the editor or lexicographer to concentrate on conceptual work in Steps F3 to F5. Step F3, "Work out the structure of the thesaurus", is mainly a "process of distillation": from among all the terms collected the preferred terms are selected. The preferred terms are in turn examined to determine whether or not they should be selected as descriptors. The concepts designated by the preferred terms are decomposed into semantic factors as far as possible. In this step the decomposition into semantic factors serves mainly the purpose of detecting elemental concepts to be included in the indexing language. The result of this distillation process is a listing of the more important preferred terms, which contains, in condensed and easily comprehensible form, most of the information that has been collected in step F1.

The result of Step F3 is a first draft of the hierarchical arrangement of the descriptors and other important preferred terms. In Step F4, "Work out first draft of the classified index", the hierarchical structure is elaborated and improved upon. Since only the more important preferred terms are retained for this step, it is possible to get a picture of the whole and to streamline the overall structure. After this step the design of the indexing language and of its structure is essentially finished. On this basis it is now possible to elaborate in Step F5, "Complete first draft of the thesaurus as a whole", the complete structure of the thesaurus, making use of the work that has already been done in Step F3. One might say that one returns from the condensed classified index to the complete mass of material.

The result of Step F5 is a first draft of the whole thesaurus. Before the thesaurus is actually used, however, it should be put to a practical test in indexing and retrieval experiments (Step F6). From these a number of modifications may arise. Only after this step is the thesaurus ready for distribution and actual use. Of course there will be further additions and modifications that come up during the use of the thesaurus. This problem is dealt with in Chapter J, "Updating and maintenance of indexing languages and thesauri".

Figure 53 gives a detailed flowchart for later reference.

F0.2 Cooperative Thesaurus Development

In many cases it is useful for a group of institutions to share efforts in thesaurus development. This cooperation may be strictly for the purpose of saving effort in such thesaurus development or with a view to sharing the results of subject indexing. These topics are dealt with in Chapter K, especially Sections K1.2, "Cooperation in the development of the terminological and classificatory structure" and K2.3.1, "Production of conversion tables. Ideal situation: the indexing languages of the cooperating institutions have yet to be built".

F0.3 Collaboration of Experts from Different Subject Areas

F0.3.0 Necessity of full-time staff and collaboration of subject experts

Thesaurus construction is *not* a task appropriate for a committee of subject experts alone; it requires an adequate staff. On the other hand, a good thesaurus can only be developed in close collaboration with experts in the appropriate subject areas and specialized fields. It is of advantage if some of these subject experts have experience in indexing documents and in searching ISAR systems and if others come to the task without having their thinking constrained by the practical limitations inherent in any ISAR system.

There are various organizational frameworks that can be used in the consultation of experts. If the thesaurus is developed for a specific institu-

F0 Overview and General Problems

tion, it may be sufficient to consult experts from only that institution. If the thesaurus is developed for a broader network or even as a national or international thesaurus, the range of experts has to be broadened accordingly. In either case one may consult individual experts (F0.3.1 and F0.3.2) and/or set up a structure of committees or panels (F0.3.3): a central or full committee for making the ultimate decisions and any number of panels to deal with specific subject fields or subfields. (There may even be a further hierarchy among these panels. Such a structure has been used in building TEST, and it is also used for updating UDC. In the development of the EJC Thesaurus (1st edition) ten committees for fields such as *Electrical and Electronic* or *Aerospace* were set up. An elaborate hierarchy of panels has been set up for the updating of UDC.)

Subject expertise is especially important for the basic decisions in developing the classificatory structure. The consultation of subject experts should therefore be especially intensive in the determination of the major areas in which the indexing language is to be divided (Steps F3.1, "Sort terms into broad subject fields"), in the elaboration and streamlining of the classificatory structure (Step F4, "Work out first draft of the classified index"), and in the review of the whole thesaurus (Step F5.5).

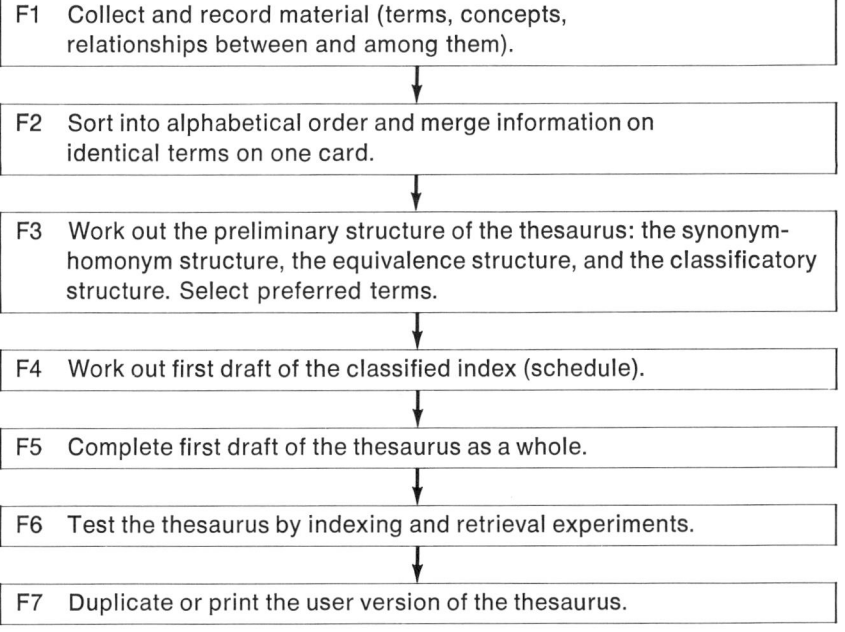

Figure 52. Flow of work in thesaurus construction: overview flowchart (F0.1).

Figure 53. Flow of work in thesaurus construction: detailed flowchart (F0.1).

Step #	To be performed by	See also Section	Work to be done
F1.1	Professional staff	F8.5	Select sources for the collection of terms, etc.
F1.2.1,0	Semiprofessional staff		Assign an abbreviated code to each source.
F1.2.1,1 F1.2.1,2	Professional staff Semiprofessional staff		Selection of terms (for part of the prearranged sources, for all open-ended sources). Assignment of an auxiliary notation (for some prearranged sources).
F1.2.2	Clerical staff	D2; F0.5; F1.2.3;	Transfer selected terms with all information on thesaurus forms.
or	Clerical staff, keying device	G1.2.2	Punch selected terms with all information.

F2.1	Clerical staff or computer	G2	Sort into alphabetical order.
F2.2	Semiprofessional staff or computer	F0.7.2; F2.4; G2; G2.2.3; G2.4	First round of merging: merge information for identical terms. Possibly "pulling" information from additional sources.
F2.3	Semiprofessional staff or computer	F0.7.2; F2.4 G2.3; G2.4	Second round of merging: merge information or terms in the same concept class. (Computer: printout on thesaurus forms)
F3.1	Professional, semiprofessional staff, or computer	C1.4.3; F0.3.2; F0.3.3; G3 excl. subsect.	Define broad subject fields and sort terms into these broad fields. (Computer: printout on thesaurus forms)

(Continued)

Figure 53. (Continued)

Step #	To be performed by	See also Section	Work to be done
F3.2	(Subject experts), professional, semiprofessional staff, ((or computer))	F0.3.2; G3 excl. subsect.	Define subfields within one broad subject field and sort terms into these subfields. (Computer: printout on thesaurus forms)
F3.3	(Subject experts), professional, semiprofessional staff, ((or computer))	B; C; F0.3.2; F0.4; F0.7; F0.8; F8.4; F8.5; G3.3; G3.4	Work out the detailed structure. Select preferred terms. Merge information for terms in the same concept class. (Computer: printout on thesaurus forms; then manual editing.)

- Same for next subfield
- Same for next broad subject field

All subfields of broad subject field finished? — No / Yes

All broad subject fields finished? — No / Yes

F8.1

F4.1	Clerical staff or computer	D3, esp. D3.1.1 G0.2(4) and (5)	Type preliminary version of classified index. Amend working file.
F4.2	Professional with semiprofessional staff or computer	B5; C	Improve classificatory structure.
F4.3	Clerical staff (computer)	F4.0; G4	Type improved version of classified index. Distribute among subject experts. Amend working file.
F4.4	Subject experts, professional, semiprofessional staff	B5; C; F0.3.3; F0.4	Discuss classified index with subject experts. Select descriptors and checklist descriptors.

Many modifications? → Yes (loop back to F4.2) / No → (Continued)

Figure 53. (Continued)

Step #	To be performed by	See also Section	Work to be done
F4.5	Semiprofessional (professional), or computer	D4; F8.2; G0.2(5)	Assign notational symbols.
F4.6	professional		Make a systematic search for additional cross-references.
F5.1	professional with semiprofessional or computer	B5; B6; C; D2 E0; E1; E2; F0.7; F0.8; F3.3.2; F4.0; G5.1	Revise all entries in the working file as follows: (a) formulate standardized abbreviation; (b) standardize form of Main Term; (c) standardize elements in BT, NT, RT to consist of notation and preferred term; (d) improve classificatory structure; (e) USE, UF, etc.
F5.2	Clerical	D2; F5.10.2; F0.8.3; F9; G0.2(6)	Produce the main part of the thesaurus in list-form.
F5.3	Semiprofessional, clerical or computer	C7; G5.3	Check inverse cross-references and insert where necessary.
F5.4	Clerical		Insert modifications in the manuscript prepared in F5.2, duplicate and distribute among subject experts.

F5.5	Subject experts, professional/ semiprofessional	F0.3.3	Review the whole thesaurus. Consult with subject experts.
F5.6	Semiprofessional with clerical or computer		Insert modifications; repeat F5.3.
F5.7	Semiprofessional with clerical or computer	E3 F9	Produce alphabetical index. Test model: produce alphabetical main part and alphabetical index.
F5.8	Professional/ semiprofessional		Check homonyms and cross-references using alphabetical index.
F5.9	Clerical	F5.10.2; F9; G7	Reproduce test version of thesaurus.
F6	Subject experts		Test the thesaurus by indexing and retrieval experiments. Insert modifications.
F7	Professional semiprofessional clerical or computer	F5.10.2; F9; G7	Duplicate or print the user version of the thesaurus.

End

334 F Flow of Work in Thesaurus Construction

It is important that the consultation of subject experts be carefully prepared by the staff so that optimal use is made of the subject experts and so that subject experts are not annoyed by trivial, unclear, or imprecise questions. Do not ask subject experts to answer questions that could be just as easily answered by looking in a dictionary or that otherwise do not really require subject expertise. Formulate questions as precisely as possible. The problems to be emphasized in the collection of information from subject experts are indicated in the description of each step of the procedure for thesaurus development.

As mentioned above, the contributions of subject experts can take three forms, which will now be discussed in detail.

F0.3.1 Supply of material

(1) *Search requests and indexed documents.* Subject experts should be asked to supply search requests and/or to index documents using free terms. Even better is the soliciting of points of interest in a discussion session, using documents as initial stimuli, to be described in Section F1.1.2(n). If this is not possible, indexing guidelines should be given to the subject experts. In these guidelines the checklist technique of indexing should be explained briefly, and the subject experts should be asked to think of all aspects for which the document might be relevant and to use appropriate terms in indexing. The guidelines should not contain rules for the form of terms or other technical details that would only distract from the major task. These details can be taken care of by the editorial staff.

(2) *Comments on draft of thesaurus.* Subject experts can be asked to give written additions to and modifications of a draft edition of the thesaurus. The easiest way for the experts to give these comments is to write them into a copy of the draft thesaurus and return this copy. Usually these written comments yield fewer suggestions from any one subject expert than the discussions described in the following sections. However, this procedure has the advantage of making it possible to secure comments from many experts.

F0.3.2 Answering questions on single problems that come up during the work on the thesaurus

Getting information from experts by asking specific questions is especially useful for the sorting of terms into broad subject fields (Step F3.1), for the individual decisions on the terminological and the classificatory structure to be made in Step F3.3, and while working out the final thesaurus structure in Step F5.1.

If possible one should not bother a subject expert with every individual question as it comes up but wait until a group of questions has been collected. In order to get different opinions it is often advisable to ask the same question of different experts in the appropriate subject fields. Questions should be asked of an expert personally or by phone, if possible, since then

F0 Overview and General Problems 335

a clarifying dialogue can take place. If this is not possible, a query-and-reply slip can be sent to the expert. For procedural details see Section F0.8.1,2.

F0.3.3 Discussion sessions for review and/or decisions on difficult problems

Discussion sessions are appropriate for the Steps F4.4, "Discussion of the classified index" and F5.5, "Review of the whole thesaurus" (and possibly for the definition of broad subject fields in Step F3.1). There are two types of discussions: "routine" discussions of the whole thesaurus and special sessions on difficult problems. The material to be discussed should be sent to the participants well in advance. (On keeping minutes see Section F0.8.1,3, "keeping track of why decisions have been made".)

(a) *Routine discussions of the whole thesaurus.* For most problems, a meeting of three to five people (2-3 subject experts, 1-2 information specialists) to discuss a certain subject field will give the best results. There are two possibilities for conducting such small group discussions:

(a1) Discuss selected problems only. These may be problems in which further clarification seems necessary to the staff responsible for the development of the thesaurus, or they might be cases in which at least one subject expert has indicated dissent from a draft version of the thesaurus.

(a2) Discuss descriptor by descriptor. Experience has shown that, in the discussion of a single descriptor or of the hierarchical arrangement in a specific area, useful revisions arise which none of the participants alone would have thought of.

If it is possible in terms of time and personnel, the discussion of a subject field should be repeated with a second group of subject experts (the information specialists being the same as in the first group). In most cases the results of both groups will agree. Many remaining differences may be resolved by a second discussion with the first group.

In developing a cumulative thesaurus that is to represent the viewpoints of different institutions the whole thesaurus should be discussed with representatives of each institution, possibly in two rounds, to make sure that the interests of each institution are represented adequately. The differences still remaining have to be resolved in a meeting of representatives from all institutions, as described in (b).

(b) *Special sessions on difficult problems.* The differences still remaining are probably major problems in their specific disciplines or reflect differences in the approach taken by different institutions. These differences have to be discussed and decided upon in a larger meeting. Such discussions in a larger group require especially careful preparation. The alternatives have to be worked out and presented very clearly, and the necessary documents should be sent to the participants well in advance. In no case should the whole indexing language or thesaurus be discussed in a larger group. The many detailed questions that are involved in such a discussion cannot be dealt with thoroughly and leisurely enough, and many ill-formed decisions will be made in a hurry. In particular, it doesn't make any sense to go through an alphabetical listing, term for term, in a larger meeting.

F0.3.4 Inter-disciplinary approach

Subject experts should also be asked to look at parts of the indexing language not falling into their specialty, at least at those parts in the neighborhood of their specialty. In particular, the indexing language as presented in the classified index should be checked in its entirety by subject experts from many different fields. It might well be that a scientist can make useful suggestions in fields that are not his own specialty because he, from the viewpoint of his specialty, may bring in aspects that have been overlooked by the experts in the field in question. This is of particular importance for the transfer of information among different disciplines. There is another advantage to this procedure: it enables one to make sure that all areas of the indexing language can be understood by all subject experts to be served by the information system, regardless of their specialty. If parts of the indexing language are comprehensible only to specialists in those particular areas, discussions with subject experts should reveal how this shortcoming can be corrected. This aspect is especially important in the discussion of the classified index (Step F4.4).

F0.3.5 Briefing of subject experts on thesaurus functions

At least the subject experts consulted regularly and/or involved in discussion sessions should have some understanding of what a thesaurus is and how it is structured. The appropriate information may be given in written form (e.g., the introduction to the thesaurus) or through briefings.

F0.3.6 Source codes for subject experts and panels

Subject experts and panels consulted should be treated as sources and assigned a code symbol accordingly, as described in Sections F0.7.5 and F1.2.1,0.

F0.4 Criteria for the Selection of Terms and Descriptors

Selection processes take place in all the steps to be described later. Selection decisions are concerned with terminological problems on the one hand and conceptual problems on the other.

In Step F1, "Collection and recording of material", only those terms should be eliminated that obviously do not fall within the scope of the thesaurus. Final selection can be made only in the framework of the classificatory structure to be developed.

There are three different kinds of selection decisions, and one should

F0 Overview and General Problems

be careful to keep them separate. First, one has to decide what terms should be included at all, if only as nonpreferred synonyms (F0.4.1). Second, one has to select a preferred term from each class of synonyms and quasi-synonyms (F0.4.2). Third, one has to select the preferred terms to be included in the thesaurus and, more important, the descriptors from among the preferred terms (F0.4.3). Most guidelines on thesaurus construction confuse selecting a preferred term from a class of synonyms and selecting descriptors; they then offer a mix between two sets of criteria that should be kept separate. (It is interesting to compare the problem of vocabulary selection for a thesaurus, to be discussed in this section, with the problem of vocabulary selection in foreign language instruction. Teachers and textbook authors have relied heavily on frequency listings to determine the vocabulary that should be taught. However, it has been argued recently that semantic considerations should take precedence over the mechanical application of frequency as a selection criterion. This is exactly the point brought out in the following discussion.)

F0.4.1 Criteria for the selection of terms (whether nonpreferred lead-in terms, preferred lead-in terms, or descriptors) to be included in the thesaurus

Include every term designating any concept that is included in the thesaurus, even if the term is outdated or seldom used or in an area marginal to the field of the thesaurus. The reason for establishing this rule is that it will make the alphabetical index more useful. The time needed to look up a term in the alphabetical index does *not* increase substantially with the number of entries contained in the index (provided the index is arranged properly). On the other hand, the average time needed to find a term in the alphabetical index decreases as the probability of the term being contained in the index increases. (TEST stipulates: "Slang, jargon, coined terms, and deprecated terminology should be excluded." However, this is not a useful restriction; on the contrary, if such terms are in current use among the user group to be served, they should be included.) On the selection of spelling variants to be included, see Section C6.2.2.

F0.4.2 Criteria for the selection of a preferred term from a class of synonyms and quasi-synonyms (arranged according to decreasing priority)

The preferred term should:

(a) be the best to reflect the meaning of the concept;
(b) be recognized in the "user community". (In science and technology this usually means recognition in the national and, if possible, international scientific

community. The term should also reflect exact scientific usage and the newest terminology of the field in question. It is to be hoped that all these criteria converge.) ("The acceptability of terms can be determined by consulting dictionaries, encyclopedias, or other indexing vocabularies, and the opinions of subject specialists.");

(c) be unambiguous (not a homonym);
(d) be simple and short in spelling.

Statistics gathered in the following way may assist in the selection of the appropriate term:

(e) Identify all sources, such as other thesauri, that mention the concept in question. Some of these sources may contain several terms to designate the concept but usually one of them will be used as the preferred term. Find the term that is used by most sources as the preferred term. The strength of the terminological consensus can be measured by the percentage of the sources using that term as the preferred term (from all sources mentioning the concept). In computing that percentage sources might be weighted. The use of a term as the preferred term in an important source may thus count 5 points while in a marginal source it would count only 1 point. As sources one might also use documents dealing with a concept to see what terms are used in the title, the abstract, or free indexing. An empirical study has shown that in the majority of cases the situation is similar to that of *Humor* (preferred term) and *Wit* (nonpreferred synonymous term). Of 14 articles indexed by *Humor*, 7 contained in their title the term *Humor*, only 1 the term *Wit*, and 6 neither term.

F0.4.3 Criteria for the selection of descriptors

The real problems arise in the selection of the descriptors, that is, the concepts to be included in the indexing language (to be used in document representations and search request formulations). The indexing language, especially the listing of the checklist descriptors, should be displayed in a form that can be grasped easily. (Checklist descriptors are those descriptors that are of special importance in searching and that, therefore, require special consideration in indexing.) Therefore, the number of descriptors in the indexing language, at least the number of checklist descriptors, has to be limited. Often there are additional considerations for limiting the size of the indexing language, especially considerations related to the technical devices used in the ISAR system. On the other hand the advantages of specific indexing, necessitating a larger indexing language, should be carefully weighed.

The selection of descriptors should be based "on their estimated usefulness in communication, indexing, and retrieval". The following criteria are helpful to determine the usefulness of a concept and for making selection decisions:

(a) *Usefulness for searching.* Is the concept likely to be used in search requests? The frequency of occurrence of a concept in previous search requests may

F0 Overview and General Problems 339

be used as an indicator on this score. Frequency data can be gathered from search requests solicited as a source for the development of the thesaurus, from search requests used in test runs, and from search requests collected during the operation of the ISAR system (for updating the thesaurus). However, one should be aware of the problem discussed in Section B5.3: useful descriptors might be omitted if indexing is too biased towards the search requests presently received or expected. (It has been suggested that "When a word appears relevant for a number of questions, however, it may decrease in value as a search word for an indexing thesaurus because its wide applicability may lead to retrieving irrelevant information." This argument is not valid because high frequency of occurrence in search requests does not necessarily mean high frequency of occurrence in indexing documents.)

(b) *Alternative solutions.* Are there alternative solutions that might be adopted instead of selecting a concept as descriptor? Possible alternatives might be:

(b1) The concept can be expressed by a combination of semantic factors already available as descriptors.

(b2) The concept can be consolidated with a closely related concept, resulting in a newly formed "ISAR concept".

(b3) A broad concept can be used in indexing and searching instead of a specific one.

The availability of alternative solutions is of utmost importance in the selection or rejection of a concept as descriptor. Therefore, meaningful selection decisions cannot be made without taking into account the classificatory structure.

(c) *Logical structure.* Does the concept have "a pertinent relationship with a broader (or narrower, D.S.) subject that was being treated whereby its selection would help to fill out a useful pattern?"

(d) *Frequency of use of a concept in indexing.* This criterion requires more elaborate consideration; therefore it is postponed until Section F0.4.4.

(e) *Number of sources* (thesauri, dictionaries, abstracts, etc.) in which the concept occurs, regardless of what terms are used in these sources to designate the concept. The number of sources in which a concept occurs indicates the importance of that concept. Again, sources might be weighted in computing the frequency. The occurrence of a concept in an important source may thus count 5 points; the occurrence in a marginal source may count only 1 point. In many cases where this criterion is used terms are counted instead of concepts.

(f) *The selection of concepts of general application* (which are often frequently used concepts) requires special considerations (see Section C4.3).

In deciding whether or not a concept should be selected as descriptor the first three criteria (usefulness for searching, alternative solutions, logical structure) are most important. The frequency criteria (d) and (e) are mainly useful in hinting at solutions that then need to be supported by other considerations.

For selecting a concept as checklist descriptor, usefulness for searching is the overriding criterion. It is even useful for this purpose to use a stricter formulation of this criterion: Is the concept under consideration of importance for the program of research and development (for the planning of the city, for preparing of political moves, etc., depending upon the purpose of the ISAR system)? Is it very likely that it is going to be important?

For the concepts to be included in the indexing language but not as checklist descriptors a less stringent selection is appropriate. If it is not too important to limit the size of the indexing language one should include very specific concepts, too.

On the problem of what compound concepts to introduce as precombined descriptors (rather than using a combination of descriptors) see Section C2.7, especially C2.7.1. The criteria given there partially overlap with the criteria for descriptor selection given here.

Only those concepts that obviously have no relation to the subject area of the thesaurus should be eliminated altogether. The corresponding terms can be left out at the collection stage (Step F1) so that one doesn't need to bother with such cases in the following steps.

In this section we have dealt with the selection of concepts and terms designating the concepts from a collection of terms gathered from different sources. It seems appropriate at this point to emphasize that a somewhat opposite activity is at least as important: the clarification of concepts and the definition and introduction of new concepts and terms to supplement the indexing language and contribute to its logical coherence. We expounded on this point in Sections B7 and C1.1.

F0.4.4 The use of frequency data in the selection of descriptors (technical)

,0 **Introduction.** Since there is much confusion about the use of frequency data, some clarification is in order. First of all, it must be clear what is being counted, terms or concepts. Second, either of these can be counted from sources like other thesauri, from search requests, or from indexing and/or occurrence in titles, abstracts, or full text documents. (If we want to count terms occurring in titles, abstracts, or full-text documents we have an additional problem: it is easy to identify single words automatically, but it is difficult to identify multiword terms. The same problem occurs in automatic indexing, as discussed in Section B6.2, but there we assumed that multiword terms were already in a thesaurus, whereas here the task is to build the thesaurus. Methods to detect multiword terms are discussed in Chapter H.)

A frequency count on terms is useful in selecting the preferred term from a class of synonyms and quasi-synonyms, as discussed in Section F0.4.2(e). In more sophisticated procedures it can also be used to detect synonyms, as described in Chapter H. For the selection of descriptors we need a frequency count on concepts.

The frequency of occurrence of a concept has to be computed as the sum of the frequencies of all the terms designating that concept. In many studies this point is overlooked, and term frequencies are used where concept frequencies would be appropriate. (A related and somewhat tricky point is the following: Suppose we have a concept A and three narrower concepts B, C, and D. If A, B, C, D are all seldom used, we may not consider them to be good descriptor candidates. However, if we do not use B, C, and D as descriptors and say "USE BT A" instead, we have to sum up all frequencies to obtain the new frequency of A. This *new* frequency may then suggest that A should in fact be a descriptor, or it may still be so low that we should rather say "USE BT A'''", A' being broader than A.)

Concept frequencies from search requests are more important for descriptor selection than concept frequencies from documents. The use of concept frequencies from search requests in descriptor selection is straight forward. Concept frequencies from documents are more difficult to interpret. Since they are usually more readily available, Section F0.4.4,2 is devoted to their interpretation. Section ,1 deals with the collection of data from search requests and from documents.

,1 Gathering of frequency and co-occurrence data. Frequency data can be gathered from:

—search request statements and search request formulations;
—the indexing done during the collection of material, from abstracts, and from full-text documents (these are types of sources mentioned in Section F1.1.2);
—the test run (discussed in Section F6);
—other operating ISAR systems;
—the operation of the ISAR system for which the thesaurus has been built (these frequencies are used for updating).

Another problem is how to actually obtain a frequency and co-occurrence count. This is very easy in mechanized ISAR systems. In manual systems it is difficult. In a card catalog one may check to see whether the volume of cards filed under a descriptor has become too large. (This procedure is facilitated if each descriptor has a guide card with a tab.) Still the catalog has to be scanned regularly. With edge-notched cards or peek-a-boo cards it is difficult to obtain any statistics at all. One possibility is monitoring the frequency of descriptors while searching. (If the search results show that a descriptor is used very frequently or very rarely, one may take action on this particular descriptor.) But this is a haphazard kind of procedure. With peek-a-boo cards descriptors that are used very frequently or very seldom can be selected just by going through and having a short glance at every card. With additional effort it is even possible to get association measures for specific pairs of descriptors. (There is an apparatus that counts holes in Termatrex cards (peek-a-boo) or combinations of those cards.)

F Flow of Work in Thesaurus Construction

The possibilities of data collection in mechanized ISAR systems are illustrated by the plans formerly developed by ASTIA to produce three listings to provide the thesaurus builder with frequency data and related information:

Example:
Descriptor frequency listing.

Descriptor	Frequency in indexing	Frequency in searching
Jet planes	2216	37
Jet sea planes	22	9

Low-frequency descriptor manual file.

Descriptor	Document numbers
Alpha chambers	AD 204 929
First aid kits	AD 219 127
	AD 222 912

This file can be used to assess the value of the infrequent descriptors by looking at the documents. (In addition this file is very useful for retrieval; in searching for infrequent concepts manual look-up is faster than computer search.)

List of context descriptor sets.

Aircraft	5325	(total frequency)
Co-occurring with		
Engine	2733	(co-occurrence frequency)
Wing	2201	
Rudder	2182	
Stabilizer	2180	
Airframe	2023	
Fusilage	1845	
Autopilot	1673	
Supersonic	1580	
Rotor	1512	

Such lists are useful for the more sophisticated methods dealt with in Chapter H.

From some mechanized ISAR systems frequency counts are available (see references in Appendix 2).

The frequency of a concept in an operating ISAR system has to be judged with a view to the following factors:

—relatedness of that system to the system for which the thesaurus is being built;
—size of the collection;

F0 Overview and General Problems 343

—age and subject field of the collection;
—time elapsed since the first use of the concept within the ISAR system and increase of the collection within that timespan;
—rules used in indexing (if generic posting in indexing is used—i.e., with a specific descriptor all the broader descriptors are to be used in indexing as well—the count of the more general descriptors is inflated);
—frequency of the concept at hand as compared with the frequency of other concepts. If the ISAR system uses very exhaustive indexing, resulting in a large number of descriptors per document, descriptor frequencies in general tend to go up. It might therefore be better to use the rank of a concept in a list arranged by decreasing frequency rather than frequency itself.

Frequency counts (for both terms and concepts from both indexing and search request formulation) can be refined if descriptors are weighted or ranked within document representations or search request formulations. For example, if a descriptor occurs in an important position it is counted 2 or 3 instead of just 1. Or one may simply select a concept as descriptor if it has been used among the four most important terms in indexing any one document.

A quite different method for weighted frequency counts is weighting by source, assigning a higher weight if the term or concept occurs in an important source than if it occurs in a marginal one. This method is particularly appropriate if statistics are based on a count of the number of other thesauri and similar sources in which the term or concept occurs.

Remark: In a situation where documents indexed by free terms serve as sources the following modified procedure for weighting by source has been used: it is possible that the term profile of a document contains only terms that, due to low frequency, would not qualify as descriptors. Thus, none of the terms used to index the document would be included in the indexing language, and the document would not be accessible at all in retrieval. In order to avoid this the weight of a document is decreased each time one of its index terms is selected as a descriptor. (In the beginning all documents have the same weight.) After each weight modification the frequency count is done all over again. This enhances the chance of documents that are indexed only by seldom-used terms to have at least some of their terms included in the indexing language. This may be useful in a fully automated selection procedure but not in the manual or computer-assisted selection procedures recommended in this book.

,2 Use of frequency data in descriptor selection. First of all, frequency data, especially those gathered from other ISAR systems, can give broad hints only. The selection decisions have to be based mainly on substantive considerations. Frequency data from the operation of one's own ISAR system are more useful and should be collected on a continuing basis (if this is possible without too much effort) as indicators of the need for thesaurus updating. The following considerations hold for initial thesaurus building as well as for thesaurus updating.

Frequency data identify concepts that occur either very frequently or very rarely.

(1) *Concepts used very frequently.* If a concept occurs very frequently in documents, it does not have much discriminatory power in searching if it is used alone. If it is also used very seldom in searching, its usefulness is in doubt. If, however, the concept is used with reasonable frequency in searching, one should investigate to determine which of the following explanations applies:

(1.1) The concept is of general application and mostly used in combination with other concepts. This type of concept can be very useful in searching, as has been discussed in Section C4.3.

(1.2) The concept pertains to a specific subject field and is often used by itself (as the "thematic" concept) in search requests. In this case further subdivision should be considered.

(2) *Concepts used very seldom.* If a concept occurs very seldom in documents, it has very high discriminatory power. If such a concept is used frequently in searching, this high discriminatory power is very welcome. For example, a concept used for indexing seven out of a hundred thousand documents (0.007%) and occurring in 5% of the search requests is of tremendous usefulness in searching and should be considered as a strong descriptor candidate. In fact, this concept is much more useful than a concept used for indexing five thousand documents (5%) and occurring in 1% (or only 0.1%) of the search requests. On the other hand, if the concept is used seldom in searching, it may be too specific, and a USE instruction to a broader concept or to a combination of semantic factors might be appropriate in order to keep the indexing language within reasonable limits. In order to achieve specific indexing it might often be useful to retain as descriptors those low-frequency concepts that belong to the central areas of the thesaurus.

Note: In the case of a concept newly introduced in the subject field no conclusions should be drawn from low frequency.

The above considerations can be formulated more precisely in terms of cost-benefit analysis: the inclusion of a concept in the indexing language incurs costs (larger files, indexing more difficult as size of indexing language increases, etc.). These costs have to be distributed over the documents indexed by that concept. If these documents are few, the cost per document is high. This cost can be justified only if there is a corresponding benefit on the searching side, that is, if the concept in question is used often in search requests.

(3) *Co-occurrence data.* If two concepts co-occur heavily, one should check to determine whether the compound concept formed by their combination should be introduced as a precombined descriptor, using the criteria given in Section C2.7.1.

The considerations of this section partly overlap with Section C2.8.2

on the optimization of an indexing language. More sophisticated uses of frequency data, both for terms and for concepts, in thesaurus-building will be described in Chapter H.

F0.4.5 Central area versus peripheral areas

In selecting the terms to go into a thesaurus, especially the descriptors, one must have a clear picture of the relative importance of the areas to be covered in the thesaurus. One should distinguish:

—central areas;
—areas of intermediate interest;
—peripheral areas.

Many specific descriptors are needed in the central areas; in the peripheral areas a few broad descriptors might do. This difference in emphasis should also be reflected in the lead-in vocabulary, but not as strongly as for the descriptors. An indexer might come across a fairly specific term of a peripheral area and will need to know what descriptor to use.

F0.5 Use of a Thesaurus Form and Related Problems

For the construction of a thesaurus, thesaurus forms on index cards are indispensable (except if very sophisticated automated methods are used). We shall refer to the use of these forms repeatedly as we describe in detail the procedures for thesaurus building. If the necessity of using a thesaurus form is accepted and if the lay-out shown in Figure 54 is deemed useful, Figure 54 may be used as a master form. Instructions for its use are given in Section F0.5.1. The interested reader will find the reasons why a thesaurus-form is needed in Sections F0.5.2–F0.5.3 and the reasoning behind the lay-out and discussion of alternatives in Sections F0.5.4–F0.5.6.

F0.5.1 Instructions on how to use the thesaurus form (technical)

Everything except the top line is self-explanatory. The hierarchical level should be marked by putting "+" (for descriptors) and "−" (for preferred terms) after the appropriate number. If the hierarchical level exceeds 6, the number has to be written in the blank box. Marking the hierarchical level provides a very easy means of giving instructions for typing the classified index from thesaurus forms.

DS (Descriptor), OP (Other preferred term) and CH (Change in existing term) have to be marked, if appropriate, no matter what procedure is followed. DS and OP may be omitted, since the same information is expressed by "+" and "−" after the hierarchical level; however, DS and OP give added protection against errors. Instead of marking NP one may merge

| 0 | 1 | 2 | 3 | 4 | 5 | 6 | check hierarchical level | 02 check type: | DS | OP | NP | EL | CH | 03 Subject Field |

05 Notation:

10 MT:

12 Stand. abbr. (AB):
20 Spellings (incl. abbr.):

30 Synonymous T. (ST) (incl. equiv. t.):

46 Related Terms (RT):

50 Translations (TR):
F:
G:
R:
S:

4 Classification:
42 Category (CA):
44 Semantic factors/Broader Terms (BT):

60 Definition, scope note (SN):

45 Is semantic factor of Narrower T. (NT)

70 Unspec. rel. (UN):

81 Editor/Date:

DS ☐ Descriptor   EL ☐ Eliminate
OP ☐ Other preferred term CH ☐ Change in existing term
NP ☐ Nonpreferred term

Figure 54. Thesaurus form (F0.5).

F0 Overview and General Problems 347

the information on the card for the preferred term and discard the card for the nonpreferred term. Instead of marking EL one may simply discard the card. However, even with manual procedures it is easier for the professional just to check EL on the thesaurus form and have it eliminated by a clerical assistant than to eliminate it himself. (Cautious people keep cards to be discarded in a back file until the thesaurus is finished; some keep them even longer.)

As with every form some procedure is needed in case the space allocated for some field is not sufficient. To indicate a continuation use a circled number and put the overflow, identified by the circled number, on the back of the card or on a second card.

For an example of a thesaurus form where the information is filled in see Figure 58 (Section F2.2) and Figure 63 (Section F5.1), where the same form is shown after it has been processed further.

F0.5.2 Reasons for having an index card for each term

In the procedure of constructing a thesaurus it is useful to have an index card for every term so that the terms can be sorted into various arrangements. This holds particularly for the manual performance of Step F2 "Sort into alphabetical order and merge information on identical terms on one card". (If F2 is performed by a computer, no cards are necessary for this step.) Other points where terms have to be sorted and where, therefore, index cards are essential are the steps F3.1, F3.2, and F3.3, where the classificatory structure is worked out.

F0.5.3 Reasons for having a form rather than blank cards

If we had all the information for each term from the beginning, then it would be easiest to use blank cards and to put down the different data elements, properly labeled, one after the other (this procedure is followed, for example, by BASF1). In reality, however, we have a quite different situation. The information to be entered for a term accumulates gradually during the construction of the thesaurus. For example, we may come across Related Terms at different points in our work. So that all these Related Terms can be entered at one place a space has to be reserved for Related Terms. The same holds for other types of cross-references and data elements Therefore, we need a thesaurus form such as the one depicted in Figure 54. However, it would not be practical to have a separate data field for each of the cross-reference types listed in the detailed subdivisions in Figure 21 (Section C7). Accordingly, rather than establish the data fields *Broader Term–Class inclusion* and *Broader Terms–Whole*, for example, and provide a space for each, we just establish one data field *Broader Terms*. If one wishes to preserve the fine subdivisions, this can be achieved by the use of the detailed labels as discussed in Section C7.

F0.5.4 Size

Letter-size (about European size DIN A4) is too large for easy handling. Four by six cards do not provide enough space. Therefore, five by eight (or European size DIN A5) cards are recommended.

If information is entered on the card mainly by handwriting or cut-and-paste techniques, the lines should be parallel to the longer edge of the form ("Querformat") (see Figure 54). This is handy and allows for easy transfer of information by cutting and pasting techniques. A disadvantage is that in typing the main part of the thesaurus one always has to think of the two columns on the form.

If a large amount of information is entered on the forms by typing, the two-column format is definitely awkward. The lines should then be parallel to the shorter edge of the form ("Hochformat"), and the data fields should be arranged sequentially. For the use of a punched paper tape typewriter, to be described in Section F9.1.1, "Hochformat" is mandatory. However, the disadvantages are that it is less handy and file drawers are not as easily available.

F0.5.5 Width of lines

The form depicted in Figure 54 uses lines corresponding to 1½ line spaces on a typewriter. This is convenient for filling in by hand. If the forms are to be filled in by typewriter, tabulator, computer printer, or other equipment, the lines have to be adjusted accordingly.

F0.5.6 Sequence of data fields

The data fields should be arranged on the thesaurus form in the sequence to be used in the user version of the thesaurus to simplify transferring the data in the production of the user version. The sequence of fields in the form depicted in Figure 54 agrees with the discussion of sequence of fields in Section D2.2.

F0.6 Working File and User Version

We have repeatedly referred to the working file and to the user version of the thesaurus. The working file is used in working out the thesaurus and updating it. It contains the most detailed information. The user version of the thesaurus, to be used by indexers and searchers, need not give that much detail, e.g., with respect to source indications or the distinction of cross-reference types. The physical form of the working file should be such that modi-

F0 Overview and General Problems 349

fications and additions can be made easily; that means either a card file on thesaurus forms or a computer-stored file. The physical form of the user version should be such that it can be easily used and that it can be reproduced at reasonable cost; that usually means book form.

More precisely, the working file corresponds to the main part of the user version. The classified index and the alphabetical index can be produced from the working file also. The working file is thus the master file of the thesaurus from which all parts of the thesaurus can be produced. Especially with computerized procedures one might consider storing only the working file and produce the classified index and the alphabetical index from the updated working file each time a revised edition of the user version of the thesaurus is prepared. This would simplify storing and updating the thesaurus. The alternative would be to maintain working copies of the classified index and the alphabetical index and insert revisions as they arise. It depends on the circumstances which of the two solutions is cheaper, but we suspect that usually it is more efficient to store and update the classified index and the alphabetical index separately. Note also that a working copy of the classified index reflecting the latest changes is very helpful in processing further revisions.

F0.7 Source Indications for Data Elements Entered in the Thesaurus

F0.7.1 Why source indications?

,1 *Use of the source indications for the elaboration of the thesaurus.* Source indications are useful for the elaboration of the thesaurus. It is, for example, possible to look up the place of a concept in the hierarchy of a classification scheme used as a source. This might give suggestions for the building of one's own hierarchy. One could look up the definition of a term, or one could check to see how a term is used in its context in the abstract that has been used as a source. Also it might be useful to look up the frequency of a terms in the ISAR system that employs a particular classification scheme or thesaurus used as a source.

,2 **Why source indications in the user version of the thesaurus?**

(1) *Reference to definitions.* Some sources contain a definition and/or further explanations of the preferred term; the user should be referred to such sources by an appropriate source indication given as part of the scope note (data field SN), as described in Section C3.2.1. (In the working file these sources appear also in the specific data field, as appropriate; see below.)

(2) Source indications in thesauri are especially important in the context of *cooperation in information services.* For example, through source indications it is possible to determine the institutions that use a particular descriptor (and are therefore likely to have material on that descriptor) and

possibly the form in which this descriptor is used in each system (cumulative thesaurus). Such sources should be given in data field SR following the scope note or, if the exact form of the descriptor as used in the source is given in a cumulative thesaurus, in the format described in K1.3.3.

F0.7.2 Keeping track of the sources in the working file (technical)

(For examples, see Figures 56–58, Section F2.2, and Figure 61, Section F2.3; it might facilitate understanding to skip Section F0.7.2 now and come back to it after reading F2.)

Recording and keeping track of the source indications is a somewhat tricky matter. First, one has to decide how detailed the source indications should be. In the detailed form the exact sources for each and every data element entered in the thesaurus are kept precisely. In a computerized procedure this is easy. However, with manual procedures the effort may be prohibitive and not worth the benefits. In this case one should use the crude form. In the crude form one only keeps track of the sources in which a concept as such occurs and what term is used in each source to designate the concept. One does not keep track where ST, BT, NT, and RT cross-references and other information on the concept come from. (If the need arises, one may check each of the sources mentioning the concept to find out the source from which a certain data element came.)

Keeping track of the sources comes in at two points in the procedure for thesaurus building:

(1) *Transfer from sources.* In the process of transferring a term and information on that term from a source to a thesaurus form it is sufficient to give a source indication after the Main Term in data field MT. It is understood that all other data elements on the card come from the same source. If the detailed form is to be used in keeping track of the sources, the source code should be underlined in this step for reasons that will become clear shortly. The following procedure is designed for the case where only entries for terms that are preferred terms in the source are transferred on thesaurus forms (this is in line with Section F1.2.1,1, "Preparation of pre-arranged sources").

The format for the source indication is as follows:
(Source code: Notation from source/frequency given in source in percent).
Notation and frequency are simply omitted if they do not appear in the source.

(2) *Merging information from different cards.* The second point is when information from several cards (thesaurus forms) is merged on one card. For simplicity we assume that there are only two cards, card 1 and card 2, and that the information is to be merged on one card. We deal with the crude form first and then proceed to the more complicated procedure needed for the detailed form.

(2a) *Crude form.*

(2a1) The Main Term on card 2 is the same as the Main Term on card 1: Enter the source indication from card 2 in data field MT of card 1. Simply transfer

F0 Overview and General Problems 351

all other data elements from card 2 to card 1 without paying attention to source indications.

(2a2) The Main Term on card 2 is a synonym of the Main Term on card 1: Enter the Main Term from card 2, together with its source indication, in data field ST of card 1. If the term is already given in field ST of card 1, just add the source indication. Transfer all other data elements as in case (2a1).

Spelling variants can be dealt with in the same way as synonyms. However, if spelling variants are not important in the thesaurus to be built, one might disregard differences in spelling.

Card 2, to be merged on card 1, might in turn be the result of an earlier merge. In this case terms from the data fields MT and ST are transferred together with any source indications that might already be attached to them.

(2b) *Detailed form*

Now the source for every single data element is kept. Therefore, before transferring any other data elements to card 1, the source code given in field MT of card 1 is added to every data element in every data field of card 1; the source code is *not* underlined.

(In most situations it is sufficient to give just the source code, not a full source indication with notation and frequency for BT, NT, and RT. In some situations it might be useful to have the notation, too, for BT, NT, and RT, at least for selected sources. In this case a source indication for each term entered in these fields has to be made while transferring entries from the source to thesaurus forms.)

The further procedure is as follows:

(2b1) The Main Term on card 2 is the same as the Main Term on card 1: The source indication from data field MT of card 2 is entered in field MT of card 2 (the source code underline is carried!). Further information from card 2 is transferred as follows (using data field RT as an example): If card 2 gives an RT already on card 1, only the source code from data field MT of card 2 is added. If card 2 gives an additional RT, that term is entered in field RT of card 1 with the source code from MT of card 2 (the underline is *not* carried in this case). In this way no confusion about the sources of a data element can occur.

(2b2) The Main Term on card 2 is a synonym of the Main Term on card 1. The Main Term from card 2 is entered in data field ST of card 1, together with its source indication. If the term is already contained in data field ST of card 1, merely the source indication is added. In either case the underline under the source code is carried to show that the term is the preferred term in the source. Further information is transferred as in case (2b1).

A special problem can occur with synonyms, as illustrated by the following.

Example:
 Card 1: Lawyer (*CT*)
  ST *Attorney (CT)*

Card 2:   *Attorney (WH)*
          ST Lawyer (WH)
After the merge, card 1 looks as follows:
          Lawyer (CT) (WH)
          ST Attorney (CT) (WH)

Card 1 or card 2 or both might be the result of a previous merge. In this case all source indications are transferred (underlines under source codes are carried).

In the description of the procedure for thesaurus building in Sections F1 ff. we shall repeat parts of this section at the appropriate points.

Special considerations on the source indications are necessary if one wants to build a cumulative thesaurus as described in Section K1.3.1.

F0.7.3 Experts and lexicographers as sources (technical)

Input into the thesaurus comes not only from other thesauri and from documents but also from consulting scientists, panel discussions, and decisions by the editor(s)/lexicographer(s). As far as practical, these sources should, for internal purposes, be treated as all other sources. Keeping track is especially difficult in these situations, however, and may not be worth the effort required.

Part of the difficulty arises from the fact that in the very important step of hierarchy building one does not deal with each term (or the card for each term) individually but with whole groups of terms that are rearranged continuously until a satisfactory arrangement is found.

F0.7.4 Keeping track of deletions (technical)

The procedures outlined above do not provide for the possibility of recording decisions on initial rejection or on deletion of data elements. If one wants to keep track of those decisions the easiest way to do so would be as follows: The data elements initially rejected or to be deleted are kept in the working file but tagged by an appropriate symbol. In typing the thesaurus (or in printing it out by a computer) these data elements are then omitted. The procedure described in Section F0.8 incorporates this feature.

F0.8 Keeping Track of Decisions and Dates

In the working file it might be useful to record who made a particular final decision on the data element (that includes decisions on the inclusion of a descriptor). In both the working file and the user version of the thesaurus it might be useful to keep the dates when a certain data element has been entered. It might also be useful to treat deletions in the same way. In many cases, however, the effort to do so is not justified; one should carefully weigh costs against benefits. The procedure described in the following makes it

F0 Overview and General Problems 353

possible to keep track of every minute detail. A less detailed procedure might be appropriate in many circumstances. Also, the procedure is described in terms most appropriate for computer applications. The principles are the same in manual application, however.

F0.8.1 Keeping track of decisions and dates in the working file (technical)

,1 Keeping track of decisions made. Whenever a decision on a record as a whole is made a fixed-field decision indicator string is entered as the active string in data field 81 "Editor and date when entered" (Figure 21, Section C7); the former active string (if any) becomes inactive. An example of a decision indicator string is:

    1   ETS   67-07   68-12 $

The elements of the decision indicator string are as follows:

—Status code;
—Initials or other code of the editor/lexicographer making the decision;
—Date when record entered into the working file;
—Date when record entered into the user version;
—End mark.

The status code is as follows:

0 to be entered into user version
1 entered in user version
4 to be deleted from user version
5 deleted from user version

(In the construction phase only, a simpler procedure can be used for the elimination of whole entries: put EL in data field 02 Type.)

    For even status codes the second date is blank. When the record is printed in or deleted from the user version, the appropriate date is entered. For all records in the first edition of the thesaurus, this is the date at which the first edition of the user version has been completed. The information contained in data field 81 for the record as a whole can be given for a single data element. The appropriate decision indicator string(s) are enclosed in brackets (or other delimiters) and follow the source indications (if any). The active decision indicator string for a single data element overrides the active decision indicator string for the record as a whole, except if the whole record is to be deleted.

    Things get just a little more complicated if one has to keep track of the inclusion of a change into a supplement, a cumulative supplement, and finally a new edition of the user version.

    The procedure described takes care of changes from descriptor to non-descriptor, and vice versa, due to the fact that, for example, "term is descriptor" is expressed by the data element DS in data field 02 Type. Note also that

EL (Eliminate) in data field 02 is allowed during the construction of the thesaurus only.

In a cumulative thesaurus the situation is more intricate, as discussed in Section K1.3.1.

,2 **Keeping track of decisions still to be made.** The data fields 82–86 provide the possibility of recording where decisions have been postponed and where necessary information may be obtained.

An X is put into data field 82 (or a paperclip on the thesaurus form) if a record is not yet final and a decision cannot be made right away. It is then possible to single out at any time those records that need further work.

The data fields 85 "Name of expert to be consulted" and 86 "Question to be asked" make the consultation of experts more efficient. A duplicate of each pair 85/86 is kept in a file sorted by experts. Experts and questions can be written on query-and-reply slips. From time to time the questions can then be asked, either orally or in writing. This procedure has the advantage that all the questions to be asked of any one expert are batched.

,3 **Keeping track of why decisions have been made.** For later reference it is useful, at least in some cases, to note down the reasons why a particular decision has been made. This type of "documentation" can take several forms. One might write an essay giving the rationale for the over-all arrangement. (It might even be useful to include such an essay in the introduction to the thesaurus.) Considerations on the subdivision of a whole subject field can be given in the scope note (data field 60 SN) if they are useful for the thesaurus-user, or in the internal scope note (data field 61 SN-IN, cf. Figure 21, Section C7) otherwise. The same holds for comments on individual descriptors.

Keeping track of the reasons for decisions is especially difficult in meetings in which the thesaurus is discussed. If it is not possible to enter a summary of the discussion on the thesaurus form during the meeting, one has to keep minutes and transfer the information to thesaurus forms later on.

F0.8.2 Giving dates in the user version of the thesaurus (technical)

Some dates are of interest to the user of the thesaurus: the date when a descriptor has been actually included in the thesaurus for use in indexing, or when a descriptor has been deleted, and possibly dates when some of the cross-references have been introduced. These dates are best given in the scope note for the descriptor. In the working file these dates are stored with the appropriate data element, as described above, in addition to their appearance in the scope note.

After the discussion of these general problems we can now go on to describe the individual steps needed in the construction of a thesaurus. Some

F1 Collect and Record Material 355

of the descriptions are rather technical. The reader might find it useful actually to work out an example in order to gain a better understanding.

F1 COLLECT AND RECORD MATERIAL (CONCEPTS, TERMS, RELATIONSHIPS BETWEEN AND AMONG THEM)

It is natural and useful to start the development of a thesaurus by gathering, from a variety of sources, information as complete as possible on concepts, terms, and all kinds of relationships between terms and concepts (synonym-homonym structure and equivalence structure) and among concepts (classificatory structure). Based on the material so collected, one can then develop the structure of the thesaurus and introduce necessary additions.

F1.1 Kinds of Sources. Criteria for Selection of Sources

F1.1.1 Sources in which terms are already arranged according to some principle (prearranged sources)

(a) Descriptor lists, classification schemes, thesauri (this includes universal classification schemes such as LCC or UDC, or parts thereof, and special classification schemes, e.g., schemes used in special libraries, patent classification schemes);

(b) Nomenclatures of single disciplines such as the nomenclature approved by IUPAC (International Union of Pure and Applied Chemistry);

(c) Treatises on the terminology of a subject field or subfield;

(d) Encyclopedias, lexica, dictionaries, glossaries (universal or discipline-oriented; mono-, bi-, or multilingual);

(e) The tables of contents and indexes of textbooks and handbooks;

(f) Indexes of journals and abstracting journals;

(g) Indexes of other publications in the field;

(h) Term-association lists produced by subjects in term association studies or similar experiments (see Section F1.1.4).

(i)–(j) (Reserved for additions).

Institutions and bibliographies that can be consulted to find prearranged sources are given in Appendix 2.

F1.1.2 Sources in which terms are not ordered or from which terms must first be derived (open-ended sources)

(k) Lists of search requests and interest profiles. Search requests can sometimes be obtained from records of operating ISAR systems. Another approach, to be used instead or in parallel, is to solicit search requests from potential users. It is also possible to have the same users select terms useful for the expression of their search requests.

(l) For ISAR systems in specific institutions: descriptions of the projects in research and development or of other activities to be supported by the ISAR system.

(m) Discussions with specialists in order to identify their interests and potential search requests. In personal interaction one might get a better idea of user needs and points of emphasis than in written answers. The result of such a discussion is a list of terms and themes recorded by the thesaurus builder.

(n) An extremely useful variant of this is the following method: A sample of about one hundred documents representing the scope of the thesaurus to be developed is selected in cooperation with a subject expert. A meeting of seven to twelve potential users is organized. The documents are presented to potential users and for each document one asks the question: What are the aspects under which this document may be of interest to your work? The sample documents serve as stimuli to elicit the explicit formulation of interests that otherwise may have remained hidden. This method yields a large number of concepts and terms that are of immediate interest to the users of the ISAR system. It might be possible to achieve similar results by sending out documents to specialists and asking for written answers.

(o) Have a number of documents indexed by experts in the field or (less desirable) by indexers in the information center or other staff using terms of their own choice; in order that many synonymous terms be collected, it is recommended that the same documents be indexed by different experts.

(p) Titles of documents.

(q) Abstracts and reviews of documents.
Conference programs provide a timely source for both titles and abstracts.

(r)-(y) (Reserved for additions).

(z) Finally, the editor(s)/lexicographer(s)) working on the thesaurus give their own input and should therefore be considered as a source.

Since the indexing language or thesaurus should tell the indexer what aspects are important for the users of the ISAR system and should therefore be considered in indexing (request-oriented indexing as implemented through the checklist technique), the study of user needs provides an input of paramount importance for thesaurus building. If general studies of user needs are available, they should be consulted. Specifically, thesaurus-directed data on user needs are contained in search requests, more generally in the sources (k)-(n). These sources should receive the greatest weight in thesaurus construction. Very often this point is neglected and thesaurus construction is mainly, if not exclusively, document-oriented. This can be justified only if it can be shown for the ISAR system in which the thesaurus is to be used that terms derived from documents are the same as those derived from search requests and that the term frequencies and other indicators of term importance are also the same.

F1.1.3 Selection of the sources to be used

The number of sources to be selected—the completeness of the coverage—is a function of the resources available. In any case one should aim to make the

F1 Collect and Record Material 357

collection of concepts and terms as complete as possible within the scope of the thesaurus. As will be shown below it is usually not possible to achieve this end by using prearranged sources only or open-ended sources only. Each type complements the other.

The two kinds of sources have the following characteristics:

(1) The *prearranged sources* require less effort in the gathering of material. Often the terms are already in a standardized form. Furthermore, these sources indicate relationships between terms and concepts and relationships among concepts in an explicit way. On the other hand, prearranged sources suffer from the following disadvantages: The viewpoints used in selecting and arranging terms and concepts are often very specific and narrow and/or do not take into account the complexity of the subject field. In most cases too few of the synonyms and quasi-synonyms are given (unless a good thesaurus in the subject field is available already).

One may rely mainly (but not only) on prearranged sources if the following conditions hold for the subject field in which the thesaurus is to be developed:

—recognized special classifications and thesauri, extensive and extensively cross-referenced indexes of abstract journals, and larger terminological works are available;

—nomenclatures for materials, living organisms, etc., are available;

—the field is not in a phase of rapid development.

(2) *The open-ended sources* require more effort in information gathering. They have the advantage of yielding a complete collection of those concepts that are necessary to express the subjects asked for in search requests. These concepts are identified in the degree of specification in which they occur in the search requests and in the documents. The terminology reflects the actual usage in the field. Furthermore, the collection reflects the current conceptual and terminological status of the field, not the status of five or fifty years ago. Therefore, these sources should be specially emphasized for mission-oriented thesauri, for thesauri in complex subject fields, and for new, highly specialized or fast-developing subject fields.

In selecting the sources one should make sure that the whole area of the thesaurus is covered. In using prearranged sources one should be careful not to neglect marginal areas.

Furthermore. the following criteria can be used for the selection of prearranged sources:

"1. They contain scientific and technical terminology. (With other thesauri the appropriate field has to be substituted here, of course. D.S.).

2. Their development was from the actual indexing (and searching, D.S.) experiences, thereby representative of storage and retrieval requirements.

3. They were strong in thesaurus-like arrangement, showing various kinds of cross-referencing data, generic relationships, scope notes, and frequencies of use."

It is important to select a representative sample of open-ended sources. With search requests or user discussions this might be difficult. With documents or abstracts it is easier. A reasonable sample size might be 1,000–2,000 abstracts. The sample may be obtained by scanning relevant journals and/or abstracting journals and/or by asking potential users to submit relevant documents.

Remark: In selecting documents to serve as sources of terms (be it from the table of contents, from an abstract, or from free indexing terms), one should take care to include both pre-research documents (proposals, descriptions of research projects) and post-research documents. It has been observed in a study in the field of neurological diseases that "it is apparent that the semantemes of high frequency in the pre-research documents and of low frequency in the post-research articles are rather general terms, while those that are of high frequency in the post-research articles but low in the pre-research documents are specific and tend to be clinically oriented." It might be possible to detect hierarchical relationships by comparing the terms used in pre- and post-research documents on the same research project.

F1.1.4 Term-association lists (special topic)

Term-association lists obtained from subjects representative of the user group are an especially useful source since they reflect the conceptual and terminological "map" of the user. Term-association lists are on the borderline between prearranged sources and open-ended sources.

There are two methods of obtaining term association lists. We might call them the *free association method* and the *bound association method*.

In the free association method each individual is presented with a number of terms, the stimulus terms, and asked to name any terms that he thinks of in connection with each stimulus term. In this method new terms are added to the initial vocabulary. In studies done with this method terms in both definitional and contextual contiguity relationship to the stimulus term are named by the subjects.

The bound association method can also be described as a brute-force approach to determine relationships between terms, once the list of terms has been established. Each ordered term-pair is presented to several (for example, 3) subjects, and the subjects are asked to determine the relationship that holds between the two terms in the pair. This procedure is, from a theoretical point of view, very much in line with our considerations on hierarchy-building in C1.2; however, it is impractical in most situations.

F1.2 Technical Procedures for the Recording of Terms, Etc.

F1.2.0 Introduction

For each term to be entered from a source into the initial collection of terms a record has to be established. This record contains the term itself as Main

F1 Collect and Record Material 359

Term and possibly other data elements, such as Broader, Narrower, and Related Terms. With manual procedures, each term and the data elements for it should be transferred to a separate index card (thesaurus form, see Figure 54, Section F0.5) so that the terms can be sorted easily. Each record thus consists of one card. Having in mind the reader who is interested mainly in manual procedures for thesaurus construction we shall generally use the term "card" instead of the more general "record" throughout Chapter F. (In Chapter D and elsewhere the term "entry" is used with the same meaning.)

Before information on terms can be transferred from sources to cards, the sources have to be prepared as described in Section F1.2.1. The actual transfer of information will be discussed in Section F1.2.2.

F1.2.1 Preparation of sources (technical)

,0 Source identification codes. Each source is identified by a short code which later serves as an indication of origin for all information taken from that source. Any system for the assignment of these codes will do. For prearranged sources the following are examples:

Examples:
(1) A combination of four letters, namely, the first three letters of the name of the author and the first letter of a word of the title. For example, Crad = Craig, R.: The Dynamics of Stratospheric Circulations.

(2) A combination of three letters arbitrarily selected among the beginning letters of authors and/or words in the title, for example, CDS.

(3) Two capitals drawn from the name of the issuing organization, e.g., BY — Boeing Company.

For open-ended sources (search requests, abstracts, etc.), sequential numbers or, if available, call numbers may be best. For scientists as sources and lexicographers as sources initials might serve as source codes as long as they are unambiguous. For purposes of machine processing it is convenient if all source codes have the same fixed length.

,1 Preparation of prearranged sources. From the prearranged sources, terms can be transferred to cards without prior scanning and selection. Prior scanning and selection is recommended only if 25% or more of the terms are likely to be eliminated right away. Otherwise more work is needed for scanning and selection then is saved by eliminating the work of transferring unwanted terms. One should keep in mind that in this phase of thesaurus development only those terms are to be eliminated that are obviously beyond the scope of the thesaurus. If cards have to be made for selected terms only, those terms have to be marked in the source—for example, by "*" or "√".

If the source in question contains USE instructions and if for every USE instruction the corresponding inverse UF statement is given, it is not necessary to prepare cards for nonpreferred terms. In fact these cards would only create work without adding any new information.

Example:
Television camera tubes
  UF Pick-up tubes
Pick-up tubes
  USE Television camera tubes.

Pick-up tubes is a synonym of *Television camera tubes*. Therefore, there is no need to make an extra card for *Pick-up tubes;* this card would only be eliminated later on when all cards referring to the same concept are merged (in Step F2.3, "Second round of merging", or in Step F3.3, "Work out detailed thesaurus structure. Select preferred terms"). However, if a USE instruction is of the USE BT type (whether or not it is explicitly so designated), one may want to have a separate card for the specific concept from the beginning.

Example:
Television camera tubes
  UF Iconoscopes
Iconoscopes
  USE Television camera tubes.

Iconoscopes are a special type of *Television camera tubes,* and a separate card should therefore be established. If this is not done in the transfer operation (where it is merely a clerical process), it has to be done later, while working on the card for *Television camera tubes*. If this case occurs often, one may include initially all terms that have a USE instruction. The cards for truly nonpreferred terms like *Pick-up tubes* are then eliminated in later editing.

Some of the prearranged sources, e.g., TEST and often special dictionaries, are usually too big to be included or even to be searched through for relevant terms. They may, however, be used to look up information on terms obtained elsewhere, as described in Section F2.2.1. Or the terms from certain sections are included (e.g., the terms listed under the appropriate subject categories in TEST).

,1.1 **Adding an auxiliary notation.** Some sources arrange terms in classified order but do not attach a notation to them. In this case an auxiliary notation is added, using the modified decimal notation described in Section D4.3.4 (the notation is used at a later stage if one wants to refer back to the source, e.g., in step F3.3.2, "Work out the classificatory structure").

,2 **Preparation of open-ended sources: mark terms to be transferred.** With open-ended sources it is necessary to identify the significant terms before

F1 Collect and Record Material 361

they can be transferred to cards. In most cases positive selection will be used: all significant terms occurring in search requests, abstracts, etc., are underlined. Even wrong, inexact, or popular terms are to be marked. The same is true for terms that belong to subject fields that are marginal for the thesaurus. Index terms that describe the content of the search requests or the document more precisely and/or on a higher level of abstraction may be added as deemed necessary by the editor. In working with full documents as sources it might be useful to use index terms only.

Terms that occur several times in the same document are taken over only once for this document (possibly recording the frequency within the document). However, if the same term occurs in several documents, several index cards are made up accordingly (compare Section F1.2.3).

Examples:
THE LOW-INCOME FARMER IN A CHANGING SOCIETY
To identify some major differences among low-income farmers, *and to delineate the group that represents the real* core of the persistently poor, *data were obtained from 189* farm operators *representing a* stratified random sample *in Fayette County, Pennsylvania, in 1957. The five main categories of individuals identified were: (1)* the aged, *(2) the* physically handicapped, *(3) the* farm operator primarily oriented to non-farm opportunities, *(4) the* farm operator oriented to commercial agriculture, *and (5)* the farm operator oriented to subsistence agriculture. *The characteristics of the core of* low income subsistence farmers *who normally do not respond to either* welfare *or* economic-development *efforts were examined in greater detail. It was found that they: (1) retained* traditional values *while having lost many* traditional subsistence skills, *(2) failed to respond to greater agricultural* efficiency *and* productivity *efforts because* commercial success *was not highly valued, (3) placed extreme emphasis on* neighborliness *and* friendliness *as their primary* goals, *and (4) must respond to an attempt to* change prestige *orientation if their* cycle of poverty *is to be broken.*

NEMATODE CONTROL IN SWEET POTATOES
The yield *and* quality *of* sweet potatoes *can be increased by* soil fumigation *or the addition of* solid nematocides *in some areas of* Mississippi. *The commercial fumigants* Vorlex, Dow W-85, *and* DD *significantly increased yields and quality in the treatments of* rows. *Vorlex or Dow-85 should be applied at 2.5 gal/acre and DD at 9-10 gal/acre, 8-10 inches deep in the center of the row, 14-30 days prior to* planting. *Broadcast fumigation was also effective, but required higher* fumigant levels. *Among the* experimental solid nematocides, Bayer 68138 *and* Dasanit *showed promise. This study of control of* rootknot nematodes *was conducted by the Truck Crops Branch Experiment Station in 1967 on three- and four-row replicated and* random-

ized field plots known to be *infested* with the nematodes. More information is deemed necessary than was obtained from this one-season field test.
Added terms: *Application dose; Application time*

,3 Pre-processing of open-ended sources. In working with open-ended sources one may also use negative selection, that is, include all terms that are not on a stop-list. This is sensible only if computer assistance is used to produce a list of all the terms occurring in a corpus of open-ended sources.

An intermediary solution in which the open-ended sources are pre-processed is also possible: a listing of all non-stop-list terms occurring in the open-ended sources is produced. From this listing terms to be included in the thesaurus are then selected, possibly using frequency criteria as discussed in Section F0.4.4. Such a listing is particularly useful if the context of each term is given. This might simply be done by producing a KWIC index (the units being titles, search request statements, or sentences from documents and/or abstracts). Such a listing is very useful for the study of homonyms and for the study of relationships between terms and for the formulation of definitions. Further elaboration of these methods leads to the automatic construction of indexing languages, to be discussed in Chapter H.

F1.2.2 Transfer of terms to cards (thesaurus forms) (technical)

After these preparations the terms and other information can be transferred to cards (thesaurus forms), as shown in Figure 55.

,1 Entering Synonymous, Broader, Narrower, and Related Terms. Together with a term, additional information, such as Synonymous or Equivalent Terms, Broader and Narrower Terms (one level up or down), and Related Terms (possibly including Coordinate Terms, i.e., brothers in a hierarchy), short definitions, etc., is transferred to the appropriate data fields of the thesaurus form. (Data fields for which no information is given in the source are simply left blank. Note that data field 05 Notation is left blank for later use; the notation from the source, if any, is given in the source indication; see section ,2.) Long definitions are only referred to. In certain situations, Broader and Narrower Terms need not be transferred from sources that have a classified arrangement, as explained in the rest of this paragraph. If the terms in a source are arranged in classified order, Broader and Narrower Terms for a term given can be easily looked up in the source, using the notation of the term (if necessary, the auxiliary notation assigned in F1.2.1,1). If keeping track of sources of relationships is not an important problem, one may therefore omit the Broader and Narrower Terms from these sources. At the stage described in F3 one consults the original source and applies the information for hierarchy-building. In those cases where the classified arrangement chosen coincides with the classified arrangement in

| 0 | 1 | 2 | 3 | 4 | 5 | 6 | check hierarchical level | 02 check type: | Color TV picture tube (TH: 659.5) | DS | OP | NP | EL | CH | 03 Subject Field |

05 Notation: _____ 10 MT: Color TV picture tube (TH: 659.5)

12 Stand. abbr. (AB): _____

20 Spellings (incl. abbr.): _____

30 Synonymous T. (ST) (incl. equiv. t.): Color kinescope

46 Related Terms (RT): Flat picture tube;
Radiation hazard

50 Translations (TR):

F:
G:
R:
S:

60 Definition, scope note (SN):

4 Classification: _____

42 Category (CA): _____

44 Semantic factors/Broader Terms (BT):
Color TV receiver

45 Is semantic factor of Narrower T. (NT)
Color TV screen

70 Unspec. rel. (UN): _____

81 Editor/Date: _____

Figure 55. Example of filled-in thesaurus form (F1.2.2).

the source, Broader or Narrower Terms need not be transferred even at this stage. In other cases Broader and Narrower Terms are transferred as is deemed useful. This procedure saves much work, both in the transfer of terms and in merging information from different cards. If, in Section F3, "Work out the structure of the thesaurus", machine processing is to be used, this procedure is not applicable. Compare Section F4.0 to the problem of transferring Broader and Narrower Terms.

If a source uses the crude lead-in method, that is, does not distinguish between UF ST and UF NT, we have the problem of where to enter the terms listed in the source under UF. One may choose between three strategies:

(1) Assume that most UF statements do in fact refer to Synonymous Terms and enter all terms from UF in field ST. Corrections will then be made in later editing.

(2) Enter all terms from UF in field UN (Unspecified relationship). Further specification is then made in later editing.

(3) Exercise judgment during transfer and put terms from UF into SP (Spelling variants), ST, or NT (or sometimes RT), as the case may be. Keeping track of the source precisely presents a problem in this case.

Relationships among terms can also be detected from open-ended sources, such as search requests/interest profiles and abstracts, and should be transferred to the thesaurus forms.

Example for the case of abstracts:
From the second sample abstract given above it can be seen that Dasanit has a broader concept (Experimental) solid nematocides. Therefore, on the card for Dasanit one should enter (Experimental) solid nematocides as a Broader Term.

Search requests are also very useful for detecting relationships, especially if they have been formulated for an ISAR system using natural language as indexing language. In this case the searcher should name as many synonyms designating a certain concept as he can think of and combine them all by OR. In the case of an inclusive search he has to add terms for narrower concepts, too. Looking at search request formulations one should therefore analyze the terms co-occurring in an OR parenthesis to see whether there are relationships of synonymity or Narrower Term-Broader Term relationships or whether a suitable Broader Term, covering all the terms combined by OR, should be introduced. Interest profiles that have been improved through feedback over a period of time are especially useful as a source for this procedure.

These sources can be exploited further by detecting term relationships through statistical methods, as discussed in Chapter H.

,2 Entering the source indication. After the term in data field MT, the source indication is given in the following format:

(Source code: Notation in source/Frequency given in source in percent)

If notation and frequency are not given in the source, they are simply omitted. (For the detailed form of keeping track of the sources only: The source code is underlined. In some cases it might be useful to give the notation for BT, NT, and RT, too. In this case a source indication, omitting frequency, is entered after each term in these data fields.)

In some cases it might be useful to add a page number to the source indication so that it is easier to find the term in the source. This is useful in the construction of the thesaurus and mandatory if it is planned to include a reference to the source in the user version of the thesaurus.

(A more detailed referencing procedure is possible but not recommended: number the entries on each page of the thesaurus and give page and entry number, together with the source indication. This procedure is not recommended, however, because the minor benefits (if any) for the later steps do not justify the major costs in the step of collection of material. Based on a notation or the alphabetical sequence, any term may be looked up rapidly in any source without having a page number—certainly without having an entry number on the page.)

Often it may save labor to stamp the source codes on the cards (e.g., using a rubber stamp printing set). In this procedure the card decks resulting from different sources are kept separate until the source code is stamped on. However, if notations or page numbers have to be added, this method is less practical. In mechanized methods the inclusion of the source codes is even easier.

,3 Transfer of terms and other information with manual procedures. Terms from the open-ended sources have to be typed or written on the cards.

For transfer of the terms from prearranged sources, two procedures are possible:

(a) type or write on cards;
(b) copy the source, cut the entries, and paste on cards. Which of these procedures is cheaper has to be decided from case to case. The following parameters have to be considered in the decision:
—how much text has to be transferred to the index cards? (text may include a definition or scope note);
—machines available (a machine may considerably speed up the pasting of entries on cards);
—clerical staff available (pasting requires less skill than typing and is therefore cheaper!).

If cutting and pasting is used, it is often not possible to fill in the in-

366   F   Flow of Work in Thesaurus Construction

formation in the proper spaces of the thesaurus form. In this phase of the thesaurus development, this is of minor importance, provided that the different data fields (such as Synonymous Terms, Related Terms) can be identified without difficulty.

F1.2.3 An alternative procedure

With the method of term collection suggested here multiple cards are made for a term occurring in several sources, and duplicates are not removed until the next step. An alternative procedure would be as follows: Make cards for the terms of the first source and alphabetize. In processing the next source look for each term in the alphabet. If the term is found, add information to the card. If it is not found, make a new card and insert into alphabet.

It is hard to say whether this method is cheaper. This depends on the number of identical terms and the arrangement of terms in the source: If the arrangement in the source is alphabetical, the look-up procedure may be cheaper; if the arrangement is hierarchical, it is cheaper first to collect and then to eliminate duplicates. An intermediate strategy is also possible: Start with the open-ended sources and with the sources that have a classified arrangement. Transfer terms to cards, as described previously. Alphabetize and eliminate duplicates. Then process further sources that are arranged alphabetically by checking and merging information on the same term and interfiling cards for new terms.

Compare Section F2.2.3 on "pulling" information from a big thesaurus.

F2 SORT INTO ALPHABETICAL ORDER AND MERGE INFORMATION ON IDENTICAL TERMS ON ONE CARD

F2.1 Sort into Alphabetical Order. Rules for Preliminary Alphabetical Sorting

Common sense alphabetical sorting can be used in this phase; consideration of complex filing rules is usually not necessary. The cards for identical or nearly identical (singular/plural or similar variations) terms are put together with a paper clip. Often terms consist of a string of terms separated by commas (for example, the term *Beer, ale, malt liquor*). In this case all terms that start with the same term are considered synonymous and these cards are clipped together. However, this is not always useful, e.g., *Roughness, smoothness* is broader than *Roughness,* not synonymous. Spelling variants should be grouped together. This sometimes requires judgment, e.g., *Automated* and *Automation* are not spelling variants. (For a more detailed discussion see Section F2.4.1.) It is advantageous to disambiguate homo-

F2 Sort into Alphabetical Order and Merge 367

nyms in this step so that, for example, *Banks (economics)* and *Banks (waterways)* do not get merged by mistake on one card (Compare the discussion on homonyms in Section F2.4.2).

With the exceptions mentioned at the end this step can be performed by clerical staff or computer. If Step F2.2 is performed as a manual procedure employing judgment, the critical problems can be resolved there.

F2.2 First Round of Merging: Merge Information for Identical Terms

In the previous step the cards have been grouped into packages. Within each package we have identical or nearly identical terms or terms starting with the same word. In a second step the information contained on the cards of each package is merged on one card (record), as illustrated in Figures 56–58.

F2.2.1 Procedure for merging cards and keeping track of sources (technical)

With manual procedures there are two possible places to put the record that results from merging: one may put it on a fresh card, or one may select a card already in the package and transfer only the information from other cards, thus saving work.

The following criteria may be used in selecting a card (listed in decreasing priority):

(a) Select the card that contains the largest amount of text (e.g., a definition). This will minimize the work needed for the transfer of information from other cards.

(b) Select the card that has been made up from a preferred source. A preferred source may be a thesaurus using structural principles similar to those to be used in the thesaurus to be developed.

(c) Select the card that is most legible.

If a nonselected card contains a lengthy definition, one may just clip it onto the selected card and establish the proper link by a circled number.

While merging cards, one has to keep track of the sources as follows (we repeat here the process already described in Section F0.7.2(2)): Assume that card 1 is the selected card and that card 2 is the card from which information is to be entered on the selected card in the operation of merging. In the crude form all one has to do is to enter the source indication from data field MT of card 2 into data field MT of card 1. If one wants to keep track of spelling variants, then one has to check first to see whether the Main Term on card 2 is a spelling variant of the Main Term on card 1. If so, the Main Term from card 2, together with its source indication, is entered into the field SP of card 1. For ST, BT, NT, and RT, one simply checks for each term given on card 2 to see whether it is already given on card 1. If so, nothing needs to be done. If not, the term is added to card 1. If the detailed form is to be used, things are more complicated. Before any information is transferred from card 2 to card 1 the source code given in data field MT is added to every term entered in any other data field of card 1. When the information from card 2 has been transferred one proceeds as follows. First the source indication (with underline) from data field MT of card 2 is entered in field MT of card 1, (or the Main Term from card 2, together with the source indication, is entered into field SP of card 1) as before. The new feature in the detailed form is that sources are given for data elements in other data fields too. Let us explain this using as an example a term in data field RT of card 2. If the term is already in the data field RT of card 1 only the source code from card 2 is added to the term. If the term is not yet contained in the data field RT of card 1, then it is entered there together with the source code from card 2. (Source codes in data fields other than MT, SP, and ST are not underlined.) An example is given in Figure 56. Further examples are given in Figure 57. Note that in example 3 the term *Attorney, lawyer* is treated as a synonym of the term *Lawyer* (this is done only during the construction phase). An example of merging on a thesaurus form is given in Figure 58.

F2.2.2 Steps after the first round of merging

In most cases one may proceed after this to Step F3, "Work out the structure of the thesaurus". However, there are two exceptions:

(1) Sometimes there is a big thesaurus or other prearranged source that cannot be included in the term collection at the beginning but that could supply useful information for the terms that have been collected from other sources. In this case one should consider "pulling" this information, as described in F2.2.3. This is particularly useful in small projects where an exhaustive collection of terms and relationships is not possible.

(2) In the first round of merging, nothing is done about synonyms. If the area of the thesaurus is not too complex and interrelated and if it may be divided into subject fields and subfields without too much overlap, synonyms will be detected later on in Step F3, "Work out the preliminary structure of the thesaurus". Synonymous and Equivalent (quasi-synonymous) Terms are very likely to be sorted into the same subject field and subfield in this case. If, on the other hand, the area of the thesaurus is complex and interrelated and not easily subdivided, Synonymous and Equivalent Terms are likely to be scattered over different subject fields and subfields during the sorting in Steps F3.1 and F3.2, and there is the danger that the synonymity will never be detected. Therefore, a second round of merging, to be described in Section F2.3, is recommended in this case. In this second round of merging, the information contained (after the first round of merging) in data field ST and possibly in data field SP (spelling variants) is used to bring together the records for Synonymous and Equivalent Terms. The procedure is rather intricate and cumbersome. It is not recommended unless it is really necessary.

```
INFORMATION RETRIEVAL
WRO800  LB05  AV    AZ    BY     AR15    DD0502
BR      EJ    CM    HI    EI     LM1506  FC
MS      IE    MR11  MZ05  NAO010 NE      NO
SP      VO
DD SNO        The use of computers, electronic accounting
   1          machines, and similar mechanical devices to
   2          organize store and retrieve recorded
   3          information. For the use of manual
   4          techniques in such activities see
   5          (documentation).
   9          DD FR    990    Frequency of term in DDC-collection
   USE        Information storage and retrieval                    BY

        UF    Document retrieval                                   EI
              Information storage and retrieval                    MZ
              Library searches                                     HI
              Records retrieval                                    EJ
              Records retrieval                                    HI
        BT    Data processing                                      AV
              Documentation                                        DD
              Documentation                                        WR
        NT    Computerized information retrieval                   AV
              Data bank                                            AV
              Data processing                                      SP
              Data recording                                       SP
              Data retrieval                                       WH
              Document retrieval                                   WH
              Environmental information retrieval                  AV
              Information dissemination                            AV
              Information storage                                  AV
              Search structuring                                   WH
              Stinfo                                               AV
              Vocabulary development                               AV
        RT    Bibliographies                                       WR
              Computers                                            BS
              Data collections                                     WR
              Data retrieval                                       EJ
              Documentation                                        EJ
              Electronic accounting machines                       BS
              Filing systems                                       EJ
              Image storage                                        SP
              Index terms                                          EJ
              Indexes (locators)                                   EJ
              Library sciences                                     EJ
              Machine translation                                  BS
              Microfilm                                            EJ
              Microfilm selectors                                  EJ
              Publications                                         WR
              Records management                                   EJ
              Records storage                                      EJ
              Search questions                                     EI
              Selective dissemination                              EI
              Translations                                         WR
              Indexing vocabulary                                  WH
```

This example is from the development of TEST. The two-letter codes stand for sources: 23 sources contained the term, and they contained further information as shown in the different fields. DD0502 means that in the DDC thesaurus the item is assigned to COSATI field 05, group 02. Note that in UF two lines could be replaced by

    RECORDS RETRIEVAL   EJ,HI
and in BT
    DOCUMENTATION   DD,WR

Figure 56. Merging of data elements from different cards for the same term (F2.2). (Source: Heald 1967, issued by the Office of Naval Research, Department of Defense.)

	Card No.	Entry on card	Comments
		Example 1	
Before merging	1	B22.cl Army (1m)	Notation after first source code omitted; assumed to be the notation that precedes the term
	2	BGH Army (2b)	
	3	15.20.1 Army (3)	
		Merged on card 3:	':' separates source code from notational symbol in that source.
After merging	3'	15.20.1 Army (3)	
		(1m: B22.cl; 2b: BGH)	';' separates different sources
		or merged on new card	
	4	Army	
		(1m: B22.cl; 2b: BGH; 3: 15.20.1)	
		Example 2	
Before merging	1	474 Attorney (1)	
	2	338 Attorney (1b2)	
	3	K51 Attorney, lawyer (2c)	

After merging	2'	338 Attorney (1b2) (1:474) ST Attorney, Lawyer (2c:K51)	Card 2 contains a definition, therefore merged on card 2 Different form of term in source (2c) treated as synonym

Example 3

Before merging	1 2 3 4 5 6 7 8	5.A.d Parliament (1h) 5.B.d Parliament (1h) 453 Parliament (2a) 453 Parliament, control of executive branch (1c) G51 Parliament, legislative assembly (2c) I42 Parliament, legislative assembly (FR) 19.83 Parliament, Parliamentarianism (3) 452 Parliament, senate, committees (1)

Merged on card 3

After merging	3'	453 Parliament (2a) (1h:5.A.d;1h:5.B.d) ST Parliament, control of executive branch (1c:453) Parliament, legislative assembly (2c:G51; FR:I42) Parliament, Parliamentarianism (3:19.83) Parliament, senate, committees (1:452)

Figure 57. Further examples to illustrate merging in the first round (F2.2).

Figure 58. Example of result of merging on a thesaurus form in the first round (F2.2). (The detailed form of keeping track of sources has been used. In the crude form only the source codes that are underlined would remain. The entry in source AR has been added to illustrate the merging procedure; it would not normally be detected in the first round.)

Entry in Source TH

    659.5 **Color TV picture tube**
              ST Color kinescope
              BT 435.7   Color TV receiver
              NT 478.2   Color TV screen
              RT 568.3   Flat picture tube
                   075   Radiation hazard

Entry in Source AR

    Color kinescopes
        UF Color TV picture tubes
        BT Kinescopes
           Color TV receiver
        NT Color TV screen

Entry in Source SK

    Color TV picture tubes
        UF Color television picture tubes
        BT Color TV receiver
        NT Lawrence tubes
           Shadow mark tubes
        RT Radiation hazards

Entry in Source KL

    TC904 Color television picture tubes
           BT TK25 Color television set

Result of Merging

| 0 | 1 | 2 | 3 | 4 | 5 | 6 | check hierarchical level | 02 check type: | DS|OP|NP|EL|CH| 03 Subject Field |

05 Notation: _____   10 MT: Color TV picture tube (TH:659.5) (AR;SK)

12 Stand. abbr. (AB): _____

20 Spellings (incl. abbr.): Color television picture tubes (KL:TC904;SK)

30 Synonymous T. (ST) (incl. equiv. t.): Color kinescope (TH) (AR); Color TV display tube (TH)

4 Classification: _____
42 Category (CA): _____

44 Semantic factors/Broader Terms (BT): Color TV receiver (TH) (AR;SK); Kinescopes (AR); Color television set (KL)

45 Is semantic factor of Narrower T. (NT) Color TV screen (TH) (AR); Chromatrons (AR); Shadow mask tubes (AR;SK); Lawrence tubes (SK)

46 Related Terms (RT): Flat picture tube (TH) (SK); Radiation hazard (TH)

50 Translations (TR):

F:
G:
R:
S:

60 Definition, scope note (SN):

70 Unspec. rel. (UN):

81 Editor/Date:

If neither (1) "Pulling" nor (2) "Second round of merging" apply the reader may turn immediately to Section F2.4.

F2.2.3 "Pulling" information from additional sources (match and merge)

In addition to the information for a term merged from the cards prepared in Step F1 one may look up the term in a big thesaurus (for example, TEST), a big dictionary, or other sources and add the information given there (match and merge). The term itself as well as the entry for the concept involved has to be found. If the Main Term given in the file cannot be found in the big thesaurus, one should try Synonymous and Equivalent Terms given in field ST or spelling variants given in field SP. If the term finally found in the big thesaurus is not a preferred term, follow the SEE ST or USE ST instruction given to obtain the entry for the concept involved.

Example:
After 1st round of merging we have
Cyclophones
    UF ST Additrons.
Looking for Cyclophones in the big thesaurus, we find nothing. Therefore, we look up Additrons. There we find
Additrons
    USE ST Trochotrons.
Therefore, we look up Trochotrons and find the entry for the concept involved. This record gives, for example, the Broader Term Counting tubes.

The information taken from the big thesaurus may be grouped into three types:

(1) *Terminological information.* New synonyms for a term may be given (these synonyms may be terms already contained elsewhere in the file or terms new to the file). One can also note which term has been selected as the preferred term in the big thesaurus and copy that decision.

(2) *New BT, NT, and RT relationships* between concepts already represented in the file. A special case in point is the introduction of finer distinctions in these relationships. For example, a source may put together into one field "see also" both NT and RT. The information from the big thesaurus can be used to distinguish between NT and RT.

(3) *Entirely new concepts.* In particular one should take care to include in the file all concepts that are broader than any concept in the file.

,1 Procedure for "pulling" (technical). To obtain new BT, NT, and RT relationships and entirely new concepts one proceeds as follows (manual procedure employing judgment; for computer procedures see Section G2.2.1).

The card for the Main Term A is being compared with the entry found

F2 Sort into Alphabetical Order and Merge

in the big thesaurus. Check each Broader Term (Narrower Term, Related Term) given in the big thesaurus to see whether it is already on the card for A. If the BT, NT, or RT cross-reference is not given on the card for A, add it in the appropriate data field and check whether or not a card for the added term or a synonym is already contained in the working file. If the added term is not contained in the working file already, one should consider including it. If the new term is a Broader Term, it should always be included. If the new term is a Narrower Term or Related Term, a decision has to be made as to whether the new term will be useful in the thesaurus to be constructed. A new term is included in the working file by transferring the entire entry from the big thesaurus onto a card. In the case of a Broader Term one should check whether it, in turn, has Broader Terms that are not yet contained in the working file. If so, the entries for these Broader Terms have to be pulled as well, and so on. The same procedure could, of course, be followed for Narrower and Related Terms, but this would lead too far. Whenever a whole entry has been pulled from the big thesaurus, the "starting term" is marked so that one knows later on why the term has been pulled. If the big thesaurus contains a cross-reference to a term not to be included in the working file, the cross-reference is not included in the working file either.

The whole process may be performed either as merging in the first round is performed for each term or as a separate step after the merging has been done for all terms in the working file.

An additional note is necessary. As long as the Main Term in the working file is the same as the Main Term in the entry being pulled from the big thesaurus, pulling corresponds to merging in the first round. But whenever we look for a synonym that occurs in the working file card and/or follow a USE instruction in the big thesaurus, we are making use of the USE instructions that are taken from the sources and included in the working file and/or the USE instructions given in the big thesaurus. This corresponds to merging in the second round, to be discussed in the next section. In doing so, we are dependent on the quality of these USE instructions. The problem of prior editing occurs in pulling as well as in the second round of merging (see Section F2.3.3).

In order not to complicate this description too much, keeping track of the sources has not been considered so far. It is rather simple: In the crude form, enter the source indication for the big thesaurus after the term that is the Main Term in the big thesaurus (this term can be MT, SP, or ST in the working file). In the detailed form underline the source code after this term. Furthermore, enter the source code for the big thesaurus after the appropriate terms in all other data fields too. (For a more detailed description of the procedure, see Section F0.7.2.)

F   Flow of Work in Thesaurus Construction

F2.3   Second Round of Merging: Merge Information for Terms in the Same Concept Class (Advanced and Technical)

The second round of merging is necessary if and only if the area of the thesaurus is complex, interrelated, and not easily subdivided. The second round of merging makes use of the information contained in the field ST (and possibly SP) after the first round of merging.

F2.3.1   The procedure (algorithm)

Basically what we want is this: Given a file like the one depicted in Figure 59 and all the synonyms for each term in the file. Create one entry (card) in which all the information given for each of the synonyms is merged. Delete all entries that are then obsolete. This is achieved in two passes through the file by the following algorithm which may be performed either manually or by computer. An example to illustrate the algorithm is given in Figure 59, a flow chart in Figure 60, and an example with actual terms in Figure 61.

Pass 1: Start with A. Look up D, flag D "to be deleted", add "ST* A" and merge information from D to A. Look up F and do the same. This brings

	Original	Added through algorithm
A	ST D,F,K	ST J,L,N,P,U
B	ST H	
C		
D—		ST * A
E		
F—	ST A,J	ST * A
G		
H—		ST * B
I		
J—		ST * A
		K — ST * A
L—	ST A,N	ST * A
M		
N—		ST * A
O		ST S
P—	ST D	ST * A
Q		
R		
S—	ST O	ST *O
T		
U—	ST K	

Figure 59. Sample file for the second round of merging (F2.3.1). (Note Minus-sign "—" is flag for entry to be deleted.)

F2 Sort into Alphabetical Order and Merge 377

a new term into data field ST of A, namely J, added at the end. The next term to be looked up is K. It is not found in the file, and a new entry K ST* A is created and flagged "to be deleted" (this will cause U to be picked up as synonym of A; in a manual procedure one might omit this additional cross-reference at the expense of not picking up U as a synonym.) Next look up J, ... Now field ST is exhausted; therefore, proceed in the list and process B in the same way. Coming to D, the flag "to be deleted" is detected and D is therefore skipped. The same is true for F and J. L does not have a flag when encountered first. However, when looking up A it is detected that A has already been processed and is not flagged "to be deleted". Therefore, L is flagged "to be deleted", "ST* A" is added and all the information is merged to A. This situation occurs if a term has an ST cross-reference to another term preceding it in the alphabetical sequence. L is added to the field ST of A and marked as processed. N is also added to the field ST of A in the merging procedure. N then has to be processed in the same way as D, F, and J. (Note that one could just as well add all information to the entry for L and flag A. Choosing routinely the term first in the alphabet is convenient in a computer program, especially with respect to keeping track of which synonyms have already been looked up. But it is less desirable in a manual procedure where the information should be added to the entry that already has more information.) If field ST of A is exhausted again, go on to M and continue. P, like L, does not have a flag when encountered first. However, when looking up its synonym D, the flag "to be deleted" is detected and "ST* A" is found. The same action as in the case of L is taken. (In this case, the synonymity between A and P is detected due to the fact that they had the Synonymous Term D in common.) This situation shows that it would not be appropriate to delete D before pass 1 is completed. When coming to U look up K, find K ST* A. Therefore, transfer all information from U to A and enter ST U with A and ST* A with U.

A special situation, not shown in the example, may also arise.

Example:

A ST D,F
K ST U
P ST A,K
U

While processing K the information from U is transferred to K, and with U the cross-reference ST* K is entered. In processing P, K is transferred to A into data field ST, and the next step is to look up K. In this case the flag with K is changed to "to be deleted", ST* A is added, and the information is cumulated to A. A double transfer of information, from U to K and then from K to A, is necessary. (In the case of L double transfer of information—

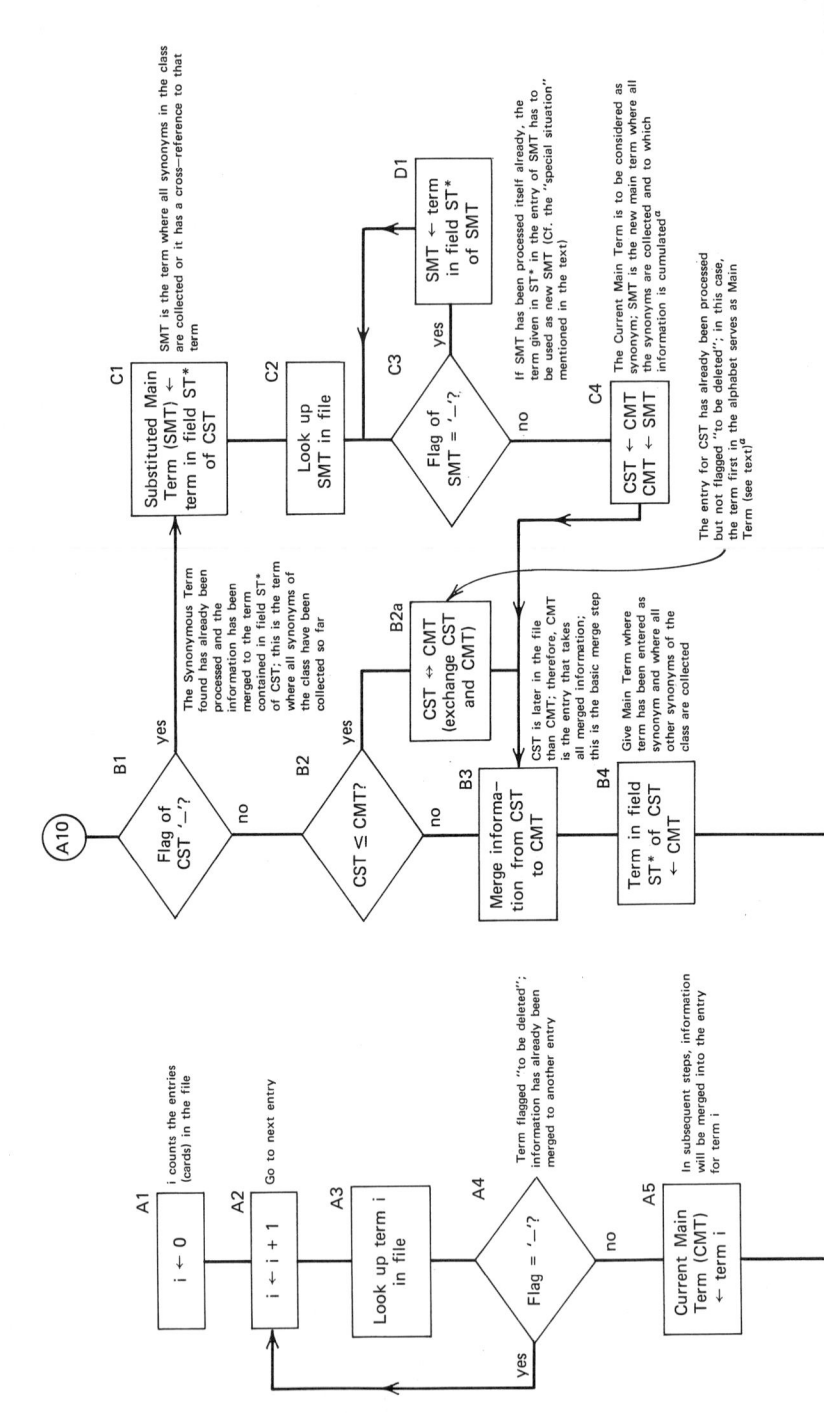

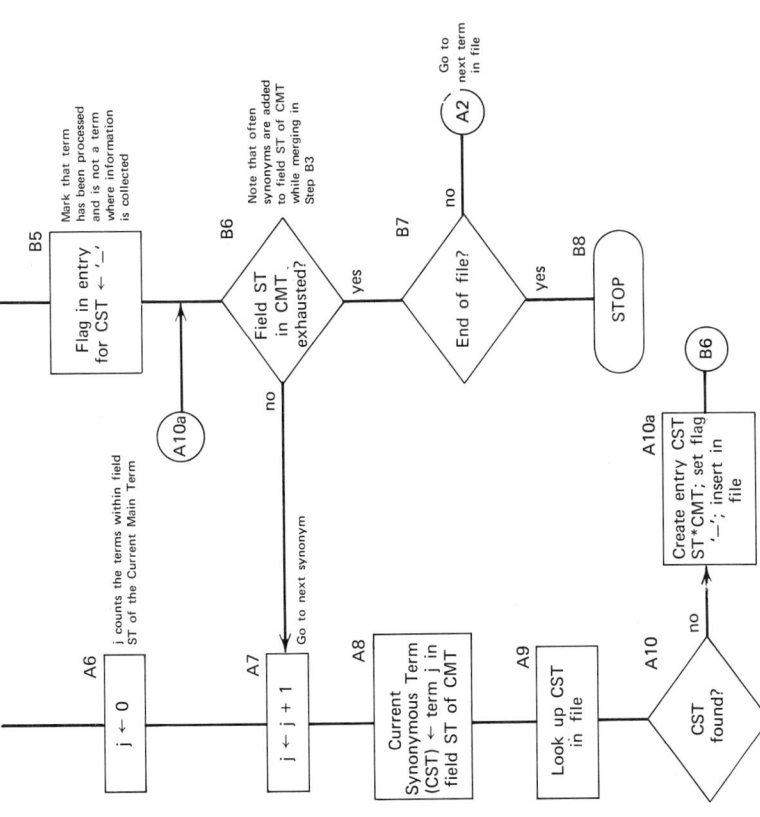

Figure 60. Flowchart for the second round of merging (identifying classes of synonyms) (F2.3.1).

from *N* to *L* and then from *L* to *A*—is avoided by processing the terms in alphabetical order.) Also, if we have *Z* ST *U*, we are referred from *U* to *K* and then from *K* to *A*

Pass 2: Delete all records flagged "to be deleted".

In manual processing the flag "to be deleted" may consist of a paper clip put on the card and the indication "ST* *A*" may be achieved by entering A in the field ST and underlining it. Cards with main records do not have a paper clip.

The algorithm described is a natural way to identify groups of synonyms in a manual procedure. Since the general problem of identifying equivalence classes in a set starting from binary equivalence relationships (of which our problem is a special case) occurs fairly often, it is quite possible that, for processing by computer, better algorithms can be found in the computer science literature.

In order not to complicate the description, details of the actual process of merging two entries and keeping track of the sources have been omitted. Refer to Sections F0.7.2 and F2.2.

F2.3.2 Treatment of terms that consist of a string of Synonymous Terms

Sometimes a term (either the Main Term in data field MT, or a synonym in data field ST) consists of a string of synonymous or quasi-synonymous words or phrases, separated by commas; for example: *Beer, ale, malt liquor*. In this case the constituents are considered to be synonymous or quasi-synonymous to the term as a whole and to each other. Therefore, starting from *Beer, ale, malt liquor,* one should look up *Beer, Ale,* and *Malt liquor* (unless one of these terms has been processed already). In a manual procedure in which a certain capability of judgment can be assumed (see below) appropriate instructions should be given that the constituents are to be treated in the same way as synonyms. (However, there are cases where the terms in a string are not synonymous; see Section F2.3.3,2.) In a purely mechanical procedure (manual or computer) the constituents should be entered into field ST prior to performing the second round of merging. The procedure is further illustrated by the examples given in Figure 61.

Of course, this procedure is not applied to multiword terms like *Gross national product* or *Electron tube* (note the absence of commas!).

F2.3.3 Editing during or prior to the second round of merging

In the algorithm described above the appearance of one wrong synonym in a source may lead to the merger of two whole series of records that actually belong to different concepts and should be kept separate. It is rather awkward to disentangle such a mess afterwards. Therefore, an editor has to exercise judgment as to what terms appearing in field ST (and possibly in field UN Unspecified relationship) should be used in the second round of merging, and what terms should not. If the second round of merging is performed manually by a person capable of making such judgments, the editing can be done during the second round of merging. If the second round of merging is performed in a merely mechanical way, especially if it is done by a computer, prior editing is necessary. The following points have to be considered in editing:

(1) Wrong synonyms are especially likely to come from sources that do not distinguish between UF ST and UF NT (use the crude lead-in form).
(2) If artificial synonyms are created from string terms as described in F2.3.2, careful editing is necessary. E.g., in *Parliament, parliamentarianism, Parliamentarianism* is not a synonym for *Parliament*. Also sometimes two specific terms are strung together to designate a broader concept, such as *Roughness, smoothness*. Again the procedure is not applicable.
(3) Often a term that is wrong as a synonym is useful if specified in some other kind of relationship. A simple change in the relationship indicator will do in this case. The term may come from a source, or it may be an artificial synonym. Whereas *Parliamentarianism* is not synonymous to *Parliament,* it is a useful Related Term.
(4) The problem of spelling and morphological variants described in Section F2.4.1 can be taken care of in this step as well by entering, for example, the relationship *Filtering* Spelling Variant *Filtration*.
(5) Homonyms can also be detected in this step of editing, as described in Section F2.4.2.
(6) If it is necessary to keep track of the sources precisely, two source codes are used for the relationships newly entered in editing: the code of the source that contributed the information being edited and the code for the editor.
(7) In a cumulative thesaurus special problems arise, as described in Section K1.3.

F2.3.4 Concluding remark

In the second round of merging, groups of synonyms and quasi-synonyms are detected in a purely mechanical way, based on ST cross-references in the sources. To keep the procedure simple the cumulated main record is kept under that term of a group that comes first in the alphabet. This in no way prejudices the selection of the preferred term. There is no guarantee that any group of synonyms is complete, especially if the ST cross-references in the sources are not very well developed. Further synonyms will then be detected later in Step F3, "Working out the preliminary structure of the thesaurus".

F2.4 Remarks Regarding Both Rounds of Merging

F2.4.1 Spelling and morphological variants

In both procedures spelling variants should be treated as identical. This does not present a problem with manual procedures as long as the spelling vari-

Figure 61. Examples illustrating the second round of merging (examples 2 and 3 from Figure 57 are continued into the second round of merging) (F2.3.1).

	Card No.	Entry on card	Comments
		Example 2	
After 1st round of merging before 2nd round of merging	2'	338 Attorney (1b2) (1:474) ST Attorney, Lawyer (2c:K51)	
	4	327 Barrister, attorney (7) (3:15.72)	
	5	U25 Lawyer (FR) ST Solicitor	
After 1st step in second round of merging → : added in first step	2''	338 Attorney (1b2) (1:474) ST Attorney, lawyer (2c:K51) → Lawyer (FR:U25) → Solicitor (FR:–U25)	Step 1: *Lawyer* appears on card 2'. Therefore, look up, find card 5, transfer into 2' resulting in 2'', tag 5 "to be deleted" (5—), add ST*Attorney. Now *Solicitor* appears on card 2'. Therefore look it up. No entry found, Step 1 finished. Go to next card. -U25 as notation for *Solicitor*, because it is not the preferred term in FR.
	4	327 Barrister, attorney (7) (3:15.72)	
	5—	U25 Lawyer (FR) ST Solicitor → ST*Attorney	
After 2nd step in second round of merging → : added in second step	2'''	338 Attorney (1b2) (1:474) ST Attorney, Lawyer (2cK51) Lawyer (FR:U25) Solicitor (FR:–U25) → Barrister, attorney (3:15.72:7:327)	Step 2: In due course, one arrives at card 4. Attorney is looked up and card 2'' found. Since 2'' has been processed and is not tagged "to be deleted", the information from 4 is transferred on it, card 4 is tagged "to be deleted" and "ST*Attorney" is added. Note that the original cards 1-5 can be completely recon-
	4—	327 Barrister, attorney (7) (3:15.72) → ST*Attorney	
	5—	As above	

Merging in second round performed until here	9	375 Congress, legislative assembly (4) ST Legislative assembly (2b : IEF) IEF Legislative assembly (2b) ST*Congress, legislative assembly	
	10—		
Merging in second round still to be performed in these cards	3'	453 Parliament (2a) (1h:5.A.d;1h:5.B.d) ST Parliament, control of executive branch (1c:453) Parliament, legislative assembly (2c:G51;FR 142) Parliament, Parliamentarianism (3:19.83) Parliament, senate, committees (1:452)	The process continues with card 3'. All terms recorded there are looked up. This leads first to card 10—. This card is flagged, and leads, in turn, to 9. Since 3' contains more data, it is retained as main card and information from 9 is transferred, 9 is flagged, etc. Next we find card 11, and transfer of information results in the last data element on card 3. Note the link between 9 and 3 established by *Legislative assembly*.
	11	414 Parliamentarianism (1c)	
Merging in second round performed for all cards of example	9—	375 Congress, legislative assembly (4) ST Legislative assembly (2b:IEF) → ST*Parliament IEF Legislative assembly (2b) ST*Congress, legislative assembly	Now, not all results of this mechanical procedure are useful. *Congress* is the legislative assembly for the U. S. and should have a separate entry. *Parliamentarianism* not a synonym of *Parliament* (source 3 is wrong) and should also retain its main entry. These are decisions to be made by the lexicographer who will also note that *Parliament* is a semantic factor of *Congress* and a Related Term of *Parliamentarianism*.
	10—		
	3"	453 Parliament (2a) 1h:5.A.d;1h:5.B.d) ST Parliament, control of executive branch (1c:453) Parliament, legislative assembly (2c:G51;FR:l42) Parliament, parliamentarianism (3:19.83) Parliament, senate, committees (1:452) → Congress, legislative assembly (4:375) → Legislative assembly (2b:IEF)	
	11—	414 Parliamentarianism (1c:414) Parliamentarianism → ST*Parliament	

ants are near neighbors in the alphabetical sequence. It does present a problem, however, in computerized processing.

There is a more fundamental problem, illustrated by pairs such as *Filtering* and *Filtration, Safe* and *Safety, Automated* and *Automation.* From a morphological point of view these are clearly spelling variants. From a semantic point of view the terms in each of these pairs might be sufficiently different to justify treating them as different descriptors or at least keeping one as a Synonymous or Equivalent Term. Intellectual judgment is necessary to make these decisions. (Compare Section C6 on the functional distinction between Synonymous Terms and Spelling Variants.)

F2.4.2 Homonyms

In all the procedures described (first round of merging, pulling from a big thesaurus, second round of merging) there is the danger that cards for homonys might be merged. In a manual procedure employing judgment this danger can be avoided easily enough once one is aware of it. In mechanized procedures things are more difficult. There is no way to avoid the merger of records for a homonymous term unless it is explicit from at least one source that the term is homonymous. In this case all records for this term can be printed out for decision by an editor. Otherwise, the homonymy must be detected later on and the wrongly merged records must be disentangled. If the first round of merging has been done in a purely mechanical way, editing should take place before the second round of merging, as discussed in Section F2.3.3. In this step it should be easy enough to detect records created by wrongly merging the records for two different meanings of a homonym. Obviously, the result of such a merge is odd, especially as there are likely to be many wrong synonyms.

F3 WORK OUT THE PRELIMINARY STRUCTURE OF THE THESAURUS: THE SYNONYM-HOMONYM STRUCTURE, THE EQUIVALENCE STRUCTURE, AND THE CLASSIFICATORY STRUCTURE. SELECT PREFERRED TERMS

Conceptually, it is very important to keep the distinction between the synonym-homonym structure, the equivalence structure, and the classificatory structure as expounded in Chapters B and C. However, in the practical development of a thesaurus problems of all three levels have to be considered in one and the same procedure. Synonymous and Equivalent (quasi-synonymous) Terms are scattered over the whole alphabet. Therefore, terms must be sorted according to a preliminary coarse classification so that groups of Synonymous and Equivalent Terms can be detected. This is the only way to deal with the terminological problems and to form new concepts by consolidating equivalent concepts. The procedure essentially consists of a "cascade-type" sorting of terms, first into broad subject fields, then into subfields, and then into small groups of terms each corresponding to an ISAR concept.

The procedure to be described can be viewed best as the interaction of two principles: (1) the "deductive" principle: start from broader concepts and subdivide them further and further according to some preselected viewpoints, arriving at specific concepts; (2) the "inductive" principle, start from specific concepts, arrange them in small groups which correspond to less specific concepts, arrange those in groups, and so forth, finally arriving at the very broadest concepts. In most practical situations, the inductive principle plays a larger role, but the interaction of both principles is always necessary.

The procedure described in the following leads to a working file in classified order. In the Roget-Soergel model this corresponds to the arrangement of descriptors in the main part. In the TEST model the main part is arranged alphabetically, and it might seem, therefore, that the procedure is not appropriate for the development of a TEST-like thesaurus. However, this is not so. For the development of the thesaurus structure, the working file should be arranged in classified sequence in any case. It will become clear in the following sections that classified arrangement is essential for a reliable detection of synonyms, for the proper definition of concepts, and for uncovering their interrelationships. Also, classified arrangement makes it much easier to discuss all terms belonging to a certain subject field with an expert in that subject field. The user version of the main part, in which terms are arranged alphabetically, should then be produced in Step F5.7 (see Section F5.7.3).

F3.1 Define Broad Subject Fields and Sort Terms into These Broad Fields

By looking at the material collected in the previous step one should get some idea of what the subject fields should be. Further information can be gathered by looking at the major divisions of existing classification schemes, or at tables of contents of textbooks or similar documents. Further clarification, especially concerning the delineation of the different subject fields, can be achieved by asking subject experts, e.g., by organizing a discussion, as described in Section F0.3.3. Terms are sorted into these broad subject fields. In the course of the development of the thesaurus a partial or complete reshuffling of the subject fields may prove necessary. If a thesaurus is developed by parallel development of constituent thesauri, the subject fields are given by the general framework of the total thesaurus (the "umbrella classification"), see Section K2.3.1. Instead of subject fields one may also choose facets as the primary subdivisions. In Step F3.2 subfacets must then be defined.

F3.2 Define Subfields within Each Subject Field and Sort Terms Accordingly

The broad subject fields are now subdivided into smaller but still sizeable subfields, and the terms are sorted into these subfields. The remarks on how to obtain suitable subject fields apply to subfields as well. However, it is usually sufficient to consult subject experts according to the procedure described in Section F0.3.2; discussions would involve too much effort for the purpose at hand. Quite often a major reshuffling of these subdivisions will prove necessary later in Step F4, "Work out first draft of the classified index".

Notes on F3.1 and F3.2:

Sorting can be done in both steps as a two-step process: A professional writes the code for the subject field or subfield on the card for the term or encircles the appropriate code as preprinted on the card. The actual sorting is then done by clerical staff (or by a computer).

If an appropriate list of fields and subfields can be drawn up from the beginning, Steps F3.1 and F3.2 may be performed at the same time. One may use the checklist technique in analyzing terms. This may be assisted by providing a form such as the one given in Figure 62. In essence this form gives the outline of a faceted classification, and terms are analyzed according to a faceted scheme. We could also say they are decomposed into semantic factors on a very broad generic level. Note that some of the downward arrows in Figure 62 correspond to autonomous subdivisions (such as the arrow going down from *Materials*). Other arrows correspond to subdivisions according to another facet; for example, the arrow going down from *Supplies*.

Step F3.1 or Step F3.2 is also the appropriate time to fill in the information in the data fields 41 Subject field and 42 Facet (of Figure 21, Section C7) if those data fields are to be used in the thesaurus to be built.

F3.3 Work Out Detailed Thesaurus Structure. Select Preferred Terms. Merge Information for Terms in the Same Concept Class

Each of the subdivisions created in the previous step contains only a limited number of terms. These terms can be kept in mind or displayed all at the same time so that it is possible to detect relationships among them and to work out the detailed structure of these relationships.

The elaboration of the detailed structure can be performed in two steps, as described in the following Sections F3.3.1 and F3.3.2. However, the functions to be performed in both steps cannot be completely separated, so that sometimes one has to go back and forth between the two steps. Sections F3.3.3 and F3.3.7 contain additional considerations to be taken into account in one or both of these steps.

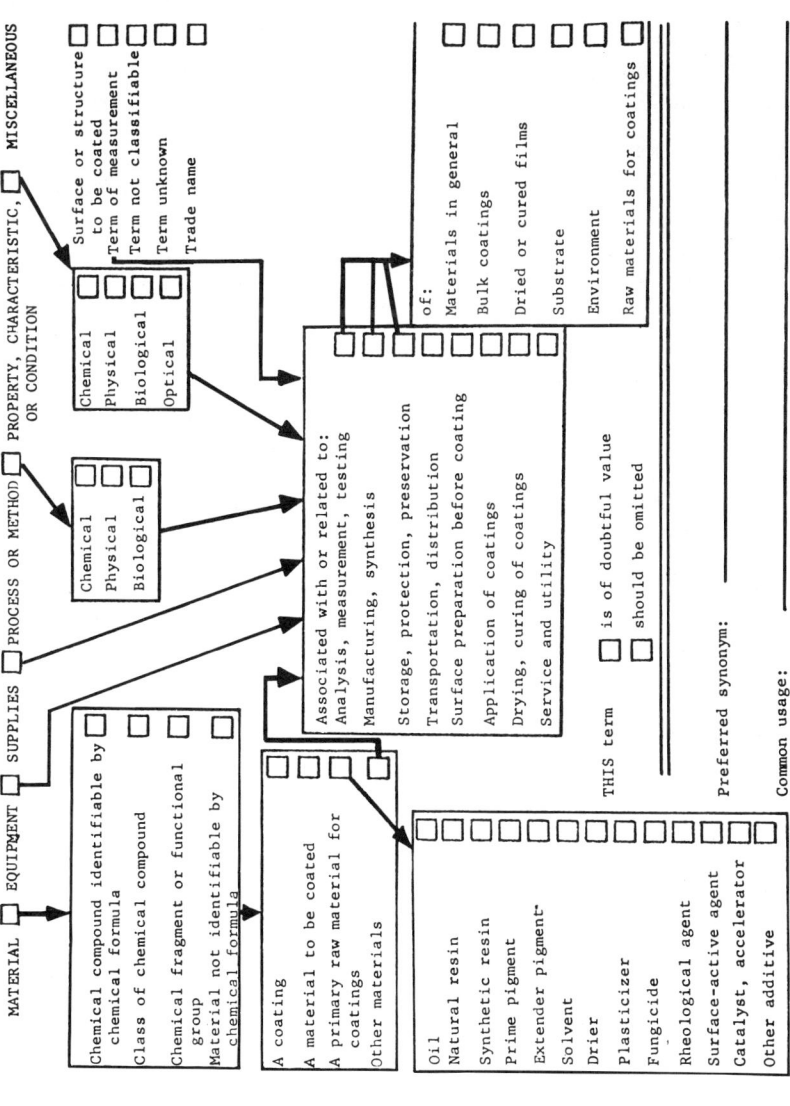

Figure 62. "Road map" for the analysis of terms (Section F3.2). (Courtesy American Society for Information Science.)

During the elaboration of the detailed structure it is useful to consult subject experts on specific topics according to the procedure described in Section F0.3.2.

F3.3.1 Work out the synonym-homonym structure and the equivalence structure

The cards of Synonymous and Equivalent Terms are grouped together. In principle this is a continuation of the "cascade-type" sorting procedure started in Step F3.1 and continued in Step F3.2. There is one difference, however: In these former steps the subject fields and subdivisions were established before the sort began. Here the groups are established during the very sorting procedure, as follows: The first card is laid on the table, thus "opening" a group. If the second card contains a term synonymous or equivalent to the term on the first card, the second card is added to that group; otherwise, a new group is opened, and so forth. All cards of a subdivision are processed in this way, that is, either added to a group already available or used for opening a new group. The viewpoints to be considered in the formation of groups of Synonymous and Equivalent Terms have been dealt with in Sections B1 and B2. Synonyms given on the card may also be helpful in the process (unless the second round of merging has been performed, in which case synonyms on the card have been used already). It is possible and even occurs frequently that a group consists of one card only. The whole process shows how important hierarchy and classified arrangement are for the detection of Synonymous and Equivalent Terms.

For each group a preferred term is selected according to the criteria set forth in Section F0.4.2. It is especially useful to consult experts in order to make correct decisions. The preferred term selected may be any term occurring in data field MT or ST (or SP) on one of the cards. The selection decision is not bound by a selection made in one of the sources (or, in case the second round of merging has been performed, by the completely arbitrary selection there). Often it will be necessary to coin a new term.

The information from all other cards of the group is merged onto the new card for the preferred term. The nonpreferred terms themselves, together with their source indication, are entered in field ST; other information is entered in the appropriate data field (see Section F0.7.2 and F2.2 for the technique of merging and keeping track of the sources). After the information has been merged on the card for the preferred term, all other cards can be eliminated, since they do not contain any information in addition to the card for the preferred term. By this procedure the number of cards is reduced considerably; they can now be surveyed much more easily in the following step.

F3.3.2 Work out the classificatory structure

The previous step was concerned with the elaboration of the synonym-homonym structure and the equivalence structure. Each of the preferred terms now corresponds unequivocally to a concept. We can now turn to the classificatory structure in the set of concepts represented by the preferred terms. In elaborating the classificatory structure, the following questions have to be answered (a full treatment of classificatory structure is to be found in Section C1):

(1) *Is it possible to decompose a concept into semantic factors?* If semantic factors are given in the input, one can draw upon the semantic factors given for different terms in a class; OR parentheses as semantic factors may often be useful to take into account several contributions. Otherwise, or in addition, it is useful to look at the Broader Terms (if any) given for the concept. For example, *Monetary policy* may have the Broader Term *Economic policy* in one of the classification schemes used as a source.

A concept to be used as semantic factor may be already available among the concepts collected so far, but it is also quite possible that semantic factoring gives rise to the introduction of a concept that did not occur explicitly in any of the sources.

Example:
 Airports = Air traffic: Traffic stations

Traffic stations is introduced as a new concept (with the editor's code as source code). Of course, a card is made up for the new concept and is filed in the appropriate subject field and subdivision (which need not be the same as the subject field and subdivision just processed). It may turn out later in the process that the concept assumed to be new was available in the collection. This doesn't do any harm, however.

(2) *What hierarchical relationships exist among the concepts?* The best way to indicate many of the hierarchical relationships is to arrange the cards in a linear sequence representing a monohierarchical structure (as described in Section D3.1.1). The hierarchical level (the number of indentions) is indicated on top of the thesaurus form by '+' (for potential descriptors) or '—' (for other preferred terms). Additional Broader Terms of the next higher, and Narrower Terms of the next lower hierarchical level that come to mind are entered on the cards. In many places it will prove necessary to introduce new broader concepts, as discussed in Section C1.4.1 (the reader is urged to reread this section).

(3) *What associative relationships exist among concepts?* In answering these questions, one uses all the information contained on the card for a concept (preferred term).

Notations given—either for the preferred term or for spelling variants

390 F Flow of Work in Thesaurus Construction

or synonyms—are especially useful in this step: they can be used to look up the concept in the corresponding source scheme; there one can see the whole context in which the source scheme places the concept. Often open-ended sources, such as search requests or abstracts, give very useful hints on the use of a term, on the context in which it occurs, and on relationships to other concepts. Furthermore, an alphabetic index in the KWIC format can be useful (see Section F5.8 for a more detailed discussion). If the terms are in machine-readable form, a KWIC index should be produced for this purpose.

F3.3.3 Use of judgment and creative thinking in processing the information collected from different sources

In steps F3.3.1 and F3.3.2 use is made of all the information on a term or concept as collected from the different sources and merged on one card. However, one is in no way compelled to include all synonyms and cross-references from each source. One may well disagree with a source on a certain relationship. That relationship may then simply be deleted (except in building a cumulative thesaurus, see K1.3). On the other hand, the lexicographer may and should introduce new relationships. If the type of the new relationship is not completely clear, the term is entered in data field 70 UN (Unspecified relationship, of Figure 21, Section C7).

Creative thinking is called for, particularly when new concepts are introduced arising from semantic factoring or needed as broader concepts. This process of concept formation results from the application of a specific way of thinking: The information scientist or classificationist developing a thesaurus is charged with the task of rendering explicit and laying down on paper the structural relationships among the concepts of a field. For achieving this end he applies the tools and the methodology developed in Chapter C. It is therefore not surprising that he sometimes comes up with the formation of concepts that have not been thought of before in that form by the experts in the particular field.

The process of concept formation aims at a complementation of the indexing language in such a way that the subject field in question is completely covered and that overlap between concepts is eliminated as far as this is possible and useful. This activity also leads to the formulation of scope notes and definitions, to be dealt with below. The whole process is continued in step F4, "Work out first draft of the classified index".

This process of concept formation is the essential and truly creative activity in thesaurus development. It is obviously not possible without developing a classificatory structure. (Compare Section C3.1, "Concept formation in thesaurus building").

The following two sections take up two specific problems in this context.

F3.3.4 Introducing more specific concepts

It might occur that one of the source schemes lumps together several related concepts that should be kept separate in the scheme to be developed. Accordingly, new cards have to be made. One may wish to retain the original concept as a broader concept for the newly created ones or one may wish to establish an associative relationship between the newly created concepts.

F3.3.5 Scope notes and definitions

In delineating concepts in step F3.3.1 it is often useful to put down the distinctions explicitly in the form of scope notes or definitions as discussed in Section C3.2. Scope notes are also needed for new concepts arising from semantic factoring or introduced as Broader Terms. In connection with the mutual delineation of concepts, numerous associative relationships will be detected.

F3.3.6 Preliminary selection of descriptors from among the preferred terms

Recall from the summary in Figure 6 (Section B4.2) that a preferred term is the term selected from a class of Synonymous and Equivalent Terms to designate the concept at hand. Only part of the preferred terms are used as descriptors, i.e., in document representations and search request formulations. In the previous steps, we were concerned only with the elaboration of the conceptual and terminological structure. Now we are faced with the problem of which concepts are important enough to be descriptors, i.e., to be included in the indexing language.

In clear-cut cases preferred terms can already be removed from the list of potential descriptors in this step, using the criteria given in F0.4.3 (the final selection takes place after step F5.1):

(1) For some concepts it may become apparent from the structure developed in this step that they fall beyond the scope of the thesaurus and therefore should not be included. The corresponding cards should be taken out of the working file but kept until the thesaurus is finished (one might reconsider some of the decisions).

(2) For less important concepts, especially if they are very specific, one may decide that a broader concept or a combination of concepts should be used in indexing and searching. OP ("other preferred term, nondescriptor") is marked on the corresponding card, and the descriptors to be used are entered in field BT together with a USE instruction. For the purpose of working out the basic hierarchical structure in step F4, one may wish to exclude these cards so that one has to deal only with the smaller set of really significant concepts. The hierarchical level is marked by '-', so that these cards are skipped over in typing the first draft of the classified index in step F4.1. (One could also remove these cards from the

working file and reintroduce them in step F5.1, "Revise main thesaurus file", but this is not recommended.)

F3.3.7 Some suggestions for the technique to be used (technical)

It has been suggested that the following technique gives a better overview during the procedure: for arriving at the groups of Synonymous and Equivalent Terms (step F3.3.1), write the terms belonging to one subdivision on a large sheet of paper in such a way that related terms appear in the same neighborhood, the closeness of the relationship being indicated by the degree of their proximity on the paper. In doing so, one obviously performs at the same time some of the functions of arranging concepts in a meaningful order (Step F3.3.2). Having finished this display, isolate groups of Synonymous and Equivalent Terms and draw a line around them. Within each group select a preferred term and underline it.

A variant of this technique is as follows: the terms are not written immediately on the large sheet of paper but on small slips of paper (2 x 1 cm.) which then can be arranged on a table or pinned onto a board. This technique has the advantage of being more flexible with respect to working out the arrangement of terms.

Methods for the display of relationships between terms by a graphical arrangement have been dealt with in detail in Section D3.

It is questionable whether the application of these elaborate techniques is worthwhile in this phase of thesaurus development. It is quite possible to isolate the groups of Synonymous and Equivalent Terms and to select the preferred terms by the method described in F3.3.1, which uses the index cards that are already prepared. Techniques similar to those described in this paragraph are more appropriate later on, as described in section F4.2.

F4 WORK OUT FIRST DRAFT OF THE CLASSIFIED INDEX (SCHEDULE)

As a result of step F3 one has a very preliminary version of the main part of the thesaurus in a classified arrangement in the form of a file of index cards, the working file. The purpose of the procedure described in this section is to improve and streamline this structure.

F4.0 Classified Index and Cross-References in BT, NT, and RT

A somewhat difficult preliminary point has to be discussed first. A classified arrangement transmits information by the very sequence of terms. As soon as the arrangement is changed, information is lost. Therefore, a preliminary step is recommended: enter the hierarchical relationships for a term as shown by the classified arrangement on the card for the term so that the classified arrangement can be changed without information loss. The Broader Term on the next higher level and the Narrower Terms on the next lower level should be entered. (One may omit the Narrower Terms since they will be introduced later on anyway as inverse cross-references. On the other hand, it is easier to work with the file if the Narrower Terms are entered from the beginning.)

This remark applies at different points of the procedure to be described. First of all, it should be followed before any changes in the arrangement arrived at in Step F3 are made. The appropriate point is after the preliminary classified index is typed because the Broader and Narrower Terms can be easily seen then. At this point one should also transfer additional hierarchical relationships to be seen from sources that have a classified arrangement (see Section F1.2.2,1. A second obvious point is after the improved classified index has been typed (F4.3). Ideally, one should also keep track of all the changes taking place in rearranging the hierarchy in steps F4.2 and F4.4; however, there are practical limits.

If few changes are expected in the classified arrangement, the effort required for this procedure might not be warranted, and one may follow a procedure otherwise recommended only for thesaurus updating and described in Section J3.2.

Similar considerations hold for Related Terms (Compare Section C1.5).

If detailed keeping track of the sources is necessary, the code of the editor or the code of a source that has a classified arrangement should be used.

F4.1 Type Preliminary Classified Index. Amend Working File

It is not easy to work with the working file in classified arrangement, as produced in F3, because it does not allow for a good overview. Therefore, a classified index should be typed now. The preliminary classified index lists only the descriptor candidates selected in Step F3.3.6, and it gives only the term as such, perhaps supplemented by a notation, but no further information, thus being much shorter and easier to peruse than the working file.

The classified index should be typed as a sequence with indentions. The number of indentions is indicated to the typist by a "+" after the hierarchical level on top of the card. Cards on which the hierarchical level is indicated by "−" and on which OP is marked are skipped in typing. (These are cards for terms that have been ruled out as descriptor candidates for example, because they are too specific. If there is a "−" and DS is indicated, there is an error that should be checked by a staff member.) If one wishes to have extra line spaces, they are indicated by an empty card. Other forms of display are possible, but usually less suitable at this stage. If such other displays are planned for the user version, they should be drawn up during or after step F4.2 or after step F4.4. (Compare Sections D3.1 and D3.2.)

After the preliminary classified index is available, the Broader and Narrower Terms that can be seen from the classified arrangement have to be entered on the cards, as described in Section F4.0.

F4.2 Improve the Classificatory Structure

The classified index is now copied on cardboard or heavy paper (if the available equipment does not allow for copying on cardboard, the following procedure may be used: type on cardboard, make a normal copy that can be retained, and then proceed as described in the following). Cut the cardboard into small slips containing one term or a group of terms each. Arrange these slips in tree form or as a network (compare sections D3.1.2 and D3.2 as to the format). Since the unqualified tree method needs much space, a modified arrangement is usually to be preferred.

Example:

		Field (Internat. politics)
subfield 1	*subfield 2*	*subfield 3 (diplomatic activities)* . . . *subfield*
xxxxxxx		*Official visits and other contacts*
xxxx		*State visits*
xxxx		*Visits of VIP's*
xxxx		*Contact of embassy*
xxxx		*with host government*
xxxx		*Exchange of notes*
xxxx		. . .

In this example the preferred terms are arranged within each subfield in a linear sequence with indentions. It would also be possible to carry the tree-type arrangement one level further and then use the linear-sequence-type arrangement. If one chooses this type of arrangement, it is advisable to leave hierarchical subgroups uncut if it seems likely that the elements of the group would be left together in any arrangement. In trying alternative arrangements one can then move the whole group as one block. The group may be cut later of course.

This technique allows one to survey the structure of a whole subject field. Therefore, the classificatory structure, especially the hierarchical relationships, can be checked. By rearranging the slips one can try out different variants of the hierarchical structure and select the best. It is useful to enlist the cooperation of subject experts for the step of trying out the different possibilities for the hierarchical structure.

F4 First Draft of the Classified Index 395

Further screening as to which preferred terms should be selected as descriptors and which of these should be selected as checklist descriptors may also take place in this step. Decisions should be recorded in the working file, thus preparing for Step F4.4.

During the whole procedure, appropriate BT and NT entries should be made in the working file to preserve information before the classified arrangement is changed, as described in Section F4.0. Additional BT, NT, and RT cross-references may evolve during the process. As a labor-saving device, all these cross-references might be recorded very sloppily in this stage until the notations are available. More thorough recording is then done in Step F4.6. If a new concept is introduced, a card has to be made up. Finally, the working file should be rearranged so as to correspond to the improved version of the classified index.

F4.3 Type Improved Classified Index and Amend Working File

The improved classified index can now be typed and copies can be produced for distribution to subject experts (if numerous copies are necessary, use of a stencil is advisable). In typing, leave enough space at the left margin so that a notation can be entered later on.

If the changing BT and NT relationships were not entered in the working file during the elaboration of the classified index, the BT and NT relationships to be seen from the improved version of the classified index should be entered now.

F4.4 Discuss Classified Index with Subject Experts. Select Descriptors and Checklist Descriptors

The classified index displaying the hierarchical structure is the backbone of a thesaurus. A thorough discussion with subject experts, as described in Section F0.3.3, is therefore in order. Separate discussions should be arranged with experts from each subject field or subfield. In each such discussion the subject field or subfield should be discussed thoroughly, concept by concept, and selected problems from other subject fields or subfields should be dealt with also. In an interdisciplinary approach one might want to discuss the whole scheme with subject experts from different areas as described in section F0.3.4.

It is possible and often useful for the preparation of the discussions to ask for written comments from subject experts as described in Section F0.3.1(2). Copies of the draft of the classified index should be distributed to gather such comments.

F Flow of Work in Thesaurus Construction

The discussion should deal with the following points:

(a) *Does the preferred term represent the concept in question adequately?* This is a terminological problem. If the need arises, recourse can be made to the corresponding card in the working file where all the Synonymous and Equivalent Terms are given.

(b) *Over-all structure of the hierarchy:* selection and delineation of the subject fields and subfields; sorting of the concepts in the subfields; helpful order in the arrangement of concepts on the same level of the hierarchy. However, experience has shown that the subdivision of a subject field into subfields cannot be meaningfully discussed without a more detailed look at the concepts listed within each subfield.

(c) *Individual hierarchical relationships.* In order to make sure that it is correct to indicate A as a Broader Term for B, ask the following question: while searching for documents on A, do you want to retrieve all or most of the documents indexed by B?

(d) *Selection of the descriptors* (preferred terms that should be included in the indexing language) and selection of the checklist descriptors (descriptors that are of particular importance in searching and therefore warrant special consideration in indexing). See Section F0.4.3 for the criteria to be applied in the selection of descriptors and checklist descriptors.

(e) *Filling in any gaps* in the indexing language (classification scheme) by introduction of new concepts; new broader concepts are introduced, as discussed in Section C1.4.1, or entirely new concepts are added that up to now have been overlooked.

The resulting modifications are recorded in the draft of the classified index and in the working file. If many modifications have been made, the modified sections of the classified index should be completely retyped. Often it will be useful to repeat the discussion after the improved version of the classified index has been typed. It may even prove necessary to go through this process several times, especially if different groups of experts are involved, as suggested in Section F0.3.3.

A special difficulty arises in these discussions from the fact that the classified index displays only part of the full classificatory structure, omitting cross-references to additional Broader or Narrower Terms, indications of semantic factors, and cross-references to Related Terms. As a result, many questions are asked that could have been avoided by displaying the full structure. On the other hand, it is very inconvenient to display the full structure without having a notation, and the notation should be assigned only after the classified index has been discussed thoroughly and has undergone major modifications arising from these discussions. So we have a vicious circle. The circle may be broken by indicating clearly that only part of the structure is displayed and by submitting additional information taken from the working file during the discussions.

F5 First Draft of the Thesaurus as a Whole 397

F4.5 Assign Notational Symbols

The result of Step F4.4 is a first draft of the classified index or schedule. Only minor revisions are to be expected in the steps to follow. Therefore, it is now possible to assign a notational symbol to every preferred term included in the classified index, especially to every descriptor. Notational symbols for very specific concepts that are included only in the working file should be assigned after the main part has been revised in step F5.1. (As has been shown in Section D1.3.4, it is very advisable to have a notation if a classified index is to be part of the user version of the thesaurus. Even if one does not plan for a classified index in the user version, a notation might be useful in the construction of the thesaurus.)

Although the classified index is typed without a notation, enough space should be left at the left margin to enter the notation later on. Besides the original or stencil, one or two copies should be available. These copies serve as working copies for the design of the notation. When the design is finished, the notational symbols can be entered on the original or on the stencil, and the necessary number of copies of the finished draft of the classified index, together with notational symbols, can be made. See Section F5.9 for technical details.

F4.6 Make a Systematic Search for Additional Cross-References

The notations can now be used to record cross-references with less effort. Cross-references recorded sloppily before should now (or in Step F5.1(c)) be recorded precisely using notations. A systematic effort should be made to detect additional cross-references, which can then be recorded by their notations.

F5 COMPLETE FIRST DRAFT OF THE THESAURUS AS A WHOLE

F5.0 Introduction

The procedures to be used in the individual steps of this phase are very dependent on the size of the thesaurus and the technical means employed in thesaurus construction. This is particularly true for steps F5.2, "Produce main part"; F5.3, "Check inverse cross-references"; F5.4, "Duplicate preliminary version"; F5.6, "Enter modifications into master copy"; F5.7, "Making the alphabetical index"; F5.9, "Reproduce test version"; and F7 "Duplicate or print the final version". (Steps F5.1, "Revise working file" and F5.5, "Consultation with subject experts" are not dependent on the technical means employed.) Where differences exist, the procedures described in the following are intended for smaller projects not using computer assistance, except possibly for the production of the alphabetical index.

F5.0.1 Special problems of smaller projects not using computer assistance (special topic)

The problem in this case is to avoid retyping the thesaurus over and over and to use at least parts of draft versions in the master copy for reproducing the final user version of the thesaurus. Therefore, the working file should not differ in its information from the main part of the user version. Accordingly, the less detailed cross-reference indicators should be used in this case, e.g., BT and not BT-WH (Broad Term-Whole). Only external spelling variants should be given in the working file; they will, of course, appear in the main part of the user version. (Internal spelling variants are needed only in computerized ISAR systems anyway. Because the size of the alphabetical index is small, external spelling variants can be used sparingly.) Furthermore, with small thesauri the working file on cards is needed only in thesaurus construction, not for updating. For updating a working copy of the user version is sufficient. On the other hand, if only very few people will be using the thesaurus, it may be possible to use the card file as main part so that retyping is not necessary at all.

The procedure described in the following is just one possibility. Alternative procedures are discussed in Section F9.

We have tacitly assumed that in smaller projects the user version of the main part will not be produced by typesetting. If, in fact, typesetting or complete retyping are envisioned, some of the restrictions mentioned disappear.

F5.1 Revise Entries in the Working File

Step F3 resulted in a preliminary main part in the form of the working file. In Step F4 much of the information in this file is disregarded in order to concentrate on the elaboration of the conceptual structure of the indexing language as represented in the classified index. We now come back to the working file in order to revise all the entries in the light of the results of Step F4. It is also appropriate at this stage to see to it that all terms conform to the rules selected for the form of entries (spelling, singular/plural, etc.). (If the cards for less important concepts have been removed from the working file in Step F3.3.6, they must be put back now at the appropriate location.)

For each card in the working file the following tasks must be performed (see the example in Figure 63):

(a) *Standardized abbreviations.* In many thesauri it is useful to use a standardized abbreviation instead of the full text of a descriptor (or even of a preferred term that is not descriptor) whenever the descriptor is referred to (as described in Section E1.8.3). If such a procedure is to be followed, one has to

| 0 | 1 | 2 | 3 | 4 | 5 | ⑥ | check hierarchical level | 10 | 02 check type: | ⑤ OP NP ELCH | 03 Subject Field: M |

05 Notation: M48.7 _____ Color TV picture tubes(TH:659.5) (AR;SK)

---

12 Stand. abbr. (AB): M48.7 Color TV pic tu

20 Spellings (incl. abbr.): Color television picture tubes (KL:TC904;SK)

30 Synonymous T. (ST) (incl. equiv. t.): Color kinescopes (TH) (AR); Color TV display tubes (TH)

46 Related Terms (RT): (M48.2) Flat picture tubes(TH) (SK); Radiation hazards (TH) -V83

50 Translations (TR):
F:
G:
R:
S:

60 Definition, scope note (SN): Descriptor introduced Jan. 1, 1960. In searching for documents indexed before that date, USE BT M48 TV picture tubes

---

4 Classification:
42 Category (CA):
44 Semantic factors/Broader Terms (BT): -F75 Color TV receivers (M48 TV picture tube) (TH) (AR;SK), Kinescopes (AR); Color television set (KL)

45 Is semantic factor of Narrower T. (NT): (M48.7.3) Color TV screens (TH) (AR); Chromotrons (AR), (M48.7.2) Shadow mask tubes) (AR;SK); Lawrence tubes ((SK))

70 Unspec. rel. (UN): _____

81 Editor/Date: AKS1959-07

Figure 63. Examples of revisions in the working file (F5.1). (The original card, as produced by merging, is shown in Figure 58 (Section F2.2). The top line and the notation have been filled in at earlier steps.)

formulate a standardized abbreviation for each descriptor and type a list of these standardized abbreviations. This task must be performed for the whole file first, before (c) can begin. (b) may be done together with (a) or together with (c).

(b) *Standardize form of Main Term.* The Main Term (the heading of the entry), as well as the terms listed in data fields ST and TRanslations, must be checked and, if necessary, changed so as to conform to the rules established for the form of terms (spelling, singular/plural, use of adjectives and verbs, etc.). If necessary, the appropriate changes should also be made in the classified index.

Depending on the use of the thesaurus it might be necessary to enter the unchanged forms of the term as external or internal spelling variants, as discussed in Section C6.2. Specifically, this is necessary in a cumulative thesaurus, as discussed in Section K1.3.

If one wants to avoid adjectives and/or verbs and if syntactical information is given for each term in the thesaurus, one may print out all entries that contain adjectives or verbs in any of the data fields MT, SP, ST, or TRanslations.

(c) *Standardize elements in BT, NT, RT.* All elements in the data fields BT, NT, RT must consist of notation (if any) and preferred term (or abbreviation of preferred term). If the notation is missing, it has to be inserted; if a non-preferred term is given, it has to be replaced by notation and preferred term. As a labor-saving device, one may put down just the notation and instruct the typist or the computer to fill in the term itself later. If the term appearing in the cross-reference cannot be found either in the classified index or the working file (blind cross-reference), a new card has to be made up and entered at an appropriate place in the hierarchy. (In big thesauri one should have a preliminary alphabetical index at this stage; this is possible if computer assistance is used.)

A somewhat tricky point arises here: While replacing non-preferred terms by preferred terms, one may detect that hierarchical relationships taken from different sources use different terms, but are the same conceptually.

Example:
On the card we have (sources 1 and 2)
Color TV picture tubes (1;2)
   NT Three-gun color picture tubes (1)
   Shadow mask tubes (2)
Since Three-gun color picture tubes is synonymous to the preferred term Shadow mask tubes, this reduces to
Color TV picture tubes (1;2)
   NT Shadow mask tubes (1;2)
One of the original entries might in fact have been
Color Kinescopes (2)
   NT Shadow mask tubes
Color Kinescopes being synonymous to the preferred term Color TV picture tubes. (Special rules hold for cumulative thesauri; see Section K1.3, esp. K1.3.1,1.3.)

All Broader Terms, Narrower Terms, and Related Terms that can be seen from

F5   First Draft of the Thesaurus as a Whole   401

the classified index are now tagged so that they do not appear in the main part of the user version of the thesaurus unless they are part of a USE instruction. An example from Figure 22 (Section D0) illustrates this point.

Example:
Vacuum tubes
   BT Vacuum devices
      (Electron tubes)
Looking up Vacuum tubes in the classified index one can see there that Electron tubes is a Broader Term; therefore, Electron tubes is enclosed in parentheses on the card. (In the TEST model, all BT, NT, and RT are listed in the main part; therefore, no tags are needed.)

   (d) *Improve classificatory structure.* Data field UN (Unspecified relationship) contains terms for which the proper type of relationship has not been determined previously; this determination should be made now. All BT, NT, and RT relationships should be checked as to their validity. The decomposition into semantic factors in particular has to be checked in view of the changes that have been made in the classified index in Step F4. This is also the time to check and/or fill in the information in the data fields 41 Subject field and 42 Facet (cf. Figure 21, Section C7).

   (e) Enter *USE, SEE, and PT (Post to) instructions* and UF (Used for), SF (Seen from), and PF (Posted from) statements. If the crude lead-in form is used, this might involve some reshuffling of the terms on the card.

   (f) *Create inverse cross-references and enter in the appropriate places.* Since these inverse cross-references are going to be checked in Step F5.3 anyway, the amount of care devoted to the task here should not be excessive. If, on the other hand, one were to delay all inverse cross-references until Step F5.3, a great many modifications would have to be made in the main part, necessitating extensive retyping. In cases illustrated by the following example cross-references can be limited (compare Figure 22a2, Section D0).

Example:
The descriptor M48.7 Color TV picture tubes has many narrower preferred terms that are not descriptors and that are listed after the descriptor in the main part. Each of them has an instruction
   USE BT   M48.7 Color TV picture tubes
Instead of entering all inverse UF NT statements, we may simply write
   UF NT*   see the following nondescriptor entries*.

The decisions made in this step may, in turn, give rise to modifications in the classified index. In principle, the situation is the same as discussed earlier: In step F3.3 the decomposition of a concept into semantic factors may give rise to the definition of a new concept, serving as a semantic factor. In the step here a concept may be used as a semantic factor in a new context, changing its definition or its place in the hierarchy. It is therefore important to list for a concept A all the compound concepts that contain A as a semantic factor. This is achieved by entering all inverse cross-references.

Despite the fact that Steps F3.3 and F5.1 are similar in principle, there is a major practical difference: In Step F3 the emphasis is on the "distillation" of the classified index, i.e., the basic structure of the indexing language out of the wealth of the material collected; the expression of concepts not to be included in the indexing language is a by-product. In Step F5.1 it is the other way around: the emphasis is on the expression of concepts not included in the indexing language by concepts included, that is, descriptors; modifications in the list of descriptors to be included in the indexing language that may arise as a result of the work in this step are a by-product. (However, the systematic introduction of relationships among descriptors is part of Step F5.1).

F5.2 Produce the Main Part of the Thesaurus in List Form

Most of the cards in the working file are now likely to be messy due to many handwritten additions and modifications. It is therefore necessary to retype the main part of the thesaurus before the later steps can be performed. Steps F5.3, "Check inverse cross-references", F5.5, "Consultation with subject experts", and F6, "Testing of the thesaurus" are much easier if the main part of the thesaurus is available in list form, every entry being compressed to its actual size (not spread over an entire thesaurus form). Also, unchanged parts of this draft can be used in reproducing the final version of the thesaurus.

The best procedure is probably to simply type the main part in list form. An alternative is to type on blank cards which can then be shingled to produce a list copy. For technical details see Section F5.10.2.

The arrangement to be followed in typing the main part is described in Section D1.1.2 (assuming the Roget-Soergel-model): All Main Terms start at the left margin. Descriptors (marked by '+' after the hierarchical level and by crossing off DS in the top line of the thesaurus form) are emphasized by a solid underline. Preferred terms not used as descriptors (marked by '—' after the hierarchical level and by crossing off OP) are indicated by a broken underline. The hierarchical level is always given at the left of the margin proper; it is copied from the top of the thesaurus form, including '+' for descriptors and '—' for preferred terms not used as descriptors. BT, NT, and RT that are tagged "not for user version of main part" are omitted.

F5.3 Check Inverse Cross-References and Insert Where Necessary

It is important that for every cross-reference the appropriate inverse cross-reference is included, as discussed in Section C7.1. Checking the completeness of inverse cross-references involves a great many look-up processes.

It is therefore advisable to perform this step only after the main part of the thesaurus is available in list form, where speedy look-up is possible. In the Roget-Soergel model, only the classificatory structure (data fields BT, NT, RT) has to be considered in this step; the inverse cross-references for variants in spellings, for Synonymous and Equivalent Terms, and for translations are taken care of in the alphabetical index. In the TEST model *all* inverse cross-references must be checked. It is recommended that two persons together perform the somewhat cumbersome task of checking inverse cross-references. The additions that result are recorded in one of the working copies.

F5.4 Duplicate Preliminary Version of the Thesaurus

Enter the additions in the master copy leaving the picture as clean as possible (it might prove necessary to retype some of the entries; compare Section F5.10.2). Reproduce the classified index and the main part of the thesaurus in the required number of copies and distribute them among all the experts to be consulted in the next step.

F5.5 Review the Whole Thesaurus. Consult with Subject Experts

The synonym-homonym and the equivalence structure, as well as the classificatory structure, as worked out in the steps F3.3 and F5.1, are now presented in a form easy to peruse. In the next step the decisions made must be checked in consultation with experts. The following procedure is recommended; this procedure may be shortened if time does not allow for the full procedure.

(a) Discuss the different subject fields or subfields with a subject expert, entry by entry. The points to be considered are essentially the same as in step F4.4. The decomposition of compound concepts into semantic factors should be checked with special care. It is of advantage if one can repeat the same procedure with a second subject expert to get different points of view. Alternatively or concurrently, one may gather written comments from a number of subject experts according to F0.2.1(2). (It may be preferable to postpone the collection of written comments, which are not likely to be sent in promptly, to Step F6).

(b) Inform the subject experts in a field about the resulting modifications in that field.

(c) Probably there will remain a small number of problems that need further discussion (compare F0.2.3(3)): perhaps there has been disagreement between two subject experts consulted or between different written comments or a problem has been suggested for further discussion by subject experts after receiving information on modifications in (b). A special meeting has to be called to decide about these problems, as described in Section F0.2.3(b).

Instead of distributing the thesaurus to all subject experts involved after Step F5.4 and informing them afterwards about the modifications made in individual discussions, one may choose the following procedure: after F5.4, copies of the thesaurus are distributed only to the experts that are to be involved in individual discussions. After this step, the master copy is revised, and the number of copies necessary for the discussion in a meeting is produced and distributed. This procedure is more convenient for the subject experts involved; it has two disadvantages, however:

(1) it does not allow the collection of written comments in F5.5(a);

(2) it does not alert the subject experts—as does the information on modifications—to specific problems that should be considered more carefully.

F5.6 Enter Modifications in the Master Copy

The modifications and additions resulting from F5.5 are again entered in the master copy. In the same step inverse cross-references for newly introduced cross-references and the deletion of inverse cross-references for deleted cross-references are checked.

F5.7 Production of the Alphabetical Index (Technical)

By far the simplest method is to produce a KWIC (Key-word-in-context) or KWOC (Key-word-out-of-context) index by computer. Since computers and the appropriate programs are easily available nowadays, this method is described first. The programs available are usually written with titles and document numbers in mind. But they work just the same way on terms (instead of titles) and notations (instead of document numbers). The following description is oriented mainly toward the Roget-Soergel model.

F5.7.1 Production of a KWIC index

Process each card contained in the working file. Punch a separate card for each of the following: the Main Term appearing in data field MT; the spelling variants appearing in data field SP; every Synonymous or Equivalent Term appearing in data field ST; every translation appearing in data field TR, and all terms that appear in a UF (Used For) statement in the data fields NT or RT if separate main part entries for these terms are not made (intermediate form of lead-in). In a type-1 (lead-in only) multilingual thesaurus, one might have a separate alphabetical index for each language (compare Section D5.1). In this case a special code has to be punched for each language, e.g., F for French, G for German, so that they can be sorted into separate alphabets.

Punch the notation on each of these cards. If the program used has an option of punching the notation (in the program description: document number) first, this is preferable because this is the sequence used in the main part. A few rules have to be followed in this process:

(1) Split composite words by inserting a hyphen or a blank so that the second component shows up in the index, too. In some cases it might even be useful to separate prefixes.

Examples:
Gold-fish
Pre-test
Over-compensation

Make sure that a hyphen is considered as a separator between two words in the KWIC program used. One should also be aware of the possibility that prefixes separated from the word stem may appear in a stop-word list; this would mean that the full term starting with the prefix would not appear in the index. If the program used allows for using a non-printing separator instead of the hyphen this is greatly preferred.

(2) If a term is longer than the space provided on one punched card and if the program does not provide for continuation cards, break the term down into several KWIC lines. The omission of parts of the term in a KWIC line is indicated by '...'.

Example:
Term: B335 Military installations strengthening the offense potential
Card 1   B335   Military installations strengthening the ...
Card 2   B335   ... offense potential
           or, even better,
Card 2   B335   ... strengthening the offense potential

(3) If a notation consists of more characters than are provided in the program for the document number, truncate it to the required length. The truncated notation will still show where to look for the term in the classified index or the classified main part. The last sign of the truncated notation is immediately followed by a number sign in order to indicate that the notation has been truncated.

Remark: Procedure for including page numbers along with the notations. According to Section D1.5 the number of the page where the term appears in the main part in addition to the notation is not particularly useful. If page numbers are wanted nevertheless, they should be introduced only for the final version of the thesaurus in step F7. For purposes of the KWIC index the page number must form part of the punched card field provided for the document numbers. The easiest way to introduce them is as follows: Leave the appropriate columns blank while punching the cards. If all the modifications introduced in step F6 have been inserted into the punched card file and if the main part of the thesaurus is available in its final form with page numbers, insert page number cards into the punched card file at the appropriate places. (Remember that the punched cards serving as input for the KWIC program are in the sequence in which the terms appear in the main part.) Gang-punch the page numbers into the appropriate packs of cards, take the page number cards out, and the punched card deck is ready for running the KWIC program. In this case, continuation cards must not be used even if the KWIC program does provide for them, and the procedure described in (2) has to be followed.

F5.7.2 Manual production of the alphabetical index

For the manual production of the alphabetical index, three steps are necessary:

(1) Produce the necessary entries;
(2) sort into alphabetical order;
(3) type the index.

The main problems arise with step (1), producing the necessary entries. There must be one entry for each form in which a term should appear in the alphabetical index, e.g., one entry for the direct form and one for the inverted form of a term (this problem is avoided in a KWIC index). Each entry must contain the information to be given in the alphabetical index, namely, the notation and/or the text of the preferred term and/or the page number of the preferred term in the main part. Sometimes it is convenient to produce the entries for the alphabetical index by copying; in this case they often contain more information than is needed. The typist must be instructed properly what information to type. In producing the entries for the alphabetical index one starts, as in F5.7.1, from the entry for the preferred term. One possibility is to write an index card or a paper slip for each entry for the alphabetical index, that is, for the Main Term itself, possibly for different forms of the Main Term (such as inverted form), for each spelling variant, and for each Synonymous or Equivalent Term (and possibly for different forms of each of these terms). The other needed information as described above is added. Another possibility is to produce a number of copies of the entry for the preferred term and underline on each copy a different spelling variant or Synonymous or Equivalent Term. The underlined term is then the entry term for the alphabetical index. In this case inverted forms have to be entered on the card; the most appropriate field is SP-EX (external spelling variants). If one uses translucent paper for the thesaurus forms, the necessary copies can be produced by diazo copying.

F5.7.3 TEST model: produce alphabetical main part and alphabetical index

As was shown in the beginning of Section F3, the development of any thesaurus should be based on a working file in classified arrangement. In the TEST model, the user version of the main part is alphabetical. To produce it, the necessary entries are created and then sorted in alphabetical order. All cards in the working file are entries. Further entries are created from the cards in the working file, as illustrated by the following examples (taken from Figure 18, Section C5.1).

Examples:
(1) Crude lead-in form
    Card in working file
        Data processing
            UF Automatic data processing
                Electronic data processing
                Data analysis
                Data management
                Data handling
            BT . . .
    Additional entries created
        Automatic data processing
            USE Data processing
        . . .
        Data handling
            USE Data processing
(2) Detailed lead-in form
    Cards in working file
        Data processing
            UF ST Automatic data processing
                  Electronic data processing
            UF NT Data analysis
                  Data management
            BT . . .
        Data analysis
            USE BT Data processing
        Data management
            SF ST Data handling
            USE BT Data processing
            SN . . .
    Additional entries created
        Automatic data processing
            USE ST Data processing
        Electronic data processing
            USE ST Data processing
        Data handling
            SEE ST Data management
            USE BT Data processing

As can be seen from these examples, elements in UF NT are not processed to result in a USE BT instruction. However, if the intermediate form of lead-in is used, the working file will not contain a card for, e.g., *Data analysis,* and the elements in UF NT must be processed to obtain the proper USE BT instruction.

In both cases entries should be made for external spelling variants.

Example:
Aesthetics
    USE Esthetics.

The alphabetical index is best produced as a KWIC or KWOC index of the Main Terms in all the main part entries (original and created). The notation is simply omitted if the thesaurus being built does not give a notation. The alphabetical index might also be produced as described in Section F5.7.2. However, in many cases the proper form of the term would have to be added in a USE instruction.

Example:
Antennas, radar   *USE Radar antennas.*

Another possibility is to include all forms of a term as entries in the main part. (This is done in the Library of Congress Subject Headings; see Section D1.7.10.)

F5.7.4 Remark

Some authors suggest establishing two card files from the very beginning of the construction of a thesaurus—one classified and one alphabetic—and the production of two cards for each of the collected terms. If the alphabetical file were to have any meaning for the production of the alphabetical index, this would mean that one would have to enter in the alphabetical file all the decisions made during thesaurus development; that obviously is not possible in terms of economics. It would be useful to have an alphabetical file during thesaurus construction so that one could see whether or not a particular term is already included in the thesaurus and to which subject field or subfield it belongs. Without the tool of an alphabetical file, one has to rely on his memory for such inquiries. But even that doesn't justify the effort of keeping a separate alphabetical file. However, if computer-assistance is used, a preliminary alphabetical index can be printed at various stages of thesaurus construction. This is very useful, especially for big thesauri.

F5.8 Check Homonyms and Improve Cross-Reference Structure Using the Alphabetical Index

If the same term has been assigned two different notations or otherwise occurs twice as preferred term or if a term has been used as a synonym of two different preferred terms, this shows up in the alphabetical index. Either the term is homonymous and should be disambiguated, or something is wrong in the synonym-homonym structure or in the equivalence structure. In a KWIC index it will also become apparent if the same word occurs with different meanings in different multiword terms.

Also the alphabetical index collocates terms that contain common or similar words. Often this indicates that there are conceptual relationships between these terms, and appropriate cross-references should be made in the thesaurus. Thus, to the extent that conceptual structure is reflected in the linguistic structure of terms the alphabetical index may be used to improve the cross-reference structure. The suggested format of the alphabetical index offers particular advantages in this connection: if two terms that appear near to each other in the alphabetical index are also collocated in the classified sequence (as may be seen from the notation), no action is necessary. If they are not collocated in the classified sequence, then one can look up one of the terms in the main part using the notation and check whether an appropriate cross-reference has been introduced. If not, it has to be decided whether it is a hierarchical or a Related Term cross-reference. One should take care to record the inverse cross-reference, too (unless an additional run using a computer program for this purpose can be made).

F5.9 Reproduce Test Version of the Thesaurus

The following parts of the thesaurus are now ready:

—classified index;
—main part;
—alphabetical index.

If one wishes to have additional displays (such as an overview of the subject fields and subfields, a display of the checklist descriptors, or graphical displays) they can be produced now. The entire thesaurus can then be reproduced in the number of copies which is required for the practical test to be performed in Step F6.

F5.10 Remarks on Some Technical Problems Arising in F5, F6, and F7 (Technical)

F5.10.1 Use of notations as "shorthand" for descriptors

Wherever a descriptor has to be entered in the process of modification, it is sufficient to give its notation. The term itself (or a standardized abbreviation) can be added later on by the typist. For this purpose the typist is provided with a listing that gives for every notation the appropriate term or standardized abbreviation. This listing is compressed into the smallest space possible to minimize page-turning.

F5.10.2 Technical considerations as to the production of the main part of the thesaurus in smaller projects without computer assistance

Since a considerable amount of clerical work goes into the production of the main part of the thesaurus, it is worthwhile considering in more detail some seemingly trivial questions connected therewith. It is best to start by listing the requirements to be met:

—Two working copies of the main part are needed for step F5.3, "Check inverse cross-references".

—A number of working copies of the main part, as modified by the results of step F5.3 "Check inverse cross-references", are needed for step F5.5, "Consultation with subject experts".

—A number of working copies of the main part, as modified by the results of F5.5, are needed in F6, "Testing the thesaurus".

—The main part, as modified by the results of F6, has to be duplicated or printed in step F7.

—The final format should be about letter size, two columns per page. Reduction by 1:1.4 should be used in preparing the final copy (linear reduction 1:1.4 makes for a reduction in area of 1:2).

A good solution for meeting these requirements is the following: In step F5.2, the first typing of the main part, a master is created that has the following characteristics:

(a) It is easy to correct, even after copies have been made.

(b) It is possible to make copies repeatedly from it (that is, the master can be stored after copies have been made).

(c) It is possible to apply photographic reproduction processes involving reduction in size.

The only materials showing these qualities are normal paper, which may be used as a master for Xerox copies or other photographic reproduction processes, and translucent paper, which can also be used for diazo copying.

In typing, a column width of 6 inches (including margins) should be used. This allows for appropriate reduction in size in reproducing the final version ($12:1.4 = 8.5$, assuming letter size for final format). It also leaves a wide margin which can be used for insertion of comments that should not show up in the final version but that are needed in the draft version for discussion, etc.

As to further procedure, one may follow one of two alternatives:

(1) In step F5.2, type the main part on sheets of paper. Modifications from checking the inverse cross-references (Step F5.3) and consultation with subject experts (Step F5.5) may be entered on the margin or, if this becomes too messy, the whole entry is retyped and pasted over the old entry (or the correct entries of the original master are cut and mounted together with the new entry on a new

sheet). If many entries on a page have to be typed, it is best to retype the whole page. The master for producing the final version is prepared as follows: Cut the entries to a width of 6 inches (including margins) and mount them in two columns on 12" × 15.4" sheets. These sheets are then ready for photographic reproduction with a reduction of 1:1.4. Of course, all entries having modifications indicated on the margin must be retyped before this step.

In this procedure the two working copies needed for checking inverse cross-references (Step F5.3) can be produced as carbon copies while typing the main part in Step F5.2. (If translucent paper is used as a master, the copies needed for the consultation with experts (Step F5.5) and for the test phase (Step F6) may be produced by diazo copying, which might be cheaper than other processes. However, this process is not compatible with the technique of mounting retyped entries described above.)

This procedure also has a major disadvantage; the replacement of entries by the technique of mounting is cumbersome. If half of the entries on a page have to be retyped, it is usually easier to retype the whole page, thus unnecessarily duplicating the typing of the correct entries.

(2) The alternative is to type each entry on a separate card. This procedure offers more flexibility in the replacement of entries. Blank cards (not thesaurus forms) are used, and the entries are typed in compact form as they should appear in the list. The master, then, is a card file. For making copies the cards are shingled so as to show the typed part only. This procedure is definitely to be preferred if the main part is to be arranged alphabetically; the cards can easily be sorted in alphabetical order.

With this procedure carbon copies and use of translucent paper for diazo copying are not feasible. In addition, the making of copies is cumbersome unless specific devices for mounting the cards are available.

F6 TEST THE THESAURUS BY INDEXING AND RETRIEVAL EXPERIMENTS

Index 1,000 to 2,000 documents with the aid of the thesaurus. In addition, collect as many potential search requests as possible (or use the search requests collected in the collection phase) and formulate these search requests with the aid of the thesaurus. Perform a number of searches in the test collection and analyze the search results with respect to search failures due to shortcomings of the thesaurus. In analyzing the search results one should keep in mind that they are dependent on many factors other than the quality of the thesaurus. The most important of these factors is the selection of documents in the test collection and the quality of indexing (which depends only in part on the quality of the thesaurus). (This is not the place to go into details of the evaluation of ISAR systems; the reader may consult the references given in the back.)

If, for reasons of time, it was not possible to collect written comments from numerous subject experts in step F5.5, "Consultation with subject experts", such a collection can be done now.

As a result of this step, new terms are entered both in the indexing language and in the lead-in vocabulary, definitions are broadened or narrowed down, new relationships between concepts are detected. All these additions and modifications are entered into the working file, the user version of the main part, the classified index, and the alphabetical index, as appropriate. (See Chapter J on thesaurus updating for procedural details.) The thesaurus is now complete. This does not mean, of course, that the thesaurus is perfect and that no further improvements and modifications are possible. On the contrary, the thesaurus has to be updated on a continuing basis, as discussed in Chapter J.

F7 DUPLICATE OR PRINT THE USER VERSION OF THE THESAURUS

F7.1 Duplication or Printing of the Main Part and the Alphabetical Index

With the main part and the alphabetical index, there are no specific problems as to layout and space limits. If the detailed scheme of cross-reference indicators has been used in the working file, one should make sure in this step that all specific cross-reference indicators are replaced by the corresponding general ones; for example, BT-CL (Broader Term - Class inclusion) is replaced by BT. Also, the working file contains BT, NT, and RT cross-references that can be seen easily from the classified index. These cross-references are tagged as "not to be included in the user version", and they are omitted accordingly. (Compare Section F4.0, "Classified index and cross-references in BT, NT, and RT in the main part".) In smaller projects projects not using computer assistance, these problems are already taken care of, as discussed in Section F5.0.1.

F7.2 Duplication or Printing of the Classified Index

The classified index, especially the list of checklist descriptors, has to be presented in such a way as to make its perusal as easy as possible. Different type fonts and other means may be used to achieve this purpose. It is often useful to introduce the requirement that the display of checklist descriptors should fit onto a sheet of double letter size. This offers the advantage that the checklist descriptors can be surveyed with one glance. This requirement becomes almost mandatory if one wants to print the checklist descriptors on the document or request analysis sheet. If one introduces this requirement, one may have to reconsider the selection of some of the checklist descriptors for reasons of space. It is recommended, therefore, that the typesetting be done before Step F6 (use monotype rather than linotype because of the many corrections to be expected). This ensures that the list of checklist descriptors (which in some systems is identical with the indexing language) can be printed in the space available. Due to many cross-references involving notational symbols and to the usage of a number of different type fonts, the typesetting is very complicated. One should therefore weigh the possibility of letting the type stand so that later revised versions can be printed.

F7.3 Proofreading

It will be necessary to be especially thorough in proofreading the thesaurus.

F8 FURTHER REMARKS CONCERNING THE WORK-FLOW AND MODIFICATIONS OF THE STANDARD WORK-FLOW

F8.0 Introduction

The optimal sequence of steps in thesaurus construction is dependent on so many factors that it has to be determined for every individual project. The sequence shown in Figure 53, Section F0.1, should be used only as a guideline, and appropriate modifications should be made as the individual case requires. The following considerations should be helpful in these decisions. It is recommended that the reader look at the flowchart in Figure 53 while going over the following discussion.

F8.1 Sequence of the Steps F3, "Work Out the Preliminary Structure of the Thesaurus" and F4, "Work Out the First Draft of the Classified Index"

One possibility is to complete step F3, "Work out the preliminary structure of the thesaurus" for all the subject fields and then move to Step F4, "Work out the first draft of the classified index". This has the following advantage: In working on subject field 3, for example, one may detect by semantic factoring concepts which belong to subject field 1 or 2. These additional concepts are then included before step F4 is performed for these subject fields. On the other hand, there is an inverse problem: in working on subject field 3, it might be necessary to use descriptors from subject field 1 as semantic factors. If the area of the thesaurus is so large that the descriptors of the previous subject fields cannot be kept in mind, this is difficult. In this case it is recommended that step F4.1 or even all steps F4.1 through F4.4 be completed for a subject field or group of subject fields before step F3 is performed for the next subject field. Then the classified index for the prior subject fields can be used to look up the descriptors needed.

Another viewpoint for the planning of the steps F3 and F4 is to make optimal use of the staff and distribute the workload evenly over time. If, for example, step F3 is completed for all subject fields before step F4 is performed, then the typist may be idle for that time and afterwards in a big rush to type the classified index.

F8.2 When Should the Notation Be Introduced?

In the standard sequence the notation is introduced after the classified index has been discussed with experts and is somewhat "stabilized". If one does not expect many modifications from the discussion with experts in Step F4.4, then it is useful to introduce the notation before this step. This would make the discussion easier because in the discussion descriptors could be cited by their notation and it would be easier to locate the descriptors in the classified arrangement.

On the other hand, it is possible to postpone the assignment of a notation until the modifications in Step F5, "Prepare first draft of the thesaurus as a whole" have been completed. Advantages of introducing the notation before Step F5 are as follows: Many procedures in F5, as well as Step F6, "Testing the thesaurus through indexing and retrieval experiments", are much easier if a notation is at hand. In Step F5.1, "Revise entries in the working file", descriptors or other preferred terms appearing in cross-references need not be written in full but can be cited by their notation. The same is true for the checking of inverse cross-references in Step F5.3 and the making of the alphabetical index in Step F5.7. The disadvantages of introducing the notation before Step F5 are as follows: In Step F5 the classificatory structure is modified, particularly in Step F5.1, "Revise entries in the working file". This means that the notations have to be modified accordingly. If the notation for a descriptor is changed, this change has to be recorded at every place where this descriptor appears in a cross-reference. This is less difficult than it might seem at first; after the check of inverse cross-references in F5.3, the entry for a descriptor gives all the places where this descriptor appears and where consequently the change in notation has to be recorded.

Of course, changes in notation necessary due to modifications of the classificatory structure in F5.1, "Revise entries in working file" are introduced before the first draft of the main part is typed in Step F5.2, and the same is done in the following steps. If one has decided not to introduce the notation before Step F5.1, one might introduce it either after Step F5.1, after Step F5.3, "Check inverse cross-references", after Step F5.5, "Consultation with subject experts", or even after Step F6, "Testing the thesaurus". The later the notation is introduced, the smaller are the advantages to be gained from the notation in thesaurus construction. At the same time, the effort for changes in notation is reduced.

F8.3 When Should the Main Part Be Typed (Smaller Projects without Computer Assistance)?

In the standard sequence, the main part or at least part of it has to be typed twice, namely, in step F5.2, "Type the main part of the thesaurus in list form" and in reproducing the user version (Step F7.1). This can be avoided if punched paper tape or punched card equipment or a computer are available. However, the following discussion deals with the case where such equipment is not available. Advantages and disadvantages of several possibilities will be considered. (It might be useful at this point to re-read Section F5.10.2.)

(1) It is not useful to type the main part before Step F5.1, "Revise entries in the working file". This step can very well be performed using the cards in the working file, so nothing is gained by prior typing. On the other hand, numerous modifications arise in Step F5.1, and all these modifications would have to be inserted into the typed version.

(2) Type the main part before Step F5.3, "Check inverse cross-references". This has the following advantage: Checking the inverse cross-references in Step F5.3 is much easier (an estimated time-saving by a factor 2 to 4) if the main part is available in list form.

(3) Type the main part after the inverse cross-references have been checked in Step F5.3. Advantage: the copies of the main part used for the discussions with experts in Step F5.5 would be more orderly, since the modifications resulting from Step F5.3 would not appear as handwritten additions. On the other hand, one would lose the advantage mentioned in (2).

(4) Type after Step F5.5, "Consultation with subject experts", before Step F6, "Testing the thesaurus". This will rarely be advisable because of the following major disadvantages: The consultation with experts would have to be based on the working file on cards, which would be rather messy due to the many modifications entered during the process; the file would have to be duplicated in the necessary number of copies, and this might be just as expensive as typing. On the other hand, this procedure would have the following advantage: the draft used for testing through indexing and retrieval experiments in Step F6 would be very orderly; in fact, it would not differ too much from the final user version because the modifications suggested by the experimental indexing are usually limited (provided the initial collection of terms has been performed adequately). This procedure would therefore have the additional advantage of minimizing the number of entries in the main part that have to be retyped in producing the user version.

(5) Type after F6, "Testing the thesaurus". From the end of the previous paragraph, it follows that this is not advisable; one would lose the advantage of having an orderly draft for testing the thesaurus without saving much work in typing.

F8.4 Drawing Up and Using a "Core Classification" Consisting of Elemental Concepts Early in the Process

(Before going further it might be advisable to reread Section C2.5 on the idea of a core classification and possibly Section C2.8 on the optimization of an indexing language where the number of descriptors is limited).

Some systems require that the indexing language consist only of a limited number of elemental or nearly elemental concepts (to give a concrete example: the indexing language for a peek-a-boo system). In this case the indexing language is restricted to a "core classification". But even in a system using many precombined descriptors, a core classification of limited size is useful for achieving compatibility and/or for establishing an auxiliary ISAR system. To keep the core classification limited, it might be necessary to force a decomposition of some concepts into semantic factors that are available in the indexing language or the core classification as discussed in Section C2.8.2. In this case it is recommended that a tentative core classification be drawn up after Step F3.3.1, "Working out the synonym-homonym structure and the equivalent structure". In Step F3.3.2, "Working out the classificatory structure", which involves the decomposition of concepts into semantic factors, the tentative core classification gives some idea what elemental concepts are available as semantic factors. Of course, new elemental concepts may still be created. A consolidation will take place in Step F4, "Work out the first draft of the classified index".

One may take an even more radical approach: A tentative list of elemental concepts is defined right at the outset after looking at some of the sources. The decomposition of compound concepts into semantic factors, resulting in a combination of elemental concepts for each compound concept, can then be done *before* Step F3, "Work out the structure of the thesaurus". This opens the possibility of grouping the terms according to the concept combinations assigned to them. For example, two terms having exactly the same concept combination are very likely to be synonymous. Of course, this is checked in an editing step: if two terms are not synonymous and have been assigned the same concept combination in spite of this, one should consider adding descriptors to the indexing language or the core classification so that a distinction between the two terms is possible. The derivation of further relationships from the concept combinations is described in C1.3. One could say that this procedure operates as follows: A combination of elemental concepts is assigned to each term; this is a *local* operation. The *global* structure is then derived automatically or, at least, with computer assistance. We shall discuss in Section G3.4.2 how this approach can be implemented in computer-assisted thesaurus construction.

F8.5 Extending the Collection of Conceptual Relationships, Especially for Cooperative Information Services

If heavy emphasis is placed on the complete collection of conceptual relationships as seen from different points of view one may proceed as follows: After the source lists of terms have been collected, they are first presented to scientists who are asked to indicate Synonymous and Equivalent Terms, Broader and Narrower Terms, Related Terms, and possibly decomposition into semantic factors, using a preliminary core classification as described in the previous section; these enriched lists of terms are then processed as described in Section F2. This approach is particularly appropriate if the task is to develop an indexing language and thesaurus that is to serve as the basis for the cooperation of a number of information service institutions. If the enrichment is done at each of these institutions (each institution processing appropriate parts of the over-all input vocabulary), all viewpoints are brought out in the indexing language. This is essential for the success of cooperation, as will be discussed in detail in Chapter K. On the other hand, this procedure means increased effort in thesaurus construction, since most terms are analyzed by at least two people.

F9 USE OF PUNCHED PAPER TAPE AND PUNCHED CARDS IN THESAURUS CONSTRUCTION (SPECIAL TOPIC, IN PART TECHNICAL)

F9.1 Use of Punched-Paper-Tape Typewriters in Thesaurus Construction

The use of punched-paper-tape typewriters for more efficient text processing is well known. Of particular interest in our context is the use of punched-paper-tape cards. These are cards that are punched on one edge like punched paper tape; they could also be called "unitized punched paper tape". Punched-paper-tape cards are easier to sort manually and to correct than punched paper tape.

F9.1.1 Modifications in the flow of work

Only small modifications are necessary. It is not worthwhile to produce a punched paper tape in the initial stages of collection of terms even if terms from different sources are typed on thesaurus forms (rather than using cut-and-paste techniques). The reason is that during the process of thesaurus construction so many modifications are introduced that an initial punched paper tape would be of no value. The main savings can be achieved in the typing of the main part of the thesaurus, as discussed in Section F8.3: The main part can be typed after Step F5.1, at the same time producing a

418 F Flow of Work in Thesaurus Construction

punched paper tape, (or, even better, punched-paper-tape cards). In later steps a modified punched paper tape can be produced without retyping the correct parts, and a modified listing can be typed automatically using the modified tape.

A number of technical notes are of interest:

(1) One can make use of a suitable control tape to enter function codes into the punched paper tape in such a way that it is possible to write on thesaurus forms with the appropriate spacing and also on paper in compact list form. This makes it possible to obtain a clean copy of the card file without much effort. This card file is convenient for updating.

At the same time, information needed for the working file but not for the user version (such as spelling variants) can be tagged by function codes so that it does not appear when writing in list form.

(2) Punched-paper-tape cards are to be preferred because only those cards where modifications have to be made need to be fed into the machine and duplicated. If punched paper tape is used, appropriate function codes should be entered so that an entry can be duplicated at high speed without typing and the machine will stop automatically before the next entry. In this way correct entries can be duplicated into the modified tape much faster.

(3) If many modifications are necessary in an entry, it is faster to retype it in its entirety than to duplicate the correct parts and insert the modifications. The limit point depends on the ability of the typist.

(4) Word of caution: The production of a corrected duplicate tape and the automatic typing from punched paper tape takes more time and effort than many sales representatives might have you believe, especially if the equipment is low-speed (a good punched-paper-tape typewriter writes about 900 characters per minute from the tape) and/or if the equipment is not suitable for continuous high-speed operation.

F9.1.2 Conversion of punched paper tape to punched cards

Punched paper tape can be converted to punched cards (for example, by the IBM 47). These cards can then be used for the following purposes:

(1) Production of various listings using conventional punched-card equipment as described below.

(2) Data input into a computer if the computer program requires card input and/or if no punched tape reader is available at the computer installation used. This can be especially useful for producing cards as input for a KWIC program. The punched paper tape is formatted as follows: the notation is preceded by a special code (start of record code); the preferred term, the spelling variants, and the Synonymous and Equivalent Terms are preceded by another special code (field delimiter code); the tape-to-card converter can be programmed to store the notation and to make up a punched card for every term, the stored notation being punched in specified columns. Very long terms should be divided by the field delimiter in the punched paper tape so that two or more punched cards are produced.

F9.2 Use of Conventional Punched Card Equipment

F9.2.1 Punched-card-controlled typewriters (for example, the IBM 870 Document Writing System)

There are punched-card-controlled typewriters that can be used in the same way as punched-paper-tape typewriters. Advantages and disadvantages are the same as in other applications. Punched cards are easier to correct but more difficult to produce because of the 80-column limit. Punched cards are also more expensive.

F9.2.2 Keypunch and unit-record equipment

A combination of keypunch and accounting machine (tabulating machine) may be used in the same way as a punched-card-controlled typewriter. Additional disadvantages are:

—limited character set (in particular, no lower case letters);
—one-to-one correspondence of punched cards and lines in the printout (the types of programming to overcome this would not be practical in our context).

An advantage is the higher speed of accounting machines in printing.

Instead of a keypunch, a punched-paper-tape typewriter and subsequent conversion of the paper tape to punched cards can also be used.

A sorter in connection with an accounting machine can be used for the production of the alphabetical index or other listings in specified order if the appropriate sort-key is punched in the cards. In the alphabetical index it would not be practical to give more information than the notation for each entry, since each entry consists of only one punched card. Inverted forms of the preferred term, as well as Equivalent or Synonymous Terms, must be entered as spelling variants in order to appear in the alphabetical index. A collator could be used to detect duplicates.

An interesting variation of the procedures described is the following: In the working file, use punched cards as thesaurus forms on which the terms and other information are transferred. Then punch part of the information. Gang-punch the source code. The cards can now be sorted, according to a subject field and subfield code, and a lexicographer can work on the cards so sorted. The cards can also be sorted by other sort-keys. The problem with this approach is that the writing space on a punched card is limited and only part of the data is machine-readable. The production of an alphabetical index, for example, would need additional punching.

(Edge-notched cards can be used in a similar way; however, the sorting operations are much slower and listings cannot be produced automatically.)

Chapter G

Use of Computers in Thesaurus Construction
(Advanced; Technical with the Exception of Sections GO.1 and GO.2)

The application of computers is of growing importance in thesaurus construction. Whereas most basic procedures and many details described in the previous chapter remain unchanged, the application of computers opens a number of additional possibilities and sets a number of additional requirements. It is therefore appropriate to set aside a separate chapter for a discussion of these problems. It starts with the rationale for computer use in thesaurus construction (G0.1) and proceeds to an overview of the steps that can be computerized and of suitable modifications of the work flow, especially the possible "entry points" for computer processing (G0.2). Record organization in the computer is discussed next (G0.3). This overview provides the basis for detailed considerations of computer applications in individual steps. All the possibilities outlined below are still only in the design stage. They should be useful in the implementation or adaptation of programs for computer assistance in thesaurus construction. No system based on these considerations has been implemented. However, some of the design principles have been taken from existing systems (see the references).

G0 RATIONALE FOR COMPUTER APPLICATION. OVERVIEW.

G0.1 Rationale for Computer Application

G0.1.1 Performing routine operations

The construction of a thesaurus requires, in addition to intellectual work, quite a number of routine operations for which rules can be precisely speci-

G0   Rationale, Overview   421

fied. These operations can be performed much faster and much more reliably by computer than by a human clerk. Such operations are, for example, check of inverse cross-references and alphabetical sorting. In the flow diagram given in Figure 53, Section F0.1, those operations that can be performed by computer have been specially marked. It is important to note that all the data the computer manipulates have been produced by intellectual work in the first place. It is man-machine cooperation rather than full automation that is promising at this time. An editor or lexicographer should do what an editor can do best, and the computer should do what a computer can do best.

Therefore, one should always be aware of the possibility of human intervention if the programming of a certain sub-task becomes too complicated. Human intervention can be either on-line or by the editing of intermediary printouts.

G0.1.2   Continuous modification of data base

In constructing a thesaurus, we have a file of data which is continuously modified and to which data are added continuously. The computer is ideally suited for such a task. Only the modifications or addenda are entered into the computer. The insertion into the file is done automatically by the program. The corrected file can be printed very fast in different forms as desired. This solves, for example, the whole problem discussed in F8.3, "When to type the main part"; when using a computer, one may print, for each step, an orderly draft. It also solves the problem discussed in F5.7.4; it is possible without much cost to print an updated alphabetical index at different stages of the work. This is very convenient, particularly in the construction of large thesauri. (Compare Section G8 on updating.)

By the same token, a computer greatly facilitates the updating and the publication of revised editions of the thesaurus. Punched paper tape and punched cards offer similar advantages in principle, but to a much lesser degree.

G0.2   Overview. "Entry Points" for Computer Processing. Modifications in Work Flow

The problem is when to convert the data into machine-readable form to create a computer-stored working file. From this point on, computer assistance can then be used. The earlier the computer file is created, the more data have to be keyed and the more tasks have to be programmed; these costs have to be weighed against the benefits to be derived from computer assistance.

(1) The *first "entry point"* for computer processing is when terms and appropriate information from the sources selected in the previous steps are recorded on thesaurus forms (Step F1.2.2); the data can be keyed in this step. All the

processes of sorting and merging can then be performed by computer. However, this approach has some very serious problems. While programs to sort the entries in alphabetical order are easily available, programs for eliminating duplicates and merging information in Steps F2.2 and F2.3 would have to be specially written unless one is fortunate enough to find a program package that performs these tasks adequately. Also, the amount of data to be keyed is much greater before all the duplicates are eliminated. It might be more economical to use a cut-and-paste technique for entering the information on thesaurus forms, then eliminate duplicates and merge information on the same term manually, and key the information at some later stage.

(2) The *second entry point* is, then, after the duplicates have been removed (that is after Step F2.2). The reduced file can be keyed, and the steps that follow can be performed by computer. Section F2.2.1 discussed the possibility of using a big thesaurus, such as TEST, or a big dictionary as a source from which additional information on terms obtained from other sources can be pulled in a matching and merging process. This can, of course, be done by computer, provided the big thesaurus is available in machine-readable form. The somewhat cumbersome second round of merging (Step F2.3) can also be performed by computer. Both procedures require a special program to merge information from different records.

(3) The *third entry point* is after all merging has been completed. After the second round of merging has been performed, the size of the file is reduced considerably due to the elimination of redundancy (there is only one card for each class of synonyms as far as synonyms have been detected already). The reduced file can be keyed.

Whichever of these entry points is chosen, inverse cross-references can be generated immediately (rather than in Step F5.1); this gives a more comprehensive view of term relationships in the steps that follow. The terms can then be printed out with the appropriate information on thesaurus forms so that Step F3, "Working out the preliminary structure of the thesaurus", can be performed manually. A big advantage is that these forms will be orderly and easy to work with, in contrast with the rather messy forms resulting from manually performing Step F2. A further advantage is that a preliminary alphabetical index can be printed (KWIC format). It is also possible to use computer assistance in working out the preliminary structure of the thesaurus (Step F3) as described in section G3. This is especially true for sorting into broad subject fields and then subfields (Step F3.1 and F3.2). The terms can then be printed so that the detailed structure can be worked out manually (Step F3.3). Even in working out the detailed structure, computer assistance is possible, as described in Sections G3.3 and G3.4. Sorting into subject fields and subfields might be done by machine even if the second round of merging has not been performed. However, since all data have to be machine-readable in order to sort into subject fields, one might as well do the second round of merging first. The only obstacle is that a special program has to be written. If computer assistance is used in working out the detailed structure (Step F3.3), the second round of merging should have been carried out prior to this step. All the modifications arising from working out the preliminary structure have to be keyed into the (computer-stored) working file which is thereby updated.

(4) The *fourth entry point* is after the detailed structure has been worked out. The working file on cards (which is still further reduced at this point) can now be keyed. Again, orderly forms may be printed for use in Step F4, "Work out first draft of the classified index", and an alphabetical index can be prepared. But the main advantage of having the working file machine-readable at this point is that Step F4.1, "Type preliminary classified index", and the clerical functions of Step F5.1, "Revise entries in working file", can be done by computer.

(5) The *fifth entry point* is while typing the preliminary classified index manually (Step F4.1). A machine-readable record can be produced at the same time so that the preliminary classified index is available in machine-readable form. Modifications arising in Step F4.2, "Improve classificatory structure", can then be keyed and inserted into the classified index as well as into the working file. An improved version of the classified index can then be printed automatically (Step F4.3). The same holds for modifications arising in the discussions with subject experts in Step F4.4.

Once the classified index is available in machine-readable form, the assignment of notational symbols to descriptors and other preferred terms can be partially automated. The assignment of a machine-internal code (which is not to be confused with the external notation) can be fully automated (Step F4.5).

With the fifth entry point only the classified index is machine readable. Step F5.1, "Revise entries in working file", has to be done manually.

(6) The *sixth entry point* is, accordingly, to key the working file after Step F4. Note that many modifications have been made in the working file in the course of working out the classified index. The classified sequence, in particular, has been modified. After the working file has been keyed, computer assistance can then be used for Step F5.1, "Revise entries in working file".

If the working file is available in machine-readable form prior to Step F5.1, then Step F5.2, "Typing the main part of the thesaurus", is practically eliminated. Only the "intellectual" corrections made in F5.1 have to be keyed. The working file is updated by the program.

(7) The *seventh entry point* is after the entries in the working file have been revised. The main part has to be typed anyway at this point, and a machine-readable record can be produced with very little additional effort. Step F5.3, "Check inverse cross-references", can now be performed by computer, and the thesaurus draft can be printed (Step F5.4). Programs to check inverse cross-references are available. Again, the computer is ideally suited to the task of inserting the modifications resulting from Step F5.5, "Consultation with subject experts", into the working file (Step F5.6). A clean copy for the testing of the thesaurus in Step F6 can then be produced. The computer can also be used to print the final user version of the thesaurus, either on a high-speed printer or by typesetting machines driven by magnetic tape or punched paper tape. Also producing updated versions is much easier.

424 G Use of Computers in Thesaurus Construction

If one intends to use a computer at all, it is not sensible to introduce automated procedures after the seventh entry point. All the programs needed after this point are general edit-and-print programs and need not be specifically written.

There is one exception to this: in almost any case it is advisable to use a computer for the production of the alphabetical index (Step F5.7). If the working file is in machine-readable form, entries in the format required by a KWIC program can be produced by an easy-to-write program. Otherwise, the entries for the KWIC program have to be keyed.

G0.3 Record Organization in the Computer

All the data elements for one Main Term (the heading of an entry or record) together form a record. Most of these data elements are cross-references. For the procedures to be described in the following, it is convenient if the cross-references can be handled as independent units, especially with a view to checking inverse cross-references. Therefore, the following record format is suggested: A record consists of a variable number of subrecords (essentially one subrecord for each cross-reference). There are three basic types of subrecords:

(1) leading subrecord, giving the Main Term;
(2) cross-reference subrecords; and
(3) other types of subrecords to be defined in the program (e.g., subrecords to accommodate the text of a scope note or a decision indicator string).

For programming convenience it is advisable to define leading subrecords and cross-reference subrecords as fixed-field subrecords of the same length. The basic format is shown below.

A	B	C

A = Subrecord type and relationship indicator.
B = Term from which cross-reference is made (Main Term).
C = Term to which cross-reference is made (empty for leading subrecords).

Examples:

MT	Vacuum tubes	(empty)

Leading subrecord

BT	Vacuum tubes	Vacuum devices
RT	Vacuum tubes	Degassing

cross-reference subrecords

Since all the B-fields are the same within one record, this form of organization is redundant. The redundancy is introduced for reasons of processing

G0 Rationale, Overview 425

that will become clear later. However, for purposes of storage, the record can be compressed as follows:

A	B

leading subrecord

A	C

cross-reference subrecord

Example:

MT	Vacuum tubes

BT	Vacuum devices

RT	Degassing

In the detailed discussion of the individual steps of processing, more features will be added to this basic format. For reference purposes a complete summary of the organization of a cross-reference subrecord is given in Section G0.3.1.

Instead of the fixed-field format described here, a variable field format with delimiters between fields or a mixed format may also be used. Details are a problem to be worked out by the programmer. The main point here, and especially in Section G0.3.1, is the information that should be contained in each record.

G0.3.1 Complete summary of the organization of cross-reference subrecords

As mentioned before, this section contains a complete summary of the organization of cross-reference subrecords. In the detailed discussion of procedures for computer assistance in thesaurus construction, the function of each data field will become apparent. In the first reading, therefore, it is advisable to skip this section and go to Section G1.

The format suggested is as follows:

A	B	C	C1	D	E	F	G	H	I	K	L	OPEN

A	Subrecord type and relationship indicator
B	Term from which cross-reference is made (Main Term)
C	Term to which cross-reference is made
C1	Pointer to other form of term
D	Additional relationship indicator
E	Recommended structure indicator
F	Source indication
G	Cross-reference status indicator
H	Cross-reference printing indicator

I   Instruction (e.g., USE) or statement (e.g., UF) indicator
K   Type of term indicator
L   Form of term indicator

Contents of the fields

A   *Subrecord type and relationship indicator*
Each relationship to be used has to be identified by a label (see Figure 21, Section C7). Additional labels are needed to identify other subrecord types.

B, C *Term fields*
Each term field may contain the following subfields:
(1) internal code of the term;
(2) notation of the term;
(3) actual text of the term;
(4) pointer to remainder of text if text does not fit into fixed field.
Either one of the subfields (1), (2), or (3) alone will do for some purposes. This fact may be used for purposes of reduction of storage space and possibly processing time.

D   *Additional relationship indicator*
This indicator is necessary because the same pair of terms may occur in different relationships in different sources. It takes the following values:
0   No additional relationships (initial value)
1   One or more other subrecords with same B and C, but different A

E   *Recommended structure indicator* (cumulative thesauri, see K1.3)
0   Relationship not in recommended structure
1   Relationship in recommended structure (initial value)

F   *Source indication*
This field contains either a source indication or a pointer to a string of source indications (see Section F0.7.2 for the format of source indications). The fields G-L are specific for each source and therefore go with the source indication. In the final version of a cumulative thesaurus, field F always contains a pointer to a list of source indications and fields G-L pertain to the recommended structure of the cumulative thesaurus.

G   *Cross-reference status indicator*
0   Cross-reference encountered in input, inverse cross-reference not yet created
1   Cross-reference encountered in input, inverse cross-reference created
2   Cross-reference created by program

H   *Cross-reference printing indicator*
0   Cross-reference to be printed
1   Cross-reference not to be printed because expressed by classified arrangement or the alphabetical index (this value may have to be changed if the classified arrangement is changed)
2   Inverse cross-reference created by program but not to be printed
3   External spelling variant, not to be printed in main part but to be used in the alphabetical index

G0 Rationale, Overview

   4 Internal spelling variant, not to be printed anywhere
I *Instruction or statement indicator*
   0 Cross-reference is not part of an instruction or statement
   1 USE
   2 SEE
   3 POST TO
   4 UF
   5 SF
   6 PF
K *Type of term indicator*
   0 Descriptor (DS)
   1 Other preferred term (OP)
   2 Nonpreferred term (NP)
   3 Eliminate whole record (EL)
   4 Change in existing term (CH)
L *Form of term indicator* (mainly for cumulative thesauri)
   0 Form same as in cumulative thesaurus
     Values other than zero are only used if the form of the term in the source differs from that given in the cumulative thesaurus
   1 Singular
   2 Plural

  Fields C1, E, F, G, K, and L are needed in the leading subrecord too (their values apply to the term in field B in this case). It is therefore best to maintain identical formats for the leading subrecord and the cross-reference subrecord. If the condensed format is to be used, one of the term fields is eliminated. The sequence of fields was chosen in order to make some external sense. It can, of course, be changed however one pleases. The length of the fields may vary from 60 ± 25 for a term field to one bit for fields that have only the values "0" and "1".

  The storage of scope notes is a special problem because of their varying length. In many systems it is best to store the scope notes in a separate file so that they are out of the way in the processing, as described in the following sections. The leading subrecord or a separate subrecord would then give the address of the scope note.

  This overview provides the basis for a detailed discussion of some of the individual steps. The section numbers parallel the section numbers of Chapter F; many section numbers will therefore be missing. The reader should keep in mind that the detailed descriptions of the functions to be performed given in Chapter F can be used as the basis for writing the appropriate computer programs. Only points specific to computer application and perhaps advantages and disadvantages of computer application need therefore be dealt with. In some tasks, however, the approach should be quite different if computer assistance is used; in those instances different approaches will also be discussed.

G1 COMPUTER ASSISTANCE IN THE COLLECTION AND RECORDING OF MATERIAL

Only Step F1.2.2, "Transfer of terms" is affected as discussed below. Any intellectual tasks (e.g., recognizing Narrower Terms from an abstract, as discussed in F1.2.2,1) have to be done before the data are keyed.

G1.2.2 Recording the data from the sources in machine-readable form

Preceding all terms taken from a source the source code is keyed. Then an input record for each term is keyed. For the identification of the data element types, appropriate labels have to be used. These may be either the labels given in Figure 21 (Section C7) or the labels used in each source; in the latter case, a translation table into standard labels has to be provided. In order to facilitate further processing, it is advisable that the terms be keyed in a form corresponding to the rules set forth for the thesaurus to be developed. This can be achieved by prior editing or by instructing the keying operator properly. If this is not done, the same term might be entered in singular form from one source and in plural form from another; unless a somewhat sophisticated computer program is used, these would be considered two different terms. If simple rules for the forms of terms are chosen, a more efficient method than manual editing might be to use an available linguistic program for the "grammatical normalization" to be discussed in Section G2.4.

If the keying operator enters all terms in a standardized form, information is lost: We do not know what form is used in the particular source.

Example:
ISAR system 1 uses   Computers;
ISAR system 2 uses   Computer.
The keying operator keys the singular form Computer in both cases.

In a cumulative thesaurus this information may be needed for the following purpose: In order to enter a search request formulation containing *Computer* into ISAR system 1, the searcher has to know the exact form of the term as used in that system. If he uses *Computer* instead of *Computers* the system will respond with the message that *Computer* is not a term in its vocabulary. The more intricate problems of cumulative thesauri will be dealt with in Section K1.3. In the case of composite words, the components should be separated (possibly by a non-printing symbol) so that the word appears

in a KWIC index under each of its components, as discussed in Section F5.7.1.
Different input devices will be discussed in Section G9.

G2 COMPUTER ASSISTANCE IN SORTING INTO ALPHABETICAL ORDER AND IN MERGING INFORMATION ON IDENTICAL TERMS INTO ONE RECORD

Steps F2.1, "Sorting" and F2.2, "First round of merging" are carried out together. In the same procedure, inverse cross-references are created. In this procedure it will become apparent how convenient it is to treat cross-reference subrecords as independent units (it makes a special merging program unnecessary). The procedure consists of three steps:

Step 1: From the records encountered in input the appropriate subrecords are produced using the following sequence of instructions: Put the cross-reference term in field C, put the Main Term in field B and put in A (relationship) and I (USE, UF, etc.) the values appropriate for the field (such as BT) that contains the cross-reference term. Put the code for the source currently being processed into F. Put "1" as the value of the cross-reference status indicator G; this shows that we have a cross-reference encountered in a source and that an inverse cross-reference has been created. For each original subrecord, except for those containing spelling variants, synonyms, or translations, an inverse subrecord is created at once by exchanging fields B and C, changing A and I to the inverse form (given in Figure 21, Section C7) and putting 2 into G (to show that this is a cross-reference created by the program).

Special rules apply to synonyms, etc.: no inverse subrecord is needed (and "1" is not put into field G) because in the working file we do not want to have entries for terms that are not preferred terms (in the construction phase this is true even for thesauri using the main-part method for all leads). If a Main Term or a synonym consists of several terms, separated by commas, each constituent term is considered as an internal spelling variant (as discussed in Section F2.3.2), and a subrecord is created accordingly.

Subrecords for external spelling variants will be marked by 3 in field H (suppress in printing main part, print in alphabetical index) and subrecords for internal spelling variants are marked by 4 in field H (always suppress in printing).

Step 2: Sort all subrecords according to field B (the Main Term) as the first sort key and according to field C (the cross-reference term) as the second sort key. (Within one record, the cross-reference subrecords are then arranged by cross-reference terms, not by relationship types.)

Step 3: Compress records. The resulting record for a term is likely to be highly redundant and can therefore be compressed. First of all, if two subrecords differ only in their cross-reference status indicator G, the cross-reference created by the program ($G = 2$) may be omitted.

Example:

A	B	C	D	E	F	G	H	I
RT	Alcohol	Solvents	0	1	CY	1	0	0

A	B	C	D	E	F	G	H	I
RT	Alcohol	Solvents	0	1	CY	2	0	0

$G = 2$ shows that the second subrecord has been created from the entry
 Solvents
  RT Alcohol
in source CY. Since this source already contains the inverse cross-reference, the cross-reference created by the program can be omitted.

Next, if two subrecords differ only in their source and possibly also in G, the common part A-E need be given only once. The two subrecords can be merged by appending the F-L field string of the second subrecord to the first subrecord. Assume the *Alcohol-Solvent* relationship is also given in source SR:

Example:

RT	Alcohol	Solvents	0	1	SR	1	0	0

Merging results in

RT	Alcohol	Solvents	0	1	CY	1	0	0	SR	1	0	0

Even in the case where the cross-reference from source SR is created by the program ($G = 2$), SR should be given as a source.

For processing another method is more convenient. F is replaced by a pointer to "daughter" subrecord that contains a number of F-L field strings. Both F-L field strings (as well as F-L field strings from later merging operations) are placed in the "daughter" subrecord. In the "parent" subrecord the fields G-L are given the following values:

$G = 1$ if it was 1 in any of the sources
$G = 2$ otherwise
$H = 0$ (cross-reference to be printed, subject to later editing)
$I = 0$ (no USE, UF, etc., subject to later editing)
$K =$ lowest value encountered in any of the sources (this is the type of term indicator)
$L = 0$ (Form of term in source same as in field C or, in the case of a leading subrecord, field B)

A special case arises if an ordered pair of terms occurs in two sources

G2 Sort into Alphabetical Order and Merge

with a different relationship in each. That means, two subrecords agree in B and C, but not in A. The subrecords must be kept separate in this case, but a note should be made and a special flag shown in printout for both subrecords. For this purpose, a "1" is put into field D.

Example:

| NT | Information retrieval | Data retrieval | 1 | 1 | WH | ... |
| RT | Information retrieval | Data retrieval | 1 | 1 | EJ | ... |

'1' in field D

(Here and in the second round of merging to be discussed below, the sorting in alphabetical order using the cross-reference term as the second sort key, rather than by the type of relationship, is intended to detect such cases. In the final working file or, at least, in the file for printout the subrecords will be arranged first by type of relationship.)

A further compression can be achieved by using the abridged subrecord format, as discussed in Section G0.3.

For each cross-reference subrecord created by the program by inversion one has to check whether the term in field B occurs as a Main Term in the same source. Otherwise we have a blind cross-reference in that source, and a leading subrecord with the same source indication and $G = 2$ has to be created.

Example:

Source SR has the entry

| RT | Alcohol | Antifreeze | D | E | SR | 1 | ... |

The program creates

| RT | Antifreeze | Alcohol | D | E | SR | 2 | ... |

No Main Term subrecord for Antifreeze with source SR is found. Therefore, the program creates

| MT | Antifreeze | Empty | D | E | SR | 2 | ... |

If we also have the subrecord

| MT | Antifreeze | Empty | D | E | CY | 1 | ... |

merging according to the procedure described above results in the new subrecord

| MT | Antifreeze | Empty | D | E | CY | 1 | ... | SR | 2 | ... |

The new subrecord tells that Antifreeze occurs as Main Term in source CY and in a blind cross-reference in source SR.

G2.2.3 Computer assistance in "pulling" information from big thesauri by computer

This is now the place to "pull" information for each term that can be found in a big thesaurus through the matching and merging operation described in Section F2.2.3. (It is advisable to re-read this section.) The best computer procedure to perform this task is probably as follows (this procedure is mandatory for magnetic tape processing): Assume that the record for term A is being processed. If term B is given as BT, NT, or RT in the big thesaurus but not in the working file, term B is written in a special file accompanied by term A. Later on this special file is sorted and compared with the working file. If term B is not contained in the working file, its record is pulled from the big thesaurus, flagged appropriately, and accompanied by a note that the "starting term" is A. Depending on the circumstances, a special procedure may be necessary to obtain the Broader Terms all the way up.

After that computer procedure is finished, it is necessary to edit the working file, as discussed in Section F2.3.3. An edit-copy has to be printed for this purpose. Subrecords within one record are arranged by type of relationship in this printout. All Main Terms and inverse cross-references created by the program are flagged so that particular attention is paid to them in editing. Due to the purely mechanical nature of the procedure, some modifications have to be introduced: First of all spelling variants present a problem, as discussed in Section F2.4.1. Second, a Broader Term, Narrower Term, or Related Term cross-reference has to be taken over even though the same cross-reference using a Synonymous Term is already contained in the working file (the redundancy thus introduced will be eliminated later in Step F5.1). The full records for all additional terms appearing in BT, NT, or RT cross-references should be pulled as described in the procedure given. If they are not wanted they can be removed in editing.

Homonymous terms present the additional problem of determining which of several records should be pulled from the big thesaurus. If parenthetical qualifiers or subject categories are given in both the working file and the big thesaurus a decision might be reached by the program based on this information. Or the program might compare the Synonymous Terms given in both files. If no decision can be reached by the program, the records of the working file and of the big thesaurus should not be merged. Instead, all the records of the big thesaurus should be pulled, tagged, and appended to the record in the working file so that later on manual editing can take place. The case is even worse if the homonymity is not detected, that is if a term

G2 Sort into Alphabetical Order and Merge 433

is used in one meaning in the big thesaurus and in another meaning in the working file. In this case errors are unavoidable. They have to be corrected in later editing.

G2.3 Second Round of Merging by Computer

The algorithm given in Section F2.3 is suitable if a large random-access device (disk, drum) is available. It is not suitable for magnetic tape processing. The most convenient way to implement the algorithm given in F2.3 is probably as follows: Scan all subrecords in a record. Put all spelling variants, synonyms, and translations into a Temporary Storage location, called Active Synonym Location, unless field E contains 0, in which case the synonym is skipped because it does not belong to the recommended structure. Then start to work through the synonyms in the Active Synonym Location, tagging those that are finished. While other records are cumulated into the record being processed, new synonyms, etc., may turn up. They are entered at the appropriate place in the record and are also added at the end of the Active Synonym Location.

G2.4 Standardization of Spelling Variants by Computer

In G1.2.2 we remarked that the keying operator should enter all terms in a standardized form corresponding to the rules set forth for the thesaurus to be developed. Otherwise, the program considers terms as different that actually are the same. This approach has two disadvantages: it puts a burden on the keying operator and it cannot be used for the construction of a cumulative thesaurus where the exact form of a term in a source matters. The best solution is a program that can perform standardization of spelling, e.g., find the nominative singular for each noun or the infinitive for each verb. Another problem occurs if the source contains inverted entries which should be transformed to direct entries. Another function of such a program could be the separation of composite words into their components (especially important for German). Obviously, such a program would be language-specific. In a more sophisticated version such a program could identify word stems. The components of compound terms or, if necessary, their stems could then be used for computer-assistance in deriving the decomposition into semantic factors, as discussed in Section G3.4.3.

G2.5 Miscellaneous Problems

G2.5.1 Cross-references given using notations

Some sources that have a notation attached to the terms use notations in cross-references (see Section D4.1) and it should be possible to key the cross-references that way. It would be awkward if the keying operator had

434 G Use of Computers in Thesaurus Construction

to look up the term each time, and even if the notation is followed by the term it would be more efficient to key only the notation. The complications arising therefrom are most easily solved as follows: Notations are treated exactly like terms synonymous to the Main Term. In order to avoid confusion of notations from different sources, an @ (or other symbol) is keyed before each notation and in processing the input (Step (1) of G2) this is expanded to:

@	Source Code	Notation

In a later step the appropriate preferred term can be added to or replace the notation.

As has been discussed in Sections F4.6 and F5.1(c), the same procedure can be used in the introduction of new cross-references by the editor/lexicographer. In Step F5.1(c) we often have the reverse problem: we have to look up the notation when the term is given. This can, of course, be done automatically. As a safety measure it might be useful to store an indication whenever the text has been inserted based on the notation or vice versa (an additional field K would have to be introduced in the cross-reference subrecord for that purpose.)

G2.5.2 Record identification

After the second round of merging (Step F2.3), each record should be given a unique identification number under which it is accessible. This temporary number can be used to identify the record for adding modifications and corrections made in editing.

In a printout with line numbers, the identification number can be the line number of the leading subrecord of a record.

G2.5.3 Substituting numbers for terms to save storage space

It is a programming option to set up an auxiliary dictionary file that contains the text of each term (on disk) and then replace the term wherever it occurs by a 2-byte number giving the address of the term in the disk file. This saves space and some processing time, but on the other hand needs processing time for look-up in input and output (where the number has to be replaced by the term itself). Furthermore, look-up is necessary each time a term has to be worked on as a linguistic entity, e.g., in grammatical standardization.

G3 COMPUTER ASSISTANCE IN WORKING OUT THE PRELIMINARY STRUCTURE OF THE THESAURUS

Working out the structure of the thesaurus is basically an intellectual task. However, if among the sources one has a classification scheme or a thesaurus

G3 Working Out the Preliminary Structure   435

that provides a good structure (a "model scheme") then this model scheme may serve as the data base for performing at least some of the steps by a computer. The options range from sorting terms into broad subject fields based on the "model scheme" (Step F3.1) to copying the classified arrangement from the model scheme (Step F3.3). Problems arise with terms that are not in the model scheme. The results of any computer procedure for this task have to be edited, of course.

Another computer-assisted method for sorting terms into subject fields and subfields is as follows:

Manual steps:
(1) Index a number of documents using free terms.
(2) Make up a list of terms that designate larger subject fields.
Computer step:
(3) For each term in the list of subject fields, look up all documents indexed by it, and prepare a list of all the terms used for indexing any of these documents. This is the list of terms belonging to that subject field.

This may be refined by giving for each term the accession numbers of the documents from which it was taken and the number of documents in which the subject field and the term co-occur. This figure may then be compared with the over-all number of documents for that term. Since each term is likely to belong to more than one subject field, this statistical information may be used to determine the "main" subject field to be used for the first sorting into subject fields (Step F3.1).

Whenever intellectual work has to take over, the terms are printed on thesaurus forms. The arrangement of terms is determined by the last step that has been performed by the computer (alphabetically within broad subject fields or within subfields after Step F3.1 or F3.2, respectively; in a more detailed classified arrangement if parts of F3.3 have been performed by computer). The remaining tasks are then performed by a human editor. In many cases it will be necessary to modify the results produced by the computer.

G3.3 Computer Assistance in Clerical Tasks to Be Performed in F3.3, "Work Out the Detailed Structure of the Thesaurus"

Assume that the working file is available in machine-readable form before Step F3.3 and that it should be available in corrected form after Step F3.3. Furthermore assume that each record is printed on a card and identified by a number, as described in Section G2.5.2, and that a human editor works on these cards. This section deals solely with clerical assistance by the computer. (More sophisticated uses of the computer in working out the detailed thesaurus structure will be discussed in Section G3.4).

G3.3.1 Merging information for each class of synonyms

When the editor has defined synonym classes and selected the preferred terms, the following input is keyed for each group.

Example:
Text of preferred term
   Number of first record in group   numbers
   .   need not
   .   be in
   .   ascending
   Number of last record in group   order

The text of the preferred term can be omitted if it is identical to the Main Term in the first record. The sequence of the groups should be as meaningful as is possible at this point.

The program then processes this input as follows: for each group, it gets all the records and merges them into one new record, headed by the preferred term. These records are then printed on cards in the input sequence so that the editor can work out the classificatory structure (Step F3.3.2).

G3.2.2 Rearranging the working file in classified order

After the editor has worked out the classificatory structure, the file has to be rearranged and updated accordingly. For this purpose, the following input is keyed: the numbers of the records in classified sequence, indicating the hierarchical level and marking descriptors by '+' and all other terms by '—' after the hierarchical level. Each number may be followed by modifications to be made in the record. For new records the text of the preferred term is used instead of a number. Using this input, the program creates an updated working file in classified order. From this file the classified index can be printed. If new cross-references have been introduced, it might also be useful to go through the routine of creating the corresponding inverse cross-references. (The merging process alone does not affect inverse cross-references; if we have A RT B and create B RT A and merge A on A', B on B', we get A' RT B, B' RT A, which later becomes (replacing A by A', B by B'): A' RT B', B' RT A'.)

G3.4 Computer Assistance for Intellectual Tasks in Working Out the Detailed Thesaurus Structure

G3.4.1 Computer assistance in hierarchy construction

If BT and NT cross-references are indicated, the computer can tentatively put together segments of the hierarchical structure by "chaining" these cross-references (see Figure 64). The result is usually a polyhierarchical structure.

Example 1:
    Cathode ray tubes
        BT Thermionic tubes
    Picture tubes
        BT Cathode ray tubes
    Thermionic tubes
        BT Electron tubes
    Electron tubes
Results in
    A   Electron tubes
       B   Thermionic tubes
          C   Cathode ray tubes
             D   Picture tubes

Example 2: (example 1 modified, added elements marked by *)
    Cathode ray tubes
        BT Thermionic tubes   turn out to be on same
        * Vacuum tubes   level. Polyhierarchy
    Picture tubes
        BT Cathode ray tubes
    Thermionic tubes
        BT Electron tubes
    *Vacuum tubes
        BT Electron tubes
    Electron tubes
Results in
    A   Electron tubes
       B   Thermionic tubes
          C   Cathode ray tubes → E
             D   Picture tubes
             E   Vacuum tubes ← C

Example 3: (example 1 modified, added elements marked by *)
    Cathode ray tubes   turn out to be in same
        BT Thermionic tubes   hierarchical chain;
        *Electron tubes   no polyhierarchy
    Picture tubes
        BT Cathode ray tubes
    Thermionic tubes
        BT Electron tubes
    Electron tubes
Results in
    A   Electron tubes ← C
       B   Thermionic tubes
          C   Cathode ray tubes → A
             D   Picture tubes

By checking both chains upward from C, it is detected that Electron tubes is in the first chain already. The cross-references are deleted.

Figure 64. Construction of a hierarchy by "chaining" hierarchical cross-references (G3.4.1).

A monohierarchical structure has to be selected for printing the classified index; a format that shows the hierarchical level by indention, as described in Section D3.1.1, is best.

The selection of a monohierarchical structure may be assisted in the following alternative ways:

(1) Print out those terms that have two or more Broader Terms (neighbors), so that one of these Broader Terms can be selected.

(2) Create all monohierarchical chains. Each such chain is headed by a term having two or more Broader Terms. Print all chains, and print all the Broader Terms for each term heading a chain, so that one of them can be selected. The chains can then be put together into one classified arrangement.

(3) Produce a classified sequence where each term appears as often as necessary. At each place in the hierarchy where a term appears, all the other Broader Terms are also given. This display gives the best overview as to the consequences of each selection. In the final version a term is retained only at the selected place and is deleted from all other places (deletion includes all Narrower Terms). Of course, a cross-reference should be retained.

(4) If one and only one subject field or main subject field is given for each term, it may be used to determine the Broader Term to be used in the monohierarchical structure.

An on-line video console would make these procedures much more effective.

If one wants to apply the chaining method some preparations are required: nonpreferred terms in the fields BT and NT have to be replaced by the corresponding preferred terms because otherwise links may be missed. (This means G5.1 has to be performed first.) Thereafter, an editing step should be inserted because one wrong hierarchical relationship may lead to very strange consequences. (In the case of a cumulative thesaurus wrong hierarchical relationships are marked as not belonging to the recommended thesaurus structure by putting '0' in field E.) It is also possible to perform the chaining algorithm without prior editing and then edit the BT - NT cross-references based on the results of the first run.

Using the same technique, one may obtain candidates for additional RT relationships: if A RT B and B RT C, then A RT C is a candidate for an RT relationship.

The "chaining" method is a special case of the graph-theoretic approach to the automatic construction of indexing languages mentioned in Section H2; for references see there.

G3.4.2 Use of the decomposition of compound concepts into elemental concepts in working out the preliminary structure of the thesaurus

Once a combination of elemental concepts has been assigned to each term one may use these combinations in a number of ways that were briefly sketched in Section F8.4. Their implementation is dependent upon computer assistance and details are therefore discussed here. In the following we assume that a core classification scheme has been defined and that the concept combinations are given as strings of notations from that core classification. Sorting rules for notations and strings of notations have been given in Section D4.3.3,2. To implement these sorting rules each number field in a notation should be expanded to its maximum possible length by leading zeros.

Example:
HC93.3.7 becomes
HC0093.03.007
(assuming that the number fields can contain 4, 2, and 3 digits, respectively).

The resulting strings can then be sorted letter by letter, using the collating sequence given in Section D4.3.3,2. To keep things simple assume furthermore that notations are arranged in ascending order (or in another fixed citation order) within one string.

,1 Use of the decomposition of compound concepts in sorting terms into subject fields and subfields, and in forming groups of synonyms (Steps F3.1, F3.2, and F3.3.1). The records for the terms are sorted in notation-string sequence and printed. Terms that have been assigned the same concept combination are flagged. If one term has been assigned different concept combinations (from different sources) it is printed at each appropriate place and flagged by a different symbol. This classified file can now be used for the following purposes:

(1) Detection of synonyms and quasi-synonyms—look for terms that have the same or nearly the same concept combination.

(2) Detection of homonyms—if a term has been assigned different concept combinations from different sources, an editor has to check whether the differences are only slight and reflect slightly different interpretations of the term or whether the differences are substantial, in which case we have a homonym that should be disambiguated.

The results of this procedure are, of course, highly dependent on the quality of the concept combinations assigned. It will usually be necessary to supplement this procedure by performing the intellectual operations described in Section F3.3.1 (which are now much easier than they would have been without prior computer assistance).

,2 Use of the decomposition of compound concepts in working out the classificatory structure (Step F3.3.2). If this procedure is to be used the concept combinations obtained from different sources should be edited, and resulting modifications punched as additional input in G3.3.1. The concept combinations may then be used for the purely automatic derivation of relationships among compound concepts, according to the rules given in C1.3.

This function is ideally suited for computer processing. The working file is thus "enriched" by the addition of many BT, NT, and RT cross-references. It should then be edited by a human editor. It can then be used, with or without prior editing, for the construction of a hierarchy by chaining BT and NT cross-references, as described in Section G3.4.1. Furthermore, if the citation order of the semantic factors within a compound concept is fixed, a monohierarchical structure is thereby defined (see Section C2.4).

As has been discussed earlier the hierarchical structure derived from the concept combinations, especially if many of them contain 4 or more components, is rather overwhelming; its display and expression by cross-references requires a good deal of space. Instead of, or in addition to, the construction of a hierarchy with elaborate BT and NT cross-references, one may then print a conceptual index using any of the methods described in D3.6. This index is to assist in editing and also to show what relationships need *not* be included as cross-references.

G3.4.3 Computer assistance in semantic factoring

To the extent that conceptual structure is reflected in the linguistic structure semantic factoring can be assisted by an analysis of the linguistic structure. The principle is as follows: A multiword term or a composite term can be analyzed as to its constituent words or word stems. These linguistic components are then looked up in a file that has been established prior to this operation. This leads to a set of suggested semantic factors. If synonyms of the term being processed are known, each synonym can be processed the same way, resulting in one additional set of semantic factors for each synonym. A scope note can also serve as a source of suggested semantic factors. Furthermore, any Broader Terms indicated in the input (or, if a Broader Term is a composite term, its semantic factors) can be added to each set. (Depending on the organization of the source, one may have to look in the classified index of the source to find all Broader Terms.)

The main question is, of course, how does one establish the file in which the linguistic components are looked up? One possibility, and the most appropriate one for the present context, is to establish a core classification scheme prior to the Step F3, "Work out the preliminary structure of the thesaurus". To the core descriptors, add all their synonyms and spelling variants. Another possibiilty is to perform Step F3.3.1, "Working out the synonym-homonym structure and the equivalence structure" first. The working file can then at the same time be used as the file for looking up the linguistic components for multi-word terms.

Two refinements can be used in the process:

(1) In looking up linguistic components one should also look for spelling variants and morphological variants.

G4 Working Out the Classified Index   441

(2) The analysis into linguistic components may be refined by looking not only for individual words, but also for meaningful phrases.

Example:
Starting term:
Social security for experts going to developing countries. *Meaningful phrases:* Social security for experts; Experts going to developing countries; Social security; Developing countries. Note that Social experts or Social security in developing countries would not be meaningful phrases.

The selection of meaningful phrases is a difficult problem. If syntactical information is available, "development rules" may be formulated to create all meaningful phrases. Incidentally, the same problem occurs with multiword terms in semi-mechanized indexing. Syntactical information can be obtained from function words and from prefixes, infixes, and suffixes. This syntactical information could also be used to derive concept combinations using roles and links.

Computer assistance in semantic factoring is particularly useful if one of the sources is of the type of the Library of Congress Subject Headings. The procedure would even be useful to process LCSH (or a similar source) as the only source with the objective of analyzing and/or revising it. The special nature of subject headings can be exploited in this case. Many subject headings consist of a main heading combined with a subheading. The list of main headings together with often used subheadings is in essence a core classification. If the structure of this core classification is worked out, the relationships between all the other subject headings may be derived fairly automatically.

The following procedure may be especially useful for processing subject heading lists: Have a person who knows the subject heading list to be analyzed set up a list of frequently used subheadings. It is then possible to write a program to identify all those subject headings that consist of a main heading combined with one of these subheadings. The list of headings that remain can then be analyzed, and thereupon one may proceed as described in the previous paragraph.

G4 COMPUTER ASSISTANCE IN WORKING OUT THE CLASSIFIED INDEX

The classified index is worked out after a preliminary hierarchical structure has been developed, possibly using the technique of chaining BT- NT cross-references described in Section G3.4.1. The improvement of the hierarchy is an intellectual task. However, computer assistance can be very helpful in alleviating some clerical problems. On a low level of sophistication updated versions of the classified index can be printed easily. If the working file is available in machine-readable form, it can be updated as the information changing one classified arrangement to another is put in, as discussed in Section F4.0 (it might be advisable to reread this section): New BT - NT cross-references can be added if they are introduced in the new classified arrangement; BT, NT, and RT cross-references shown in the new classified arrangement can be tagged accordingly; and references that were shown in the old classified arrangement but are not shown in the new one can be untagged. Changes that are made tentatively but revised again before the next version of the classified index is prepared and that, therefore, never show up as computer input, cannot be captured in this manner. Also the editor still has to work with slips of paper containing the terms and move them around on a table. Both problems can be solved by using a video-screen on which the hierarchy can be displayed and on which changes can be indicated by a light pen. However, this is a rather sophisticated technique and at this time it is hardly applicable in an operational environment.

G5 COMPUTER ASSISTANCE IN COMPLETING THE FIRST DRAFT OF THE THESAURUS AS A WHOLE

G5.1 Computer Assistance in Revising Entries in the Working File

The revision of the entries can be automated in part. The form of the terms (e.g., singular versus plural, use nouns only, etc.) can be checked automatically if the rules chosen for the particular thesaurus are simple enough and if an appropriate linguistic program (for example, to recognize plural forms) is available. The replacement of nonpreferred terms by notation and preferred term can be fully automated. (Compare Section G2.5.1, "Cross-references given using notations".) The improvement of the classificatory structure, on the other hand, is a solely intellectual task.

The easiest way to replace nonpreferred terms by notation and preferred term is as follows: An internal alphabetical dictionary is created that gives for each term the appropriate notation and preferred term (or standardized abbreviation). This dictionary is maintained on a direct access device so that replacement can be done simply by look-up in this dictionary. (The working file may be on magnetic tape!) If storage space is a problem, only the notation is given in the dictionary and the text or standardized abbreviation is looked up in a second file, using the notation.

However, a less direct method based on sorting operations may be faster. It is mandatory if no direct access devices are available.

G5.3 Check of Inverse Cross-References by Computer

This is straightforward and needs no further discussion. Most programs for computer assistance incorporate this feature.

G7 PRINTING THE FINAL THESAURUS BY COMPUTER

The computer offers considerable advantages for printing the thesaurus. The terms and the data elements given for each term can be arranged as needed for the different parts of the thesaurus. The thesaurus can then be printed on a high-speed printer and duplicated by photoreproduction. Much better results can be achieved by typesetting machines driven on-line by computer or off-line by a magnetic tape or a punched paper tape. Furthermore, a computer can perform some of the tasks of proofreading.

While no conceptual difficulties are involved there are many details to be taken care of, so that the printing programs may get rather lengthy.

G8 UPDATING A COMPUTER-STORED THESAURUS

Updating of the computer-stored thesaurus is necessary in thesaurus construction as well as in thesaurus updating. The usual operations are required: additions, deletion, and replacement, applied to a record as a whole or to parts of a record. However, this is only the smaller part of the story. Due to the strong interconnectedness of thesaurus data, a change in one place usually requires changes at many other places. For example, the insertion UF *Lawyer* with the Main Term *Attorney* requires that *Lawyer* be inserted into the alphabetical index or that a record *Lawyer* USE *Attorney* be prepared (depending on the thesaurus format). In the latter case one might enter with equal justification 'insert the record *Lawyer* USE *Attorney*', in which case the UF subrecord would have to be created.

In this section it is assumed that the following files are stored in the computer:

—the working file containing all information in the thesaurus;
—the classified index file;
—the alphabetical index file.

As discussed in Section F0.6 it would be possible, but usually less efficient, to store only the working file and to produce the classified index and the alphabetical index whenever a new user version is prepared. If this alternative is used, changes in the classified index and in the alphabetical index mentioned in the following description do not apply. However, this remark does not affect the interaction between changes in the classified index and changes in BT, NT, and RT cross-references discussed in Section F4.0.

It is useful to divide the following discussion into types of changes to be made (G8.1) and format for the input of updating information (G8.2).

G8.1 Types of Changes

Only the major types are discussed in the following:

(1) *Insertion of one or more cross-reference subrecords.* Other changes required: Insert inverse cross-references (for ST cross-references these might be entries in the alphabetical index). Possibly changes in the classified index.

(2) *Insertion of a whole record.* This is operation (1) for all subrecords of the new record and additionally the insertion of the Main Term. In addition the Main Term itself has to be inserted into the alphabetical index and into the classified index.

(3) *Replacement of one subrecord; specifically, change of a Main Term.* Often it is convenient to delete one subrecord and at the same time insert a new subrecord (rather than perform a sequence of two operations). A frequent special case is the change of the Main Term. Specific cases of Main Term change are: (i) a term previously listed as a synonym or a spelling variant is now selected as the preferred term; (ii) the notation is changed. Other changes to be made: The old Main Term has to be replaced by the new form in all cross-references to it as well as in the classified index. If standardized abbreviations given in data field AB rather than the Main Term given in field MT are used in cross-references, these remarks apply to the standardized abbreviation.

(4) *Change in relationship type.* Change in instruction (USE, UF, SEE, SF, PT, PF). Other changes required: Appropriate changes with the inverse cross-references. Possibly changes in the classified index and/or in the alphabetical index depending on the type of relationship involved.

(5) *Deletion of one or more cross-reference subrecords.* This operation is inverse to operation (1). See the remarks there.

(6) *Deletion of a whole record.* This is the inverse of operation (2). Note that by deleting each inverse cross-reference, the Main Term is deleted wherever it occurs in the main part. In addition, it has to be deleted from the alphabetical index and from the classified index.

(7) *Insertion, deletion or changes in other types of subrecords, e.g., in the scope note.*

(8) *Insertion of source indications.* Such insertions occur when an additional source is incorporated into a cumulative thesaurus. They are usually not keyed as such, but generated by a computer program.

In order to achieve better consistency in the intellectual preparation of the updating information, cross-references involving a lead to a preferred term should always be entered at the preferred term, that is, at the UF (Used for) or SF (Seen from) end. Similarly, cross-references involving posting should always be entered at the PF (Posted from) end. The exchange of a preferred term against a synonym is achieved easily by the series of operations demonstrated below.

Example:
    Attorney
        UF ST Lawyer.
1. *Replace UF ST Lawyer by UF ST Attorney (operation (3))*
2. *Change the Main Term from Attorney to Lawyer (also operation (3))*

G8 Updating a Computer-Stored Thesaurus   445

(Note that the program does not permit putting Attorney as a Synonymous Term into the record for Attorney unless we do something specific to prevent that; and why should we? If USE ST instructions are part of the main part, the program will generate Attorney USE ST Attorney as a result of step 1, and it will replace Attorney in the cross-reference by Lawyer in step 2, resulting in Attorney USE ST Lawyer.)

Changes in BT/NT and RT cross-references may lead to changes in the classified arrangement. In most cases these changes will lead to changes in notation and operation (3) will have to be performed for the preferred terms affected.

Up to now we have dealt with changes in the working file and how such changes might affect the classified index and the alphabetical index. Changes may also originate in the classified index. Introducing the changes in the classified index itself is basically a text-editing procedure. The text editor program should be able to move whole blocks of lines from one position to another (the number of indentions of the first line of the block being specified). The text editor should also be able to move a line to a specified position in terms of number indentions. Any changes in the notations are dealt with as changes in the Main Term. Changes in the classified index may also mean new BT, NT, and RT cross-references to be entered in the working file and they affect the BT, NT, and RT cross-references to be printed in the user version of the main part, as discussed in Sections F4.0 and G4. This problem is rather intricate.

G8.2 Input of Updating Information

There are two methods which are called here *line-oriented* and *term-oriented* input of updating information.

G8.2.1 Line-oriented input of updating information

A printout of the file to be updated is produced and the lines are numbered in that printout. For simplicity's sake assume that each subrecord consists of one line. It is not difficult to modify the procedure described in the following to overcome this restriction. Reference to subrecords to be deleted is made by the first and last line of the section to be deleted; if only one line is to be deleted, the last-line field should be blank (or repeat the number of the line to be deleted). As a convenient convention one should stipulate that whenever a Main Term line is deleted the whole record is deleted. Lines to be changed are referenced by their line number (only one line can be changed at a time). If the line changed contains the Main Term (or the standardized abbreviation, depending on which is used in cross-references), appropriate action is taken (see G8.1(3)). If one or more lines have to be inserted, the insertion point is referenced by the line preceding the first line to be inserted. Note that only the "to-part" of a cross-reference (field C, G0.3) has to be given. The preceding Main Term can be "picked up" as the "from-part" (field B).

In a system with a little more sophistication, one may provide for the replacement of a group of one or more lines by another group of one or more lines. One may also provide for the insertion, replacement, and deletion of character strings within a line.

The place where subrecord(s) are inserted into a record does not matter as long as the sequence of subrecords within a record follows strict rules so that a computer program can restore order after the update.

G8.2.2 Term-oriented input of updating information

In this method an "updating record", i.e., a record containing the updating information, is created for each record to be changed (any number of subrecords within that record may be involved). The structure of updating records is exactly the same as that of an original input record (described in Section G1.2.2), except that a special code precedes elements to be deleted. The updating record must be identified by the Main Term (the notation is sufficient). A special problem arises if the Main Term has to be changed. A field "New Main Term" has to be introduced in the updating record format, since the Main Term field must contain the *old* Main Term for identification purposes.

Updating a record is nothing other than merging the updating record into the old record, except that in this merge elements can be deleted.

G8.2.3 Comparison of the two methods

In line-oriented input reference is made to a certain status of the working file; it is only for that status of the working file that the line numbers have their meaning. In an off-line situation, everyone who prepares input for updating has to have a printout of the whole file with line numbers. Updating suggestions coming in on thesaurus forms and based on the published version of the thesaurus have to be processed by look-up of the line numbers in the printout before they can be keyed for input. Updating has to be done in batches and after each updating the whole file has to be printed again. In an on-line situation, one may have a display of that portion of the file that contains the lines of interest. However, this involves keying the Main Term affected so that the program can search the file for that record. If no visual screen is available and the display has to be done by teletype printout, it is rather slow. In term-oriented input all these difficulties are avoided. The only thing that one needs to know is the current form of the Main Term at hand (even that requirement can be waived if the program goes automatically from a synonym to the preferred term). This may be paid for by an increase in the keying necessary: The Main Term (or its notation) has to be keyed in each case, and elements to be deleted have to be keyed in full. On the other hand keying of verbal information is less error-prone then keying of line numbers.

As to the programming effort the term-oriented method can use the program for merging two records (needed in G2.2.3 and G2.3) with few modifications. If no program for merging is available it is much easier to program for the line-oriented method.

G9 DEVICES FOR THE INPUT (KEYING) OF THESAURUS DATA

The device to be used to produce a machine-readable record will depend mostly on what is available in the institution. *Punched cards* are most common. In some respects *punched paper tape* is easier to use; most punched-paper-tape typewriters also allow for upper- and lower-case characters which punched cards do not (unless specific coding is used which is inconvenient). Also, if the tape typewriter has a reader, a master tape with the input format can be prepared. Typewriters using *magnetic tape cassettes* (e.g., the IBM MT Selectric) are very similar to punched-paper-tape typewriters. The cassettes are easier to handle than paper tape. On the other hand, most paper-tape typewriters have a number of non-printing codes that are convenient for formatting; such codes are missing on the IBM MT Selectric. Both paper tape and magnetic tape cassettes require special reading equipment for input into the computer. This equipment is not available in most computer installations, so one may have to use a service bureau. The same is true for input via *machine-readable typescript*, which otherwise is very convenient. Then there are devices for keying directly on magnetic tape, thus speeding up input into the computer and avoiding any conversion problems. Most convenient, especially for input of updating information, is *on-line* input via remote terminal. Since in this case input is directly into the computer, the operator is free from handling cards, tapes, cassettes, etc. Data stored in the computer (e.g., the input format) can be copied into the input file. Any mistakes can be easily corrected. Also, the operator may request a printout of a line or a number of lines he just typed in order to check for errors.

Before deciding about the input device in a medium- or large-scale project of thesaurus construction, one should consult an expert. The following criteria might be useful for a decision:

(1) Character set available on the device.
(2) Possibility of having a master tape or equivalent containing the input format.

(3) Ease of use (the keyboard should feel and look similar to a typewriter keyboard).
(4) Ease of detecting errors.
(5) Ease of correction (especially useful is a buffer that can be read and corrected before the line is transferred to the machine-readable record).
(6) Ease of handling the medium used, e.g., punched cards, paper tape.
(7) Ease of further processing.

Chapter H

Automatic Methods in the
Construction of Indexing Languages
and Thesauri, Starting from the Texts
of Documents and/or Search
Requests. Automatic Classification
(Advanced)

H0 INTRODUCTION

The relationships that exist between terms based on their meaning result in certain statistical patterns of occurrence and co-occurrence of these terms in text. Conversely, we should be able to conclude from observed statistical patterns of the occurrence and co-occurrence of terms what these conceptual relationships are. This idea is the basis for automatic methods in thesaurus construction. These automatic methods can assist in, but not replace, the intellectual effort needed for the construction of an indexing language or a thesaurus. "Statistics should not take precedence over human judgment in the evaluation of vocabulary, but these studies and other provide the basis for some useful decisions." In other words, the identification of terms and relationships by automatic methods should be considered as a kind of pre-processing of open-ended sources, especially abstracts and full-text documents, before transferring terms onto thesaurus forms (in Step F2.2). The results of this pre-processing are then used in the further steps of thesaurus building. Fully automatic thesaurus building may be attractive as an idea, but it is not feasible.

Section F0.4.4 dealt with the use of frequency and co-occurrence data in the selection of preferred terms and descriptors. The present chapter is a continuation of these considerations on a more sophisticated level. The major thrust of Section F0.4.4 was on frequency data collected for terms that at one point or another have been picked or assigned by a human editor or indexer; the major thrust of this chapter is the fully automatic processing of text. However, many of the methods to be described are also applicable for the analysis of frequency data on descriptors, for example, the automatic derivation of a classificatory structure.

The chapter starts with an exploration of the units from which frequency and co-occurrence data may be gathered and of different kinds of counting (H1). It proceeds to methods by which promising descriptor candidates can be identified from frequency patterns (H2) and how relationships between terms can be detected from co-occurrence patterns (H3). Both sections are concerned with "local" information. Section H4 turns to the automatic derivation of classification schemes, i.e., "global" structures, from co-occurrence data or from the indication of relationships between terms.

The reader is advised to re-read Section F0.4.4, especially F0.4.4,0, before going further in this chapter.

H1 DEFINITION OF UNITS OF TEXT AND COUNTING METHODS

"Units of text" can be any of the following:

—search request statements;
—search request formulations in terms of descriptors;
—sets of indexing terms contained in document representations;
—abstracts of documents;
—individual sentences of documents or abstracts;
—paragraphs of documents;
—full text of documents.

"Corpus of text" is any assembly of units of text of one or more types.

There are two main methods of counting frequencies and instances of co-occurrence.

(1) *Total count:* a term or concept occurring nine times in one unit is counted nine times to obtain the total count.

(2) *Unit-wise count:* a term or concept is counted only once for each unit, even if it occurs nine times in the unit.

Instead of just counting unit-wise, one can assign weights according to within-unit frequency.

H3 Relationships from Co-Occurrence Patterns

Recall from Section F0.4.4 two major problems that should be kept in mind throughout the following considerations:

(a) A computer program can only recognize words as strings of characters between two blanks. It cannot recognize multi-word terms immediately, unless such terms are identified prior to computer processing by an editor, as for example in free term indexing. To a certain extent, multi-word terms can also be identified through syntactical analysis of a sentence and through statistical analysis (see Section H3.1(3)).

(b) We have to distinguish between the plane of terms and the plane of concepts. It is often useful to get frequency data and data of co-occurrence for concepts rather than for terms. The frequency of a concept is computed as the sum of the frequencies of all terms designating that concept.

H2 IDENTIFICATION OF DESCRIPTOR CANDIDATES FROM FREQUENCY PATTERNS

Elementary methods have been discussed in Section F0.4.4,2. A more sophisticated procedure is as follows: Determine concepts that occur with high within-unit frequency in a few units. These concepts have more discriminatory power than concepts that occur in many units with about the same frequency. (The total count for both concepts may be the same.) Some statistical measure has to be established to determine that the deviation from equal distribution over documents is big enough to make a useful descriptor. This type of analysis is more appropriate for concepts than for terms.

H3 DETECTION OF TERM OR CONCEPT RELATIONSHIPS FROM CO-OCCURRENCE PATTERNS

H3.0 Nearness Measures

We want to determine quantitatively which pairs of terms co-occur more often than others. For this purpose we must define a measure of co-occurrence (association, nearness). A very simple and often-used measure is the following.

Example:

$$r(A,B) = \frac{2c}{a+b},$$

where:
$a =$ *number of units in which A occurs,*
$b =$ *number of units in which B occurs,*
$c =$ *number of units in which both A and B occur.*

There are many other nearness measures, many of them more complicated and some of them more appropriate. In some systems a relationship between two terms is introduced in the thesaurus whenever the nearness measure is above a certain threshold. These relationships are then used indiscriminately in retrieval. However, a high nearness measure can mean many different things and it is therefore advisable to make sure first how the relationship between two terms should be interpreted.

H3.1 Interpretation of High Association between Two Terms A and B

High association between two terms A and B can mean any of the following.

(1) Definitional relationship.
(1a) A and B are synonymous.
(1b) A and B are quasi-synonymous (designate equivalent concepts).
(1c) A and B designate concepts that are similar in meaning.
(1d) A and B designate concepts that are in a class-inclusion or topic-inclusion relationship.
(2) A and B designate concepts that are in a relationship of contextual contiguity.
(2a) Part-whole relationship.
(2b) Other connected hierarchical relationships.
(c) Empirically connected.
(3) Two words form a multi-word term; for example, *Information* and *Retrieval* co-occur heavily.

The synonymity interpretation is highly unlikely if the units are sentences because two synonyms are seldom used in one sentence. It is also unlikely if the units are abstracts or sets of indexing terms because an abstracter is unlikely to use Synonymous Terms within an abstract. Synonymity is likely, however, if the units are paragraphs and even more so if the units are full-text documents because people tend to use synonyms in order to achieve variety. Synonymity is also very likely if the terms co-occur in search requests or interest profiles where the users have been instructed to include all synonyms they can think of as OR-combinations. In fact, if two terms occur in an OR-combination in *one* search request one should immediately consider the possibility that they are synonymous or nearly related; see F1.2.2. Interpretation as equivalence, similarity in meaning, class inclusion or topic inclusion and as contextual contiguity may be appropriate whatever the units are. However, if the units are sentences the relationship "empirically connected" is the most likely unless we have a multi-word term. The interpretation as a multi-word term makes sense only if the units on which the computations are based are sentences.

In dealing with similarity in meaning, class inclusion, topic inclusion, and contextual contiguity it is more appropriate to use concepts instead of terms and compute co-occurrence data accordingly.

H3 Relationships from Co-Occurrence Patterns

H3.2 Second-Order Associations for the Detection of Definitional Relationships

The associations, as measured by the nearness measure in the previous paragraph, are called first-order associations. A second-order association can be defined as follows (compare Figure 65): The list of terms associated in first order with *Airplanes* is called the association profile of *Airplanes*. In the same way, we have an association profile for *Aircraft*. The degree of similarity between the two association profiles is called the second-order association between the two terms. If we have a situation where the first-order associations mostly correspond to contextual contiguity then similarity in the association profiles of *A* and *B* means that the concepts designated by the terms *A* and *B* tend to occur in the same empirical context. This we would expect if *A* and *B* were synonymous or in a class inclusion relationship. We therefore conclude the other way around: if two terms *A* and *B* have similar association profiles, then they are expected to be in a definitional relationship. That means they are either synonymous or quasi-synonymous or they designate concepts that are similar in meaning or in a class inclusion or topic inclusion relationship.

Airplanes
  Associated terms:
  Wing
  Engine
  Rudder
  Airframe
  Stabilizer
  Autopilot
  Jet
  Supersonic

Aircraft
  Associated terms:
  Engine
  Wing
  Rudder
  Stabilizer
  Airframe
  Fusilage
  Autopilot
  Supersonic
  Rotor

Figure 65. Example of second-order association (H3.2).

One may also obtain association profiles directly by asking individuals to name terms associated with a similar term. Terms related by definition as well as terms related by contextual contiguity are obtained by this method (compare F1.1.4).

H3.3 The Use of Inconsistent Association Profiles for the Detection of Homonyms

"Consistent association of a given term with two groups of terms, each representing an entirely different discipline, may indicate that a homograph exists and that separate terms should be established. For example, if the term

Precipitation were frequently associated with such terms as *Climate, Clouds, Temperature, Humidity, Solutions, Chemical reactions,* and *Solubility,* it is evident that two separate concepts are being indexed as one; therefore, two terms should be established or the one term redefined."

H3.4 Detection of Hierarchical Relationships

Earlier it was mentioned that a high second-order association between two terms A and B may mean that they are synonymous or that the concepts designated by the two terms are in a class-inclusion relationship. A hierarchical relationship may be surmised especially if there is a one-sided overlap. This means if term B is considerably less frequent than term A and if almost all units containing term B also contain term A we may suspect that B designates a concept that is narrower than the concept designated by A. However, B may just as well be a rarely used synonym of A.

The one-sided overlap criterion can be applied also to concepts, and this application is even more useful. We can suspect that a concept B is narrower than concept A if almost all units dealing with concept B also deal with concept A and if the number of units dealing with A is much larger than the number of units dealing with B (compare the definition of hierarchical relationship in Section C3.2). (Note that it is quite likely that a specific concept is used more often than a more general concept. For example, there may be many articles dealing with a certain biological species, few of which bother to mention the genus to which the species belongs. However, in this case the same genus will usually co-occur with a number of other species so that we do not have the situation of one-sided overlap between the genus and one species.)

For this kind of analysis it is useful to use as units either search requests (where the searchers have been instructed to include Narrower Terms in their requests if they want to retrieve material on Narrower Terms also) or sets of indexing terms (if the indexers have been instructed to use Broader Terms for which the document may be of interest, too).

H3.5 Combined Application of Different Methods

If full-text documents are used as units, high first-order association may mean any type of relationship. We could now proceed to compute second-order associations. Two terms that have a high second-order association are likely to be in a definitional relationship. We could subtract from the list of pairs with high first-order association those pairs with a high second-order association. The remaining pairs should be in a relationship of contextual contiguity.

Since the detection of contiguity relationships should be based on a

H4　Derivation of Classification Schemes

count of concepts rather than a count of terms the following procedure might be useful: Detect synonymity relationships by second-order associations and form classes of synonymous and quasi-synonymous terms accordingly. Each class corresponds to a concept. It is now possible to obtain a frequency count on concepts and determine contiguity relationships between them.

H4　AUTOMATIC DERIVATION OF CLASSIFICATION SCHEMES ("GLOBAL" STRUCTURES)

The previous section was concerned with the identification of terms and their pairwise interrelationships. This could be called "local" information. A next step is the automatic derivation of a "global" structure (a classification scheme) to obtain the overall picture. There are two interrelated tasks:

(a) Find useful groupings of concepts.
(b) Find a pattern of subdivision of the set of documents into non-overlapping classes.

There are two main methods to perform these tasks:

(1) Clustering methods.
(2) Graph-theoretical methods.

To some extent these methods overlap; one might even say that the clustering method is a special case of methods based on graph theory.

H4.1　Automatic Derivation of Classification Schemes by Clustering Methods

The basic idea is to define a nearness measure in the set of concepts (such as the nearness measure defined in Section H3.0) or in the set of documents, respectively, and then derive clusters of near concepts or near documents, respectively. A cluster of concepts can be defined roughly as a set of concepts that tend to be nearer to each other than to concepts outside the cluster. Various cluster definitions and various clustering procedures are used.

H4.2　Automatic Derivation of Classification Schemes by Graph-Theoretical Methods

These methods are probably more appropriate to the relational nature of thesaurus data. In this approach one starts with a set of concepts (the nodes of the graph), and relationships between the concepts (the connections between the nodes called the arcs of the graph). Thus, the input consists of "local" information, namely, terms and pairwise relationships between them (the terms and the interrelationships may have been derived by the automatic methods discussed in Sections H2 and H3). Algorithms derived from graph theory make it possible to put together the over-all structure, the total graph, as in a jigsaw puzzle. One example of this is computer-assisted hierarchy construction by chaining BT-NT cross-references, as discussed in Section G3.4.1. Application of graph theory might lead to more efficient procedures for this purpose. In this case the graph is based on hierarchical relationships. It is also possible to use RT relationships as the base for the graph. In either case one might look for relatively close (strongly connected) subgraphs; these would then correspond to subdivisions of the classification scheme to be developed.

A simple-minded method, based on RT relationships, is as follows: pick any term A. $R(1,A)$ is the set of all terms related to A. $R(2,A)$ is the set of all terms that are related to any term in $R(1,A)$. If $R(n,A) = R(n+1,A)$, then clearly $R(n+1,A) = R(n+2,A)$ and $R(n,A)$ is a closed subset. If the difference between the number of elements in $R(n+1,A)$ and the number of elements in $R(n,A)$ reaches a minimum then $R(n,A)$ is relatively closed, the closure being sharper as the minimum is smaller.

Chapter J

Updating and Maintenance of Indexing Languages and Thesauri

J0 INTRODUCTION

Unless the subject field of the indexing language or thesaurus is at a complete standstill the indexing language or thesaurus must be updated on a continuing basis: new concepts and terms arise, terms become outmoded, concepts lose their importance. And even if no such developments take place, it is likely that while indexing a large number of documents and formulating many search requests, one encounters many terms that have not been noticed in the first construction of the indexing language or thesaurus. It is expected that 1,200 terms will change per year in the 25,000-term TEST.

As we shall see, the procedures for the updating of a thesaurus are closely intertwined with the operation of the ISAR system as a whole.

J1 TYPES OF CHANGES

(1) First, there may be *changes in the synonym-homonym structure* and in the equivalence structure. New synonyms and quasi-synonyms may be added, a new preferred term may be selected, or it may be detected that a term is homonymous and has to be disambiguated. These changes do not cause trouble except that the addition of a quasi-synonym may result in a change in the definition of a descriptor (see below).

(2) Second, there may be *changes in the lead-in part of the classificatory structure*. New concepts may be added, or the Broader Terms given in the USE instruction for an existing concept may be changed. By themselves these changes do not cause trouble either, but they often result in a change in the usage of a descriptor.

(3) Third, there may be *changes in the indexing language* itself. These changes are serious in that they affect retrieval and possibly make it necessary to reindex

457

a number of documents (these problems will be discussed in Section J6). These changes may involve the following:

(3.1) Introduction of a new descriptor.
(3.2) Elimination of a descriptor.
(3.3) Subdivision of an existing descriptor into a number of narrower descriptors.
(3.4) Change in the definition or usage of a descriptor, especially changing the delineation between two descriptors, changing the definition of both.
(3.5) Addition or elimination of a hierarchical relationship, especially assigning a descriptor to another group in the hierarchy.
(3.6) Addition or elimination of an RT relationship.

One change often involves several of these features. Subdivision of a descriptor, for example, involves the introduction of new descriptors and possibly the elimination of the old one (unless the descriptor to be subdivided is retained as a broader descriptor, in which case its usage for indexing changes, as discussed in Section D1.4.6,1). A change in the definition of a descriptor often affects the definition of broader descriptors. A change in hierarchical relationships affects the definition of the old and/or new broader descriptors.

J2 SOURCES FOR NEW TERMS, CONCEPTS, AND RELATIONSHIPS TO BE INCLUDED IN THE THESAURUS

In general, the same kinds of sources can be used for updating as for the construction of a new thesaurus. Most important are the following sources:

J2.1 Sources within the ISAR System

J2.1.1 Search request statements, search request formulations, and search performance

Again the importance of search requests as a source of updating information can hardly be overemphasized. Search request statements submitted in free language give the terminology that is actually used by people in searching. New terms that are synonymous and quasi-synonymous to terms already in the thesaurus should be included in the lead-in vocabulary. The same is true for terms designating new compound concepts that can be expressed by combining existing descriptors. Sometimes one will find that a concept needed in the formulation of the search request cannot be expressed by the available descriptors. In this case, a new descriptor should be introduced. The need for a new descriptor may become apparent only after the search has been performed and the results have proved unsatisfactory with regard to recall and precision.

While formulating search requests one often detects that new relationships between terms should be introduced or that existing relationships should be eliminated. Observing search performance is also useful for the detection of relationships, especially of hierarchical relationships to be introduced or to be eliminated. If documents are missed in an inclusive search for A, missing hierarchical relationships may be the reason: documents on B should have been retrieved automatically but were not. Contrariwise, if many irrelevant documents are retrieved by an inclusive search for C, a faulty hierarchical relationship might be the reason: if we have C NT D and most of the irrelevant documents have been retrieved because they are indexed by D, then C NT D is faulty. These considerations show that continuous monitoring of the search performance is a useful source for thesaurus updating.

J2.1.2 Documents and indexing of documents

The considerations that apply to search requests apply to the indexing of documents with obvious modifications. Two additional points should be mentioned. If an appropriate descriptor for indexing cannot be found, the indexer should use the nearest descriptor, which will often be a descriptor "..., *other*". The documents indexed by "..., *other*" should be examined periodically to detect new descriptor candidates, as discussed in Section C1.4.7. If a new concept is especially significant, a tentative descriptor can be introduced on the spot and used instead of or in addition to "..., *other*" (for details on tentative descriptors see Section J6.1(2)).

J2.1.3 Collection of updating information from sources within the ISAR system

The collection of updating information should be an integral part of the process of search request formulation and of indexing, respectively. If indexing and search request formulation are done manually, instruct the indexers and searchers to report terms and relationships between terms that are needed. Provide appropriate space on the request analysis sheet and the document analysis sheet. Note that searchers and indexers will report terms that are synonymous or quasi-synonymous to an existing term only if they have tried to locate a term via the alphabetical index. Compound concepts also present a special problem in updating. If the indexing language contains numerous precombined descriptors then the probability is high that a compound concept not contained in the indexing language will be suggested for inclusion as a precombined descriptor. If, on the other hand, the indexing language consists mainly of elemental or nearly elemental descriptors then the situation is different: The indexer or searcher encountering a compound concept forms immediately the appropriate combination of descriptors, often without looking into the thesaurus. A new compound concept that can be expressed easily as a combination of existing descriptors will therefore not be suggested for inclusion in the thesaurus. Only those compound concepts that are difficult to express by existing descriptors are mentioned and suggested for inclusion.

If automatic indexing is used, all terms not yet contained in the thesaurus must be listed for processing.

In addition to the kind of information discussed so far, data on frequency and co-occurrence of descriptors can be gathered. These data can then be used in the decisions on the introduction or elimination of descriptors, as has been described in Section F0.4.4, or for the more sophisticated automated methods of index language construction discussed in Chapter H.

J2.2 Sources Outside the ISAR System

J2.2.1 Information on changes in user needs

The search requests asked of an ISAR system often do not exhaust the range of user needs the ISAR system could serve. The reason for this is that users often are not aware of all the capabilities of an ISAR system. Therefore, it is important to get an independent assessment of user needs. If the ISAR system is serving a specified clientele, such as a research laboratory or a company, one may obtain information on changing tasks (such as changes in the research program or changes in the production program) from the management of the organization. If the clientele is not defined well enough for this approach, specific studies on user needs may be necessary at regular intervals.

J2.2.2 Information on new developments in the subject fields of the ISAR system

Such information can be obtained, for example, from state-of-the-art reports, informal discussions, and meetings.

J3 PROCEDURES FOR REGULAR UPDATING

J3.1 Use of Thesaurus Forms in Updating

Information on new terms and concepts as well as on relationships between terms and concepts already in the thesaurus is collected on thesaurus forms. The forms are either filled in directly by the person making the suggestion or the staff person responsible for updating transcribes suggestions contained in request analysis sheets or document analysis sheets on thesaurus forms. To indicate changes in existing terms 'CH' is checked on the top of the thesaurus form. New synonyms are best dealt with as a change in field ST in the entry for the appropriate preferred term.

Example:
> *Attorney*
> > *UF ST Counsel*

(Counsel is the new synonym.)

This is most compatible with the method for thesaurus construction suggested here. The alternative method is the following.

Example:
> *Counsel*
> > *USE ST Attorney*

(this alternative is not applicable in the Roget-Soergel model.)

J3.2 Processing of Updating Information

For the incorporation of this information into the thesaurus, the procedure described for thesaurus building applies with appropriate modifications. It is especially important to keep in mind that a thesaurus is a highly interrelated structure and that changes in one place lead to changes at other places. If a cross-reference is added or deleted, the appropriate inverse cross-reference has to be added or deleted. If the classified arrangement is changed the appropriate changes in the fields BT, NT and RT have to be made (for details see Section F4.0). For a more detailed discussion see Section G8.

J3.3 Issuing Supplements and/or Revised Versions

J3.3.1 Time schedule for updating

The working file should be updated continuously. Every data element is accompanied by the date it has been entered into the working file and by a special flag showing that it is not contained in the current printed version. (Different flags may be necessary for supplements and the full edition of the thesaurus.)

The updating of the copies of the thesaurus actually used is more complicated. It should be done at regular intervals, the length of the interval depending on the circumstances. In one company the indexers get the information on modifications of the thesaurus immediately on a continuing basis. In general, if the thesaurus is used in a medium-size information center where the indexers are all at one location and under full administrative control and where the number of copies of the thesaurus actually used is relatively small, the intervals may be short (two weeks to three months). On the other hand, if one has an operation based on cooperation among several institutions and

J Updating and Maintenance

possibly using scientists as part-time indexers, then longer intervals (a year or more) are necessary, at least for the list of checklist descriptors, in order to maintain a certain continuity of the work, in spite of the disadvantages of such slow updating. If a thesaurus has a wide distribution (such as the TEST thesaurus) and, in particular, if it is in the form of a bound book, the updating intervals may be even longer. This poses particular problems for information centers concentrating on a rapidly developing field and using such a thesaurus. These problems can be solved as follows: The information center develops modifications in its special area in accordance with the body responsible for the updating of the thesaurus and updates the copies used by its own indexers at short intervals. When the next edition of the whole thesaurus is printed these modifications are included. Another possibility would be for each institution to introduce tentative descriptors as needed. At regular intervals, say every 6 months, the lists of these tentative descriptors are merged and the merged list is used for updating the central thesaurus.

J3.3.2 Physical form of supplements

The techniques suitable for updating depend on the number of copies used. If there are only a few copies, they may all be kept as card files and immediate updating is no longer a problem. For big thesauri the size of the card file would be forbidding. However, loose-leaf binders might be useful. If there is one change on a page, the whole page should be replaced. Another method is a cumulative supplement; this can be sent out at regular intervals, say 30 days, provided that a sufficient number of new descriptors, say 25, has been accumulated since the last cumulative supplement. The most convenient method for the issuing agency and at the same time the most cumbersome for the user is simply to issue individual supplements (for example, additions and changes to LCC or the P-notes issued by FID to update UDC) and to issue complete revised editions only at longer intervals. Contrariwise, complete revised editions of DDC are published fairly frequently.

J3.3.3 Listing of changes made

In a revised edition one should take care to list all changes in one place. Also the date when a descriptor was introduced should be given in the scope note. If possible, descriptors that should be used instead of a newly introduced descriptor for searching the old part of the collection should be given in the scope note.

J3.4 Organization for and Decision-Making in Thesaurus Updating

Special problems of coordination and decision-making arise if an indexing language is used for shared subject indexing or if a widely used indexing language allows the users to take part in the decisions on updating (such as UDC). In these cases the decisions cannot be made by a central body alone but it is necessary to discuss them with all participants. In most cases it will be sufficient to send the modifications around and get written agreement. For difficult problems and far-reaching decisions, however, meetings are necessary.

This procedure does not apply to decisions relating to how the existing indexing language should be used in indexing. These decisions, usually referring to the usage of a descriptor, have to be made quickly and should therefore be made by the central body responsible for the updating of the thesaurus.

Two widely used classification schemes, DDC and LCC, are updated by a central body meant to represent the users, without too much other user participation in decision-making.

J3.5 "Interactive" Updating of Thesauri

In on-line computerized ISAR systems arrangements can be made for indexers and searchers to enter their suggestions for updating the thesaurus immediately via a computer terminal. However, terms and relationships to be included should undergo the editorial process described above in this case, too. This method is particularly useful in ISAR systems that exert terminological control in searching. In such systems the thesaurus grows continually from the inception of the system (rather than being updated at intervals or not being updated at all).

J4 REVISION OF THE INDEXING LANGUAGE OR THE THESAURUS AT LONGER INTERVALS

After a number of years so many changes have accumulated within the thesaurus that the physical presentation becomes more or less unreadable and the logical structure deficient at many places. Then it becomes time for a major revision. The procedure is the same as that described in Chapter F for the construction of a new thesaurus with appropriate modifications. In most cases considerably less effort will be needed for the major revision than for the initial construction. Before undertaking the revision, one should find out whether in the meantime new thesauri or classification schemes or other sources have appeared and decide which ones should be used as sources in the revision.

It is quite possible that new developments require major revisions in the hierarchical structure of the indexing language. To the extent that descriptors are merely rearranged and no descriptors are eliminated or added, the indexing done using the prior indexing language is not affected. On the conceptual level, this is true even if the notational symbols for the descriptors have to be changed. (Compare Section J6, "Problems of re-indexing".)

J5 REMARKS ON THE FLEXIBILITY OF STRUCTURED INDEXING LANGUAGES (CLASSIFICATION SCHEMES)

It is often stated that updating an alphabetical descriptor list or an alphabetically arranged thesaurus is much easier than updating a structured indexing language or classification scheme of the type recommended in this book. From this it is quickly concluded that structured schemes should be discarded in favor of alphabetically arranged thesauri. There is no doubt that updating a structured indexing language requires more effort. Before drawing any conclusions, one has to ask two questions, however: What are the benefits of a structured indexing language? and How much more effort is needed for updating a structured indexing language? We have dealt at length with the first question in Section B5, and we repeat only one key point: The structure of the indexing language is the device that makes sure that the interests and needs of the users are considered in indexing; a well-structured indexing language is essential for the application of the checklist technique of indexing.

In answering the second question the following points have to be considered: It is obviously true that the difficulties in updating such schemes as UDC, DDC, or LCC are enormous. This is a result of the structure of these schemes: They try to express the relationships between numerous compound concepts in a monohierarchy—an impossible task as we have seen in Section C1. Additional difficulties arise from the type of notation used, which is rather inflexible, especially in UDC and DDC. In UDC these difficulties are enhanced by the principle that a notational symbol that has become free through a change in the classified arrangement is not to be re-used for a long period of time. In UDC enormous organizational difficulties are involved on top of all that.

However, these difficulties do not apply to the type of indexing language proposed here, which has a quite different structure and notation:

(a) In Sections C1 and C2 we have seen that the structure of an indexing language or a classification scheme may be best understood as follows: First, there is a core classification consisting of elemental or nearly elemental concepts of a not too specific nature. This core classification can be expanded to an "extended classification" by adding compound concepts or other very specific concepts. However, depending on the ISAR technique used, many compound concepts will not occur in the indexing language at all but will be included only in the lead-in vocabulary. The important point is now the following: Experience shows that the overwhelming majority of modifications and additions affects compound concepts only, that is either the extension part of the scheme or the lead-in vocabulary. In both parts the system is flexible and no serious problems arise from changes. If the core classification has been worked out thoroughly from the beginning it will not require many changes. An example is provided by the Euratom Thesaurus: Changes from 1st ed. (Nov. 63) to 2nd ed. (1966): Among 1,200 "General purpose" core descriptors, a few were discarded and 24 added. The list of non-core descriptors grew from about 1,500 to about 11,000. Data from PRECIS also corroborate the statement.

There is a widespread belief that if a scheme has a hierarchy, this hierarchy must never be changed. This belief is to a large measure not warranted. If a more meaningful hierarchical arrangement is detected, then the hierarchy can and should be changed.

(b) If a flexible system of notation, such as the one described in Section D4.3.3, is used, many changes and additions can be made in the core classification without changing the notations of descriptors already in the core classification. And if notations have to be changed this is quite possible (see Section D4.1.1).

There are serious difficulties arising from changing hierarchy or notation in ISAR systems that arrange documents by subject, be these documents books on shelves or clippings in a clipping file. But for these systems classified arrangement is essential, and the question "alphabetical versus classified" never arises. The only question there is how long to stick with the old hierarchy if a new and better one is found. In other ISAR systems, particularly mechanized systems, changes in the hierarchy create no serious problems.

We conclude that the higher costs involved in updating a structural indexing language are outweighed by the benefits to be derived from a structured indexing language in the ISAR system.

J6 PROBLEMS OF RE-INDEXING (RE-CLASSIFICATION)

This section is concerned with re-indexing that is necessary due to changes within one indexing language or classification, not with re-indexing from one indexing language or classification into another to be discussed in Section K2.

J6.1 Re-Indexing Problems Due to Introduction of New Descriptors

Most problems of re-indexing arise from the introduction of a new descriptor. The new descriptor has not been used in indexing the documents acquired prior to its introduction; therefore, it cannot be used for searching through this part of the collection. The following procedures can be used to solve this problem:

(1) Stipulate that the newly introduced descriptor can be used only for retrieving documents processed after the introduction of the descriptor, and include a statement to that effect in the scope note. Descriptors to be used in searching

for the same topic in the earlier part of the collection should also be given in the scope note. This procedure requires less effort in indexing and correspondingly more effort in searching.

(2) Re-index all documents already in the store. In many cases this is not as impossible a task as it may seem at first. It is often possible to define a search request in terms of the existing descriptors so that only the documents retrieved by that search request have to be considered for re-indexing, whereas all other documents are known not to be relevant for the new descriptor anyway. Such a situation occurs, for example, if an existing descriptor is subdivided into a number of narrower descriptors. One may also provide for newly created terms to be used as "tentative" descriptors in indexing. If a final decision on a new descriptor is made at least some of the relevant documents can then be retrieved by tentative descriptors. Note, however, that one cannot rely on the use of tentative descriptors since they are not part of the indexing language and may therefore easily be omitted in indexing.

(3) In most cases an intermediary solution is to be recommended: Re-indexing is done when the newly introduced descriptor is used the first time for searching the old part of the collection. In this case the relevant documents have to be retrieved some way or other anyway, and re-indexing becomes a by-product of the search.

J6.2 Re-Indexing Problems Due to Changes in Descriptor Usage

If descriptor usage changes, it is obviously a fiction to assume that the descriptor could be used to search the old part of the collection as well as the new part. If the meaning of a descriptor is broadened there may be documents in the old part of the collection that are relevant for the new, broadened meaning but that are not indexed by the descriptor. If the meaning of a descriptor is narrowed down, documents not relevant to the new, narrower meaning will be retrieved. The problem and the possible solutions are the same as described in Section J6.1.

Note that changes in the hierarchy may lead to changes in descriptor usage, if in a more subtle way. If A has been established originally as a descriptor broader than B, then A would be redundant for a document indexed by B; in an inclusive search for A, the documents indexed by the narrower descriptor B will be retrieved anyway. Therefore, if a document has been indexed by B it will not also be indexed by A. If it is detected later on that in searching for A one does not really want to retrieve all or almost all the documents indexed by B, then the hierarchical relationship should be deleted. Those documents indexed by B that should still be retrieved while searching for A must then be indexed by A in addition. (See Section C1.4.1,6 and Section C1.4.6,1 for a more detailed discussion of this problem.)

J7 THESAURUS UPDATING AND THESAURUS COMPATIBILITY: COMMON PROBLEMS (ADVANCED)

The re-indexing problems discussed in the previous section are problems of the compatibility of the old version of an indexing language with the updated version, and of the conversion from one to the other. This is particularly conspicuous when a major revision has taken place. For example, a study has been done on how to search documents indexed by the (old) NASA Subject Authority List using the (new) NASA Thesaurus. The problem is no different from the problem of establishing a searching conversion table or an indexing conversion table between any two indexing languages, to be discussed in Section K2. The degree of compatibility is likely to be high, of course.

We shall encounter the solutions, (1) formulation of the search request in the old indexing language, and (2) re-indexing all documents in the store, again in Section K2 on shared subject indexing where they take the following form: (1) Referral of a search request from information center A to information center B, implying the translation of the search request formulation from indexing language A into indexing language B. (2) Re-indexing of the documents indexed by B, using the indexing language of A. Whether we have re-indexing due to updating or due to shared subject indexing, things are much easier in mechanized than in manual systems.

Another commonality is in the comparison of different indexing languages or thesauri. The basic ideas underlying the typology of changes made in updating as presented in Section J1 are equally valid for the comparison between different indexing languages or thesauri.

The common features of updating and compatibility problems are especially apparent in the use of classification schemes for the collection and presentation of statistical data. The updating problem affects the compatibility of data collected at different times by, for instance, the US Bureau of the Census. The compatibility problem affects the compatibility of data collected by the census bureaus in different countries.

Part IV

Thesauri as a Basis for Cooperation in Information Services

Chapter K

Thesauri as a Basis for Cooperation in Information Services

K0 INTRODUCTION

This is a rather complex subject with many intertwined aspects. This chapter will unfold these aspects as clearly as possible. As usual, it starts with the purposes to be achieved through cooperation. There are two:

(1) *Save work in the construction of indexing languages and thesauri.*
(2) *Share the results of subject indexing.* This can be done in three ways:
(2a) *Referral of search requests.* If a search request cannot be adequately satisfied by information center A, it is also run in information center B (none of the information centers alone may be able to provide an adequate answer). Organizationally, the search in information center B need not be performed by the staff of information center B. It can be initiated and/or performed by the user himself or by the staff of information center A. We may even have a complete duplicate of the catalog (or other retrieval tool) of B available at A (for example, Chemical Abstracts available at a library). In either case the additional search has to be performed in terms of the indexing language of B.

(2b) *Shared subject indexing on a specific level*: document representations prepared by information center B are incorporated into the store of information center A. The descriptors used in indexing by B are converted into the appropriate descriptors of the indexing language of A. In this case only one search has to be performed using the indexing language of A.

(2c) *Shared subject indexing on a general level*: Finally, A may make use of the subject indexing done by B on a very broad generic level. This may take the form of using B's indexing for SDI or for assigning an article to the proper group in an announcement service. It may also simply take the form of B notifying A of articles that fall into a subject category of interest to A, and that A might miss otherwise.

Obviously, both the referral of search requests and shared cataloging

471

are much easier if information centers A and B use the same, or at least highly compatible, indexing languages.

Purpose (1), saving work in the construction of indexing languages and thesauri, is easier to achieve than purpose (2), sharing the results of subject indexing. Therefore, we shall first deal with purpose (1) and develop the concept of a source thesaurus (K1). We shall then see that such a source thesaurus can also contribute to sharing the results of subject indexing but that additional aspects have to be considered if sharing the results of subject indexing is to work properly (K2). And lastly, we shall introduce the idea of a Universal Source Thesaurus (UST) which would take the functions of a universal classification but avoid many of the problems militating against the success of a Universal Classification (K3).

K1 COOPERATION IN THE CONSTRUCTION OF INDEXING LANGUAGES AND THESAURI

Cooperation can be limited to the strictly clerical tasks of material collection and merging information (Steps F1, "Collecting of material" and F2, "Sort into alphabetical order and merge information on identical terms") or it can be extended to the intellectual tasks of actually developing the terminological and classificatory structure. (Steps F3-F5 of thesaurus development.)

K1.1 Cooperation in Material Collection and Merging Only

This may be done on an *ad hoc* basis between two thesaurus development projects that have a large overlap in the sources to be used. The sources in common to both projects are processed as described in Sections F1 and F2. The result is an alphabetic list of terms, and for each term the merged information contained in the sources processed is given. This file is duplicated. Each project now adds its own additional sources and can then proceed to step F3, "Working out the classificatory structure".

If a computer is used a modified and more efficient method can be used. All sources used by either project are processed first. A selective listing is prepared giving all the terms with all the information from all sources used by project 1, and the same for project 2. For the convenience of further processing each listing should be given on thesaurus forms and/or on magnetic tape.

This leads to a more generalized approach. One could set up a data bank containing terms and information on these terms from a great many sources. If someone wants to build a thesaurus, he submits a bibliography of sources to be used. A list of those terms that are contained in any of the sources is then extracted from the data bank; the information given in any of

K1 Cooperation in the Construction Only 473

the sources is included for each term. (This list is identical to the list produced from the original sources using the sorting and merging procedures described in sections F2.1 and F2.2.) If the bibliography contains sources not yet in the data bank, these sources might be processed first for the data bank; otherwise, the thesaurus builder has to process these missing sources himself.

The data bank created and updated in this way is a cumulative thesaurus. The concept of a cumulative thesaurus and the data structure needed for a cumulative thesaurus will be dealt with in detail in Section K1.3.

K1.2 Cooperation in the Development of the Terminological and Classificatory Structure

K1.2.1 Cooperation between two (or a few) institutions

Again, we could have cooperation between just two projects. This means that the two groups join efforts in Steps F3-F5 where the terminological and classifiactory structure is developed. This by no means implies that a common thesaurus has to be developed. In fact, this would be impractical in many cases. Instead, one can proceed as follows: Whenever the groups disagree on a specific point, an appropriate note is made in the common working file. From this file two user versions of the thesaurus, one for each institution, can then easily be produced especially if a computer is used. If there are very few differences, only one user version of the thesaurus could be produced with the differences indicated.

The "qualified USE instructions", discussed in Section C5.5.1, are an example of this.

Example:
Claw
    USE Nail
    VETDOC USE Hoof

K1.2.2 Generalized cooperation: the concept of a source thesaurus (advanced)

If a number of institutions wish to cooperate in this way, the most obvious thing to do is to construct a common thesaurus for all of them. However, as we have seen in the discussion of the checklist technique of indexing, it is absolutely essential that an indexing language or thesaurus be geared specifically to the interests of the user group to be served, and a common thesaurus would in many cases make it impossible for the participating institutions to follow this principle. This is a major obstacle to a universal classification, as will be further expounded in Section K3.0. If a common thesaurus is ruled out for this reason. the best method is to construct a *source thesaurus* from which the indexing languages and thesauri to be used in each institution can then be extracted. A source thesaurus is thus not an indexing tool in itself but rather a data bank from which an indexing tool can be extracted. A source thesaurus contains a recommended or "guidance" structure with respect to terminology and classification. In extracting a thesaurus, this structure can be overriden by other specifications. (The concept of a source thesaurus has essentially been described already by Kyle, who thinks of it as a "do-it-yourself-kit" and who says about the creation of special schemes: "Just as with many 'do-it-yourself kits', the economical and efficient compromise may be to 'do-it-yourself' from professionally prefabricated parts." Kyle gives an illustration using a faceted classification as example. Klingbiel also has seen this problem very clearly: "A National Thesaurus of any real depth would surely be a multi-volume compendium. As such it could not function as an effective indexing or search tool for anyone. A National Thesaurus, therefore, must be thought of as an authoritative reference from which selected subsets, in the form of agency (specialized subject area) thesauri, would be drawn, uniquely tailored to the document collection it is to serve, yet compatible with all other microthesauri since all would draw from the same source." This quote already alludes to the concept of a Universal Source Thesaurus, to be discussed in Section K3.)

The construction of a source thesaurus does not differ from the construction of any other thesaurus, except that no descriptors are selected from among the preferred terms. Descriptor selection is determined by the specific task to which an indexing language is to be put and is therefore part of the extraction of an indexing language for a specific institution. A source thesaurus can be constructed starting from a data bank cumulating the information contained in a number of sources such as other classification schemes and thesauri, as described in Section K1.1. Whereas in Section K1.1 we merely accumulated information from a number of sources, we now have to work out the recommended structure of the thesaurus (Steps F3-F5 of thesaurus development). Especially, decisions in the following areas are necessary:

(1) Definition of classes of Synonymous and Equivalent Terms (quasi-synonymous) and selection of preferred terms representing each class.

(2) What BT/NT and RT relationships are to be part of the recommended structure. In particular, each concept would be expressed by a combination of elemental concepts.

(3) Working out a monohierarchical structure for the printing of the recommended or guidance classificatory structure.

Once constructed, a source thesaurus can be used to extract indexing languages (classification schemes) or thesauri for special applications, at the same time making all modifications required by the situation in which the extracted indexing language is to be used. The indexing language extracted may be broad in scope, e.g., for a general library, or very specialized, e.g., for a specialized information analysis center. Similarly a source thesaurus can be used in the revision of existing specialized indexing languages or thesauri. Efficient methods for extraction and revision are described in Section K1.2.2.,2 and K1.4, respectively.

A source thesaurus would not only reduce the effort in constructing new indexing languages for specific applications and increase the quality of such new indexing languages but it would also lead to increased similarity and, therefore, compatibility between indexing languages constructed with its help. If a source thesaurus is used for the revision of two existing indexing languages, it may lead to an increase in their compatibility, too. This increase in compatibility is not achieved by forcing everyone into a straightjacket but by avoiding unnecessary and unfunctional differences. On the other hand, there are fortunate situations where it is possible to develop a common thesaurus for a number of institutions and thereby enable unimpeded shared subject indexing as described in Sections K2.3.1 and K3.3.

Cooperation in the development of the terminological and conceptual structure need not be an all-out affair. A participating institution may decide to develop from scratch those parts of the thesaurus that pertain to its main subject field and use the source thesaurus for marginal areas only. If all participating institutions want to proceed that way it is sufficient to keep the source thesaurus on a rather broad level; it could then be called an "umbrella thesaurus" (for details see Section K2.4). Furthermore, areas such as bibliographic descriptors, geographical names, and nomenclatures are more amenable to standardization than others, and it is therefore useful to develop "adjunct thesauri" for such areas cooperatively. These adjunct thesauri can then be used by each participating institution. Adjunct thesauri will be discussed in detail in Section K1.2.3.

The following sections deal with the structure of a source thesaurus (K1.2,1) and the highly technical question of how to extract indexing languages and thesauri for special application (K1.2.2,2).

,1 The structure of a source thesaurus.

(1) A source thesaurus should be a cumulative thesaurus; that means, it should contain the appropriate source information (a) for the thesauri and other sources that served as input into the construction phase *and* (b) for the thesauri that have been extracted (with new information coming from the modifications that have been introduced) *and* (c) for the thesauri that have been revised using the source thesaurus. A source thesaurus thus becomes more complete and more useful as it is used.

(2) A source thesaurus must contain concepts down to the deepest level of specificity needed by any one of the cooperating institutions. Otherwise it would not be possible to extract a complete indexing language for each institution or to use the source thesaurus as a switching language.

(3) The information for each preferred term should be as complete as needed by any of the cooperating institutions. Scope notes, in particular, should be added whenever appropriate.

(4) A monohierarchical structure should be marked out so that the recommended classificatory structure (guidance classification) can be printed out. In fact, one might work out two arrangements; one subject-oriented, the other based on facets.

A source thesaurus is not tied to any specific ISAR system. Therefore, it does not specify which of the preferred terms are to be descriptors and which are to be in the lead-in vocabulary only. Consequently, there are no USE instructions. There are only SEE instructions from non-preferred synonyms to the appropriate preferred term, and even these can be omitted if the alphabetical index method for lead-in is used. Descriptors are selected and the appropriate USE instructions are introduced as a thesaurus for a specific application is extracted. Preferred terms from the source thesaurus that are not used as descriptors may still be included together with their synonyms in the lead-in vocabulary.

Example:
Source thesaurus, classified index:
   Aircraft
      Airplanes
         Subsonic airplanes
         Supersonic airplanes
      Helicopter
Source thesaurus, main part:
   Aircraft
      BT   :Vehicles
      and :Air transport
(The ":" designates Broader Terms that are semantic factors).
Thesaurus A may use all concepts as descriptors. Thesaurus B may give:
   Supersonic airplanes
      USE BT Airplanes
Theasurus C may give:
   Supersonic airplanes
      SEE BT Airplanes
      USE BT Aircraft

Thesaurus D may even give:
>Aircraft
>>USE BT :Vehicles
>>and :Air transport

(*i.e., use the combination of the descriptors Vehicles and Air transport to index documents on Aircraft*).

A related problem is illustrated by the following.
Source thesaurus:
>Locomotive engines
>>BT :Vehicles
>>and :Rail transport
>>and :Engines

Thesaurus D:
Rail transport is not a descriptor and Ground transport is to be used instead; therefore, we have:
>Locomotive engines
>>SEE BT :Vehicles
>>and :Rail transport
>>and :Engines
>>USE BT :Vehicles
>>and :Ground transport
>>:Engines

,2 Extraction of indexing languages or thesauri for special applications from a source thesaurus. There are two methods of extraction, *specific extraction* and *general extraction*.

In specific extraction the segments or even the individual terms to be extracted, terms to be added, and the sequence in which all these elements are to be arranged are exactly specified in an "extraction specification". To put it in another way: the source thesaurus is considered a series of building blocks that can be taken out and put together in any way. A format that can be used for specific extraction is shown in Section ,2.1.

In general extraction one simply asks for an indexing language or thesaurus for, say, a "medium-sized political science collection", and the system extracts an appropriate indexing language and thesaurus. Details of general extraction are discussed in ,2.2.

Finally a source thesaurus can be used in the revision of existing indexing languages and thesauri as discussed in ,2.3. All the methods are described with a view to computer processing. However, some of the functions could also be performed manually.

,2.1 Specific extraction of indexing languages from a source thesaurus.
In this method a guidance classification (in either a faceted or a more tradi-

tional arrangement) is first printed out in whole or in selected parts. Since concepts up to a high level of specificity should be included in a source thesaurus, it would seldom be practical to print the whole guidance classification. One may print out, for example, "the part *Electrical engineering* and concepts from other fields important for *Electrical engineering*, in faceted arrangement". One may do the same for the field of psychology. The command may also be given to "omit very specific concepts" (very specific concepts are marked as such in the source thesaurus and there is no absolutely fixed relationship between hierarchical level and being very specific.)

Based on this printout an "extraction specification" is written using a simple format described in Section ,2.1.1. Note that any modification desired can be included in this specification: the order of facets or of subject fields or the order of subfields within a subject field or the sequence of the sons of the same father can be changed. Concepts can be deleted or new concepts can be added. All these changes are very easy due to the format used in writing the specification. The major question is, of course, what modifications should be made in the first place. This has to be determined by a careful study of user needs, by collection of actual and expected search requests and by discussion of the scheme with the users.

The extraction specification is then processed by a computer program resulting in the following products:

(a) The classified index (or the schedule) as specified. A tentative notation reflecting the specified arrangement has been assigned by the computer program.

(b) The main part of the specialized thesaurus containing for each term all information available in the source thesaurus, such as Synonymous and Equivalent Terms, additional Broader and Narrower Terms, scope note.

(c) An alphabetical index.

The main part should now be studied in detail in order to determine whether the information contained in it is acceptable and sufficient. Again, all desired modifications can be entered in a specialized format. The classified index should also be checked because it is now easier to see whether it really reflects the needs of the specific environment.

The modifications are entered into the computer which thereupon produces final versions of (a)-(c).

Instead of starting with the guidance classification scheme developed for the source thesaurus at hand, one might start with any classification scheme that has been used as a source in building the source thesaurus and use the same procedure.

,2.1.1 Format for "extraction specifications" (technical). The format is explained using an example which is simple yet elaborate enough to show the potentialities of the method. The guidance classification is given in Figure

66. Two examples of an extraction specification and the resulting classified index are shown in Figures 67 and 68. The figures do not show the main part and the alphabetical index.

This format addresses only one problem, the extraction of the classified index (the schedules). It is given to represent the general idea. In any real implementation more elaborate rules would have to be worked out. For example, one might want to include a concept, but not as descriptor, etc.

,2.2 General extraction of indexing languages from a source thesaurus. Specific extraction is somewhat cumbersome. It would be much more convenient if one could extract simply an indexing language for, say, a "medium-sized political science collection". As is well known one needs descriptors from fields other than political science in order to index such a collection properly. For example, terms from psychology are also needed. Also, for a big political science collection, more terms from psychology are needed than for a medium-sized political science collection. Basically, this is a retrieval problem. We want to retrieve all descriptors necessary to index a medium-sized political science collection. In order to do so we first have to tag the descriptors accordingly. This could be done as follows: Define, for example; five levels of specificity, 1-5. 3 may designate the level of specificity needed for a medium-sized collection. Therefore, each descriptor needed to index a medium-sized political science collection is tagged as *Political science 3*. Note that this descriptor will be needed in indexing a bigger collection anyway so that it is not necessary to tag it as *Political science 4* as well. It should be clear that a number of terms from psychology, economics, sociology, and other fields are tagged as *Political science 3*. The same term from psychology might be tagged as *Psychology 1*, meaning that this term is necessary to index a small psychology collection. While searching for *Political science 3*, we have to retrieve all descriptors tagged as *Political science 2* or *Political science 1* as well. We might also specify that our collection consists of a medium-sized political science collection and a medium to small sociology collection in which case we would search for *Political science 3* OR *Sociology 2*. The appropriate place to store these subject field and level indications is data field 41, "Subject field" of Figure 21, Section C7. The considerations of this section could be reformulated as follows: a source thesaurus comprises many specialized indexing languages that can be extracted on demand. This is more economical than storing many specialized indexing languages separately.

,2.3 Use of a source thesaurus in the revision of existing indexing languages and thesauri. Essentially this means "pulling" information from the source thesaurus for each term in the existing thesaurus by the matching and merging process described in Section F2.2.1. After this step manual editing is required. A detailed procedure is described in Section K1.4. As the existing

WU		DOCUMENT REPRODUCTION
WU2		*Photocopying*
WU3		Basic photocopying techniques
WU4		Direct photocopying
WU5		Reflex photocopying
WUA		Photographic photocopying
WUB		Silver halide processes
WUJ		Diazo process
WUL		Thermography
WUN		Adherography
WUQ		Dual spectrum process
WUR		Infrared reflex process
WUS		Infrared transfer process
WUT		Infrared sublimation process
WUV		Electrostatic copying
WUX		Xerography
WUY		Electrofax
WV		*Microphotography*
WV2		Microforms
WV3		Flat microforms
WV4		Microtransparencies
WV9		Microopaques
WVD		Roll microforms
WVE		Microfilm
WVG		Microform equipment
WVH		Microfilm cameras
WVHB		Planetary microfilm cameras
WVHE		Rotary microfilm cameras
WVHM		Step and repeat microfilm cameras
WVI		Microform processors
WVJ		Microform mounters
WV		Microform printers
WVM		Microform readers
WVQ		Micropublishing
WVS		*Duplicating*
WVT		Carbon copy duplicating
WVU		Stencil duplicating
WVV		Typing stencils
WVV1		Writing on stencils
WVV2		Electronic stencil cutting
WVW		Spirit duplication

Figure 66. Sample guidance classification scheme of a source thesaurus (K1.2.2, 2.1.1). (Taken from Thesaurofacet, with modifications.) (Courtesy English Electric Co. Ltd., Whetstone, Leicester LE8 3LH, England, and American Society for Information Science.)

a: Extraction specification

	Comment:
WU#111	Take WU itself and all the descriptors being one or two levels below (each 1 after # stands for one level, the first level being WU itself)
*NOTATION TYPE 1	Assign notation of type 1, using range K00-K99
USE K00-K99	

b: Resulting classified index with tentative notation

K00 DOCUMENT REPRODUCTION
  K30 *Photocopying*
    K32 Basic photocopying techniques
    K34 Photographic photocopying
    K36 Thermography
    K38 Electrostatic copying
  K50 *Microphotography*
    K53 Microforms
    K55 Microform equipment
    K57 Micropublishing
  K70 *Duplicating*
    K73 Carbon copy duplicating
    K75 Stencil duplicating
    K77 Spirit duplication

Figure 67. Simple extraction specification and resulting classified index (K1.2.2, 2.1.1). (Courtesy American Society for Information Science.)

thesaurus is processed, the source thesaurus is updated. Where the two are in agreement, the appropriate source code is added in the source thesaurus; new information contained in the existing thesaurus is added to the source thesaurus. New synonyms designating concepts already in the source thesaurus and terms designating new concepts are added to the source thesaurus, thus increasing its usefulness for the processing of further schemes. The effort needed for manual editing after the computer processing of the existing thesaurus against the cumulative source thesaurus will thus decrease with every new thesaurus processed.

K1.2.3 Adjunct thesauri

Some areas or facets are more amenable to standardization and uniform treatment than others. It would be foolish to develop a new scheme for such areas in each thesaurus construction project.

a: Extraction specification

Instruction No.		Comments
1	WU#1	Take WU itself
2	WVS#11 (WU,01)	Starting one level below WU (therefore '(WU,01)') take WVS and all descriptors one level below
3	WU2#111	Starting on the same level as WVS, take WU2 with all descriptors one or two levels below
4	(/WUBa,01/)	( ) signifies a modification. Between / / the place is given. Here something has to be inserted after WUB (therefore 'WUBa'), starting one level below WUB (therefore ',01')
	Photostat process	
	Photostabilization process	This is the block to be inserted
	Direct positive process	
	Diffusion transfer process	
	Gelatin transfer process)	
5	(/WUN-WUT/==)	Take the block starting with WUN and ending with WUT and eliminate it (== stands for a block containing nothing, replacing the original block)
6	WV#2	Starting on the same level as WU2 take WV and all narrower descriptors ('#2')
7	(/WV3-WVE,1/)	Take the block WV2-WVE and replace it by the following block, starting on the level of WV3 (therefore ',1')
	Microtransparencies	Replacing block. Note that indentations signifying hierarchy are allowed in writing blocks
	Microfilm (roll)	
	Flat microtransparencies	
	Microfiches	
	Aperture cards	
	Film strips	
	Microopaques)	
8	*NOTATION TYPE 1 USE K00-K99	Assign notation of type 1, using range K00-K99

Figure 68. More elaborate extraction specification and resulting classified index (K1.2.2, 2.1.1). (Courtesy American Society for Information Science.)

Figure 68. (Continued)

b: Resulting classified index

K00 DOCUMENT REPRODUCTION
  K20 *Duplicating*   This division has
    K23 Carbon copy duplicating   been moved from the
    K25 Stencil duplicating   bottom to the top
    K27 Spirit duplication   (instruction no. 2)
  K30 *Photocopying*
    K35 Basic photocopying techniques
      K37 Direct photocopying
      K38 Reflex photocopying
    K40 Photographic photocopying
      K42 Silver halide processes
        K42.2 Photostat process
        K42.4 Photostabilization process   Insert (instruction
        K42.5 Direct positive process   no. 4)
        K42.7 Diffusion transfer process
        K42.8 Gelatin transfer process
      K44 Diazo process
      K46 Thermography   Omission (instruc-
      K48 Electrostatic copying   tion no. 5)
        K48.3 Xerography
        K48.5 Electrofax
  K50 *Microphotography*
    K60 Microforms
      K62 Microtransparencies
        K63 Microfilm (roll)
        K64 Flat microtransparencies   Replacement
          K65 Microfiches   (instruction no. 7)
          K66 Aperture cards
          K67 Film strips
      K68 Microopaques
    K70 Microform equipment
      K72 Microfilm cameras
        K72.3 Planetary microfilm cameras
        K72.5 Rotary microfilm cameras
        K72.7 Step and repeat microfilm cameras
      K74 Microform processors
      K75 Microform mounters
      K77 Microform printers
      K78 Microform readers
    K85 Micropublishing

K   Thesauri as a Basis for Cooperation

Examples:
Form descriptors (bibliographical descriptors)
Concepts of general application
Chemical compounds
Names of plants and animals
Geographical names
Role indicators and/or relators.

For such areas the procedures described in Section K1.2.2 are particularly appropriate, and usually extraction without much modification will be sufficient.

These considerations give rise to the definition of the concept of an "adjunct thesaurus". An adjunct thesaurus is defined by the following characteristics:

(a) It deals with a specific facet that is relatively "closed", i.e., there are not many relationships between concepts within the facet and concepts outside the facet (the concepts within the facets may be combined with concepts from other facets without any restriction). It follows that an adjunct thesaurus may be added to another thesaurus without requiring major changes in the structure and in the relationships between concepts either in the adjunct thesaurus or in the main thesaurus.

(b) An adjunct thesaurus cannot be used independently of a main thesaurus.

There are two ways of using an adjunct thesaurus: Implicit inclusion and explicit inclusion.

(1) In *implicit inclusion* one simply declares that the adjunct thesaurus is a part of the thesaurus and uses the adjunct thesaurus as available, for example, in published form. This saves a lot of work in the preparation of the thesaurus because it is not necessary to type or otherwise process the elements of the adjunct thesaurus. In many systems, particularly in systems using subject headings, implicit inclusion is often by a general note, for example, "subdivide by place", without an adjunct thesaurus of place names actually being given. As the reader may have gathered implicit inclusion is most appropriate for proper names and elements of nomenclatures. For the classified index and the main part there are no disadvantages with implicit inclusion: The indexers know that this part of the hierarchy is to be found in the adjunct thesaurus. The only disadvantage is that one has two alphabetical indexes, e.g., a general alphabetical index not including chemical compounds and an alphabetical index for chemical compounds (as available in the published adjunct thesaurus).

(2) In *explicit inclusion* one includes explicitly all the terms contained in the adjunct thesaurus in the thesaurus to be built, preserving as far as possible the hierarchy and the notation of the adjunct thesaurus (see Section D4.4.1 for the notational problems involved).

Implicit inclusion is possible only if one agrees completely or almost completely with a given adjunct thesaurus, for example, with a nomenclature for the designation of chemical compounds or a nomenclature of hierarchical species or a classification of bibliographical forms. Preferably one should select nomenclatures that are internationally accepted. Explicit inclusion allows for modifications in the adjunct thesaurus. Actually explicit inclusion is only a special case of using another thesaurus as a source.

Obviously, the acceptance of an adjunct thesaurus by two institutions means high compatibility of their indexing languages at least in that specific area.

The following two sections, K1.3 and K1.4, deal with the special problems of a cumulative thesaurus and its application in the revision of indexing languages and thesauri. Due to the complexity of the files required only procedures using computer assistance are considered. The technical considerations contained in Sections F0.7, "Source indications" and F0.8, "Keeping track of decisions and dates" as well as in Chapter G, "Use of computers in thesaurus construction", and especially Section G0.3, "Record organization in the computer", are necessary to understand these sections.

K1.3 The Concept of a Cumulative Thesaurus (Advanced)

K1.3.0 Definition and use

A cumulative thesaurus is a thesaurus that cumulates the information contained in a number of thesauri or classification schemes serving as sources in its construction. Its distinguishing characteristics are:

(1) Every minute detail from every source is retained so that each source can be reconstructed.

(2) Commonalities among different sources are exhibited and utilized to reduce the storage space needed.

A cumulative thesaurus may contain a recommended or "guidance" structure. In the following we assume a cumulative thesaurus with a recommended structure.

A cumulative thesaurus can be used simply as a data base bringing together several sources as discussed in Section K1.1, or it can be used as a source thesaurus for extracting specific indexing languages for thesauri, thus using the recommended structure too. Section K2.3.2 will discuss the use of a cumulative thesaurus for the extraction of conversion tables between pairs of indexing languages and as a guide to information centers likely to have information on a specific topic. A cumulative thesaurus can also be used to print out any specific thesaurus that has been used as a source in its construction, either in the form of the complete working file or in the form of the user version.

K   Thesauri as a Basis for Cooperation

In order that a cumulative thesaurus can serve these purposes it has to meet the following requirements:

(a) For each concept each source is given together with the preferred term used in that source in the exact form in which it is used in that source. (The sources are important if one wants to know which institutions to approach for material on a certain subject and the exact form of the term is important for the formulation of a search request.)

(b) In the entry for each concept all data elements contained in any of the sources are given. In cross-references the exact form of the term used in the source is given. (This is done so that each source can be printed out.)

(c) Information on decisions and dates, as described in Section F0.8, is given for each source separately. (Again, this is needed for printing out a specific source.)

(d) The recommended structure is clearly marked.
(For further considerations see Section K3.1, "The structure of UST.")

With the increase in cooperation between information services and the simultaneous use of several data bases, cumulative thesauri become more and more important. It is, therefore, worthwhile to consider their organization in some detail.

K1.3.1   Record organization for a cumulative thesaurus (technical)

The record organization described in Section G0.3 and the procedures for keeping track of the sources and of decisions and dates described in Sections F0.7 and F0.8 respectively, provide all the machinery that is needed to accommodate all the detailed data described in the previous section. This section shows how this can be done.

,1 **Treatment of the recommended structure and of source indications in a cumulative thesaurus.**

,1.1 **Treatment of the recommended structure.** First each data element belonging to the recommended structure must be clearly marked. The preferred term, as well as the form of a term used in a cross-reference, can be seen immediately from the way they are entered in the record; they are marked implicitly. Other data elements must be marked explicitly. The most direct way to do so is to treat the recommended structure in the same way as any other source and identify each data element in it by a source indication. However, this would have disadvantages with respect to both storage space and processing. Therefore, data field E, "Recommended structure indicator", is included in the subrecord format. E is '1' if the data element is included in the recommended structure and '0' otherwise.

,1.2 **Group of data fields F-L.** Next, recall from Section G0.3 that the data fields

    G   Cross-reference status indicator,

K1 Cooperation in the Construction Only

H Cross-reference printing indicator,
I Instruction (e.g., USE) or statement (e.g., UF) indicator,
K Type of term indicator, and
L Form of term indicator

are specific for each source and, therefore, form a group with the data field F "Source indication". In the first group field F always contains a pointer to a place where the source indications can be found, and fields G-L refer to the recommended structure unless the recommended structure indicator (field E) is 0, in which case fields G-L are empty. In fact, field I in the first group will be mostly empty since instructions like USE and statements like UF are usually not part of a recommended structure unless a thesaurus following that structure is actually used by an ISAR system.

,1.3 Use of the data fields C1, K, and L for increasing the precision of source indications. The first problem to be dealt with is this: if a source contains several terms designating a concept, which term is used as the preferred term in that source? Field K, "Type of term indicator" is used for that purpose.

Example:
  Source ZX
     Attorney
        UF ST Lawyer
  Source WH
     Lawyer
        UF ST Attorney
Record in the cumulative thesaurus:

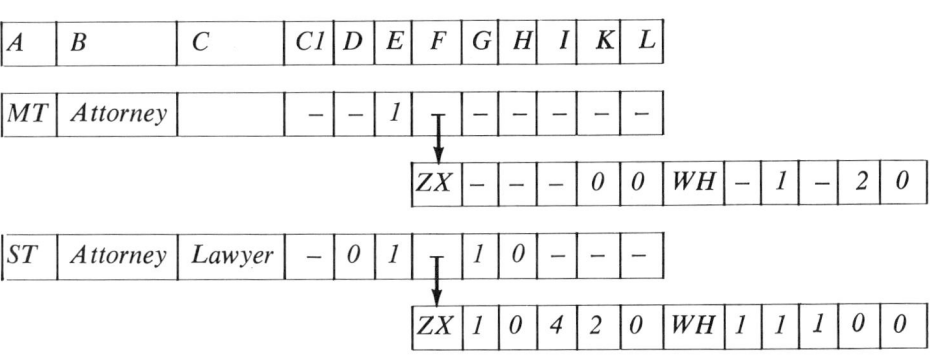

(A dash in a data field means that the content of that field is not of interest in the discussion at hand.)

The Main Term *Attorney* has a group of fields F-L for source ZX and field K is 0 to indicate that *Attorney* is descriptor in source ZX. For source WH, field is 2 to indicate that *Attorney* is a nonpreferred term in source WH. With the Synonymous Term *Lawyer* it is just the other way around.

The second problem is the treatment of spelling variants. The simplest solution is to treat spelling variants in the same way as synonyms. However, the connection between different forms of a term would be lost. A more sophisticated method makes use of the pointer field C1.

Example:
Let us assume the entry in source WH is as follows:
   Lawyers
      UF ST Attorney
The second subrecord would then be modified as follows:

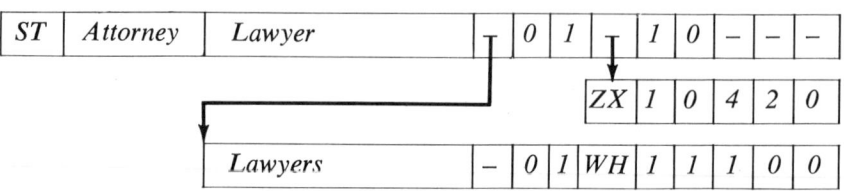

The C1-field in the "daughter subrecord" for *Lawyers* could point to another spelling variant. One might also put a pointer in field F rather than giving the source code in order to be consistent with the parent subrecord.

Actually, in the case where the variation in spelling concerns only singular and plural, a simpler procedure is possible; in the source indications for the second subrecord write:

| WH | – | – | – | 0 | 2 |

The '2' in field L form of term indicates that source WH uses plural; it is not necessary to create a daughter subrecord. Other morphological variations can possibly be dealt with in the same way.

The third problem is how to show the exact form of a term in a cross-reference as it is used in a source so that any specific thesaurus can be printed.

Example:
   Source KT
      Judge
         RT Attorney
   Source WH
      Judge
         RT Lawyer
One might do with

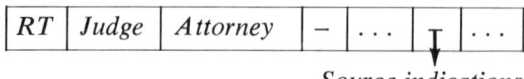

Source indications

Looking up *Attorney*, one would find out that in source WH *Lawyer* is the preferred term. However, this is cumbersome for processing. If one is willing to use more storage space, one can use the pointer field C1 and create a daughter subrecord.

Example:

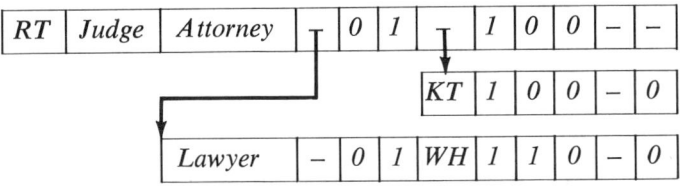

,1.4 Further refinements. One might want to distinguish in the source indication between the following two cases:

(1) The source institution suggested or already used the term or the concept in question.

(2) The source institution included that concept in its thesaurus through the mediation of the cumulative thesaurus. The format for source indications would have to be amended accordingly.

,2 Keeping track of decisions and dates in a cumulative thesaurus. Decisions and dates must be kept for the recommended structure as well as for each source. Since information on decision and dates is source-specific, it is always preceded by the appropriate source code. The format used for decision indicator strings is described in Section F0.8.1,1. If the string pertains to a record as a whole, it is put into a separate subrecord. In this case the information on decision and dates pertains to the record as valid for the source preceding the decision indicator string, omitting data elements not marked by the code of that source. If the decision indicator string pertains to a specific data element only it follows the appropriate source indication for that data element.

For the purpose of keeping track of decisions and dates, the recommended structure is treated as a source with a source code like all other sources. If such information has to be given for a specific data element, a separate group of fields F-L is needed. It is not necessary to keep the date when a data element has been entered into the cumulative thesaurus because that can be seen from the sources.

K1.3.2 Development of a cumulative thesaurus

The development of a cumulative thesaurus from a number of sources is basically no different from the construction of any other thesaurus as described in Chapter F, except that keeping track of the sources has to be more careful and elaborate, as discussed in the previous section. A slightly different problem arises if an additional source has to be worked in later on. The procedure described in Section K1.4, or a simplified version of this procedure, can be used for this task.

It is also possible to proceed as follows: At the beginning consider source 1 as the cumulative thesaurus. Incorporate source 2. Consider the result as the cumulative thesaurus. Incorporate source 3, etc. If a number of sources are known from the beginning it is usually more efficient to process all these sources together as described in Chapter F.

In editing and updating a cumulative thesaurus no relationship taken from a source can be deleted or changed. "Deletion" then means, in effect, to set the recommended structure indicator (field E) to 0. Change in a relationship indicator means: set the recommended structure indicator in the original relationship to 0, create a new subrecord for the relationship as changed; in the new subrecord set the recommended structure indicator to 1 and give the appropriate source indication (who suggested the change?); in both subrecords, set the additional relationship indicator (field D) to 1.

K1.3.3 Display of a cumulative thesaurus

The user version of a cumulative thesaurus must serve the same purposes as the user version of any other thesaurus. Therefore, the considerations dealt with in Chapter D apply. The classified index of a cumulative thesaurus would follow the recommended classificatory structure.

The most important additional function of the user version of a cumulative thesaurus is to show the searcher looking up a certain concept what descriptor(s) to use in each source and what the exact form of the descriptor is. One way to achieve this is as follows: after the Main Term (heading of an entry) insert for each source a line of the form

Source: Descriptor in source.

The source should be given in an abbreviation that can be immediately recognized by the user. If the descriptors are the same in all or almost all sources, many lines can be replaced by the following.

Example:
  All sources
or
  All sources except
    Source: Descriptor in source.

In order not to confuse the user, it would seem best to omit any further source indications. However, in many cases the searcher should know which of the hierarchical relationships given in the cumulative thesaurus are used in a given indexing language that has been incorporated in the cumulative thesaurus. One may either include source indications for data elements in data fields BT and NT or else refer the user to the user version of the specific

K1 Cooperation in the Construction Only 491

thesaurus. A more satisfactory solution can be achieved through on-line display.

K1.4 Incorporation of an Additional Thesaurus into a Cumulative Thesaurus and/or Analysis and Improvement of That Thesaurus Using a Cumulative Thesaurus (Advanced and Technical)

In Chapters F and G we discussed procedures to construct a new indexing language or thesaurus from a number of sources that are processed simultaneously. Here we deal with two other tasks that occur often and that require very similar procedures. First, we may want to simply incorporate an additional thesaurus into a cumulative thesaurus. Second, we may have a specific indexing language or thesaurus for a specific institution that needs revision. For this revision we can use the information contained in a cumulative thesaurus. At the same time, the cumulative thesaurus can be updated, taking in new information provided by the specific indexing language or thesaurus processed. The following procedure performs both tasks at once. It can be simplified if only one task is to be performed. Some of the procedures could be performed manually, while others require computer assistance.

Step 1: *Preparation of the thesaurus to be incorporated* (This step corresponds to F1.2.1, "Preparation of sources".)

Introduce inverse cross-references within the thesaurus to be processed. This is done for two reasons. First, new Main Terms may turn up. Secondly, this makes sure that for every cross-reference added to the cumulative thesaurus the inverse cross-reference is added, too.

Step 2: *Match terms and merge information* (This step corresponds to F2, "Sort into alphabetical order and merge information on identical terms", especially F2.2.3, "pulling information from additional sources".)

Look up each preferred term in the cumulative thesaurus, and "pull" information from the cumulative thesaurus through the matching and merging procedure described in Sections F2.2.3 and G2.2.3. In case the thesaurus to be processed does not have a detailed distinction in its cross-reference (for example, confounds NT and RT as "see also"), the proper distinction can be obtained from the cumulative thesaurus. Also, if the thesaurus/indexing language to be revised does not have a classified arrangement, pertinent information can be extracted from the cumulative thesaurus and a tentative classified arrangement can be printed. Information from the thesaurus being processed which is not contained in the cumulative thesaurus is transferred there tentatively. The following files are created as a result of this step:

File 1: The thesaurus to be processed with the additions extracted from the cumulative thesaurus.

File 2: Preferred terms for which no record can be found in the cumulative thesaurus.

File 3: Records found in the cumulative thesaurus that have been changed by transferring information from the thesaurus being processed.

File 1 is printed for further editing; the complete working file, a classified index and an alphabetical index are printed. New cross-references that have been introduced by inversion in Step 1 and modifications and additions taken from the cumulative thesaurus are flagged appropriately in this printout.

File 2 is printed for further processing in Step 3. File 3 is also printed for editing.

File 1 and file 3 can now be edited and the resulting corrections inserted into the thesaurus processed and the cumulative thesaurus, respectively. Alternatively, one can postpone printing and editing of files 1 and 3 until at least parts of Step 3 have been performed.

Step 3: *Process the preferred terms not found in the cumulative thesaurus* (File 2) (This step corresponds to F3, "Work out the preliminary structure of the thesaurus" and partly also to F4, "Work out first draft of the classified index" and F5, "Complete first draft of the thesaurus as a whole".)

First determine for each of the remaining preferred terms whether the cumulative thesaurus contains a synonym not detected in the pulling procedure. The hierarchical structure and the classified arrangement of the cumulative thesaurus can be used for that purpose. For example, we might have the source term *Lawrence tubes* with the Broader Term *TV color picture tubes*. Looking in the cumulative thesaurus under *TV color picture tubes*, we find a number of Narrower Terms, among them *Chromatrons*. Either from knowledge or from a dictionary we find that this is a synonym of *Lawrence tubes*. We can now pull the records for all terms for which synonyms have been identified and update files 1-3 before we proceed further. This might be a good point to print and edit files 1 and 3.

The preferred terms from the source scheme that still remain have to be worked into the recommended structure of the cumulative thesaurus. If part of the revision task is to create or revise the hierarchical structure of the indexing language being processed these terms have to be placed into the tentative classified arrangement produced in step 2, and additional Broader and Narrower Terms have to be identified.

It is possible to partially mechanize this step by assigning a combination of elemental concepts to each preferred term and derive hierarchical relationships therefrom, as described in Section G3.4.2. The procedure for this option is as follows:

Step 3a: *Express the preferred terms contained in file 2 by combinations of elemental concepts*

This is usually done manually but computer assistance can be used, as described in Section G3.4.3 (the reader is advised to re-read that section). Since the file where components of composite or multi-word terms are looked up is the cumulative thesaurus we have an advantage over the case of Section G3.4.3: for each component, we find not only an appropriate preferred term but also a combination of elemental concepts; both are included in the list of suggested semantic factors. We can also take Broader, Narrower, and Related Terms from the thesaurus being processed, look them up in the cumulative thesaurus and find a combination of elemental concepts. After all this information has been extracted and inserted into file 2, file 2 is printed for editing. The editing refers mainly to the concept combination assigned but deals also with the rest of each record (these records were not included in file 1 and have therefore not been edited in step 2).

Step 3b: *Use the concept combinations to detect synonyms and hierarchical relationships* (as described in Section G3.4.2)

Given the concept combinations assigned to a term, one can look for a term with the same concept combination in the cumulative thesaurus. Such a term is likely to be a synonym. Furthermore, the concept combination can be used for a thorough analysis of the hierarchical structure of the thesaurus being processed as follows: Create all Broader, Narrower and Related Term cross-references that can be derived from the concept combination according to the rules discussed in Section C1.3 (it is possible to include in this step *all* the preferred terms from the thesaurus to be processed). For each preferred term the list of relationships derived from the concept combination is now merged into the original record. Each relationship is marked as belonging to one of the following groups:

—both original and derived;
—only original;
—only derived.

This new file 4 can then be used for editing. For example, a concept combination assigned to a term may lead to a hierarchical relationship that is not in the original thesaurus and that does not make sense either. In this case we probably have a homonym that is used in one meaning in the thesaurus being processed and in another meaning in the cumulative thesaurus. Or we might have the following case: the term is a homonym and it is included in the cumulative thesaurus in all of its meanings. Consequently, several concept combinations have been pulled in Step 2. There should be one concept combination that leads to hierarchical relationships that are in agreement with the original hierarchical relationships or make sense otherwise. The proper meaning of the term in the thesaurus being processed can thereby be determined. All decisions made in editing have to be inserted into the thesaurus being processed. The result is the final improved version of the thesaurus.

Step 4: *Final comparison with the cumulative thesaurus*

The final revised thesaurus should now be compared again with the cumulative thesaurus. Information flow in this step is one-directional from the final version of the improved thesaurus into the cumulative thesaurus. The records of the cumulative thesaurus that have been changed in this procedure are printed out so that they are edited properly.

K2 COOPERATION THROUGH SHARING THE RESULTS OF SUBJECT INDEXING (SPECIAL TOPIC)

Recall from the introduction of Chapter K that there are three ways to share the results of subject indexing:

(a) *Referral of search requests*: If a search request cannot be answered adequately by information center A, it is also processed in information center B. None of the information centers alone may be able to provide an adequate answer.

Organizationally, the search of the store of information center B need not be performed by the staff of information center B; it can be initiated and/or performed by the user himself or by the staff of information center A (A may have available for this purpose a complete duplicate of the catalog or other searching tools of B; for example, a library may have available Chemical Abstracts). In either case the search request formulation has to be converted from the indexing language A into indexing language B.

(b) *Shared subject indexing on a specific level*: Document representations prepared by information center B are incorporated into the store of information center A. The descriptors used in indexing by B are converted into the appropriate descriptors of the indexing language of A. In this case only one search has to be performed, using indexing language A.

(c) *Shared subject indexing on a general level*: Document representations prepared by B are used by A for SDI or for assigning the document to the appropriate group in an announcement service but not for retrospective searching involving specific descriptors. Or the document representations prepared by B are simply used to determine whether or not the document falls into the scope of A.

Referral of search requests and shared subject indexing on a specific level will be discussed in more detail below, shared subject indexing on a general level in Section K2.4.

Sharing the results of subject indexing is dependent upon the compatibility of the indexing languages used. (Incidentally, compatibility is even more important if one wants to compare, for example, census data, since the very definition of the data is dependent on the definition of the descriptors.)

This section explores the problems arising from the requirement of compatibility and examines possible solutions. A note of caution is in order to put this rather technical exposition in perspective: Compatibility is not an absolute goal. By adjusting to other systems and thus achieving compatibility, a system may be less suited to fulfill its specific functions. So there might not be an increase in benefits, there might even be a decrease. And there is a cost in achieving compatibility. As always, the potential benefits have to be weighed against this cost.

K2.1 Introduction. Statement of the Problem. Searching Conversion Versus Indexing Conversion

Assume that two information centers A and B that have been operating for some time, each using its own indexing language, want to start cooperating through sharing the results of subject indexing. Obviously, the problem of converting from indexing language A into indexing language B and vice versa occurs whether: (a) A wants to run a search request formulated in A-descriptors against B's store or whether: (b) A wants to translate document representations produced by B into its own indexing language and incorporate them into its own store. The basic test of whether A can use B's indexing results is retrieval: is it possible to convert search requests formulated in indexing language A into indexing language B and retrieve the relevant documents indexed by B? Retrieval also remains the basic test if A converts B's document representations. It follows that conversion of search requests from A to B is the basic problem. We shall deal with this problem first.

A is the source language, B the target-language. The B-descriptor or combination of B-descriptors used to express an A-descriptor in the search request formulation is called the searching equivalent of that A-descriptor. Target language B is said to be fully compatible with source language A if every descriptor of A has a precise searching equivalent in B. Note that compatibility is a directed relationship. B may be fully compatible with A, but A may not be fully compatible with B. This happens if B is more specific than A.

These considerations lead to the concept of a searching conversion table (also called *concordance*). This is simply a list that gives the nearest searching equivalent in B for every descriptor of A or indicates that no such searching equivalent exists. Note again that a searching conversion table is unidirectional from A to B.

Let us illustrate these concepts through an example.

Example:

	Indexing language A	*Indexing language B*
	A1 Vehicles	B1 Vehicles
	A2 Cars	B2 Cars
	A3 Ships	B3 Ships
Restricted version	A4 Aircraft	B4 Aircraft
		B4.2 Airplanes
		B4.4 Subsonic planes
		B4.6 Supersonic airplanes
		B4.8 Helicopter
	A5 Passenger versus freight transport	
	A6 Passenger transport	
Extended version	A7 Freight transport	
	A7.3 Light weight cargo	
	A7.7 Heavy weight cargo	

B is fully compatible with the restricted version of A: every A-descriptor has a searching equivalent in B, the searching equivalent for *A4 Aircraft* being *B4 Aircraft, inclusive* (that is, retrieving documents indexed by *B4.2-B4.8* as well). Contrariwise, A is not compatible with B, since for example, *B4.6 Supersonic airplanes* does not have a precise searching equivalent in A; the best we can do is to search for *A4 Aircraft*. If we go to the extended version of A, then B is no longer compatible with A since, for example, *A6 Passenger transport* does not have a searching equivalent in B. If a document is in fact on *Passenger ships* (as opposed to *Freighters*), this is not brought out in the indexing done in B. We shall come back to this point shortly. In this example the searching conversion table is trivial; real-life cases will be discussed later.

One should be aware of the following points: *A4* means *Aircraft, inclusive*, whereas *B4* actually means *Aircraft, general references*. The position of a descriptor in the hierarchy affects how it should be used in indexing (these points have been discussed in detail in Sections C1.4.6,1 and C1.4.1,6, respectively).

To sum up: The problem is to retrieve documents indexed by B, starting from a search request formulated in the indexing language A. The approach described up to now is as follows: The descriptors used by B (and inscribed, for example, on catalog cards) are left unchanged. If A receives a search request and formulates it in its indexing language, this search request must be converted to the indexing language B, using a searching conversion table (see Figure 69a). This approach is called searching conversion.

Searching conversion is awkward, especially if manual searching is used. We would like to retrieve all documents, whether originally indexed by A or by B, with one search request formulation expressed in indexing language A. In order to achieve this purpose, we obviously must convert the B-descriptors used in indexing by B to the appropriate A-descriptors and inscribe these A-descriptors on the catalog cards for the documents (Figure 69b). This approach is called indexing conversion.

For example: In searching conversion, *B3 Ships* remains unchanged on the catalog card and the search request *A3 Ships* is converted to *B3 Ships*. In indexing conversion, *B3* is converted to *A3* on the catalog card, and conversion of the search request is not necessary. The next example is less trivial: In searching conversion, *B4.4 Subsonic airplanes* remains unchanged on the catalog card and the search request *A4 Aircraft* is converted to *B4 Aircraft, inclusive,* retrieving, among others, documents indexed by *B4.4*. In indexing conversion, *B4.4 Subsonic airplanes* is converted to *A4 Aircraft* on the catalog card, and conversion of the search request is not necessary.

Conceptually, both approaches are the same; only the implementation is different. The conversion of document representations from B to A in indexing conversion corresponds to the conversion of search requests from A to B

K2 Sharing the Results of Indexing 497

in searching conversion. (In a sense, searching conversion corresponds to the use of the lead-in structure in searching, as discussed in Section B6.3, and indexing conversion corresponds to the use of the lead-in structure in indexing. Indexing conversion could also be characterized as semi-mechanized indexing by A based on the descriptors assigned by B; the indexing conversion table takes the role of the lead-in structure.)

In indexing conversion we need for each B-descriptor an *indexing equivalent* in A.

Examples:
*B3 Ships; indexing equivalent is A3 Ships
because A3 has B3 as its searching equivalent.
B4.4 Subsonic airplanes; indexing equivalent is A4 Aircraft*
Reason: *There is no A-descriptor that has B4.4 as searching equivalent. In A, we always have to search for Aircraft, inclusive, which is A4, and A4 has B4 as its searching equivalent.*

In general, the indexing equivalent for a descriptor *Bx* is determined as follows: Look for an A-descriptor *Ax*, so that *Ax* has *Bx* as its searching equivalent. If no such A-descriptor is found, go to the next broader term *Bx'*, and look for an A-descriptor that has *Bx'* as its equivalent and so on. In this way we can construct an *indexing conversion table* from B to A that corresponds to the searching conversion table from A to B. Note that A does not need to distinguish between different kinds of aircraft and that therefore, *A4 Aircraft* is just as good an indexing equivalent for *B4.4 Subsonic airplanes* as *A3 Ships* is for *B3 Ships*. (Of course, indexing information is lost while converting *B4.4 Subsonic airplanes* to *A4 Aircraft*. But we can assume that A does not need that information; otherwise, it would provide the specific descriptor. And even if some users of A would like to search for *Subsonic airplanes*, it would not make much sense in most cases to provide the capabilities of specific searching if only documents indexed by B can be retrieved with such high specificity. Special action is necessary in multilateral cooperation, see Section K2.1.1.) If we were looking for searching equivalents from B to A, things would be different.

The reader should keep in mind that our definition of compatibility is based on conversion tables for searching, not on conversion tables for indexing. B is not compatible with the extended version of A, in spite of the fact that every B-descriptor has an indexing equivalent in A. Nor is the restricted version of A compatible with B, in spite of the fact that each A-descriptor has an indexing equivalent in B.

The reason is clear in each case: If A (extended) receives document representations prepared by B, an indexer at A still must look at each document to determine whether it deals with *A6 Passenger transport* or *A7*

498 K Thesauri as a Basis for Cooperation

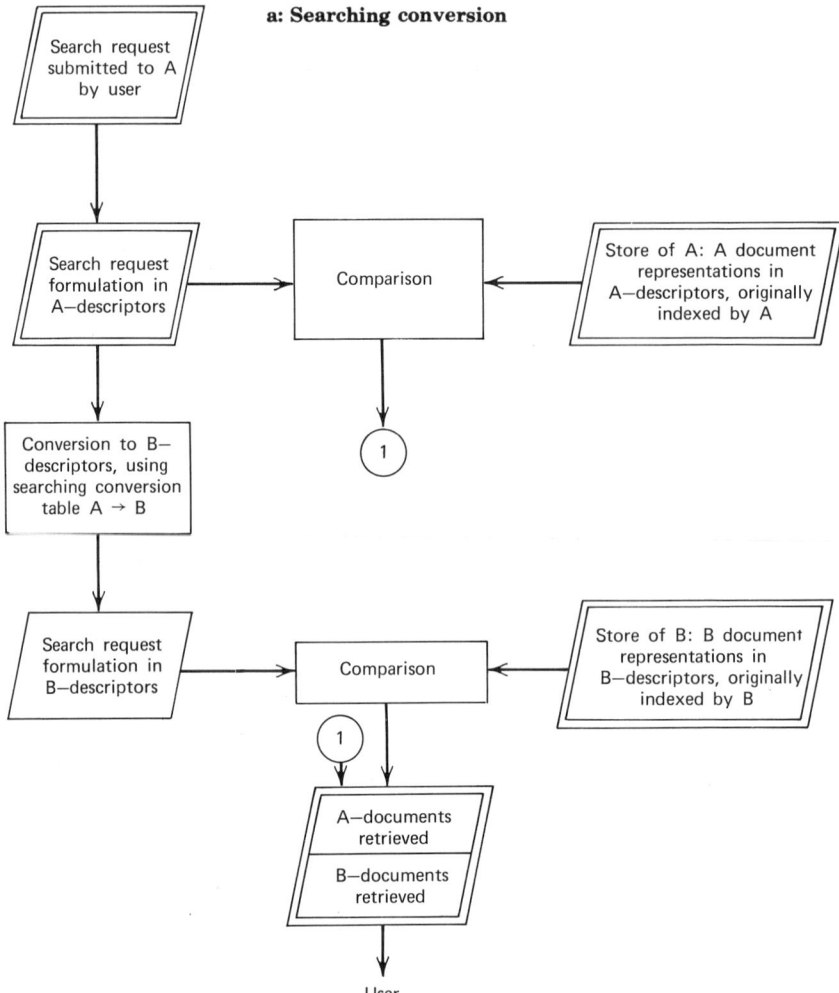

Figure 69. Searching conversion and indexing conversion (K2.1). (Note: The task is the same in both cases, as illustrated by the doubly-framed boxes: Given a search request expressed in A-descriptors and stores of A and B, find the relevant A documents and the relevant B documents.)

Freight transport (and if so, whether light or heavy weight). If B receives document representations prepared by A, an indexer at B has to look at all documents indexed by *A4 Aircraft* to find out whether they deal with *B4.2 Airplanes* (and if so, what kind) or with *B4.8 Helicopters*. Otherwise, a reliable search of the store of A or B, respectively, is not possible. Again, it is useful to compare an indexing conversion table, in this case from A to B,

K2 Sharing the Results of Indexing   499

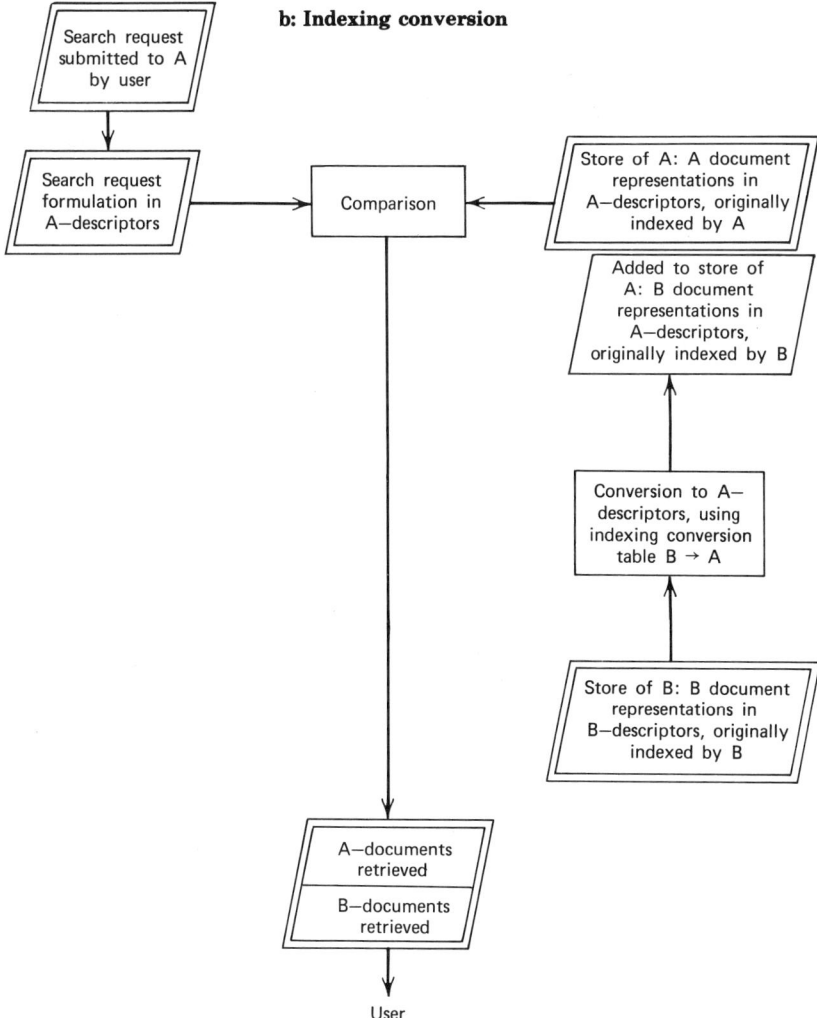

Figure 69. (Continued)

with the lead-in structure within one thesaurus. As we have seen in Section C5.0.3, the USE instruction does not always lead to the descriptor to be used but only to the proper entry point in the indexing language. A more specific descriptor may then have to be selected. Likewise, an indexing conversion table from A to B leads to an entry point in B's indexing language, in this case *B4 Aircraft*. All B descriptors narrower than B4 must then be considered. This is nothing but an application of the checklist technique of indexing to the problem of shared subject indexing: Information center (or Library) A can use the indexing results of information center B if and only if the viewpoints important for A have been considered in indexing by B, and vice versa. Both information centers have to communicate these viewpoints to one another. Often it will not be possible for B to use all the specific descriptors that A would like to have used in indexing, and vice versa. Instead of many specific descriptors, a smaller number of broader descriptors is used. In searching for documents indexed by B, A must then replace the specific descriptor by a more general descriptor. An over-all classification scheme or a conversion table insures that the appropriate broader descriptors are used in each information center.

The important function of hierarchy comes again to light. The question, "Is it necessary for cooperation that information center B consider the specific A-descriptor *A7.7 Transportation of heavy weight cargo?*" need not be answered with either 'yes' or 'no'. There is the intermediate answer that B should at least use *A7 Freight transport*. A would then not re-index documents indexed by B. Instead, A would use the following search request formulation in searching for *A7.7.*

Example:
A.7.7 OR (A7 AND Indexed by B).

That is, in searching for documents indexed by B, *A7.7* would be replaced by the broader descriptor *A7*. Conversely, A might agree to use at least *B4.2 Airplanes* and *B4.8 Helicopters* in indexing, even though *B4.4 Subsonic airplanes* and *B4.6 Supersonic airplanes* would be too specific. We have a bargaining situation between the two information centers. In practical situations more hierarchical levels are involved. Only such a flexible give-and-take procedure can solve the problems arising from shared subject indexing.

But even if such agreed-upon indexing languages are used in information centers A and B, there still exists a problem: one has to make sure that in day-to-day indexing each descriptor is used in the intended and agreed-upon meaning. Otherwise, any compatibility is fictitious. It has been observed that "where the interests of two institutions are similar, the indexing is similar; where the interests are different, indexing is different, even if the same terms are available to the indexers of both institutions." In addition to this interest bias, indexers within one institution develop a kind of oral tradition or "lore" that more or less ensures a consistent usage of descriptors in indexing within that institution. In shared subject indexing, where indexers work at different institutions, this informal system does not work; it has to be replaced by a formal system, that is, the extensive use of scope notes. More general, indexing rules, such as rules on exhaustivity of indexing, time to be

K2 Sharing the Results of Indexing

spent, and special aspects to be considered, affect the results of indexing and their exchangeability. This has to be kept in mind while establishing cooperation in subject indexing. Furthermore, classified arrangement, by displaying the viewpoints to be considered in indexing, plays a major role in the determination of the descriptors for which a document is relevant. If two indexing languages contain exactly the same descriptors with exactly the same relationship and exactly the same scope notes, indexing results may still differ due to a different arrangement of the descriptors.

The discussion up to now was concerned with conceptual compatibility. In an abstract sense, conceptual compatibility is all that matters. Once the concepts for which a document is relevant have been determined and expressed by terms or notational symbols from indexing language B, it is a purely mechanical matter to look up the terms or notational symbols to be used with indexing language A, provided indexing language B is compatible with indexing language A on a conceptual level. As we have seen, conceptual compatibility is dependent mainly on the availability of the individual descriptors in indexing language B. The hierarchical structure established between these descriptors and the arrangement chosen are important only insofar as they influence descriptor usage. How the descriptors are expressed —by natural language terms or by notational symbols—is of no consequence on the conceptual level. Therefore, shared subject indexing does not require a common indexing language or classification scheme.

However, if we come down to day-to-day work, we encounter limiting technical factors that require compatibility in the designation of concepts as well. If information centers A and B both use computerized systems, then there is no problem in replacing the terms or notational symbols used by B by those used by A. But if we have a medium-sized library using conventional methods and receiving Library of Congress catalog cards and/or books that are already labeled by the call number according to Library of Congress Classification, then the situation is very different, and cooperation in subject indexing does indeed require a common indexing language.

K2.1.1 Multilateral shared subject indexing using a "switching language"

If several, say 5, information centers or libraries want to organize a mutual exchange of indexing results, each needs indexing conversion tables, and for each conversion the appropriate table has to be selected. Altogether, 20 indexing conversion tables are needed. Obviously, the system of conversion tables could be simplified by establishing a "switching language" S. Indexing conversion from B to A, for example, is then done in 2 steps: (1) from B to S (performed by B); (2) from S to A (performed by A). In this case, each institution, for example A, needs only two conversion tables, from A to S and from S to A. Altogether 10 conversion tables are needed. With more participants, the savings are even more conspicuous. These savings are paid for by having two steps in the conversion instead of one.

It is obvious that for shared subject indexing on a specific level all indexing information must be preserved while converting into the switching language S. Therefore, S must be as specific as the most specific indexing language involved in every area. In no case may S be less specific than any of the indexing languages involved. An indexing language for shared subject indexing on a specific level must *not* be an umbrella classification.

On the other hand if the purpose of the cooperation is only shared subject indexing on a general level (for announcement purposes, for example), then the switching language can be less specific. However, there might be a problem if the schemes of announcement categories used by the participating institutions are built upon different principles of subdivision. A considerable amount of indexing information has to be preserved so that a document can be assigned to the proper announcement category in *each* of the schemes involved.

Remark: It has been asserted that "In all these cases, the transfer (of indexing done in B to A, D.S.) should proceed unimpeded provided that the units of the switching language—the concepts isolated there—are not more composite than the units which make up the least composite of the inputting and receiving languages." The discussion in this section leads to different conclusions. Unimpeded exchange of the results of indexing is possible if, and only if, each participating institution uses an indexing language that represents in every area the maximum detail (which may mean the maximum degree of compoundness) desired by any participating institution—a situation not likely to occur except in small networks. The best we can do is to construct a switching language that will minimize impediment, given the varying levels of specificity of the different indexing languages involved. This objective can be achieved only if the switching language is as specific as the most specific of the indexing languages involved in every area. It follows that a compound concept must be included in the switching language if it is used as a descriptor in any of the indexing languages involved.

K2.2 Framework for the Comparison of Two Indexing Languages or Thesauri

The comparison of two indexing languages or thesauri involves more than just establishing a conversion table. A conversion table merely presents a concept-by-concept comparison. It does not, by itself, involve a structural comparison of the two indexing languages or thesauri (the structure is considered only insofar as it affects the usage of individual descriptors). A conversion table may be said to give a local comparison, as opposed to a global

K2 Sharing the Results of Indexing 503

comparison that would also consider the structural differences and similarities. However, only convertibility categories in conversion tables will be discussed in detail.

The differences that may exist between two indexing languages or thesauri are much the same as the changes within one indexing language or thesaurus in updating, as discussed in Section J1.

K2.2.1 Convertibility categories (advanced)

In building a searching conversion table from indexing language A to indexing language B, one will find that some A-descriptors have precise searching equivalents in B while others have only an approximated searching equivalent or none at all. Also some searching equivalents consist of only one B-descriptor while others have to be formed by a combination of several B-descriptors. The same is true for indexing equivalents in building the corresponding indexing conversion table from B to A. It follows that in building a conversion table one must have a clear scheme of convertibility categories. Since searching conversion is more basic, it is logical to discuss searching convertibility categories first. But since in practice indexing conversion is more frequent, a scheme of indexing convertibility categories will also be derived. The entire discussion is centered around examples taken from the conversion between the indexing languages A and B given in Figure 70. The same examples are used for searching convertibility and for indexing convertibility. They are displayed in a systematic and parallel arrangement in Figures 71 and 72. From this, the relationship between searching convertibility categories and indexing convertibility categories should become clear.

,1 **Searching convertibility categories** (for examples see Figure 71). The suggested scheme is based on the two facets already alluded to above:

Facet 1: Degree of equivalence
(S1) The A-descriptor has a precise searching equivalent in B.
(S2) The A-descriptor has only an approximate searching equivalent in B. Within this category the following cases can be distinguished:
(S2.1) The approximate searching equivalent is broader than the A-descriptor.
(S2.2) The approximate searching equivalent is narrower than the A-descriptor.
(S2.3) The approximate searching equivalent is related to the A-descriptor.
(S3) The A-descriptor does not have a searching equivalent. No corresponding concept at a useful generic level or in sufficiently near relationship can be expressed in B.

Facet 2: Way in which the searching equivalent is expressed in B
(a) The searching equivalent is expressed by one B-descriptor.
(a1) B uses the same term as A.
(a2) B uses a different term from A.

(b) The searching equivalent is a combination of B-descriptors:
(b1) An OR combination.
(b2) An AND combination.
(b3) A combination using both AND and OR.

(If A and B use different spelling variants of the same term, then so far as human processing is concerned, we deal with it as if it were an example of (a1), whereas in computer processing it needs to be treated as an example of (a2).)

The basis for this scheme of convertibility categories is conceptual, except for the distinction between (a1), "Same term in A and B" and (a2), "Different terms in A and B". The searching convertibility categories that result from the combination of these two facets are shown in Figure 71. Note the examples for (S2.3a1) and (S3a1): the same term may be used by both A and B, but in different meanings. It follows that in establishing a conversion table one must analyze the actual usage of descriptors, a difficult task. The distinction between (S1), "Precise searching equivalent" and (S2.3), "Related searching equivalent" is often blurred, especially if one thinks of the problem of quasi-synonyms.

If no precise searching equivalent can be found, then approximate searching equivalents in categories (S2.1), (S2.2), and (S2.3) should be looked for. All searching equivalents found in any of the categories should be given (with obvious restrictions: if there is an upward chain of broader searching equivalents or a downward chain of narrower searching equivalents, only the first element of the chain is given; if there are two related B-descriptors and if in all possible conversion situations the first one should be used, only the first one is given). The searching equivalents should be ranked by "closeness" to the A-descriptor. If it is found necessary to classify each case into one category, this should be done based on the closest searching equivalent.

,2 **Indexing convertibility categories** (see Figure 72). Indexing convertibility categories are more difficult to define than searching convertibility categories. Not only do we have to consider how a B-descriptor is converted into the A-indexing language, but we must be even more concerned with the retrievability of a document indexed by B after all its descriptors have been converted, as compared to its retrievability had it been indexed originally by A. For this purpose it is necessary to analyze the process of index conversion for a document: A set of B-descriptors is assigned to the document. Based on this, a set of A-descriptors is generated by conversion. This generated set of A-descriptors has to be compared to a potential set of A-descriptors that would have been produced by indexing the document originally in A. The basic question is: Do the B-descriptors assigned to the document provide enough information that the generated set of A-descriptors can be made as

A	B
Vehicles	Vehicles
Cars	Cars
	Passenger cars
	Busses
	Cargo cars
Ships	Ships
	Passenger ships
	Cargo ships
Aircraft	Aircraft
Civilian aircraft	
Military aircraft	
	Passenger aircraft
	Cargo aircraft
	Cargo airplanes
	Cargo helicopters
	Airplanes
	Helicopters
Combat vehicles	
Tanks	
Passenger vs. freight transport	
Passenger transport	
Freight transport	
Light weight cargo	
Heavy weight cargo	
Rail transport	Rail transport
Rolling stock	
Locomotives	
Traffic simulation	
	Traffic connection
Offices	
(Office) Furniture	
	Home
	(Home) Furniture
Pest control	Pest control
Pesticides	
	Herbicides
	Insecticides
	Rodenticides
	(Molluscacides missing)
Astrology	
	Stars
	Popular ideas

Figure 70. Two sample indexing languages for the illustration of convertibility categories (K2.2.1).

Expression of searching equivalent: to the A-descriptor corresponds	Degree of equivalence					
	(S1) Precise searching equivalent in B	(S2) Approximate searching equivalent in B				(S3) No searching equivalent in B
		(S2.1) Searching equivalent broader	(S2.2) Searching equivalent narrower	(S2.3) Searching equivalent related		
(a) One B-descriptor						
(a1) Same term	A: Ship B: Ship	A: Radar (for traffic control) B: Radar		A: Furniture (meaning office) B: Furniture (home)		A: Tanks (combat vehicles) B: Tanks (containers)
(a2) Different terms	A: Ship B: Vessel	A: Military aircraft B: Aircraft A: Pesticides B: Pest control		A: Office Furniture B: Home Furniture		A: Traffic simulation B: —
(b) A combination of B-descriptors						
(b1) OR-combination of B-descriptors	A: Aircraft B: Aircraft OR Airplanes OR Helicopters OR ... A: Passenger transport B: Passenger cars OR Busses OR Passenger ships OR Passenger aircraft	A: Heavy weight cargo transport B: Cargo cars OR Cargo ships OR Cargo aircraft OR Cargo airplanes OR Cargo helicopters	A: Pesticides B: Herbicides OR Insecticides OR Rodenticides (Molluscacides omitted from B)			—
(b2) AND-combination of B-descriptors	A: Rolling stock B: Vehicles AND Rail transport	A: Locomotives B: Vehicles AND Rail transport		A: Astrology B: Stars AND Popular ideas		—
(b3) Combination of B-descriptors using both AND and OR	A: Animal food products B: Food AND (Hunting OR Animal husbandry)	A: Meat as food B: Food AND (Hunting · Animal husbandry)				—

Figure 71. Searching convertibility categories (conversion from A to B) (K2.2.1.1).

Expression of indexing equivalent to the B-descriptor corresponds		Degree of equivalence					
		(I1) Precise indexing equivalent in A		(I2) Approximate indexing equivalent in A			(I3) No indexing equivalent	
		(I1.1) A-indexing equivalent same level as B-descriptor	(I1.2) A-indexing equivalent broader than B-descriptor	(I2.1) Indexing equivalent in A, but original indexing n A might be more specific		(I2.3) Related indexing equivalent	(I3.1) Aspect not of interest to A	(I3.2) There is a narrower A-descriptor
				(I2.1.1) A-index. equivalent same level as B-descr.	(I2.1.2) A-index. equivalent broader than B-descriptor			
(a) One A-descriptor	(a1) Same term	(S1a1) Doc: Ships B : Ships A : Ships A¹ : Ships		(S2.1a2) Doc: Military aircraft B : Aircraft A : Aircraft A¹ : Military aircraft Doc: Molluscacides B : Pest control A : Pest control A¹ : Pesticides		(S2.3a1) Doc: Home furniture B : Furniture (home furniture) A : Furniture (office furniture) A¹ : Furniture (office furniture)	(S3a1) B: Tanks (containers) A: Tanks (combat vehicles)	(S2.1a1) B: Radar A: Radar (for traffic control)
	(a2) Different terms	(S1a2) Doc: Ships B : Vessels A : Ships A¹ : Ships	(S2.2b1) Doc: Helicopter B : Helicopter A : Aircraft A¹ : Aircraft		(S2.1b1) Doc: Military helicopter B : Helicopter A : Military aircraft	(S2.3a2) Doc: Home furniture B : Home furniture A : Office furniture A¹ : Office furniture	(S3a2) B: Traffic connections A: —	
(b) A combination	(b1) AND – combination of A-descriptors	(S1b1) Doc: Passenger cars B : Passenger cars A : Cars AND Passenger transport A¹ : same	(S1b1) Doc: Busses B : Busses A : Cars AND Passenger transport A¹ : same	(S2.2b1) Doc: Herbicides B : Herbicides A : Pesticides A¹ : Pesticides	(S2.1b1) Doc: Heavy cargo aircraft B : Cargo aircraft A : Aircraft AND Cargo transp. A¹ : Aircraft AND Heavy weight cargo transp.			

Legend:
Doc: concept dealt with in the document;
B : descriptor used by B;
A : A-descriptor generated by conversion;
A¹ : A-descriptor that would have been assigned in original indexing by A.

Figure 72. Indexing convertibility categories (conversion from B to A) (K22.1,2). (Note: The examples are the same as the ones used in Figure 71 for searching convertibility categories. For each example, the S-category is given so that the relationship between I and S convertibility categories can be seen. (I2.2) is missing because there is no indexing convertibility category corresponding to (S2.2).).

specific and exhaustive as the potential set of A-descriptors? The reader should keep in mind that our task here is not to find out what B-descriptor(s) would have been used in indexing a document that has been indexed by the A-descriptor, say, *Rolling Stock*. That is the problem of finding searching equivalents. Our task here is to generate a set of A-descriptors from the given set of B-descriptors. The following scheme is restricted to a conversion table that gives for each single B-descriptor the appropriate A-descriptor(s). As we shall see, that is not enough; we may also have to use combinations of B-descriptors as entry points in the indexing conversion.

There is also the question of whether all the information provided by B is preserved while translating into A. This question is not important if system A is considered in isolation. If A does not use a specific descriptor that is used by B, the reason presumably is that A does not need that descriptor in searching. The question is important, however, in multilateral schemes of shared subject indexing, as discussed in Section K2.1.1.

The following scheme for indexing convertibility is derived from the one for searching convertibility. It is also based on two facets:

Facet 1: Degree of equivalence
(I1) The B-descriptor has a precise indexing equivalent in A. That means, the A-descriptor(s) generated by conversion is (are) the same as the A-descriptor(s) that would have been assigned in the original indexing by A.
(I1.1) The indexing equivalent is on the same level as the B-descriptor.
(I1.2) The indexing equivalent is broader than the B-descriptor.
(I2) The B-descriptor has an approximate indexing equivalent in A.
(I2.1) The B-descriptor has an indexing equivalent in A, but original indexing in A might have resulted in the use of a more specific A-descriptor or combination of A-descriptors.
(I2.1.1) The indexing equivalent is on the same level as the B-descriptor.
(I2.1.2) The indexing equivalent is broader than the B-descriptor.
(I2.2) A category corresponding to (S2.2) is not useful.
(I2.3) The B-descriptor has a related indexing equivalent in A.
(I3) The B-descriptor has no indexing equivalent in A.
(I3.1) The aspect covered by the B-descriptor is not of interest for A (and is not necessary for searches in A).
(I3.2) There is a narrower A-descriptor.

Facet 2: How is the indexing equivalent expressed in A?
(a) The indexing equivalent is expressed by one A-descriptor.
(a1) A uses the same term as B.
(a2) A uses a different term from B.
(b) The indexing equivalent is expressed by a combination of B-descriptors.
(b1) An AND combination. (As may be seen from Figure 72, we have an OR combination in searching conversion if we have an AND combination in indexing conversion; therefore both are labeled (b1). An OR combination or an AND/OR combination would be of limited value as indexing equivalent.)

The indexing convertibility categories resulting from the combination of these two facets are shown in Figure 72. Examples for the more frequent combinations are also given, and relationships to the searching convertibility categories are indicated.

A further discussion of these indexing convertibility categories is in order. In case there is a precise indexing equivalent (I1), indexing conversion can be fully automatic; the descriptor used in indexing by B provides enough information to derive the appropriate A-descriptor(s). However, the occurrence of *Pesticides* as target descriptor in one (I1)-case does not guarantee complete retrieval performance in A. The B-descriptor *Herbicides* has the precise indexing equivalent *Pesticides*. But a document on *Molluscacides* is indexed by *Pest control* in B, therefore ends up under *Pest control* in A, and would consequently be missed in a search for *Pesticides* in A. In general formulation: (S2.2b1) cases show up as (I1) cases in the same way as (S1b1) cases.

In case (I2.1) automatic indexing conversion will result in failures with respect to the specificity of indexing. Take a document on military aircraft. In B, this document will be indexed by *Aircraft*, and in automatic indexing conversion this will become the A-descriptor *Aircraft*. This is a specificity failure, since the document should be indexed by the A-descriptor *Military aircraft*. Human intervention would be required to achieve the proper specificity in A. If automatic indexing conversion is used, a search for documents on military aircraft in A must be formulated as follows: *Military aircraft* OR (*Aircraft* AND *Indexed by B*), as has been pointed out in Section K2.1. In case (I2.3), "Related indexing equivalent", human intervention is necessary, too. Automatic index conversion in this case would mean that the definition of the A-descriptor, say, *Furniture [office]* is in fact broadened to include also the B-descriptor *Furniture [home]*. On the other hand if no descriptor to express the concept *Home furniture* or a broader concept is available in A then human intervention wouldn't help either. In case (I3.1) no harm is done by simply omitting the B-descriptor, for example, *Traffic connections*, in which A is not interested anyway. Case (I3.2) is different; here human intervention is required in order to determine whether a document indexed by the B-descriptor *Radar* actually deals with *Radar* as meant by A, namely, *Radar for traffic control*. In automatic descriptor-to-descriptor conversion, two possibilities exist: Omit *Radar*, which leads to recall failures, or convert *Radar (B)* to *Radar (A)*, which leads to precision failures. If (and only if) B has a descriptor *Traffic control* then the documents on *Radar (A)* can be found automatically by looking for the combination *Radar (B)* AND *Traffic control*, as described in the next paragraph.

The method of indexing conversion dealt with so far leads from single B-descriptors to indexing equivalents in A; the entries in the indexing conversion table are for single B-descriptors only. This method will never lead to the A-descriptors *Rolling Stock* or *Animal food products* because these concepts are expressed by an AND or AND/OR combination of B-descriptors, respectively. There are no indexing convertibility categories corresponding to the rows (b2) and (b3) in Figure 71. Apart from human intervention, A has two strategies available: Strategy 1 is to scan each document representation provided by B to determine whether it contains the two descriptors *Vehicles* and *Rail transport* and if so, assign the A-descriptor *Rolling stock* to the document. Note that this procedure will lead to some irrelevant documents (corresponding to "false drops" in combination indexing) while searching for *Rolling stock* in A, unless a human indexer checks the conversion. What actually happens here is this: If a precombined A-descriptor is not explicitly available in B, A formulates an appropriate search request and then scans all document representations provided by B against all these search requests. Strategy 2 is to translate each B-descriptor individually but tell a searcher in A who is looking for documents on *Rolling stock* that he has to use the combination *Vehicles* AND *Rail transport* in order to retrieve those documents that were originally indexed by B.

Strategy 2 can be used only if the individual B-descriptors all have indexing equivalents in A. This is not the case in *Animal food products*; *Animal husbandry* is not a descriptor in A. The whole problem gets further compounded in cases like *Locomotives* where the combination of B-descriptors is less specific than the A-descriptor.

K2.3 Production of Conversion Tables

Recall the definition of a conversion table: A *searching conversion table* from A to B is a list of A-descriptors together with their searching equivalents in B. The corresponding *indexing conversion table* from B to A is a list of B-descriptors with their indexing equivalents in A.

If we have a cumulative thesaurus with a recommended terminological and classificatory structure, as described in Section K1.3, conversion tables between each pair of sources can easily be extracted. The production of a conversion table thus boils down to the construction of a cumulative thesaurus. Often it will be useful to have, in addition to the conversion table, a common alphabetical index for the two (or more) indexing languages or thesauri involved. This would eliminate the necessity for separate alphabetical indexes, and it would also increase the consistency of indexing between institutions.

In the actual development of conversion tables we have to deal with two situations: the ideal situation, where the indexing languages of the cooperating institutions are still to be built, and the usual situation, where the indexing languages of the cooperating institutions are already long in use.

K2.3.1 Ideal situation: the indexing languages of the cooperating institutions are still to be built

In this case it is possible to develop a unified "total thesaurus" which contains all the specific descriptors needed by any of the cooperating institutions (strong coordination). For each information center an appropriate "constituent thesaurus" is extracted. This constituent thesaurus contains all the specific descriptors in the special field of the information center; for other fields it contains more general descriptors only, the specificity decreasing with increasing distance of a field from the main interest of the information center (see the examples in Section K1.2.2,2). A minimal set of general descriptors, called an "umbrella classification", is used by all institutions. It also serves as a common framework. This procedure guarantees optimal compatibility. The resulting system of thesauri may be depicted as shown in the diagram. The total thesaurus (outer circle) contains all descriptors in the system, that is, any descriptor used by any participating institution. The center (inner circle) contains the descriptors used by all institutions, that is, the umbrella classification and at least the more gener¹ descriptors from the adjunct thesauri in the system. Constituent thesaurus A (sector including the inner circle) contains the descriptors used by A.

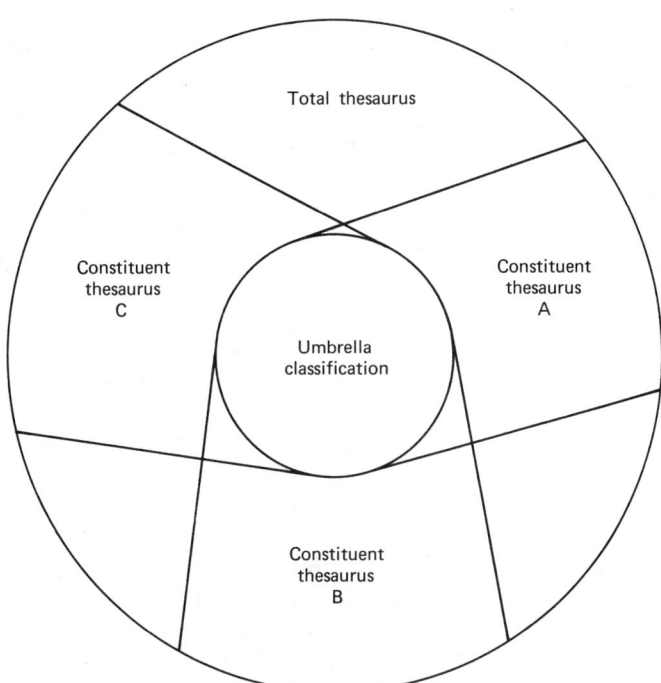

K   Thesauri as a Basis for Cooperation

For each descriptor in one indexing language, a precise or at least a broader searching equivalent can be expressed in any other language. The case where we have only an approximate searching equivalent or no searching equivalent at all and the impediments to cooperation connected with this case are avoided.

In the formulation of Section K1.2.2 we can say that the total thesaurus serves as a source thesaurus for the cooperating institutions. The recommended structure is mandatory in this case. Being a source thesaurus, the total thesaurus would not contain USE or SEE instructions. These have to be created while extracting the individual constituent thesauri.

,1 The development of a total thesaurus through parallel development of constituent thesauri. There are situations where it is useful to divide the work of the development of a total thesaurus among different organizations and where it is difficult to coordinate the effort during all the phases of the work. In such a situation one can proceed by assigning to each organization the task of developing a constituent thesaurus in one area. In a second step, these constituent thesauri can then be put together into a total thesaurus. In order to achieve compatibility among the constituent thesauri, it is necessary to develop a preliminary outline of the hierarchy or umbrella classification to be used in Step F3, "Work out the preliminary structure" in the development of all constituent thesauri. This umbrella classification should subdivide the entire scope of the total thesaurus into broad areas and then go down three or four hierarchical levels as appropriate. Of course, this outline of the hierarchy has to be modified later on. It is further recommended that adjunct thesauri, such as a thesaurus of geographical names, be developed only once for the whole system.

While putting together the constituent thesauri to obtain the total thesaurus one has to watch for conflicts in the selection of preferred terms and for disagreements with respect to the monohierarchical structure that is to serve as the basis for the classified arrangement. To a limited extent, the process of bringing together Synonyms and Equivalent Terms and of merging all information for the same concept has to be performed again because different terms designating the same concepts may be contained in different constituent thesauri (the boundaries of the areas for the constituent thesauri will always be fuzzy, so that a little overlap can never be avoided). In summary, the same steps have to be performed as in the development of a thesaurus starting from different sources, but the task will be much easier.

,2 Alphabetical index for the total thesaurus. It has been suggested that a separate alphabetical index for each of the constituent thesauri be prepared. However, such a procedure is hardly useful: It would not involve a lot of space to include an alphabetical index to the total thesaurus in the published version of each of the constituent thesauri; this might even be cheaper in production. In addition, this serves to stress the relationships between the constituent thesauri.

K2.3.2 Usual situation: each of the cooperating institutions already has its own indexing language long in use

In this case it is usually neither possible nor desirable to make major changes in the indexing languages of the cooperating institutions because major collections would have to be reclassified. (However, in many American libraries changing from DDC to LCC, this is exactly what is done.) Instead, conversion tables from one indexing language to another as described above should be produced. This is most easily done as follows: A cumulative thesaurus is constructed, using at least the indexing languages and thesauri of the cooperating institutions as input. Or, even better, these indexing languages and thesauri are incorporated into an existing cumulative thesaurus, as described in Section K1.4. For sorting the terms into subject fields and subfields (Steps F3.1 and F3.2 of thesaurus construction), a coarse classification scheme is needed. An available umbrella classification can serve this purpose (compare Section K2.4.2). From this cumulative thesaurus, conversion tables are then extracted. It is no longer possible to avoid the case where there is only an approximate searching equivalent or no searching equivalent at all. However, it is possible to alleviate the worst problems by appropriate revisions in the indexing languages of the participating institutions (if these revisions are very extensive, we approach the case in which new indexing languages are built for the participating institutions, as described in Section K2.3.1). Also, the updating of the indexing languages and thesauri should be coordinated so that no new incompatibility is introduced.

The cumulative thesaurus is also useful in itself, as discussed in Section K1.3: From the source indications given in each entry, one can see at which institution to look for material on a certain subject. The cumulative thesaurus can also be used to formulate search requests in any of the indexing languages that are contained in it. This is valuable for users who regularly search collections at different institutions. It is important to record in the cumulative thesaurus each term in exactly the form it is used in the indexing languages of any participating institution. These exact forms are needed for automatic conversion of search request formulations or document representations from one indexing language into another. They are also needed if one wants to formulate a search request in any indexing language by using the cumulative thesaurus (see Section K1.3 for a discussion of what this requirement means for file organization.)

,1 **The local approach and the global approach to the construction of conversion tables.** The construction of a cumulative thesaurus to obtain conversion tables can be characterized as the "global" approach. Contrasted to this is the "local" approach where each term of the source thesaurus is processed individually against the target thesaurus. Two points can be made for the global approach. First, the construction of a searching conversion table or an indexing conversion table requires not only a term-to-term comparison but also a comparison between the structures of the two vocabularies. Second, source terms for which an appropriate target term cannot be found immediately are all processed together, making the procedure more efficient. If more than two indexing languages are processed or, particularly, if an existing cumulative thesaurus can be used as a base, more problems can be solved in a merely mechanical way by making use of the ST relationships given. A global procedure can be used without actually constructing the cumulative thesaurus. In case the target language is a faceted classification, the construction of conversion tables is greatly simplified. To each descriptor of the source indexing language being processed, the appropriate combination of core descriptors of the faceted classification is assigned (see Section C2.5 on core classification and extended classification). This is done, for example, in the framework of PRECIS, the new system used to produce the index of the British National Bibliography. Conversion tables from DDC and from LCC into the PRECIS indexing language are developed as new Dewey numbers and new LC class numbers are found in documents or their representations that are processed for BNB. Using the thesaurus building procedure described in Section G3.4.2, one could easily develop a full-fledged cumulative thesaurus of all three schemes based on the concept combinations assigned to the classes in DDC or LCC.

K2.3.3 Updating of the individual indexing languages or thesauri

In both the ideal and the usual situation, updating should be done by a central institution that receives input from all participants. This insures that at least no new incompatibility is introduced. New descriptors and other new information would be communicated rapidly to the participants on a need-to-know basis. Only at longer intervals would the entire set of revised conversion tables be re-issued. (Compare Section J3.3 and J3.4 on the organizational problems of updating.)

K2.4 Compatibility on a General Level. The Concept of an Umbrella Classification

K2.4.1 Shared subject indexing on a general level

Up to now we have dealt with the referral of search requests and shared subject indexing on a specific level. Both require compatibility on a specific level. A third mode of cooperation is shared subject indexing on a general level. The problem can be stated as follows: Institution A has an announcement service in which documents are grouped into broad subject categories, for example, using the COSATI scheme (see Section C1.4.3,1). A wants to include in this service documents indexed by B without having to re-index manually. There are two ways to do this:

(1) *Conversion from B-descriptors to A subject categories*. The B-indexer indexes as usual but marks the one most important descriptor from which the subject category of the document is to be derived. A then determines the (general) announcement category, using an indexing conversion table from the B indexing language to the A announcement scheme. This approach is satisfactory if most B-descriptors can be assigned uniquely to one A announcement category. We call this compatibility on a broad generic level. Compatibility on a broad generic level should be much greater than descriptor-to-descriptor compatibility. In principle the structure and general outline of the indexing language B may be quite different from the structure and general outline of the announcement scheme of A. All that is required is that each B-descriptor can be assigned uniquely to an A announcement category. In practice compatibility should be greater if both indexing languages are built upon a common umbrella classification. In multilateral cooperation of this type, an umbrella classification might serve as a switching language.

(2) *Explicit assignment of A subject category by B-indexer*. The second approach requires additional work from the B-indexer. He is now required to assign explicitly the appropriate A announcement category to the document indexed. This approach avoids all compatibility problems. In practice, however, it is feasible only if A and B can agree on a common "umbrella classification" to be used for announcement purposes by both A and B. With respect to the amount of work involved, such an umbrella classification is easier to construct than a full-blown cumulative thesaurus or a set of conversion tables. On the other hand it is often much harder to find agreement on general outlines than on specific descriptors. Also, categories in an announcement service should be geared specifically to the needs of the user group to be served, and this often precludes the use of the same scheme by both A and B.

K2.4.2 The concept of an umbrella classification

In the foregoing considerations we repeatedly encountered the concept of an umbrella classification. By this is meant a coarse classification scheme having only 2-4 hierarchical levels (as discussed in Section C1.4.3,1) and accepted by a number of institutions. Such an umbrella classification is useful for the following purposes:

(1) An umbrella classification is needed as the basis for the development of a total thesaurus, as discussed in Section K2.3.1,1.

(2) An umbrella classification can be used in the construction of a cumulative thesaurus from which conversion tables are to be extracted, as discussed in Section K2.3.2.

(3) An umbrella classification can be used as a switching language for shared subject indexing on a general level, as discussed in Section K2.4.1(1).

(4) If the interests of the users of two information centers are sufficiently similar, an umbrella classification can be used for shared subject indexing on a general level, as discussed in Section K2.4.1(2).

(5) An umbrella classification can be used as the indexing language for a directory of information centers or similar directories.

As can be seen from these and previous considerations, an umbrella classification does play a role in sharing the results of subject indexing. But it is not a panacea as is sometimes claimed. In particular, it cannot be used as a switching language for shared subject indexing on a specific level.

K3 THE IDEA OF A UNIVERSAL SOURCE THESAURUS (UST) (SPECIAL TOPIC)

K3.0 Universal Source Thesaurus Versus Universal Classification

There is an increasing discussion, stimulated by the necessity for cooperation in information services, on the possibility of a truly universal classification or indexing language. Some authors suggest that the Universal Decimal Classification (UDC) should take this role. Others propose a complete rebuilding of UDC. The Classification Research Group has suggested a faceted approach without agreeing on a set of facets to be applied to a universal scheme. It is very unlikely that agreement on the principles on which a universal classification should be based will ever be reached.

The advocates of a universal classification argue that it would serve extremely well the two purposes of cooperation mentioned in the introduction; namely,

(1) Save work in the construction of indexing languages and thesauri;
(2) Share the results of subject indexing;
(2a) Facilitate the running of a search request in different ISAR systems (in particular, the user would need to learn only one scheme in order to find his way through all the information systems he uses);
(2b) Shared subject indexing on a specific level;
(2c) Shared subject indexing on a general level.

These points are valid. But on the other hand, we have the advocates of special indexing languages/classification schemes. They argue as follows: Each company or research laboratory has its own specific problems. An information service in such an environment has to be based on an indexing language that reflects the interests and viewpoints important in this environment. Also subject indexing has to be done especially for that environment. In other words, a universal classification and universal subject indexing would not help in these circumstances.

K3 Universal Source Thesaurus

How can these opposite viewpoints be reconciled? It should be obvious from the previous sections, and it is the main thrust of this section, that there need not be an either/or in this question. There are gradations along two dimensions; namely,

(a) The scope of cooperation—the cooperation among weather bureaus around the world is much more feasible than cooperation among all scientific information services, not to speak of cooperation among all information services;

(b) Purpose and extent of cooperation—common indexing language versus conversion tables.

It would be wrong to do all or nothing in any of these dimensions. A common indexing language for the weather bureaus around the world is feasible; a universal indexing language or universal classification is not. Where a common indexing language is out of the question, conversion tables or a switching language can still be very useful. Instead of aiming for unfeasible all-out solutions, one should concentrate on feasible partial solutions. In Sections K1 and K2 we discussed how effort can be saved through partial solutions in a limited environment. Even more effort could be saved by extending the scope of cooperation to a universal frame. This leads to the idea of a "Universal Source Thesaurus" (UST). The concept of a source thesaurus has been discussed in Section K1.2.2, and we refer to that discussion. UST would be a source thesaurus universal in scope, containing a vast amount of (multilingual) terminological and classificatory information in machine-readable form, ready to use by anyone for the following purposes:

(1) Extracting indexing languages or thesauri for specific applications or revising an existing indexing language, as described in Section K1.2.2,2;

(2) Comparing any two indexing languages or thesauri that have been merged into UST, especially extracting conversion tables;

(3) Using UST as a switching language between a number of indexing languages.

K3.1 The Structure of UST

UST may be characterized best by "extremely complete" and "extremely specific". Its structure is further defined by the following points (partly repeated from Section K1.2.2,1):

(1) UST would be a cumulative thesaurus, using a great number of existing indexing languages and thesauri as input and precisely storing each bit of information contained in them. Therefore, UST could be used as a data base of terms as described in Section K1.1.

(2) UST would contain concepts down to the very deepest level of specificity useful for any specialized library or information center in any field. Otherwise, it would not be possible to extract specialized indexing languages, to extract con-

version tables between any two indexing languages, or to use UST as a switching language. Furthermore, one should consider expressing the equivalence structure as described in Section C5.2.2, that is, treating the Equivalent Term relationship in the same way as the BT, NT, and RT relationships (and not in the same way as ST relationships).

(3) For each preferred term very complete and detailed information would be given.

(3.1) A complete-as-possible list of synonyms. In addition, translations into a variety of languages, giving a preferred term for each language, so that UST would be a truly multilingual thesaurus. Note that the selection of the preferred term determines the recommended terminological structure.

(3.2) In the BT/NT and RT relationships the different kinds (class inclusion, part-whole, etc.) would be distinguished. Any relationship contained in any of the sources (or suggested by any serious user) would be included. However, some of them might be excluded from the recommended classificatory structure. The tags "needed for field X in depth y", discussed in Section K1.2.2,2.2, would also be given.

(3.3) Special care would be taken in the addition of scope notes and references to works where the concept is defined and explained in more detail. This information will be of tremendous value in constructing a specialized scheme, as anybody who has been involved in such work will acknowledge.

(4) A monohierarchical structure would be marked out so that the recommended classificatory structure can be printed out. One might mark out two arrangements, one subject-oriented, the other based on facets. This would also allow printing a mixed arrangement by broad subject fields and within these subject fields by facets. Again, information on the arrangement used in any of the sources would be stored in addition to the recommended arrangement.

(5) UST would contain a number of special sections, such as geographical terms, concepts of general application, and nomenclatures of all kinds, the recommended structure giving the most universally agreed-upon version. These sections could be used as adjunct thesauri, even if one does not make further use of UST.

(6) UST would contain a series of indexing languages, each common to a group of institutions facing a similar situation. The scope of these schemes may be either universal (as in the case of academic libraries) or specific (as in the case of the weather bureaus) (see K3.3 for further elaboration).

(7) UST would, due to its hierarchical structure, contain an umbrella classification (or, more properly speaking, several umbrella classifications) that can be extracted as needed.

K3.2 Neutrality of UST with Regard to Classification Principles

The recommended structure would reflect the best knowledge of the full-time specialists working on UST and all the subject experts asked to advise and review. It would, however, in no way be compulsory; it would represent merely suggestions to people constructing an indexing language for a special application. Above all, UST would avoid arguments over the relative merits of different principles of classification by including all the information from any existing scheme. Further, any new classification scheme based on any principle whatever, could be included. As a result UST could be used to construct any new indexing language, no matter on what classification principle it is based. Only by this neutrality with regard to the principles of classification is it possible to achieve universality.

K3.3 UST as a Framework for 'Semi-Universal" Indexing Languages for Shared Subject Indexing

The information needs of the clientele of public libraries or academic libraries or school libraries are fairly similar within each type, at least within the same type of community. Therefore, there is no good reason why each type of library should not apply a common indexing language, and it would even be of advantage if the indexing languages for different types of libraries had a common basis. The same is true for the libraries and information systems of, say, the weather bureaus around the world or any other group of institutions with similar purposes. Common "semi-universal" indexing languages or classification schemes could be constructed in these cases so as to accommodate the viewpoints important for any of the institutions in the group, thus ensuring request-orientation of indexing. The creation of common semi-universal indexing languages for thematic groups of institutions could thus completely facilitate the cooperation in subject indexing within those groups —and it is here that the bulk of cooperation would take place in any case. Embedding these semi-universal indexing languages in UST would be more economical than storing and maintaining them separately.

Of course in each case a major discussion would arise on the subject of what principles should be at the basis of the common, semi-universal indexing language. It seems to us, however, that this problem could be solved much more easily in a limited context than in the broad context of a universal classification.

K3.4 Implementation of a Universal Source Thesaurus

A Universal Source Thesaurus could assume the functions of a universal classification, as envisioned by the founders of UDC and by many contemporary authors, without sharing its pitfalls. Obviously, the creation of UST would be a major undertaking, but thanks to today's knowledge of the structure of indexing languages and thesauri and the procedures available through today's computer technology, UST is quite feasible from a technical point of view.

(It has been argued that a UST produced by the cumulation of a multitude of indexing languages and thesauri as suggested here would be too complex to serve as a common descriptor language (CDL) because the Special Descriptor Languages (SDLs) are too divergent. However, a CDL that does not contain *all* the distinct features of the different SDLs is not a true CDL. So we have to handle the complexity, and modern techniques allow us to do so. The following alternative is offered: study existing SDLs, detect common principles, use these for constructing a CDL, derive new SDLs from this, if needed, by selection and/or extension.)

The organizational side of the problem is quite another matter. The benefits to be derived from UST cannot be obtained for nothing. The construction and maintenance of a UST would require considerable organizational background. First of all, a central organization would be needed, staffed by classification theorists, subject experts in the different disciplines, systems analysts, computer programmers, keying typists, and other clerical staff (one could easily imagine a staff of 250 people) and equipped with sufficient computer facilities. In addition, there should be regional offices in all parts of the world which would make the services available to libraries/information centers. The same organization would take care of the administration of the various semi-universal indexing languages that are embedded in UST.

When all existing indexing languages and thesauri have been included, one has to keep track of the new indexing languages being developed. There are now centers in Cleveland, Ohio, and Warsaw, Poland, trying to do this. However, the incentives to submit a newly developed thesaurus are not very great. With UST and the organization backing it, the situation would be very different. Anyone building a new scheme would want to use UST and its services because he would save substantially in doing so. Thus UST would be informed of nearly all projects of constructing a new special classification and, what is more, since UST programs and computers would be used in many of these projects, the new classification scheme or thesaurus would automatically be included in UST.

Appendices

Appendix 1

Thesaurus Guidelines and Thesaurus Books

1. THESAURUS GUIDELINES

This section gives a list of documents called "thesaurus guidelines", "thesaurus rules" or similar. Only the newest edition is given in each case; reference to older edition is made in the bibliography if appropriate. Revised and new documents appear at a constant rate, and if one intends to follow one of these guidelines, one should contact the appropriate institution to obtain the newest version; a list of these institutions is also given below. A remark of caution should be added: Many of these documents neglect much of the reasoning set forth in this book. Their usefulness seems, therefore, rather questionable. Some of the documents have been incorporated in this book; that means, they have been quoted as source for every rule stated in them, and rules with which this author disagrees have at least been quoted in a footnote. For other documents, such detailed treatment was not possible; they are quoted as source only for rules that have been included in the book and that are unique.

List of Documents

ANSI Z39-1973.2 (draft)   (It was not possible to consider this document.)
BASF1/2 (good, incorporated)
DGD/ET 1966.7 (reasonable, incorporated)
DIN 1463: 1971.10 (draft)
EJC 1965.6 (incorporated)
NORDFORSK 1970.1 (not considered)
TEST 1967.12 (incorporated)
UNESCO 1971.12 (also ISO DIS2788)
UNESCO 1970.12
USCOSATI 1967.9
USERIC 1969.9
ZIID 1967.2 (reasonable, incorporated)
    The ISO and DIN standards on vocabularies are also relevant.

Appendix 1

Partial List of Institutions

International
  ISO/TC37 Terminology (principles and coordination)
  Secretariat: Österreichisches Normungsinstitut
    A-1020 Wien
    Leopoldgasse 4
    Austria
  ISO/TC46/WG5 Guidelines for Thesauri
  Secretariat: Leitstelle Politische Dokumentation
    D-1000 Berlin 45
    Paulinenstr. 22
    Germany

For further details see ISO 1972. The secretariat of the ISO group can also give information on corresponding national groups. UNESCO is also active in this area, but it works with and through ISO.

Germany
  Deutsche Gesellschaft für Dokumentation/Komitee
  Thesaurus forschung
  6 Frankfurt 1
  Westendstr. 19
  Germany

Great Britain
  Classification Research Group
  (see Wilson 1972)

United States
  ANSI (American National Standards Institute)
  1430 Broadway
  New York, N.Y. 10018
  (212) 868-1200
  Committee Z39 (Chairman: Jerrold Orne, The University of North Carolina Library, Chapel Hill, N.C. 27514)

2. THESAURUS BOOKS

There are two books on thesauri and their role in information retrieval, namely Lancaster 1972 "Vocabulary control in information retrieval" and Gilchrist 1971 "The thesaurus in retrieval." In addition, there is a short guide to thesaurus construction, namely Aitchison et al. 1972.

For the convenience of the reader, the tables of contents of these books are reprinted here.

Contents of Lancaster 1972 Vocabulary Control in Information Retrieval

  Some Abbreviations and Acronyms Commonly Used in This Book   xi

1 Why Vocabulary Control?   1

2 Vocabulary Types: Pre-coordination and Post-coordination, Enumeration and Synthesis   5

3 The Classification Scheme in Vocabulary Control   8

		Appendix 1	525
4	Vocabulary Control by Subject Heading		14
5	Vocabulary Control in Post-coordinate Systems: The Thesaurus		22
6	Generating the Controlled Vocabulary		27
7	Organizing and Displaying the Vocabulary		38
8	The Thesaurofacet		66
9	Some Thesaurus Rules and Conventions		70
10	The Reference Structure of the Thesaurus		77
11	Computer Manipulation of Thesaurus Data		90
12	Vocabulary Growth and Updating		98
13	The Influence of System Vocabulary on the Performance of a Retrieval System		107
14	Characteristics and Components of an Index Language: The Vocabulary		115
15	Characteristics and Components of an Index Language: Auxiliary Devices		121
16	Searching Natural-Language Data Bases		135
17	Creating Index Languages Automatically		153
18	Compatibility and Convertibility of Vocabularies		161
19	Some Further Controlled Vocabularies		177
20	The Role of the Controlled Vocabulary in Indexing and Searching Operations		185
21	Supplementary Vocabulary Tools		191
22	Vocabulary Use and Dynamics in a Very Large Information System		204
23	Vocabulary in the On-Line Retrieval Situation		211
24	Some Cost-effectiveness Aspects of Vocabulary Control		218
25	Synopsis		223
	Appendix: Some Controlled Vocabularies for Study or Examination		227
	Index		229

Contents of Gilchrist 1971 The Thesaurus in retrieval

1	BACKGROUND TO THE INDEXING PROCESS	1
2	THE THESAURUS AND ITS TERMS Thesaurus—Terms—Subject headings—Uniterms—Term selection—Lexical resources—Compiler produced—User-produced—Literature as source	4
3	SYSTEMS DESIGN Indexing devices	12

Appendix 1

4	RECALL ORIENTED DEVICES Synonym control—Word form control—Classification—Semantic factors—Clumps and clusters	18
5	PRECISION ORIENTED DEVICES Coordination—Links—Roles—Relationships—Weighting	41
6	CODING	57
7	FORMATS AND AIDS Form—The term—Alphabetization—Scope notes—Syndetics—Classification displays—'Programmed' thesauri—Specialized vocabularies	64
8	CASE STUDIES Shell—Lloyds—Hutton & Rostron—FAIR—Euratom—McClelland—Hoffer—TEST—Thesaurofacet—BIM	80
9	SEARCHING Query formulation—Venn diagrams	112
10	EVALUATION Size—Retrieval effectiveness—Cranfield—MEDLARS—Case Western—Costs	125
11	CONCLUSIONS	136
	APPENDIX: PRINTED INDEXES AND HARDWARE	140
	BIBLIOGRAPHY	154
	INDEX	177

Contents of Aitchison et al. 1972

A	INTRODUCTION	1
B	SYSTEM DESIGN	2
B1	Information System Considerations	2
B2	Operational Considerations	4
B3	Thesaurus Considerations	5
B3.1	New thesaurus versus adaptation	5
B3.2	Controlled versus 'free language' thesaurus	6
B3.3	Thesaurus design elements	7
B4	Thesaurus Design Data for Specific Systems	12
C-G	THESAURUS FEATURES	
C	*Standardization and Control of Terms*	13
C1	Nouns and Adjectives	14
C2	Singular and Plural Forms	14
C3	Direct and Indirect Entry	16
C4	Spelling, Capitalization and Transliteration	17
C5	Abbreviations, Initials and Acronyms	17
C6	Punctuation	18
C7	Homographs	18
C8	Scope Notes and Definitions	19

Appendix 1

D	*Specificity and Pre-coordination Level*	19
D1	Vocabulary Specificity	19
D1.1	Compressed vocabularies	21
D2	Pre-coordination Level of Index Terms	21
E	*Structure, Interrelationships and Classification*	26
E1	Structural and Classificatory Elements	27
E1.1	Equivalence relationships, synonyms	27
E1.2	Hierarchical relationships	28
E1.3	Non-hierarchically related terms	29
E1.4	Clusters and clumps	30
E1.5	Faceted classification	31
E1.6	Notation	37
F	*Auxiliary Precision Devices*	39
F1	Coordination	39
F2	Links	40
F3	Roles	40
F4	Inter-term Relationships—Relational Indicators	43
F5	Weighting	46
G	*Special Purpose Thesauri*	47
G1	Free Language Thesauri	47
G2	Convertible Thesauri	48
H	THESAURUS PRESENTATION	50
H1	Alphabetical Thesaurus	50
H1.1	Layout and reference structure	50
H1.2	Entry vocabulary	51
H1.3	Alphabetization	52
H2	Classified Thesaurus	55
H2.1	Alphabetical thesaurus with broad subject classification	55
H2.2	Alphabetical thesaurus with clusters and arrowgraphs	55
H2.3	Alphabetical thesaurus with hierarchical displays	55
H2.4	Alphabetical thesaurus with hierarchical classification	55
H2.5	Alphabetical thesaurus with faceted classification—broad groups	57
H2.6	Alphabetical thesaurus with faceted classification—detailed	61
H2.7	Systematic thesaurus with alphabetical index	62
J	CONSTRUCTION TECHNIQUES	67
J1	Definition of Subject Field	67
J2	Selection of Thesaurus Characteristics and Layout	68
J3	Establishment of Basic Structural Divisions	68
J4	Selection of Terms	69
J4.1	Manual selection	69
J4.2	Machine selection	70
J5	Recording of Terms	70
J6	Classificatory Aids	72
J6.1	Advantages of classification	78
J7	Incorporation of Existing Index Languages	79
J8	Finalization of Alphabetical Thesaurus	79
J9	Finalization of the Classified Thesaurus	81

Appendix 1

J10	Checking with Subject Experts	83
J11	Addition of Notation to Classified Thesaurus	83
J12	Writing of Introduction	83
J13	Editing	83
J14	Testing	84
J15	Production	84
J16	Computer Aids	84
K	UPDATING	86
K1	Machine Updating	87
	BIBLIOGRAPHY	88
	INDEX	91

Appendix 2

Bibliographies of Subject Access Vocabularies and Dictionaries. Specific Subject Access Vocabularies and Documents on Specific Subject Access Vocabularies Included in the Bibliography

1. LIST OF INSTITUTIONS AND BIBLIOGRAPHIES

General

Barske et al. 1969
BN (Deposit for French thesauri)
CIINTE (Collection center for non-English material)
CIINTE 1969–
CWRU/BSC (Collection center for English material)
CWRU/BSC 1969.
Denison 1968 (giving an inventory of the holdings of CWRU/BSC as from 1967)
DGD Bibliothek 1969
Fachwörterbucher 1971
Gueniot 1969.5 (with descriptions)
ICTSS
IICT
Laureilhe 1969 (with descriptions)
UNESCO 1969 (interlingual dictionaries)
UNESCO 1959 (monolingual dictionaries)
Walkley 1971.6 (with annotations)

Appendix 2

Specific Topics

Fuelhart 1968.6 (Information science, with descriptions)
Heald 1967.11a (Science and technology)
Hyslop 1965.12 (Science and technology, 23 sources)
Lewis 1968.4 (Language sciences)
MeSH 1972 (Medicine)
Miller 1966.9 (Pulp and paper)
Rosenbaum 1966.x (Science and technology)
U.S. ERIC 1972 (Education and related fields, 102 sources)
Wagner 1970 (Multilingual rehabilitation terminology tools)

Furthermore, it might be useful to contact special libraries in the subject field in question directly and ask them for their classification scheme/thesaurus. Any directory of special libraries may be consulted. Of particular usefulness might be Ash et al. 1967.

2. LIST OF SUBJECT ACCESS VOCABULARIES AND OF DOCUMENTS ABOUT SUCH VOCABULARIES CONTAINED IN THE BIBLIOGRAPHY

This list is not meant to replace any of the bibliographies listed in the first part of this bibliography. Its value is mainly in the listing of articles describing specific subject access vocabularies. A comprehensive bibliography worked out along these lines would certainly be useful.

The entries have been grouped by *ad hoc* subject categories. Subject access vocabularies are cited by a descriptive title, followed by the proper reference to the bibliography in ( ). Documents *on* a subject access vocabulary are indented.

Items marked * are listed only in the extended version of the bibliography available from ERIC.

General

UDC
DDC
LCC
See Section D1.7.3
LCSH   See Section D1.7.10
*Sears List of Subject Headings (Sears 1972)
RAND Subject Heading List (no reference)
   Way 1968.4

Science and Technology in General

ASTIA Thesaurus (USASTIA 1962.12)
   USDDC 1966.5 (Descriptor frequencies)
   Caponio 1964.1
   Gillum et al. 1961
   Klingbiel 1964.8
   Klingbiel 1963.10
   Wall 1962.8
EJC Thesaurus (EJC 1964)
   EJC 1965.6 (rules)
   Campbell 1965.6
   Wall 1965.12; 1963.10; 1962.11—63.10; 1963.8; 1962.10

TEST (TEST 1967.12a; see Section D1.2)
TEST 1967.12 (rules)
Gillum 1969.10
Dovel 1966.10
Heald 1967.11
Klingbiel 1964.8
Peirce 1969.10
Rainey 1970.1
Schön 1970
Speight 1969.10; 1966.10; 1964.9
USDOD 1965.12; 1965.10
NASA Thesaurus (no reference)
Manheimer 1969.x
Rainey 1970.1
Polytechnical thesaurus (Norway, no reference)
Schanche 1968.8; 1966
TDCK thesaurus (TDCK 1966.5)
Koekkoek 1962.12
Schüller 1968.6; 1966.10; 1963.10
Engineering Index thesaurus (no reference)
Whaley et al. 1966.10
Hammond et al. 1964.4 is a cumulative scientific-technical thesaurus.
COSATI subject category list (USCOSATI 1964.12)
*Science Citation Index 1967–
*North American Rockwell thesaurus (North American Rockwell 1966)
*Nova Scotia Research Foundation thesaurus (... 1966)
Semantic Code Dictionary (Melton 1958c)
Melton 1962 and other articles by Jessica or John Melton

Physics

Faceted scheme of plasma physics (in Lerner 1968.3b)
Euratom thesaurus (Section D1.7.6)
*ZAED descriptor list (ZAED 1963)
Documents on other subject access vocabularies in physics
Uhlmann 1967. (Nuclear science and technology)
Cheng 1968 (Rheology)
Herrmann 1967.4 (Diffusion)

Chemistry

Chemical Engineering Thesaurus 1961
Chemical kinetics index (USNBS 1971.7)
Faceted scheme for chemical physics (in Lerner 1968.3a)
Documents on other subject access vocabularies in chemistry
BASF1/2 (chemistry)
Bauer 1969.x and many other articles by Bauer (total thesaurus chemistry with various constituent thesauri)
Dym 1967.10
Fichte et al. 1968 (Silico-organic compounds)
Green 1966.3 (Physical chemistry)

Petroleum

API Thesaurus (API 1971.1) see Section D1.7.8
Exploration and production thesaurus (Univ. of Tulsa/ . . . 1968, used for Petroleum Abstracts)
    Martinez 1969.10; 1968.10
    University of Tulsa
Documents on other subject access vocabularies on petroleum
    Marlot 1970
    Neumann 1967.4 (petroleum refining)

Civil Engineering

International road research documentation thesaurus (OECD/IRRD 1971.11)
    Dijk 1966.10
Water resources thesaurus (Water 1971)
    *Bellport 1966.10
    Hersey *et al.* 1967.10
*Thesaurus of soil mechanics (American Society of Civil Engineers 1967)
Documents on other subject access vocabularies in this area:
    Roberts 1971 (Construction industry)
    Thomas 1971.11 (Transportation and planning)

Other Areas in Science and Technology

Thesaurofacet (Electrical engineering) (see Section D1.7.4)
U.S. Bureau of Ships thesaurus (. . . 1966)
    Nicolaus 1966.10
*Thesaurus of terms on copper technology (Copper Development Association 1966)
*Textile technology terms (Institute of Textile Technology 1966)
Documents on subject access vocabularies in other areas of science and technology
    DGD/ET 1966.7 (Electrical engineering)
    Frank 1967.4 (Mechanical engineering)
    Rosemann 1967.4 (Explosives)
    Miller 1966.9 (Pulp and paper)
    Nobbs 1966.12; *1966.10; 1962 (Pulp and paper)
    Hanicke 1967.4 (Wood technology)
    Kimlicek 1966.6 (Wood technology)
    Gravenstein 1968 (Earth sciences)
    Smorodinova 1966.6 (Gyroscopic devices)

Information Science

Thesaurus of information Science technology (Schultz 1968)
On a cumulative information science thesaurus
    Gardin 1969.3
    Levy 1967.9
On an information science thesaurus
    Buntrock *et al.* 1963.10

Life Sciences, Biology, and Related Areas

MESH   see Section D1.7.5

On a cumulative biomedical thesaurus in English and Spanish
  Muench 1971.7
Ringdoc codeless scanning thesaurus (Ringdoc 1968.3)
  Wegmueller *et al.* 1964.10
Thesaurus of the Vision information center   see Section D1.7.1
*Biomedical engineering information retrieval language (in Pickford et al. 1968–)
  Pickford *et al.* 1968.10
Documents on other subject access vocabularies in the area of medicine
  Hübner 1967.4
  McClelland *et al.* 1966 (Anaesthetics)
  McGee *et al.* 1963.10 (Medicine in general)
  Schneider 1968.2 (Cancer)
  Smilari *et al.* (Biochemistry and medicine)
  Wolff-Terroine *et al.* 1969.1 (Cancer)
Agricultural/Biological Vocabulary (NAL)
  Schactman 1967.10
*Thesaurus on Biodeterioration (Willsher *et al.* eds. 1967)
On other thesauri in this area
  Blankenstein 1967.4 (Food and nutrition)
  Kleeberg 1970.x (Agriculture and Food)
  Rudolph 1970 (Bio-environment and Radiological Safety)
  Weinstein 1966.10 (Biology)

Social Sciences

FR Thesaurus (Section D1.7.2)
Cumulative multilingual thesaurus on problems of developing countries
  (OECD/Development Center 1969)
*Thesaurus on problems of developing countries (DSE 1966.2)
  Rieck 1967.2
Human factors data thesaurus (Oller 1968.3)
Classification scheme for labor market research (Soergel *et al* 1970.8)
*Descriptor list for labor problems (ILO 1965.10)
International Standard Industrial Classification (ISIC 1968)
Thesaurus of education terms (Section D1.7.7)
ERIC thesaurus (Section D1.7.9; descriptor frequencies available)
Classification scheme for a management information system in education
  (Thomas 1969.10)
*British Institute of Management thesaurus (Blagden 1969)
  Blagden 1971.3
Faceted classification of occupational safety (Foskett 1957.5)
Descriptor list for social welfare (Hoffer 1962.4)
Descriptor list for history (in Boehm ed. 1965.7)
Geographical subdivision of the US (in U.S. Bureau of the Census 1962)
*Land Tribunal Index (Roberts *et al.* 1969)
Documents on other subject access vocabularies in the social sciences
  Gershon 1969 (Management services)
  Hecking et al. 1969 (Urban planning)
  Rahman et al. 1968.12 (Agricultural economics)
  Seiden 1966.6 (Economics)

Appendix 2

Adjunct Thesauri

A thesaurus-classification for the physical forms of media (Croghan 1970)
Thesaurus of microform terms (Williams 1969)
Documents on subject access vocabularies, area unknown
    Aires 1966.10
    Kerckhove 1969
See also the note to Section K2.3.2,1, where projects comparing subject access vocabularies are listed.

Chapter Notes

CHAPTER A

A. Halkin 1966.10 gives a similar overview of the functions and the structure of a thesaurus.

A1.1. The overview of the requirements follows BASF 1, p. 1. This and the following section draw partly on Wall 1963.10, Section IV.

A1.3. The first paragraph (thesaurus in context) follows ZIID 1967.2, Section 3.3.1.

A1.3.1. The list of parameters determining thesaurus size is adapted from ZIID 1967.2, Section 2 p. 4–5; similar list by Preisler 1970, p. 6. For more detailed considerations see Vickery 1965, chapter 9, p. 154–178.

A1.3.2. The dangers of an inappropriate thesaurus are pointed out in Fugmann 1966.6; compare also Blankenstein 1967.x, p. 177–178.

A1.4. Thesauri are used in preparing the indexes to the abstracting/indexing services published by API, USERIC, NLM, NASA, to name a few. This use of thesauri is described, for example, in Whaley *et al.* 1966.10, p. 47, Schultz *et al.* 1962.10 and Sheperd 1963. The system for computer-assistance in the construction and maintenance of thesauri described in Hines *et al.* 1971.6 pays particular attention to the requirements of alphabetical subject indexes.

A1.5. On (1): for an example of a classification scheme for a MIS see Thomas 1969.10–. The use of classification schemes in the collection of census data and the like needs no further elaboration. On the use of the classification schemes in research see Soergel 1971, sections A3.1.5, p. 90–99, and C1.0-C1.4, p. 273–282. On (2): for a good example of a classification of decision alternatives see Ott 1967.x. Oller 1968.3 might also be relevant. On (b): for a good article on dictionaries for content analysis see Dunphy 1966.

A1.6. The treatment of intellectual problems in thesaurus development follows BASF1 , p. 13.

A1.7. Compare the longer list of criteria for thesaurus evaluation in Preisler 1970.x, section 5.1, p. 7. We do not agree with all of his criteria.

A2. Administrative problems of thesaurus development are also dealt within TEST 1967.12, p. 1–2, "The Making of an Inter-Disciplinary Thesaurus" and Heald 1967.11.

A2.1. There are two centers maintaining collections of classification schemes and thesauri: For English language material: CWRU/BSC; for material in other languages: CIINTE. For further sources see Appendix 2. That plans for the construction of a thesaurus should be communicated to one of these centers is stated in DIN 1463: 1971.10, sections 5.1 and 5.2, p. 18.

A2.3. Speed of development to insure continuity is mentioned in ZIID 1967.2, section 3.1, p. 6. On the use of experimental indexing in thesaurus construction see, for ex-

Chapter Notes

ample, USOE 1966.2, where the guidelines for the first phase of the development of the USERIC thesaurus are given. ISAR systems that take care of the synonym-problem in searching and their thesaurus requirements are dealt with in Levery 1968.3, p. 7. For data on resources and time needed in the development of the TEST thesaurus, see Heald 1967.11, section VI, p. 13–15. The special thesaurus mentioned is Abbots biological dictionary, see Weinstein 1966.10.

ZIID 1967.2, p. 6 gives the following data:

(1) Thesaurus "Wood technology" (GDR) 24 months
(2) Thesaurus "Road technology" (France) 8 months
(3) "Polytechnical thesaurus" (Norway) 36 months
(4) "Thesaurus of Engineering terms" (EJC, USA) 18 months

CHAPTER B

B1.1. Common origin criterion for homonyms mentioned in ZIID 1967.2, 3.3.4, p. 15–16. For a detailed discussion of the synonym-problem see, for example, Kocourek 1968 and Kocourek 1968a.

B2.0. On the rationale consolidating for quasi-synonyms compare TEST 1967.12, T–7, p. 674–675; also T–1b, p. 674.

B2.1. That a preferred term should be selected is stated in TEST 1967.12, T–6, p. 674.

B2.3. Compare Kochen et al. 1968.9,4. (b) "Synonyms", p. 182–183, for a further discussion of these problems.

B2.4. On dealing with the complexities of language compare Deese 1965. On the related problem of concept formation see Klausmeier et al. 1965 and Klausmeier et al. 1969.

B3.0. On the Semantic Code see Perry et al. ed. 1958. The faceted classification example is from Vickery 1966, p. 67–71. On role indicators and especially on hierarchical relationships between them see Soergel 1967.12.

B4.2.1. The term "descriptor" was first used by Mooers with the connotation that a descriptor stands for a broad (elemental) concept (Mooers 1951.1, Mooers 1958). TEST 1967.12, defines as follows: ". . . , terms selected to be entered into the thesaurus for use as indexing terms will be called 'descriptors' ". These are understood to be mainly terms designating concepts rather than proper names (/C4.0). For other defiinitions, see, for example, USERIC 1972, 1969.4 edition, p. VII. Compare also the discussion in Autopolskii 1967, which concentrates mainly on the Russian usage. Compare also the discussion in Brenner 1964.10, with which we do not agree at all, ICTB 1970.3, item 2b, p. 4–5, and DGD/KT 1967.9. The quotation is from TEST 1967.12, p. 438.

B4.2.3. Our definition of indexing language is in agreement with the considerations by Gardin in Cros et al. 1964, chapter 2,A, paragraphs 1 and 2. Gardin's "lexique" corresponds to the indexing language (system vocabulary). Compare to the whole problem Gardin 1966.5. The quotation from the Elsinore Conference is found in Atherton ed. 1965, p. 544.

B4.2.4. Our definition of "thesaurus", especially the requirement that a thesaurus must contain a lead-in vocabulary, follows Vickery 1960.12 and Gardin in Cros et al. 1964, Glossary. Further references related to this problem of definition and terminology are: Gueniot 1969.5, p. 182: "There comes a point where it is impossible to distinguish (thesauri from subject heading lists, D.S.) and even though a thesaurus reviewed below is called thesaurus because the author has labeled the title that way, it is not at all dif-

Chapter Notes 537

ferent from a list of subject headings like that of the Library of Congress, or of Biblio." Gardin 1966.5 gives his own system of definitions for glossary, thesaurus, vocabulary, and classification. Brenner *et al.* 1965.10 suggests that subject heading lists and thesauri are basically the same. Most of the thesaurus guidelines listed in Appendix 1 give a definition. USERIC 1972, 1969.4 edition, p. VII lists several definitions. A list of (rather inadequate) definitions is also found in ICTB 1970.3, section 1.1, p. 1–2; more elaborate definitions are given on p. 21–26. The term "subject access vocabulary" has been suggested by Angel 1967.9.

B5.2. An excellent and probably the first explicit description of request-oriented indexing is to be found in Mooers *et al.* 1958, p. 350 ff; Mooers uses the term "filtering technique". The technique is also suggested by Hörig 1967.4, p. 156.

B5.2.1 Example (2) "Seismonastic movements of plants" is from Scheele 1969.4, p. 79, question 13.

B5.2.2(1.2). The importance of the descriptor display for indexer consistency is stressed in ZIID 1967.2, 3.3.5, p. 19 and in Detant 1966.7, p. 5–7 'arrowgraphs'.

B5.2.3. For references to document analysis sheets geared to request-oriented indexing see Section D1.1.2,1.

B5.2.4. The check-list technique of search request formulation is proposed in Lancaster 1968, p. 186–189.

B5.4.1(4b). Change from manual to mechanized system is mentioned in Blankenstein 1967.4, p. 114.

(7b). The format *Vegetable*beans* is used by Ringdoc 1968.3; the possibility of using *Beans*vegetables* instead is also mentioned there (p. 13). Compare also Hines *et al.* 1971.6, p. 43.

B5.4.3(c). This procedure is used in Ringdoc, as described in Ringdoc 1968.3, p. 3–5. The advantages (1), (3), and (4) from B5.4.1 are mentioned there. The broad descriptors used in the manual index are called *index terms*, the specific descriptors not admitted for the manual index are called *standardized free terms*. It is also mentioned there that two specific descriptors may lead to the same filing descriptor; this filing descriptor is then written on the card only once, of course. Descriptors on the catalog cards are written as follows: *Small Airports*Aquadromes.

B5.4.4. How confusing things can get if one does not clearly distinguish between truly free terms and terms to be used for retrieval may be seen from Detant 1966.7, sections "Additional terms" and "The Dictionary", p. 7–11. In Martinez 1968.10, p. 282–283, the problem has been recognized in the course of the use of free terms, and a "supplementary list", containing proper names (in three sections) and very specific, seldom used "concept descriptors" is issued as a supplement to the thesaurus. Another system that started out to use free terms in addition to the system vocabulary and then switched to standardize the free terms and thus, in effect, incorporate them into the system vocabulary, is Ringdoc (see Ringdoc 1968.3, p. 3–5).

B5.5. The functions of hierarchy are also discussed in McClelland 1966.10.

(b). Assist in proper level of generality: TEST 1967.12, C-6, EJC 1965.6, C-6, BASF2, A.

B5.6. The sample abstracts (3a) and (3b) are from Weil 1970.9, p. 356; see there for further examples.

B5.7(a). High sepecificity is recommended in BASF1, p. 1.

(b). Use roles and links only if high precision is a must. ZIID 1967.2, section 2., point 4, p. 3.

B6.1. The discussion of the use of the lead-in vocabulary in manual indexing follows closely BASF1, p. 1–2. The importance of the lead-in vocabularly for system performance is brought out in Lancaster's study of MEDLARS (Lancaster 1969.4; Lancaster 1968.1).

B6.2. Some of the considerations on mechanized indexing, especially the distinction between semi-mechanized and fully-mechanized indexing draw on BASF1, p. 3–4; BASF uses semi-mechanized indexing based on term lists. Partially mechanized indexing based on term lists and titles has been done in a project described by Schultz *et al.* 1962.10, Schultz 1963.10, and Shepherd 1963. An interesting project in fully mechanized indexing is described in Amacher 1967.9. The most advanced system in this area is the SMART system developed at Harvard and Cornell. It uses fully mechanized indexing and fully mechanized search request formulation. For general descriptions see Salton 1964.1, Salton 1964.6 (both overlap to a great extent), Salton 1965.6, Salton *et al.* 1966.6 and Salton 1967.6. For details see ISR (Information Storage and Retrieval) reports; a selection of the studies contained in these reports is reprinted in Salton ed. 1971. On computer-stored dictionaries to assist in translation see Schuck 1969.2 and Winkler 1969.2. These references are for purposes of illustration only; they were selected for their emphasis on thesaurus problems. There is an enormous literature on mechanized indexing, and a small portion of it deals with thesaurus usage also. See Stevens 1970.2 for a state-of-the art report.

B6.2.1. The problem of translating search requests entered into an inter-active ISAR system in free terminology into the indexing language using a notation is described in Cain 1969.7 in the framework of the SUNY Biomedical Communication Network. A number of actual examples are given. However, it is suggested in this article to include for all nouns singular and plural, etc., not taking into account the remark in section B6.2.2(1) below.

B6.2.2(2). The problem of multi-word terms is dealt with in SMART (see note to B6.2 above), and in Shepherd 1963; Amacher 1967.9 and Winkler 1969.2.

B6.2.2(5). Cue-words are used in the method for mechanized abstracting described by **Rush** *et al.* 1971.7.

B6.3. Compare to this section and to section B6 in general Jaster *et al.* 1962, section 5.3, p. 59–64. They say that the lead-in structure can be applied (1) in (manual) indexing, (2) in "posting" (roughly our semi-mechanized indexing) and (3) in searching. (Compare the note to section C1.4.5 on the similar situation in the application of the hierarchical structure.)

B7. The quotation is from Gillum 1969.10, slightly modified.

CHAPTER C

C. Kochen *et al.* 1968.9,4, "Types of relations found in cross-reference structures", p. 180–189, provides useful complementary reading even though it overlaps with our discussion. Furthermore, the following are useful as background reading especially for Section C1:

Becker *et al.* 1963, esp. Part III;
Coates 1960;
Cros *et al.* 1964;
Cuadra ed. 1966-ARIST, esp. the chapter "Document description and representation";
Lancaster 1972;
Lancaster 1968;
Meadow 1967;
Mills 1960;
Needham 1971;
Sayers 1967;
Shera *et al.* 1956;
Soergel 1967.7;
Vickery 1965;
Vickery 1959.

Chapter Notes 539

Other readings can be found in Denison 1968 and in Richmond 1972.8. Another general article, perhaps useful for its references, is Jones 1971.11.

C1.0. The scatter of concepts of general application in traditional classifications is brought out by deGrolier 1962, p. 22–42, with numerous examples from UDC.

C1.1.0. On theories of semantic factoring connected to theories of definition see Pshenichnaya 1967. On links and roles see Soergel 1967.12 (or Soergel 1971, part C, for an updated German version). Many references are given in this article. See also the references to Section D4.3.6. On faceted classification see (in order of priority) Vickery 1960, Vickery 1966 or Vickery 1959.

C1.2. The definition of "Broader than" is modified from Needham 1961, p. 6, 10. In the words of Joyce *et al.* 1958.7, p. 195: "If you ask for A you musn't complain if you get (B if A broader than B. D.S.)." The pragmatic nature of hierarchical relationships is also emphasized by Barhydt *et al.* 1968, p. 12. The cross-references in the API-thesaurus are explained in Mulvihill *et al.* 1966.10, p. 181.

C.1.2. The fact that a concept may have two or more broader concepts is also stated in TEST 1967.12, C-7, p. 678. TEST calls this situation "hierarchy overlap". The terms "strong hierarchy" and "weak hierarchy" are from Mooers 1959, p. 1344.

C1.3. That UDC leaves out many hierarchical relationships has been very aptly pointed out by Fairthorne 1955.10.

(b). That compound concepts expressed by similar combinations of elemental concepts are related is pointed out by Levery 1968.3, p. 11.

C1.3.2. On a detailed treatment of faceted classification see Vickery 1960 or Vickery 1966, a short account is given in Foskett 1959.

C1.4.1,2. That broader concepts useful for searching often have no term in the discipline in question is pointed out by Halkin 1966.10.

C1.4.1,4. On organizational headings USERIC 1972, 1969.4 edition, p. XII, "Organizational terminology."

C1.4.1,5. For a more detailed discussion of Antonyms compare Kochen *et al.* 1968.9,4.(c) "Antonyms" p. 183–184. A meaningless discussion is to be found in Mandersloot 1970.1, p. 54. TEST 1967.12, T-7, p. 674–675 allows for the treatment of antonyms as quasi-synonyms, for example, *Smoothness* USE *Roughness*; in fact, the broader concept is used here and designated by *Roughness*. EJC 1965.6, T-7, p. 2 and DGD/ET 1966.7, 4. p. 4 have the same rule as TEST.

C1.4.2. Kochen *et al.* 1968.9, 4.(e), "Inclusion relations", p. 185–189 provides useful complementary reading on the kinds of hierarchical relationships; especially (2) "Topic inclusion" is defined there. (1)-(3) including Figure 14 follow BASF1, p. 7–11; BASF1 in turn cites Wüster 1959 as source. The quotation is from TEST 1967.12, C-4, p. 677; other part-whole relationships are treated as RT relationships in TEST (C-8d, p. 678). EJC 1965.7 gives the same rules (C-4, p. 4).

C1.4.3,1. On coarse hierarchy compare Jaster 1963.2 and Hammond 1963.12 who use the term "subsumption scheme" and discuss the application dealt with here. BASF1, p. 6 uses the term "Grobklassifizierung" and mentions its use for sorting terms. The examples are taken from the COSATI Subject Category List as printed in TEST 1967.12, p. 565–567. The middle way between coarse and fully detailed hierarchy is followed in DGD/ET 1966.7, 2.2, p. 1 and Anhang 2, p. 8.

C1.4.4. The headings "General descriptors" and "Other descriptors" are used by DGD/ET 1966.7, Anhang 2, point 3, p. 7.

C1.4.5. Implementation of inclusive searching in the searching line and the storage line, respectively (methods (1) and (2)) are mentioned in Jaster *et al.* 1962, Section 5.3, p. 59–64. They deal with the lead-in problem in the same context: (1.1) corresponds to completely manual indexing, (1.2) corresponds to semimechanized indexing and (2) corresponds to the application of the lead-in structure in searching. (Compare the note to section B6.3.)

C1.4.6(2). The term "general references" in this connection has been suggested by K. P. Jones in McClelland *et al.* 1966.10, p. 302.

C1.4.7. The U.S. Bureau of the Census example for the use of descriptors "..., other" is from Priebe 1968.7.

C1.5. The definition of "is related to" follows TEST 1967.12, C-8, p. 678. Kochen *et al.* 1968.9, 4.(8) "Other relations", p. 188–189 and Barhydt *et al.* 1968, p. 15–18 provide complementary reading and further examples for associative relationships. The possibility of reducing the number of RT-cross-references in the presence of a classified index is mentioned in Barhydt *et al.* 1968, p. 15, point (2).

C1.5.1. RT-cross-references based on similarity in meaning are used in TEST 1967.12, C-8a and b, p. 678.

C1.5.2,1. The treatment of contiguity based on definition follows ZIID 1967.2, 3.3.5, p. 17 (example (2) is ours).

,2. The *Alcohol* examples are taken from TEST 1967.12, C-8c., p. 678, "descriptors that have viewpoint interrelationships, such as a relationship based on usage."

,3. RT cross-references based on frequent usage in combination are suggested by Smorodinowa 1966.6, who also mentions advantage (b).

C1.5.3. The idea of the "instructional scope note" is mentioned in Wall 1962.11, C; the disease example is from there. Using a suitable arrangement of the descriptors instead of an instructional scope note and using a rudimentary form of an instructional scope note by writing *** are both described in Weinstein 1966.10, p. 191–192 and p. 193, respectively.

C1.7. On psychological dimensions of relationships compare Richards *et al.* 1970.5, Section 3. "Centers of interest", p. 6–8, Deese 1965, and possibly Bourne 1966.

C2.3 The quantitative view of post-combination and pre-combination forming a continuous scale has first been set forth in Jonker 1959; Jonker speaks of a "descriptive continuum." The ideas of Section C2.3 form the basis, if implicitly, for the procedure of converting a subject heading list into a system vocabulary consisting of elemental concepts only described in Thomas *et al.* 1953. By now this paper is outdated.

C2.3.1. The Unemployment insurance example for precombination vs. colon is from Wellisch 1971.6, p. 15a. On the use of syntax versus the use of compound concepts, compare USERIC 1972, 1969.4 edition, p. XI, "Descriptor construction". Maixner 1970.12 makes the same point.

C2.3.2. The idea of an auxiliary ISAR system that retrieves compound descriptors based on their semantic factors occurs repeatedly in the literature. See Cordonnier 1960, p. 1102, "Syntermation", Libbey 1966.10 and 1967.1 (while we agree with Libbey in principle, he makes a number of rather odd points), and Levery 1968.3, p. 11.

C2.3.3. The two-step procedure for searching in an ISAR system for biology has been developed by Scheele (1964.3, p. 3, II 2.C).

C2.4. On the problem of citation order in subject headings compare Coates 1960, ch. VI, p. 50–64.

C2.5. On the PRECIS-system see, for example, Austin 1972. Some experiments with a unified scheme that would establish a correspondence between an alphabetical subject catalog, a classified subject catalog and a shelving classification are reported in Dehnhard 1968.x.

C2.6.1(2). Reducing the size of the indexing language through avoiding precombined descriptors is mentioned in TEST 1967.12, T-11, p. 676.

C2.7. The following sources have been used in elaborating the rules for the use of precombined descriptors in Section C2.7: TEST 1967.12, T-11, p. 676; EJC 1965.6, T-5, p. 2; ZIID 1967.2, Sections 3.2, p. 7 and 3.3.2.2/3, p. 11. The rules given by Mandersloot *et al.* 1970.1, "Term-splitting", p. 53–54 do not make much sense. TEST gives reasonable rules under the unreasonable heading "multi-word terms" which really should be "specific terms" (Gillum 1969.10, p. 10–11). All the rules given by Jones 1971.7 are based on the linguistic structure of words and are accordingly deficient. As far as they make sense, they can all be replaced by the simple rule: Split concepts, not terms. Note that none of the rules that follow and that are aimed at improving retrieval performance are included in Jones' rules. The quotation in (1) is from TEST 1967.12, T-11, p. 676. Checking the decisions by practical indexing and retrieval experiments is recommended by ZIID 1967.2, section 3.3.2.3, p. 11. The rule on decomposition of multiword terms is slightly modified from UNESCO 1971.12, section 3.22, p. 9.

C2.7.1. TEST 1967.12 addresses the problem of when to use a precombined descriptor in rule T-11, p. 676, EJC 1965.6 in rule T-5, p. 2. In detail, sources for the rules are as follows: (a) Frequency in indexing and/or searching: TEST, T-11(b), first half; EJC, T-5d; BASF2, E3.2, p. 8. (b) Frequency of components: Our first sentence only: TEST, T-11(b), second half and T-11(d); EJC, T-5e; the student teacher example is from Eller 1968.7, p. 214. (c) Syntactical relationship of components: DGD/ET 1966.7, 3.4, p. 2. (f) Doubtful cases: TEST, T-11; EJC 1965.6, T-5f.

C2.7.2. Sources for the two rules on when to use a combination of descriptors are as follows: (a) Object—material: TEST 1966.4 version: T-12h, p. 13; EJC 1965.6, T-5h, p. 2. (b) Chemical compounds: TEST 1967.12, T-10a, p. 676; ZIID 1967.2, 3.3.2.3, p. 11.

C2.7.2(c). The additional rules mentioned in the footnote are from TEST 1967.12, T-11a. and c., p. 676.

C2.8.1. For a generalized treatment of superimposed coding, see Soergel 1967.7, chapter 3. For random superimposed coding as applied to edge-notched cards, see Mooers *et al.* 1958; Mooers 1951.1.

C2.8.1. The quotation on random superimposed coding and inclusive searching is from Hayne *et al.* 1957, p. 247. For an example of "two-stage" superimposed coding see Mooers *et al.* 1958. For an example of the simultaneous application of semantic and random superimposed coding, see the system of Inter Nationes, described in Arntz 1964.3.

C2.8.2. Compare to this discussion on how to reduce the number of concepts Soergel 1967.7, Chapter 5, especially 5.2, "Reduction of the number of terms", p. 168–170. To (a1) and (a2): compare Wall 1962.8, p. 12–13. On negation as retrieval operation see Soergel 1967.7, section 2.3, p. 151. On implementation with peek-a-boo cards, see for example Pietsch in Casey *et al.* ed. 1958, p. 609. The Inter Nationes system is described in Arntz 1964.3.

C3.1. The quotation on concepts useful in several disciplines is from Singer 1968.6, p. 2.

C3.2.1. Compare to (1) and (2) Friedrich 1963, p. 2ff, where the problem of definition is dealt with in more detail.

C3.2.2. The necessity for scope notes is also pointed out by Heald 1967.11, p. 30. For a more detailed exposition and examples see Mulvihill 1968.10; the quotation is from Mulvihill, p. 4. The importance of scope notes for terms, the meaning of which varies over time or from country to country pointed out in UNESCO 1971.12, Section 5.5.2, p. 25. For an inventory of pictorial symbols see Dreyfuss 1972.

C4.0(a). Form descriptors are mentioned in ZIID 1967.2, 3.3.2, point 6., p. 12. TEST 1967.12, p. 673, says ". . . (b) bibliographic terms—terms that describe the document itself, not the information in the document. Bibliographic terms, examples of which are personal authors, corporate authors, and publication dates, should not be included in the thesaurus." While these examples suggest that "bibliographic terms" is used in a narrow sense and does not refer to what we call "form descriptors", such descriptors are not included in TEST (a few exceptions like *Bibliography* and *Handbook* not withstanding).

C4.0(b). Content descriptors are discussed in TEST 1967.12, p. 673, (a). TEST lists the following types, given after our number: (b1.2): project names; (b1.4): "(5) geopolitical names"; (b1.10): "(7) other proper names"; (b2.4): "(6) trademarks" and "(2) military nomenclature". Furthermore, TEST mentions "(3) identification symbols or numbers" and "(4) nicknames or jargon". TEST does not distinguish between (b2) Elements of nomenclature and (b3) Other concepts. It subdivides by another criterion, namely "(8) terms of an analytical nature. . ." and "(9) terms of an abstract nature. . .". The quotations (b3.1) and (b3.2) are from TEST.

C4.1. The division of proper names into categories is from Martinez 1968.10, p. 282–283. Another list is given in USERIC 1969.9, section 3, "Identifier guidelines", p. 12–19; the example is from USERIC 1971.6a.

C4.2.2. The quotations on biological and chemical nomenclature are from TEST 1967.12, T-10c for (1) and (2.2) and T-10a for (2.1) (all p. 676).

C4.3. The usefulness of concepts of general application for forming combinations is mentioned in TEST 1967.12, 1966.4 version, IA3f., p. 3. BASF2, A, p. 2 is skeptical about the use of concepts of general application for the reasons mentioned in the first paragraph of C4.3. Point (3) is mentioned in TEST 1967.12, C-6, p. 678; EJC 1965.6, C-6, p. 4. The example is from TEST (selection of example due to Heald 1967.11, p. 30), modified according to the rule set forth in C5.3(2). TEST actually says "consult the terms listed below" and then just lists the terms, *not* marking them NT. As a consequence, *Losses* does not appear in the hierarchical index.

C5.0.1(2). The alphabetical index method for lead-in is used, for example, in DDC. The main part method for lead-in is used in TEST 1967.12, C-2, p. 677; EJC 1965.6 C-2, p. 3; DGD/ET 1966.7, 4., p. 4; ZIID 1967.2, 3.3.3, p. 12ff. Note that all these sources use the crude lead-in form. Compare the descriptions of various thesauri in Section D1.7.

C5.0.2. The description of the crude lead-in form follows TEST 1967.12, C-2 "USE" (the list a.-1. of situations when a USE cross-reference is used is rather unsystematic) and C-3 "Used for", both page 677. The whole problem is dealt with by Angell 1967.9. He analyzed several thesauri as to their treatment of that problem, and gives numerous examples in his table. He also mentions the problems of compatibility between different thesauri created by the crude form. His position is that all preferred terms should be used as descriptors.

,1. Examples 1 and 2 are from USERIC 1972, slightly modified, example 3 is from Schultz 1968a.

C5.2.2. The examples illustrating the more detailed lead-in form are from USERIC 1972, slightly modified. ST and ET, as appropriate, were added by us.

C5.3. Ringdoc 1968.3 uses OR-type USE-instructions designated by SEE . . . OR . . . OR . . . (p. 8). Some of our examples are from this thesaurus.

C5.3.1. The example for a homonymous lead-in term is modified from the EURATOM Thesaurus, 1967, Part 1.

C5.3.2. The scope note solution to remind the indexer to use more specific descriptors is chosen in Barhydt *et al.* 1968 "Scope note*", p. 10–11. The ASTIA example is from Wall 1962.8, p. 8.

Chapter Notes 543

C5.4.1. The idea of qualified USE-instructions has first been used in Ringdoc 1968.3, p. 7. The examples were taken from p. 9–10 and modified. See also Ringdoc 1968.3, p. 17, on the "Roche-version" of the Ringdoc thesaurus.
C6. Part of the considerations on synonyms and spelling variants follows BASF2, B, p. 3–4.
C6.1. That synonyms should appear in the main part entry is stipulated in TEST 1967.12, C-3, p. 677; EJC 1965.6, C-3, p. 4; DGD/ET 1966.7, 2.1, p. 1; Wall 1962.11, B-1. The latter two sources also mention the reason that synonyms convey additional information.
C6.2. For a more detailed discussion of spelling variants see Kochen *et al.* 1968.9, 4. (a) "Morphological and grammatical relations", p. 180–182.
C6.2.2(3). The inclusion of frequent erroneous forms has been done by Schultz *et al.* 1962.10, p. 422 and is planned by Cain 1969.7, p. 253.
C7.1. . .Inverse cross-references are prescribed in TEST 1967.12, C-9, "Reciprocal entries", p. 678. Their use in thesaurus updating is mentioned by Wall 1962.11, B-1.

CHAPTER D

D. Compare on the presentation of vocabularies in general ISO/R919 and DIN2334.
D0. Figure 22b3 is an extract from TEST 1967.12a, p. 591–592.
D1. The subject of the different parts of a thesaurus and their functions receives a thoroughly confused treatment in Surace 1970.3. However, this paper contains a useful collection of sample pages from different thesauri (TEST, NASA, FAA, NAL, AEC and Tancredi 1968.10). See also Infodata Systems 1971.6, ch. 1, p. 1–14, where options for several parts of a thesaurus are discussed.
D1.0. Slamecka did some experiments on the impact of display on indexer performance, but Slamecka 1963.1 is purely a discussion of what he thinks is plausible; we disagree with most of it. Compare also Herner *et al.* 1964.5.
D1.1. A thesaurus format basically similar to the Roget-Soergel model has also been suggested by London 1965.11. ICTB 1970.3 also recommends priority of a classified listing over alphabetical listing (p. 17–18). The Smithsonian Science Information Exchange is an example of a large-scale operating ISAR system where the philosophy expounded in this section (which is based on Section B5) is applied, see Hersey *et al.* 1968.7.
D1.1.0,2. It is mentioned repeatedly in the literature that the indexer or searcher considering the use of a descriptor should be aware of its broader, narrower, and related descriptors. The point is made especially clear by Barhydt 1968, p. 27, "Use of the faceted display". In connection with TEST, it is recommended to the user "that after he finds the descriptor he believes is proper he should confirm his selection by consulting the actual treatment in the thesaurus of terms (the main part, D.S.)" (Heald 1967.11, p. 39). The quotations are from Pickford 1971.3, p. 135, 136.
,3. On the arrangement of entries in a subject catalog see Coates 1960, especially chapters 1, 3, and 13.
D1.1.1,1. Document analysis sheets on which some or all of the descriptors are printed, are used by Tancredi 1968.1, p. 67, Weinstein 1966.10, FR, API 1970.5, USNBS 1971.7 and Hoffer 1962.4, p. 171. In the document analysis sheet used by Weinstein, additional descriptors taken from a larger list can be entered. On the document analysis sheet used by FR, the entire classification scheme is printed (see Figure 35, Section D3.1.1,3). The API indexing form lists a few very frequently used descriptors, namely temperature ranges and chemical aspects. All other descriptors have to

be written down (API 1970.5, Fig. 2, p. 7–8). USNBS 1971.7 lists frequent descriptors in groups headed by questions, such as "Kinetic effects studied?". Search request forms on which some descriptors are printed in order to remind the user of their usefulness in limiting search requests are described in Lancaster 1968, p. 186–189.

D1.2. On the format of TEST compare the description given in TEST 1967.12a itself, p. 3–5, and Gillum 1969.10.

D1.3.3,1. LCSH systematically includes spelling variants, especially inverted forms, into the main part. In a rather incomplete manner this is also done in Thesaurofacet. Neither of these thesauri has a separate alphabetical index.

D1.4(1a). The fact that in the presence of a good classified index the number of RT cross-references can be reduced is mentioned by Barhydt et al. 1968, p. 15.

D1.4(2). (2c) is used in ZIID 1967.2, 3.3.5, p. 21–22. TEST lists all BT in alphabetical sequence. The problem of path tracing following cross-references has been stated (but solved only for a trivial case) by Reisner 1965c. The rules for EJC are given in EJC 1965.6, C-6, p. 4 and in TEST 1967.12, C-6, p. 678. Actually, the rule C-6 of TEST prescribes (2bNT), but it is not followed. BASF1, p. 7 suggests, as we do, (2aBT)-(2aNT).

D1.4.1. The quotation on omitting certain inverse cross-references is from TEST 1967.12, C-6, p. 678. Same rule in EJC 1965.6, C-6, p. 4.

D1.4.2. Thesaurofacet agrees with our recommendation and does not list coordinate terms. TEST lists coordinate terms as RT if deemed useful enough. In Barhydt et al. 1968, 1966.6 version, there is the rule to list coordinate terms as RT-RF (related term-reflexive) without @. (@ is the sign to distinguish RT-RF from RT-TO.) In Barhydt et al. 1968, the listing of coordinate terms has been completely abandoned.

D1.5.1(a). Inverted entries and connected rule: EJC 1965.6, T-4, p. 2.

(b). In Infodata Systems 1971.6, p. 3 an alphabetical index in KWOC-format giving USE instructions and UF statements is suggested. An example is given there in Fig. 6, p. 12. OECD/Development Center 1969 has a KWIC-Index giving USE instructions.

D1.5.2. The KWIC-format is used frequently, for example by USERIC 1972 (Fig. 25a is from the 1969 version, p. 259) and by Verevcenko 1968.10. Originally it was also planned for TEST (see TEST 1967.12, 1966.4 version, IA6., p. 4); however TEST uses a sophisticated KWOC format (Fig. 25c is from TEST 1967.12a, p. 495).

D1.7.1. A description of the Thesaurus of the Vision Information Center is to be found in Eichhorn et al. 1970.1, or in Eichhorn et al. 1969.5.

D1.7.2. Only German unpublished documents are available on the FR Thesaurus. A general description is given in FWZ 1966.4. The classified index is printed on the document analysis sheet (FWZ 1966.5; for an extract translated into English and printed in the proper format see Figure 35, section C3.1.1,3), the main part is FWZ 1964.3. FWZ 1964.9 a and b are auxiliary descriptor listings.

D1.7.3. From the vast literature on these schemes we can only give a few important items. For a good short description of all three thesauri see Needham 1971 (UDC: p. 152–156; DDC: p. 140–152; LCC: p. 163–168). UDC: For a complete listing of the editions of UDC, see FID 1971.1, p. 23–49, and supplement, p. 7–10. Some texts on UDC are: Wellisch 1970; Mills 1964; Fill 1969; Herrmann 1965. An interesting application of UDC is described in Dehnhard 1971. See also Ungurian 1966.6. Compare also the references to Section K2.3.2,1. On mechanized procedures for maintaining UDC see Freeman et al. 1968.5 and other reports by Freeman and/or Atherton, *Caless 1970.12, Cook et al. 1971.6. DDC: Our comments refer to the 17th edition (DDC 1965) or earlier editions. The 18th edition is changed considerably and approaches a faceted classification. Volume 1 of the 18th edition contains an extensive introduction by Benjamin A. Custer (p. 13–66). Another text is Batty 1967. LCC: For an outline and information on the schedules see LCC 1970. A good text is Immroth 1968. See also Angell 1965. There are at least two alphabetical indexes to the LCC outline, namely Newman 1969.11 and Nitecki 1967.

D1.7.4. The thesaurus itself is Thesaurofacet 1969. It contains a detailed introduction on p. XIV-XXV. Two references are: Aitchison 1970.9; Aitchison 1972. Fig. 26 shows parts from pp. 95 and 96, Fig. 27 from p. 463.

D1.7.5. The thesaurus itself is MeSH 1972, amended by the other documents listed under MeSH. On MeSH see, for example, Lancaster 1969.4 or Lancaster 1968.1. Figure 28a shows p. 242, Figure 28b shows p. 491 of the Tree structures, and Figure 29 shows shows parts of pp. 65 and 109.

D1.7.6. The thesaurus itself is EURATOM 1967. For a sample page see Figure 46, Section D3.2. Some papers about the thesaurus are: Detant 1966.7; Rolling 1970.10; Rolling 1965; Rolling 1963; Rolling 1962.8; Marosi 1969.9.

D1.7.7. The Thesaurus of Education Terms itself is Barhydt et al. 1968; it contains a detailed introduction.

D1.7.8. The thesaurus itself is API 1971.1; the introduction is API 1970.5; on the thesaurus see Mulvihill et al. 1966.10. Also Moureau 1968.5.

D1.7.9. The thesaurus itself is USERIC 1972; it contains a detailed introduction. Statistics on descriptor and identifier usage are contained in USERIC 1971.6 and USERIC 1971.6a, respectively. Thesaurus rules are given in USERIC 1969.9. The introductory steps of thesaurus construction are described in USOE 1966.2. Two other references are Eller et al. 1968.7 and Eller.

D1.7.10. The thesaurus itself is LCSH 1966. On the thesaurus see Haykin 1951 (a fairly outdated book, but still followed by LC to a considerable extent).

D1.8. Points (1.1)-(1.4) of the introduction are required by DIN 1463, section 4.1, p. 15; (1.1)-(1.3): TEST 1967.12, 1966.4 version, IA1, p. 2. To (1.1) and (1.2) compare Malkiel 1960.x. (2.1) Explain relationship to other thesauri: DIN 1463, section 5.1, p. 18. (2.2) Explain conceptual structure: TEST 1967.12, 1966.4 version, IA2., p. 2.

D2.1. The sample thesaurus entry in Figure 32 is from TEST 1967.12a, p. 9. The USERIC thesaurus uses the same arrangement, except that the sequence of BT and NT is reversed. Figure 33 is from BASF1, p. 16, translated and adapted.

D2.3.2,3. The "†" is used by TEST 1967.12, C-3, p. 677, but only in the case UF NT†, which in TEST is simply UF†. Listing narrower terms in an indented format is recommended in Hammond 1968.1, p. 10–11 and in Infodata Systems 1971.6, p. 4–5. An example of this format is given in Infodata Systems 1971.6, Figure 4A, p. 10. This format is used in the Water Resources Thesaurus (Water 1971). The 1.3 times more space is for TEST from Hammond 1968.1.

,5. Barhydt et al. 1968 gives RT-RF and RT-TO in one alphabetical sequence and marks RT-RF by @. LCSH lists both RT-TO (as "see also") and RT-FR (as "xx"), listing terms belonging to both twice.

,7. TEST 1967.12, C-4, paragraph 3, p. 677–678 prescribes that a '-' precede every descriptor having narrower descriptors; however, in TEST this rule is not followed for descriptors entered in field BT. '#' is used in the NASA thesaurus to mark the broadest term in a hierarchical chain (according to Hammond 1968.1, p. 11). The more elaborate system of signs is from Infodata Systems 1971.6, p. 3–4.

D3.0. For numerous examples of subject arrangement versus facet arrangement see Barhydt et al. 1968, p. 4–6; for further examples see Steinweg 1950.1. That a subject-oriented arrangement is easier to grasp for the user is argued by Nenninger 1967.4, p. 148.

D3.1.1,2.1. The list of criteria for helpful arrangements follows largely Needham

1971, p. 115 (1964, p. 75). Needham summarizes Ranganathan 1962, Chapter E, "Helpful sequence within groups" (p. 30–44); this chapter gives many examples but does not make for very clear reading. See also Palmer *et al.* 1951, Chapter 2, p. 23–34. On the theory of integrative levels see Feibleman 1968.

D3.1.1,3. Figure 35 is a translated segment of the document analysis sheet used in FR. Figure 36 is extracted and translated from Soergel *et al.* 1970.8.

D3.1.2,1. That the tree method is suitable for a small number of terms is mentioned in ZIID 1967.2, Section 3.3.5, p. 19. Further references for D3.1.2 in general can be found with D3.2. Figures 37–38 are from Syntol 1964, vol. 3D, p. 40 and p. 43. Figure 39 is from Mostecky 1956.10, p. 104.

,2. For another example of a horizontal tree see Blankenstein 1967.4, p. 116–117.

,3. Figure 41 illustrating the circular display of hierarchical relationships is from TDCK 1966.5, circle 112.

D3.2. Part of the discussion of network displays follows ZIID 1967.2, 3.3.5, p. 19–21. A summary display of the descriptor groups is given in EURATOM 1967, 1964 ed., p. 37. Further references are: Aitchison 1972; Doyle 1961.10; Hanicke 1967.4; Hirsch 1967.4; Rolling 1965; Rolling 1971.11. A discussion of the computer-assigned development of network displays is to be found in Garfield *et al.* 1967.9, which also gives many further references; the *diagonal display* explained in this paper seems less useful for our purposes, however. Related material on the graphical representation of data can be found in Feitscher 1967, especially the appendix. Figure 42 (EURATOM 1) is from EURATOM 1967, 1964 ed., Group 15. Figure 43 is from OECD/IRRD 1971.11, frame 36. Figure 45 showing metallurgical processes is from Henglein 1969, p. 500. Figure 46 is from EURATOM 1967, pt. 2, frame 05.

D3.5. Six-letter abbreviations for descriptors are suggested in Dobrowolski 1964.

D3.6.0. The quotation elaborating on the idea of an auxiliary ISAR system is from Korotkin *et al.* 1965.4, p. 53.

,1. The use of a peek-a-boo system as auxiliary ISAR system has been proposed by Cordonnier 1960, p. 1104, 2.06, and p. 1119, 3.3.

D3.6.1,2. Other examples of one-component-entry indexes are: Foskett's rotated index (Foskett 1963, p. 165ff); the Semantic Code Dictionary (Melton 1958c); the Precis system (Austin *et al.* 1969; Austin 1972; Needham 1971, p. 186–193). On the SLIC index see Sharp 1966.1. On entering "useful" combinations only see Dehnhard 1968.x. On the chain indexing method see Needham 1971, p. 182–186.

D4. On notation in general, see the following references: Vickery 1960, Chapter N; Vickery 1952–59; Foskett 1963, chapter 9; Needham 1971, p. 125–131. For further references see there. The discussion draws heavily on these sources.

D4.0. The example in Figure 48 is from Soergel *et al.* 1970.8, translated.

D4.3.1(a4). Tables of pronounceable syllables are given in Leiner 1961.1.

(d). This author could not find a good survey article on check digits. A brief illustration is therefore in order. Take the notation 713. We want to detect input errors like 731 or 714. This can be achieved by computing a check-digit as follows:

$$\begin{array}{ccc} 7 & 1 & 3 \\ \times & \times & \times \\ 3 & 2 & 1 \\ 21 & + \ 2 \ + & 3 \ = \ 26 \end{array}$$

Subtract the nearest smaller multiple of 10, in this case 20; the check digit is 6. The check digit is appended to the notation which then reads 7136 (or, alternatively, 713/6 or 713-6). If the input is 7316, computation of the check-digit results is 8:

Chapter Notes 547

$$\begin{array}{ccc} 7 & 3 & 1 \\ \times & \times & \times \\ 3 & 2 & 1 \\ 21 \ + \ 6 \ + \ 1 & = & 28; \ 28\text{-}20 \ = \ 8. \end{array}$$

Since this is different from the check-digit keyed in input, the notation is marked as erroneous. (Instead of multiples of 10, multiples of 11 or any other number can be used. If 11 is used one can express the check-"digit" 10 by the single character A.) If letters are used in notations, this procedure can be modified as follows: Assign the numerical values 11-36 to the letters A-Z. Instead of multiples of 10 use, say, multiples of 33 for subtraction. For example:

$$\begin{array}{ccccc} C & W & 3 & 4 & 6 \\ \times & \times & \times & \times & \times \\ 5 & 4 & 3 & 2 & 1 \\ 65 \ + \ 132 \ + \ 9 \ + \ 8 \ + \ 6 & = & 221; \ 221\text{-}198 \ = \ 23. \end{array}$$

The check-"digit" or better the check-character, is the thirteenth letter, M. The notation with check-character is CW346M.

D4.3.2,1(b1). The octavizing device was introduced by Ranganathan.

D4.3.2,2.1. The intercalating device is described in Perreault 1965.7.

D4.3.3,2(c). Compare Hines 1967.9 for a (rather difficult to understand) discussion of computer sorting of notations.

D4.3.4. This notation follows the German standard DIN 1421 for the numbering of divisions and subdivisions of written document, which is in agreement with ISO R2145.

D4.3.6. On relational indicators in notations for compound concepts see, for example, Farradane 1955.12 (or Farradane 1967.12 or Farradane 1966.3) or Perreault 1965 (both are discussed in Soergel 1967.12).

D4.4.1. The geographical sub-division of the US is from the US Bureau of the Census 1962; ISIC is ISIC 1968. For references on adjunct thesauri see the note to K1.2.3.

D5. Compare to the discussion of multilingual thesauri ISO R1149, "Layout of multilingual classified vocabularies" and Melton et al. 1958e. A thoroughly confused account of multilingual thesauri and their development is to be found in UNESCO 1970.12. Worthwhile considerations, along with some confused notions, are to be found in Beling 1971.10. For language symbols to be used in multilingual thesauri, see BS3862:1965, DIN2335 ISO R639-1967. Compare also Wagner 1970, and Brendler 1970.x.

D5.0. The distinction between type 1 and type 2 multilingual thesauri is taken from Beling 1971.10, p. 4.

D5.1. Ringdoc 1968.3, basically a TEST-type thesaurus with English as the main language, has a few French and German terms in the lead-in vocabulary. They are interfiled in the English alphabet and marked by a language code (p. 13).

D5.2.1 and D5.2.2. An example of a multilingual thesaurus in the format recommended is the OECD/IRRD 1971.11 (Thesaurus on road research). Another format is illustrated by the OECD/Development Centre 1969, which is a multilingual cumulative thesaurus. Another example of a bilingual cumulative thesaurus is described in Muench 1971.7. While deciding on the format of a multilingual thesaurus it is also useful to look at multilingual dictionaries; examples: Haensch 1965 which comes nearest to a type 1 (lead-in only) multilingual thesaurus in the Roget-Soergel format; the multilingual dictionaries published by Elsevier, which are also type 1 and resemble our recommended format (e.g. Clason 1955, the format varies within the series);

Neidhardt 1964 or others in the same series which resemble the format D5.2.2, not recommended here; Back *et al.* 1964 which also resembles format D5.2.2.
D5.3. ISO R919-1969, 1.2.1, p. 7 recommends having scope notes in one language only.
D5.4. A special source for social science terminology in different languages is ICTSS. The use of an alphabetical index for the detection of homonyms is mentioned in Beling 1971.10, p. 12.
D5.5. The difficulties likely to arise in an interlingual thesaurus due to the different thought structures underlying and represented in different languages may be seen from Glenn 1954.3.

CHAPTER E

E. Most of the rules for the form of terms given in Grosch 1969.2, table 2, p. 90, do not seem to make much sense and have not been included in the following compilation. ISO R919-1969 and ISO R1149-1969 give some rules on the layout of vocabularies which might also be of interest in the context of this chapter. For the specific problems connected with subject headings, compare Coates 1960, Harris 1969, Harris 1969.3 (formulating entries for computer sort), Daily 1957, Haykin 1951.
E1.0.3(1). Retaining of spelling variants mentioned in BASF2, Vorbemerkung, p. 0.
E1.1. Most of the introductory considerations on why and how to formulate terms more precisely are also covered in TEST 1967.12, T-5, paragraph 1 and T-5d, p. 674; EJC 1965.6, T-2 paragraphs 1 and 3, p. 2 and partly in ZIID 1967.2, 3.3.3, p. 13–15.
E1.1.1. Parenthetical qualifiers are used by TEST 1967.12, T-5b, p. 674; EJC 1965.6, T-2a, p. 2; BASF2, C-2, p. 5; ZIID 1967.2, 3.3.4, points 1 and 2, p. 16. EJC 1955.6, T-2b, p. 2 wrongly uses parenthetical qualifiers for compound concepts whereas TEST 1967.12, T-5a, p. 674 rightly uses multi-word terms. Numbers for distinguishing homonyms are used by ZIID 1967.2, 3.3.4, point 2, p. 16. The use of parenthetical qualifiers for "lonely homonyms" is prescribed in ZIID 1967.2, 3.3.4, point 1, p. 16.
E1.1.2. BASF2, E4, p. 8 suggests to avoid homonymous composite terms.
E1.2.1. BASF2, D3, p. 6 allows adjectives; ZIID 1967.2, 3.2, p. 9 permits all but prefers the noun form over verbs.
E1.2.2. Only nouns are allowed in EJC 1965.6, T-8, p. 3 and, with limitations, in TEST 1967.12, T-2, p. 674 (the quotation is from there) and in USERIC 1972, 1969.4 edition, p. XII-XIII, where adjectives such as *Disadvantaged* are used in the sense of *Disadvantaged people*, but no other adjectives are used. DGD/ET 1966.7 avoids adjectives (3.5, p. 4), but allows for verbs (3.2, p. 3).
E1.2.3. Adverbial form for adjectives: ZIID 1967.2, 3.2, p. 9. Forms of verbs: ZIID 1967.12, 3.2, p. 9 and DGD/ET 1966.7, 3.2, p. 3 use infinitive, TEST 1967.12, T-2, p. 674 uses the gerund form.
E1.3.1,1. The verb-noun rule to distinguish processes from products is used by DGD/ET 1966.7, 3.2, p. 3 and BASF2, D-4, p. 6.
,2. The ". . . ing"-". . . ation" rule is given in TEST 1967.12, T-5c, p. 674 when a clear distinction is necessary; however, according to Gillum 1969.10 this rule has not been followed in TEST. The rule is also prescribed by EJC 1965.6, T-3, p. 2.
,3. Explicit disambiguation is used in BASF2, D4, p. 6.
,4. The recommended rules are used in BASF2, D4, p. 6.
E1.4.1,2. On pluralia tantum: DGD/ET 1966.7, 3.1, p. 3; BASF2, D-1, p. 6 (the X-ray example is from there). On terms that have a different meaning in singular and plural, respectively: BASF2, D-2, p. 6.

E1.4.2. The simple rule "use singular" is used by DGD/ET 1966.7, 3.1, p. 3 and by BASF2, C1, p. 6. ZIID 1967.2, 3.2, p. 9 uses the simple rule with the exception for terms designating generic concepts. The reasons for the simple rule "use singular", including those given by us, are advanced in ISO/TC46 (Germany-2) 1036E.

E1.4.3. The quotation on singular/plural usage and Figure 51 are from TEST 1967.12, T3, p. 674 and Table 1, p. 675. The same rule is used by EJC 1965.6, T-10, p. 3.

E1.5. There exists a vast mass of literature on direct versus inverted entry. Classic is Coates 1960, especially chapters 3–5. For more references see Harris 1969. An interesting approach is described in Austin et al. 1969 and Austin 1972. On the underlying linguistic problems see Daily 1957 and Lees 1960.

E1.5.1. Direct entry is used in TEST 1967.12, T-4, p. 674; EJC 1965.6, T-4, p. 2; BASF2, A3, p. 2; ZIID 1967.2, 3.2, p. 9; DGD/ET 1966.7, 3.3, p. 3 for composite one-word terms.

E1.5.2. Inverted entry is prescribed by DGD/ET 1966.7, 3.6 and 3.5, p. 4 for type (1.1.1) and type (1.2) multiword terms, with the exceptions mentioned by us and prescribed in section 3.9, p. 4.

E1.6. Strings of terms to designate newly formed concepts have been extensively used by Brisch, as described in Kyle 1956.3, where numerous examples are given.

E1.7. BASF2, p. 5, 10 allows for symbols of chemical elements. The simple rule for numerals in chemical names is from Ringdoc 1968.3, p. 9. There is a vast amount of literature on chemical nomenclature where this problem is treated. The *Grade 4* example and the corresponding rule is from USERIC 1969.9, section 1.2.4, p. 7.

E1.8.1(a). Well-known acronyms used as descriptors: TEST 1967.12, T-9, p. 675–676.

E1.8.2. For rules for English see Bourne et al. 1961. The rule for German abbreviations is from BASF2, F2, p. 10. For a set of rules for German see DIN2340. For standards giving abbreviations for often used words see ANSI Y1.1-1972; ANSIZ39.5-1969; BS4148:1967; DIN1502:1955 Beiblatt 1; ISO DR1278:1967; ISO R4-1954; ISO R832-1968; ISO R83-1968; ISO R1043-1969.

E1.8.3. The abstract journal America–History and Life uses standardized abbreviations, called *cues*. See Boehm ed. 1965.7, p. IX and 70.

E1.9. The quotation on term length is from TEST 1967.12, T-1d., p. 674; EJC 1965.6, T-9, p. 3 prescribes 34 characters.

E1.10. For a list of language symbols, see BS3862:1965; DIN 2335; ISO R639-1967.

E1.11. Ringdoc 1968.3 uses /R/ (p. 11), TEST 1967.12, p. 4 uses ®; TEST 1967.12, T-5e, p. 674 prescribes (trademark).

E2.1. E2.1 on authorities for spelling draws on ZIID 1967.2, 3.2, p. 9. DGD/ET 1966.7, Anhang 3, p. 9–10, lists the rules to be used for chemical terms in this German thesaurus.

E2.2. The quotation on punctuation is from TEST 1967.12, T-8, p. 675. DGD/ET 1966.7, 5.2, p. 5 has a similar rule: Composite words are written without hyphens, periods or unnecessary spaces because otherwise errors in alphabetization will occur. This rule holds even for longer words containing 4 or more stems.

E2.3. Rule (a), capitalize each word in a term, is used by Hines 1971.6, p. 49. Most thesauri use rule (b), capitalize the first word in a term. (dG1) is prescribed in DIN 2334, 3.3; (dG2) follows BASF2, F1, p. 11, modified.

E2.5. There are national and international standards on transliteration; see the American National Standard Institute Catalog (it includes ISO standards) and Eggert 1968.8. In the US, the rules used by the Library of Congress (to be published) are widely followed. Compare also Osterman 1959 and Schneider et al. 1966. For a comprehensive bibliography of transliteration and transcription see Wellisch 1973. The use of standards is also mentioned in ZIID 1967.2, 3.2, p. 9, modified. Prefer transliteration without diacritical marks: DIN 1463, 3.2.3(c), p. 7. Writing out of Greek characters: BASF2, F3, p. 10 (Lower case prescribed for first letter); ZIID, 3.2, p. 9. E3. Computer sort is mentioned in USCOSATI 1970.9. The quoted rules are from TEST 1967.12, A-1, p. 679; compare also Heald 1967.11, p. 21–22. Further rules and other considerations on alphabetization may be found in the following documents: BS 1749:1969; DIN 5007:1962; ALA 1968; Harris 1969.3; Hines et al. 1966; US Library of Congress 1956.

CHAPTER F

F. Compare to this chapter in general ISO R919, Schirmer 1967.5.

F0.1. DGD/ET 1966.7 and ZIID 1967.2 describe a general flow of work very similar to the one shown in Figure 52. In detail, the correspondence is as follows: Step F1: DGD/ET, 6.1.1, p. 5; ZIID, 3.2, p. 7–10. Step F2: DGD/ET, 6.1.2, p. 5; ZIID, 3.3.1, p. 10–11. Step F3: DGD/ET, 6.1.3 and 6.1.4, p. 6; ZIID, 3.3.5, p. 17–23. Step F6: DGD/ET, 6.1.5, p. 6; ZIID, 3.5, p. 23. Another detailed flowchart covering the steps F3 through F5 of Figure 53 is given in Preisler 1970.x, Fig. 3, p. 14.

F0.3. Compare to the discussion of how to consult subject experts and especially to F0.3.4 the use of working panel sessions in the development of TEST as described in Heald 1967.11, p. 25–34. It seems to us that some tasks assigned to the panels should have been performed by the central staff. This is reflected in the outline for the panel briefings (p. 26–27). On the use of panels in the development of the EJC thesaurus see Wall 1963.10, p. 37.

F0.3.1(1). On the use of subject experts for free indexing of documents see, for example, Pickford 1968.3, p. 21, and app. 1 and 7. However, the guide for indexers given there is not recommended, since it does not take into account the checklist technique of indexing. Another shortcoming of the guide is that the subject experts must be bothered with rules for the form of terms.

(2). Nobbs 1966.12 describes plans to solicit suggestions of new terms and changes in old terms and their relationships from readers of an abstract journal. Suggestions were to be submitted on 4 x 6 cards.

F0.4. On the vocabulary selection problem in foreign language instruction see Richards 1970.5.

F0.4.2. Criteria (a)-(c) for the selection of preferred terms are given in ZIID 1967.2, 3.3.3, p. 14, points 1. and 2. and 3.3.4, p. 16, point 3. The elaboration of criterion (b) including the quotation is from TEST 1967.12, T-1(c), p. 674. Criterion (e) is used Rubinoff 1966.7, p. 8–9; in particular, he describes the weighting of sources. The study on the occurrence of terms in the titles is reported in Kochen 1968.9, 4.(d) "The preferred term", p. 184–185.

F0.4.3. For the development of criteria for descriptor selection TEST 1967.12, T-1, p. 673–674 and EJC 1965.6, T-1, p. 1 have been used. The quotation is from TEST.

(a). Usefulness for searching. First sentence: DGD/ET 1966.7, 6.1.4, p. 5; also contained in TEST 1967.12, T-1a., p. 673. The quotation is from Greer 1965.12, p. 833.

(b). Alternative solutions. In the development of the EJC thesaurus, forerunner of TEST, each committee charged with a given subject field developed an ad hoc hierarchical framework for that purpose (Wall 1963.8, p. 4). In the final thesaurus, this framework does not appear explicitly. Same point in TEST T-1(c), p. 673 and T-1b, p. 674.

(c). The quotation on logical structure is from Heald 1967.11, p. 28.

(e). The number of sources (based on a count of terms instead of a count on concepts) has been used as a criterion for descriptor selection in the development of the EJC thesaurus: only those terms that occurred in at least two sources were considered for inclusion into this thesaurus as described by Wall 1963.10, p. 37. The criterion is also mentioned in EJC 1965.6, T-1, p. 1 and in TEST 1967.12, 1966.4 version, T-1a., p. 17. The weighting of sources is described in Rubinoff 1966.7, p. 8–9.

F0.4.4. In the discussion of the use of frequency data in descriptor selection TEST 1967.12, T-1a, p. 673 and EJC 1965.6, T-1, p. 1 have been used.

,1. The device for counting holes in Termatrex cards is described in Doudnikoff 1965.12. The listing of frequency data and related information was planned in ASTIA as described in Jaster *et al.* 1962, section A2, p. 98–100, modified, especially other example for (3).

,1. Refinement of frequency data by weighting descriptors in document representations is used in Pickford 1968.3, p. 23, point 3. The weighting of sources is described in Rubinoff 1966.7, p. 8–9. The modification described at the end is due to Pickford, p. 22, point 2.

,2. The treatment of high-frequency concepts in (1) follows ZIID 1967.2, 3.3.3, p. 14. (2): Retain newly introduced low frequency concepts: ZIID 1967.2, 3.3.2.1, p. 11; TEST 1967.12, T-1a, p. 673. Retain low frequency concepts in the central area: ZIID 1967.2, 3.3.2.1, p. 11.

F0.4.5. On central vs. peripheral areas compare UNESCO 1971.12, Section 5.5.3, p. 26 and Cros *et al.* 1964, p. 96–97, 'echelles'.

F0.5. The thesaurus form shown in Figure 54 was developed by the author in cooperation with I. Dahlberg. Other thesaurus forms see: Descriptor justification form (form no. OE6016 (1066)) used in USERIC and printed in Eller 1968.7, Fig. 7, p. 218 and in USERIC 1972, 1969.4 edition, p. IX, Fig. 1. The form is 8½ x 11 and designed for easy punching of cards. Blankenstein 1967.4, p. 112. Nobbs 1966.12 (4 x 6 cards). Wall 1962.8, p. 10–11 also used a thesaurus form (not shown). He uses the back for scope notes. In the development of TEST, 8 x 14 cards were used. Even so, several cards were necessary for some terms (Heald 1967.11, p. 17).

F0.7.1,1. Second sentence on the use of source indications: BASF1, p. 7.

,2. The FR-Thesaurus (FWZ 1964.3) uses source indications; Ringdoc 1968.3 uses source indications for drug names.

F0.8.1,2. Query and reply slips are suggested by ISO R1149-1969, 2.1.4, p. 13.

F0.8.2. Dates in the user version are suggested in DIN 1463, section 3.3.2, p. 10.

F1.1. In the discussion of kinds of sources F1.1.1 and F1.1.2 TEST 1967.12, 1966.4 version, I, para. 4, p. 1–2, and DGD/ET 1966.7, 6.1.1, p. 4 have been used.

F1.1.2(k). Use of search requests as sources: Greer 1965.12, section "User approach mode", p. 830–834.

(n). Use of sample documents to elicit formulation of interests: Mooers *et al.* 1958, p. 348–350.

F1.1.3. The selection of sources is discussed following ZIID 1967.2 as follows: Use both prearranged and open-ended sources: 3.3.2, point 5., p. 12; (1): 3.2.2, p. 7; (2): 3.2.1, p. 7. The additional criteria are quoted from Heald 1967.11, p. 16. A sample of 1,500 documents was used by Pickford 1968.3, p. 20; 1,000 documents were purposively selected by scanning relevant journals and 500 were obtained by asking potential users to submit relevant documents. The difference between pre-research and post-research documents stated in the remark has been observed by Lunin *et al.* 1967.10.

F1.1.4. On the free association method see Richards *et al.* 1968, section 3, p. 6–8 and Deese 1965. This method of source data collection has been used by Reisner

552 Chapter Notes

1966.8 (this is the most complete account of Reisner's work). The bound association method has been used by Rubinoff *et al.* 1967.6. An association study has also been done by Papier *et al.* 1962.12, but for the wrong purpose.

F1.2.1,0. The types of source codes have been suggested in the following publications (1): DIN 2333, 3.1.5; (2): London 1966.10, p. 17; (3): Used in TEST, see Heald 1967.11, p. 18; for examples see Fig. 56 (section F2.2).

,2. On the selecting and marking of terms: ZIID 1967.2, 3.2., p. 8–9; on the transfer of terms: ZIID 1967.2, 3.3.1, p. 10. The examples are from Weil 1970.9, p. 355–356.

,3. On the use of a KWIC index for the study of homonyms see Stone *et al.* 1966.6; Dunphy 1966, p. 166–167. On the use of a KWIC index for the derivation of definitions see Werner 1967.1.

F1.2.2,1. The use of OR combinations in search request formulations for the detection of synonyms and narrower terms is described in Levery 1968.3, p. 10 and p. 11, respectively. Levery uses interest profiles improved over a period of 3 years.

,2. Indication of the page number within the source is prescribed by DIN 2333, 3.1.5. Numbering of the entries on each page is used by London 1966.10, p. 17.

F2.2.1. The sample entry illustrating merging shown in Fig. 56 is from Heald 1967.11, Fig 2, p. 19–20. For an example of a merger of four large vocabularies and partial cumulation see Hammond *et al.* 1964.4, vol. 1.

F2.2.3. The idea of "pulling" information from a big thesaurus is described by Hammond 1969.10, p. 16–17 and Miller 1966.9, p. 81A. Point (3) "With a new concept include all its broader concepts" is from Miller.

F2.3.1. The idea of detecting synonymity between two terms due to the fact that they have a synonym in common is from Levery 1968.3, p. 9.

F2.4.1. On spelling and morphological variants compare Wall *et al.* 1969.5, section 5.2, p. 5-2 - 5-4.

F2.4.2 On homonyms compare Wall *et al.* 1969.5, section F5.2, p. 5–2.

F3. Cascade-type sorting is also mentioned in Tancredi 1968.1, p. 67. That classification is needed in the construction of thesauri that rely mainly on alphabetic arrangement is clearly stated by Vickery 1959, p. 4–5 (citing Pettee 1946); it is also an underlying theme of Coates 1960.

F3.2. The "road-map" for the analysis of terms shown in Fig. 62 is from Dym 1967.10, p. 128.

F3.3.7. Writing terms in groups on a large sheet of paper is suggested in ZIID 1967.2, 3.3.3, p. 13–14.

F5.8. The use of the alphabetical index for detecting homonyms has been suggested in Verevcenko 1968.10 and also in Beling 1971.10.

F6. The first three sentences of the discussion of thesaurus testing follow ZIID 1967.2, 3.3.5, p. 18 and 3.5, p. 23, modified. For more detailed suggestions how to perform such a test see Snow 1965.9 and Gehring 1970.2. For a flowchart see Preisler 1970.x, Fig. 14, p. 15. We do not fully agree with that flowchart, however. On the testing of ISAR systems see King 1971, especially chapter 2, 4, and 5 and the references given there; Lancaster 1970.9; Lancaster 1969.4; Lancaster 1968.1.

F8.4. Detecting synonyms by looking for terms expressed by the same combination of semantic factors is also mentioned by Levery 1968.3, p. 11; Levery talks about "definition" (= formal representation) and "definisseurs" (= elemental concepts). He applies this method to analyze the names of diseases.

F9.1. The first paragraph on the use of punched paper tape follows BASF1, p. 11.

F9.1.2. Conversion of punched paper tape to punched cards is used in ZMD 1966.1.

F9.2.2. Projects using punched card and unit record equipment are mentioned in the following references: Bauer 1967.2; DGD/ET 1966.7, section 6.3, p. 5; Finger 1967.9 (use of punched cards in the working file); Tinker *et al.* 1963.10 (rather sophisticated); ZMD 1966.1. On the use of edge notched cards see Kreusler *et al.* 1963.3.

CHAPTER G

G. The following is a list of references in which computer application to thesaurus construction is described.
Program packages: Hines *et al.* 1971.6 (IBM 360/75); Infodata Systems 1971.3 (the same package is described in Hammond 1969.10) (COBOL F for IBM 360, OS and DOS; ANSI COBOL for UNIVAC 1100 Series EX VIII); Owens-Illinois 1969 (COBOL for IBM 360/30, 64K, DOS, or upward; also OS; also RCA Spectra 70/45); Wong *et al.* 1969.9.
Other references: Amacher 1967.9; Bailey *et al.* 1969.10 (survey of computer application in the related field of lexicography); BASF (360/65 or RCA Spectra 70/46); Caless *et al.* 1970.12 (UDC); Cassidy *et al.*; Cooke *et al.* 1971.6; Eichhorn *et al.* 1970.1 (good); Eller 1968.7; Feinberg; Findler *et al.* 1969.7 (deals with the related problem of the analysis of kinship structure); Freeman *et al.* 1968.5 and other reports by Freeman or Atherton on the UCD-project at AIP; Freeman 1967.12; Ginsberg 1967.11; Harris 1969.3 (styling and formatting of subjecting headings for computer sort); Hayes 1968, section 3, p. 178–190 (construction and modification of hierarchies); Heald 1967.11, especially appendix 10; Henderson 1964.5 (bad, mainly on how to program the IBM 7094); Hersey *et al.* 1967.10 (bad); Honecker *et al.* 1967.10; Horvath *et al.* 1967.8; Klingbiel 1963.10; Larousse/Redaction 1960 (using punched cards and computers in lexicography); Manheimer 1969.x (360/20); Martinez 1969.10; McGee *et al.* 1963.10; Nicolaus 1966.10 (UNIVAC-LARC); Pickford 1968.3 (ATLAS computer); Quemada 1959 (not recommended); Ringdoc 1968.3 (360/40, 128K, assembler program); Schirmer 1967.5 (only elimination of duplicates); Smilari *et al.* 1968.10 (mainly updating, very unclear); Szigethy 1970.6; Way 1968.4 (not recommended); Whaley *et al.* 1966.10 (updating); Wolff-Terroine 1969.1 (not recommended).
Further work in this area has been done or is underway at the following institutions: American Petroleum Institute (API); Auerbach Corporation (programs for EJC-thesaurus); Badische Anilin-und Soda-Fabrik (BASF) 360/65 or RCA Spectra 70/46; see also BASF1 and BASF2); Food and Drug Administration/Bureau of Foods; Library of Congress/Information Systems Office (especially printing LCSH).
G0.1.2. Ease of updating by computer mentioned in TEST 1967.12, 1966.4 version IC(4), p. 5.
G0.2. Assignment of internal code by computer mentioned in TEST 1967.12, 1966.4 version, IC1, p. 5; BASF1. Check of inverse cross-references mentioned in TEST 1967.12, 1966.4 version, IC2, p. 5; BASF1, p. 12.
G0.3. The type of file organization and record organization described has been developed by Hammond for application in developing the TEST thesaurus and the Water Resources Thesaurus. See Heald 1966.11, appendix 10; Hammond 1969.10; and Infodata Systems 1971.6.
G2.2.3. "Pulling" information from a big thesaurus using a computer program is described in Hammond 1969.10, p. 16–17.
G2.4. The program described in Hines *et al.* 1971.6 can transform inverted entries to the direct form, and vice versa (p. 48).

G3. The method to sort terms into subject fields based on their use in indexing documents is described in Ginsberg 1967.11, the same basic idea is used in Maron 1961.7.
G3.4.1. One method for "chaining" BT (or NT) cross-references to construct the hierarchy is described in Hammond 1968.1, p. 4–6 and p. 10–14; the same method has probably been used in TEST, see TEST 1967.12, 1966.4 version, IC3, p. 5; there are more elegant methods based on graph theory. See also Hayes 1968, section 3, p. 178–190. Programs for this purpose have also been developed at BASF (see BASF1, p. 12).
G3.4.3. Development rules: Cros *et al.* 1964, chapter 3, A2.5 "Règles de developpement", p. 66.
G5.1. The replacement of non-preferred terms by the appropriate preferred term is mentioned in TEST 1967.12, 1966.4 version, IC2, p. 5 and BASF1, p. 12.
G7. Variability of arrangement for printing is mentioned in TEST 1967.12, 1966.4 version, IC3, p. 5; computer typesetting is mentioned in TEST 1967.12, p. 2, and in Freeman 1967.12.
G8. Section G8 on updating owes much to the description of MODIFILE in Hammond 1968.1, p. A7 - A-11. MODIFILE is a program for updating based on line-oriented input. A user description of a newer version of MODIFILE is found in Infodata Systems 1971.6, Ch. 4, p. 21–23. (However, this description is less clear than the earlier one.)

CHAPTER H

H. The following is a selected list of references on automatic methods in the construction of indexing languages and thesauri. It contains all the references given in Batty 1969.6 and in Dahlberg 1971.4, section 2.2.4.

Abraham 1965a
Abraham 1965c
Abraham 1964.10
Abraham 1963.
Arthur D. Little 1963.7
Atherton *et al.* 1965.1
Auguston *et al.* 1970.3
Baker 1968.8
Baker 1965.12
Baker 1962
Batty 1969.6
Blomgren *et al.* 1966.6
Borko 1965
Borko 1965.
Borko 1965.12
Borko 1964.2 (many examples)
Borko 1963.11
Borko 1963.10
Borko 1963.4
Borko 1962.5
Crouch 1971.10 (bibliography)
Dale *et al.* 1965.1
Dale *et al.* 1964.10
Dattola 1969.3
Dattola *et al.* 1967.12
Dennis 1967
Dennis 1965.12
Doyle *et al.* 1966.10
Doyle 1966.7
Doyle 1965.12
Doyle 1964.3 (good overview, many examples)
Doyle 1962.10
Doyle 1961.10
Edmundson *et al.* 1969.9
Edmundson 1965
Giuliano 1965.12
Giuliano 1963
Giuliano 1963.4
Gotlieb *et al.* 1968.10
Harary 1960.7
Hill 1968
Hillman 1965
Hillman 1964.7
Honecker 1967.10
Houston *et al.* 1964.4
Hülck *et al.* 1967
ISR (Information Storage and

Retrieval) V.1 (1961)—contains many papers on the subject. See further references on SMART in the note to Section B6.2
Jackson 1969.4
Jones et al. 1969 (contains empirical raw data)
Jones et al. 1967.7
Jornagin 1962
Lance et al. 1966.5
Lazarsfeld 1950
Lefkovitz 1963.9
Lefkovitz 1963
Lesk 1969.1
Lewis et al. 1967.1
Litofsky 1969
Luhn 1957.10
Lustig 1968
Lustig 1965.9
Maron 1961.7
Maron 1960.7
Maron 1959
Masterman 1956.10
McQuitty 1970.4
Meetham 1964.4
Meetham 1963.1
Needham 1965.6
Needham et al. 1964.9
Needham 1961
Parker-Rhodes et al. 1960
Price et al. 1968
Salton 1971.1
Salton et al. 1966.6
Salton 1962
Schiminovich et al. 1968.4
Soergel 1967.7, Ch. 4–5
Sparck Jones 1971
Sparck Jones 1970.6
Sparck Jones 1970.5
Sparck Jones et al. 1970.2
Sparck Jones 1968.8
Sparck Jones et al. 1968.6
Sparck Jones et al. 1967.6
Sparck Jones et al. 1967.5
Sparck Jones 1965.11
Sparck Jones 1965.6
Sparck Jones 1964.6
Sparck Jones 1961
Stevens 1970.2
Stevens et al. ed. 1965.12
Stone 1967.12
Tauber 1968.10
Ward 1963
Williams 1968
Williams 1966.2
Williams 1965.12
Winters 1965.7
Wolff-Terroine 1971.6

A number of studies have been done in connection with the SMART system. See Salton ed. 1971 and the ISR reports.

H0. The quotation putting automatic methods in perspective is from Gillum 1964.1, p. 32. On the statistical analysis of vocabulary usage compare Schultz et al. 1961.4; Schultz et al. 1961.10 and Soergel 1965.5, Chapter V, p. 25–30.

H1. A sophisticated program for doing frequency counts is described in Baker et al. 1968.8.

H2. On detecting descriptor candidates from frequency patterns see Dennis 1965.12; Dennis 1967.

H3. The discussion dealing with the interpretation of term associations owes much to Giuliano 1965.12.

H3.2. The example of second-order association in Figure 65 is from Giuliano 1963.4, p. 223, modified.

H3.3. The quotation on detection of homonyms through inconsistent association profiles is from Gillum 1964.1, p. 32.

H4.1. For a short discussion of the basic problems of the automatic derivation of classification schemes see Soergel 1967.7, ch. 4, especially section 4.4. For individual studies see the references given at the beginning of Chapter H.

H4.2. Methods based on graph theory are described in Abraham 1965a and Abraham 1964.10, based on the graph-theoretic work in Abraham 1965c and 1963. Related graph-theoretical work has been done by Harary; see for example, Harary 1960.7. A very interesting study using a graph-theoretical approach starting from the cross-references in the LC Subject Headings is described in Gottlieb *et al.* 1968.10. See also Rapoport *et al.* 1966.11. Related work on the computer analysis of PERT networks might also be useful; see, for example, Jornagin 1962.

CHAPTER J

J. Some sources dealing with thesaurus updating are: Heald 1967.11, p. 44–45 and app. 9, p. 161–170, especially V "Conclusions"; Speight 1969.10; both on updating TEST, including details of the administrative arrangements (Heald). Eller 1968.7 on updating of the USERIC-thesaurus. Of special interest is the administrative procedure described; indexing and further processing of abstracts and thesaurus updating are intertwined in this procedure. Klingbiel 1963.10 on the revision of the ASTIA-thesaurus. ZIID 1967.2, section 3.6, p. 23–24 (general guidelines) and DGD/ET 1966.7, section 7, p. 6 on updating the "Thesaurus Elektrotechnik"; both publications also deal with the necessary administrative arrangements. Chapter G on computerized procedures deals with the use of computers in updating also; the references given at the beginning of Chapter G are, therefore, also relevant.

J0. The data on the updating of TEST are from Heald 1967.11, p. 44.

J1. The types (3.1)-(3.6) of changes in a thesaurus are given in Priebe 1968.7.

J2.1. Detection of needed descriptors from unsatisfactory search results also mentioned in DIN1463, section 6.1, p. 23. The general point of monitoring the search performance to obtain updating information is made in Lancaster 1970.9.

J3.1. In USERIC the indexers are to fill in thesaurus forms for updating information (Eller 1968.7, p. 217–219). Nobbs 1966.12 asks users to submit updating information on thesaurus forms.

J3.3.1 and J3.3.2. Continuous updating of thesaurus copies in form of card files is used by Weinstein 1966.10. Cumulative supplements are used in USERIC (every 30 days, provided 25 new descriptors have accumulated) (Eller 1968.7, p. 217–219). API sends change notices between yearly revised editions. Non-cumulative supplements are used by UDC (see Freeman 1967.12 for a description of the procedures used for updating UDC), and LCC. Hammond 1963.12 suggests the use of provisional descriptors in cooperative documentation.

J3.3.3. For a model solution of listing descriptor changes see MeSH 1972. API 1971.1, p. 432–453 lists new descriptors, but no other changes. For another more elaborate example involving the listing of other changes, too, see Priebe 1968.7. Change information in scope notes is given in API 1971.1.

J3.4. References describing the administrative arrangement are given at the beginning of Chapter J.

J3.5. On-line updating has been suggested by Reisner 1963.10.

J4. The API thesaurus and MeSH are issued yearly. The USERIC thesaurus (USERIC 1972) is issued approximately every two years. For TEST, a 4-year period has been envisioned for the issuing of a completely revised edition (Heald 1967.11, p. 168, e.); as of today, no updated version of TEST is planned at all.

J5(a). The data on changes in the EURATOM thesaurus are from EURATOM 1967, pt. I, p. VI-VII. The data on PRECIS are from Austin 1972 and Austin, private communication.

J6(2). Tentative descriptors are used in MEDLARS.

J7. The study on the NASA thesaurus is Manheimer 1969.x.

CHAPTER K

K. General issues of thesauri in cooperation are dealt with in Blankenstein 1967.x, p. 178–180. The ideas of Soergel 1972.9 have been completely absorbed in this chapter.
K0. On shared subject indexing ((2b) and (2c)) compare Soergel 1971, Section B6.0.4,2, p. 200–208.
K1.2.1. For a common thesaurus for two institutions in which slight variations are indicated see Ringdoc 1968.3. The method is described on p. 17.
K1.2.2. The "do-it-yourself kit" formulation is from Kyle 1960.9. The quotation on the role of a national thesaurus is from Klingbiel 1964.8, p. 256.
K1.2.2,2.1.1. The format for writing extraction specifications has first been described in a slightly different version in Soergel *et al.* 1970.10. The format as given here is described in Soergel 1972.9; Figures 66–68 are from this article.
K1.2.3. For an example of an adjunct thesaurus see Croghan 1970 and Wagner 1970 (both give a scheme of form descriptors). Implicit inclusion is also described by Hines *et al.* 1971.6, p. 42. Implicit inclusion of place names and other names for which an adjunct thesaurus does not actually exist is used in LCSH 1966, p. III. To the whole problem compare Atanasiu *et al.* 1966.6, p. 92–95. Explicit inclusion has been used in the Vision Information Center of the Harvard Medical School, as described in Eichhorn 1970.1, especially p. 24–25.
K1.3.0. References to actual cumulative thesauri using source indications see with K2.3.2,1.
K1.4. The procedure for incorporating an additional thesaurus into a cumulative thesaurus, taken together with Sections F2.2.3 and F2.4 which are to be used in it, has much in common with an algorithm for the construction of conversion tables given in Wall *et al.* 1969.5, ch. 6, p. 6–1 - 6–15.
K2. For the general problem of cooperation with emphasis on thesaurus problems compare Soergel 1971, section B6.0.4,2, p. 200–208. Compare also, especially to Section K2.2 Hammond 1963.12 and Henderson *et al.* 1966.6, Section 3.7.3, p. 78–83, where Hammond's work is summarized. Compare also Sukiasjan 1968.7. Further references not mentioned with any specific section are: Hammond 1965; Hammond 1962; Painter 1963.3; Painter 1963.7; Harrish 1967.10; Hoffman 1968.10; Kulik 1969; Vcerasnij, R.P.
K2.1. The term *conversion table* is used by Henshaw 1967.11. The quotation on the effect of the interest of an institution on indexing is from Hammond 1963.12, p. 63–64. The effect of indexing rules is mentioned in Klingbiel 1964.8, p. 256.
K2.1.1. Problems of a switching language are dealt with in Neville 1970.12. The quotation on unimpeded transfer is from Coates 1970.6.
K2.2. Compare to the whole problem of convertibility Perreault 1967 and Öhmann *et al.* 1971.6.
K2.2.1. Other lists of convertibility categories can be found in the following references: Hammond *et al.* 1962.8, app. II, p. II; Henshaw 1967.11 (gives many examples); Neville 1970.12; Perreault 1967; Vickery 1960a. The list given in Soergel 1965, p. 22–23 is superseded by this section. We do not enter into a comparison of the different lists.
,1. For an example where combinations were not considered in determining searching equivalents, see Vickery *et al.* 1969.6. For a good example where this point has been considered see Öhmann *et al.* 1971.6; see also Wellisch 1971.6. The notion "closest searching equivalent" is used in Hammond 1962.8.
K2.3.1. On building a total thesaurus comprised of several constituent thesauri see

Preisler 1970.x, second half of section 4, p. 67, and Fig. 4 and 5, p. 69; also Rosenbaum 1967.4, p. 46–53; Bauer 1967.4 and other publications by Bauer. All these references deal with plans for the German Democratic Republic.

,1. On parallel development of constituent thesauri see DGD/ET 1966.7, 2.2, p. 1 and 6.2, p. 5; and ZIID 1967.2, 3.1, p. 5.

,2. A separate alphabetical index for each constituent thesaurus has been suggested by ZIID 1967.2, 3.4, p. 23.

K2.3.2. On re-indexing (reclassification) mainly from DDC to LCC see, for example, Perreault ed. 1968.4 and Dougherty 1967.7; also Perreault n.d. That conversion tables are often the best solution has been stated numerous times. For example: Pietsch 1960, p. 496: "that concordances are the best solution to the problem discussed here." Compare also Kent *et al.* 1958, "Encoding of information previously indexed", where an actual experiment is described.

,1. For an example of the local approach to the construction of conversion tables, see the algorithm described in Wall *et al.* 1969.5, ch. 6, p. 6–1 - 6–15. A global procedure is used by Hammond *et al.* 1962.8, p. 3–6, even though a cumulative thesaurus is not constructed explicitly in this case. In a later study of conversion tables construction (Hammond *et al.* 1964.4, vol. 1 and vol. 2) the first steps in the explicit construction of a cumulative thesaurus from four large vocabularies are taken. The PRECIS system is described in Austin 1972. A similar experimental study is described in Melton 1958b (UDC vs. Semantic Code). Other studies on the construction of conversion tables are: Öhmann *et al.* 1971.6 (Thesaurus Documentaire d'Economie vs. UDC; MeSH vs. UDC); Wellisch 1971.6 (TEST vs. UDC); Földi *et al.* 1970.10 (Thesaurus documentaire d'economie vs. UDC); Goltdamer *et al.* 1967.4 (suggests to base conversion tables on the Soviet Library Classification); Gardin 1969.3 (Information Science); Levy 1967.9 (same project as Gardin 1969); Melton 1960 (Colon Classification vs. Semantic Code); Wilson *et al.* 1969.11; Comparison 1967. Two examples of actual cumulative thesauri are the thesaurus described in Muench 1971.7 and OECD/Development Centre 1969; both are multilingual.

K2.4.2. The use of a coarse classification scheme, called subsumption scheme, for the construction of conversion tables and shared subject indexing on a general level is discussed in Hammond 1963.12, especially p. 63ff. A preliminary report on "subsumption schemes" is Jaster 1963.2.

K3. On the concept of UST compare Atanasiu *et al.* 1966.6.

K3.0. A few references on the idea of universal classification may suffice; Classification Research Group 1969; Classification Research Group 1968.12; Foskett 1970; Austin 1969.7; Dahlberg 1971.10.

K3.1. The suggestion to process a great many existing indexing languages and thesauri into a common data base has been made by Mooers 1959.3.

K3.4. The parenthetical remark on the feasibility of UST refers to Vickery 1960a, p. 1160, II A(1). The centers collecting thesauri are CIINTE and CWRU/BSC.

Bibliography

Scope. This bibliography emphasizes documents on thesaurus format and on procedures used in thesaurus construction. Documents important for specific aspects (e.g. alphabetical sorting) and selected documents on background needed (e.g. classification theory, testing of ISAR systems) have also been included.

Coverage. The coverage is extensive but it is by no means comprehensive. In order to combine the advantages of extensive bibliography with the advantages of a selective bibliography, the individual items are evaluated with respect to topicality and quality, as explained below.

Information Given for Each Entry

Bibliographic information. The usual bibliographic information is given. The publication date is given including the month, e.g., 1967.5 (1967 May). If the month is unknown, we write 1967.; if the document should have a month but doesn't (e.g. an article that appeared in a journal giving only no. and year, but not the month for each issue) we write 1967.x. A document that does not have a period in its date is, then either a book or a paper originally printed in a book.

An effort has been made to include AD, PB, and ED numbers as well as reprint information in order to facilitate access to the documents cited. However, completeness is not guaranteed.

For standards only number, date, and title are given. Standards can be obtained from the issuing institution (see App. 1).

Citation information. For each document the section(s) where it has been cited is (are) given at the end of the entry. If the document has been included only because it appeared in another bibliography (see "Coverage"), this other bibliography is given.

Evaluation information. Evaluation information is printed in boldface at the bottom right. The following codes are used:

Topicality (Codes a-e)

a   The document is within the scope of the bibliography, and it contains material not covered in this book.

b   The document is within the scope of the bibliography, but it does not contain general material beyond what is covered in this book. Description of specific thesauri are labeled **b** if the format and the procedures described do not go beyond what is covered in this book.

c   The document is presumably or possibly within the scope of the bibliography, but it was not possible to consider the document in writing the book (relevance judged from title only).

e The document contains an actual indexing language or thesaurus or dictionary or a bibliography of such sources. These documents are not evaluated as to quality.

Quality (Codes 1 and 2)

1 Good or very good
2 Reasonable

These codes are used only in conjunction with **a** and **b**. Documents labeled **c, d,** or **e** are not evaluated.

Other

n Used where an evaluation is not appropriate or not feasible. This includes items that could not be obtained by this author.

More Comprehensive Version

A more comprehensive version of this bibliography has been submitted to ERIC under the title

    Soergel, Dagobert
        Indexing Languages and thesauri: Construction and maintenance. Extended bibliography.

Several other bibliographies on thesaurus construction have been worked completely into the extended version so that the need to consult these earlier bibliographies is eliminated. As a result of this procedure, quite a few items have been included that do not, in our judgment, fall in the scope of this bibliography. Those items have been marked by 'd,' as will be explained below.

The bibliographies given in the following documents have been worked in completely:

BASF 1/2
Batty 1969.6
Blagden 1968.8
Dahlberg 1971.4, sections
    2.2.4, 2.2.7, and 4.2.3
Gaster 1967.9

Gilchrist 1971
Soergel 1969
Soergel 1965.5
USDOD/ONR/LEX 1966.4
ZIID 1967.2

All articles contained in the following documents have been included:

Bull. A.I.D. v. 5, n. 4 (1966.10)
ZIID 1967.4

ZIID 1966.6

Further Evaluation Code Used

d The document is not within the scope of the bibliography but is included to achieve 100% coverage of other bibliographies as explained above or because the title might suggest that the document is relevant whereas in reality it is not. (These documents are not evaluated as to quality.)

Continuing Bibliography

A continuing bibliography on classification, indexing languages, and thesauri will appear in the new journal *International Classification*, edited by Ingetraut Dahlberg and

Bibliography 561

published by Verlag Dokumentation, München-Pullach. The author is planning a supplement to the bibliography in this book, including older material not captured here, and will submit it to the same journal and/or to ERIC.

Abraham, C. T. 1963: *Graph-theoretic techniques for the organization of linked data.* Cambridge, Mass.: Air Force Cambridge Research Laboratories 1963. H; H4.2. **cn**

Abraham, C. T. 1964.10: *Techniques for thesaurus organization and evaluation.* In: ADI Proc., v.0 (1964.10), p. 485–497. H; H4.2. **al**

Abraham, C. T. 1965a: *Techniques for thesaurus organization and evaluation.* In: Kochen ed. 1965, ch.II E, p. 131–150. H; H4.2; Batty 1969.6. **al**

Abraham, C. T. 1965c: *Graph-theoretic techniques for the organization of linked data.* In: Kochen ed. 1965, ch.V A, p. 229–251. H; H4.2. **al**

ADI 1963.10; Luhn, H. P., ed.: *Automation and scientific communication.* Pt. 1 and 2. Papers pres. at the ADI annual meeting, Chicago, 1963.10.6–11. Washington, D.C.: ADI 1963. Source. **n**

ADI 1964.10: *Parameters of information science.* Papers pres. at the ADI annual meeting, Philadelphia, Pa., 1964.10.5–8. New York: MacMillan 1964, 519 p. ADI Proceedings, v.1. Source. **n**

ADI 1965.10: *Proceedings of the 1965 FID Congress.* Papers pres. at the Meeting and Congress, International Federation for Documentation, Washington, D.C., 1965.10.7–16, in cooperation with ADI. Washington, D.C.: Spartan Books, 1966. ADI Proceedings, v.2. Source. **n**

ADI 1966.10: *Progress in information science and technology.* Papers pres. at the ADI annual meeting, Santa Monica, Calif. 1966.10.3–7. Woodland Hills, Calif.: Adrianne Press 1966, 494 p. ADI Proceedings, v.3. Source. **n**

ADI 1967.10: *Levels of interaction between man and information.* Papers pres. at the ADI annual meeting, New York, 1967.10.23–30. Washington, D.C.: Thompson Book Company 1968. ADI Proceedings, v.4. Source. **n**

AFOSR 1965.5; SDC: *Workshop on working semi-automatic documentation systems.* Warrenton, Va. 1965.5. Proceedings. Warrenton, Va.: Airlie Foundation 1965, 106 p. AD 620 360. **n**

Aitchison, Jean 1970.9: *The thesaurofacet: a multipurpose retrieval language tool.* In: J. Doc. v.26, n.3 (1970.9), p. 187–203. (Abbr. and slightly modified version of the introduction to Thesaurofacet, p. XIX-XXV). D1.7.4. **al**

Aitchison, Jean 1972: *Thesaurofacet—a new concept in subject retrieval schemes.* In: Wellisch et al. ed. 1972, p. 72–98. D1.7.4; D3.2. **a2**

Aitchison, Jean 1972; Gilchrist, Alan: *Thesaurus construction—A practical manual.* London: Aslib 1972, 95 p. (Table of contents reproduced in App. 1). **cn**

Akhmanova, O. S. 1965.11; Nikitina, S. E.: *Some linguistic problems of compiling descriptor languages.* In: Voprosy Yazykoznaniya v.14, n.6 (1965.11), p. 111–115. **cn**

ALA 1968: *ALA filing rules for filing catalog cards.* 2nd ed. Chicago: American Library Association 1968. E3. **an**

Amacher, Peter 1967.9: *A natural-language glossary for an automated bibliographic-retrieval system.* In: FID 67.9, III-g-1, 14 p. Abstr. in: Doc. Absn. v.1/2, n.4 1967.12). B6.2; B6.2.2(2). **al**

Angell, Richard S. 1965: *On the future of the Library of Congress classification.* In: Atherton ed. 1965, p. 101–112. D1.7.3. **a2**

Angell, Richard S. 1967.9: *The specific-to-general see reference in thesaurus construction.* In: FID 1967.9, III-g-4, 21 p. Repr. in Angell 1968. B4.2.4; C5.0.2. **a2**

Angell, Richard S. 1968: *Two papers on thesaurus construction: a. the language of term-relation designations in subject access vocabularies. b. the specific-to-general see reference in thesaurus construction.* Copenhagen: Danish Center for Documentation 1968, FID/CR Report no. 8. **n**
ANSI Y1.1–1972: *Abbreviations* (Revision and consolidation of Z10.1–1941 and Z132.13–1950). E1.8.2. **an**
ANSI Z39–1973.2 (draft): *Guidelines for thesaurus structure, construction and use.* (Standard to be in effect before June 1, 1973.) App. 1. **an**
ANSI Z39.4–1968: *Indexes, basic criteria for.* In partial agreement with ISO R999. **cn**
ANSI Z39.5–1969: *Abbreviation of titles of periodicals.* The list of abbreviations given in this standard is updated through the following publication: National Clearinghouse for Periodical Title Word Abbreviations (NCPTWA): Quarterly supplement to the revised and enlarged word-abbreviation list for the "American Standard for Periodical Title Abbreviation" USAS12395–1963. Columbus, Ohio: Chemical Abstracts Service, v.1, n.1 (1967). A consolidated list was published in 1971 under the title NCPTWA word-abbreviation list. E1.8.2. **cn**
API/Central Abstracting and Indexing Service 1970.5: *Indexers manual.* New York: American Petroleum Institute 1970.5, 47 p. D1.1.1; D1.7.8. **an**
API 1971.1: *Subject authority list.* New York: American Petroleum Institute 1964.1, 245 p. 5th ed.: 1971.1, 516 p. (New editions appear yearly.) D1.7.8; J3.3; J3.3.3; J4; App. 2. **e**
Aries, Philippe 1966.10: *Un lexique par phrases descriptives* (the lexicon of IFAC). In: Bulletin de l'A.I.D., v.5, n.4 (1966.10), p. 99–101. **b**
ARIST: *Annual review of information science and technology.* See Cuadra.
Arntz, H. 1964.3: *Dokumentation mit Sichtlochkarten.* Ringtausch mit Lochkarten im Dienst der auswärtigen Vertretungen der Bundesrepublik Deutschland. In: Nachr. Dok., v.15, n.1 (1964.3), p. 18–27. C2.8.1; C2.8.2. **a2**
Artandi, Susan 1970: *Document description and representation.* In: Ann. Rev. of Info. Sci. and Tech., v.5 (1970), p. 143–168. **a1**
Arthur D. Little, Inc. 1963.7: *Centralization and documentation.* Cambridge, Mass.: Arthur D. Little 1963.7, 70 p. Final report to the NSF. 2 ed. 1964, 49 p. H. **a1**
Ash, Lee 1967; Lorenz, Denis: *Subject collections: a guide to special book collections and subject emphases as reported by university, college, public, and special libraries in the United States and Canada.* New York: Bowker 1967. App. 2. **e**
Ashworth, Wilfred, ed. 1955–1967: *Handbook of special librarianship and information work.* 3 rev. ed. London: ASLIB 1967, 624 p. Source. **n**
ASIS 1968.10: *Information transfer.* Papers pres. at the ASIS annual meeting, Columbus, Ohio, 1968.10.20–24. New York: Greenwood Publ. Corp. 1968, 362 p. ASIS Proceedings, v.5. Source. **n**
ASIS/Annual Meeting 32/Thesaurus workshop 1969.10: *The thesaurus in action.— Background information for a thesaurus workshop at ASIS/annual meeting 32.* Washington, D.C.: Dept. of the Army, Information Systems Office 1969.10, 42 p. AD 694 590; ED 038 983. Source. **n**
ASIS 1969.10a: *Cooperating information societies.* Papers pres. at the ASIS annual meeting, San Francisco, 1969.10.1–4. Westport, Conn.: Greenwood Publ. Corp. 1969, 432 p. ASIS Proceedings, v.6. Source. **n**
ASIS 1970.10: *The information conscious society.* Papers pres. at the ASIS annual meeting, Philadelphia, Pa., 1970.10.11–15. Washington, D.C.: ASIS 1970, 348 p. ASIS Annual Proceedings, v.7. Source. **n**
ASIS 1971.11: *Communication for decision-makers.* Papers pres. at the ASIS annual

meeting, Denver, Col., 1971.11.7–11. Westport, Conn.: Greenwood 1971.11, 413 p.
ASIS proceedings, v.8. Source. **n**
Atanasiu, P. 1966.6; Bazareson, G.: *Vergleichende Analyse von Thesauri and Möglichkeiten ihrer Vervollkommung (Comparative analysis of thesauri and possibilities for their improvement)*. In: *ZIID 1966.6, p. 87–109. K1.2.3; K3. **a1**
Atherton, Pauline, ed. 1965: *Classification research*. Proc. 2nd Internat. Study Conf., Elsinore, 1964.9.14–18. Copenhagen: Munksgaard 1965, 563 p. FID publ. 370. B4.2.3. Source. **n**
Atherton, Pauline 1965.1; Borko, Harold: *A test of the factor-analytically derived automated classification method applied to descriptions of work and search requests of nuclear physicists*. New York: American Institute of Physics 1965.1, 11 p. + app. Report AIP/DRP-65-1. Santa Monica, California: System Development Corp. 1965.1. SDC-SP-1905. H. **an**
Auguston, Gary J. 1970.3; Minker, Jack: *Deriving term relations for a corpus by graph theoretical clusters*. In: JASIS, v.21, n.2, (1970.3), p. 101–111. H. **a1**
Augustson, J. Gary 1970.10; Minker, Jack: *An analysis of some graph theoretical cluster techniques*. In: J. ACM, v.17, n.4 (1970.10), p. 571–588. **an**
Austin, Derek 1969.7: *Prospects for a new general classification*. In: J. Librarianship, v.1, n.3 (1969.7), p. 149–169. K3.0. **an**
Austin, D. 1969; Butcher, P.: *PRECIS: a rotated subject index system*. London: BNB 1969. D3.6.1, 2; E1.5. **an**
Austin, Derek 1969.11: *Development of a new general classification: a progress report*. In: Inform. Scientist, v.3, n.3 (1969.11), p. 95–115. **an**
Austin, Derek 1972: *The PRECIS system for computer-generated indexes and its use in the British National Bibliography*. In: Wellisch et al. ed. 1972, p. 99–115. C2.5, D3.6.1,2; E1.5; J5(a); K2.3.2,1. **a2**
Autopol'skii, A.B. 1967; Boldov, V. B.: *Some definitions of basic concepts in information retrieval languages*. In: Naucno-Tekn. Informatsiya, series 2, n.5 (1967), p. 5–8. Trans. in: Automated Documentation and Math. Linguistics, v.1, n.2 (1969.x) p. 14–17. B4.2.1. **a2**
Avramescu, A. 1969: *Descriptor vocabulary for covering a special field*. In: Stud. & Cercetari Doc. & Bibliog., v.11, n.1 (1969), p. 3–22. **cn**

Back, Harry 1964; Cirullies, Horst; Marquard, Günter: *Polec. Dictionary of politics and economics*. Berlin: de Gruyter 1964, 961 p. D5.2. **e**
Backer, S. 1967: *The thesaurus as a first step in an information retrieval system*. In: Textile Inst. Ind., v.5, n.4 (1967), p. 91–96. **cn**
Bailey, Richard W. 1969.10; Robinson, Jay L.: *The computer in lexicography*. Ann Arbor, Mich.: Univ. of Michigan 1969.10, 21 p. G. **a1**
Baker, F. B. 1962: *Information retrieval based on latent class analysis*. In: J. ACM, v.9, n. (1962), p. 512–521. H; Batty 1969.6. **an**
Baker, F. B. 1965.12: *Latent class analysis as an association model for information retrieval*. In: Stevens et al. ed. 1965.12, p. 149–156. H; Batty 1969.6. **an**
Baker, F. T. et al.: *Research on automatic classification, indexing and extracting. Annual progress report*. (No bibliographic data available.) **an**
Baker, F. T. 1968.8; Williams, John H. Jr.: *Research on automatic classification, indexing and extracting: a general-purpose frequency program*. Bethesda, Md.: IBM 1968.8, 52 p. AD 673 428, ED027919 (but not available from EDRS). H; H1. **an**
Bakewell, K. G. B., ed. 1968: *Classification for information retrieval*. . . . London: Clive Bingley; Hamden, Conn.: Archon Books 1968, 100 p. Source. **n**

Balazs, S. 1966.6; Orosz, G.: *Übersicht über die Arbeiten an Deskriptorsystemen in der Ungarischen Volksrepublik.* In: ZIID 1966.6, p. 110–119.
Ball, Geoffrey H. 1970.11: *Classification analysis.* Menlo Park, Calif.: Stanford Research Inst. 1970.11, 120 p. AD 716 482. **cn**
Ball, N. T. 1958: *Making classification systems for punched-card coding.* In: Casey et al. ed. 1958, ch.5, p. 528–541. **b2**
Barhydt, Gordon C. 1968; Schmidt, Charles T.; Chang, Keel T.: *Information retrieval thesaurus of education terms.* Cleveland, Ohio: Case Western Reserve Univ. Press 1968, 133 p. (p. 1–28 introductory material, p. 29–133 actual thesaurus). *The preparation of a thesaurus of educational terms. Final report.* Cleveland, Ohio: CWRU/ Center for Documentation and Communication Research 1966.6, 98 p. (p. 1–8 text, p. 9–98 thesaurus). ED 010 239. C1.2(5); C1.5; C5.3.2; D1.1.0,2; D1.4 (1a); D1.4.2; D1.7.7; D2.3.2,5; D3.0. **a2/e**
Barske, I. L. 1969; Tschache, L.: *Thesauren und ähnliche Bergriffslisten.—Berichtszeit 1960–1968.* (Thesauri and similar concept lists—1960–1968). Dresden: Technische Universität/Bibliothek 1969, 134 p. TU Dresden/Bibliothek. Bibliotheksarbeit No. 4. App. 2. **e**
BASF 1/2: Unpublished papers that have been produced within BASF (Badische Anilin- und Soda-Fabrik). The material is to be published by E. Meyer and R. Jansen. Part is published in Jansen 1970.4. A1.6; B5.5(b); B5.7(a); B6.1; B6.2; C1.4.2; C1.4.3,1; C2.7.1; C4.3; C6; D1.4, Fig. 4; D2.2, Fig. 33; E passim; F0.7.1,1; F9.1; G; G0.2; G3.4.1; G5.1; App. 1. **b1**
Batty, C. D. 1967: *Introduction to the seventeenth edition of Dewey decimal classification.* London: Bingley 1967 (a programmed text). D1.7.3. **an**
Batty, C. David 1969.6: *The automatic generation of index languages.* In: J. Doc., v.25, n.2 (1969.6), p. 142–151. H. This is a merely indicative report, useful mainly for its bibliography. All items of the bibliography are included in our bibliography. **a2**
Bauer, Gerd 1960: *Einige Gedanken über den Aufbau eines Thesaurussystems für das Gesamtgebiet der Chemie.* (Some thoughts on the development of a thesaurus system for the total field of chemistry.) In: Biul. Osrodka Dok. i Inform. Nauk. PAN, Warszawa (1960), p. 9–16. App. 2. **cn**
Bauer, Gerd 1965.6: *Der Grundthesaurus "Chemie"—Probleme des Aufbaus und der Ergänzung durch Fachthesauri.* (The base thesausus "Chemistry"—Problems of Development and of supplementation through special thesauri.) In: ZIID 1965.6. App. 2. **cn**
Bauer, Gerd 1965a: *Probleme und Erfahrungen beim Aufbau von Fachthesauri für die Chemie.* (Problems and experiences with the development of special thesauri for chemistry.) In: Wiss. Z. TH Ilmenau, v.11 Sonderheft (1965), p. 89–104. App. 2. **cn**
Bauer, Gerd 1966.3: *Alphabetische Liste der wichtigsten Termini zum Begriff "Deskriptor."* (Alphabetical List of the most important terms relating to the concept "descriptor.") Berlin: Dt. Akad. d. Wiss., Wiss. Redaktion der Zentralblätter, Abt. Forschung und Entwicklung 1966.3. **cn**
Bauer, Gerd 1966.6: *Gedanken zur Theorie des Aufbaus und der Funktionsweise der in einem Thesaurussystem zusammengefassten Thesaurusarten.* (Thoughts on the theory of the structure and functions of the different types of thesauri comprised in a thesaurus system.) In: ZIID 1966.6, p. 1–52. **cn**
Bauer, Gerd 1967; Maneck, Martin: *Probleme der chemischen Information und ihre Lösungmoglichkeiten mit Hilfe eines Thesaurussystems.* (Problems of chemical information and possibilities of their solution through the use of a thesaurus system.) In: Z. Chemie, v.7, n.9 (1967), p. 338–339. App. 2. **cn**
Bauer, Gerd 1967.x: *Anwendung des Prinzips des Facettenklassifikation für den Aufbau*

von Thesauri.—Erläutert am Beispiel "Thesaurussystem Chemie." (Application of the principles of faceted classification in the construction of thesauri.—Described with reference to the "Thesaurus system chemistry.") In: ZIID-Z., v.14, n.3 (1967.x), p. 72–81. App. 2. **b**

Bauer, Gerd 1967.1; Maneck, Martin; Schoenberg, D.: Ergebnis der Voruntersuchungen zum klassifikatorischen Gerüst des Grundthesaurus Chemie MEF 1/67. (Result of the preliminary investigations on the classificatory structure of the base thesaurus chemistry MEF 1/67.) Berlin: Dt. Akad. d. Wiss., Wiss. Redaktion der Zentralblätter, Forschungsgruppe TSC 1967.1. App. 2. **cn**

Bauer, Gerd 1967.3; Maneck, M.; Schoenberg, D.: Die Anwendung des Prinzips der Facettenclassifikation beim Aufbau des Thesaurussystems Chemie. 1. Teil: Einführung in die allgemeine Problemstellung und die Grundlagen der Facettenklassifikation MEF 3/67. (Application of the principles of faceted classification in the construction of the thesaurus. Part 1: Introduction to the problem in general and to the principles of faceted classification. MEF 3/67.) Berlin: Dt. Akad. d. Wiss., Wiss. Redaktion der Zentralblatter, Forschungsgruppe TSC 1967.3. App. 2. **cn**

Bauer, Gerd 1967.3a: Stellungnahme zum DK-Abschnitt 661 "Chemische Erzeugnisse." (Comments on the UDC-Section 661 "Chemical products.) Berlin: Zentrale Leitstelle fur Information und Dokumentation der chem. Industrie und Forschungsgruppe TSC der Wiss. Redaktion der Zentralblätter 1967.3.9. **cn**

Bauer, Gerd 1967.4: Zur Methodik des Aufbaus "koordinierfähiger" Fachthesauri im Rahmen des Thesaurussystems Chemie. (On the methodology of the construction of "compatible" special thesauri in the framework of the thesaurus system chemistry.) In: ZIID 1967.4, p. 207–209. K2.3.1; App. 2. **a2**

Bauer, Gerd 1968.x: Die Bedeutung der Kategorien als "Ordnungsmittel" in Thesauri und Speichern der elektronischen Datenverarbeitungsanlagen. (The importance of categories as ordering device in thesauri and in computer storage.) In: ZIID-Z, v.15, n.2 (1968.x), p. 61–65. **cn**

Bauer, Gerd 1969.x: Zur geeigneten Bergriffsordnung im Thesaurussystem Chemie. (On the suitable conceptual structure in the thesaurus system chemistry). In: Informatik, v.16 (1969) p. 1: Nichtstrukturchemische Begriffe. (Concepts not from structural chemistry). n.2 (1969.x), p. 35–41. p. 2: Strukturchemische Begriffe (Concepts from structural chemistry). n.5 (1969.x), p. 11–16. **b**

Bauer, H. 1967.2: Aufstellung eines Thesaurus für Elektrotechnik mit Hilfe von Maschinenlochkarten. (Compilation of a thesaurus for electrical engineering with the aid of machine punched cards.) In: Nachr. Dok. v18, n.1 (1967.2), p. 6–12. F9.2.2. **a**

Baxendale, Phyllis 1966: Content analysis, specification and control. In: ARIST, v.1 (1966), p. 71–106. **a1**

Becker, J. 1963; Hayes, R. M.: Information storage and retrieval: tools, elements, theories. New York: Wiley 1963, 448 p. Information Sciences Series. v. I. C. **a1**

Beling, G. 1971.10: Übersetzung von Thesauri (translation of thesauri). First draft. Wachtberg-Werthoven: Forschungsinstitut fur Funk und Mathematik 1971.10, 17 p. D5; D5.0; D5.4; F5.8. **a2**

Bergmann, S. 1966.6: Die Ausnutzung logischer Deskriptorenfunktionen in Notationssystemen. (The use of logical descriptor functions in notational systems). In: ZIID 1966.6, p. 161–168.

Bernier, Charles L. 1956.10—1964. et al.: Correlative indexes. 1–6 In: Amer. Doc. 1: Alphabetical correlative indexes. v.7, n.4 (1956.10), p. 283–288. 2: Correlative trope indexes. v.8, n.1 (1957.1), p. 47–50. 3: with: Heumann, Karl F.: Semantic relations among semantemes—the technical thesaurus. v.8, n.3 (1957.7), p. 211–220. 4: Chemical group indexes. v.8, n.4 (1957.10), p. 306–313. 5: The Blank sort. v.9, n.1 (1958.1), p. 32–41. 6: *Serendipity, suggestiveness, and display.* v.11, n.4 (1960.10), p. 277–287. 7–10: In: J. Chem. Doc. 7: *Trope vocabularies and trope indexes for chemistry.* v.2, n.2 (1962.4), p. 93–102. 8: With: Crane, E. J.: *Subject indexing vs. word indexing.* v.2, n.2 (1962.4), p. 117–122. 9: *Vocabulary control.* v.4, n.2 (1964), p. 99–103. 10: *Subject-index qualities.* v.4, n.2 (1964), p. 104–106. cn

Bernier, Charles L. 1968.2: *Indexing and thesauri.* In: Special Libraries, v.59, n.2 (1968.2), p. 98–103. a

Blagden, John F. 1968.8: *Thesaurus compilation methods: a literature review.* In: Aslib Proc., v.20, n.8 (1968.8), p. 345–359. (Incomplete survey of who did what. Bibliography completely incorporated in extended version of this bibliography.)

Blagden, John F. 1971.3: *Structured thesauri.* In: Aslib Proc., v.23, n.3 (1971.3), p. 139–143. (Description of Brit. Inst. of Management thesaurus.) App. 2. a

Blankenstein, G. 1967.x: *Erarbeitung von Thesauri unter Berücksichtigung der zukünftigen Entwicklung. (The construction of thesauri with a view to future developments.)* In: ZIID-Z., v.14, n.6 (1967.x), p. 177–180. A1.3.2; K. a2

Blankenstein, G. 1967.x: *Hierarchische Struktur eines Thesaurus, Fachsystematik und Klassifikation. (Hierarchical structure of a thesaurus, taxonomy of a field, and classification.)* In: ZIID-Z., v.14, n.5 (1967.x), p. 138–140. cn

Blankenstein, G. 1967.4: *Konzeption zur Erarbeitung eines Thesaurus auf dem Sachgebiet Nahrung und Ernährung. (Design for the development of a thesaurus in the area of food and nutrition.)* In: ZIID 1967.4, p. 111–117. Unpublished version: *Die Erarbeitung eines Thesaurus auf dem Gebiet von Nahrung und Ernährung und ein Versuch zur Verallgemeinerung der methodischen Konzeption.* B5.4.1 (4b); D3.1.2,2; F0.5; App. 2. a2

Blomgren, G. et al. 1966.6: *An experimental investigation of automatic hierarchy generation.* In: ISR-11 (1966.6). H; Batty 1969.6. an

BN: *Bibliothèque Nationale*, 58, Rue de Richelieu, Paris 2e, France. Depository of French thesauri, etc. (In charge Marie-Therese Laureilhe). App. 2. e

Boaz, M. 1959: *Modern trends in documentation.* Oxford, New York: Pergamon Press 1959, 103 p. Proc. Symposium Univ. Southern Calif. 1958.4. Source. n

Boehm, Eric H. ed. 1965.7: *America.—History and life. A guide to periodical literature.* Santa Barbara, Calif.: Clio Press. Here v.5, n.1 (1965.7). E1.8.3. e

Borko, Harold 1962.5: *The construction of an empirically based mathematically derived classification system.* In: Proc. SJCC, v.21 (1962.5), p. 279–289. Also Santa Monica, Calif., System Development Corp. 1961.10.26, 23 p. SDC-SP 585; AD 267 901. H; Batty 1969.6. a1

Borko, Harold 1963.4; Bernick, Myrna D.: *Automatic document classification.* In: J. ACM, v.10, n.2 (1963.4), p. 151–162. Repr. in: Saracevic ed. 1970, paper 36, p. 411–418. H; Batty 1969.6. an

Borko, Harold 1963.10; Bernick, Myrna D.: *Automatic document classification. Part II. Additional experiments.* Santa Monica, Calif.: Systems Development Corp. 1963.10.18, 33 p. SDC TM-771-001-00. H. an

Borko, Harold 1963.11: *Research in document classification and file organization.* Santa Monica, Calif.: Systems Development Corp. 1963.11.13, 12 p. SDC-SP 1423; AD 425 531. H. an

Borko, Harold 1964.2; Bernick, Myrna D.: *Toward the establishment of a computer based classification system for scientific documentation.* Santa Monica, Calif.: SDC 1964.2.19, 47 p. SDC TM-1763. (Many examples.) H. a1

Borko, Harold 1965: *Research in computer based classification systems.* In: Atherton ed. 1965, p. 220–257. H. an

Borko, Harold 1965.: *A factor analytically derived classification system for psychological reports.* In: Perceptual and Motor Skills, n.20 (1965.), p. 393–406. H. **an**
Borko, Harold 1965.12: *Studies on the reliability and validity of factor-analytically derived classification categories.* In: Stevens et al. ed. 1965.12, p. 245–258. H; Batty 1969.6. **an**
Borko, Harold 1967: *Indexing and classification.* In: Borko ed. 67, p. 99–125. Gilchrist 1971. **cn**
Borko, Harold, ed. 1967: *Automated language processing.* New York: Wiley 1967, 386 p. Information Science Series. Source. **n**
Bourne, Charles P. 1961.; Ford, Donald F.: *Study of methods for systematically abbreviating English words and names.* In: J. ACM, v., n. (1961.), p. 538–552. E1.8.2. **an**
Bourne, L. E. 1966: *Human conceptual behavior.* Boston: Allyn and Bacon, Inc. 1966, 139 p. C1.7. **an**
BPA 1965; Arntz, Helmut; Kümmel, Hiltburg: *Ringtausch mit Lochkarten. Sachlogisches Gesamtregister. (Information exchange with peek-a-boo cards. Classified index.)* Bonn: Presse- und Informationsamt der Bundesregierung 1965, 87 p. **e**
Brendler, Gerhard 1970.x: *Der Mehrsprachige Thesaurus: ein Instrument zur Rationalisierung des Informationflusses. (The multilingual thesaurus: an instrument for increasing the efficiency of information flow.)* In: Informatik, v.17, n.4 (1970.x), p. 19–24. D5. **cn**
Brenner, Everett H. 1964.10: *Descriptors, terms, subject heading, term-indexing, subject indexing—definitions.* In: ADI Proc., v.1 (1964.10), p. 387–388. B4.2.1. **a**
Brenner, Everett H. 1965.10; Hines, T.: *Thesaurus construction—historical background and use considerations.* New York: American Petroleum Institute 1965.10, 24 p. Abstract in FID 1965.10, p. 63. B4.2.4. **a2**
Brenner, Everett H. 1966.10; Mulvihill, J. G.: *American Petroleum Institute information retrieval project subject authority list.* In: Bull. de l'A.I.D., v.5, n.4 (1966.10), p. 81–84. (Summary of Mulvihill et al. 1966.10). **b2**
BS 1749:1969 *Specification for alphabetical arrangement and filing order of numerals and symbols.* E3. **an**
BS 3862:1969 *Symbols for languages, geographical areas, and authorities.* D5; E1.10. **an**
BS 4148: 1967 *The abbreviation of titles of periodicals.* E1.8.2. **an**
Bud'ko, N. S. 1966.6: *Methodik der Ausarbeitung von Deskriptorverzeichnissen für Recherchesysteme. (Methodology for the development of descriptors lists for information storage and retrieval systems.)* In: ZIID 1966.6, p. 53–62. **en**
Buntrock, Herbert 1963.10; Meyer-Uhlenried, K. H.: *Terminology work for the preparation of natural language expressions and approached expressions for mechanised and semi-mechanised documentation systems, demonstrated by "Documentation of Documentation" in EURATOM/CETIS.* In: ADI Proc, v.0 (1963.10), p. 19–20. App. 2. **b**
Buntrock, H. 1963.5: *Zur Kompilation von Thesauri. (On the compilation of thesauri.)* In: Serbanescu 1963.5. Also: Brussels: EURATOM 1964., 16 p. EUR 558.d. reprint. **b2**

Cain, A. M. 1969.7: *Thesaural problems in an on-line system.* In: Bull. Med. Lib. Assoc., v.57, n.3 (1969.7), p. 250–259. B6.2.1; C6.2.2(3). **a**
Caless, T. W. 1970.12: *Strategies for manipulating Universal Decimal Classification relationships for computer retrieval. Final report.* Washington, D.C.: George Washington Univ./Biological Sciences Communication Project 1970.12, 40 p. AD 717 212. D1.7.3; G. **an**

Campbell, D. J. 1965.10: *Application of classificatory methods to radical revision of thesauri or lists of keywords.* An expanded and revised version of the paper read at FID Congress 1965.10. Unpublished. cn

Campbell, D. J. 1965.6: *EJC thesaurus of engineering terms* (review). In: J. Doc., v.21, n.2 (1965.6), p. 136–139. App. 2. cn

Campbell, D. J. 1963.10: *Making your own indexing system in science and technology (classification and keyword systems.)* In: Aslib Proc., v.15, n.10 (1963.10), p. 282–303. (Outdated). b

Caponio, J. F. 1964.1; Gillum, T. L.: *Practical aspects concerning the development and use of ASTIA's thesaurus in information retrieval.* In: J. of Chem. Doc., v.4, n.1 (1964.1), p. 5–8. App. 2. b2

Casey, R. S. et al. ed. 1958: *Punched cards: their applications to science and industry.* 2nd ed. New York: Reinhold 1958, 697 p. C2.8.2; Source. n

Cassidy, F. G. et al.: *Data processing system for the Dictionary of American Regional English.* Madison, Wis.: Dept. of English, Univ. of Wisconsin. G. cn

Castner, W. G. 1968: *The MECCA vocabulary control system for library collections.* Seattle: Boeing Co. 1968, 21 p. cn

Cernjavskij, V. S. 1966.6; Kusnecov, V. I.: *Die Erarbeitung automatisierter Recherchesysteme vom Deskriptortyp. (The development of automated retrieval systems of the descriptor type.)* In: ZIID 1966.6, p. 141–151. cn

Cernyj, A. I. 1968: *General methods of IR thesaurus compilation.* (orig. Russ.) In: Naucno-Techn. Inform., series 2, n.5 (1968.), p. 9–32. cn

Chemical Engineering Theasurus 1961: *Chemical Engineering Thesaurus.* New York: American Institute of Chemical Engineers 1961. App. 2. e

Cheng, D. C. 1968.: *Some thoughts on the preparation of a thesaurus for rheological information retrieval.* In: Bull. Br. Soc. Rheology, n.2, p.29–34. App. 2. cn

CIINTE: Centralny Instytut Informacji Naukowo Techniczenej i Ekonomicznej, A1. Niepodleglosci 188, Warszawa, Polen. Center for the collection of classification schemes and thesauri in languages other than English. A2.1; K3.4; App. 2. e

CIINTE 1969: *The holdings of the Clearinghouse for Scientific and Technical Classification Schedules.*—Keywords, subject-heading and descriptor lists, thesauri, indexes and other means of information retrieval in languages other than English. Warszawa: CIINTE 1969, 140 p. Bibliographic Bulletin of the Clearinghouse at CIINTE. (Annual supplements are planned.) App. 2. e

Clason, W. E., comp. 1955: *Elsevier's dictionary of television, radar and antennas in six languages.* Amsterdam: Elsevier 1955, 760 p. D5.2. e

Classification Research Group 1955.7; *The need for a faceted classification as the basis of all methods of information retrieval.* (Memorandum of CRG received for information by Library Association Library Research Committee.) In: Lib. Assoc. Rec., v.57, n.7 (1955.7), p. 262–268. Also: Paris: UNESCO/Dept. of Natural Sciences 1955. Doc. 320/5515. Repr. in: International Study Conference 1957.5, p. 137–147. K3.0. a

Classification Research Group 1968.12: *Classification Research Group Bulletin no. 9.* In: J. Doc., v.24, n.4 (1968.12), p. 273–298. K3.0. cn

Classification Research Group 1969: *Classification and information control.* London: The Library Association 1969, 130 p. K3.0. cn

Claus, F. 1966.6: *Die hierarchisch gegliederten Klassifikationssysteme als Basis für die Begriffslisten beim Sichlockkartenverfahren. (The hierarchically structured classification schemes as basis for descriptor lists used with peek-a-boo cards.)* In: ZIID 1966.6, p. 149–155. cn

Claus, F. 1967.4: *Der Fachthesaurus und die einzelnen Betriebe. (The special thesaurus and individual companies.)* In: ZIID 1967.4, p. 261–265. **b**
Cleverdon, Cyril 1966.; Mills, Jack; Keen, Michael: *Factors determining the performance of indexing systems.* V.1. Design. Pt. 1. Text. Pt. 2. Appendices. V.2. Test results. Cranfield: Aslib Cranfield Research Project 1966, 378 p. (v.1), 299 p. (v.2). Gilchrist 1971; Blagden 1968.8. **cn**
Cleverdon, Cyril 1967.6: *The Cranfield test on index languages.* In: Aslib Proc., v.19, n.6 (1967.6), p. 173–194. Gilchrist 1971; Blagden 1968.8. **cn**
Coates, Eric James 1960: *Subject catalogues. Headings and structures.* London: The Library Association 1960, 186 p. C; C2.4; D1.1.0,3; E; E1.5. **a1**
Coates, Eric James 1970.6: *Switching languages for indexing.* In: J. Doc., v.26, n.2 (1970.6), p. 102–110. K2.1.1. **b2**
Colbach, R. 1970.2: *Thesaurus structure and generic posting.* In: IAEA 1970.2, p. 585–595. **cn**
Collison, Robert L. 1969: *Indexes and indexing: guide to the indexing of books.* 3. rev. ed. London: Ernest Benn; New York: John de Graaf 1969. 1.ed.1962. **cn**
Comparison of UDC with descriptor systems. In: FID Bull., v.17, n.10 (1967.10), p. 106. K2.3.2,1. **cn**
Cooke, Geraldine A. 1971.6; Heaps, Doreen M.; Mercier, Marcel: *The study of UDC and other indexing languages through computer manipulation of machine-readable data bases.* In: UDC 1971.6, paper 1, 24 p. C1.7.3; G. **cn**
Cordonnier, G. 1960: *Metalangage pour les traductions d'intercommunications entre hommes et son adaptation dans le domaine des machines pour recherches documentaires. (Metalanguage for the translation of communications between men and its adaptation to the field of mechanized information storage and retrieval.* In: Kent ed. 1960, p. 1091–1137 (ch.51). C2.3.2; D3.6.0,1. **a1**
Costello, J. C. Jr. 1966: *Coordinate indexing.* New Brunswick, N.J.: Rutgers Univ./ Graduate School of Library Service 1966, 224 p. Rutgers Series on Systems for the Intellectual Organization of Information VII. **a2**
Croghan, Antony 1970: *A thesaurus-classification for the physical forms of media.* London: Antony Croghan 1970, 47 p. K1.2.3. **e**
Cros, René Charles 1964; Gardin, Jean Claude; Levy, Francis: *L'automatisation des recherches documentaires.—Un modèle général "le SYNTOL." (The automation of information storage and retrieval.—A general model: SYNTOL.)* Paris: Gauthier-Villars 1964 (2nd. ed. 1968), 260 p. Documentation et Information. B4.2.3; B4.2.4; C; F0.4.5; G3.4.1. **a1**
Crouch, Donald B. 1971.10: *Cluster analysis: bibliography.* In: ACM/SIGIR Forum, v.6, n.3 (1971.10), p. 11–14. H. **an**
Cuadra, Carlos A. ed.: *Annual review of information science and technology* (ARIST). v1. New York: Wiley 1966. v.8. Washington: ASIS 1973. C. **n**
CWRU/BSC 1971.9: Bibliographic Systems Center, School for Library Science, Case Western Reserve University, Cleveland, Ohio 44106. Center for the collection of English language classification schemes and thesauri. A2.1; K3.4; App. 2. **e**
CWRU/BSC 1969: *Bibliographic Systems Center subject index.* Cleveland, Ohio: Case Western Reserve University 1969. Computer printout. App. 2. **e**

Dahlberg, Ingetraut 1966.10: *Thesaurus research: Deutsche Gesellschaft für Dokumentation e.V.* In: Bull. de l'A.I.D., v.5, n.4 (1966.10), p. 103–106. (News item.) **cn**
Dahlberg, Ingetraut 1971.10: *Principles for the construction of a universal classification system.—A proposal.* Frankfurt: the author 1971.10, 23 p. 1. Ottawa Conference

on the Conceptual Basis of the Classification of Knowledge, Ottawa 1971.10.1–5, paper. K3.0. **a2**
Dahlberg, Ingetraut 1972.4: *Das Informationsbankensystem. (The information bank network.)* Band III: *Literatur zu den Informationswissenschaften.—Annotierte Auswahlbibliographie internationaler Fachliteratur, 1960–1971. Information sciences literature.—An annotated bibliography of selected international literature 1960–1971.* Köln, etc.: Heymanns 1972, 472 p. **n**
Daily, Jay Elwood 1957: *The grammar of subject headings: a formulation of rules for subject headings based on a syntactical and morphological analysis of the Library of Congress list.* Columbia University 1957. D.L.S. thesis. E; E1.5. **an**
Dale, A. G. 1964.10; Dale, N.; Pendergraft, E.D.: *A programming system for automatic classification with applications in linguistic and information retrieval research.* Austin, Texas: University of Texas, Linguistics Research Center 1964.1, 19 p. Report LRC-64-WTM-4. H. **an**
Dale, A. G. 1965.1; Dale, N.: *Some clumping experiments for associative document retrieval.* In: Amer. Doc., v.16, n.1 (1965.1), p. 5–9. H. **an**
Daniels, Parmely C. 1969.10: *Identifying information.* In: ASIS 1969.10, p. 3–6. **b2**
Dattola, R. T. 1969.3: *A fast algorithm for automatic classification.* In: J. Lib. Automat., v.2, n.1 (1969.3), p. 31–48. Also in: ISR 14 (1968.10). H; Batty 1969.6. **an**
Dattola, R. T. 1968.1; Murray, D. M.: *An experiment in automatic thesaurus construction.* In: ISR-13 (1968.1). H; Batty 1969.6. **an**
DDC 1965: *Dewey decimal classification and relative index.* 17th ed. Lake Placid, N.Y.: Forest Press Inc. of Lake Placid Club Educational Foundation 1965, 2 v., 2153 p. 18th ed. 1971, 3 v., 2692 p. D1.7.3. **e**
Deese, J. 1965: *The structure of association in language and thought.* Baltimore: The Johns Hopkins Press 1965. B2.4; C1.7; F1.1.4. **an**
Dehnhard, Hans 1968.x: *Probleme einer simultanen Bearbeitung alphabetischer und systematischer Sachkataloge mit Hilfe der elektronischen Datenverarbeitung.* (Problems of processing alphabetical and classified subject catalogs simultaneously with computer.) In: Pflug ed. 1968.x, p. 86–104. C2.5; D3.6.1,2. **a2**
Dehnhard, H. 1971: *Aufbau und Bentutzung eines DK-Thesaurus (Construction and use of a UDC thesaurus).* Bochum: Ruhr-Universität 1971, 59 p. D1.7.3. **an**
Denison, B., comp. 1968: *Selected materials in classification. A bibliography.* New York: Special Libraries Assn. 1968, 142 p. (Earlier edition with slightly different title and without theoretical works on classification 1961.) C; App. 2. **e**
Dennis, Sally F. 1965.12: *The construction of a thesaurus automatically from a sample of text.* In: Stevens et al. ed. 1965.12, p. 61–148. Also: Chicago: IBM, 40 p. H; H2. **a1**
Dennis, S. F. 1967: *The design and testing of a fully automatic indexing-searching system for documents consisting of expository text.* In: Schecter ed. 1967, p. 67–94. H; H2. **a2**
Detant, Marcel 1966.7: *The terminological problems facing EURATOM's nuclear documentation service.* Brussels: EURATOM 1966, 13 p. EUR/C/3201/66e; ED-030463. B5.2.2(1.2); B5.4.4; D1.7.6. **b2**
Detant, Marcel 1966.10: *Les problemes terminologiques dans la documentation nucleaire de l'Euratom.* In: Bull. de l'A.I.D., v.5, n.4 (1966.10), p. 67–77. (French version of Detant 1966.7). **cn**
DGD/Bibliothek und Dokumentationsstelle 1969: *Thesauri in der Bibliothek der DGD. Bestandsliste Nr. 2. (Thesauri in the Library of the DGD. Holdings List*

no. 2.) Frankfurt/M: Deutsche Gesellschaft fur Dokumentation 1969. Nachtrag 1.12.1970. App. 2. **e**

DGD/ET 1966.7: *Richtlinien zur Aufstellung eines Thesaurus für die Dokumentation Elektrotechnik. (Guidelines for the development of a thesaurus in electrical engineering.)* Frankfurt/M: Deutsche Gesellschaft für Dokumentation e.V., Hauptausschuss Elektrotechnik 1966.7.15, 10 p. C1.4.1,5; C1.4.3,1; C1.4.4; C2.7.1; C5.0.1(2); C6.1; E passim; F0.1, Fig. 52; F0.4.3(a); F1.1; F9.2.2; J; K2.3.1,1; App. 1; App. 2. **bn**

DGD/Komitee Terminologie und Sprachfragen 1967.9: *Definitionen zum Begriffsfeld "Schlüsselwort," "Schlagwort," "Stichwort," "Deskriptor etc." (Definitions in the concept field "key word," "subject heading," "cue word," "descriptor," etc.)* In: Nachr. Dok., v.18, n.5 (1967.9), p. 206–208. B4.2.1. **a2**

Dijk, Marcel van 1966.10: *Un thesaurus multilingue au service de la cooperation internationale. (A multilingual thesaurus in the service of international cooperation.)* In: Bull. de l'A.I.D., v.5, n.4 (1966.10), p. 85–87. (On OECD/IRRD 1971.11.) App. 2. **b**

DIN 1421: *Abschnittsnumerierung in Schriftwerken. (Numbering of divisions and subdivisions in written documents.)* Berlin: Beuth-Vertrieb 1964. D4.3.4. **an**

DIN 1463:1971.10: *Richtlinien fur die Erstellung und Weiterentwicklung deutschsprachiger Thesauri. (Guidelines for the development and updating of thesauri in the German language.)* Mimeographed version: Berlin: Deutscher Normenausschuss/ Fachnormenausschuss Bibliotheks-und Dokumentationswesen 1971.9, 24 p. (Page numbers refer to the mimeographed versions.) A2.1; D1.8(1); D1.8(2); E2.5; F0.8.2; J2.1; App. 1. **an**

DIN 1502:1955 Beiblatt 1: *Zeitschriftenkurztitel.—Internationale Regeln für die Kürzung der Zeitschriftentitel. Wörter aus Sprachen mit lateinischen Schriftzeichen. (Abbreviations of titles of periodicals.—International code for the abbreviation of periodicals. Words from languages using the Latin alphabet.)* (Gives a list of abbreviations of words from languages written in the Latin alphabet; new edition in preparation.) E1.8.2. **an**

DIN 2330: *Begriffe und Benennungen. Allgemeine Grundsätze. (Terms and concepts. General rules.)* Berlin: Beuth-Vertrieb 1961.7. **an**

DIN 2331–1971.10: *Begriffssysteme und ihre Darstellung (Entwurf). (Concept systems and their representation (draft.))* 12 p. **an**

DIN 2332:1965.12 (draft): *Internationale Angleichung von Fachbegriffen und ihren Benennungen. (International unification of concepts and terms.)* Also in: DIN Mitt., v.44, n.12 (1955.12), p. 649–655 (compare Kübler 1965.12). **an**

DIN 2333:1964.4 (draft): *Ausarbeitung von Fachwörterbüchern. Arbeitsstufen und technische Einzelheiten (Richtlinien). Beiblatt: Anregungen für das organisatorische Verfahren (Verteilung der Aufgaben). (Preparation of special dictionaries. Work phases and technical details (guidelines). Appendix: Suggestions for the organizational procedure—task assignment).* In: DIN-Mitteilungen, v.43, n.4 (1964.4), p. 161–168; 169–172. F1.2.1,0; F1.2.2,2. **an**

DIN 2334:1965.10 (draft): *Gestaltung von Fachwörterbüchern und von Wörterbuchmanuskripten. (Layout of special dictionaries and of dictionary manuscripts.)* Bl. 1: *Wörterbücher* (Dictionaries). Bl. 2: *Wörterbuchmanuskript* (Dictionary manuscript). Bl. 3: *Belegzettel* (Index cards or forms for terms). In: DIN-Mitt., v.44, n.10 (1965.10), p. 480–487; 488–495; 496–407. D; E2.3. **an**

DIN 2335:1965.11 (draft): *Sprachenzeichen, Länderzeichen, Autoritätszeichen. (Symbols for languages, countries, and authorities).* D5; E1.10. **an**

DIN 2338:1971.10 (draft): *Begriffssystem Zeichen. (Concept system symbols.)* Berlin: Beuth-Vertrieb 1971.10, 17 p.. **an**

Bibliography

DIN 2340:1967.9 (draft): *Kurzformen von Benennungen für Fachbegriffe. Begriffe, Regeln. (Abbreviation of technical terms. Principles, rules.)* E1.8.2. **an**

DIN 5007:1962: *Regeln für die alphabetische Ordnung* (ABC-Regeln). *(Rules for alphabetical arrangement and filing order.)* E3. **an**

DK See UDC

Dobrowolski, Zygmut 1964: *Etude sur la construction des systèmes de classification. (Study on the construction of classification schemes.)* Paris: Gauthier-Villars/ Warsaw: PWN-Editions Scientifiques de Pologne 1964, 301 p. Documentation et Information. D3.5. **a**

Doudnikoff, Basil 1965.12; Conner, Arthur N. Jr.: *Statistical vocabulary construction and vocabulary control with optical coincidence.* In: Stevens ed. 1965.12, p. 177–180. F0.4.4,1. **a**

Dougherty, Richard M. 1967.7: *The realities of reclassification.* In: Coll. and Res. Libr., v.28, n.4 (1967.7), p. 258–262. K2.3.2. **a2**

Dovel, J. A. 1966.10; Heald, J. H.: *Project LEX status.* In: ADI Proc., v.3 (1966.10), p. 357–365. (Outdated.) App. 2. **b**

Doyle, Lauren B. 1961.10: *Semantic road maps for literature searchers.* In: J. ACM, v.8, n.4 (1961.10), p. 553–578. Repr. in: Saracevic ed. 1970, paper 22, p. 223–239. Also: Santa Monica, Calif.: Systems Development Corporation 1961.1.23, 29 p. SDC-SP 199. H. **a1**

Doyle, Lauren B. 1962.10: *Indexing and abstracting by association.* In: Amer. Doc., v.13, n.4 (1962.10), p. 378–390. Also: Santa Monica, Calif.: Systems Development Corporation 1962.4, 27 p. SDC-SP 718/001/00. H. **an**

Doyle, Lauren B. 1964.3: *Some compromises between word grouping and document grouping.* Santa Monica, Calif.: Systems Development Corp. 1964.3.26, 22 p. SDC SP-1481; AD440044. (Good overview, many examples.) H. **a1**

Doyle, Lauren B. 1965.12: *Is automatic classification a reasonable application of statistical analysis of text?* In: J. ACM, v.12, n.4 (1965.12), p. 473–489. Also: Santa Monica, Calif.: Systems Development Corporation 1964.8.31, 34 p. SDC SP 1753. **an**

Doyle, L. B. 1966.7: *Breaking the cost barrier in automatic classification.* Santa Monica, Calif.: System Development Corp. 1966.7, 67 p. SDC SP-2516; AD636837; ED 027 023. H; Batty 1969.6. **an**

Doyle, L. B. 1966.10; Blankenship, D. A.: *Technical advances in automatic classification.* In: ADI Proc. v.3 (1966.10), p. 63–71. H; Batty 1969.6. **an**

Dreyfuss, Henry 1972: *Symbol sourcebook.* New York: American National Standards Institute 1972, 288 p. C3.2.2. **e**

Duden 1961: *Rechtschreibung der deutschen Sprache und der Fremdwörter. (Spelling of the German language and of the foreign words.)* Mannheim: Bibliographisches Institut 1961. Der Grosse Duden Bd. 1. **e**

Dunphy, Dexter C. 1966: *The construction of categories for content analysis dictionaries.* In: Stone et ed. 1966, p. 134–168, ch.4. A1.5(b); F1.2.1,3. **a1**

Dux, W.: *Regeln für die Aufstellung einer Begriffsliste auf dem Gebiet Korrosion und Korrosionsschutz. (Rules for the development of a descriptor list in the area of corrosion and corrosion prevention.)* (Report prepared in the GDR.) **cn**

Dym, Eleanor D. 1967.10: *A new approach to the development of a technical thesaurus.* In: ADI Proc., v.4 (1967.10), p. 126–131. F3.2; App. 2. **b1**

Dyson, G. M. 1967.4: *Computer input and the semantic organization of scientific terms-I.* In: Inform. Storage and Retr., v.3, n.2 (1967.4), p. 35–115. **a**

Edmundson, H. P. 1965: *Mathematical models of synonymy.* Los Angeles, Calif.: UCLA 1965, 19 p. AFOSR 65-1387. AD 621 160. H. **an**

Edmundson, H. P. 1969.9; Epstein, M. N.: *Computer-aided research on synonymy and antonymy.* College Park, Md.: University of Maryland Computer Science Center 1969.9, 24 p. AD 699 197. H. **an**
Eggert, J. 1968.8: *Normen als Arbeitsmittel für die Dokumentation. (Standards as working aids in documentation.)* In: Nachr. Dok., v.19, n5 (1968.8), p. 181–187. E2.5. **an**
Eichhorn, Mary M. 1969.5; Reinecke, Robert D.: *Development and implementation of a thesaurus for the visual sciences.* In: J. Chem. Doc., v.9, n.2 (1969.5), p. 114–118. D1.7.1. **an**
Eichhorn, Mary M. 1970.1; Reinecke, R. D.: *Development and implementation of a thesaurus for the visual sciences.* In: Bull. Med. Libr. Assoc., v.58, n.1 (1970.1) p. 23–29. D1.7.1; G; K1.2.3. **al**
EJC 1964: *Thesaurus of engineering terms: a list of engineering terms and their relationships for use in vocabulary control in indexing and retrieving engineering information.* New York: Engineers Joint Council 1964. **e**
EJC 1965.6: *Rules for preparing and updating engineering thesauri.* New York: Engineers Joint Council 1965.6, 4 p. B5.5(b); C1.4.1,5; C1.4.2; C2.7 passim; C4.3; C5.0.1(2); C6.1; D1.4 fu. 4; D1.4.1; D1.5.1(a); E passim; F0.4.3 passim; F0.4.4; App. 1. **n**
Eller, James L.: *The development and potentials of the ERIC thesaurus for educators.* In: J. Educ. Data Process., v.7, n.2, p. 74–80. D1.7.9. **cn**
Eller, James L. 1968.7; Panek, Robert L.: *Thesaurus development for a decentralized information network.* In: Amer. Doc., v.19, n.3 (1968.7), p. 213–220. C2.7.1; D1.7.9; F0.5; G; J; J3.1; J3.3. **b**
ERIC See USERIC
EURATOM 1967: *EURATOM-Thesaurus.* Pt. 1: *Indexing terms used within EURATOM's nuclear documentation system.* 2nd ed. Brussels: EURATOM 1966.12, 90 p. Pt. 2: *Terminology charts used in EURATOM's nuclear documentation system.* 2nd ed. Brussels: EURATOM CID 1967, 57 p. EUR500e. Newer edition 1969. C5.3.1; D1.7.6; D3.2, Fig. 46; J5(a); App. 2. **e**

Fachwörterbücher 1971: *Fachwörterbücher und Lexika.*—Ein internationales Verzeichnis. 5.ed. München-Pullach, Berlin: Verlag Dokumentation 1971, ca. 800 p. Handbuch der technischen Dokumentation und Bibliographie. Bd. 4. App. 2. **e**
Fairthorne, Robert A. 1955.10: *Essentials for document retrieval.* In: Special Libr., v.46, n.10 (1955.10), p. 340–353. C1.3. **al**
Fairthorne, Robert A. 1969: *Content analysis, specification and control.* In: Ann. Rev. of Info. Sci. and Tech., v.4 (1969), p. 73–109. **al**
Farradane, J. E. L. 1955.12: *The psychology of classification.* In: J. Doc., v.11, n.4 (1955.12), p. 187–201. D4.3.6. **al**
Farradane, J. 1965.12; Poulton, R. K.; Datta, S.: *Problems in analysis and terminology for information retrieval.* In: J. Doc., v.21, n.4 (1965.12), p. 287–290. **a**
Farradane, J. 1966.3; Datta, S.; Poulton, R. K.: *Report on research on information retrieval by relational indexing. Part 1: methodology.* London: City University 1966.3. D4.3.6; Gilchrist 1971. **a2**
Farradane, J. 1967.12: *Concept organization for information retrieval.* In: Info. Stor. & Retr., v.3, n.4 (1967.12), p. 297–314. D4.3.6. **a2**
Feibleman, J. K. 1968: *Integrative levels in nature.* In: Kyle ed. 1968, p. 27–41. D3.1.1,2.1. **an**
Feinberg, H.: *Innovations in a thesaurus.* (Cited in Hines 1971.6). G. **cn**
Feitscher, Wolfgang 1967: *Graphische und tabellarische Wissensspeicher. (Graphical*

and tabular knowledge stores). Berlin: ZIID 1967, 84 p. ZIID Schriftenreihe No. 14. D3.2. **an**

Fichte, B. 1968.; Bauer, Gerd: *Der Fachthesaurus "Siliciumorganische Chemie" als integrierbarer Bestandteil eines Thesaurusssystems Chemie. (The special thesaurus "silico-organic chemistry" as a component that can be integrated in a thesaurus system chemistry.)* In: ZIID-Z, v.15, n.6 (1968.), p. 259–264. App. 2. **n**

FID 1965: *International Federation for Documentation* (FID). *1965 Congress,* Washington, D.C., 1965.10.10–15. *Abstracts.* Washington, D.C.: Secretariat, FID Congress, 94 p. Source. **n**

FID 1967.9: *Proceedings of the 33rd conference of FID and International Congress on Documentation, September 12–22, 1967.* **n**

FID 1971.1: Publications catalogue 1971. FID 474. Supplement 1972, 1972.2, FID 474a. D1.7.3. **e**

FID 1971.6: *UDC in relation to other indexing languages. Proceedings of the International Symposium, Herceg Novi, Yugoslavia, 1971.6.28–7.1.* Beograd: Yugoslav Center for Technical and Scientific Documentation; the Hague: FID 1971.6, separately paged. Source. **n**

Fill, Karl 1969: *Einführung in das Wesen der Dezimalklassifikation. (Introduction to the UDC).* Berlin: Beuth-Vertrieb 2nd ed. 1960; 3rd ed. 1969, 102 p. 3rd ed. FID-Nr. 437. D1.7.3. **cn**

Findler, Nicholas V. 1969.7; McKinzie, Wiley R.: *On a computer program that generates and queries kinship structures.* In: Behavioral Science, v.14, n.4 (1969.7), p. 334–343. G. **an**

Finger, M. A. 1967.9: *Lexikologisches Material auf Lochkarten. (Lexicographic information on punched cards.)* In: Nachr. Dok. v.18, n.5 (1967.9), p. 194–196. F9.2.2. **a2**

Földi, T. 1970.10; Sommer, K.: *Konkordanz zwischen Thesaurus documentaire d'économie und Universelle Dezimalklassifikation (fasc. 8, 9, 14, and 17). Concordance between thesaurus documentaire d'économie and the Universal Decimal Classification.)* Report to FID/C3 Arbeitsgruppe für Planung und Organisation 1970.10.30. K2.3.2,1. **cn**

Foskett, A. C. 1970: *A guide to personal indexes using edge-notched and peek-a-boo cards.* 2nd ed. London: Bingley 1970. Gilchrist 1971. **cn**

Foskett, D. J. 1959: *The construction of a faceted classification for a special subject.* In: ICSI 1959, v.2, p. 867–888. C1.3.2. **a2**

Foskett, D. J. 1959.12: *Comparative classification.* In: Ann. Libr. Sci., v.6, n.4 (1959.12), p. 105–112. **cn**

Foskett, D. J. 1963: *Classification and indexing in the social sciences.* London: Butterworth 1963, 190 p. D3.6.1,2; D4. **a2**

Foskett, D. J. 1970: *Classification for a general indexing language.* London: Library Association 1970, 48 p. Library Association Research Publication 2. Report on the studies of the Classification Research Group 1963–1969. K3.0. **a**

Foskett, D. J. et al. ed. 1970: *Library systems and information services. Proceedings of the second Anglo-Czech Conference of Information Specialists.* London: Crosby Lockwood 1970. Source. **n**

Foskett, D. J. 1970.3: *Classification and indexing in the social sciences.* In: Aslib Proc., v.22, n.3 (1970.3), p. 90–100. **a2**

Fossum, Earl G. 1966.5: *Associations and thesaurus—implicit relationships.* Paper presented at 3rd Ann. Coll. on IR, Philadelphia, Pa. 1966.5.12–13. (Not printed in the proceedings.) **cn**

Freiburger Ring für sozial-und kulturwissenschaftliche Entwicklungsländer-Dokumen-

tation. (Freiburg network for documentation on socio-cultural problems of developing countries.) See FWZ 1966.4 for a description. D1.1.1,1; D1.7.2; F0. **n**

Frank, W. 1967.4: *Erste Erfahrungen bei der Aufstellung eines Fachthesaurus auf dem Gebiet Verzahnmaschinen unter Beachtung der Auswertung der gesamten Fachliteratur einschliesslich Patentschriften.* (First experiences in the development of a special thesaurus in the area of toothed wheelwork machines based on an analysis of all special literature including patents.) In: ZIID 1967.4, p. 266–270. App. 2. **cn**

Freeman, Robert R. 1966.10: *Modern approaches to the management of a classification.* New York: American Institute of Physics 1966.10.1, 29 p. + app. Report AIP/UDC-3. Basis for Freeman 1967.12. **al**

Freeman, Robert R. 1967.12: *The management of a classification: modern approaches exemplified by the UDC project of the American Institute of Physics.* In: J. Doc., v.23, n.4 (1967.12), p. 304–320. Based on Freeman 1966.10, Report AIP/UDC-3. J3.3; G; G7. **al**

Freeman, Robert R. 1968.5; Atherton, Pauline: *Final report of the research project for the evaluation of the UDC as the indexing language for a mechanized reference retrieval system.* New York: American Institute of Physics 1968.5.1, 31 p. Report AIP/UDC-9; LI 000 583 (ERIC). D1.7.3; G. **an**

Fried, C. 1966.10; Prevel, J. J.: *Effects of indexing aids on indexing performance.* General Electric Co. 1966.10, 192 p. RADC-TR-66-525; AD 804 298 (not available NTIS). **an**

Friedrich, Carl J. 1963: *Man and his government.—An empirical theory of politics.* New York, etc.: McGraw-Hill 1963, 737 p. C3.2.1. **an**

Fuellhart, Patricia O. 1968; Weeks, David C.: *Compilation and analysis of lexical resources in information science.* Final report. Washington, D.C.: George Washington Univ. 1968, 46 p. AD 671 148; ED 021602. App. 2. **e**

Fugmann, R. 1966.6; *Der Weg in die Sackgasse bei der mechanisierten Dokumentation.* (The way into the dead end street in mechanized documentation.) In: Nachr. Dok., v.17, n.3 (1966.6), p. 79–83. A1.3.2. **b1**

FWZ 1964.3: *Vorläufiger Thesaurus (Fachwörter-Verzeichnis) für die sozial- und kulturwissenschaftliche Entwicklungsländer-Dokumentation.* (Preliminary thesaurus for documentation on socio-cultural problems of the developing countries). Freiburg/Br.: Forschungsstelle für Weltzivilisation 1964.3, 40 p. with CWRU/BSC; call no. S678.F73. D1.7.2; F0.7.1,2. **e**

FWZ 1966.4: *Freiburger Ring für sozial- und kulturwissenschaftliche Entwicklungsländer-Dokumentation.—Prospekt.* (Freiburg network for documentation on socio-cultural problems of the developing countries.—Prospectus.) Freiburg/Br.: Forschungsstelle fur Weltzivilisation 1966.4, 10 p. D1.7.2. **e**

FWZ 1966.5: *Meldeformular. (Document analysis sheet.)* 5. veränderte Auflage, Freiburg/Br.: Forschungsstelle fur Weltzivilisation 1966.5, 4 p. 1963 version with CWRU/BSC, call no. S678.F73. D1.7.2. **e**

Gardin, J. C. 1965: *SYNTOL.* New Brunswick, N.J.: Rutgers Univ. Graduate School of Library Science 1965. Rutgers Series on systems for the intellectual organization of information, v.II. (Cros et al. 1964 is preferable.) **an**

Gardin, Jean-Claude 1966.5: *Elements d'un modèle pour la description des lexiques documentaires.* (Elements of a model for the description of lexica for information storage and retrieval.) In: Bull. des Bib. de France, v.11, n.5 (1966.5), p. 171–182. B4.2.3; B4.2.4. **al**

Gardin, Natacha 1969.3: *The intermediate lexicon. A new step towards international cooperation in scientific and technical information.* In: UNESCO Bull. Lib., v.23, n.2 (1969.3), p. 58–63. K2.3.2,1. **e**

Garfield, Eugene 1967.9; Sher, Irving H.: *Diagonal display—a new technique for graphic representation of complex topological networks.* Philadelphia, Pa.: Institute for Scientific Information 1967.9, 92 p. AD 664 059. D3.2. **a1**

Gaster, Kathleen 1967.9: *Thesaurus construction and use: a selective bibliography based on material in the ASLIB library in July 1967.* In: Aslib Proc., v.19, n.9 (1967.9), p. 310–317. (Completely incorporated in extended bibliography.) **n**

Gehring, G. 1970.2: *Indexing Test zur Prüfung der Brauchbarkeit eines Dokumentationssystems. (Indexing test to evaluate the adequacy of a documentation system.)* In: Nachr. Dok., v.21, n.1 (1970.2), p. 8–13. F6. **a2**

General Electric/Apollo Support Department 1963.4: *Thesaurus development and guides for indexing and search functions.* **cn**

Gershon, M. R. 1969.: *Building a management services thesaurus.* In: O & M Bull., v.24, n.1 (1969.), p. 19–26. App. 2. Gilchrist 1971. **cn**

Gilchrist, A. 1971: *The thesaurus in retrieval.* London: Aslib 1971, 184 p. App. 1 (table of contents is given there). **an**

Gillum, T. L. 1961; Klingbiel, P. K.; Mooers, C. N.; Wall, E.: *Philosophy and guidelines for revision of the ASTIA thesaurus.* Arlington, Va.: ASTIA 1961. App. 2. **cn**

Gillum, Terry L., 1964.1: *Compiling a technical thesaurus.* In: J. Chem. Doc., v.4, n.1 (1964.1), p. 29–32. Also: Alexandria, Va.: Defense Documentation Center 1963.1.14. AD 420 504. H; H0; H3.3. **b2**

Gillum, Terry L. 1969.10: *Comments on the TEST conventions.* In: ASIS 1969.10, p. 7–13. B7; C2.7; D1.2; E1.3.1,2; App. 2. **a2**

Ginsberg, H. F. 1967.11; Schmitz, R. F.; Holman, W. K.; Hall, M. D.: *Computer aids in the evaluation of indexing terminology.* In: J. Chem. Doc., v.7, n.4 (1967.11), p. 237–239. G; G3. **b2**

Giuliano, Vincent E. 1963; Jones, P. E.: *Linear associative information retrieval.* In: Howerton et ed. 63, ch. 2. Also: Cambridge, Mass.: Arthur D. Little 1962.8.13, 23 p. Working Memorandum ACORN-O. H. **a1**

Giuliano, Vincent E. 1963.4: *Analog networks for word association.* In: IEEE Transactions on Military Electronics, v.MIL-7, n.2–3 (1963.4-7), p. 221–234. H, H3.2.**a1**

Giuliano, Vincent E. 1965.12: *The interpretation of word associations.* In: Stevens et ed. 1965.12. H; H3. **a1**

Glenn, Edmund S. 1954.3: *Semantic difficulties in international communication.* In: ETC: A Review of General Semantics, v.11, n.3 (1954.3), p. 163–180. D5.5. **an**

Goethals, F. 1969.: *Rôle et élaboration d'un thésaurus. (Role and development of a thesaurus.)* In: Cah. Docum., v.23, n.1/2 (1969.), p. 20–39. **cn**

Goltdammer, I. 1967.4; Stein, G.: *Thesauri—Koordinierung—sowjetische bibliothekarisch-bibliographische Klassifikation—elektronische Datenverarbeitung. (Thesauri—coordination—Soviet Library—bibliographic classification—electronic data processing.)* In: ZIID 1967.4, p. 252–266. K2.3.2,1. **a2**

Goodman, Frederick 1970: *The role and function of the thesaurus in education.* In: USERIC 1972, 1970 edition, p. 1–28 (appears also in 1972 edition). **b2**

Gotlieb, C. C. 1968.10; Kumar, S.: *Semantic clustering of index terms.* In: J. ACM, v.15, n.4 (1968.10), p. 493–513. Repr. in: Saracevic ed. 1970, paper 25, p. 264–278. H; H4.2. **a1**

Gravenstein, J. 1968.: *Présentation d'un thésaurus des sciences de la terre sous forme de schèmes flèches. (Presentation of an earth sciences thesaurus in arrow diagrams.)* In: A.N.R.T. Inf. Docum., n.8 (1968.), p. 21–28. App. 2. **cn**

Grecu, Natalia 1965.6: *Information retrieval thesaurus—a basic tool in scientific information* (in Rumanian). In Studii si Cercetari-de Documentare si Bibliologie, v.7, n.2 (1965.6), p. 145–153. **cn**

Grecu, Natalia 1966.3; and others: *Experienta in alcatuirea unui vocabular de termeni di chimie fizica. (Experience in working out a vocabulary of terms in physical chemistry.)* In: Studii si Cercetari de Documentare si Bibliologie, v.8, n.1 (1966.3), p. 11–15. App. 2. **cn**

Grecu, N. 1966.6; Kuiban, L.; Dantschu, V.; George, I.; Michelis, A.: *Erfahrungen bei der Zusammenstellung eines terminologischen Rohvokabulariums auf dem Gebiet der physikalischen Chemie und seine Anwendung beim Wiederauffinden von Informationen. (Experiences in the development of a terminological raw vocabulary in physical chemistry and its application in information retrieval.)* In: ZIID 1966.6, p. 88–98. **cn**

Greer, F. Loyal 1965.12: *User vocabulary in thesaurus development.* In: Perceptual and Motor Skills, v.21, n. (1965.12), p. 827–837. F0.4.3(a); F1.1.2(k). **a1**

Grolier, Eric de 1962: *A study of general categories applicable to classification and coding in documentation.* Paris: UNESCO 1962, 248 p. (French version 1960.) C1.0. **a1**

Grosch, Audrey N. 1969.2: *Thesaurus construction.* In: Special Libr., v.60, n.2 (1969.2), p. 87–92. E. **a**

Gueniot, Yvonne 1969.5; Laureilhe, Marie-Thérèse: *De quelques thesauri. (On some thesauri.)* In: Bull. des Bibl. de France, v.14, n.5 (1969.5), p. 181–218. Continuation v.15, n.1 (1970.1), p. 5–19. B4.2.4; App. 2. **b2/e**

Gull, C. D. 1966.10: *Structure of indexing authority lists.* In: Libr. Resources and Techn. Services, v.10, n.4 (1966.Fall), p. 507–511. **a**

Haensch, Gunther 1965: *Wörterbuch der internationalen Beziehungen und der Politik. —Systematisch und alphabetisch. (Dictionary of international relations and politics. —Systematic and alphabetical.)* München: Hueber 1965, 638 p. D5.2. **e**

Hähnel, H.-R. 1966.6; Neumann, Ch.: *Erste Erfahrungen bei der Aufstellung eines Fachthesaurus für das Gebiet "Erdölverarbeitung auf Kraftstoffe und Heizöle." (First experiences in the development of a special thesaurus "crude oil refining into gasoline and heating oil.")* In: ZIID 1966.6, p. 191–194. App. 2. **n**

Halkin, Jacques E. J. 1966.10: *Les vocabulaires documentaires: formation, utilisation et crise de croissance. (Information storage and retrieval vocabularies: development, use, and growth crisis.)* In: Bull. de l'A.I.D., v.5, n.4 (1966.10), p. 19–28. A; C1.4.1,2. **a2**

Hammond, W. 1962: *Convertibility of indexing vocabularies.* In: USAEC 1962, p. 223–234. K2. **cn**

Hammond, W. 1962.8; Rosenborg, S.: *Experimental study of convertibility between large technical indexing vocabularies with table of indexing equivalents.* Silver Spring, Md.: Datatrol Corp. 1962.8, 297 p. Datatrol Technical Report IR-1. K2.2.1; K2.2.1,1; K2.3.2,1. **a2/e**

Hammond, William 1963.12: *Common vocabulary approaches for government scientific and technical information systems.* Silver Spring, Md.: Datatrol Corp. 1963.12, 108 p. Datatrol Technical report no. IR-10; AD 430 000. C1.4.3,1; J3.3; K2; K2.1; K2.4.2. **a1**

Hammond, W. 1964.4; Rosenborg, S.: *Indexing terms of announcement publications for government scientific and technical research reports.* 2v. Silver Spring, Md.:

Datatrol Corp. 1964.4. Datatrol Technical Report IR-15. Vol. 1: Alphabetic listing, 439 p. PB 181 712. Vol. 2: Structural listing, 457 p. PB 181 713. F2.2.1; K2.3.2,1; App. 2. **e**

Hammond, William 1965: *Dimensions in compatibility.* In: Newman ed. 1965, p. 7–20. K2. **b2**

Hammond, William 1965.5: *Vocabulary construction and control. Panel summary.* In: AFOSR 1965.5, p. 71–76. **b**

Hammond, William 1968.1: *Construction of the NASA thesaurus: computer processing support.* McLean, Va.: Aries Corp. 1968.1.5, 14 p. N68-28811; ED 025 282. (See Infodata Systems 1971.6 for a newer publication on the same system.) D2.3.2,3; D2.3.2,7; G3.4.1; G8. **a1**

Hammond, William 1969.10: *Satellite thesaurus construction.* In: ASIS 1969.10, p. 14–20. (Esp. details of procedure on p. 16–17.) F2.2.3; G0.3; G2.2.3. **a2**

Hanicke, P. 1966: *Erarbeitung eines Fachwörterverzeichnisses (Thesaurus) über das Gebiet der Holztechnik, in welchem die Wörter nach der Verwandtschaftsbeziehung ihrer Bedeutung zusammengestellt sind.* (Development of a thesaurus in which the terms are ordered according to the relationships of their meanings.) Dresden: Zentralinstitut für Holztechnologie 1966. ZIHT Abschlussbericht 16 90 01/6-207/5. **cn**

Hanicke, P. 1966.6: *Schlagwortverzeichnisse — Deskriptorsysteme — Thesauri. Wie macht man das?—Eine Arbeitsanleitung für die Praxis.* (Subject heading lists—descriptor systems—thesauri. How is it done?—A practical guide.) In: ZIID 1966.6, p. 63–86. **cn**

Hanicke, P. 1967.4: *Erfahrungen beim Aufbau des Fachthesaurus "Holztechnologie."* (Experience from the development of the special thesaurus "wood technology.") In: ZIID 1967.4, p. 91–107. D3.2; App. 2. **b2**

Harary, F. 1960.7: *On the consistency of precedence matrices.* In: J. ACM, v.7, n. (1960.7), p. 255–259. H; H4.2. **an**

Harris, Jessica 1969: *Subject headings: factors influencing formation and choice, with special reference to Library of Congress and H. W. Wilson practice.* New York: Columbia University, School of Library Service 1969, 284 p. E; E1.5. **an**

Harris, Jessica L. 1969.3: *A study of the computer arrangeability of complex terms occurring in a major tool used in subject analysis. Final report.* New York: Columbia Univ./School of Library Service 1969.3, 55p. E; E3; G. **an**

Harrish, Barbara A. 1967.10: *A comparison of Library of Congress and National Library of Medicine subject headings.* Detroit, Mich.: Wayne State University, School of Medicine Library and Biomedical Information Service Center 1967.10, 21 p. Report No. 39. K2. **a**

Hayes, R. M. 1968: *The decomposition of vocabulary hierarchies.* In: Samuelson ed. 1968, p. 160–191. G; G3.4.1. **a2**

Haykin, David J. 1951: *Subject headings: a practical guide.* Washington, D.C.: U.S. Govt. Print. Off. 1951, 140 p. D1.7.10; E. **a**

Hayne, R. L. 1957; Turim, F.: *Machine retrieval of pharmacological data.* In: Shera 1957, p. 240–249. C2.8.1. **a2**

Heald, J. Heston 1966.3: *Project Lex. Compilation of a Department of Defense thesaurus.* 3rd draft. Washington, D.C.: U.S. Office of Naval Research 1966.3.9, 21 p. (Outdated by USDoD/ONR/LEX 1966.4, which in turn is outdated by TEST 1967.12.) **b**

Heald, J. Heston 1960.: *Project MARS.* In: Spec. Libr., v.51, n.3 (1960.), p. 115–121. Gilchrist 1971. **cn**

Heald, J. H. 1967.11: *The making of TEST. Thesaurus of engineering and scientific terms.* Springfield, Va.: CFSTI 1967, 176 p. AD 661 001; ED 016 500. A2; A2.3;

C3.2.2; C4.3; D1.1.0,2; E3; F0.3; F0.4.3(c); F0.5; F1.1.3; F1.2.1,0; F2.2.1; G; G0.3; J; J0; J4. **a2**
Heald, J. H. 1967.11a: *Bibliography of reference material used by project Lex.* In: Heald 1967.11, app. B, p. 113–138. App. 2. **e**
Hecking, Georg 1969; Jaeschke, Hildburg: *Die Entwicklung eines Thesaurus Stadtplanung-Raumordnung. (The development of a thesaurus urban and regional planning.)* In: Bauen und Wohnen, n.11 (1969), p. 8, 10, 12, 14, 16, 18. App. 2. **b2**
Henderson, M. M. et al. 1966.6: *Cooperation, convertibility and compatibility among information systems; a literature review.* Washington, D.C.: U.S. Dept. of Commerce, Natl. Bureau of Standards 1966.6.15, 140 p. K2. **a2**
Henderson, Paul B. Jr. 1964.5: *A computer-generated thesaurus.* Pittsburgh: Advanced Data Systems, Westinghouse Electric Corp. 1965.5.27–29. Paper given at the CORS-ORSA Conf., Montreal, May 27–29, 1964. (Mostly programming the IBM 7094.) G. **a**
Henglein, F. A. 1969: *Chemical technology.* Oxford, etc.: Pergamon 1969, 894 p. (Original in German: *Grundriss der chemishen Technik.* Weinheim/Bergstr. 1968. The English translation is based on the 11th ed. which appeared in 1963.) D3.2, Fig. 45. **e**
Henshaw, Marie 1967.11: *Conversion sampler. Principles, examples and a design for developing conversion tables for book classification schemes.* In: Libr. J., v.92, n.19 (1967.11), p. 3964–3966. (Examples are useful.) K2.1; K2.2.1. **b1**
Herner, Saul 1963.10: *The role of thesauri in the convergence of word and concept indexing.* In: ADI Proc, v.0 (1963.10). Pt. 2, p. 183–184. (Outdated.) **a**
Herner, Saul 1964.5; Johanningsmeier, Walter F.; Campbell, David T.: *A use evaluation of the AIChE bibliographic descriptions and the Chemical Engineering Thesaurus.* Washington, D.C.: Herner 1964.5.1, 60 p. PB 164 505. D1.0. **a1**
Herrmann, P. 1967.4; Löschner, G.: *Thesaurus zur Erschliessung der Literatur über Diffusion. (Thesaurus for indexing the literature on diffusion.)* In: ZIID 1967.4, p. 69–90. App. 2. **b2**
Herrmann, Peter 1965: *Praktische Anwendung der Dezimalklassifikation. (Practical application of the Universal Decimal Classification.)* Klassifizierungstechnik. 5. erw. u. verb. Aufl. Leipzig: VEB Bibliographisches Institut 1965. ZIID-Schriftenreihe Bd. 5. D1.7.3. **an**
Hersey, David F. 1967.10; Hammond, William: *Computer usage in the development of a water resources thesaurus.* In: Amer. Doc., v.18, n.4 (1967.10), p. 209–215. G; App. 2. **b**
Hersey, D. F. 1968.7; Foster, W. P.; Snyderman, M.; Kreysa, F. J.: *Conceptual indexing and retrieval of current resarch records: an analysis of problems in large scale information system.* In: Methods of Info. in Med., v.7, n.3 (1968.7), 172–187. D1.1. **a1**
Hill, D. R. 1968: *A vector clustering technique.* In: Samuelson ed. 1968, p. 225–234. H. **an**
Hillman, Donald J. 1964.7b: *Study of theories and models of information storage and retrieval. Report No. 7: Graphs and algorithms for term relations.* Bethlehem, Pa.: LU 1964.7.30, 21 p. GN-283. H; Batty 1969.6. **an**
Hillman, Donald J. 1965.: *An algorithm for document characterisation.* Bethlehem, Pa.: Lehigh Univ./Center for the Information Sciences 1965., 56 p. Mathematical theories of relevance with respect to the problems of indexing. Report No. 2. H. **an**
Hines, Theodore C. 1963.10: *Machine arrangement of alphanumeric concordance, thesaurus, and index entries, the need for compatible standard rules.* In: ADI Proc., v.0 (1963.10), p. 7–8. **b**

Hines, Theodore C. 1966; Harris, Jessica L.: *Computer filing of index, bibliographic and catalog entries.* Newark, N.J.: Bro-dart Foundation 1966. E3. **a2**

Hines, Theodore C. 1967.9: *Computer manipulation of classification notations.* In: J. Doc., v.23, n.3 (1967.9), p. 216–223. D4.3.3,2(c). **a2**

Hines, Theodore C. 1971.6; Harris, J. L.: *Columbia University School of Library Service system for thesaurus development and maintenance.* In: Info. Stor. & Retr., v.7, n.1 (1971.6), p. 39–50. A1.4; B5.4.1(7b); E2.3; G; G2.4; K1.2.3. **a1**

Hirsch, S.: *Methode zur Aufstellung von Deskriptorsystemen in Komplexwissenschaften mit starkem gesellschaftswissenschaftlichem Anteil (vorzugsweise unter Verwendung der Sichtlochkartei.)* (Method for the development of descriptor systems in complex fields of science with a strong social science component (especially for a peek-a-boo system.)) **cn**

Hirsch, S. 1967.4: *Der Thesaurus zwischen Fachwissenschaft und Informationsspeicher.* (The thesaurus between subject discipline and information store). In: ZIID 1967.4, p. 54–68. D3.2. **b2**

Hoffer, Joe R. 1962.4: *Information retrieval in social welfare: experiences with an edgenotched information retrieval system.* In: Amer. Doc., v.13, n.2 (1962.4), p. 169–175. **a2**

Hoffman, Günter 1966.6: *Erkenntnisse und Erfahrungen bei der Aufstellung von Teilthesauri.* (Experiences in the development of constituent thesauri.) In: ZIID 1966.6, p. 174–184. **cn**

Holland, H. G. 1969.x: *Thesaurusarbeiten im Post- und Fernmeldewesen.* (Thesaurus work in postal service and telecommunication.) In: Informatik, v.16, n.3 (1969.x), p. 52–53. **b2**

Holm, Bart E. 1961.7; Rasmussen, L. E.: *Development of a technical thesaurus.* In: Amer. Doc., v.18, n.3 (1961.7), p. 184–190. (Outdated.) **b**

Holm, Bart E. 1966.3: *Source and vocabulary control.* In: Nat. Symposium on Engineering Info. 2. Proceedings. **cn**

Holst, W. 1966.10: *Problems connected with the use of a polytechnical thesaurus.* In: Bull. de l'A.I.D., v.5, n.4 (1966.10), p. 105–109. **a**

Honecker, Walter 1967.10; Newmark, Mark: *Automated maintenance of a highly structured thesaurus at Engineering Index.* In: ADI Proc., v.4 (1967.10), p. 132–136. G. **b2**

Hörig, J. 1967.4: *Erfahrungen aus der praktischen Arbeit mit Maschinenlochkarten und Konsequenzen fur ein verallgemeinertes Recherchesystem.* (Experiences from practical work with machine-punched cards and consequences for a generalized information storage and retrieval system.) In: ZIID 1967.4, p. 155–165. B5.2. **b2**

Hörig, J. 1966.6: *Grundsätze und Erfahrungen bei der Aufstellung von Begriffsschlüssellisten für die Information eines wissenschaftlichen Industriebetriebes.* (Principles and experiences in the development of descriptor lists for the information services of a scientific company.) In: ZIID 1966.6, p. 208–226. **n**

Horvath, Paul J. 1967.8; Chamis, Alice Yanosko; Carroll, Robert F.; Dlugos, Joyce: *The BF Goodrich information retrieval system and automatic information distribution using computer-compiled thesaurus and dual dictionary.* In: J. Chem. Doc., v.7, n.3 (1967.8), p. 124–130. G. **b**

Houston, N. 1964.4; Wall, E.: *The distribution of term usage in manipulative indexes.* In: Amer. Doc., v.15, n.2 (1964.4), p. 105–114. H; Gilchrist 1971. **cn**

Howerton, Paul ed. 1963; Weeks, D. ed.: *Vistas in information handling.* Washington, D.C.: Spartan Books 1963, 233 p. Source. **n**

Howerton, Paul W. 1965: *Organic and functional concepts of authority files.* In: Newman ed. 1965, p. 47–54. **a**

Bibliography 581

Hübner, W. 1967.4: *Methodische Probleme bei der Erarbeitung eines Systems medizinischer Fachthesauri. (Methodological problems in the development of a system of special thesauri in medicine.)* In: ZIID 1967.4, p. 118–123. **b**

Hülck, Klaus 1967; Klugmann, Dietrich; Peetz, Günter: *GOLEM. Ein allgemein anwendbares Verfahren für die Dokumentation und das Wiederauffinden von Informationen. (GOLEM. A procedure of general application for the storage and retrieval of information.)* München: Siemens 1967, 12 p. Siemens Schriftenreihe data praxis; Siemens Best. Nr. 2-2600-418. H. **an**

Hungermann, Erich H. 1964: *Auswertungs- und Ordnungsverfahren in der Patentdokumentation. Analyse von Dokumentationssystemen, insbesondere der Auswertungs- und Begriffsordnungsverfahren, sowie der maschinellen Herstellung von Sachregistern und Thesauri. (Procedures for indexing and ordering of material in patent documentation. Analysis of documentation systems, in particular procedures for indexing and ordering of concepts and of mechanized production of subject indexes and thesauri.)* Frankfurt/M: Deutsche Gesellschaft für Dokumentation 1964, 76 p. Nachrichten für Dokumentation, Beiheft Nr. 10. **b2**

Hutton, Geoffrey 1968.; Rostron, Michael: *The construction of a thesaurus.* In: Building, n.215 (1968.), p. 111–112. **cn**

Hyslop, M. R. 1965.12: *Sharing vocabulary control.* In: Special Libraries, v.56, n.10 (1965.12), p. 708–714. App. 2. **b**

IAEA 1970.2: *Handling of nuclear information.* Proc. of the Symposium on . . . IAEA, Vienna, 1970.2.16–20. Vienna: International Atomic Energy Agency 1970.2, 676 p. Proceedings Series. Source. **n**

ICSI 1959: *International Conference on Scientific Information.* Washington, D.C. 1958.11.16–21—Proceedings. 2v. Washington, D.C.: National Academy of Sciences/National Research Council 1959, 1635 p. Source. **n**

ICTB 1970.3: *Proceedings of the International Conference on General Principles of Thesaurus Building.* Warsaw: Documentation and Scientific Information Center of the Polish Academy of Science 1970.3, 186 + 20p. (Papers not individually included in this bibliography; see Dahlberg 1972.4, p. 213, for table of contents. Our citations refer to the mimeographed version of the "Minutes of the conference," a rather confused and useless document also included in the Proceedings.) B4.2.1; B4.2.4; D1.1. **n**

ICTSS 1966.9: *The International Centre for the Terminology of the Social Sciences* (26, route de Malagnou, Geneva, Switzerland). In: Soc. Sc. Info., v.5, n.3 (1966.9), p. 88–90. D5.4; App. 2. **e**

IICT: International Information Center for Terminology, affiliated with the Austrian Standards Institute, Vienna, Austria. App. 2. **e**

Immroth, John Philip 1968: *A guide to Library of Congress classification.* Rochester, N.Y.: Libraries Unlimited 1968, 350 p. D1.7.3. **an**

Infodata Systems 1971.6: *AVOCON. Infodata Systems Inc.'s thesaurus processing system.—Users guide.* Arlington, Va.: Infodata Systems Inc. 1971.6, 23 p. (The system is a further development of the system described in Hammond 1968.1. The earlier report is more detailed in describing program operations, esp. with respect to the "hierarchical display generator". The description of the updating program is also much clearer in the older publication, but it refers to the state of 1967.) D1; D1.5.1(b); D2.3.2,3; D2.3.2,7; G; G0.3; G8. **a2**

International Computer Centre 1962: *Symbolic languages in data processing.* ICC 1962. **n**

International Study Conference 1957.5: *International study conference on classification for information retrieval, 1957, Dorking, England. Proceedings.* London: Aslib 1957.5, 151 p. Source. n

Internationale Richtlinien jür Thesauri: Beschreibung des dritten Entwurfs der UNESCO. (International guidelines for thesauri: description of the third draft of UNESCO.) In: Nachr. Dok., v.21, n.2 (1970.4), p. 72–75. (Abridged German translation of UNESCO 1971.12, 1970.2 version.) Gilchrist 1971. b

ISI/DRTC 1969: *Subject analysis for document finding systems.* Annual Seminar. 7. Bangalore: Indian Statistical Institute/documentation Research and Training Center. Source. n

ISIC 1968: United Nations/Department of Economic and Social Affairs/Statistical Office. *International Standard Industrial Classification of all Economic Activities (ISIC).* New York: United Nations 1968, 48 p. UN/ST/STAT/Ser.M/4/Rev. 2. D4.4.1. e

ISO 1972: *Memento 1972.* Geneva: International Organization for Standardization 1972, 96 p. (ISO Handbook.) e

ISO DR1278:1967: *International code for the abbreviation of periodicals.* E1.8.2. an

ISO DR1951 (draft): *Lexicographical symbols, particularly for use in classified defining vocabularies.* an

ISO R4-1954: *International code for the abbreviation of periodicals.* (Newer: ISO DR1278:1967). E1.8.2. an

ISO R639–1967: *Symbols for languages, countries, and authorities.* Geneva: ISO 1967, 15 p. D5; E1.10. an

ISO R 704–1968: *Naming principles.* an

ISO R832–1968: *Abbreviations of typical words in bibliographical references.* E1.8.2. an

ISO R833–1968: *Abbreviations of generic names in titles of periodicals.* E1.8.2 an

ISO R860–1968: *International unification of concepts and terms.* an

ISO R919–1969.1: *Guide for the preparation of classified vocabularies (example of method.)* D; D5.3; E; F. an

ISO R999–1969: *Index of a publication.* an

ISO R1043–1969: *Abbreviations (symbols) for plastic.* E1.8.2. an

ISO R1087–1969: *Vocabulary of terminology.* an

ISO R1149–1969e: *Layout of multilingual classified vocabularies.* D5; E; F0.8.1,2. an

ISO R2145 (draft): *Numbering of divisions and subdivisions of written documents.* D4.3.4. an

ISR 1961; Salton, Gerard, project director: *Information storage and retrieval. Scientific report to the National Science Foundation.* No. 1–10: Cambridge, Mass.: Harvard Univ./Computation Lab. 1961.11–1966.3. No. 11–: Ithaca, N.Y.: Cornell Univ./Dept. of Computer Science 1966.6–The reports contain descriptions of the various stages of SMART which is an automatic text processing information storage and retrieval system. Tables of contents appear in Information Science Abstracts and, for the following volumes, in Dahlberg 1972.4: 11 (p. 106), 12–13 (p. 181), 14 (p. 106), 16 (p. 107), 18 (p. 206). The volumes are available from NTIS or ERIC at least as follows:

1. 1961.11 = AD 274 816	7. 1964.6 = PB 166 210	
2. 1962.9 = AD 287 945	8. 1964.12 = PB 166 807	
3. 1963.4 = AD 408 934	9. 1965.8 = PB 168 499	
4. 1963.8 = PB 164 184	10. 1966.3 = PB 170 702	
5. 1964.1 = PB 164 464	11. 1966.6 = PB 173 196	
6. 1964.4 = PB 164 572	12. 1967.6 = ED 020 748; PB 176 536	

13. 1968.1 = ED 019 091
14. 1968.10 = PB 180 931
15. 1969.1 = ED 032 217; PB 184 246
16. 1969.9 = PB 188 957
17. 1969.9

B6.2; H.

18. 1970.10 = ED 048 910; PB 198 069
    (Parts I-IV available individually
    as ED 048 911 - ED 048 915)
19. 1971.2 = PB 204 946
20. 1972.6 = PB 211 061
21. 1973.2 = PB 214 020

an

Jackson, David M. 1969.4: *The construction of retrieval environments and pseudo-classifications based on external relevance.* Columbus, Ohio: Computer and Info. Sci. Research Center, Ohio State University 1969.4, 74 p. PB 184 462; ED 032 216; ED 031 288. H. **a1**

Janning, E. A. 1965: *The modification of an information retrieval system by improving vocabulary control, indexing consistency and search capabilities.* Springfield, Va.: NTIS 1965. AD 613 301. Gilchrist 1971. **cn**

Jansen, Rolf 1970.4: *Sachverhaltsdokumentation und Thesaurus-Entwicklung.* Ludwigshafen: BASF 1970.4, 28 p. Revised and expanded version of: *Some observations on thesaurus problems.* In: ICTB 1970.3, p. (Contains in part the information from BASF1/2.) **b1**

Jaster, Josephine J. 1962; Murray, Barbara R.; Taube, Mortimer: *The state of the art of coordinate indexing.* Washington, D.C.: Documentation Inc. 1962. AD 275 393. NSF-C-147. B6.3; C1.4.5; F0.4.4. **n**

Jaster, Josephine 1962.10: *A note on descriptors.* In: Amer. Doc., v.13, n.4 (1962.10), p. 433–434. **cn**

Jaster, J. J. 1963.2: *Subsumption scheme for dictionary of indexing equivalents.* Silver Spring, Md.: Datatrol Corp. 1963.2, ca.25 p. Technical rept. No. IR-3, Contract NSF C-295. AD 299 236. C1.4.3,1; K2.4.2. **a2**

Jones, Kevin P. 1971.7: *Compound words: a problem in post-coordinate retrieval systems.* In: J. ASIS, v.22, n.4 (1971.7), p. 242–250. C2.7. **a**

Jones, Kevin P. 1971.11: *Basic structures for thesaural systems.* In: Aslib Proc., v.23, n.11 (1971.11), p. 575–590. C. **a**

Jones, Paul E. 1967.7; Curtice, Robert M.: *A framework for comparing term association measures.* In: Amer. Doc., v.18, n.3 (1967.7), p. 153–161. H. **a1**

Jones, Paul E. 1969; Guiliano, Vincent E.; Curtice, Robert E.; Arthur D. Little, Inc.: *Automated language processing.* Detroit, Mich.: American Data Processing 1969, 481 p. Information Technology Series. H. **a2**

Jonker, Frederick 1959: *A descriptive continuum: a "generalized" theory of indexing.* In: ICSI 1959, v.2, p. 1291–1311. C2.3. **b2**

Jonker, Frederick 1964: *Indexing theory, indexing methods and search devices.* New York: Scarecrow Press 1964. **an**

Jornagin, M. P. 1962: *Automatic machine methods of testing PERT networks for consistency.* U.S. Naval Weapons Lab 1962. Tech. Memo. K-24-60. H; H4.2. **an**

Joyce, T. 1958.7; Needham, R. H.: *The thesaurus approach to information retrieval.* In: Amer. Doc., v.9, n.3 (1958.7), p. 192–197. C1.2. **b2**

Kaiser, J. 1926.9: *Systematic indexing.* In: Aslib Rep. of Proc. of 3rd Conf. 1926.9.24–27, p. 20–44. Rep. in: Olding ed. 1966, p. 145–162. **a1**

Kent, Allen 1958; Perry, J. W.: *Encoding of information previously indexed.* In: Perry et al. ed. 1958, p. 343–360. K2.3.2. **a2**

Kent, A., ed. 1960: *Information retrieval and machine translation.* New York: Interscience 1960/61, 1376 p. Advances in Documentation and Library Science, v.3, pt.

1-2. *Int. Conf.f.Standards on a Common Language for Machine Searching and Translation, Cleveland, Ohio, 1959.9.6–12* proceedings. Source. **n**

Kerckhove, P. 1969.: *Elaboration du thésaurus du C.R.I.C.* In: Cah. Docum., v.23, n.1/2 (1969.), p. 5–14. App. 2. **cn**

Kerckhove, P. 1970.: *Critères de sélection et de rédaction des mot-clefs d'un thésaurus encyclopédique. (Criteria for the selection and editing of the keywords of an encyclopedic thesaurus.)* In: Cah. Docum., v.24, n.2 (1970.), p. 49–77. **cn**

Kimlicek, O. 1966.6: *Konzeption und Aufstellung eines Thesaurus für das Fachgebiet "Holz" in der CSSR. (Design and development of a thesaurus for "wood" in the CSSR.)* In: ZIID 1966.6, p. 185–190. App. 2. **cn**

King, Donald W. 1971; Bryant, Edward C.: *The evaluation of information services and products.* Washington, D.C.: Information Resources Press, 1971, 306 p. F6. **a1**

Klausmeier, Herbert J. et al. 1965: *Concept learning and problem solving: a bibliography, 1950–1964.* Madison, Wisc.: Univ. of Wisconsin/Wisconsin Research and Development Center for Cognitive Learning 1965. WRDCCL Technical Report. 1. B2.4. **an**

Klausmeier, Herbert J. et al. 1969.4–1970.11: *Concept learning: a bibliography.* Madison, Wisc.: Univ. of Wisconsin/Wisconsin Research and Development Center for Cognitive Learning. WRDCCL Technical Report. v.1: 1950–1967. 1969.4, 177 p. TR-82; ED 035 954. v.2: 1968. 1969.11, 62 p. TR-107; ED 036 865. v.3: Jan.-June 1969. 1970.3, 36 p. TR-120; ED 043 092. v.4: Jul.-Dec. 1969. 1970.11, 37 p. TR-147; ED 046 033. B2.4. **an**

Kleeberg, Werner 1970.x: *Erarbeitung und Vervolkommung des Thesaurus Landwirtschaft und Nahrungsgüterwirtschaft. (Development and improvement of the thesaurus agriculture and food.)* In: Informatik, v.17, n.6 (1970.x), p. 19–20. App. 2. **cn**

Klingbiel, Paul H. 1962: *Language oriented retrieval systems.* AD 271 600. Gilchrist 1971. **cn**

Klingbiel, Paul H. 1963.10: *The revision of the thesaurus of Astia descriptors.* Alexandria, Va.: DDC 1963.10, 5 p. **b2**

Klingbiel, Paul H. 1964.8: *The DDC thesaurus: past, present and future.* In: Aslib Proc., v.16, n.8 (1964.8), p. 252–257. K1.2.2; K2.1; App. 2. **b2**

Klingbiel, Paul H. 1970.11: *The future of indexing and retrieval vocabularies.* Alexandria, Va.: DDC 1970.11, 31 p. DDC-TR-70-4; AD 716 200. **cn**

Knight, G. Norman ed. 1969: *Training and indexing: a course of the Society of Indexers.* Cambridge, Mass.: MIT Press 1969. Gilchrist 1971. **cn**

Kochen, Manfred, ed. 1965: *Some problems in information science.* New York, London: Scarecrow Press 1965, 309 p. Source. **n**

Kochen, M. 1968.9; Tagliacozzo, R.: *A study of cross-referencing.* In: J. Doc., v.24, n.3 (1968.9), p. 173–191. Also: Springfield, Va.: CFSTI 1968.3, 31 p. PB 179 752; ED 030 455. B2.3; C; C1.4.1,5; C1.4.2; C1.5; C6.2; F0.4.2. **a1**

Kocourek, R. 1968: *Synonymy and semantic structure of terminology.* In: Travaux linguistiques de Prague, n.3 (1968), p. 131–141. B1. **an**

Kocourek, R. 1968a: *Synonymes en terminologie. (Synonyms in terminology.)* In: Studies in Terminologie, Prague, v.2 (1968), p. 49–64. B1. **an**

Koekkoek, M. 1962.12; Schüller, J. A.: *The TDCK—compact system.* In: J. Doc., v.18, n.4 (1962.12), p. 176–182. App. 2. **cn**

Korotkin, Arthur L. 1965.4; Oliver, Lawrence H.; Burgis, Donald R.: *Indexing aids, procedures and devices.* Bethesda, Md.: General Electric Co. 1965.4, 106 p. RADC-TR-64-582; AD 616 342. D3.6.0. **a2**

Kravets, L. G. 1965.: *(On the quantitative evaluation of the terminology of a vocabulary).* In: Nauchno-Tek, Inform., n.2 (1965.), p. 27–29. AD 662 574; ED 017 285. **a**

Kreusler 1963.3; Rothkirch-Trach, K. Ch., Graf: *Randlochkarten als Sprachwörterkartei. (Edge-notched cards as terminological file.)* Brussels: EURATOM 1963.3, 6 p. EUR 187d. F9.9.2. **a2**
Krieg, H. 1964: *Anforderungen der Praxis an die Begriffsordnung einer Fachdokumentation. (Practical requirements for the concept classification of a special information storage and retrieval system.)* In: Nachr. Dok., v.15, n.1 (1964), p. 5–12. **b**
Kübler, G. 1965.12: *Terminologie.—Erlaüterungen zum Norm-Entwurf DIN 2332 Internationale Angleichung von Fachbegriffen und ihren Benennungen. (Terminology.—Comments on draft standard DIN 2332 International unification of concepts and terms.)* In: DIN Mitt., v.44, n.12 (1965.12), p. 647–655. **an**
Kulik, A. N. 1969.: *On the feasibility of connecting the different descriptor information retrieval systems on the basis of common language.* In: Nauchno-Techn. Inform., series 2, n.11 (1969.), p. 18–21. K2. **cn**
Kurmey, William: *Construction of thesauri entries.* Chicago: Univ. of Chicago/Graduate Library School Thesis. **an**
Kyle, B. 1956.3: *E. G. Brisch, something new in classification.* In: Special Libraries, v.47, n.3 (1956.3), p. 100–105. E1.6. **b1**
Kyle, B. 1960.9: *Classification: adopt, adapt, or create? A discussion point.* In: Aslib Proc., v.12, n.9 (1960.9), p. 317–320. K1.2.2. **al**
Kyle, Barbara ed. 1968: *Focus on information and communication.* London: Aslib 1968. Source. **n**

Lancaster, F. W. 1968: *Information retrieval systems: characteristics, testing and evaluation.* New York: Wiley 1968, 222 p. B5.2.4; C; D1.1.1,1. **a2**
Lancaster, F. W. 1968.1: *Evaluation of the MEDLARS demand search service.* Washington, D. C.: National Library of Medicine 1968.1, 278 p. PB 178 660; ED 022 494. B6.1; D1.7.5; F6. **al**
Lancaster, F. W. 1969.4: *MEDLARS: Report on the Evaluation of its Operating Efficiency.* In: Amer. Doc., v.20, n.2 (1969.4), p. 119–142. Repr. in: Saracevic ed. 1970, paper 60, p. 641–664, B6.1; D1.7.5; F6. **al**
Lancaster, F. W. 1970.9; Jenkins, Grace T.: *"Quality control" applied to the operations of a large information system.* In: JASIS, v.21, n.5 (1970.9), p. 370–371. F6; J2.1. **al**
Lancaster, F. Wilfrid 1972: *Vocabulary control for information retrieval.* Washington, D.C.: Information Resources Press 1972, 233 p. C; App. 1. **al**
Lance, G. N. 1966.5; Williams, W. T.: *Computer programs for hierarchical polythetic classification ("similarity analyses").* In: Computer J., v.9, n.1 (1966.5), p. 60–64. H. **an**
Larkey, S. V. et 1951: *Categorisation as a basis for machine coding.* Johns Hopkins Library Project 1951. Unpublished. **cn**
Larousse/Rédaction 1960: *Essais de classification lexicographique. (Essay on lexicographic classification.)* In: Cahiers de Lexicologie, v.2 (1960), p. 98–151. D3.1.2,2, Fig. 40; G. **a2**
Laureilhe, M. T. 1969.: *Essai de bibliographie (des thésauri) et index par matières parus depuis 1960. (Bibliographic essay (of thesauri) and index for material published since 1960.)* In: Bull. Bibl. France, v.14, n.5 (1969.), p. 203–218. 1. Complement (au 1er dec. 1969): v.15, n.1 (1970.1), p. 21–26. 2. Complement (au 1er dec. 1970): v.16, n.1 (1971.1), p. 33–38. App. 2. **e**
Larzarsfeld, P. F. 1950: *Latent structure analysis.* In: Stouffer ed. 50 p. H; Batty 1969.6. **al**
LCC 1970: Library of Congress/Processing Department/Subject Cataloging Division.

Outline of the Library of Congress Classification. 2.ed. Washington, D.C.: Library of Congress/Card Division 1970, 22 p. The schedules themselves consist of 30 volumes, issued in a various number of editions at different times with many supplements. They are also available from Gale Research Comp., Detroit, Mich. D1.7.3; J3.3. **e**

LCSH 1966; Quattlebaum, Marguerite V., ed.: *Subject headings used in the dictionary catalogs of the Library of Congress (from 1897 through June 1964)* 7th ed. Washington, D.C.: Library of Congress 1966, 1432 p. Additions and changes are published in supplements, issued monthly and in cumulations since July 1964. D1.3.3,1; D1.7.10; D2.3.2,5; K1.2.3. **e**

Lebrun, Y. ed. 1966: *Linguistic research in Belgium.* Belgium: Universa Wetteren 1966. Source. **n**

Lees, Robert B. 1960: *The grammar of English nominalizations.* In: Internat. J. Appl. Ling., v., n. (1960.), p. E1.5. **an**

Lefkovitz, D. 1963; Prywes, N. S.: *Automatic stratification of information.* In: AFIPS Conf. Proc., v.23 (1963.), p. H. **an**

Lefkovitz, David 1963.9: *Automatic stratification of descriptors.* Philadelphia, Pa.: Univ. of Pennsylvania/Moore School of Electrical Engineering 1963.9.15, p. Rept. No. 64–03. AD 423 647. H. **an**

Leiner, A. L. 1961.1; Youden, W. W.: *A system for generating "pronounceable" names using a computer.* In: J. ACM, v.8, n.1 (1961.1), p. 97–103. D4.3.1(a4). **a2**

Leont'eva, P. M. 1968; Margaritov, V. B.: *A method for construction and use of a descriptor dictionary.* In: Nauchno-Techn. Inform., series 2, n.8 (1968), p. 19–22, 25. (Orig. Russ.). **cn**

Lerner, Rita G. 1968.3a: *Development of a multi-coordinate vocabulary, chemical physics.* New York: American Institute of Physics 1968.3, 4 p. + 20 p. app. AIP-ID68-3. (Gives a good scheme). App. 2. **b2/e**

Lerner, Rita G. 1968.3b: *Development of multi-coordinate vocabulary, plasma physics.* New York: American Institute of Physics 1968.3, 3 p. + 10 p. app. AIP-ID68-4. (Gives a good scheme). App. 2. **b2/e**

Lesk, M. E. 1969.1: *Word-word associations in document retrieval systems.* In: Amer. Doc., v.20, n.1 (1969.1), p. 27–28. Repr. in: Saracevic ed. 1970, paper 29, p. 312–323. H. **a1**

Leski, K. 1966: [*Descriptors and thesauri seen in terms of the exchange of information and the processing of materials.*] (In Polish) In: Aktualne Problemy Informacji i Dokumentacji, v.11, n.6 (1966), p. 14–18. **cn**

Leski, K. 1966.6: *Einige Prinzipien der Schaffung von Deskriptoren and Thesauri. (Some principles of the development of descriptors and thesauri).* In: ZIID 1966.6, p. 33–52. **cn**

Levery, F. 1968: *Les problèmes posés par le vocabulaire et l'organisation des dictionaires et thésaurus. (Problems encountered in the area of vocabularies and in the organization of dictionaries and thésauri).* In: Vessey ed. 1968, p. 23–29. **cn**

Levery, F. 1968.3: *Rôle et constitution du thésaurus. (Role and constitution of the thesaurus).* In: Documentaliste, v.3, n. (1968.3), p. 3–13. A2.3; C1.3(b); C2.3.2; F1.2.2,1; F2.3.1; F8.4. **a2**

Levy, F. G. 1967.9: *Compatibility between classifications and thesauri: first evaluation of a study in the field of information storage and retrieval.* In: FID 67.9, III-g-2, 15 p. K2.3.2,1; App. 2. **b**

Lewis, Kathleen P. comp. 1968.4: *Indexing tools and terminology sources in the language sciences, a bibliographical listing.* Washington, D.C.: Center for Applied Linguistics 1968.4, 22 p. ED 021 245. App. 2. **e**

Lewis, P. A. W. 1967.1; Baxendale, P. B.; Bennett, J. L.: *Statistical discrimination of the synonymy/antonymy relationship between words.* In: J. ACM, v.14, n.1 (1967.1), p. 20–44. H. **an**
LEX see USDoO/ONR/LEX 1966.4.
Libbey, Miles A. 1966.10: *The representation of meaning to computers.* In: ADI Proc., v.3 (1966.10), p. 43–49. C2.3.2. **b**
Libbey, Miles A. 1967.1: *The use of second order descriptors for document retrieval.* In: Amer. Doc., v.18, n.1 (1967.1), p. 10-20. Full version: Redford, Mass.: MITRE 1966.2, 41 p. MTP-26. C2.3.2. **b**
Litofsky, Barry 1969: *Utility of automatic classification systems for information storage and retrieval.* Philadelphia, Pa.: Univ. of Pennsylvania 1969. Ph.D. Thesis. H. **an**
London, Gertrude 1965.11: *A classed thesaurus as an intermediary between textual, indexing and searching languages.* In: Revue Internationale de la Documentation, v.32, n.4 (1965.11), p. 145–149. D1.1. **b2**
London, Gertrude 1966.10: *A classed thesaurus as an aid to indexing, classifying and searching.* New Brunswick, N.J.: Rutgers Univ. 1966.10, 96 p. F1.2.1,0; F1.2.2,2. **a**
London, Gertrude 1969: *Glossary-based classed thesauri as the core of modern reference systems.* In: Michajlov et al. ed. 1969, p. 286–315. **cn**
Long, John M. 1967.1; Barnhard, Howard J.; Levy, Gertrude C.: *Dictionary buildup and stability of word frequency in a specialized medical area.* In: Amer. Doc., v.18, n.1 (1967.1), p. 21–25. **a**
Loosjes, Th. P. 1967: *On documentation of scientific literature.* London: Butterworth 1967, 165 p. Not revised German edition: *Dokumentation Wissenschaftlicher Literatur.* München: BLV 1962, 144 p. **a2**
Lunin, Lois F. 1967.10; Shepard, Richard H.: *Differences between vocabularies used in pre- and post-research documents: preliminary observations.* In: ADI Proc., v.4 (1967.10), p. 137–141. F1.1.3. **a1**
Lüpnitz, F. 1966.6a: *Verschlüsselte oder unverschlüsselte Systeme? Die natürliche Sprache. (Encoded or not encoded systems? The natural language).* In: ZIID 1966.6, p. 169–173. **cn**
Lüpnitz, F. 1966.6b: *Einsatz technischer Hilfsmittel bei der Erarbeitung von Thesauri. (Use of technical aids in the development of thesauri).* In: ZIID 1966.6, p. 250. **cn**
Lustig, G. 1965.9: *Statistische Beziehungen zwischen Schlagwörtern und ihre Verwendung im Information Retrieval. (Statistical relationships between terms and their use in information retrieval).* Vortrag auf der 17. Jahresversammlung der Dt. Ges. f. Dokumentation, Konstanz, 1965.9.27. (See Lustig 1968 for paper in English on same content). H. **a1**
Lustig, G. 1968: *A new class of association factors.* In: Samuelson ed. 1968, p. 213–224. H. **a1**

Maixner, V. 1969.10: *On some general methodological problems of retrieval languages.* In: Info. Storage and Retrieval, v.5, n.3 (1969.10), p. 143–144. **a**
Maixner, V. 1970.12: *Towards compensation laws in constructing thesauri.* In: Info. Storage and Retrieval, v.6, n.5 (1970.12), p. C2.3.1. **b**
Malkiel, Yakov 1960.x: *A typological classification of dictionaries on the basis of distinctive features.* Bloomington, Ind.: Indiana Univ. 1960.x, 28 p. D1.8(1). **a2**
Mandersloot, W. G. B. 1970.1; Douglas, E. M. B.; Spicer, N.: *Thesaurus control—the selection, grouping, and cross-referencing of terms for inclusion in a coordinate index word list.* In: J. ASIS, v.21, n.1 (1970.1), p. 49–57. (Only the material on role indicators is useful). C1.4.1,5; C2.7. **a2**
Maneck, Martin 1966.6: *Thesaurussystem "Chemie"—ein Beitrag zur Schaffung eines*

einheitlichen Dokumentations- und Informationssystems auf dem Gebiet der Chemie. (Thesaurus system chemistry—a contribution to the creation of a unified documentation and information system in chemistry). In: ZIID 1966.6, p. 53–72. **cn**

Manheimer, Martha L. 1969.x: *The applicability of the NASA Thesaurus to the file of documents indexed prior to its application.* Pittsburgh: Univ./USA: Pittsburgh/ Graduate School of Library and Information Sciences 1969, 206 p. G; J7. **a**

Marlot, L. 1970; Moureau, M.: *Elaboration d'un thésaurus pétrolier.* Paris: CNSR 1970. App. 2. **cn**

Maron, M. E. et al 1959: *Probabilistic indexing: a statistical technique for document identification and retrieval.* Los Angeles, Calif.: Thompson Ramo Woodridge 1959. TM n. 3. H. **an**

Maron, M. E. 1960.7: *On relevance, probabilistic indexing and information retrieval.* In: J. ACM, v.7, n.3 (1960.7), p. 216–244. H. **a1**

Maron, M. E. 1961.7: *Automatic indexing: an experimental inquiry.* In: J. ACM, v.8, n.3 (1961.7), p. 404–417. Also in: 3rd Ind. Info. Stor. and Retr. 1961, papers presented, p. 236–265. H. **a1**

Marosi, A. 1969.9: *Euratom thesaurus and UDC: combined use for the subject organization of a small information service.* In: J. Doc., v.25, n.3 (1969.9), p. 197–213. (Has many examples). D1.7.6. **b**

Martinez, Samuel J. 1968.10; Jelander, Donald P.: *The development and maintenance of a specialized, controlled vocabulary thesaurus.* In: ASIS Proc., v.5 (1968.10), p. 279–283. B5.4.4; C4.1. **b2**

Martinez, Samuel J. et 1969.10: *Computer processing of thesaurus data.* In: ASIS Proc., v.6 (1969.10), p. 269–275. G; App. 2. **cn**

Masterman, Margaret 1956.10: *The potentialities of a mechanical thesaurus.* Cambridge: Language Research Unit 1956, 17 p. Also: 2nd Int. Conf. on Machine Translation, M.I.T. 1956.10. Summary in: ICSI 1959, p. 929–934. H. **an**

McClelland, R. M. A. 1966.10; Mapleson, W. W.: *Construction and usage of classified schedules and generic features in coordinate indexing.* In: Aslib Proc., v.18, n.10 (1966.10), p. 290–302. B5.5; C1.4.6(2). **b2**

McGee, L. L. et al 1963.10: *Compilation and computer updating of a medical sciences thesaurus.* In: ADI Proc., v. 0 (1963.10), p. G; App. 2. **cn**

McQuitty, Louis L. 1970.4: *Hierarchical classification by multiple linkages.* In: Educ. Psychol. Meas., v.30, n.1 (1970.1 Spring), p. 3–19. H. **an**

Meadow, C. T. 1967: *The analysis of information systems. A programmer's introduction to information retrieval.* New York: Wiley 1967, 301 p. (2nd ed. 1973.) **a1**

Meetham, A. R. 1963.1: *Preliminary studies for machine generated index vocabularies.* In: Language and Speech, v.6, pt. 1 (1963.1), p. 22–36. H. **a1**

Meetham, A. R. 1964.4: *Probabilistic pairs and groups of words in a text.* In: Language and Speech, v.7 pt. 2 (1964.4), p. 98–106. H. **an**

Meier, G. 1966.6: *Linguistische, besonders semantische Probleme der Informationsverarbeitung. (Linguistic, especially semantic problems of information processing).* In: ZIID 1966.6, p. 120–140. **cn**

Melton, Jessica 1958b: *Encoding of information previously classified.* In: Perry et al ed. 1958, p. 361–378. K2.3.2,1. **a2**

Melton, Jessica 1960: *A note on the compatibility of two information systems. Colon Classification and Western Reserve University (Encoded Telegraphic Abstracts) and the feasibility of interchanging their notations.* Cleveland, Ohio: West. Res. Univ. Cent. Doc. & Commun. Res. 1960, 7 p. Tech. Note 13. K2.3.2,1. **a2**

Melton, John 1958e; Melton, Jessica: *A method for automatic encoding for languages other than English.* In: Perry et ed. 58, p. 327–340. D5. **a2**

Melton, John L. 1958c: *The semantic code dictionary.* In: Perry et al. 1958, p. 603–964. D3.6.1,2; App. 2. **e**
Melton, J. L. 1962. *The semantic code today.* AD 263 126. **a2**
MeSH 1972: National Library of Medicine: *Medical subject headings 1972.* Washington, D.C.: Government Printing Office 1972, 436 p. DHEW Publication No. (NIH) 72-265. Index Medicus, v. 13, pt. 2 (1972.1). (Contains the alphabetical main part as well as the subject category listing; appears yearly.) Newer editions are available: *Medical subject readings 1974.* Bethesda, Md.: NLM 1973.7 *Alphabetic list.* 715 p. NLM-MED-74-01; PB 221 326/2. *Tree structures.* 343 p. NLM-MED-74-02; PB 221 327/0. (Better quality copy from GPO, 1972 no. is GPO 926-425.) *Permuted medical subject headings.* 747 p. NLM-MED-74-03; PB 221 463/3. Furthermore, *Medical subject headings.—Provisional headings.* 1972.4, 131 p. D1.7.5; J3.3.3; J4; App. 2. **e**
Metcalfe, J. W. 1959: *Subject classifying and indexing of libraries and literature.* Sydney: Angus and Robertson 1959. **cn**
Metcalfe, J. W. 1963: *Alphabetical subject indication of information.* New Brunswick, N.J.: Rutgers Univ./Graduate School of Library Services 1963. Rutgers Series on Systems for the Intellectual Organization of Information, v.III. **cn**
Michajlov, A. I., ed. 1969; Cernyj, A. I., ed.; Giljarevskij, R. S., ed.: *International forum for informatics. Mezdunarodnyj forum po informatike.* 2 v. Papers submitted for the FID conference planned in Moscow 1968.9. Moscow: VINITI 1969, 656 + 603 p. Source. **n**
Miller, George B. 1966.9: *Storage and retrieval of technical information in laboratories. Generation of thesauri of technical terms.* In: Tappi, v.49, n.9 (1966.9), p. 79A–82A. F2.2.3; App. 2. **b2**
Mills, J. 1960: *A Modern outline of library classification.* London: Chapman and Hall 1960, 198 p. C. **an**
Mills, J. 1964: *The Universal Decimal Classification.* New Brunswick, N.J.: Rutgers Univ. Press 1964, 132 p. D1.7.3. **an**
Model, Fr. 1966.3: *Thesaurus in der Dokumentation—Vielschichtigkeit des Begriffes und historische Entwicklung (The thesaurus in documentation—multiple aspects of the concept and its historical development).* In: Nachr. Dok., v.17, n.1/2 (1966.3), p. 5–11. **a**
Mooers, Calvin N. 1951.1: *Zatocoding applied to mechanical organization of knowledge.* In: Amer. Doc. v.2, n.1 (1951.1), p. 20–32. C2.8.1. **a1**
Mooers, Calvin N. 1958; Brenner, C. W.: *A case history of a Zatocoding IR system.* In: Casey et al. ed. 1958, p. 340–356. B5.2; C2.3.1; F1.1.2(n). **a1**
Mooers, Calvin N. 1959.3: *The next twenty years in information retrieval. Goals and predictions.* In: Proc. Western Joint Computer Conf. (1959.3.3-5), p. 81–86. Also: Cambridge, Mass.: Zator Company 1959.3, 18 p. ZTB-121a; AD 212 225. K3.1. **a1**
Mooers, Calvin N. 1959: *A mathematical theory of the use of language symbols in retrieval.* ZTB No. 122 (1959); In: ICSI-Proceedings, 1959, p. 1327–1364. Also: Zator Technical Bulletin No. 122, 1959. C1.2. **a1**
Mooers, Calvin N. 1963: *The indexing language of an information retrieval system.* In: Simonton ed. 63. **cn**
Moss, R. 1964: *Vocabularies for Batten card ("Peek-a-Boo") indexing.* Paper from proceedings of Aslib 38th annual conference, University of Exeter, 1964, p. 2–55 — 2–62. Full version: Liverpool Library School Occasional Papers. 2. **a**
Moss, R. 1967.9: *Minimum vocabularies in information indexing.* In: J. Doc., v.23, n.3 (1967.9), p. 179–196. Repr. in: Saracevic ed. 1970, paper 24, p. 254–263. **a**

Moss, R. 1970.3: *Analysis of indexing terms for plastics.* In: JASIS, v.21, n.2 (1970.3), p. 164–165. Gilchrist 1971. **b**
Mostecky, V. 1956.10: *Study of the "see also" reference structure.* In: Amer. Doc., v.7, n.4 (1956.10), p. 294–314. D3.1.2,1, Fig. 39. **a2**
Moureau, M. 1968.5: *Problèmes posés par la structure d'un thésaurus. Exemple d'un système à facettes (Problems posed by the structure of a thesaurus. Example of a faceted scheme).* In: Bull. Bibl. France, v.13, n.5 (1968.5), p. 201–210. (As far as useful, this is the same as Mulvihill 1966.10). D1.7.8. **a**
Muench, Eugene V. 1971.7: *A computerized English-Spanish correlation index to five biomedical library classifications.* In: Bull. Med. Libr. Assoc., v.59, n.3 (1971.7), p. 404–411. D5.2; K2.3.2,1; App. 2. **b2**
Mulvihill, J. G. 1966.10; Brenner, E. H.: *Faceted organization of a thesaurus vocabulary.* In: ADI Proc., v.3 (1966.10), p. 175–183. (Summary in Brenner et al. 1966.10). C1.2(5); D1.7.8. **b2**
Mulvihill, John 1968.10: *Supplementing thesaural relationships with usage notes.* Abstract in: ADI Proc. v.5 (1968.10), p. 41. (Full version av. from API). C3.2.2. **a1**

Natason, E. A. 1966.: *Requirements made on scientific and technical terms.* In: Nauchno-Techn. Inform., n.1 (1966.), p. 23–25. German: Die an wissenschaftliche und technische Benennungen zu stellenden Auforderungen. (av. DGD/ZDOK, Sdr. 1729).
NCPTWA. see ANSIZ39.5–1969. **a**
Neametu, O. 1969.: *Towards new types of thesauri.* In: Stud. & Cercetari Doc. & Bibliolog., v.11, n.1 (1969.), p. 35–40. **cn**
Needham, C. D. 1971: *Organizing knowledge in libraries: an introduction to classification and cataloguing.* 2nd ed. London: Deutsch 1971, 448 p. (1st ed. 1964, 259 p.) (An excellent textbook.) C; D1.7.3; D3.1.1,2.1; D3.6.1,2; D4. **a1**
Needham, R. M. 1961: *Research on information retrieval, classification and grouping 1957–61.* Cambridge: CLRU 1961, 177 p. CLRU ML 149. C1.2; H. **a1**
Needham, R. M. 1964.9; Sparck, J.: *Keywords and clumps.* In: J. Doc., v.20, n.1 (1964.9), p. 5–15. H; Batty 1969.6. **an**
Needham, R. M. 1965.6: *Applications of the theory of clumps.* In: Mech. Transl., v.8, n.3–4 (1965.6–10), p. 113–127. H. **an**
Neidhardt, Peter 1964: *Technical dictionary of television engineering—television electronics....* Berlin: VEB Verlag Technik; London: Pergamon; New York: MacMillan 1964, 340 p. D5.2. **e**
Nenninger, U. 1967.4: *Erste Erfahrungen beim Aufbau eines Fachthesaurus für Informations- und Dokumentationswissenschaft. (First experiences in the development of a special thesaurus for information science.)* In: ZIID 1967.4, p. 143–152. D3.0. **b2**
Neumann, C. 1967.4: *Aufstellung eines Fachthesaurus für das Gebiet der Erdölverarbeitung auf Kraftstoffe und erste Erfahrungen bei der Klassifizierung wissenschaftlich-technischer Fachliteratur.* In: ZIID 1967.4, p. 138–142. App. 2. **b**
Neville, H. H. 1970.12: *Feasibility study of a scheme for reconciling thesauri covering a common subject.* In: J. Doc., v.26, n.4 (1970.12), p. 313–336. K2.1.1; K2.2.1. **a1**
Newman, Lois 1969.11: *A general index to the Library of Congress classification.* Santa Monica, Calif.: Rand Corp. 1969.11, p. AD 698 181. D1.7.3. **e**
Newman, Simon M. ed. 1965: *Information systems compatibility.* New York: Spartan Books; London: Macmillan 1965, 184 p. Technology of Management Series, No. 1. Source. **n**
Nicolaus, John J. 1966.10: *Description of the Bureau of Ships thesaurus of descriptive*

terms and code book. In: Bull. de l'A.I.D., v.5, n.4 (1966.10), p. 59–65. G; App. 2. **b**
Nitecki, Andre 1967: *Index to the Library of Congress classification outline.* Syracuse, N.Y.: Syracuse Univ./School of Library Science 1967, 91 p. D1.7.3. **e**
Nobbs, Peter M. 1965.: *Coordinate indexing and the pulp and paper thesaurus as tools in information retrieval.* In: TAPPI, v.48, n.9 (1965.), p. 136–141A. **cn**
Nobbs, Peter M. 1966.12: *Progress with keyboard indexing and the updating of the Thesaurus of Pulp and Paper Terms.* In: Tappi, v.49, n.2 (1966.12), p. 58A–59A. F0.3.1(2); F0.5; J3.1. **a2**
Noel, J. 1966: *Le rôle de la définition dans une étude sémantique preparatoire a l'indexation mécanisee. (The role of definition in a semantic study for the preparation of mechanized indexing.)* In: Lebrun ed. 1966, p. 87–97. **cn**
NORDFORSK Arbeitsgruppe for thesaurussporsmal 1970.1: *Regler for bygging av thesauri pa nordiske sprak. (Rules for developing thesauri in nordic languages.)* Stockholm: NORDFORSK 1970.1, 20 p. App. 1. **cn**
Nouveau Petit Larousse 1968: *Nouveau Petit Larousse.* Paris: Librairie Larousse. **e**
NPL 1961: *National Physics Laboratory conference on automatic translation and applied language analysis.* Teddington: NPL 1961. Source. **n**

OECD/Development Centre 1969: *Liste commune de descripteurs. Aligned list of descriptors. Gemeinsames Schlagwortverzeichnis.* 2nd ed. Paris: OECD 1969. v.1: Introduction (in F, E, G) and list of descriptors. 53, 307 p. v.2: Annexes; List of countries and regions; institutions: titles and abbreviations, 77 p. v.3: Aligned list of descriptors—alphabetical order (English alphabetical index), 97 p. v.4: Liste commune des descripteurs—classement alphabetique (French alphabetical index), 87 p. v.5: Gemeinsames Schlagwortverzeichnis—Alphabetische Ordnung (German alphabetical index), 82 p. D1.5.1(b); D5.2; K2.3.2,1. **e**
OECD/IRRD 1971.11: *International Road Research Documentation Thesaurus* 1972, 2 ed., 6 vol. Paris: OECD 1971.11 (1. ed. 1967). Numerical list and English arrowed diagrams; English alphabetical list. Same for French and German. D3.2, Fig. 43; D5.2. **e**
Öhmann, Einar 1971.6: Olivecrona, Christina: *Some notational, hierarchic and syntactic problems in connection with concordances between UDC and thesauri.* In: FID 1971.6, paper 13, 48 p. K2.2; K2.2.1,1; K2.3.2,1. **al**
Olding, R. K., ed. 1966: *Readings in library cataloging.* Melbourne: Cheshire; London: Crosby Lockwood; Hamden, Conn.: Archon 1966, 278 p. Source. **n**
Oller, Robert G. 1968.3: *Human factors data thesaurus, an application to task data. Final report, January 2, 1967 - October 31, 1967.* Dayton, Ohio: SDC 1968.3, 71 p. AD 670 578. A1.5(2); App. 2. **e**
Orosz, G. 1966.6; Patsky, E.: *Ein Deskriptorsystem für die Informationsrecherche mittels Maschinenlochkarten. (A descriptor system for information retrieval with machine punched cards.)* In: ZIID 1966.6, p. 201–209. **cn**
Ostermann, Georg F., von 1959: *Manual of foreign languages.* 4. rev. and enl. ed. New York: Central Book Company 1959 (c.1952), 414 p. E2.5. **an**
Ott, Jack M. 1967.x: *A decision process and classification system for use by Title I project directors in planning educational change.* Columbus, Ohio: Ohio State Univ./College of Education/Evaluation Center 1967.x, 102 p. A1.5(2). **al/e**
Ovčinnikov, V. G. 1969.: *Some aspects of the evaluation of classifications used for information retrieval.* In: Nauchno-Techn. Inform., series 2, n.7 (1969.), p. 23–29. **cn**
Ovčinnikov, V. G. 1966.: *Tezaurus i nekotorye metode ego postroenija. (The thesaurus*

and some methods of its development.) In: Nauchno-Techn. Inform. (1966). I. *A Thesaurus as a classification scheme of facts.* n.8 (1966.), p. 24–28. II. *The methods of thesaurus development.* n.9 (1966.), p. 20–26. **cn**

Owens-Illinois, Inc. 1969: *Thesaurus software system. An introduction.* Toledo, Ohio: Owens-Illinois 1969, 7 p. G. **an**

Painter, A. F. 1963.3: *An analysis of duplication and consistency of subject indexing involved in report handling at the Office of Technical Services:* Washington, D.C.: Office of Technical Services 1963.3, 135 p. PB 181 505. K2. **a**

Painter, Ann F. 1963.7: *Convertibility potential among government information agency indexing systems.* In: Libr. Res. & Tech. Serv., v.7, n.3 (1963.7), p. 274–281. More detailed: Painter 1963.3, ch. 4 + 5. K2. **a**

Painter, Ann F. 1968.10: *Flexibility of the thesaurus structure for information control.* Indiana University: Graduate Library School 1968.10, 4 p. Abstract in: ASIS Proc., v.5 (1968.10), p. 341. Full paper: Bloomington, Ind.: Indiana Univ./Graduate Library School 1968.10, 4 p. **b**

Palmer, B. I. 1951; Wells, A. J.: *The fundamentals of library classification.* London: Allen & Unwin 1951, 114 p. D3.1.1,2.1. **an**

Pandex 1967–: *Index to the world's scientific and technical periodicals.* New York: Pandex Inc 1967–. Gilchrist 1971. **e**

Papier, Lawrence S. 1962.12; Cortelyou, E. H.: *Use of a technical word association test in the preparation of a thesaurus.* In: J. Doc., v.18, n.4 (1962.12), p. 183–187. F1.1.4. **a2**

Parker-Rhodes, A. F. 1960; Needham, R. M.: *The theory of clumps.* Cambridge: Cambridge Language Research Unit 1960. Rep. ML126. H; Batty 1969.6. **an**

Peirce, James G. 1969.10: *The use of TEST in the preparation of the Research and Development Capability Index.* In: ASIS 69.10, p. 26–32. (A history of committees for vocabulary building in the US Army.) **a**

Perreault, J. M.: *Re-classification: some warnings and a proposal.* Urbana: Univ. of Illinois/Graduate School of Library Science. Occasional papers no. 87. K2.3.2. **an**

Perrault, Jean M. 1965.: *Categories and relators: a new schema.* In: Rev. Int. Doc., v.32, n.4 (1965.), p. 136–144. Repr. in: Perreault et al. 1967. D4.3.6. **a1**

Perreault, Jean M. 1965.7: *A new device for achieving hospitality in an array.* In: Amer. Doc., v.16, n.3 (1965.7), p. 245–246. D4.3.2,2.1. **b1**

Perreault, Jean M. 1967; Wesseling, J. C. G.: *On the Perreault scheme of relators, and the rules of formation in UDC.* Copenhagen: Danish Centre for Documentation 1967. FID/CR Report Series, no. 405. **an**

Perreault, Jean M. 1967.: *On concordance between classifications.* College Park, Md.: University of Maryland/School of Library and Information Services 1967., 8 p. K2.2; K2.2.1. **a2**

Perreault, J. M., ed. 1968.4: *Reclassification. Rationale and problems. Proceedings of a Conference on Reclassification held at the Center of Adult Education, University of Maryland, College Park, April 4 to 6, 1968.* College Park, Md.: Univ. of Maryland 1968, 191 p. K2.3.2. **n**

Pettee, Julia 1946: *Subject headings.—The history and theory of the alphabetic subject approach to books.* New York: M. W. Wilson 1946, 195 p. F3. **an**

Pflug, Günther ed. 1968: *Elektronische Datenverarbeitung in der Universitätsbibliothek Bochum- Ergebnisse—Erfahrungen—Pläne. (Electronic data processing in the university Library Bochum.—Results, experiences, plans.)* Bochum: Pressestelle der Ruhr-Univ. Bochum 1968, 148 p. Source. **n**

Pickford, A. G. A. 1967.3: *FAIR (Fast Access Information Retrieval) project; aims and methods.* In: Aslib Proc., v.19, n.3 (1967.3), p. 79–95. (The same material as in Pickford 1968.3 in less detail.) **a2**
Pickford, A. G. A. 1968.3: *An objective method for the generation of an information retrieval language.* In: Information Scientist, v.2, n.1 (1968.3), p. 17–37. F0.3.1(1); F0.4.4,1; F1.1.3; G. **a2**
Pickford, A. G. A. 1971.3: *Some problems of using an unstructured information retrieval language in a coordinate indexing system.* In: Aslib Proc., v.23, n.3 (1971.3), p. 133–138. D1.1.0,2. **a2**
Pietsch, Erich 1960: *Current research efforts and trends in storage and retrieval in Western Europe.* In: UNESCO 1960, p. 496. K2.3.2. **an**
Pilz, J. 1967.4: *Probleme des Aufbaus eines Thesaurussystems "Technologie und Organisation der Produktion im Maschinenbau." (Problems in the development of a thesaurus system "technology of and organisation of production in mechanical engineering.)* In: ZIID 1967.4, p. 230–251. **a**
Pollard, A. F. C. 1930; Bradford, S. C.: *The inadequacy of the alphabetical subject index.* In: Aslib, Rep. of Proc. of Fifth Conf. 1930, p. 39–54. **cn**
Preisler, Werner 1970.x: *Bedeutung, Aufbau und Prüfung eines Thesaurus. (Importance, construction and evaluation of a thesaurus.)* In: Informatik, v.17, n.6 (1970.x), p. 4–18. A1.3.1; A1.7; F0.1, Fig. 53; F6; K2.3.1. **a2**
Price, N. 1968.8; Schiminovich, S.: *A clustering experiment: first step towards a computer-generated classification scheme.* In: Info. Stor. & Retr., v.4, n.3 (1968.8), p. 271–280. H. **an**
Priebe, John A. 1968.7: *Changes between the 1950 and 1960 occupation and industry classifications, with detailed adjustments of 1950 data to the 1960 classifications.* Washington, D.C.: U.S. Bureau of the Census, GPO 1978.7, 35 p. U.S. Bureau of the Census Technical Paper 18. C1.4.7; J1; J3.3.3. **a1**
Pshenichnaya, L. E. 1966.: *One method of coding meanings for an information language.* In: Nauchno-techn. Inform., series 2, n.7 (1966). **cn**
Pshenichnaya, L. E. 1967.6: *(Construction of semantic trees for term definitions.)* In: Nauchno-techn. Inform., series 2, n.6 (1967.6), p. 12–16. Translation in: Automated Documentation and Math. Linguistics, v.1, n.3 (1971.x), p. 17–21. C1.1.0. **a2**

Quemada, Bernard 1959: *La méchanisation dan les recherches lexicologiques. (Mechanization of lexicological research.)* In: Cahier de Lexicologie, v.1 (1959), p. 7–46. G. **b**

Rahmann, Manfred 1968.12; Samulowitz, Hansjoachim: *Planung und Aufstellung eines Fachthesaurus. (Planning and development of a special thesaurus.)* In: Nachr. Dok., v.19, n.6 (1968.12), p. 222–226. App. 2. **b**
Rainey, Laura 1970.1: *Experience with the new TEST thesaurus and the new NASA thesaurus.* In: Special Libraries, v.61, n.1 (1970.1), p. 26–32. App. 2. **an**
Ranganathan, S. R. 1962: *Elements of library classification.* 3rd ed. Bombay, New York: Asia Publishing House 1962, 168 p. Ranganathan Series in library science v.8. 2nd ed.: London: Association of Assistant Librarians 1959, 108 p. D3.1.1,2.1. **an**
Ranganathan, S. R. 1967: *Prolegomena to library classification.* 3rd ed. Gilchrist 1971. **an**
Rapoport, Anatol 1966.11; Rapoport, Ammon; Livant, William P.; Boyd, John: *A study of lexical graphs.* In: Foundations of Language, v.2, n.4 (1966.11), p. 338–376. H; H4.2. **an**

594 Bibliography

Reed, Gordon E.: *Analysis of the dictionary at the General Electric Company.* Bethesda, Md.: General Electric Company. Unpublished. (Some results summarized in Schultz et al. 1961.4.) **an**

Reich, Peter A.: *Competence, performance and relational networks.* New Haven, Conn.: Yale University/Linguistic Automation Project. **cn**

Reich, Peter A. 1968: *Symbols, relations, and structural complexity.* New Haven, Conn.: Yale Univ./Linguistic Automation Project 1968. **cn**

Reisner, Phyllis 1963.10: *Construction of a growing thesaurus by conversational interaction in a man-machine system.* In: ADI Proc., v.0 (1963.10), p. 99–100. Also: Yorktown Heights, N.Y.: IBM Th. Watson Research Ctr. 1963, 9 p. Full version see Reisner 1965a. J3.5. **a**

Reisner, Phyllis 1964.2: *Constructing an adaptive thesaurus by man-machine inter-* Yorktown Heights, N.Y.: IBM Th. Watson Research Ctr. 1963. AF 19 (626)–10. Preliminary report: 1963.2. Final report: 1964.2. **an**

Reisner, Phyllis 1965: *Construction of authority files.* In: Newman ed. 65 p. 55–68. **a**

Reisner, Phyllis 1965a: *Semantic diversity and a growing man-machine thesaurus.* In: Kochen ed. 65, p. 117–130. **a1**

Reisner, Phyllis 1965c: *A note on minimising search and storage in a thesaurus network by structural reorganization of the net.* In: Kochen ed. 65, ch. IVC, p. 265–270. (More recent version in Reisner 64.2, app. IVF.) D1.4. **a2**

Reisner, Phyllis 1966.8: *Evaluation of a "growing" thesaurus.* Yorktown Heights, N.Y.: IBM Watson Research Center 1966.8.9, 19 p. IBM-RC-1662. (Most complete account of Reisner's work, supersedes other papers by Reisner.) F1.1.4. **a1**

Richards, Jack C. 1970.5: *A psycholinguistic measure of vocabulary selection.* In: Internat. R. of Appl. Ling. in Language Teaching, v.8, n.2 (1970.5), p. 87–102. Also: Quebec: Laval University/International Center for Research on Bilingualism 1969.8, 25 p. ED 035 860 (this version cited). Not rev. version: Annual meeting of the Canadian Linguistic Assoc., York University, Toronto, 1969.6, paper. C1.7; F0.4. **a1**

Richmond, Phyllis 1965: *Aspects of recent research in the art and science of classification.* Copenhagen: Danish Center for Documentation 1965, 65 p. FID/CR report n.3, 56 p. **cn**

Richmond, Phyllis A. 1972.8: *Reading list in classification theory.* In: Libr. Resources and Technical Services v.16, n.3 (1972.Summer), p. 364–382. C. **an**

Rieck, J. 1967.2: *Thesauri fur die Entwicklungsländer-Dokumentation. (Thesauri for documentation on developing countries.)* In: Nachr. Dok., v.18, n.1 (1967.2), p. 32–34. App. 2. **a**

Ringdoc 1968.3: *Ringdoc codeless scanning thesaurus.* 3rd ed. London: Derwent Publications Ltd.; Basel: Hoffmann-La Roche 1968.3, 508 p. Suppl. 1: 1968.9. Suppl. 2: 1968.11. Suppl. 3: 1969.2. *For a description of the philosophy behind and applications of this thesaurus see Wegmueller et al. 63.10/64.10.* B5.4.1 (7b); B5.4.3(c); B5.4.4; C5.3; C5.4.1; D5.1; E1.7; E1.11; F0.7.1,2; G; K1.2.1; App. 2. **b1/e**

Roberts, Michael 1971: *Thesaurus for the construction industry.* In: Conrad, v. 2, n.4 (1971.), p. 189–193. App. 2; Gilchrist 1971. **cn**

Robinson, F. 1970.6: *A computer based retrieval system using a reactive thesaurus.* In: Info. Stor. & Retr., v.6, n.2 (1970.6) p. 171–177. Gilchrist 1971. **cn**

Roget's international thesaurus 3rd ed. New York: Crowell 1962, 1258 p. D1.1. **e**

Rolland, M. Th. 1971: *Grundriss eines Thesaurus als funktionsfähiges Hilfsmittel für Indexierung und Recherche. (Application of a thesaurus for information indexing and retrieval.)* München-Pullach: Verlag Dokumentation 1971, 68 p. Studiengruppe fur Systemforschung e.V., Heidelberg, Report No. 104. **cn**

Bibliography 595

Rolling, Loll N. 1962.8: *Ein Schlagwörterverzeichnis für die maschinelle Dokumentation der Kerntechnik.* Brussel: EURATOM 1962.8, 42 p. EUR/C/3663/62d. *A keyword index for machine documentation in the nuclear field.* Brussels: EURATOM 1962.8. EUR/CID/4243/10/62/e. D1.7.6. **cn**
Rolling, L. 1963.: *Un répertoire de mots-clés pour la documentation méchanisée dans le domaine de la technique nucleaire.* In: Bull. Bib. France, v.8 (1963.), p. 11–25. D1.7.6. **a2**
Rolling, L. 1965: *The role of graphic display of concept relationships in indexing and retrieval vocabularies. Including a thesaurus of documentation terms.* In: Atherton ed. 1965, p. 325–370. Also: Brussels: EURATOM 1965.3, 14 p. EUR 2291.e. D1.7.6; D3.2. **a2**
Rolling, L. 1970.10: *Compilation of thesauri for use in computer systems.* In: Information Storage and Retrieval, v.6, n.4 (1970.10), p. 341–350. D1.7. **a**
Rolling, L. 1971.11: *Graphic display devices in thesaurus construction and use.* In: Aslib Proc., v.23, n.11 (1971.11), p. 591–594. D3.2. **b2**
Roloff, Heinrich 1954: *Lehrbuch der Sachkatalogisierung. (Textbook of subject cataloging.)* Leipzig: Harrassowitz 1954. Source. **n**
Roloff, Heinrich 1954a: *Der Schlagwortkatalog. (The subject heading catalog.)* In: Roloff 1954, p. 87ff. **cn**
Rosemann, S. 1967.4: *Über erste Erfahrungen beim Aufbau einer Begriffsschlüsselliste für das Gebiet "Explosivstoffe." (On first experiences in the construction of a descriptor list in the area of explosives.)* In: ZIID 1967.4, p. 124–137. (Describes sources to be used in the development of this thesaurus.) App. 2. **e**
Rosenbaum, Hans-Dieter 1966.8: *Technische Thesauri in Westeuropa. (Technical thesauri in Western Europe.)* In: ZIID-Z., v.15, n.4 (1966.8), p. 114–116. (This is the first of a series of articles.) App. 2. **e**
Rosenbaum, H.-D. 1967.4: *Probleme der Thesaurusarbeit und die nächsten Aufgaben zu ihrer Lösung in der DDR. (Problems of thesaurus work and the next tasks to solve them in the GDR.)* In: ZIID 1967.4, p. 35–53. K2.3.1. **cn**
Rostron, R. M. 1968.3: *The construction of a thesaurus.* In: Aslib Proc., v.20, n.3 (1968.3), p. 181–187. **b**
Rothkirch-Trach, Karl-Christoph, Graf 1964.9; Rothkirch-Trach, Malve, Gräfin. *Erfahrungen und Erkenntnisse bei der Aufstellung von Thesauren. (Experiences in the development of thesauri.)* In: Nachr. Dok., v.15, n.3 (1964.9), p. 118–121. **a**
Rothkirch-Trach, Karl-Christoph, Graf von 1970: *Prinzipien der Thesauruserstellung. (Principles of thesaurus development.)* 2nd ed. München-Pullach, Berlin: Verlag Dokumentation 1970, 87 p. Studiengruppe fur Systemforschung. Bericht Nr. 93. **cn**
Rubinoff, Morris 1966.7: *A rapid procedure for launching a microthesaurus.* In: IEEE Trans. on Eng. Writing & Speech, v.9, n.1 (1966.7), p. 8–14. F0.4.2; F0.4.3(e); F0.4.4,1. **b2**
Rubinoff, Morris 1967.5; Stone, Don C.: *Semantic tools in information retrieval.* Philadelphia, Pa.: University of Pennsylvania/Moore School of Electrical Engineering, 26 p. AD 660 087; ED 027 915. Abridged in: ADI-Proc. v.4 (1967.10), p. 169–174. **a1**
Rubinoff, Morris 1967.6; Franks, Winifred; Stone, Don C.: *Description of an experiment investigating term relationships as interpreted by humans.* Arlington, Va.: Air Force Office of Scientific Research; Philadelphia, Pa.: University of Pennsylvania 1967.6, 29 p. AD 671 906; ED 023 432. F1.1.4. **a1**
Rush, J. E. 1971.7; Salvador, R.; Zamora, A.: *Automatic abstracting and indexing. II. Production of indicative abstracts by application of contextual inference and syntactic coherence criteria.* In: JASIS v.22, n.4 (1971.7), p. 260–274. B6.2.2(5). **a1**

Bibliography

Salton, Gerard 1962: *The identification of document content: a problem in automatic information retrieval.* In: Proc. Harv. Symp. on Comp. (1962), p. 273–304. H. **al**

Salton, Gerard 1964.1: *A flexible automatic system for the organization, storage and retrieval of language data (SMART).* In: ISR-5 (1964.1), Section I. B6.2. **al**

Salton, Gerard 1964.6: *The SMART system.—An introduction.* In: ISR-7 (1964.6), Section I. B6.2. **al**

Salton, Gerard 1965.6; Lesk, M. E.: *The SMART automatic document retrieval system.—An illustration.* In: Comm. ACM v.8, n.6 (1965.6), p. 391–398, 10 Lit. NSF–GN–245. B6.2. **al**

Salton, Gerard 1966.6; Lesk, Michael: *Information analysis and dictionary construction.* In: ISR-11 (1966.6), Section II. Repr. in: Salton ed. 1971, p. 115–142. Somewhat altered version: *Information dissemination and automatic information systems.* In: Proceedings of the IEEE, v.54, n.12 (1966.12), p. 1663–1678. B6.2, H. **al**

Salton, Gerard 1967.6: *The SMART project.—Status report and plans.* In: ISR-12 (1967.6), Section I. Later version in: Salton ed. 1971, p. 3–11. B6.2. **al**

Salton, Gerard, ed. 1971: *The SMART retrieval system.—Experiments in automatic document processing.* Englewood Cliffs, N.J.: Prentice-Hall. Prentice-Hall Series in Automatic Computation. B6.2; H. **n**

Salton, Gerard 1971.1: *Experiments in automatic thesaurus construction for information retrieval.* New York: Cornell Univ./Computer Science Dept. 1971.1, 27 p. H. **al**

Saracevic, Tefko et al. 1968: *An inquiry into testing of information retrieval systems.* Cleveland, Ohio: Case Western Reserve Univ./Center for Documentation and Communication Research 1968. pt 1: Objectives, methodology, design, and controls. 272 p. PB 179290. pt 2: Analysis of results. 226 p. PB 180951. **al**

Saracevic, Tefko, ed. 1970: *Introduction to information science.* New York: Bowker 1970, 751 p. Source. **n**

Saussure, F. de 1959: *Course in general linguistics.* New York: Philosophical Library 1959. Gilchrist 1971. **cn**

Sayers, W. C. B. 1967: *Manual of library classification.* 4th ed. revised by Maltby. London: Deutsch 1967, 404 p. C. **an**

Schactman, Bella E. 1967.10: *Agricultural/Biological vocabulary.* In: Libr. Resources and Techn. Services, v.11, n.4 (1967.Fall), p. 443–450. App. 2; Gilchrist 1971. **cn**

Schanche, Grete 1966.: *Erfaringer fra arbeidet med en polyteknick Thesaurus som indeksoringsgrunnleg. (Experience derived from work with a polytechnical thesaurus as an index basis.)* In: Tidskrift for Dokumentation, v.22, n.3 (1966.), p. 18–40. App. 2. **cn**

Schanche, Grete 1968.8: *Erfahrungen mit dem polytechnischen Thesaurus im Vergleich zu den spezialisiterten Fachthesauren (Satellittthesauren) als Wörterkontrolle für die koordinierte Indexierung. (Experience with the polytechnical thesaurus compared with the specialized subject thesauri (satellite thesauri) for word control in coordinate indexing.)* In: Nachr. Dok., v.19, n.5 (1968.8), p. 171–173. App. 2. **b**

Scheele, Martin 1964.3: *Thesaurus—Baustein jeder Fachdokumentation. (Thesaurus—building block of each special documentation.)* In: Nachr. Dok., v.15, n.1 (1964.3), p. 1–4. C2.3.3. **bl**

Scheele, Martin 1965.3: *Ein Verfahren zur automatischen Klassifizierung für Veröffentlichungswesen, Bibliothekswesen und Dokumentation. (A procedure for automatic indexing for bibliography, librarianship, and documentation.)* In: Naturwissenschaften, v.52, n.1 (1965.3), p. 1–10. **cn**

Scheele, Martin 1969.4: *Ergebnisse eines Retrievaltestes der Dokumentationsstelle für Biologie. (Results of a retrieval test of the information service for biology.)* In: Nachr. Dok., v.20, n.2 (1969.4), p. 73–80. B5.2.1. **al**

Schiminovich, S. 1968.4; Lieberman, N.: *A clustering experiment: first step toward a computer-generated classification scheme.* New York: American Institute of Physics/ Information Div. 1968.4.17, 43 p. PB 178 370. H. **an**

Schirmer, Robert F. 1967.5: *Thesaurus analysis for updating.* In: J. Chem. Doc., v.7, n.2 (1967.5), p. 94–98. F; G. **b2**

Schneider, John H. 1968.2: *Hierarchical decimal classification of information related to cancer research.* Bethesda, Md.: National Cancer Institute 1968.2.2, 124 p. PB 177 209. **e**

Schneider, Klaus 1966; Holl, L.: *Behandlung von Sonderbuchstaben. (Treatment of special characters.)* Frankfurt/M: Zentralstelle für Maschinelle Dokumentation 1966, 29 p. ZMD-A-8. Berichtigter Nachdruck der Veröffentlichung: Zurückführung von Sonderbuchstaben auf normale Buchstaben. Frankfurt 1961. AED-M-3. E2.5. **an**

Schön, J. 1970.: *Der Thesaurus of Engineering and Scientific Terms (TEST). Entstehungsgeschichte und Aufbau. (TEST. History and structure.)* In: Nachr. Dok., v.21, n.3 (1970.), p. 110–113. (Essentially a German translation of the introduction to TEST.) App. 2. **b**

Schreiber, Herbert 1971.: *Optimierung von Schlagwortverzeichnissen. (Optimization of descriptor lists.)* In: Informatik, v.18, n.1 (1971.), p. 17–21. **cn**

Schuck, J.-J. 1969.2: *Zusammenarbeit Mensch/Maschine beim Umgang mit elektronisch gespeicherten Wörterbüchern. (Man-machine cooperation in consulting computer-stored dictionaries.)* In: Nachr. Dok., v.20, n.1 (1969.2), p. 10–16. B6.2. **a2**

Schüller, J. A. 1963.10: *The TDCK circular thesaurus system.* In: ADI Proc., v.0, (1963.10), p. 13–14. (All material is covered in Schüller 1966.10). **a2**

Schüller, J. A. 1966.10: *TDCK—Organisation und Systeme. Das wissenschaftliche und technische Dokumentations- und Informations-Zentrum der holländischen Wehrmacht. (TDCK—organization and systems. The scientific and technical documentation and information center of the Dutch armed services.)* In: Nachr. Dok., v.17, n.5 (1966.10), p. 153–162. **a2**

Schüller, J. A. 1968.6: *Manual systems—TDCK circular thesaurus system.* In: Vessey et al. ed. 1968.6, p. 101–110. **cn**

Schultz, C. K. 1960.7; Shepherd, C. A.: *The 1960 Federation meeting: a study in programming and indexing by computer.* Federation Proceedings, vol.19, no.2, (1960.7), p. 682–699. Mimeographed version also 1960.7. **a1**

Schultz, Claire K. 1961.4; Shepherd, Clayton A.: *A computer analysis of the Merck, Sharp, and Dohme Research Laboratories indexing system.* In: Amer. Doc., v.12, n.2 (1961.4), p. 83–92. H; H0. **a1**

Schultz, Claire K. 1961.10; Schwartz, Phyllis D.; Steinberg, Leon: *A comparison of dictionary use within two information retrieval systems.* In: Amer. Doc., v.12, n.4 (1961.10), p. 247–253. H; H0. **a1**

Schultz, Claire K. 1962.10; Schwartz, Phyllis A.: *A generalized computer method for index production.* In: Amer. Doc., v.13, n.4 (1962.10), p. 420–432. (Compare Shepherd 1963.) A1.4; B6.2; C6.2.2(3). **a1**

Schultz, Claire K. 1963.10: *Editing author-produced indexing terms and phrases via a magnetic-tape thesaurus and a computer program.* In: ADI Proc. v.0 (1963.10), p. 9 (Basically the same as Schultz 1962.10 and Shepherd 1963.) B6.2. **a2**

Schultz, Claire K. 1968a: *Thesaurus of information science technology.* Rev. ed. Washington, D.C.: Communication Service Corp. 1968. C5.0.2,1; App. 2. **e**

Sechser, O. 1966.6.: *Welche Variablen müssen sich in einem Mass für die Vollkommenheit einer Recherchesprache widerspiegeln? (Erläutert am Beispiel einer Recherchesprache vom Deskriptortyp.) (What variables must be reflected in a measure for the quality of a retrieval language. Illustrated with reference to a retrieval language of the descriptor type.)* In: ZIID 1966.6, p. 156–160. cn

Sechser, O. 1968; Mojzisek, J.; Konigova, M.: *Selecni jazyk a jeho popis. (The indexing language and its description.)* (orig. Cs) Prag: Ustredi Vedeckych, Techn. a Ekonom. Inform. 1968, 219 p. cn

Seiden, W. 1966.6: *Erfahrungen über Versuche zur Bildung von Deskriptoren für Rechercheverfahren mit Maschinenlochkarten auf dem Gebiet der Wirtschaftswissenschaften. (Experience with descriptor formation for retrieval procedures with machine-punched cards in the area of economics.)* In: ZIID 1966.6, p. 132–148. cn

Serbanescu, V. F. ed. 1963: *Information retrieval/Recherche de la documentation/Dokumentation*. Blaricum, Holland: IBM European Education Centre 1963, var pag. Source. n

Sharp, Harold S., ed. 1964: *Readings in information retrieval*. New York: Scarecrow 1964, 759 p. Source. n

Sharp, John R. 1964.2: *The SLIC index*. Paper presented at Aslib 38th Annual Conference, University of Exeter, 1964.2.11–2.16. an

Sharp, John R. 1966.1: *The SLIC index*. In: Amer. Doc., v.17, n.1 (1966.1), p. 41–44. D3.6.1,2. al

Sharp, John R. 1967: *Content analysis, specification and control*. In: Ann. Rev. of Info. Sci. & Tech., v.2 (1967), p. 87–122. al

Shepard, R. N. 1961: *Learning and memorization of classifications*. Psychological Monographs, n.517 (1961). cn

Shepherd, C. A. 1963.: *The computer-stored thesaurus and its use in concept processing*. In: AFIPS Conf. Proc., v.24 (1963), p. 389–395. (Basically the same as Schultz 1963.10 and Schultz 1962.10.) A1.4; B6.2; B6.2.2(2). al

Shera, Jesse H. 1956; Egan, Margaret: *The classified catalog*. Chicago: ALA 1956, 130 p. C. al

Shera, Jesse H. ed., 1957.4; Kent, A., ed.; Perry, J. W., ed.: *Information systems in documentation*. New York: Interscience 1957, 639 p. Advances in documentation and library science, v.2. *Symp. Systems for Information Retrieval, WRU/CDCR, Cleveland, Ohio, 1957.4.15–17* proceedings. Source. n

Shumway, N.: *Medlars: vocabulary construction and medical subject headings*. Nolte Center for Continuing Education. App. 2. cn

Silar, F.: *Thesaurus as an aid for increasing the efficiency of classification of information*. In: Féderation Internationale Des Geomètres, Information and documentation, v.1 (n.d.), p. 26–40. cn

Silbernagel, G. 1967.x: *Anwendung der Logik auf die Lösung von Thesaurusproblemen. (Applications of logic to the solution of thesaurus problems.)* In: ZIID-Z., v.14, n.5 (1967.x), p. 140–142. cn

Singer, David J. 1968.6: *A general systems taxonomy*. Ann Arbor, Mich.: Mental Health Res. Inst. 1968.6, 41 p. (First draft of ch. 3 of a book by Singer.) C2.8.2. al

Skolnik, Hermann 1970.: *The multiterm index: a new concept in information storage and retrieval*. In: J. Chem. Doc., v.10, n.2 (1970.), p. 81–84. Gilchrist 1971. cn

Slamecka, V. 1963.1: *Indexing aids*. Bethesda, Md.: Documentation Inc. 1963.1, 33 p. AD 294 859. D1.0. a

Slamecka, Vladimir 1963.7: *Classificatory, alphabetical and associative schedules as aids in coordinate indexing*. In: Amer. Doc., v.14, n.3 (1963.7), p. 223–228. a

Slype, G. van 1964.: *Comment réaliser une liste des mots-clés et la transformer en un thesaurus de termes normalisés. (How to create a list of keywords and transform it into a thesaurus of standardized terms.)* In: CNOF, v.38, n.6 (1965.), p. 21–27.

Übersetzung Nr. 880 des Instituts für Verwaltungsorganisation und Bürotechnik, Leipzig. **cn**

Smilari, Sonia 1968.10; Delfino, Allan: *Structure, preparation and computer input of a biochemical and medical thesaurus for Syntex research.* In: ASIS Proc., v.5 (1968.10), p. 289–292. G; App. 2. **a**

Smorodinova, E. V. 1966.6: *System der mechanisierten Patentrecherche auf dem Gebiet gyroskopischer Geräte. (A system for mechanized patent search in the area of gyroscopic devices.)* In: ZIID 1966.6, p. 73–87. C1.5.2,3. **cn**

Snow, D. C. 1965.9: *Development and monitoring of indexing systems: evaluation of term lists by comparison with a sample of claims in new patent applications.* London: U.K. Patent Office 1965.9. F6. **an**

Society of Automotive Engineers 1966.1: *Automotive engineering congress.* SAE 1966.1. Source. **n**

Soergel, Dagobert 1965.5: *Outline of an algorithm for the analysis and comparison of classification systems.* Freiburg i. Br.: the author 1965.5, 30 p. mimeo. (Superseded by the present work, except for ch. V "Statistical Investigations," p. 25–30 and some outdated details.) H; H0; K2.2.1. **an**

Soergel, Dagobert 1967.7: *Mathematical analysis of documentation systems.—An attempt to a theory of classification and search request formulation.* In: Info. Storage & Retr., v.3, n.3 (1967.7), p. 129–173. Revised version of a mimeo paper dated 1965.9. C; C2.8.1; C2.8.2; H; H4.1. **an**

Soergel, Dagobert 1967.12: *Some remarks on information languages, their analysis and comparison.* In: Info. Storage & Retr., v.3, n.4 (1967.12), p. 219–291. (Proceedings, Int. Symp. on Relational Factors in Classification, Univ. of Maryland, 1966.6.8-11. paper.) B3.0; C1.1.0; D4.3.6. **an**

Soergel, Dagobert 1969: *Klassifikationssysteme und Thesauri. (Classification schemes and thesauri.)* Frankfurt/M: Deutsche Gesellschaft für Dokumentation e.V. 1969. (All material is included in the present work except table Anh./1, giving a comparison of field labels used in different thesauri (p. 192), table Lit./1 "Standards and other selected publications on transliteration" (p. 209) and the glossary (p. 210–217). **bn**

Soergel, Dagobert 1970.8; Furmaniak, Karl: *Klassifikationssystem der für die Arbeitsmarktforschung relevanten Sachverhalte. (Classification scheme for labor market research.)* Bad Godesberg: DATUM 1970.8, ca. 200 p. Fundortkatalog für Daten des Arbeitsmarktes. Projektreport Nr. 5(3). D4.0, Fig. 48; App. 2. **e**

Soergel, Dagobert 1970.10; Furmaniak, Karl: *The description of statistical tables. A problem in data documentation.* In: ASIS Proc., v.7 (1970.10), p. 331–336. K1.2.2,-2.1.1. **an**

Soergel, Dagobert 1971: *Dokumentation und Organisation des Wissens.—Versuch einer methodischen und theoretischen Grundlegung am Beispiel der Sozialwissenschaften. (Documentation and organization of knowledge.—An inquiry into the methodological and theoretical foundations with particular reference to the social sciences.)* Berlin: Duncker u. Humblot 1971, 380 p. A1.5(1); C1.0; K0(2C); K2. **an**

Soergel, Dagobert 1972: *A general model for indexing languages: the basis for compatibility and integration.* In: Wellisch et al. ed. 1972, p. 36–61. (This paper is a condensed version of Section C1 and C2.) **bn**

Soergel, Dagobert 1972.9: *A universal source thesaurus as a classification generator.* In: JASIS v.23, n.5, p. 299–305. (This paper is a condensed version of some of the the ideas in Chapter K.) **bn**

Bibliography

Sparck Jones, Karen 1961: *Mechanised semantic classification.* In: NPL 1961, p. 417–436. H. **an**

Sparck Jones, Karen 1964.6: *Synonymy and semantic classification.* Cambridge: Cambridge Language Research Unit 1964.6. CLRU M.L. 170. H. **an**

Sparck Jones, Karen 1965.6: *Experiments in semantic classification.* In: Mechanical Translation, v.8, n.3–4 (1965.6/10), p. 97–112. H. **an**

Sparck Jones, Karen, 1965.11: *Semantic markers.* Cambridge: Cambridge Language Research Unit 1965.11, CLRU M.L. 181. M. **an**

Sparck Jones, Karen 1967.5; Jackson, D. M.: *Current approaches to classification and clump-finding at the Cambridge Language Research Unit.* In: Computer J., v.10, n.1 (1967.5), p. 29–37. H; Batty 1969.6. **an**

Sparck Jones, Karen 1967.6; Jackson, D. M.: *The use of the theory of clumps for information retrieval.* Cambridge: Cambridge Language Research Unit 1967.6. CLRU M.L. 200. H; Batty 1969.6. **an**

Sparck Jones, Karen 1968.6; Needham, R. M.: *Automatic term classifications and retrieval.* In: Info. Stor. & Retr., v.4, n.2 (1968.6), p. 91–100. H; Batty 1969.6. **an**

Sparck Jones, Karen 1968.8: *Automatic term classification and information retrieval.* In: IFIP Proc., v. (1968.8), p. G5–G9. H. **an**

Sparck Jones, Karen 1970.2; Jackson, D. M.: *The use of automatically obtained keyword classifications for information retrieval.* In: Info. Stor. & Retr., v.5, n.4 (1970.2), p. 175–201. H. **an**

Sparck Jones, Karen 1970.5: *Automatic thesaurus construction and the relations of a thesaurus to indexing terms.* In: Aslib Proc., v.22, n.5 (1970.5), p. 226–228. H. **a2**

Sparck-Jones, K. 1970.6: *Some thoughts on classification for retrieval.* In: J. Doc., v.26, n.2 (1970.6), p. 89–101. H. **an**

Sparck Jones, Karen 1971: *Automatic keyword classification and information retrieval.* London: Butterworths 1971, 253 p., 135 lit. H. **an**

Speight, Frank Y. 1964.9: *Procedures for revision of the Thesaurus of Engineering Terms.* New York: EJC 1964.9.23 (draft). *Memorandum to W. M. Carlson.* **cn**

Speight, Frank Y. 1966.1: *Engineering society cooperation in improving dissemination of engineering information.* In: Society of Automotive Engineers 1966.1. **cn**

Speight, Frank Y. 1966.10: *What is "the Thesaurus of Engineering Terms" developed by the Engineers Joint Council (EJC).* In: Bull. de l'A.I.D., v.5, n.4 (1966.10), p. 29–43. **cn**

Speight, Frank Y. 1969.10: *Plans for updating the Thesaurus of Engineering and Scientific Terms.—Survey of users.* In: ASIS 1969.10, p. 33–8. J. **b2**

Steinweg, Hilda 1950.1: *Thoughts on subject headings.* In: J. of Cat. and Class., v.6, n.1 (1950.1), p. 40–45. D3.0. **a2**

Stevens, Mary E. 1965.12; Giuliano, V. E.; Heilprin, L. B. eds: *Statistical association methods for mechanized documentation.* Proceedings Symp. USNBS and ADI, Washington, 1964.3. Washington, D.C.: U.S. Govt. Print. Off. 1965.12, 261 p. National Bureau of Standards Misc. Publication 269. H. **n**

Stevens, Mary E. 1970.2: *Automatic indexing: a state-of-the-art report.* 2nd ed. Washington, D.C.: National Bureau of Standards 1970.2, 298 p. (1st ed. 1965.3, 220 p.) USNBS Monograph 91; ED 041 610. B6.2; H. **a1**

Stone, Don C. 1967.12: *Word statistics in the generation of semantic tools for information systems.* Philadelphia, Pa.: Pennsylvania Univ./Moore School of Electrical Engineering 1967.12, 94 p. AD 664 915; ED 017 295. H. **an**

Stone, Philip 1966.6; Woodhead, Louise: *(Rules for the disambiguation of homonyms.* —Internal working paper.) Cambridge, Mass.: Harvard Univ./Lab. f. Soc. Rel. 1966.6, 3 p. F1.2.1,3. **a1**

Stouffer, S. A. ed. 1970: *The American soldier. v.4: measurement and prediction.* Princeton, N.J.: Princeton Univ. Press 1950. Source. **n**

Stransky, Jiri 1966.: *Das Kategorieprinzip in der landwirtschaftlichen Klassifikation. (The principle of categories in agricultural classification.)* In: DK-Mitt., v.11, n.5 (1966.), p. 21–24. **cn**

Sukiasjan, E. R. 1968.7: *Centralized classification: achievements and problems in regard to future development.* In: Unesco. Bull. Libr., v.22, n.4 (1968.7), p. 189–195. K2. **a2**

Surace, Cecily J. 1970.3: *The display of a thesaurus.* Santa Monica, Calif.: Rand 1970.3, 37 p. RAND P-4331; ED 039 002. D1. **a**

Svankmajer, M. 1966.6: *Der Grundtyp der Codes und die logische Struktur der Inhaltsregistrierung der Dokumente. (The basic type of codes and the logical structure of indexing documents.)* In: ZIID 1966.6, p. 160–167. **cn**

SYNTOL 1964; EURATOM; Association Marc Bloch: *Le SYNTOL (Syntagmatic Organisation Language). Etude d'un systeme général de documentation automatique.* Paris: Association Marc Bloch 1962.7. v.1: *Aspects théoriques*, par Gardin, J. C., 120 p. v.2: *Problèmes de programmation*, par Cros, R. C. v.3: *Exemples de lexiques.* 3A: *Champ commun*, par Levy, F., 44 p. 3B: *Physiologie*, par Gardin, Natacha; Zygouris, Radmilla, ca. 200 p. 3C: *Psychologie*, par Levy, F., ca. 150 p. 3D: *Sociologie.* v.4: *Analyse automatique*, par Coyaud, M. Luxembourg; Office des Ventes des Publications des Communeautés Européennes. (See also Cros et al. 1964.) D3.1.2,1, Fig. 37 and 38. **a1/e**

Szigethy, M. 1970.6: *Computer-produced thesaurus for the clipping file.* Paper presented at the Special Libraries Association Convention, Detroit, June 1970. G. **cn**

Tancredi, Samuel A. 1968.1; Nichols, Owen D.: *Air pollution technical information processing: the microthesaurus approach.* In: Amer. Doc., v.19, n.1 (1968.1), p. 66–70. D1.1.1,1; F3. **a1**

Taube, Mortimer et al. ed. 1953–65: *Studies in coordinate indexing 1–6.* Washington, D.C.: Documentation Incorporated. (These volumes contain original material and reprints from journals by a number of authors) Source. **n**

Taube, Mortimer ed. 1958; Wooster, H. ed.: *Information storage and retrieval.* New York: Columbia University Press 1958. Gilchrist 1971. **n**

Taube, Mortimer, ed. 1959: *Emerging solutions for mechanising the storage and retrieval of information.* Washington, D.C.: Documentation Inc. 1959. **an**

Taube, Mortimer 1963.7: *Extensive relations as the necessary condition for the significance of "thesauri" for mechanized indexing.* In: J. Chem. Doc., v.3, n.3 (1963.7), p. 177–180. **a2**

Tauber, Stephen J. 1968.10: *Statistical generation of a technical vocabulary.* In: Amer. Doc., v.19, n.4 (1968.10), p. 411–412. H. **a1**

Taulbee, Orrin E. 1968: *Content analysis, specification and control.* In: Ann. Rev. of Info. Sci. & Tech., v.3 (1968), p. 105–136. **a1**

TDCK 1966.5: *TDCK—Circular thesaurus system.* 4th ed. The Hague: Netherlands Armed Forces Scientific and Technical Documentation and Information Service 1966.5, 841 p. D3.1.2,3, Fig. 41. **e**

TEST 1967.12: *Thesaurus rules and conventions.* Approved Nov. 1, 1966. In: TEST 1967.12(a), app. 1, p. 673–679. Repr. in Hanmond 1968.1, App. B. Outdates USDOD/ONR/LEX 1966.4. B2.0; B2.1; B4.2.1; B5.5(b); C1.2; C1.4.1,5; C1.4.2; C1.4.3,1; C1.4.3,2; C1.5; C1.5.1; C1.5.2,2; C2.6.1(2); C2.7 passim; C4.0(a); C4.0(b); C4.2.2 C4.3; C5.0.1(2); C5.0.2; C6.1; C7.1; D1.4 fn 4; D1.4.1; D1.5.2; D1.8(1);

D1.8(2); D2.2, Fig. 33; D2.3.2,3; D2.3.2,7; E passim; F0.4.2; F0.4.3 passim; F0.4.4; F0.4.4,2(2); F1.1; G0.1.2; G0.2; G3.4.1; G5.1; G7; App. 1. **bn**
TEST 1967.12a: *Thesaurus of engineering and scientific terms. A list of engineering and related scientific terms and their relationships for use as a vocabulary reference in indexing and retrieving technical information.* New York: Engineers Joint Council 1967.12, 690 p. A2; D1.2; D1.4(2); D1.4.2; J4; App. 2. **a2/e**
Thesaurofacet 1969: Aitchison, J. ed. & comp.; Day, P. ed.; Gomersall, A. comp.; Ireland, R. comp.: *Thesaurofacet. A thesaurus and faceted classification for engineering and related subjects.* Whetston, Leicester: The English Electric Co. 1969, 491 p. D1.3.3,1; D1.4.2; D1.7.4; App. 2. **a2/e**
Thesaurusfragen und Thesauri 1966.10: *Thesaurusfragen und Thesauri.* (Thesaurus problems and thesauri.) In: Bull. de l'A.I.D., v.5, n.4 (1966.10), p. 3–109. (All papers contained in this issue are included individually in the extended bibliography.) **n**
Thomas, Charles R. 1969.10: *Data element dictionary: X. A technical report concerning X related data elements in the WICHE management information systems program (X varies from section to section).* Boulder, Col.: Western Interstate Commission for Higher Education WICHE Technical Report. Section 1: Student. 1st ed. 1970.4, 45 p. TR-7; ED 042 431. Section 2: Staff. 1st ed. 1970.4, 35 p. TR-8; ED 042 430. Section 3: Facilities. 1st ed. 1970.4, 30 p. TR-9; ED 042 432. Section 4: Course. 1st ed. 1970.5, 22 p. TR-11; ED 042 429. Section 5: Finance. 1st ed. 1970.5, 21 p. TR-12; ED 042 433. A1.5(1). **e**
Thomas, Peter A. 1971.11: *Some problems in compiling a thesaurus of transportation and planning terms.* In: Aslib Proc., v.23, n.11 (1971.11), p. 595–606. App. 2. **b2**
Thomas, Richard B. 1953; Gull, C. D.: *The choice of terms for a Uniterm coordinate index of scientific and technical reports.* In: Taube et al. ed. 1953, v.1 (1953), p. 47–55. C2.3. **b2**
TICA 1965: *Conference on Technical Information Center Administration.* 2nd. St. David's, Pa.: 1965.6.14–17. Source. **n**
Tinker, J. F. 1963.10; Smith, R. B.: *Producing indexing aids such as a dictionary or thesaurus from a single punched card deck.* In: ADI Proc., v.0 (1963.10), p. 173–174. F9.2.2. **a1**
Toman, J. 1966.6: *Vergleich der modernen alphabetischen Ordnungssysteme und Klassifikationssysteme. (Comparison of the modern alphabetical ordering systems with classification systems.)* In: ZIID 1966.6, p. 17–32. **cn**
Toman, J. 1970: *The influence of information retrieval on the structure of indexing and classification systems.* In: Foskett, D. J. et ed. 1970. **cn**

Uhlmann, Wolfram 1967: *A thesaurus "Nuclear science and technology"; principles of design.* In: TVF/Stockholm, v.28, n.2 (1967.), p. 46–52. **b**
Ullman, Hans C. 1965: *Descriptor relationships.* Santa Monica, Calif.: Systems Development Corp. 1965. SDC SP-2203. **cn**
UNESCO 1959; Wüster, Eugen, ed.: *Bibliography of monolingual scientific and technical glossaries.* Vol. 1: *National standards.* 1955, 219 p. Vol. 2: *Miscellaneous sources.* 1959, 146 p. Paris: UNESCO. Supplements published in Babel, International Journal of Translation published by the International Federation of Translators with the assistance of Unesco. Avignon, France. App. 2. **e**
UNESCO 1960: *Information processing.* Proceedings of the International Conference on Information Processing, Paris, UNESCO, 1959.6.15–20. Paris: UNESCO; London: Butterworths; Munich, Oldenbourg 1960, 520 p. Source. **n**

UNESCO 1969: *Bibliography of interlingual scientific and technical dictionaries.* 5th ed. Paris: UNESCO 1961, 250 p. App. 2. **e**

UNESCO 1970.12: *Guidelines for the establishment and development of multilingual scientific and technical thesauri for information retrieval.* 2nd draft. Paris: UNESCO 1970.12.22, 20 p. German translation 20 p., available from DNA. D5; App. 1. **an**

UNESCO 1971.12: *Guidelines for the establishment and development of monolingual thesauri for information retrieval.* Paris: UNESCO 1971.12.22, 30 p. (earlier version 1970.7). *UNESCO* SC/WS/500. (This document is also an ISO draft proposal, ISO DIS 2788). C2.7; F0.4.5; App. 1. **an**

Ungurian, O. 1966.6: *Aufbau eines alphabetischen Sachregisters zur DK, das den an Thesauri gestellten Anforderungen und ihren Begrenzungen entspricht. (Construction of an alphabetical index to the Universal Decimal Classification that corresponds to the requirements and limitation of thesauri.)* In: ZIID 1966.6, p.118–131. **cn**

University of Tulsa/Information Services Department: *Report on basic and indexing services. App. III: Thesaurus philosophy.* Tulsa, Okla.: The University 1968, 16 p. App. 2. **cn**

University of Tulsa/Information Services Department 1968: *Exploration and production thesaurus: listing of scientific and engineering terms and their relationships for use in vocabulary control in indexing and retrieving Petroleum Abstracts.* 3rd ed. Tulsa, Okla.: The University 1968. App. 2. **e**

USASTIA 1962.12: *Thesaurus of ASTIA descriptors.* 2nd. ed. Arlington, Va.: US ASTIA 1962.12, 591, 82 p. PB 181 457. App. 2. **e**

USAEC 1962: *The literature of nuclear science: its management and use.* 1962. Source. **n**

US Bureau of Ships/Technical Library 1965: *Thesaurus of descriptive terms and code book.* 2nd ed. Washington, D.C.: the Bureau. NAVSHIPS 0900-002-000. **e**

US Bureau of the Census 1962: *County and city data book.* Washington, D.C.: Govt. Printing Office 1962, 669 p. A statistical abstract supplement. D4.4.1. **e**

USCOSATI 1964.12: *COSATI subject category list.* Washington: COSATI of the Fed. Council for Science and Tech. 1964.12. **e**

USCOSATI 1967.9: *Guidelines for the development of information retrieval thesauri.* Washington, D.C.: U.S. Govt. Print. Off. 1967.8, 9 p. E3(a); App. 1. **n**

USDDC 1966.5; Klingbiel, Paul M., ed.; Jacobs, Charles R.: *DDC descriptor frequencies.* Alexandria, Va.: Defense Documentation Center 1966.5, 58 p. AD 632 600. App.2. **e**

USDOD 1965.10: *Memorandum from the Director of Defense Research and Engineering, dated 12 Oct 1965, subject:DoD-wide Technical Thesaurus.* **a2**

USDOD 1965.12: *Memorandum from the Deputy Assistant Secretary of Defense (Comptroller), dated 2 Dec. 1965, subject: Assignment of data elements and data codes standardization responsibility—DoD-wide Technical Thesaurus.* Reprinted in Heald 67.11, p. 63–64. **a2**

USDOD/ONR/LEX 1966.4: *Manual for building a technical thesaurus.* Washington: Dept. of Defense, Office of Naval Research, Project LEX 1964.4, 21 p. USDoD/ONR 25. AD 633 279; ED 017 302. (Earlier version: Heald 1966.3; newer version: TEST 1967.12.) **bn**

USERIC 1969.9: *Rules for thesaurus preparation.* Washington, D.C.: U.S. Govt. Print. Off. 1969.9, 20 p. ED 033 740. C4.1; D1.7.9; E1.7; App. 1. **bn**

USERIC 1971.6: *ERIC descriptors. Term usage postings and term usage statistics.* Bethesda, Md.: U.S. ERIC Processing and Reference Facility 1971.6, 691, 112 p. D1.7.9. **e**

USERIC 1971.6a: *ERIC identifiers. Term usage postings and term usage statistics.* Bethesda, Md.: U.S. ERIC Processing and Reference Facility 1971.6, 322, 303 p. C4.1; D1.7.9. **e**
USERIC 1972: *Thesaurus of ERIC descriptors.* 4. ed. New York: CCM Information Corporation 1972, 330 p. 1 ed.: Washington, D.C.: Government Printing Office (for USOE) 1967.12, 15 + 309 p. OE 12031. Contains an introduction including the descriptor justification form. Supplement no. 1 1968.3. 2. ed. as 1. ed., 1969.4, 28 + 32 + 289 p. OE 12031-69. 3. ed., as 4. ed., 1970, 546 p. The original introduction is replaced by a special chapter on The role and function of the thesaurus in education by Frederick Goodman. B4.2.1; B4.2.4; C1.4.1,4; C2.3.1; C5.0.2,1; C5.2.2; D1.5.2; D1.7.9; D2.2; E1.2.2; F0.5; J4; App. 2. **b2/e**
US Library of Congress/Processing Dept. 1956: *Filing rules for the dictionary catalogs of the Library of Congress.* Washington, D.C.: GPO 1956. (Newer edition in preparation.) E3. **an**
USNBS 1971.7: *Chemical kinetics index. (Document analysis sheet for use of checklist technique.)* Washington, D.C.: U.S. National Bureau of Standards 1971.7, 4 p. Form NBS-194 (rev. 7-71). D1.1.1.1, App. 2. **e**
USOE 1966.2: *Guidelines for the development of a thesaurus of education terms.* Washington, D.C.: U.S. Office of Education 1966.2, 13 p. A2.3; D1.7.9. **an**
USOE 1966.10: *Rules for thesaurus preparation.* Washington, D.C.: U.S. Office of Education 1966.10, 12 p. Repr. in: Eller et al. 1968.7. Superseded by: U.S. ERIC 1969.9. **bn**

Valov, Yu. I. 1968.; Vinogradov, V. I.; Sokolov, A. V.: *Some problems in the development and introduction of information retrieval systems based on descriptors.* (In Russian.) In: Nauchno-Techn. Inform., series 2, n.7 (1968.), p. 27–30. **cn**
Valov, Yu. I. 1968.; Sokolov, A. V.: *Opyt razrabotki, vnedreniyai ekspluatatsii deskriptornykh IRS v usloviyakh NII. (Experience with development and operation of descriptor IRSs at a research institute.)* In: Nauchno-Techn. Inform., series 1, n.2 (1968.), p. 22–26. **cn**
Vcerasnij, R. P. 1966.: *O vozmoznosti avtomaticeskoj reklassifikacii opicanij izobretanij. (Possibilities for the automatic reclassification of patent disclosures.)* In: Nauchno-Techn. Inform., n.9 (1966.), p. 16–19. K2. **cn**
Vejsova, A. 1966.6: *Deskriptorsystem eines universal-technischen Fonds. (Descriptor system of a store on all of technology.)* In: ZIID 1966.6, p. 107–117. **cn**
Verevcenko, A. P. 1968.10; Petrov, Ju. G.: *Anwendung eines permutierenden Registers zur Analyse und Vervollkommnung von Thesauri. (Application of a permuted index for the analysis and improvement of thesauri.)* In: ZIID-Z., v.15, n.5 (1968.10), p. 206–209. Orig. in: Nauchno-Techn. Inform., series 2, v.3, n. (1968.), p. 12–14. D1.5.2; F5.8. **b2**
Vernimb, C. 1969.6: *Die Bedeutung des Thesaurus fur das Retrieval. (The importance of the thesaurus for retrieval.)* In: Nachr. Dok. v.20, n.3 (1969.6), p. 128–134. **a**
Vessey, H. F., ed. 1968.6; Gabelunan, I. J., ed.; NATO/AGARD: *Storage and retrieval of information. A user-supplier dialogue.* Proc. of a symposium, Munich 1968.6.18–30. 1968.6, 197 p. AGARD Conf. Proc. 39; AD 697 621. Source. **n**
Vickery, B. C. 52–59: *Notational symbols in classification. Parts 1–6.* In: J. Doc. I. (no subtitle), v.8, n.1 (1952.3), p. 14–32. II. Notation as an ordering device, v.12, n.2 (1956.6), p. 73–87. III. Further comparisons of brevity, v.13, n.2 (1957.6), p. 72–77. IV. Ordinal values of symbols, v.14, n.1 (1958.3), p. 1–11. V. Signposted and

retroactive notation, v.15, n.1 (1959.3), p. 12-13. VI. Pronouncable retroactive ordinal notation, v.15, n.1 (1959.1), p. 14-16. D4. **a1**
Vickery, B. C. 1959: *Classification and indexing in science.* London: Butterworths 1959, 235 p. C; C1.1.0. **a1**
Vickery, B. C. 1960.12: *Thesaurus—a new word in documentation.* In: J. Doc., v.16, n.4 (1960.12), p. 181-189. B4.2.4. **a1**
Vickery, B. C. 1960: *Faceted classification. A guide to construction and use of special schemes.* 2nd impr. ed. London: Aslib 1960, 70 p. Reprint 1968, 70 p. (references 15-20 and minor notes referring to these added). German translation: Lutterbeck, E., transl.: *Facetten klassifikation.* München-Pullach: Verlag Dokumentation 1969, 72 p. C1.1.0; C1.3.2; D4. **a1**
Vickery, B. C. 1960a: *Coding for interconvertibility.* In: Kent ed. 1960, pt. 2, p. 1159-1174. K2.2.1; K3.4. **a2**
Vickery, B. C. 1963.6: *Vocabularies for coordinate systems.* In: Aslib Proc., v.15, n.6 (1963.6), p. 170-176. **a2**
Vickery, B. C. 1965: *On retrieval system theory.* London: Butterworths 2nd ed. 1965, 191 p. (1st ed. 1961, 159 p.) German ed.: Berlin: Verl. Dokumentation 1970, 247 p. A1.3.1; B5.4.1(6); C. **a1**
Vickery, Bryan C. 1966: *Faceted classification schemes.* New Brunswick: Rutgers Univ./Grad. School of Lib. Sci. 1966, 108 p. Rutgers Series of Systems for the Intellectual Organisation of Information. 5. B3.0; C1.1.0; C1.3.2. **an**
Vickery, B. C. 1969.6; Slater, M.; Pesanis, A.; Reynolds, R.: *Classification in science information. A comparative study undertaken by Aslib for the International Council of Scientific Unions.* London: Presented as document UNISIST/CSI/5.8 at the Fourth Session of the Central Committee to study the feasibility of a world science information system at Unesco House, Paris, 15-17 December 1969. (Critically reviewed in Öhman et al. 1971.6.) K2.2.1,1. **cn**
Voieulescu, M. 1966.6: *Ein mit Hilfe von Lochkartenmaschinen und eines Thesaurus aufgestelltes alphabetisches Sachregister. (An alphabetical subject index produced with the aid of punched card machines and of a thesaurus.)* In: ZIID 1966.6, p. 243-249. **cn**
Vygotsky, L. S. 1962: *Thought and language.* Cambridge, Mass.: MIT Press 1962, 168 p. Esp. ch. 2, p. 9-24, and ch. 5, p. 52-81. **an**

Wagner, Elizabeth M. 1970: *Multi-lingual rehabilitation terminology; a preliminary study.* New York: International Society for Rehabilitation of the Disabled 1970, 58 p. ***Technical paper, 27, ED 044 878. D5; App. 2. **e**
Wahrig, Gerhard 1967.6: *Neue Wege in der Wörterbucharbeit. Gleichzeitig ein Beitrag zu einer strukturalistischen Bedeutungslehre. (New ways in dictionary work. Also a contribution to a structuralist semantic theory.)* Hamburg: Verl. f. Buchmarktforschung 1967.6, 101 p. **cn**
Walkley, Janet 1971.6; Hay, Barbara: *An annotated list of thesauri held in the Aslib library.* In: Aslib Proc., v.23, n.6 (71.6), p. 292-300. App. 2. **e**
Wall, Eugene 1962: *Small-scale information retrieval systems.* Chicago: Engineers Council 1962. Gilchrist 1971. **cn**
Wall, E. 1962.8: *Final report. First revision of the Thesaurus of ASTIA descriptors.* New York: Engineers Joint Council 1962.8.6, 19 p. AD 278 168. C2.8.2; C5.3.2; F0.5; App. 2. **b1**
Wall, Eugene 1962.10: *Engineering terminology study committee. Minutes of meeting.* New York: Engineers Joint Council 1962.12.10. App. 2. **cn**

Wall, Eugene 1962.11: *Information retrieval thesauri.* New York: Engineers Joint Council 1962.11. C1.5.3; C6.1; C7.1. **b1**

Wall, Eugene 1963.8: *Study of engineering terminology and relationships between engineering terms. Final report.* New York: Engineers Joint Council 1963.8. AD 432 231. Short version see Wall 1963.10. F0.4.3(b); App. 2. **b2**

Wall, Eugene 1962.11–63.10: *Action plan for improved dissemination of engineering information. Progress report.* New York: Engineers Joint Council. No. 1 (revised): 1962.11.23. No. 2: 1963.1.7. No. 3: 1963.4.2. No. 4: 1963.7.1. No. 5: 1963.10.1, 9 p. PB 169 320. (The material presented in no. 5 is essentially covered in Wall 1963.8, see there.) App. 2. **an**

Wall, Eugene 1963.10: *A unified engineering vocabulary for use in information dissemmination, indexing, storage and retrieval.* In: ADI Proc., v.0 (1963.10), p. 37–38. This is basically a short version of Wall 1963.8. Wall 1963.8 is recommended for the reader interested in depth. A1.1; F0.3; F0.4.3(e); App. 2. **b2**

Wall, Eugene 1964.6: *Indexing control in the technical information center.* In: TICA, v.1 (1964.6), p. 72–103. **a2**

Wall, Eugene 1965.12: *(Thesaurus of engineering terms—letter following review by Dr. Campbell, June 1965.)* In: J. Doc., v.21, n.4 (1965.12), p. 296–298. App. 2. **cn**

Wall, Eugene 1969.4: *Vocabulary building and control techniques.* In: Amer. Doc., v.20, n.2 (1969.4), p. 161–164. **b**

Wall, E. 1969.5; Barnes, J.: *Intersystem compatibility and convertibility of subject vocabularies.* Philadelphia, Pa.: Auerbach 1969.5.8, 138 p. PB 184 144; ED 032 106. F2.4.1; F2.4.2; K1.4; K2.3.2,1. **a2**

Ward, J. H. Jr. 1963; Hook, M. E.: *Application of a hierarchical grouping procedure to a problem of grouping profiles.* In: Educational and Psychological Measurement, v.23 (1963), p. 69–82. H; Batty 1969.6. **an**

Water 1971: *Water resources thesaurus.* 2nd ed. Washington, D.C.: U.S. DI/Office of Water Resources Research/Water Resources Scientific Information Center 1971, 375 p. D2.3.2,3; App. 2. **e**

Way, William 1968.4: *Subject heading authority list, computer prepared.* In: Amer. Doc., v.19, n.2 (1968.4), p. 188–199. Also: Santa Monica, Calif.: RAND 1966.12, p. ED 015000. G; App. 2. **a**

Webster's Third New International Dictionary. Springfield, Mass.: Merriam 1964. **e**

Wegmueller, F. 1964.10; Becher, R.; Guetlin, K.: *Codeless scanning—ein Verfahren zur Literaturdokumentation. (Organisation der Dokumentationsarbeit mit Lochstreifenmaschinen.) 1. (Codeless scanning—a method for literature documentation. Organisation of documentation work with punched paper tape equipment.)* Basel: Hoffman-La Roche/Literaturabteilung 1964.10, 44 p. 2. Arbeitstagung der Dokumentationszentrale des Forschungsrates fur Ernahrung, Landwirtschaft und Forsten, Bad Godesberg 1963.10.2–3. App. 2. **a1**

Weil, Ben H. 1970.9: *Standards for writing abstracts.* In: JASIS v.21, n.5 (1970.9), p. 351–357. B5.6; F1.2.1,2. **an**

Weinstein, S. Jane 1966.10: *Biological dictionary preparation, control and maintenance.* In: Amer. Doc., v.17, n.4 (1966.10), p. 190–198. A2.3; C1.5.3; D1.1.1,1; J3.3; App. 2. **b1**

Wellisch, Hans 1973: *Bibliography on transliteration and transcription.* Unpublished. E2.5. **n**

Wellisch, Hans, ed. 1972; Wilson, Thomas D. ed.: *Subject retrieval in the seventies. New directions.* Westport, Conn.: Greenwood; College Park, Md.: University of Maryland/School of Library and Information Services *Proceedings of an Inter-

national Symposium, University of Maryland, College Park, 1971.5.14–15* 1972, 180 p. Contributions in Librarianship and Information Science. 3. **n**
Wellisch, Hans 1971.6: *A concordance between UDC and Thesaurus of engineering and scientific terms (TEST)*. Results of a pilot project. In: UDC 1971.6, paper 20, 33 p. C2.3.1; K2.2.1,1; K2.3.2,1. **a2**
Wellisch, Hans 1970: *The Universal Decimal Classification.—A programmed instruction course*. College Park, Md.: University of Maryland/School of Library and Information Services 1970, 195 p. D1.7.3. **an**
Werner, Oswald 1967.1: *Systematized lexicography or 'ethnoscience': the use of computer made concordances*. In: Amer. Behav. Scientist, v.10, n.5 (1967.1), p. 5–8. F1.2.1,3. **a1**
Whaley, Fred R. 1966.10; Flanagan, Carylun M.: *The Engineering Index thesaurus*. In: Bull. de l'A.I.D., v.5, n.4 (1966.10), p. 45–52. A1.4; G; App. 2. **b2**
Williams, B. J. S. 1969: *Thesaurus of microform-terms*. Hatfield, Herts.: National Reprographic Centre for Documentation 1969. App. 2. **e**
Williams, John H., Jr. 1968: *Computer classification of documents*. In: Samuelson ed. 1968, p. 235–246. H. **an**
Williams, John H., Jr. 1966.2: *Discriminant analysis for content classification*. Griffiss Air Force Base, New York: Rome Air Development Center 1966.2. ED 027 917. H. **an**
Williams, John H., Jr. 1965.12: *Results of classifying documents with multiple discriminant functions*. In: Stevens et al. ed. 1965.12, p. 217–224. AD 612 272. H. **an**
Wilson, Paul T. 1969.11; Spitzer, Robert L.: *A comparison of three current classification systems for mental retardation*. In: Amer. J. Ment. Deficiency, v.74, n.3 (1969.11), p. 428–435. **cn**
Wilson, Thomas D. 1972: *The work of the British Classification Research Group*. In: Wellisch et al. ed. 1972, p. 62–71. A2 **a2**
Winkler, U. 1969.2: *AUTOQEST—ein Verfahren der automatischen Abfragengenerierung. (AUTOQUEST—a procedure for the automatic generation of queries.)* In: Nachr. Dok., v.20, n.1 (1969.2), p. 16–20. B6.2; B6.2.2(2). **a1**
Winters, W. K. 1965.7: *A modified method of latent class analysis for file organization in information retrieval work*. In: J. ACM, v.12 (1965.7), p. 356–363. H; Batty 1969.6. **an**
Wolff-Terroine, M. 1969.1; Simon, N.; Rimbert, D.: *Use of a computer for compiling and holding a medical thesaurus*. In: Meth. Inf. Med., v.8, n.1 (1969.1), p. 34–40. G. **a**
Wolff-Terroine, M. 1971.6; Rimbert, D.: *Computer-aided automatic generation of a structured documentary language: preliminary study*. In: J. Doc., v.27, n.2 (1971.6), p. 111–125. H; App. 2. **an**
Wong, A. L. S. I. 1969.9; Heaps, D. M.: *Thesauri, an on-line program for constructing a thesaurus*. Alberta, B.C.: *Univ./Canada: Alberta/Dept. Comp. Sci. 1969.9. ***Publ. 20. New edition in preparation. G. **an**
Wüster, Eugen 1959.: *Die Struktur der sprachlichen Begriffswelt und ihre Darstellung in Wörterbüchern. (The structure of the conceptual system of language and its representation in dictionaries.)* In: Studium generale, v.12, n.10 (1959.), p. 615–627. C1.4.2. **an**

Yakushin, B. V. 1967.; Bitman, V. B.: *On an approach to a method of thesaurus construction. (Ob odnom podkhode k razrabotke metodiki postroeniya tezaurusa.)* In: Nauchno-Techn. Inform., series 2, n.7 (1967.), p. 8–11. **cn**

Bibliography

Zavada, J. 1966.6: *Einfluss der Konstruktion eines Thesaurus auf die Effektivität der mechanisierten Dokumentenverarbeitung. (Influence of the construction of a thesaurus on the effectivity of mechanized document processing.)* In: ZIID 1966.6, p. 152–159.   cn

ZIID 1965: *Symposium der Mitgliedsländer des RGW. Komplexe Mechanisierung und Automatisierung von Prozessen der Verarbeitung, des Wiederauffindens, der Herausgabe und Fernübertragung wissenschaftlich-technischer Informationen. Referate von DDR-Wissenschaftlern, Moskau, 10–14 Juni 1965. (Symposium of the member countries of the COMECON. Complex mechanization and automation of processes of processing, retrieving, editing and telecommunication of scientific-technical information. Papers of scientists from the GDR, Moscow, June 10–14, 1965.)* Berlin: ZIID 1965. ZIID Schriftenreine. 7. Source.   n

ZIID 1966.6: *RGW-Symposium. Entwicklung von Deskriptorsystemen und ihre Nutzung beim Wiederauffinden von Informationen. Teil 1 u. 2. (Symposium. Development of descriptor systems and their use in the retrieval of information. Parts 1 and 2.)* Berlin: ZIID 1966.6, 265 p., 283 p. ZIID Schriftenreihe 12/1, 12/2. Source.   n

ZIID 1967.2: *Methodische Richtlinie für die Erarbeitung eines Thesaurus. Entwurf. (Methodological guideline for the development of a thesaurus. Draft.)* Berlin: Zentralinstitut für Information und Dokumentation 1967.2, 25 p. Reprinted (with very minor modifications) in ZIID 1967.4, p. 3–26. A1.3; A1.3.1; A2.3; B1.1; B5.2.2(1.2); B5.7(b); C1.5.2,1; C2.7 passim; C4.0(a); C5.0.1(2); D1.4 fn. 3; D3.1.2,1; D3.2; E passim; F0.1, Fig. 52; F0.4.2; F0.4.4,2(1); F0.4.4,2(2); F1.1.3; F1.2.1,2; F3.3.7; F6; J; K2.3.1,1; K2.3.1,2; App. 1.   bn

ZIID 1967.4: *Nationales Symposium. Thesauri für mechanisierte Informations recherchesysteme. (National symposium. Thesauri for mechanized information storage and retrieval systems.)* Berlin: ZIID 1967.4, 279 p. ZIID Schriftenreihe 16. Source.   n

ZMD 1966.1: *Aufnahme der Katalogbegriffe aus dem VDG-Schlagwortkatalog mit einer Lochstreifenschreibmaschine auf 8-Kanal-Lochstreifen. (Recording of the subject headings used in the VDG subject catalog with a punched paper tape typewriter on 8-track punched paper tape.)* Frankfurt: Zentralstelle fur maschinelle Dokumentation 1966.1.7, 19 p. F9.1.2; F9.1.2.   a2

Zunde, Pranas 1967.4; Slamecka, Vladimir: *Distribution of indexing terms for maximum efficiency of information transmission.* In: Amer. Doc., v.18, n.2 (1967.4), p. Repr. in: Saracevic ed. 1970, paper 26, p. 279–283.   cn

Zunde, Pranas 1968.10; Dexter, Margaret E.: *Statistical models of index vocabularies.* In: ASIS Proc., v.5 (1968.10), p. 73–78.   a

Index

INTRODUCTION

This alphabetical subject index should be seen in conjunction with the full table of contents which serves as classified index. The bibliography is at the same time the author index: all the places where a document is referred to in the book are listed with the document. If the reader wants to know, for example, where all the different rules and procedures used in the TEST thesaurus are referred to in the book, he should also consult the bibliography under TEST 1967.12 and other documents pertaining to TEST (those documents can be found in App. 2). Other supplementary tools are Fig. 21 *Types of cross-references....*(p.176) and App. 2 (p. 529). Important abbreviations used in the text are included in this index.

A fairly extensive structure of cross-references between the terms has been introduced, but due to space limitations only the cross-references most useful for this index could be considered. As a rule, the direct form of a term is preferred; a cross-reference from the inverted form is made if deemed useful. Lead-in terms have *see* instructions to the appropriate descriptors, e.g.,

Schedule, *see ST* Classified index

The entry for a descriptor gives all the lead-in terms associated with it and, for synonyms, the page where the synonymity is established, e.g.,

Classified index, 183, 184*, 194
ST Schedule, 183

For major concepts that have several page numbers associated with them (and only for these), the most important page number is marked by an asterisk (*); this page number usually leads to a section that gives a definition.

The following symbols are used:

see
s.a.   see also   NT   Narrower Term
BT   Broader Term   SP   Spelling variant
ET   Equivalent Term   ST   Synonymous Term

609

610   Index

Abbreviations, 314
  standardized, 315
Abstract terms, 149
Abstracting, automatic, 64
Abstracting services, indexes to, to be
    improved by thesaurus, 8
  as a source in thesaurus construction, 355
Abstracts, controlled vocabulary in
    writing, 60
  economy measure in ISAR systems, 41
Accounting machine, 419
Acquisition of documents as ISAR system
    function, 18
Actions and processes, designation, 305
Adjunct thesaurus, 289, 475, 481*, 512
  and nomenclature, 152
Administrative problems, see ET Organizational problems
Alloys, 153
Alphabetical array (Thes. of Ed. Terms), 221
Alphabetical catalog, see ST Alphabetical
    subject catalog
Alphabetical index method for lead-in,
    156*, 193, 211
Alphabetical index of a thesaurus, 62, 183,
    193, 207*, 309, 390, 412
  preliminary, 422
  production, 404
    computer assistance, 404
    manual, 406
    use of punched cards, 419
  TEST model, 406
  total thesaurus, 512
  use of the rules for form of terms, 300
Alphabetical main part (TEST model), 197
  production, 406
Alphabetical order of descriptors, 125
Alphabetical subject catalog or index, 8, 31,
    55, 117, 127, 535
  ST Catalog, alphabetical
Alphabetical sorting (step in thesaurus
    construction), 366
  computer assistance, 429
  punched cards, 419
Alphabetization, 320
  word-by-word vs. letter-by-letter, 320

Alternate classified index, 207, 237*
Alternate notation, 207, 237*
Alternative lead-in forms, 165
Alternatives in decision-making, classification of, 8
American Petroleum Institute, see SP API
Analytical terms, 149
Announcement service, 471, 494
Anticipated search requests, economy
    measure in ISAR systems, 41
API (American Petroleum Institute), 8
  subject authority list (API Thesaurus),
    79, 221*
Archives of newspaper clippings, 51, 276
Arrangement, s.a. NT Classified arrangement
  Filing arrangement
  Helpful arrangement
  Linear sequence
  Orderly arrangement
  Shelf arrangement
  RT Display
  Sequence
  of concepts, 9
  of descriptors, 9, 122, 124, 125
  of documents, see BT Filing arrangement
  of entries in the main part, 198
  of independent elements (criterion in the
    typology of indexing languages), 125
  of notations in linear sequence, 285
  of terms within one data field, 232
Art, works of, names, 148
Artificial homonyms, 303
Artificial monohierarchical structure, 45
Artificial synonyms, 381
Assistance programs, names of, 148
Association between two terms, association
    profiles, 452
  inconsistent (detection of
    homonyms), 453
  psychological, 112*, 358
    bound association method, 358
    term association lists, 355, 358
    free association method, 358
  second order (detection of synonyms), 453
  statistical, 452
    interpretation, 452

Index   611

Associative relationships, 107*, 389
  vs. hierarchical relationships in indexing and searching, 98
ASTIA (Armed Services Technical Information Agency), thesaurus, 342, 530
Attributes, common, *see ST* Concepts of general application
Authorities for spelling, 317
Authority list, *see ST* Thesaurus
Authorized term, *see ST* Descriptor
Automatic classification, 449
  ET Statistical methods in the construction of indexing languages
Automatic indexing, *see ST* Mechanized indexing
Auxiliary ISAR system, 77, 119*, 127, 203, 239, 263*
  ST Conceptual Index, 119
  ISAR system for descriptors, 264
  Mechanized, 265, 272
  Manual, 265
Auxiliary notation, 360

BASF (Badische Anilin und Soda Fabrik), 232
Batch search requests, economy measure ISAR system, 40
Biased indexing (by anticipated search requests), 50
Bibliographical form as descriptor, 148
Big thesaurus as source for pulling, 374
Biological nomenclatures, 153
Biological taxonomy, 148
Biomedical communication network of SUNY, 538
Blind cross-reference, 400
  in mechanized processing, 431
BNB (British National Bibliography), 129, 514
Books, names of, 148
Bound association method, 358
Brevity of notation, 278
Briefing of subject experts on thesaurus functions, 336
British National Bibliography, *see SP* BNB
Broad descriptor, connection from specific descriptor, 53

Broad descriptor *(continued)*
  for filing arrangement, 51*, 52, 59, 292
  inverse cross-references to, 205
  for peek-a-boo cards, 55
Broad lead-in terms, 168
Broad subject fields for sorting terms, 385
Broader concepts, as headings, 97
  introducing broader concepts, 95*, 99
  to replace a number of specific concepts, 97
  for searching, 95
Broader Term (BT), *s.a. RT* Hierarchical relationship, 78*, 79
  inclusion in data field BT, 202*, 233
  and classified index, 392
  transfer from sources, 362
BT *see SP* Broader Term

Capitalization (form of term), 318
Card (thesaurus form), *see SP* Index card
Card catalog, 51, 72
  s.a. RT Alphabetical subject catalog
Cascade-type sorting, 385
Catalog, *see NT* Alphabetical subject catalog
  Card catalog
  Subject catalog for manual use
Categories of terms, 94
Census data, *see BT* Collecting data
Central area vs. peripheral areas, 345
Central organization for UST, 520
Chain, hierarchical, *see SP* Hierarchical chain
Chain indexing, 265
Change in instruction, 444
Changes in thesaurus, *see ST* Updating
Changes in information needs, 460
Characteristic, specific (in definitions), 312
Characteristics of subdivision, 91
  s.a. NT Facets
Charts, terminology (EURATOM Thesaurus), 220
Checklist descriptors, 47*, 192, 338, 396
  display, 47, 193*, 263
  selection, 395
Checklist technique of indexing and search request formulation, 43, 45*, 97, 154, 184, 473, 500

Checklist *(continued)*
  ST Filtering technique of indexing, 537
  ET Request-oriented indexing
  cost-benefit considerations, 50
  hierarchy to facilitate, 47, 48, 51, 59, 81
  indexer consistency, 47, 193
  and logical structure of indexing language, 49, 66*
  search request formulation, 49
  tailored to needs of specific institution, 49
Chemical substances, 148, 153
CIINTE (European thesaurus collection center), 529, 535, 558, 568
Citation order, 125, 126, 312
Class inclusion, 99, 112
  automatic detection, 452
Class number, *see ET* Notation
Classification, *ET* Classification scheme
  System vocabulary, 4, 28, 29, 34
  s.a. ET Indexing languages, 4, 29, 34
  s.a. NT Automatic classification
    Coarse classification
    Core classification
    Dewey Decimal classification, *see SP* DDC
    Extended classification
    Library of Congress classification, *see SP* LCC
    Shelf classification
    Special classification
    Standard classification
    Umbrella classification
    Unified classification
    Universal classification
    Universal Decimal Classification, *see SP* UDC
  BT Subject access vocabulary, 35
  of alternatives for decision-making, 8
  definition, Elsinore conference, 34
  enumerative vs. synthetic, 123
  for purposes other than ISAR, 8
  and file organization, 112, 113
  for shelf arrangement
  see ST Shelf classification
  for statistical data, 467
  synthetic vs. enumerative, 123
Classification principles, neutrality of UST, 518
  vs. relational display, 236
Classification scheme, *see ET* Classification
Classificatory structure, 23*, 32, 69*, 110, 390

Classificatory *(continued)*
  changes in lead-in part, 457
  working out, 389*, 394*, 401
  computer assistance, 434
  s.a. RT Automatic classification
Classified arrangement, 125, 237*, 501
  function, rationale
    in cooperation between information services, 501
  for indexing, 59, 184
  for thesaurus construction, 388
  look-up of descriptors, notation, 275
  main part, 183, 194
  omission of parenthetical qualifiers, 302
Classified index, 183, 184*, 194
  ST Schedule, 183
  alternate classified index, 207, 237*
  and cross-references in BT, NT, RT, 392
  design, *see ST* Display
  printing, 412
  in TEST, 196
  typing, 393, 395
  working out, 392, 413
    computer assistance, 441
    discuss with experts, 395
Classified order, *see ST* Classified arrangement
Classified sequence, *see ST* Classified arrangement
Classifying, 43
Clerical staff in thesaurus construction, 12, 328
Clerical tasks, computer assistance, 420*, 435
  speeding up through notation, 275
Clippings, newspaper, *see SP* Newspaper clippings
Clue word, *see ST* Descriptor, 31
Clustering methods for automatic classification, 455*
Co-occurrence data, collection, 341
  use in thesaurus construction, 344
  s.a. RT Co-occurrence patterns
  use in updating, 460
Co-occurrence measures, 451
Co-occurrence patterns, 451
Coarse classification scheme, 102*, 384, 513, 515
  ST Coarse hierarchy
Code, semantic, 28, 531
Code for source identification, 336, 359*
  s.a. RT Source indication

Code for term, machine internal, 275, 276*, 426
Coding, superimposed, 135*, 142
Coined terms, 301, 388
Collateral terms, see ST Coordinate terms
Collecting data (MIS, research, statistics), role of classification, 8, 467, 494
Collecting material for thesaurus building, 355*, 417
   s.a. RT Sources used
   cooperation in, 472
   from subject experts, 334
   for updating, 459
Collection size, 6
Collocation, 59, 312
Combination indexing, 30, 73*
   s.a. RT Combination of concepts
Combination of concepts, s.a. RT Combination of descriptors
   interaction of hierarchy and concept combination, 83
   narrower due to combination, 92*, 116
   search for combination of concepts, 78
   use in constructing hierarchy, 91*, 438*, 439
   use in detecting synonyms, 439
Combination of descriptors, 30, 72, 74 117, 134
   consistency indexer-searcher, 130
   as searching equivalent, 504
Combinatorial indexes as auxiliary ISAR systems, 265
Comments on draft of thesaurus by subject experts, 334
Common attributes, see ST Concepts of general application
Common words, 65
Common working file, 473
Companies, names of, 148
Company, reference storage and retrieval system (example of request-oriented indexing), 46
Comparative research, 143
Comparison, match (function in ISAR system), 19
Comparison of two indexing languages, 502
   concept-by-concept comparison, 502
   local comparison, 503
   structural comparison, 502
Compatibility, 494
   conceptual, 501
   in designation of concepts, 501

Compatibility *(continued)*
   different kinds of file organization, 114, 126
   on a general level, 514
   relation to thesaurus updating, 467
Complex thesaurus structures, 36
Complexity of subject field, 6
Components of search request, 44
Composite word, 74, 207, 405, 428
   ET Composite term
   homonymous, 301
   in a KWIC index, 300
   separation into components by computer, 433
   sequence of components, 308
Compound concept, 34, 74*, 134, 459, 464
   s.a. NT Precombined descriptor
   decomposition, see ST Semantic factoring
   notation, 285
   used only as lead-in terms, 134
   used as precombined descriptor, 132
Computer as retrieval device, 72
Computer assistance in thesaurus construction, 328, 420*
   clerical tasks
      check inverse cross-references, 442
      complete first draft, 442
      merging, 429, 433
      pulling information from big thesaurus, 432
      printing, 443
      recording material, 428
      revising entries in working file, 442
      sorting into alphabetical order, 429
      standardization of spelling variants, 433
      working out detailed structure, 435
   entry points, 421
   intellectual tasks
      s.a. RT Automatic classification
      hierarchy construction, 436, 441
      semantic factoring, 440
      sorting terms into subject fields and subfields, 430
      working out detailed structure, 434, 435, 436
   rationale for, 420
   record organization, 424
   updating, 443
Concept, 17, 26*, 34
   s.a. RT Preferred term
   Descriptor
   s.a. NT Broader concept

Concept *(continued)*
   Compound concept
   Elemental concept
   Equivalent concepts
     see *ET* Equivalent terms
   General concepts
   ISAR concept
   Narrower concept
   Nearly related concepts
     see *ET* Equivalent terms
   Specific concepts
   Widely overlapping concepts
     see *ET* Equivalent terms
   collection of (sources for), 355, 417
   connected empirically, 108
   decomposition, *see ST* Semantic factoring
   definition, 9
     extending the definition, 95
   designation, 20
   of general application, 71, 153*, 205
     selection, 339
   plane of concepts vs. plane of terms, 17*, 34
   similar in meaning, 108
   and terms, 17, 26*
   terms in same concept class, 376, 386
   types, 147
   used very frequently, 344
   used very seldom, 344
Concept combination, *see ET* Combination of concepts
Concept coordination, *see ET* Combination of concepts
Concept formation, 9, 76, 142*, 390
Concept relationships, detection in automatic classification, 451
Conceptual compatibility, 501
Conceptual completeness, 9
Conceptual index, *see ST* Auxiliary ISAR system
Conceptual relationships, 5
Conceptual structure, 4, 7
   s.a. *RT* Classificatory structure
   and file organization, 113
   of indexing languages and thesauri, 15
   reflected in linguistic structure, 440
   representation, 81
   requirements of ISAR system, 3
   role in indexing, 4
   role in retrieval and searching, 4
   and terminological control, 4
Concordance, *see ST* Conversion table

Conference programs as source in thesaurus construction, 356
Conferences, names of, 148
Connected empirically, 108*, 112, 452
   s.a. *RT* Contiguity
Consistency indexer-searcher, 130
Consistency of indexing, 47, 194
Consolidation of equivalent terms, 22, 23*, 24
Consolidation of synonymous terms, 21*, 24
Constituent thesaurus, 511
   parallel development, 385, 512*
Constituent symbols (designation of descriptors), 125
Consultation of subject experts, 12, 326, 403
Content analysis, dictionaries, 8
Content descriptors, 148
Contextual contiguity, *see BT* Contiguity
Contiguity, 108, 112*, 358, 452
   and frequency of combination, 109
   based on definition, 108
   based on empirical knowledge, 109
Continuum, descriptive, 540
Control tape (punched tape typewriter), 418
Control, terminological, *see SP* Terminological control
Controlled vocabulary, *see ET* Terminological control
Conversion from B-descriptors to A subject categories, 515
Conversion from one indexing language to another, 494
Conversion method of indexing, 45
Conversion of punched paper tape to punched cards, 418
Conversion tables, 495
   construction, 102, 510*
   global approach, 513
   local approach, 513
   indexing conversion table, 497
   searching conversion table, 495
Convertibility categories, 503
   indexing convertibility categories, 504
   searching convertibility categories, 503
Cooccurrence, *see SP* Co-occurrence
Cooperation in construction of indexing languages, 326, 472*
   between two (or a few) institutions, 473

Index   615

Cooperation *(continued)*
  in development of terminological and classificatory structure, 473
  generalized cooperation, 473
  in material collection and merging, 472
Cooperation of subject experts, *see ST* Consultation of subject experts
Cooperation through sharing the results of subject indexing, 493
Cooperation in information services, 147, 417, 471*
Coordinate indexing, *see ST* Combination indexing
Coordinate terms, 207
  ST Collateral terms, 207
Coordination, concept, *see ET* Combination of concepts
Core classification, 126*, 264, 416, 439, 440, 464, 514
  s.a. RT Core descriptors
Core descriptors, 120, 123, 126*
  s.a. RT Core classification
Corpus of text, 450
COSATI (Committee for Scientific and Technical Information), 515
COSATI Subject Category List, 515, 531, 539
Cost-benefit considerations, design of indexing language, 61
  request-oriented indexing, 50
Counting methods (counting terms or concepts in text), 341, 450*
Creative thinking in thesaurus construction, 99, 390
  s.a. RT Concept formation
Cross-reference, 180*, 237
  blind, 400, 431
  and classified index, 237, 392*
  given using notations, 433
  vs. instruction, 162
  inverse, 180*
    ST Reciprocal, 180
    to broader descriptor, 205
    check and create, 401, 402
    computer assistance, 442
    printing indicator, 425
    status indicator, 425
  structure, 73
    improvement, 397, 468
    subrecords, 424, 425, 443
  types, *see ET* Data fields

Crude form for keeping track of sources, 350*, 367
Crude form for lead-in, 158*, 196, 209
Cue word, *see ST* Descriptor
  for fully mechanized indexing, 65
Cumulative supplement, 362
Cumulative thesaurus, 335, 473, 485*, 486
  adding an additional thesaurus, 491
  development, 489
  improvement of a thesaurus using a cumulative thesaurus, 491
  keeping track of decisions and dates, 489
  recommended structure, 474*, 486
    ST Guidance structure, 474
  record organization, 486
  source indications, 486
  structure, 486
Curriculum development, ISAR system (example of request-oriented indexing), 47
CWRU/BSC (Case Western Reserve University/Bibliographic Systems Center), 529, 535, 558, 569

Data, *see ET* Collecting data
Data as retrieval objects, 8
Data base of terms, 421, 472*, 485, 517
Data element representation, 19
Data elements in thesaurus record, 174
Data field (in notation), 291
  numerical, 291
  proper name, 292
Data field in thesaurus record, 174
  sequence of data fields, 228
Data recording format, 19
  as ISAR system component, 19
  in thesaurus construction, 174, 428
Date when descriptor was introduced, 352
  keeping track of dates, 352
  in a cumulative thesaurus, 489
  in the user version of the thesaurus, 354
DDC (Dewey Decimal Classification), 129, 211*, 462, 463, 514, 530, 558
  s.a. BT Traditional classification schemes
  relative index, 265, 303*
Decimal classification, *see NT* DDC, UDC
Decision making, classification of alternatives, 8
Decision making in thesaurus updating, 462
  keeping track of decisions on terms, 352*, 354, 489

Decomposition, linguistic, 74
Decomposition of compound concepts into semantic factors, *see ST* Semantic factoring
Deductive principle in developing the classificatory structure, 385
Definition of a concept, 9
  contiguity based on definition, 108
  extending the definition, 95
  focus of definition, 312
  formal definition, 145
  language of definition, 295
  theories of definition and concept combination, 76
  and use as a problem in convertibility, 485
Definitional relationship, 112*, 358, 452
  detection, 453
Deletion of terms or cross-references, 443
  keeping track of deletions, 352
Derivation rules (hierarchical relationships from combination of concepts), 84
Descriptive continuum, 540
Descriptive indexing, relationship to subject indexing, 149
  thesaurus approach, 149
Descriptor 1 (retrieval cue), 26*, 149
Descriptor 2 (subject descriptor), 27*, 31*, 58*
  ST Authorized term, 36
    Clue word, 31
    Cue word, 31
    Index term, 31
    Key word, 31
  s.a. RT Concept, 34
    Preferred term, 31, 34
  s.a. NT Broad descriptor
    Checklist descriptor
    Content descriptor
    Core descriptor
    Elemental descriptor
    Filing descriptor
    Form descriptor
    Indexing descriptor
    Precombined descriptor
    Subject heading
    Tentative descriptor
  arrangement, *which see*
  candidates, *see ET* Selection of descriptors
  combination, 30, 72, 117
    s.a. BT Combination of concepts
    indexer-searcher consistency, 130

Descriptor 2 *(continued)*
  with data field, 291
  designation, 125
  display, *which see*
  "General descriptors" as heading, 103
  "..., general references," 105
  "..., inclusive," 105
  ISAR system for descriptors
    see ST Auxiliary ISAR system, 264
  limited number of, 134
  linear arrangement in classified sequence, 237
  list of
    ST System vocabulary
    see ET Indexing language, 35
  mutual exclusivity, 70
  number of descriptors included in indexing language, 118, 130
  number of descriptors to be used for indexing, 130
  "..., other," 106
  "other descriptors" as heading, 103
  selection, *which see*
  short denotation, 275, 409
  specificity, 61
  types of descriptors, 147
  usage change, 465
  usage depending on hierarchy, 106, 465, 496
Design, typographical, 235
Design criteria for notation, 278
Design of classified index, 235
Design of indexing languages and thesauri, *s.a. RT* Evaluation and testing
  cost-benefit considerations, 61
  disadvantages of shelf classification, 45
  parameters, 5
Design of notation, 277
Designation of actions and processes and results, 305
Designation of chemical substances, 148
Designation of concepts, 20, 125
  compatibility, 235
Detailed form for keeping track of sources, 350*, 367
Detailed lead-in form, 159, 162*, 166, 193
Detailed thesaurus structure,
  construction, 386
  computer assistance, 435, 436
Development rules, 441
Dictionaries, for content analysis, 8

Dictionaries *(continued)*
   for machine translation, 8
   monolingual, bilingual, or multilingual, 8
   multilingual thesaurus as multilingual
      dictionary, 8
   as sources for thesaurus construction, 355
DIN (Deutsche Industrie Norm, German
   industrial standard)
Direct entry, 308, 309*, 406
Direct hierarchical subdivision, 117
Disambiguation of homonyms, 20, 301*,
   306, 366
Display
   ET Representation
   of check list descriptors, 47, 193*, 263
   of descriptors and their interrelation-
      ships, 193, 235*, 237
     hierarchical relationships, 82, 86-89,
       203, 235*
       different kinds, 234
       graphical, including tree, 82, 243*, 292
       through linear sequence with
          cross references, 82, 237*
   on line, 272
   of the thesaurus, 9
Doctrines, names of, 148
Document analysis sheet, 459, 460
Document representation, 19, 53, 114
   vs. filing, *see SP* Filing vs. representation
   indicative vs. informative, 60
   more informative through use of specific
      descriptors, 53*, 292
Document-oriented indexing, disadvantages, 45
   relation to shelf classification, 45
   supplementary, 50
Documents as input for information
   system, 18
Documents as source in thesaurus construction, indexed documents,
   334, 356
   post-research documents, 358
   pre-research documents, 358
Do-it-yourself kit for thesaurus construction, 474
Duplicate, *see ET* Print

Economy measures, ISAR system, 40
Edge-notched cards, as ISAR
   device, 72
   in thesaurus construction, 419

Educational objectives, hierarchy of
   (example of request-oriented
   indexing), 47
EJC thesaurus, 530
Elemental concepts, 34, 74*
   combination of, *see ST* Combination of
      concepts
Documentary language, *see ST* Indexing
   language
Elsinore conference, definition of
   classification, 34
Empirical connectedness of concepts, 108*,
   112, 452
Encyclopedias as source in thesaurus
   construction, 355
Entry for a term, *see ST* Record, 358
Entry (form of term), direct, 308, 309*, 406
   inverted, 208, 308, 312*, 406
Entry for a document, multiple, *see SP*
   Multiple entry
Enumerative vs. synthetic classification
   schemes, 123
Equivalence (comparison of indexing
   languages), 494*, 503*, 508
   s.a. RT Indexing equivalent
      Searching equivalent
Equivalence structure (within one thesaurus),
   Equivalent Terms, 22*, 24, 32, 110,
      112, 166, 232, 388, 452
   ST Equivalent concepts, 22
      Nearly related concepts, 22
      Quasi-synonyms, 22
      Widely overlapping concepts, 22
ERIC (Educational Resources Information
   Center), 8
ERIC Thesaurus, 223
Error detection, notation, 275, 278
EURATOM-thesaurus, 220*, 258, 262, 465
Evaluation and testing of indexing languages
   and thesauri, 9, 10, 411*
   NT Testing a thesaurus
   s.a. RT Design of indexing languages and
      thesauri
   in updating, 458
Events, historical, names of, 148
Excludes (data field), 147
Exclusivity of descriptors, 70
Exhaustivity of indexing, 6, 58, 71, 119
Experts, *see ST* Subject experts
Explicit inclusion of an adjunct
   thesaurus, 484

Explode (inclusive searching), 103, 105
Expressive notation, 278*, 282, 286
Extended classification vs. core classification, 126
Extending the collection of conceptual relations, 417
Extending the definition of concepts, 95
External spelling variants, 172
Extraction and conversion method of indexing, 45
Extraction of indexing languages or thesauri from a source thesaurus, 477
    format for extraction specifications, 478
    general extraction, 479
    specific extraction, 477

Facet analysis, 76, 91*, 144
    faceted array (Thes. of Ed. Terms), 221
    faceted classification, 28, 77, 114, 123*, 125, 128, 129, 130
    facets, 84, 85, 94*
        s.a. BT Characteristics of subdivision
    as primary subdivisions, 236, 385
Factoring, semantic, see SP Semantic factoring
Field 1, see ST Data field
Field 2, see ST Subject field
File, see NT Index file (ISAR system)
    Master file (thesaurus)
    Working file (thesaurus)
File organization, and classification theory (and conceptual structure), 112, 113*, 114
    compatibility of different kinds, 114, 126*
Filing, NT Grouping
    use of broad descriptors, 51*, 52, 59, 292
    vs. representation of documents, 39, 51*, 69*, 73
Filing order of notations, 285
    ST Linear sequence of notations
Filtering technique of indexing, see ST Checklist technique of indexing
Flexibility, of structured indexing languages, 464
    of notation, 278, 465
Flow of work, see SP Work flow
Focus of definition, 312
Foreign languages, 316
Form descriptors, 148
Form of term, check automatically, 442
    grammatical, 304

Form (continued)
    s.a. RT Spelling variants
    indicator, 426
    pointer to other, 425
    rules, 299
    standardize, 400
Format, see SP Thesaurus format
FR (Freiburger Ring fuer kultur- und sozial-wissenschaftliche Entwicklungslaender-Dokumentation)
FR thesaurus (problems of developing countries), 211
Fragments (in concept combination), 69
Free association method, 358
Free terms, 29, 57*, 325, 356
    ST Open-ended terms, 57
Frequency of combination and contiguity, 109
Frequency of components, 132
Frequency of concepts or terms, as aid in descriptor selection, 132, 338, 339, 340, 345*, 460
    in automatic classification, 451
    data collection, 341, 450
Frequency of search requests as parameter for thesaurus size, 6
Fully mechanized indexing, 63, 65
Full-time staff, 10, 326
Functions and structure of a thesaurus in an ISAR system, 3, 17
    hierarchy and classified arrangement, 59, 500
    indexing language, 39

Gaps in notation, distribution, 281
General application, concepts of, see SP Concepts of general application
General concepts, detection through semantic factoring, 77
    for filing arrangement
    see ET Broad descriptors for filing arrangement
"General descriptors" (heading in display of indexing language), 103
General extraction of indexing languages from a source thesaurus, 479
". . . , general references," 105
Generality, choice of the appropriate level (in indexing or search request formulation), 59
Generalization (in concept formation), 140

Generalized cooperation: the concept of a source thesaurus, 473
Generation of hierarchical structures, *see* BT Hierarchy building
Generic posting, 103, 104
Geographical names, 148
Geographical subdivision of the US, 290
Geopolitical names, 542
Global approach to the construction of conversion tables, 513
Global structures of classifications, automatic construction, 455
Glossaries as sources in thesaurus construction, 355
Grammatical form, 304
  s.a. BT Form of term
  s.a. RT Spelling variants
Graphical display of hierarchical relationships, 243
Graph-theoretical methods for automatic classification, 455
Grobklassifizierung, 539
Grouping of documents or substitutes, *see BT* Filing
Guidance devices to facilitate look-up, 209
Guidance structure, *see ST* Recommended structure
Guidelines, *see NT* Thesaurus guidelines

Handbooks as sources in thesaurus construction, 355
Heading, *see NT* Subject heading
Headings, organizational, 97
Helpful arrangement, 239
Hierarchical chains, 203, 233, 234
  hospitality in (notation), 279, 281
Hierarchical index (TEST thesaurus), 196
Hierarchical relationships, 78*
  s.a. RT Broader term
  vs. associative relationships, role in indexing and searching, 98
  detection, *see RT* Hierarchy building
  different kinds, 99*, 112, 452
  display, *which see*
Hierarchical subdivision, direct, 117
Hierarchy, 78*
  s.a. NT Monohierarchy
    Polyhierarchy
  Strong hierarchy, *see ST* Monohierarchy
  Weak hierarchy, *see ST* Polyhierarchy
  s.a. RT Hierarchical relationships

Hierarchy *(continued)*
  building, 80*, 91, 95
  ST Hierarchy construction
  NT Generation of hierarchical structures
    automatic classification, 454, 455
    computer assistance, 436, 438, 493
    use of combinations of concepts, 83*, 438, 493
    limitations of model, 93
  and checklist technique of indexing, 47*, 51, 81
  changes in, 458, 465
  coarse, 102
  and descriptor usage, 106, 465, 496
  functions, 59, 500
  logical completeness, 133
  role in thesaurus construction, 388
    detection of synonyms, 388
    selection of descriptors, 396
Historical events, names of, 148
Homographs, *see ET* Homonyms
Homonyms, 20*, 362, 384, 493
  ET Homographs, 20
  artificial, 303
  check through alphabetical index, 408
  detection through inconsistent association profiles, 453
  disambiguation through parenthetical qualifiers, 20, 301*, 366
  as lead-in terms, 168
  lonely, 301
  in mechanized indexing, 65
  multiword or composite homonyms, 301
  preferred term—avoid homonyms, 301
Hospitality of notation, 278
  in chain, 279, 281
Human groups, names of, 148

IBM MT Selectric, 447
IBM 47 punched tape to card converter, 480
IBM 870 document writing system, 419
Identical terms, merge information, 367
Identification symbols or numbers, 542
Identification codes for sources, 359
Identifiers, 151, 152
Implicit inclusion of an adjunct thesaurus, 484
Inclusion, class inclusion, 99, 112
  inclusion, adjunct thesaurus, explicit, 484
  topic inclusion, 99, 112
". . . inclusive" descriptors, 105

Inclusive search, 59, 78, 103*, 276, 279
Inconsistent association profiles, use for detecting homonyms, 453
Incorporating standard classification, notation, 289
Independent elements, 125
Independent symbols for concepts, 125
Index, *see NT* Alphabetical index
   Classified index
   Conceptual index
   see ST Auxiliary ISAR system
   Combinatorial index
   Hierarchical index (TEST)
   KWIC index
   KWOC index
   Printed index
   Relative index (DDC)
   SLIC index
   Subject category index (TEST)
   Subject index
Index cards for terms, 347*, 359
   s.a. RT Record
Index files as ISAR system component, 19
Index term, *see ST* Descriptor
Indexed documents as source in thesaurus construction, 334, 355
   s.a. RT Free term indexing
Indexer consistency and checklist technique, 47
Indexer-searcher consistency, 130
Indexes of handbooks, journals, abstracting journals, and textbooks as source in thesaurus construction, 355
Indexing (manual subject indexing unless stated otherwise), *ET* Search request formulation
   s.a. NT Descriptive indexing
   Document-oriented indexing
   Exhaustivity of indexing
   Experimental indexing
   Extraction-and-conversion method of indexing
   Free term indexing
   Mechanized indexing
   Shared subject indexing
   Request-oriented indexing
     see ET Checklist technique of indexing
   Specificity of indexing
s.a. RT Document representation
biased by anticipated search requests, 50
day-to-day, 62

Indexing *(continued)*
   disadvantages shelf classification, 45
   vs. filing of documents
     see ST Filing vs. representation of documents
   as ISAR system operation (descriptive and subject), 3, 19
   lead-in structure in indexing, 29, 62*, 63, 161, 497
   relation to descriptive indexing, 149
   role of associative relationships, 98
   role of hierarchical relationships, 98
   role of conceptual structure, 66
   s.a. RT Checklist technique of indexing rules, 19, 500
Indexing conversion table, 497
Indexing conversion vs. searching conversion, 494
Indexing convertibility categories, 504
Indexing descriptor, 52
Indexing equivalent, 497, 508
Indexing experiments for testing thesaurus, 411
Indexing language, 19, 26*, 32
   ST Documentary language, 27
   ET Classification scheme, 29, 34
   Descriptor list, 35
   System vocabulary, 29, 34
   s.a. RT Thesaurus, 35
   Subject access vocabulary, 35
   NT Subject heading list, 35
   adaptation to needs of specific institution, 49
   changes in, 457
   conceptual structure, 15, 69*
   design, 61
   disadvantages shelf classification, 45
   extraction from source thesaurus, 477
   flexibility, 464
   functions, 17, 39
   as ISAR system component, 19
   optimization, 134
   number of descriptors contained, 118
   structure, 39, 44, 69*, 112
   updating, 457
Indicative vs. informative representation of documents, 60
Inductive principle in thesaurus construction, 385
Information needs, 18
   ST User needs

Information needs *(continued)*
    changes, 460
    of specific institutions and request-
        oriented indexing, 49, 499, 500
    as source in thesaurus construction, 356
Information services, cooperative, 147,
        349, 471*
    thesauri as basis for, 471
Information scientists/librarians (staff for
        thesaurus construction), 12, 328
Information storage and retrieval system,
        see SP ISAR system
Information system, structure, 18
Informative representation of documents, 60
Infrequent concepts, 344
Input of thesaurus data, *see ST* Recording
Institutions, names of, 148
Instruction, change in, 444
Instruction vs. cross-reference, 162
    s.a. NT POST TO instruction
        USE instruction
        SEE instruction
Instruction or statement indicator, 426
Instructional scope note, 109
Integrative levels, 240
Intellectual decisions recorded in
        thesaurus, 62
Interaction of hierarchy and concept
        combination, 83
Interactive updating of thesauri, 463
Intercalating new serial numbers, 282
Intercultural research and concept
        formation, 143
Interdisciplinary approach, 336, 395
Interdisciplinary research and concept
        formation, 143
Interest profile, *s.a. RT* Search request
        formulation, 19
    as sources in thesaurus construction, 355
    statement, 18, 19
Interlingual thesauri, 296
Intermediate form for lead-in, 218
Internal code for a term or descriptor,
        275, 426
Internal spelling variants, 172
International standard industrial
        classification (ISIC), 290
Inverse cross-reference, 180
    ST Reciprocal cross-reference, 180
        Tracing, 180
    to broad descriptors, 205

Inverse *(continued)*
    check, 402
    by computer, 442
    create, 401
Inverted entry, 208, 308, 312, 406
    ST Inverted form of term
Inverted form of term, *see ST*
        Inverted entry
ISAR system, 3
    SP Information storage and retrieval
        system, 3
    s.a. NT Auxiliary ISAR system
        Mechanized ISAR system
    for curriculum development (example of
        request-oriented indexing), 47
    for descriptors, *see ST* Auxiliary ISAR
        system
    requirements for conceptual structure, 3
    structure, 19
Isolates, common, *see ST* Descriptors of
        general application

Jargon, 542
Journal indexes as sources in thesaurus
        construction, 355
Judgment and creative thinking in
        thesaurus construction, 390
Justifying the development of a new
        thesaurus, 10

Keeping track of decisions and dates, 352
    in a cumulative thesaurus, 489
    of decisions still to be made, 354
    of deletions, 352
    of reasons for decisions, 354
Keeping track of the sources used, 350*, 367
Keypunch and unit-record equipment, 419
Keyword, *see ST* Descriptor
KWIC index, 197, 209*, 211, 265, 362,
        390, 404*
    ET KWOC index
    s.a. BT Alphabetical index
    composite words, 300
    production, 404
    paper tape to card conversion for input
        of data, 418
KWOC index, *see ET* KWIC index

Labels for data fields, 174
Language, foreign, 316
Language of definition (for scope notes), 295

Language of document as form
 descriptor, 148
Language symbol, 316
LCC (Library of Congress Classification),
 123, 125, 211*, 265, 355, 462,
 463, 514
 s.a. BT Traditional classification schemes
 notation, 279
 reclassification from DDC, 513, 514
LCSH (Library of Congress Subject
 Headings), 114, 223*, 441, 530, 544
 s.a. BT Subject headings
Lead-in form, 158
 crude lead-in form, 158*, 196, 209
 detailed lead-in form, 158, 162*, 193, 212
 intermediate lead-in form, 165*, 218
 other lead-in forms, 165
Lead-in method, 156
 alphabetical, 156*, 211
 main part, 156*, 193, 196, 212
Lead-in structure, 130, 155*, 184, 497
 s.a. RT terminological control, 36
 changes in, 457
 use in indexing and searching, 29, 36, 62,
  63, 66, 161, 497
Lead-in term, *ST* Nondescriptor
 broad, 168
 homonymous, 168
 notation, 288
Lead-in vocabulary, 19, 29, 30, 32, 35,
 38, 61
Leads to related terms, 169
Legislation, names of specific, 148
Length of terms, 316
Letter-by-letter alphabetization, 320
Level of generality, choice of appropriate
 in indexing, 59
Level of precombination, 130
Level of treatment as form descriptor, 148
Levels, integrative, 240
Lexicographers as sources in thesaurus
 construction, 352
Lexicon 1 (encyclopedia) as source for
 thesaurus construction, 355
Lexicon 2, *see ST* System vocabulary, 28
Librarians and information scientists, staff
 for thesaurus construction, 12, 328
Library of Congress Classification, *see SP*
 LCC
Library of Congress Subject Headings,
 see SP LCSH

Limited number of descriptors, 134
Line-oriented input of updating
 information, 445
Linear sequence of notations, *see ST*
 Filing order of notations
Linear arrangement of descriptors in classi-
 fied sequence with cross-references,
 86, 237*
 s.a. BT Display
Linguistic decomposition, 74
 and conceptual structure, 74, 440
Links, *see BT* Syntactical devices
Local approach and global approach to the
 construction of conversion tables, 513
Local comparison of indexing languages, 503
Logical completeness of hierarchy, 133
Logical structure as descriptor selection
 criterion, 339
Logical structure and request-oriented
 indexing, 66
Lonely homonym, 301
Look-up problem, 198
 in descriptor lists arranged in classified
  sequence, 275
 guidance devices to facilitate look-up, 209
 in the Roget-Soergel model, 199
 role of notation, 202, 275
 in the TEST model, 200

Machine internal code for terms or
 descriptors, 275, 276
Machine translation, dictionaries for, 8
Machine-readable typescript, 447
Magnetic tape cassettes, 447
Main classes, *see ET* Main fields
Main fields
 ET Main classes
 summary, 193
Main heading, 126
Main part method for lead-in, 156*, 193,
 196, 212
Main part of the thesaurus, 194*
 arrangement of entries, 198
 classified, 183
 duplication or printing, 410, 412, 415
 format of entries, 228
 inclusion of spelling variants, 202
 production, 397
 in TEST model, 406
Main subject or theme of the document, 56
Main Term (MT), 400

Index 623

Maintenance, *see ST* Updating
Man-machine cooperation, 421
Management information system (MIS), 8
Manual procedures for transferring terms, 365
Manual production of the alphabetical index, 406
Master file of the thesaurus, 349
Match and merge procedures, *see ST* Pulling
Match document representations with search request formulations, 19
Material collection, 355
　cooperation, 472
　from subject experts, 334
Meaning, similarity, 108, 112, 452
Measures for term or concept association, 451
Mechanical devices available in the ISAR system, 130
Mechanized auxiliary ISAR system, 265
Mechanized indexing and search request formulation, 63, 265
　collecting updating information, 460
　cue-words, 65
　fully mechanized, 63
　homonyms in mechanized indexing, 65, 301
　semi-mechanized, 63
Mechanized ISAR system, 56, 57
　change to, 53
　and printed index, 8
　spelling variants, 173
Mechanized searching, importance of thesaurus, 5
Medical Subject Headings (MeSH), 216
MEDLARS, MEDLINE, 8, 538
Merging information from different records, 367
　s.a. NT Pulling
　cooperation, 472
　first round: identical terms, 367
　　by computer, 429
　procedure for keeping track of sources, 350*, 367
　second round: synonymous terms, 376
　　by computer, 433
　while working out the detailed structure: synonymous and equivalent terms, 388
　computer assistance, 436
MeSH, *see SP* Medical Subject Headings
Military nomenclature, 148

MIRACODE, 277
MIS, *see SP* Management information system
Mixed notation, 282
　small indexing languages, 282
　large indexing languages, 283
Mixed super-imposed coding, 142
Moderately precombined descriptors, 117
Modern technical devices in ISAR system, 72
Modification of data base, 421
Monohierarchical structure for linear arrangement, 237*, 518
　computer assistance, 438
Monohierarchy, 43, 45, 70*, 71, 80
　ST Strong hierarchy, 81
　s.a. BT hierarchy
Morphological variants of terms, *see ET* Spelling variants
Multi-purpose systems, 58
Multi-word term, in alphabetical index, 195, 207
　automatic classification, 452
　and conceptual structure, 74
　homonymous, 30
　mechanized indexing, 64
　sequence of words, 308
Multilateral shared subject indexing, 501
Multilingual thesaurus, 293*, 404, 518
　as multilingual dictionary, 8
Multiple entry, 43, 69
　ET Single entry
　vs. entry under a precombined descriptor, 116, 117, 128
　faceted classification, 129
Mutual exclusivity of descriptors, 70

Names, 148
Narrower due to combination, 92, 116
Narrower due to substitution, 92, 116
Narrower term (NT), 79
NASA, 8, 531
Nationalities, names of, 148
Nearly related concepts, *see ET* Equivalent Terms
Nearness measures, 451
Negation as a retrieval operation, 140
Negative selection of terms, 362
Newspaper clippings, 51, 276
Nicknames, 542
Nomenclature, 148*, 152, 355
　as adjunct thesaurus, 152

Nomenclature *(continued)*
  biological, 153
  military, 148
Nondescriptor, *see ST* Lead-in term
Notation, *ET* Class number, 27, 34, 273*
  alternate, 207, 237*
  assigning, 397, 414
  auxiliary, 360
  changes, 275
  for compound concepts, 285
  expressive, 278, 286
  with data field, 291
    numerical, 291
    proper name, 292
  design, 277
  filing order, 285
  flexibility, 275, 277, 465
  incorporating standard classification, 289
  and machine internal code, 276
  in machine record, 426
  mixed, 282
  necessity of, 202
  ordinal, 280
  overstressing notation, 277
  for precombined descriptors, 286
  for preferred lead-in terms, 288
  purpose, 275
  shorthand for descriptors, 409
    in type-1 systems, 298
    in cross-references, 433
    in source indications, 350
  types of, 278
  use in working out the detailed structure, 389
Note *see NT* Scope note
Number, class, *see ET* Notation, 34
Number of descriptors contained in indexing language, 118
  limitation, 134, 137
Number of descriptors to be used for indexing, 130
Numbers, intercalating, 282
Numerals as components of terms, 313
Numerical data field in the notation, 291

Octavizing device, 279
On-line display of thesauri, 272
On-line input of thesaurus data, 447
Open stacks, 51
Open-ended sources, 355, 357, 390
  preparation, 360

Open-ended *(continued)*
  pre-processing, 362
  relationships among terms from open-ended sources, 364
Open-ended terms, *see ST* Free terms
Optimization of an indexing language, 134
OR-combination of descriptors as semantic factor, 170
OR-type use instructions, 167
Order, *see NT* Alphabetical order
  Citation order
  Classified order
  Filing order
Ordinal notation, 280, 282
Organization, *see NT* file organization
  Record organization
Organizational headings, 97
Organizational problems of thesaurus construction and maintenance, 10*, 462, 520
  ET Administrative problems
Organizations, names of, 148
Over-all structure of the hierarchy, 396
Overlapping concepts, *see ET* Equivalent terms, 22
Overstressing notation, 277

Panels of subject experts, 327
  source codes, 336
Paper tape, *see SP* Punched paper tape
Para-professionals, staff needed for thesaurus construction, 12, 328
Parallel development of constituent thesauri, 385, 512
Parameters determining thesaurus size, 6
Parenthetical qualifier for the disambiguation of homonyms, 20, 301*, 302, 306
Part-whole relationship, 99, 101*, 112, 452
Parts of thesaurus, 183
  in the Roget-Soergel model, 193
  in TEST, 196
Parts of speech, 303
Peek-a-boo cards, 72
Performance of the ISAR system, *see RT* Evaluation and testing
Peripheral areas versus central area, 345
Persons, names of, 148
Pictures in scope notes, 147
Pigeonholing, 45, 73
Plane of concepts vs. plane of terms, 17*, 34
Plural, *see BT* Singular vs. plural

Plural only terms *(Pluralia tantum)*, 307
Pointer (computer record)
  to other form of term, 425
  to remainder of text, 426
Polyhierarchy, 78*, 80, 81
  ST Weak hierarchy, 81
  s.a. BT Hierarchy
  and checklist technique of indexing, 48
Polysemous terms, 21
Positive selection of terms, 361
POST TO instruction, 103
Post-combination vs. pre-combination, 6, 115*, 124, 130
Post-coordination, *see ST* Post-combination, 115
Post-research documents, 358
Posting, generic, 103, 104
Pre-combination, *see ET* Post-combination
Pre-combined descriptors, 74*, 116, 117, 131*, 132, 134
  vs. multiple entry, 128
  notation, 286
Pre-coordination, *see ET* Post-combination
Pre-processing of open-ended sources, 362
Pre-research documents, 358
Prearranged sources, 355, 357
  preparation, 359
PRECIS, 129, 465, 514
Precise formulation of terms, 300
Precise searching equivalent, 495
Precision of search results, 6
  s.a. RT Evaluation and testing
Preferred monohierarchical structure and cross-references, 237
Preferred term, 23*, 32, 487
  s.a. RT Concept, 34
  Descriptor, 31, 34
  ISAR concept, 23
  notation for preferred lead-in terms, 288
  selection, *which see*
Print user version of thesaurus, 412
  by computer, 443
Printed index, improvement through thesaurus, 8, 31
  and mechanized ISAR system, 8
Printing indicator for cross-references, 425
Processes, designation, 305
Profile, *see NT* Association profile
  Interest profile
Projects, names of, as descriptors, 148

Proofreading, 413
Proper names, 148
  data field in notation, 292
  form of term, 316
  as subject descriptors, 151
Proposals as sources in thesaurus construction, 358
Psychological dimensions of relationships, 112
Public relations as information system operation, 18
Pulling information from additional sources (match and merge), 368, 374*
  computer assistance, 432, 491
Punched cards, 419*, 447
Punched paper tape, 417*, 447
Punctuation (form of terms), 317
Purposes of a thesaurus, 8

Qualified use instructions, 17*, 473
Qualifier, parenthetical, *see SP* Parenthetical qualifier
Quasi-synonyms, *see ST* Equivalent terms
Query-and-reply slip, 335, 354

Random superimposed coding, 135, 136
Range of the thesaurus, 226
Rank of descriptor in frequency list as selection criterion, 343
Re-indexing, *ST* Reclassification
  due to changes in descriptor usage, 465
  due to introduction of new descriptors, 465
  from DDC to LCC, 558
Rearrangement of a file, use of specific descriptors, 53
Reasons for decisions, keeping track of, 354
Recall and precision of search results, 6
  s.a. RT Evaluation and testing
Reciprocal cross-reference, *see ST* Inverst cross-reference
Reclassification, *see ST* Re-indexing
Recommended structure, 474, 485
  ST Guidance structure, 474
  indicator in a cumulative thes., 425, 486
Record, 228, 345, 358
  ST Entry, 359
  ET Card, 359
  s.a. RT Thesaurus form
  deletion, 444
  identification, 434

Record *(continued)*
  insertion, 444
  organization in the computer, 424
  for a cumulative thesaurus, 486
  updating record, 446
Recording of material from sources, 355
  ST Input of thesaurus data
  computer assistance, 428, 447
  s.a. RT Updating, computer assistance
Redundancy for purposes of error detection in a notation, 278
Reference to definitions, 349
Referral of search requests, 471, 493
Related concepts, nearly, *see ET* Equivalent Terms
Related items in files, collocation of, 59
Related Terms (RT), 107*, 112, 234, 362
  entering from sources, 364
  leads to, 169
Relational displays vs. classification principles, 236
Relational indicators, *see BT* Syntactical devices
Relationships, *s.a. NT* Associative relationships
  Class inclusion relationships
  Conceptual relationships
  Contextual contiguity relationships
  Definitional relationships
  Hierarchical relationships
  Part-whole relationships
  Relevance relationships
  Syntactical relationships
  see RT Syntactical devices
  Topic inclusion relationships
  additional relationship indicator, 425
  analysis of, *see ST* Detection of
  change in relationship type, 444
  collection of, 355, 417, 458
    from open-ended sources, 364
    from search requests, 364
  detection of, 77
    automatic classification, 451
  display, 193
  kinds of, 99
  psychological dimensions of, 112
  summary, 174
Relators, *see BT* Syntactical devices
Relevance coefficient, 37
Relevance relationship, 37
Remainder of text, pointer to, 426

Replacement of one subrecord (in updating), 444
Representation of documents, *see SP* Document representation
Representation of relationships, *see ET* Display
Request, *see ST* Search request
Request-oriented indexing, *see ET* Checklist technique of indexing
Research, collecting data, 8
  comparative research, 143
Research projects as source in thesaurus construction, 356
Resources and work required for thesaurus construction, 10
Results of actions and processes, designation, 305
Retrieval, *see ET* Search, searching
Retrieval cue, *see ST* Descriptor
Retrieval experiments for testing the thesaurus, 411
Retrieval objects, 3, 6
Retrieval problem, solutions, 39
Retrieval system, *see ST* ISAR system
Retrieval techniques and devices, 6
Retrospective searching, 40
Review of the whole thesaurus, 403
  discussion sessions, 335
Reviews of documents as source in thesaurus construction, 356
Revised versions of the thesaurus, 461
Revising entries in the working file, 398
  computer assistance, 442
Revision of the indexing language or thesaurus, 463
Roget-Soergel model of thesaurus format, 184, 193
  look-up, 199
  parts of thesaurus, 193
Roget's thesaurus, 183
Role indicators, *see BT* Syntactical devices
Routine operations, *see ST* clerical tasks
RT, *see SP* Related Term
Rules of the game as ISAR system component, 19

Scanning, sequential, 42
Schedule, *see ST* Classified index
Schedule for updating, 461
Scheme, *see NT* Classification

Scheme *(continued)*
  Subsumption scheme
Science Information Exchange (SSIE), 543
Scope and complexity of subject fields, 6
Scope note, 146*, 391, 500
  instructional, 109
  pictures in, 147
Scope of cooperation, 517
SDI (Selective dissemination of information), 4, 40, 41, 59, 471, 494
Search request, analysis sheet, 49, 459, 460
  components of, 44
  for detecting relationships, 364
  formulation, *see ET* Indexing
  frequency, 6
  previous, 338
  referral, 471, 493
  as source in thesaurus construction, 334, 335
  statement, 18, 19, 458
Search, searching, *ET* Retrieval
  additional broader concepts for, 95
  associative relationships, use of, 98
  for any combination of elemental concepts, 78
  frequency of a descriptor in, 132
  hierarchical relationships, role of, 98
  inclusive, 59, 78, 103*, 276, 279
  mechanized, importance of thesaurus, 5
  performance, *see ST* Performance of ISAR system
  retrospective, 40
  role of conceptual structure, 4
  steps involved, 121
Searching conversion, 494
Searching conversion table, 495
Searching equivalent, 495, 503
Second round of merging, 376
  computer assistance, 433
  editing, 380
Second-order association, 453
SEE instruction, 155
Select descriptors for indexing, 192
Selection of descriptors, etc.,
  descriptors, 474
    ET Descriptor candidates
    criteria, 131, 338*
      frequency criterion, 340, 343
      frequency patterns, 451
      principle in typology of indexing languages, 122, 123
    process, 123, 391, 395*, 474

Selection *(continued)*
  negative selection, 362
  positive selection, 361
  preferred terms
    criteria, 337
      avoid homonyms, 301
    process, 388
Selection of sources, 355, 356
Selective dissemination of information, *see SP* SDI
Semantic Code, 128, 531
Semantic factoring, semantic factors, 74*
  ST Decomposition of concepts
  s.a. RT Combination of concepts
  advantages, 77
  applications, 112, 129
  and concept formation, 143
  OR-combination of descriptors as semantic factor, 170
  process, 389
    computer assistance, 440
    questions useful for, 76
Semi-mechanized indexing, 83*, 497
Semi-universal indexing languages, 519
Separation of composite words into their components, computer assistance, 433
Sequence, *see NT* Alphabetical sequence
  Classified sequence
  s.a. RT Arrangement
  of data fields in the thesaurus form, 228*, 348
  of descriptors on the same level, 239
  of words in multiword or composite terms, 308
Sequential scanning, 142
Shared subject indexing, 54, 59, 493*, 519
  on a general level, 471, 494, 514*
  multilateral, 501
  on a specific level, 471, 494*
Shelf classification, 43
  disadvantages, 45, 70
  document-oriented indexing, 45
Short denotation of descriptors through notation, 75
Significant word, entry for multiword term, 195
Similarity in meaning, 108*, 112, 452
Simple thesaurus structure, 37
Simplicity of notation, 278
Single entry, *see ET* Multiple entry
Singular vs. plural, 306, 308
Singular only terms, 307

628 Index

Size of the collection, 6
Size of the thesaurus form, 348
Size of thesaurus, parameters, 6
SLIC Index, 265
Small projects in thesaurus development,
 specific procedures, 398, 410, 415
Smithsonian Science Information Exchange
 (SSIE), 543
SN, see SP Scope note, 354
Sorting terms, into alphabetical order, 366
 computer assistance, 429
 into broad subject fields and subfields,
  385, 386
 computer assistance, 435, 439
 cascade-type sorting, 385
Source codes, 359
 for subject experts and panels, 336
Source indication, 349*, 365
 in computer records, 425
 in cumulative thesaurus, 486
 in updating, 443
Source thesaurus, 473*, 477, 485
 universal source thesaurus (UST), 516
Sources used in thesaurus construction, 349*
 s.a. NT Open-ended sources
  Pre-arranged sources
 experts and lexicographers as sources, 352
 keeping track of the sources, 350*, 367
 list of sources used, 227
 preparation, 359
 selection, 355, 356
 sources for definitions, 338
 transfer from sources, 350
 for updating information, see SP
  Updating, sources
Special classification, as source in thesaurus
 construction, 355
 extracted from a source thesaurus, 477
Species, designations of, 148
Specific characteristic or difference, 312
Specific concepts, in document representation, 52, 292
 introduction of specific concepts, 391
 replaced by one broader concept, 97
Specific descriptor, connection to broad
 descriptor, 53
Specific extraction of indexing language
 from a source thesaurus, 477
Specific indexing—more general filing,
 see ST Filing vs. representation of
 documents

Specificity of indexing, 6, 58
Specificity of the descriptors, 61
Spelling and transliteration, 317
Spelling variants, 64, 172*, 195, 197,
 207, 300, 341, 366, 381
 ET Morphological variants
 in a cumulative thesaurus, 488
 external, 172
 internal, 172
 in the main part, 202
 standardization by computer, 433
Staff needed in thesaurus development,
 10, 326
Standard, terminological, 8
Standard classification, incorporation, 289
Standard geographical subdivision of the
 U.S., 290
Standard subheadings, 154
Standardize form of terms, 400
 computer assistance, 433
Standardized abbreviations, 315, 398
State-of-the-art report as a source of
 updating information, 460
Statistical analysis of vocabulary usage, 555
Statistical data, see BT Collecting data
Statistical methods in the construction of
 indexing languages, see ET Automatic
 classification
Statistical patterns of occurrence and
 co-occurrence of terms, 449
Stems, 433
Stop-words, 65
String of constituent symbols, 125
String of notational symbols, 265
String of terms, 265, 313, 366, 380
Strong coordination between information
 centers, 511
Strong hierarchy, see ST Monohierarchy
Structural comparison of indexing
 languages, 502
Structure, see NT Classificatory structure
 Conceptual structure
 Detailed structure
 Equivalence structure
 Global structure
 Hierarchical structure
 Lead-in structure
 Local structure
 Logical structure
 Monohierarchical structure
 Recommended structure

Structure *(continued)*
   Synonym-homonym structure
   cumulative thesaurus, 486
   indexing language, 15, 69*
   and flexibility, 464
   information system, 18
   ISAR system, 19
   source thesaurus, 475
   thesaurus, 39, 68*
     working out, 384*, 413
       computer assistance, 434, 438
     universal source thesaurus, 516
Subdivision, characteristics of, 91
Subfield, *see BT* Subject field
Subheadings, 126, 154
Subject access vocabulary, *see NT* Classification scheme
   Indexing language
   Thesaurus
Subject authority list (API), 221
Subject catalogs for manual use, 51
Subject category index (TEST), 196
Subject category list (COSATI), 531, 539
Subject descriptor, *see ST* descriptor
Subject experts, briefing on thesaurus functions, 336
   consultation with, 12, 326*, 334, 336, 395, 403
   material collection from, 334
   as sources in thesaurus construction, 336, 352, 356
   source codes, 336
Subject field, 93, 385
   scope and complexity, 6
   sorting terms into subject fields and subfields, 385, 386
   computer assistance, 435, 439
   subdivision into subject fields and checklist technique of indexing, 47
Subject heading, 31, 123, 125, 126
   s.a. BT Descriptor
   main heading and subheading, 126
Subject heading catalog, *see ST* Alphabetical subject catalog
Subject heading list, 35
   s.a. BT indexing language
   s.a. NT LCSH
   processing by computer, 441
Subject indexing, *see BT* Indexing
Subject-oriented arrangement vs. faceted arrangement, 236

Subrecord, 424
   cross reference subrecord, 424, 425
   deletion, 444
   insertion, 444
   leading, 424
   replacement, 444
Substances, chemical, 153
Substances, designation of, 148
Substitution, narrower due to substitution, 92, 116
Subsumption scheme, 539*, 558
Summary of the main fields, 193, 341*
   ST Overview, 193
   Synopsis, 193
SUNY biomedical communication network, 538
Superimposed coding, 135
Supplementary document-oriented indexing, 50
Supplements to the thesaurus, 461
   cumulative, 462
   physical form, 462
Switching language, 501
Symbols, 20
Synonym-homonym structure, 17*, 32, 110
   changes in, 457
   development of, 384, 388
Synonyms, 17*, 20, 24, 110, 112, 171, 232
   artificial, 381
   detection of, through concept combinations, 439, 493
     through hierarchy, 388
     automatic classification, 452
   merging information on synonyms, *see* Merging
   string of synonyms, *see* String of terms
Syntactic information, for analysis of composite terms by computer, 441
   for mechanized indexing, 65
Syntactical devices in the indexing language, 28, 77, 118, 130, 131, 132, 155
   NT Links
   Relational indicators
   Relators
   Role indicators
   expression in notation, 289
Syntactical relationship of components, 132
Synthetic classification schemes, 123
System vocabulary, 4, 28, 29, 34*
   ST Lexicon, 28
   List of descriptors, 28

System vocabulary *(continued)*
  ET Classification scheme, 34
  see *ET* Indexing language, 34

Table of contents of textbooks as sources in thesaurus construction, 355
Taxonomy, biological, 148
TDCK, 531
Tentative descriptors, 462, 465
Term, *see NT* Authorized term
  Broader Term
  Composite term
  Coordinate term
  Equivalent term
  Free term
  Index term
  Lead-in term
  Multi-word term
  Narrower Term
  Preferred term
  Quasi-synonymous Term
  Related Term
  Synonymous Term
  s.a. RT Concept, 17, 26
  Descriptor
  coined term, 301, 388
  collection of terms, 355
  form of term, *which see*
  formulating terms more precisely, 300
  plane of terms, 17, 34
  string of terms, 265, 313, 366, 380
Term association, *see SP* Association
Termatrex cards (peek-a-boo), frequency count, 341
Terminological completeness, 9
Terminological control, 4*, 23, 24, 27, 29, 34, 36, 39, 66
  s.a. RT Lead-in structure, 36
  ST vocabulary control, 36
  in searching, 36, 66
  in writing abstracts, 60
Terminological treatises as sources in thesaurus construction, 355
Terminology charts (EURATOM thesaurus), 220
Terminology, problems, 20
TEST (Thesaurus of Engineering and Scientific Terms)
TEST model, TEST thesaurus, 196*, 531
  classified index, 196
  look-up, 200

TEST *(continued)*
  main part entry, 231
    alphabetical main part, production, 406
  parts of TEST, 196
  variations, 202
Testing a thesaurus, *see BT* Evaluation and testing of a thesaurus
Text, actual text of terms, 426
  corpus of text, 450
  units of text, 450
Text editing procedure, 435
Textbooks as sources in thesaurus construction, 355
Thesaurofacet, 212*, 544
Thesaurus, 32, 38*
  ET Authority list
  s.a. NT Adjunct thesaurus
    Constituent thesaurus
    Cumulative thesaurus
    Interlingual thesaurus
    Multi-lingual thesaurus
    Source thesaurus
    Total thesaurus
    Umbrella thesaurus
    Universal source thesaurus
  BT Subject access vocabulary, 35
  complex thesaurus structures, 36*
  functions in an ISAR system, 3, 17*
  functions other than ISAR, 8
  mechanized searching, importance, 5
  simple thesaurus, 29*, 37
  size, 8
  as store of intellectual decisions, 62
Thesaurus approach to descriptive indexing, 149
Thesaurus collection center, 10, 520, 529
Thesaurus form, 345*, 359
  punched cards used as thesaurus forms, 419
  sequence of data fields, 348
  size, 348
  use in updating, 460
Thesaurus format, 183
Thesaurus guidelines, 523
Thesaurus of Education Terms, 221
Thesaurus of terms (main part) (TEST), 197
Time, UDC method of handling, 219
Time available to do a search, 6
Time schedule for updating, 461
Titles of documents as source in thesaurus construction, 356
Topic inclusion, 99, 112, 342

Index 631

Total count, 450
Total thesaurus, 511
  alphabetical index, 512
  development through parallel development of constituent thesauri, 512
Tracing, see ST Inverse cross-reference
Trade names, 148
Trademarks, 316
Traditional classification schemes such as LCC, DDC, or UDC, 34, 35, 63, 71, 73, 83, 114, 129, 211, 265, 303, 355, 462, 464, 513, 514, 530, 539, 558
Transfer of terms to cards (thesaurus forms), see BT Recording of material from sources
Translation, dictionaries for machine translation, 8
  translation of thesaurus, 296
Transliteration, 317
Treaties, names of, 148
Treatises on terminology as source in thesaurus construction, 355
Tree display of hierarchical relationships, 82, 243*
Type 1 (lead-in only) multilingual thesaurus, 293*, 294
Type 1 systems using notational symbols in the document representations, 193, 298*, 306, 309, 317
  alphabetical index, 404
Type 2 multilingual thesaurus, 293*, 294, 295
Type 2 systems using terms in the document representations, 298*, 307, 309
Typists as staff for thesaurus construction, 12, 326
Typographical design of entries, 235
Typology of concepts, descriptors, terms, 148

UDC (Universal Decimal Classification), 211*, 277, 462, 463, 516, 530, 539
  s.a. BT Traditional classification schemes
UDC method of handling time (modified), 292
Umbrella classification, 385, 475, 511*, 512, 513, 515, 518
  ET Umbrella thesaurus
Unified classification scheme for different types of file organization, 126
Uniterms, 76
Unit record equipment, 419

Units of text, 450
Unitwise count, 450
Universal classification, 128, 355, 516
Universal Source Thesaurus (UST), 516*
  as framework for semi-universal indexing languages, 519
  structure, 517
Unspecified relationship (data field UN), 364, 380, 390, 401
Updating, 457
  ST Maintenance
  collection of updating information, 459
  and compatibility, 467
  computer assistance, 443
    line-oriented input, 445
    on-line (interactive), 463
    term-oriented input, 446
  cooperation, 514
  description of procedure in introduction to the thesaurus, 227
  necessity of, 13
  organization, 462
  procedures, 460
  sources, 458
    outside the ISAR system, 460
    within the ISAR system, 458
  thesaurus forms used, 460
  time schedule, 461
USE instructions, 155*
  OR-type, 167
  qualified, 171, 473
  in a source thesaurus, 476
Usefulness for searching as selection criterion for descriptors, 338
User needs, see ST Information needs
User version, 183, 348
  dates given in user version, 354
  printing, 412
  source indication, 349
UST, see SP Universal source thesaurus

Variant forms of term, see ST Spelling variants
Verbs, 303
Vision Information Center Thesaurus, 211
Vocabulary, see NT Controlled vocabulary
  Lead-in vocabulary
  Subject access vocabulary
  System vocabulary
Vocabulary control, see ST Terminological control
Vocabulary usage, statistical analysis of, 555

Weak hierarchy, *see ST* Polyhierarchy
Weighting by source in frequency count, 338, 339, 343
Weighting descriptors in indexing, 56
Whole-part relationships, *see ST* Part-whole relationships
Widely overlapping concepts, *see ET* Equivalent terms
Within-unit frequency, 451
Word, *see NT* Common words
    Composite words
    Cue words

Word *(continued)*
    Significant words
Word stems, 453
Work flow in the construction of indexing languages and thesauri, 325
    modifications in work flow, 413
    with computer assistance, 421
Work required for thesaurus development, 10
Working file, 348*, 350, 398, 442, 461
    amend working file, 393, 395
    common working file, 473
Works of art, names of, 148

DISCARDED

JUN 2 2025